Get an inside look at what it's like to be on an archaeological dig with

P9-CDM-286

Doing Fieldwork: Archaeological Demonstrations CD-ROM

Experience the excitement of the field without ever leaving your chair! While there's nothing like learning field techniques from participating in a real dig, this CD-ROM does the next best thing. With **Doing Fieldwork: Archaeological Demonstrations**, you will see archaeologists involved in actual excavations using a number of the field techniques covered in this text.

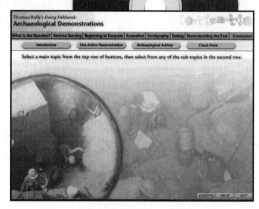

Organized according to the various stages of a live excavation, **Doing Fieldwork** presents hands-on activities, live-action demonstration videos from the authors' fieldwork, and quizzes to help you better understand the processes and techniques that are important to an excavation.

By showing archaeologists involved in various excavations, this CD-ROM illustrates important field techniques, reinforces concepts via examples, and encourages you to participate in a dig yourself.

References to the CD-ROM, like the one at right, appear in relevant chapters. These references direct you to the activities relevant to material you are studying in the text.

Preview

ASK MOST PEOPLE what archaeologists do, and they'll tell you this: "They dig." And that's true. Despite what we have seen in the preceding two chapters about archaeological survey techniques and remote sensing technology, digging up old stuff remains at the heart of archaeology—and probably always will.

But excavation is a more complex and sophisticated venture than throwing a shovel into a pickup and heading off for the mountains. Archaeologists are well aware of the fact that as they gather data from a site, they are also destroying that site, because once a site is excavated, it can never be excavated again. Therefore, it's essential that archaeologists record as much detail as possible, so that future archaeologists can reconstruct what earlier archaeologists did and use the records to answer new questions. This means that you dig slowly and take excruciatingly careful and detailed notes. Nonetheless, as Kent Flannery (University of Michigan) once said, "Archaeology is the most fun you can have with your pants on." And he's right, as anybody who has ever participated in a dig will tell you. Thomas joined his first archaeological expedition as a college junior; Kelly as a high school sophomore. We were both hooked from the start.

We warned earlier about the problems of learning archaeological field techniques from a book (even this one): you just can't do it. But in this chapter we describe common archaeological field methods, and we do hope to show you how fieldwork is done and what it really feels like.

Doing Fieldwork CD-ROM: Archaeological Demonstrations
See the "What Is the Question?" "Beginning to Excavate," "Excavation," and "Stratigraphy" sections of the CD-ROM to learn more about topics covered in this chapter.

Introduction

In Chapter 3, we talked about how archaeologists go about finding sites, such as Gatecliff Shelter. But locating sites is only the beginning; excavating these sites can be far more time consuming. Along with fields such as geology and paleontology, the science of

provenience An artifact's location relative to a system of spatial data collection.

archaeology destroys data as it is gathered—for once we excavate a site, nobody can ever dig it again. This is why archaeologists are compulsive about field notes—recording, drawing, and photographing everything we can about an artifact or a feature before removing it. This is also why we usually try to leave a portion of a site unexcavated for the future.

This chapter can be reduced to one simple point: An artifact's **provenience**, its location and context within a site, is the most important thing about that artifact;

David Hurst Thomas
AMERICAN MUSEUM OF NATURAL HISTORY

Robert L. Kelly
UNIVERSITY OF WYOMING

ARCHAEOLOGY

Third Edition   DOWN TO EARTH

THOMSON
━━━━━✦━━━━━ ™
WADSWORTH

Australia • Brazil • Canada • Mexico • Singapore • Spain
United Kingdom • United States

Archaeology: Down to Earth
Third Edition
David Hurst Thomas, American Museum of Natural History
Robert L. Kelly, University of Wyoming

Publisher: Eve Howard
Anthropology Editor: Lin Marshall
Development Editor: Julie Cheng
Assistant Editor: Leata Holloway
Editorial Assistant: Danielle Yumol
Technology Project Manager: Dee Dee Zobian
Marketing Manager: Lori Grebe Cook
Marketing Assistant: Teresa Jessen
Marketing Communications Manager: Linda Yip
Project Manager, Editorial Production: Emily Smith
Creative Director: Rob Hugel
Art Director: Maria Epes

Print Buyer: Doreen Suruki
Permissions Editor: Kiely Sisk
Production Service: Melanie Field, Strawberry
    Field Publishing
Text Designer: Gopa & Ted2, Inc
Photo Researcher: Terri Wright
Copy Editor: Pam Suwinsky
Compositor: Lachina Publishing Services
Cover Designer: Gopa & Ted2, Inc.
Cover Image: Robert L. Kelly
Text and Cover Printer: Transcontinental Printing/
    Louiseville

Thomson Higher Education
10 Davis Drive
Belmont, CA 94002-3098
USA

For more information about our products, contact us at:
Thomson Learning Academic Resource Center
1-800-423-0563

For permission to use material from this text or product,
submit a request online at **http://www.thomsonrights.com**.
Any additional questions about permissions can be submitted by e-mail to **thomsonrights@thomson.com**.

Library of Congress Control Number: 2005931608

ISBN 0-495-00858-3

For LSAP(T), colleague, companion, advocate, and mother of my son.
And, most significantly, she's still my very best friend.
—D. H. T.

For Matt and Dycus, for their love of big piles of dirt.
—R. L. K.

Brief Contents

Contents

Chapter 3
Doing Fieldwork: Surveying
for Archaeological Sites   48

Chapter 4
Doing Fieldwork: Why
Archaeologists Dig Square Holes   73

Preface

ARCHAEOLOGY: DOWN TO EARTH, Third Edition, is a user-friendly introduction to archaeology: what it is, who does it, and why we should care about it. This text addresses archaeological methods and theory, and yet it departs, in some important ways, from the standard introductory textbook.

Students tell us that they sometimes don't bother reading the introductory textbooks they've purchased—whether the books are about archaeology, chemistry, or whatever. We've heard several reasons for this paradox: the instructor covers exactly the same material, or uses the same examples as the text—so why bother reading what you can get condensed in a lecture? Or their textbooks are deadly dull, written in arcane academic jargon that nobody (including the professor) really understands. Still others tell us that they take an archaeology course just because it sounds like a fun way to fulfill a distribution requirement—but the textbook actually has nothing to say to them.

We want students to know that we've heard them.

Personal Examples, High-Interest Topics

In most archaeology texts, the approach is encyclopedic and dispassionate. But we can't do it that way. To be sure, modern archaeology is a specialized and complicated academic discipline, with plenty of concepts, several bodies of theory, and a huge array of analytical methods—all things we'd like students to learn about. But we think that the best way for students to begin to understand archaeology (or any subject, for that matter) is through a few well-chosen, extended, personalized examples—stories that show how archaeologists have worked through actual problems in the field and in the lab. So that's the approach we take here.

Writing an introductory textbook is not easy. Authors must provide a solid foundation for students who intend to become professional archaeologists. This requires a thorough review of the discipline, including all its major concepts and jargon. But we must also write for the many students who will *not* become professional archaeologists. Accordingly, we picked many of the book's topics and examples with the nonprofessional in mind.

As it turns out, these are the very subjects that the budding career archaeologist should know. In nearly all the chapters, we touch upon sensitive subjects that influence both the professional archaeologist and the public (who pays for most of the archaeological research in the United States). Many archaeological texts avoid these sensitive issues, such as the excavation of the dead, repatriation of artifacts, and working with descendant communities. But we think that these are precisely the issues that matter most to students and to instructors, so we've not backed away from them.

In fact, instructors tell us they have used previous editions of this text precisely because their students actually *read* it.

About This Edition

The first edition of *Archaeology: Down to Earth* was published back in 1991; the second edition retained the coverage and writing style that users praised and ensured that the book reflected up-to-the-minute changes in the discipline.

Confronted with the need for the present revision, David Hurst Thomas decided one person couldn't adequately cover the field any more, and he invited Robert Kelly to join in the project. These two first met more than 30 years ago, when Thomas was excavating Gatecliff Shelter in Nevada and Kelly was a gangly, enthusiastic high school kid.

They continued to work together for several years, after which their careers diverged. When the time came to expand the authorship, Thomas turned to Kelly as the obvious choice for coauthor. Thomas and Kelly recently wrote *Archaeology,* Fourth Edition, a full-length presentation of the topics summarized here. This new partnership means that the third edition of *Archaeology: Down to Earth* is more than a polishing and updating of the old. The better parts of the second edition have survived here, and a newer, fresher perspective has emerged.

Aids to Learning, Old and New

- *Archaeological Ethics.* We are especially proud of this new series of boxes, which address critical issues of archaeological ethics, such as whether archaeology puts Native Americans on trial, the ethics of studying modern people from an archaeological perspective (*ethnoarchaeology*), and whether archaeologists have the right to excavate human skeletons. We think that students will find these topics thought provoking (and these essays could easily form the basis of writing assignments or group discussions). Reviewers were enthusiastically unanimous in their support of this new feature. "Keep them at all costs," wrote one.
- *Looking Closer.* A new feature, "Looking Closer," covers ancillary topics in each chapter. For example, in Chapter 6, we discuss how the *Hunley,* a Civil War submarine, is being preserved after its recovery; in Chapter 8, we examine how theories of human behavioral ecology are being applied to understand ancient hunter-gatherers. Another looks at the proper usage of the terms "American Indian" and "Native American."
- *In His/Her Own Words* and *Profile of an Archaeologist.* We think it's important for students to meet some real archaeologists, so we have included several "In His/Her Own Words" boxes, in which our archaeological colleagues express ideas "in their own words." We also include several "Profile of an Archaeologist" boxes to emphasize the diversity of today's working archaeologists and to illustrate the varied ways in which archaeologists can make a living.

These features combine with the following learning aids to help students master the complex, fascinating discipline of archaeology:

- Chapter Outlines at the beginning of each chapter
- Bulleted Summaries at the end of each chapter
- Running glossaries in each chapter (with glossary terms defined on the page on which the term is introduced) plus an alphabetized Glossary at the end of the text
- Rapid Reviews, midchapter bulleted or tabular features that summarize especially important key concepts
- Photographs and figures that were carefully chosen or created to give students a visual sense of a case study and to act as integrated pedagogical aids to the text
- Media Resources at the end of each chapter to remind students of resources available—including practice quizzes and exercises—on the text's website
- A chapter-by-chapter Bibliography, located at the end of the text, that provides an easy way to find references and additional reading on each chapter's subjects. We have stayed away from in-text citations, but students will be able to locate material discussed in the text, as well as additional readings, in a chapter's bibliography. Page references for the few longer quotes that appear are noted in the relevant bibliographic entry.

A Distinctive Approach

The following strategies all contribute to a fuller, more up-to-date exploration of the field:

Discussions of archaeological objects in context. You'll notice that there is no chapter on "archaeological objects"—stone tools, ceramics, metals, architecture, and so forth (and what archaeologists can do with them). We've never found this encyclopedic approach especially useful in teaching, because it tends to encourage students to simply memorize a laundry list of techniques without context. Instead, we've embedded and contextualized discussions of things like stone tools and ceramics in other substantive examples. This presentation ensures that students learn about these basic archaeological objects in ways that carry significance for them.

Expanded coverage of key methods and technologies topics. We've expanded coverage to reflect the growing importance of certain methods and technologies. For instance, geographic information systems (GIS) technology now has its own section in Chapter 3. And Chapter 5's discussion of dating techniques gives more space to trapped-charge dating methods, such as optically stimulated luminescence. We've also completely rewritten the material on stratigraphy to emphasize geoarchaeology and site formation processes (Chapter 4). Chapter 7 updates explanations of taphonomy, experimental archaeology, and ethnoarchaeology with new examples and a discussion of the difference between analogy and middle-range theory.

Streamlined presentation. To make this text more amenable to semesters and quarters, we have condensed some topics, relocated vital discussions, and removed other material. So, if you think we've left something out from the second edition, look around first: it may be in a different chapter.

Balanced Coverage: Depth, Breadth, Theory

The text covers the field in a comprehensive manner. Given the background knowledge that a first- or second-year college student brings to an introductory course, this text strikes a first-rate balance among the different directions that archaeologists can take. We do believe that this text is the most readable one available and also the most "intellectual": we know of no other textbook that provides extended discussions of theoretical paradigms, the nature of science (what it can and cannot do) and of the humanities, and the intellectual process of learning about the past. Students will learn a bit about the Enlightenment and the origins of postmodernism in these pages. And students can apply the topics in this textbook—especially those in the first three chapters—to virtually any area of study.

Expanded Geographic Coverage

Many of the examples used in this text are drawn from the archaeology of western North America. Between us, we've spent seven decades working there and, frankly, it's what we know best. But we've expanded the geographic coverage as well, drawing upon work in the eastern United States, Central and South America, Egypt and the Near East, Madagascar, France, and other places. Although the text is focused, it is not provincial—and should thereby inspire classroom discussions of research projects from around the world.

All in all, we think this text is one that both instructors and students will appreciate.

Organization of the Text

We constructed this text so that various ideas build upon one another. We know that each archaeologist teaches his or her introductory course differently, so many chapters in the book cross-reference material discussed in other chapters. We note each instance within the text.

Chapter 1, "Meet Some Real Archaeologists," begins with a discussion of the Kennewick Man case—a purposeful selection, because this textbook makes an explicit point of discussing the ethical matters that confront modern archaeology. We thus use the Kennewick controversy to set the tone (and we return to that subject in Chapter 13). The remainder of Chapter 1 addresses the history of American archaeology, with an emphasis on several individual archaeologists who have defined the field.

Chapter 2, "The Structure of Archaeological Inquiry," relates archaeology to the rest of anthropology and wrestles with the diversity of theoretical paradigms evident in contemporary archaeology. We've introduced this diversity not as the interbraided stream that it really is—with all its side channels, backwaters, eddies, and periodic flash floods—but rather in terms of simple dichotomies: science and humanism, adaptive and ideational approaches, processual and postprocessual archaeology. We hope that our discussion of paradigms and of low-, middle-, and high-range theory will help organize the rest of your course. This somewhat simplified presentation provides an easy entry into the diversity of contemporary archaeology. And rather than come down on the side of processual or postprocessual archaeology, we take a centrist position that we believe characterizes the majority of working archaeologists today: There is something to be gained from looking at prehistory through both of these paradigms—each of which is well suited for answering a particular kind of question.

Chapters 3 and 4, "Doing Fieldwork: Surveying for Archaeological Sites" and "Doing Fieldwork: Why Archaeologists Dig Square Holes," respectively, provide the nuts and bolts of archaeology, explaining how archaeologists go about doing surface survey, using remote sensing equipment, and excavating sites. We give students some sense of how much fun fieldwork can be, but we also deal with issues such as sampling bias, the cost of dating methods, and the utility of GIS to modern archaeology. In Chapter 4, we also discuss the field of geoarchaeology, with emphasis upon site formation processes. This chapter also addresses archaeological stratigraphy, beginning with the law of superposition, and shows students how a site's stratigraphy can be "read" to provide a context to the artifacts contained there.

Chapter 5, "Chronology Building: How to Get a Date," covers dating methods used in prehistoric and historic archaeology. The range of dating technology seems to increase annually, and we had to make some tough choices about what to include. The major purpose of this chapter is not to write an encyclopedia of available methods, but instead to provide enough information about key techniques so that students can relate dating technology to ancient human behavior.

Chapter 6, "The Dimensions of Archaeology: Time, Space, and Form," discusses various archaeological concepts—types, cultures, and phases—that help construct large-scale patterns in space and time. Our goal is to help the student see the world as an archaeologist views it, as an ever-changing spatial and temporal mosaic of material culture.

The chapters in the second half of the book consider how archaeologists go about breathing some anthropological life into this spatial and temporal mosaic—how they use material remains to infer something about past human behavior.

Chapter 7, "Taphonomy, Experimental Archaeology, and Ethnoarchaeology," is about middle-range theory—how it is different from standard analogy and how archaeologists construct it through taphonomic, experimental, and ethnoarchaeological research. Our goal here is to convince students that archaeologists don't just make stuff up, but instead give plenty of thought to how they infer ancient behavior from material objects and their contexts.

Chapter 8, "People, Plants, and Animals in the Past," recounts how archaeologists reconstruct diet from faunal and floral remains and how they infer hunting strategies and symbolic meanings attributed to the natural world.

Chapter 9, "Bioarchaeological Approaches to the Past," considers what we can learn—about diet, disease, and workload—from human skeletal remains and explores the relatively new field of molecular archaeology.

Chapter 10, "Reconstructing Social and Political Systems of the Past," shows how archaeologists can reconstruct social and political systems and looks at gender, kinship, and social hierarchies.

Chapter 11, "The Archaeology of the Mind," presents how archaeologists address the symbolic meanings once attached to the material remains; here, we look at the nature of symbols and what archaeologists can realistically hope to learn about them.

Chapter 12, "Historical Archaeology: Insights on American History," explores historical archaeology, especially those aspects that set the field apart from prehistoric archaeology—the ability to uncover "hidden history," the ability to provide a near-forensic analysis of historical events, and the ability to present alternative perspectives on American history.

Chapter 13, "Caring for America's Cultural Heritage," examines the legal structure of modern archaeology, emphasizing the field of cultural resource management (how it came to be and the critical role it plays in archaeology today). This chapter also covers the subjects of reburial and repatriation in some detail. It also looks at the future of archaeology, especially the ways in which archaeologists apply their knowledge to contemporary problems. We conclude by discussing the increased involvement of indigenous peoples in their own archaeology and asking whether we are on the brink of another revolution—one that might produce a newer "new" archaeology.

A Note about Human Remains

In several instances, this book discusses important new frontiers of bioarchaeological research. But we also recognize the need to deal with human remains in a respectful and sensitive manner. Several Native American elders have requested that we refrain from publishing photographs or other depictions of American Indian human remains. Although not all Native Americans feel this way, no images of Native American skeletal remains appear in this book. Should other groups express similar concerns, their requests will be addressed in succeeding editions as appropriate.

About the Petroglyphs

Boxes used throughout this text are highlighted with several rock art symbols. To the best of our knowledge, they do not infringe on anyone's intellectual property rights. They are not intended to suggest a cultural or religious connotation.

Supplemental Materials

This text also comes with a strong supplements program to help instructors use their class time most effectively and to aid students in mastering the material.

- *Online Instructor's Manual with Test Bank.* The instructor's manual offers chapter outlines, learning objectives, key terms and concepts, and lecture suggestions. The test bank consists of 40–60 test questions per chapter, including multiple choice, true/false, and essay questions.
- *Doing Fieldwork: Archaeological Demonstrations CD-ROM.* Granted that students can learn field techniques only from actually participating, this CD shows professional archaeologists involved in various digs (many of which are referenced in the text), illustrates field techniques, gives students perspective about what they're learning, reinforces concepts and techniques via live examples, and encourages students to participate in a dig themselves. The presentation is organized by the main techniques that one uses on a dig. Users are taken through each step automatically or can navigate to any point via the navigation bar. Students review illustrations and video clips of each technique. After reviewing a step in the dig process, students are taken to "check points," which are concept questions about each step of the dig. Students can see the answers, receive their score, and e-mail the score to the instructor.

Throughout the book, we have integrated the *Doing Fieldwork* CD-ROM with the topics as discussed in the text. In Chapter 4, where we discuss the stratigraphy of Gatecliff Shelter (Nevada), students can find footage of the Gatecliff excavations on the CD-ROM. Similarly, our discussion of remote sensing (in Chapter 3) is augmented in the CD-ROM with video of archaeologists using this new technology in the field.

- *ExamView Computerized Test Bank.* Create, deliver, and customize tests and study guides (both print and online) in minutes with this easy-to-use assessment and tutorial system. *ExamView* offers both a Quick Test Wizard and an Online Test Wizard that guide instructors step-by-step through the process of creating tests, and its unique WYSIWYG capability allows you to see the test you are creating on the screen exactly as it will print or display on-line. You can build tests of up to 250 questions using up to 12 question types. Using *ExamView*'s complete word processing capabilities, you can enter an unlimited number of new questions or edit existing questions.
- *Companion Website.* The companion website includes the following for each chapter of the text: tutorial practice quizzes that can be scored and e-mailed to the instructor, Internet links and exercises, flashcards of the text's glossary, crossword puzzles, essay questions, learning objectives, and much more. From this site, students can link to Wadsworth's exclusive Anthropology Resource Center, which includes an Archaeology section with enriching exercises and sites such as the "Earthwatch Journal," "Applying Anthropology," and "The Latest Dirt."

Who Helped Out?

Despite the personal flavor of these pages, this text was created by more than four hands. Many people helped out, and we'd like to thank them here.

The overall presentation was vastly improved by a contingent of top-notch colleagues and friends who provided advice and critical reviews of the manuscript. We are particularly grateful to Jaclyn Jeffrey (Texas A&M International University), Rosemary A. Joyce (University of California, Berkeley), Elizabeth Leach

(Metropolitan State University), Christopher N. Matthews (Hofstra University), Randall H. McGuire (Binghamton University), Mark Schurr (University of Notre Dame), each of whom slogged through the revised manuscript and contributed immeasurably to the final product. We are most grateful for their advice and suggestions.

Many others commented on portions of chapters or entire chapters, answered questions, provided photographs or text for sidebars, and checked facts for us. We gratefully acknowledge timely and sometimes detailed assistance on this and previous editions from

Larry Babits
Mary C. Beaudry (Boston University)
Richard Berger
Lewis Binford (Truman State University)
Michael Blakey (College of William and Mary)
Ama Badu Boakyewa
Rob Bonnichsen (Center for the Study of the First Americans, Texas A&M University)
Bruce Bradley (Exeter University, UK)
Jack Broughton (University of Utah)
Jane Buikstra (University of New Mexico)
Catherine Cameron (University of Colorado)
Robert Carneiro (American Museum of Natural History)
Cheryl Claassen (Appalachian State University)
C. William Clewlow (Ancient Enterprises)
Margaret Conkey (University of California, Berkeley)
the late Don Crabtree
Jay Custer (University of Delaware)
William Davis (formerly University of California, Davis)
Phil Da Vita, Kathleen Deagan (Florida State Museum of Natural History)
Jeffrey Dean (University of Arizona)
Rob DeSalle (American Museum of Natural History)
Robert Elston (formerly Intermountain Research)
Clark Erickson (University of Pennsylvania)
T. J. Ferguson (Anthropological Research, Tucson)
Kent V. Flannery (University of Michigan)
Don Fowler (University of Nevada, Reno)
Anne Fox (University of Texas, San Antonio)
George Frison (University of Wyoming)
Robert Gargett (San Jose State University)
Ervan Garrison (University of Georgia)
Joan Gero (American University)
Diane Gifford-Gonzalez (University of California, Santa Cruz)
Dean Goodman (University of Miami, Japan Division)

Martha Graham (National Park Service)
Donald K. Grayson (University of Washington),
David Grimaldi (American Museum of Natural History)
the late Marvin Harris
Christine Hastorf (University of California, Berkeley)
William Haviland (University of Vermont)
Brian Hayden (Simon Fraser University)
Richard Holmer (Idaho State University)
Robert L. Humphrey
the late Cynthia Irwin-Williams
Gregory Johnson (Hunter College of CUNY)
Kevin Johnston (Ohio State University)
William Kelso (Jamestown Rediscovery Archaeological Project)
Thomas King (National Park Service)
Stephen Kowalewski (University of Georgia)
the late Charles Lange
Clark Spencer Larsen (Ohio State University)
Robert Leonard (University of New Mexico)
Mark Leone (University of Maryland)
Janet Levy (University of North Carolina, Charlotte)
the late Scotty MacNeish
David B. Madsen (formerly Utah State Archaeologist)
the late William Maples
Joyce Marcus (University of Michigan)
Alexander Marshack (Harvard University)
Randall McGuire (State University of New York, Binghamton)
Heather McInnis (University of Oregon)
Frank McManamon (National Park Service)
George Miller (California State University, Hayward)
Paul Minnis (University of Oklahoma)
Craig Morris (American Museum of Natural History)
Michael J. O'Brien (University of Missouri)
James O'Connell (University of Utah)
Christopher Peebles (University of Indiana)
Kathy Place

Stephen Plog (University of Virginia)
Robert Preucel (University of Pennsylvania)
William Rathje (Stanford University)
Elizabeth Reitz (University of Georgia)
John Rick (Stanford University)
Thomas Riley
Anibal Rodriguez (American Museum of Natural History)
Nan Rothschild (Columbia University)
Irwin Rovner (North Carolina State University)
Ralph Rowlett (University of Missouri)
Michael Schiffer (University of Arizona)
Enid Schildkrout (American Museum of Natural History)
Payson Sheets (University of Colorado)
Theresa Singleton (Syracuse University)
Stanley South (University of South Carolina)

Janet Spector (formerly University of Minnesota)
Charles Spencer (American Museum of Natural History)
the late William Tallbull
Ian Tattersall (American Museum of Natural History)
Anya Taylor (John Jay College of CUNY)
Mark Taylor (Manhattan College)
the late W. W. Taylor
Ruth Tringham (University of California, Berkeley)
Donald Tuohy (formerly Nevada State Museum)
Mary Vermillion (University of Illinois, Chicago)
Patty Jo Watson (Washington University)
John Weymouth (University of Nebraska)
the late Joe Ben Wheat
Mary Whelan (University of Iowa)

Each contributed worthwhile suggestions, which we often followed. We alone, however, are responsible for any errors of commission or omission.

Thomas also wishes to thank others in the American Museum of Natural History, especially Lorann S. A. Pendleton, Matt Sanger, and Molly Trauten, each of whom cheerfully helped out with dozens of details.

Kelly is grateful to his colleagues at the University of Wyoming, many of whom supplied photographs, answered innumerable questions about archaeological and anthropological trivia, and generally provided support. He is especially grateful to Lin Poyer, who, once again, has shown her unbounded patience and thoughtfulness.

We are also grateful to the crew at Wadsworth—Anthropology Editor Lin Marshall, Development Editor Julie Cheng, Production Project Manager Emily Smith, Technology Project Manager Dee Dee Zobian, Assistant Editor Leata Holloway, Permissions Editor Stephanie Lee, and Marketing Manager Lori Grebe Cook. We thank the production team: production manager Melanie Field (Strawberry Field Publishing), copy editor Pam Suwinsky, and photo researcher Terri Wright. We also gratefully acknowledge Dennis O'Brien, who created many of the illustrations used in this edition, as well as the contributions of the illustrators Diana Salles and the late Nicholas Amorosi, both of the American Museum of Natural History.

Keeping in Touch with Your Authors

We see this textbook as an opportunity to become more available to both instructors and students. With e-mail, we can have casual conversations with people around the globe, in more or less real time. We want to know what you think about this text and about archaeology—what you like and what you don't care for—so we can improve future editions. We encourage you to write us at the e-mail addresses following. Provided that we're not off on some remote dig somewhere, we'll get back to you right away. Drop us a line—we'd enjoy hearing from you.

D. H. T.
New York, New York
thomasd@amnh.org

R. L. K.
Laramie, Wyoming
RLKELLY@uwyo.edu

September 2005

About the Authors

DAVID HURST THOMAS has served since 1972 as Curator of Anthropology at the American Museum of Natural History in New York City. A specialist in Native American archaeology, Thomas discovered both Gatecliff Shelter (Nevada) and the lost sixteenth- and seventeenth-century Franciscan mission Santa Catalina de Guale on St. Catherines Island, Georgia. Since 1998, he has led the excavation of Mission San Marcos near Santa Fe, New Mexico. A founding trustee of the National Museum of the American Indian at the Smithsonian since 1989, he has published extensively, including 100 papers and 30 books—most recently, the best-selling *Skull Wars: Kennewick Man, Archaeology, and the Battle for Native American Identity.*

ROBERT KELLY began collecting arrowheads in farmers' fields when he was 10 years old and has participated in archaeological research since 1973 when he was a high school sophomore. He has worked on excavations in North and South America and conducted ethnographic research in Madagascar. He is currently conducting research into the Paleoindian archaeology of Wyoming's Bighorn Mountains. A former president of the Society for American Archaeology and a past secretary of the Archaeology Division of the American Anthropological Association, Kelly has published nearly 100 articles and books, including the 1996 *Choice* magazine Outstanding Academic Book *The Foraging Spectrum: Diversity in Hunting and Gathering Societies.* Dr. Kelly is Professor and Head of the Department of Anthropology at the University of Wyoming.

1

Meet Some Real Archaeologists

Outline

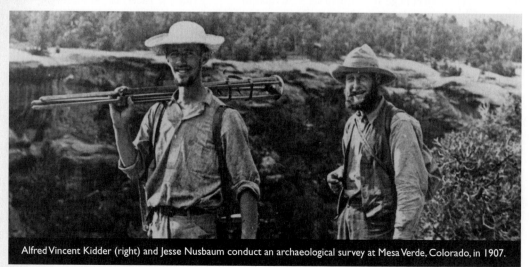

Alfred Vincent Kidder (right) and Jesse Nusbaum conduct an archaeological survey at Mesa Verde, Colorado, in 1907.

© Faith Kidder Fuller/School of American Research

Preview

This book is about what archaeologists want to learn, how they go about learning it, and what they do with what they have learned. These tasks require archaeologists to piece together a picture of the past from scraps of bone, rock, pottery, architecture, and other remains that are hundreds, thousands, or tens of thousands of years old. And, as we will see, the very nature of archaeology carries with it some serious ethical dilemmas.

In this book, we look at some of the perspectives that characterize today's archaeology: scientific and humanistic, objective and subjective, ecological and ideational. Sometimes these approaches coexist; sometimes they clash. As we discuss these various perspectives, you should keep a couple of things in mind: First, no archaeologist fits perfectly into any of these named categories, and second, there is more than one way to do good archaeology.

This chapter looks at how archaeology has evolved. Archaeology is a relatively young discipline, still going through some growing pains. To raise some key issues that define the way modern archaeologists practice their craft, we begin with an example that illustrates some of the ethical dilemmas that archaeologists face today.

 Doing Fieldwork CD-ROM: Archaeological Demonstrations
See the "What Is the Question?" section of the CD-ROM to learn more about topics covered in this chapter.

Introduction

July 1996: The two college students never intended to make a federal case out of the day's fun. They never meant to rock the ethical foundations of American archaeology, either. All they wanted was to see hydroplane boat races for free.

The month of July in the city of Kennewick (Washington) is a month of festivals topped off by hydroplane races on the Columbia River. To avoid paying admission to the races, two young men snuck through a brushy area of riverbank. There, they could get a good view, even if it meant getting wet. Trudging along the river's edge, they spied a smooth white rock. One of them picked it up and jokingly pronounced it a skull. Imagine his surprise when he saw two dark eye sockets staring back at him. It *was* a skull.

After the races, the students reported their find to police, who called in the coroner to see if the remains were those of a murder victim. The coroner eventually called in archaeologist James Chatters. Although there was no evidence of a burial pit, the skull's near-pristine condition suggested that it had eroded from the riverside only days earlier; in fact, Chatters eventually found much of the skeleton in the shallow water.

Who Was "Kennewick Man"?

Chatters's preliminary analysis showed that the individual was male and roughly 45 years old when he died. He stood about 5 feet 8 inches high. Subsequent laboratory analysis showed that two-thirds of his protein probably came from fish and that he ate limited amounts of starchy foods. In his time, the man might have been considered healthy, but today we would call him a "survivor." He suffered from severe disease or malnutrition when he was about 5 years old. He had minor arthritis in his knees, elbows, lower back, and neck from a lifetime of daily, intense physical activity. As a young adult, he had damaged the nerves to his left arm. He'd also suffered a serious chest injury, a blow to the head, and an injury to his right shoulder and left elbow. And, as if that weren't enough, he had a stone spear point embedded in his hip. He had survived this injury, too—although it left him in constant pain.

Chatters knew spear points like the one in the skeleton's hip were manufactured thousands of years ago, but he was still surprised when a radiocarbon date indicated that the man had died 9400 years ago. So-

called Kennewick Man was one of the oldest human skeletons ever found in the Americas.

Even more intriguing was that the skull did not look like other Native American skulls; some experts even thought it might be European! (See "Looking Closer: American Indian or Native American?") It's not, but that suggestion titillated the media, who created sensationalist stories of how Europeans, rather than the ancestors of American Indians, first colonized the Americas. One group, the Asatru Folk Assembly, which says it practices an ancient Celtic religion, even claimed that Kennewick Man was their ancestor.

Who Controls Human Remains?

Many federal and state laws govern archaeology in the United States (we examine some of these in Chapter 13).

LOOKING CLOSER
American Indian or Native American?

Some years ago, as Thomas was telling his son's third grade class what it's like to be an archaeologist, a small (but adamant) voice of protest came from the back of the room.

"How come you keep saying 'Indians'? Don't you know they want to be called 'Native Americans'?" a girl asked.

She had a good point. Many people are confused about these terms. In fact, our Native American colleagues tell us that people often correct them when they say "Indian," as if the term has become a dirty word.

Names are important because they are power; the people who name things are generally the people who control them. Throughout this text, therefore, we discuss the names we use, because a discussion of names is also a discussion of people's rights.

The word *Indian,* of course, is a legacy from fifteenth-century European sailors, who mistakenly

believed they'd landed in India. *Native American* arose among Indians in the 1960s and 1970s, during the civil rights movement. But many Indians point out the ambiguity in this term. Although your authors are not American Indians, we are native Americans (because we were born in the United States).

Most indigenous people of North America today simply accept the imprecision of today's terms and use *American Indian, Canadian Native, First Nations, Native American* (or *Native Hawaiian*), *Indian,* and *Native* interchangeably; we follow this lead.

Of greater concern to most Indian people is the tribal name. Many Navajo people, for instance, wish to be known as *Diné* (a traditional name meaning "The People"). When discussing particular tribes, whenever possible we use the term preferred by the tribe in question.

One such law, the 1990 Native American Graves Protection and Repatriation Act (NAGPRA) provides for the repatriation of Native American human remains to their culturally affiliated tribes. Several tribes from the Kennewick area claimed the new find to be their ancestor and requested that the remains be turned over to them under this law. Kennewick Man had been discovered on lands administered by the U.S. Army Corps of Engineers, and that agency quickly agreed to halt all scientific studies and return the skeleton to the tribes.

But then a group of eight archaeologists and biological anthropologists filed a lawsuit, arguing that handing over the bones would actually violate NAGPRA—not only because the skeleton was not affiliated with the modern tribes, but also because it might not even be Native American. The scientists also claimed that their First Amendment rights would be violated if the government kept them from studying the remains.

The Corps turned to the U.S. Department of Interior for guidance, which commissioned a set of studies. Relying heavily on oral history from the tribes, Bruce Babbitt, then Secretary of the Interior, declared that Kennewick Man was indeed culturally affiliated with the tribes and should be returned to them.

In protest, the eight plaintiffs reopened their suit, and the case was heard by the Ninth District Circuit Court (in Oregon). The judge faced uncharted legal waters: Was this 9400-year-old man a Native American or not? And, if so, was he culturally affiliated with the five modern tribes who claimed him as an ancestor? These are tough questions, both legally and scientifically. And the answers could potentially change forever the direction of American archaeology.

Five years after the boys found the skull, the judge ruled that Kennewick Man was not Native American. And even if he were, the judge ruled, the bones could not be culturally affiliated with the consortium of five tribes. The judge also granted the plaintiffs the right to study the remains. The tribes, along with the Department of Interior, appealed the ruling. And, in February 2004, the appeals court upheld the district court's ruling: Kennewick is not Native American. The tribes have promised to try and strengthen NAGPRA by amending the law.

Kennewick and American Archaeology

The Kennewick decision is a landmark, and it raises important questions that we address throughout this book. How did archaeologists know that the bones are 9400 years old? How did Chatters know that the spear point was ancient? How do we know that Kennewick Man ate a lot of fish? Can he really *not* be Native American? Answering questions like these is what archaeologists do: they reconstruct the human past from the crumbling remains that survive.

But Kennewick also raises some difficult ethical questions: What gives archaeologists the right to poke into the past, the right to study the dead? Who owns the past, anyway? And who gets to decide? This is also what archaeologists do: they make difficult ethical and moral decisions about the past (and the present).

The discipline of archaeology is presently experiencing some growing pains. With more than 7000 practicing archaeologists in the United States alone, the discipline harbors a host of diverse and sometimes conflicting perspectives. Some believe that archaeology is a science, pure and simple; others argue that archaeology must be responsive to humanistic concerns.

We argue that both statements are true. Scientists insist on high standards of evidence, and they also continually examine their methods of making inferences from evidence. Science in this sense is self-correcting, making the approach essential to most inquiry (including archaeology). But even scientific inquiry is susceptible to cultural biases. Alternatively, humanistic approaches downplay scientific standards of evidence to explore new ideas and perspectives and to examine the biases and larger agenda of science. The ongoing dialogue about the ethics of archaeology will ultimately benefit scientific perspectives by pinpointing some biases that may hold us back from achieving a more complete understanding of humanity's shared past.

Archaeologists often say that we study the past in order to avoid repeating it and that understanding where humanity has been helps us to chart the future. But the Kennewick case points up the dilemma buried in both these aphorisms. By claiming the skeletal remains as their own, the Indian tribes asserted that no scientific studies should be conducted. The tribes believed that they already understood their own past

Figure 1-1 Americanist archaeology today confronts both scientific and ethical challenges. Yet, there are many signs that archaeology need not be antagonistic to indigenous peoples. Here, Bryceson Pinnecoose (Hopi/Cheyenne, on right) and Kevin Woolridge map buried structures at Mission San Marcos, New Mexico.

and resented attempts by non-Indian scientists to probe the remains of their ancestors. Although not all Native Americans agree with this position, many do, and this dispute underscores the important point that archaeology is not just about the dead; it is also about the living. How can we justify "studying the past to create a better tomorrow" if the very act of conducting research offends the living descendants of the ancient people being studied? Our position is that archaeologists must work closely with indigenous peoples and descendant communities to achieve the goals of a scientific archaeology (as in Figure 1-1, which shows a working example of this compromise).

Rather than sweep the ethical dilemmas that confront modern archaeology under the rug, we highlight them in the "Archaeological Ethics" boxes that appear in several place in this text. And, after we learn something more about the practice of archaeology, we return in Chapter 13 to the case of Kennewick Man to explore its implications for the future of the past.

We now turn to a brief history of archaeology. This will help set the stage for an understanding of modern archaeological approaches explored in the next chapter.

The Western World Discovers Its Past

Most historians ascribe the honor of "first archaeologist" to Nabonidus (who died in 538 BC), the last king of the neo-Babylonian Empire (see "Looking Closer: AD/BC/BP . . . Archaeology's Alphabet Soup"). A pious man, Nabonidus's zealous worship of his gods compelled him to rebuild the ruined temples of ancient Babylon and to search among their foundations for the inscriptions of earlier kings. We are indebted to the research of Nabonidus's scribes and the excavations by his subjects for much of our modern picture of the Babylonian Empire. Though nobody would call Nabonidus an "archaeologist" in the modern sense of the term, he remains an important figure for one simple reason: *Nabonidus looked to the physical residues of antiquity to answer questions about the past.* This may seem like a simple step, but it contrasted sharply with the beliefs of his contemporaries, who regarded tradition, legend, and myth as the only admissible clues to the past.

For archaeology to become an intellectual field, scholars first had to recognize the idea of "the past." A major contribution of the Renaissance (approximately AD 1300 to 1700), particularly in Italy, was the distinction between the present and the past. Classical Greeks and Romans recognized only a remote past, which they reified through myth and legend. Because Europeans of the Middle Ages likewise failed to distinguish between themselves and ancient populations, it fell to Renaissance scholars to point up the differences between classical and medieval times.

Francesco Petrarch (1304–1374), perhaps the most influential individual of the early Renaissance, defined an intellectual tradition that continues to be important in today's archaeology. Beyond his considerable talents as poet and linguist, Petrarch also provided strong impetus for archaeological research. To him, the remote past was an ideal of perfection, and he looked to antiquity for moral philosophy. Of course, to imitate classical antiquity, one must first study it. In a real sense, Petrarch's approach led to a rediscovery of the past by those in the Western European intellectual tradition. Petrarch's influence can best be seen in the work

© David Hurst Thomas

LOOKING CLOSER
AD/BC/BP . . . Archaeology's Alphabet Soup

In anything written by archaeologists, you'll encounter a blizzard of acronyms that refer to age. Let's clear the air with some concise definitions of the most common abbreviations:

- **BC** ("before Christ"): For instance, 3200 BC; note that the letters follow the date.
- **AD** (*anno Domini*, meaning "in the year of the Lord"): Indicates a year that falls within the Christian era (that is, after the birth of Christ).

Given the English translation of the phrase, archaeologists place the "AD" prior to the numerical age—we say the Norman Invasion occurred in "AD 1066" rather than "1066 AD." The earliest AD date is AD 1; there is no AD 0 because this year is denoted by 0 BC, and double numbering is not allowed.

- **AC** ("after Christ"): Basically the same as AD, except that it's written AC 1066 (with the abbreviation written before the number). This usage is confusing, and hardly anybody uses it anymore. Neither do we.

- **BP** ("before present"): Many archaeologists feel more comfortable avoiding the AD/BC split altogether, substituting the single "before present" age estimate (with AD 1950 arbitrarily selected as the zero point; we explain why in Chapter 5). By this convention, an artifact from the Hastings battlefield would be dated 884 BP (1950 − 1066 = 884).

Note that all the abbreviations used so far are capital letters. Just in case you're not confused enough, you may also run into a date written in lowercase, such as 3200 b.c. This convention denotes that a date was derived by radiocarbon methods and reflects radiocarbon years rather than calendar years (we explain the difference in Chapter 5). So the term "3200 b.c." would be read "3200 radiocarbon years before Christ." We find this usage confusing and don't employ it here.

---

of his close friend Giovanni Boccaccio (1313–1375), who wrote extensive essays on classical mythology, and also in that of Giovanni Dondi (1318–1389), who is generally credited with the first systematic observations on archaeological monuments.

But it remained for the fifteenth-century Italian scholar Ciriaco de' Pizzicolli (1391–1455) to establish the modern discipline of archaeology. After translating the Latin inscription on the triumphal arch of Trajan in Ancona, Italy, he was inspired to devote the remainder of his life to studying ancient monuments, copying inscriptions, and promoting the study of the past. His travels took him into Syria and Egypt, throughout the islands of the Aegean, and finally to Athens. When asked his business, Ciriaco is said to have replied, "Restoring the dead to life"—which today

remains a fair definition of the everyday business of archaeology.

Archaeology and Society

From the beginning of Renaissance Europe's interest in the past, however, it was clear that not everyone wanted the dead to be restored to life. In 1572, Matthew Parker, Queen Elizabeth's archbishop of Canterbury, formed the Society of Antiquaries, devoted to the study of Anglo-Saxon law and writings.

At the same time, Parliament upheld English Common Law, said to have been granted by William the Conqueror upon his conquest of England in 1066. English Common Law was based on the laws and customs of the Anglo-Saxons. Unfortunately, British kings had persistently claimed that their authority to rule—the "divine right of kings"—originated in their descent from the legendary King Arthur (who probably lived about AD 500, but no one really knows). King James therefore asserted that Common Law did not apply to the Anglican Church or to the king, because it originated with William rather than with Arthur. But the Society of Antiquaries used ancient documents to demonstrate that William the Conqueror did not actually create English Common Law—instead, he had simply allowed it to stand and to be fused with his own ideas of justice. This was a problem for King James, for in English Common Law the people had the right to rebel against an unlawful and unjust king. King James saw that meddling with this particular piece of the past had too much potential to start riots in the streets, and so he ordered the dissolution of the Society of Antiquaries. The study of the past often is controversial.

But the die was cast, and the Society of Antiquaries was only the first of many British scholarly societies interested in the past. Of course, many private collectors were concerned only with filling their curio cabinets with *objets d'art,* but the overall goal of British antiquarianism was to map, record, and preserve national treasures. By the late eighteenth century, members of Europe's leisure classes considered an interest in classical antiquities to be an important ingredient in the "cultivation of taste," hence the non-scientific bent implied in the term **antiquarian.**

The Discovery of Deep Time

Archaeological research until the eighteenth century proceeded mostly within the tradition of Petrarch—that is, concerned primarily with clarifying the picture of classical civilizations. This lore was readily digested by the eighteenth- and early nineteenth-century mind, because nothing in it challenged the Bible as an authoritative account of the origin of the world and humanity.

A problem arose, however, when very crude stone tools like that shown in Figure 1-2 were discovered in England and continental Europe. About 1836, a French customs official and naturalist, Jacques Boucher de Crèvecoeur de Perthes (1788–1868), found ancient axe heads in the gravels of the Somme River. Along with those tools, he also found the bones of long-extinct mammals. To Boucher de Perthes (as he is more com-

© American Museum of Natural History

Figure 1-2 Boucher de Perthes found Paleolithic handaxes like this in the Somme River gravels.

monly known), the implication was obvious: "In spite of their imperfection, these rude stones prove the existence of [very ancient] man as surely as a whole Louvre would have done."

But few contemporaries believed him, in part because prevailing religious thought held that human beings had been on Earth for only 6000 years. Why? Some 200 years before Boucher de Perthes's discoveries, several scholars had calculated the age of the Earth as no more than about 6000 years. Perhaps the most meticulous of these calculations was that of James Ussher (1581–1656), Archbishop of Armagh, Primate of All Ireland, and Vice-Chancellor of Trinity College in Dublin. Using biblical genealogies and correlations of Mediterranean and Middle Eastern histories, Ussher concluded in 1650 that Creation began at sunset on

antiquarian Originally, someone who studied antiquities (that is, ancient objects) largely for the sake of the objects themselves—not to understand the people or culture that produced them.

Saturday, October 22, 4004 BC. His effort was so convincing that the date 4004 BC appeared as a marginal note in most Bibles published after 1700.

This reckoning, of course, allowed no chance of an extensive human antiquity; there simply wasn't enough time. Therefore, the thinking went, Boucher de Perthes must be mistaken—his rude implements must be something other than human handiwork. Some suggested that the "tools" were really meteorites; others said they were produced by lightning, elves, or fairies. One seventeenth-century scholar suggested that the chipped flints were "generated in the sky by a fulgurous exhalation conglobed in a cloud by the circumposed humour," whatever that means.

But customs officials have never been known for their reserve, and Boucher de Perthes stuck to his guns. More finds were made in the French gravel pits at St. Acheul (near Abbeville), and similar discoveries turned up across the channel in southern England. The issue was finally resolved when the respected British paleontologist Hugh Falconer (1808–1865) visited Abbeville to examine the disputed evidence. A procession of esteemed scholars followed Falconer's lead and declared their support in 1859; the idea that humans had lived with now-extinct animals in the far distant past was finally enshrined in Charles Lyell's 1865 book *The Geological Evidences of the Antiquity of Man.*

The year 1859 turned out to be a banner year in the history of human thought: not only was the remote antiquity of humankind accepted by the scientific establishment, but Charles Darwin published his influential *On the Origin of Species.* Although Darwin mentioned humans only once in that book (on nearly the last page he wrote, "Much light will be thrown on the origin of man and his history . . ."), he had suggested the process by which modern people could have risen from ancient primate ancestors. In the beginning, though, Darwin's theory (which had to do with the transformation of species) was unconnected to the antiquity of humanity (which was a simple question of age).

Nonetheless, the discovery of deep time—the recognition that life was far more ancient than biblical scholars argued and that human culture had evolved over time—opened the floodgates. British archaeology soon billowed out across two rather divergent courses. One direction became involved with the problems of remote geological time and the demonstration of long-term human evolution. Others continued the tradition of Petrarch and focused on classical studies, particularly the archaeology of ancient Greece and Rome, a field now known as **classical archaeology.** This philosophical split has continued into modern times, although some signs hint that these fields are coming back together.

Archaeology and Native Americans

Across the Atlantic, American archaeology faced its own vexing issues of time and cultural development. How, nineteenth-century scholars wondered, could regions such as the Valley of Mexico and Peru have hosted the civilizations of the Aztecs and the Inkas while people in many other places—such as the North American West—seemed impoverished, even primitive? When did people first arrive in the New World? Where had these migrants come from, and how did they get here?

Speculation arose immediately. One idea held that Native Americans were one of the Lost Tribes of Israel. Another suggested that Indians came from Atlantis. Others said they were voyaging Egyptians, Vikings, Chinese, or Phoenicians.

Gradually, investigators came to realize the considerable continuities that existed between the unknown prehistoric past and the Native American population of the historic period. As such knowledge progressed, profound differences between European and American archaeology became more apparent. While Europeans wrestled with their ancient flints—without apparent modern correlates—American scholars saw that living Native Americans were relevant to the interpretation of archaeological remains. In the crass terms of the time, many Europeans saw Native Americans as "living fossils," relics of times long past.

New World archaeology thus became inextricably wed to the study of living Native American people. Whereas Old World archaeologists began from a baseline of geological time or classical antiquity, their

classical archaeology The branch of archaeology that studies the "classical" civilizations of the Mediterranean, such as Greece and Rome, and the Near East.

American counterparts developed an anthropological understanding of Native America. The **ethnology** of American Indians became an important domain of Western scholarship in its own right, and Americanist archaeology became linked with anthropology through their mutual interest in Native American culture.

Let us stress an important point here: As Europeans refined the archaeology of Europe, they were studying their own ancestors (Anglo-Saxons, Celts, Slavs, Franks, and so forth). But New World archaeology was a matter of Euro-Americans digging up somebody else's ancestors. This fundamental difference explains the following elements peculiar to New World archaeology:

- The racist, anti–American Indian theories that dominated the thinking of early nineteenth-century American scholars
- The form of antiquity legislation in North America, and
- The fact that many contemporary Native Americans still do not trust conventional Western scholarship to interpret their past

We return to these issues in later chapters.

Founders of Americanist Archaeology

We are now prepared to look more closely at how Americanist archaeology is currently practiced. Although many other terms—such as "scientific archaeology," or "anthropological archaeology"—are used, we prefer Robert Dunnell's phrase **Americanist archaeology** because it is descriptive, yet it contains the many perspectives that constitute American archaeology today. Let us also emphasize that archaeologists working in the Americanist tradition practice their craft around the world, and not only in North America.

The history of Americanist archaeology (all history, really) is a commingling of tradition and change—illustrated here by a few individuals whose lives and careers typify archaeology of their time. These individuals were by no means the only ones practicing archaeology over the past 150 years. However, their stories demonstrate stages in the growth of Americanist archaeology and show how goals and perspectives have changed.

C. B. Moore: A Genteel Antiquarian

Clarence Bloomfield Moore (1852–1936) was born into an affluent family of Philadelphia socialites. After receiving his BA degree from Harvard University in 1873, Moore followed the social circuit, rambling through Europe and joining safaris into exotic Africa. By 1892, however, Moore found the well-to-do socialite lifestyle to be shallow and boring. Somewhere along the line, Moore was introduced to American archaeology and, at age 40, he transformed himself from gentleman socialite into gentleman archaeologist.

Smitten by his new pastime, he purchased a specially equipped flat-bottomed steamboat, which he christened the *Gopher*. With it, Moore explored the seemingly endless waterways of America's Southeast, excavating the major archaeological sites he encountered. Particularly drawn to ancient cemeteries, Moore enlisted the services of Dr. Milo G. Miller as secretary, physician, and colleague.

From the outset, Moore's annual archaeological campaigns were models of organization and efficiency. Aboard *Gopher,* Moore and Miller conducted preliminary investigations so that likely sites could be located and arrangements could be made with landowners; actual excavations began in the spring. Moore hired and supervised the workers and kept the field notes. As human skeletons were located, Dr. Miller examined the bones to determine sex, age, probable cause of death, and any unusual pathologies. They spent the summers cleaning and repairing the finds and then photographing and analyzing the collection. Moore prepared detailed excavation reports for publication and distributed the more unusual **artifacts** to major archaeological institutions.

ethnology That branch of anthropology dealing chiefly with the comparative study of cultures.

Americanist archaeology The brand of archaeology that evolved in close association with anthropology in the Americas; it is practiced throughout the world.

artifact Any movable object that has been used, modified, or manufactured by humans; artifacts include stone, bone, and metal tools; beads and other ornaments; pottery; artwork; religious and sacred items.

Moore's first investigations concentrated on the shell **middens** and the sand burial mounds sprinkled along the Gulf Coast of Florida. Year after year, Moore worked his way around to Florida's eastern shore and eventually to the Sea Islands of coastal Georgia and South Carolina. In 1899, Moore returned to the Gulf Coast, traveled up the Alabama River, and examined the coast of northwest Florida. He excavated dozens of archaeological sites on each expedition.

Finally, in 1905, Moore paused on the Black Warrior River, Alabama, to excavate the ruins known as Moundville (we return to this site in Chapter 10). Working with several trained assistants and a crew numbering 10 to 15, Moore explored the large temple mounds to examine the human burials and unearth spectacular pieces of pre-Columbian art. Moore concluded that Moundville had been a prominent regional center. He further surmised from the varied art forms that the ancient people of Moundville worshiped the sun, and that motifs such as the plumed serpent and eagle suggested strong ties with contemporaneous Mexican civilizations.

By 1916, Moore concluded that the *Gopher* had explored every southeastern river then navigable by steamer. In fact, once a sandbar was removed, Moore promptly piloted the *Gopher* up the newly navigable Chocktawatchee River in northern Florida. He had truly exhausted the resources available for riverboat archaeology. Of course, archaeological techniques have improved markedly since Moore's time, and many a contemporary archaeologist wishes that Moore had been somewhat less thorough.

Moore typifies archaeology's roots because he was an antiquarian, more interested in the objects of the past than in reconstructing the lives of the people who produced them or in explaining the past. We should not hold this against Moore's generation because, frankly, you can't move to understanding the past until you have some idea of what that past was like. Antiquarians like Moore helped to lay the groundwork for the archaeology that was to follow.

Nels Nelson: America's First-Generation "Working" Archaeologist

Whereas C. B. Moore was born into a wealthy family, Nels Nelson (1875–1964), shown in Figure 1-3, grew up on a poor farm in Jutland, Denmark. Although first a farmhand and a student only in his spare time, he stumbled onto James Fenimore Cooper novels—*The Last of the Mohicans* and *The Deerslayer*—while still quite young and became fascinated with the lore of Native Americans. Several of his relatives had already emigrated to America, and, in 1892, Nelson's aunt in Minnesota sent him a steerage ticket to New York. On his way westward, he worked at a number of jobs (including driving a six-mule team and butchering hogs) and finally saved enough money to enroll at Stanford University, where he studied philosophy by day and took odd jobs at night to pay his expenses.

Quite by accident, someone invited Nelson to attend an archaeological excavation in Ukiah, north of San

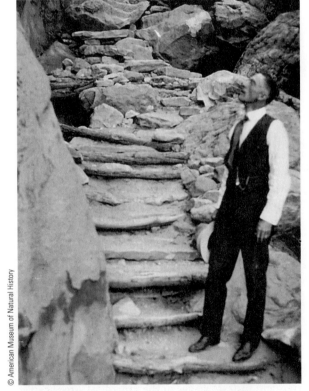

© American Museum of Natural History

Figure 1-3 Nels Nelson, one of the first professional archaeologists, stands on the stone steps leading to Acoma Pueblo, New Mexico.

midden Refuse deposit resulting from human activities, generally consisting of sediment; food remains such as charred seeds, animal bone, and shell; and discarded artifacts.

Francisco. He was immediately hooked. The dig apparently rekindled the same fascination with Indian lore he had first experienced while reading the pages of Cooper. Nelson immediately enrolled in all the archaeology courses available at the University of California.

Nelson's MA thesis was an archaeological survey of the shell middens surrounding San Francisco Bay. He walked more than 3000 miles during his reconnaissance and recorded 425 prehistoric shell mounds. His report discussed the location of these sites relative to available natural resources, listed the animal bones found in the shell heaps, and pondered the ecological adaptation implied by such a bayside lifeway. Urban sprawl has today destroyed all but a handful of these sites, and Nelson's map, originally published in 1909, remains an irreplaceable resource to modern archaeologists interested in central California prehistory.

Then, in 1912, the American Museum of Natural History in New York City launched an archaeological campaign in the American Southwest, and Nelson was engaged to oversee this influential research program. Nelson's stratigraphic excavations in New Mexico were a breakthrough in archaeological technique (we discuss **stratigraphy** in more detail in Chapters 4 and 5). By looking at the kinds of artifacts found in different, superimposed layers of earth at a site, Nelson could document culture change over time. In the next few years, Nelson broadened his experience by excavating shell mounds in Florida and caves in Kentucky and Missouri. In 1925, Nelson accompanied an American Museum of Natural History expedition to Central Asia; his North American and European fieldwork continued until his retirement in 1943.

Nels Nelson typifies the state of Americanist archaeology during the first quarter of the twentieth century. Although receiving better archaeological training than did his predecessors, such as C. B. Moore, Nelson nevertheless learned largely by firsthand experience. Archaeology was still in a pioneering stage, and no matter where Nelson turned, he was often the first archaeologist on the scene. Like others of his generation, his first responsibility was to record what he saw, then to conduct a preliminary excavation where warranted, and finally to proffer tentative inferences to be tested and embellished by subsequent investigators. Nelson also typified the new breed of early twentieth-century museum-based archaeologists, who strongly believed that the message of archaeology should be brought to the public in books, popular magazine articles, and, most of all, interpretive displays of archaeological materials.

Today, archaeologists acknowledge Nelson's 1912 excavations in New Mexico's Galisteo Basin as the first significant stratigraphic archaeology in the Americas. At that time, the cultural chronology of the American Southwest was utterly unknown, and Nelson's painstaking excavations and analysis of the pottery recovered provided the first solid chronological framework.

A. V. "Ted" Kidder: Founder of Anthropological Archaeology

Although he was born in Michigan, the life and career of Alfred V. Kidder (1886–1963) revolved about the academic community of Cambridge, Massachusetts. Kidder's father, a mining engineer, saw to it that his son received the best education available. First enrolled in a private school in Cambridge, Kidder then attended the prestigious La Villa, in Ouchy, Switzerland, after which he registered at Harvard. Kidder soon joined an archaeological expedition to northeastern Arizona, exploring territory then largely unknown to the Anglo world. The southwestern adventure sealed his fate.

When Kidder returned to Harvard, he enrolled in the anthropology program and in 1914 was awarded the sixth American PhD specializing in archaeology—and the first with a focus on North America. Kidder's dissertation examined prehistoric southwestern ceramics, assessing their value in reconstructing culture history. Relying on scientific procedures, Kidder demonstrated ways of deciphering meaning from one of archaeology's most ubiquitous items, the **potsherd.** Urging accurate description of ceramic decoration, he explained how such apparent minutiae could help determine cultural relationships among various prehistoric groups. Kidder argued that only through controlled excavation and analysis could inferences be drawn about such anthropological subjects as acculturation, social organizations, and prehistoric religious customs.

stratigraphy A site's physical structure produced by the deposition of geological and/or cultural sediments into layers, or *strata*.

potsherd Fragment of pottery.

In 1915, the Department of Archaeology at the Phillips Academy in Andover, Massachusetts, was seeking a site of sufficient size and scientific interest to merit a multiyear archaeological project. Largely because of his anthropological training, Kidder was selected to direct the excavations. After evaluating the possibilities, he decided on Pecos Pueblo, a massive prehistoric and historic period ruin located southeast of Santa Fe, New Mexico. Kidder was impressed by the great diversity of potsherds scattered about the ruins and felt certain that Pecos contained enough stratified debris to span several centuries. Kidder excavated at Pecos for ten summers.

The excavations at Pecos were consequential for several reasons. Kidder modified Nelson's stratigraphic method of digging to construct a cultural chronology of the Southwest. He went beyond the pottery to make sense of the artifact and architectural styles preserved at Pecos. His intensive artifact analysis, done before the advent of radiocarbon dating or tree-ring chronology (methods that we discuss in Chapter 5), established the framework of southwestern prehistory, which remains intact today.

Kidder then joined the Carnegie Institution of Washington, D.C., as director of the Division of Historical Research. He launched an ambitious archaeological program to probe the Maya ruins of Central America. Kidder directed the Carnegie's Maya campaigns for two decades, arguing that a true understanding of Maya culture would require a broad plan of action with many interrelated areas of research. Relegating himself to the role of administrator, Kidder amassed a staff of qualified scientists with the broadest possible scope of interests. His plan was a landmark in archaeological research as it enlarged traditional archaeological objectives to embrace the wider realms of anthropology and allied disciplines. Under Kidder's direction, the Carnegie program supported research by ethnographers, botanists, geographers, physical anthropologists, geologists, meteorologists, and, of course, archaeologists.

Kidder even proved the potential of aerial reconnaissance by convincing Charles Lindbergh, already an international figure, to participate in the Carnegie's Maya program. Early in 1929, Lindbergh flew Kidder throughout British Honduras, the Yucatán Peninsula, and the Petén Jungle of Guatemala. Beyond discovering new ruins, the Lindbergh flights also generated a wealth of previously unavailable ecological data, such as the boundaries of various types of vegetation. Today, the interdisciplinary complexion of archaeology is a fact of life. But when Kidder proposed the concept in the 1920s, it was revolutionary.

In addition to his substantive Maya and southwestern discourses, Kidder helped shift Americanist archaeology toward more properly anthropological purposes. Unlike many of his contemporaries, Kidder maintained that archaeology should be viewed as "that branch of anthropology which deals with prehistoric peoples," a doctrine that has become firmly embedded and expanded in today's Americanist archaeology. To Kidder, the archaeologist was merely a "mouldier variety of anthropologist." Although archaeologists continue to immerse themselves in the nuances of potsherd detail and architectural specifics, the ultimate objective of archaeology remains the statement of anthropological universals about *people*.

James A. Ford: A Master of Time

Born in Water Valley, Mississippi, James A. Ford's (1911–1968) major research interests centered on the archaeology of the American Southeast. While Ford was attending Columbia, Nels Nelson retired from the Department of Anthropology at the American Museum of Natural History, and Ford was chosen as the new assistant curator of North American archaeology.

Ford came of age during the Great Depression, part of an archaeological generation literally trained on the job. As the Roosevelt administration created jobs to alleviate the grim economic conditions, crews of workmen were assigned labor-intensive tasks, including building roads and bridges and general heavy construction. One obvious make-work project was archaeology, and thousands of the unemployed were set to work excavating major archaeological sites. This program was, of course, an important boost to Americanist archaeology, and data from government-sponsored, Depression-era excavations are still being analyzed and published.

Ford worked at Poverty Point, a Louisiana site explored 40 years earlier by C. B. Moore. Poverty Point is a large, 400-acre site that dates to the first and second millennia BC. It contains a number of large earthen mounds, one in the shape of a bird that is 70 feet high and 700 feet wide. Lying before this mound, like a gigantic amphitheater, is a set of concentric 5-feet-high semicircles, three-quarters of a mile in diameter. We still don't fully understand their purpose. After mapping these and the site's other mounds, Ford launched a series of stratigraphic excavations, using Nelson's principles, designed to define the prehistoric sequence.

Ford's objective was to learn what Poverty Point had to say about the people who lived there, a considerably more ambitious goal than that of C. B. Moore, who dug primarily to unearth outstanding examples of artwork. Ford continually asked, What does archaeology tell us about the people? As he excavated the mounds, he tried to recreate the social and political networks responsible for this colossal enterprise. In this regard, his approach typified the overarching anthropological objectives of mid-twentieth-century Americanist archaeology.

The unprecedented accumulation of raw data during the 1930s was a boon for archaeology, but it also created a crisis of sorts: What was to be done with all these facts? Ford and his contemporaries were beset by the need to synthesize and classify and by the necessity to determine regional sequences of culture chronology. Unlike Kidder and the others working in the American Southwest, Ford did not have access to deep, well-preserved refuse heaps; southeastern sites were more commonly shallow, short-term occupations. To create a temporal order, Ford relied on an integrated scheme of surface collection and classification.

Ford refined techniques to place the various stages of pottery development in sequential order, a process known as *seriation* (which we discuss further in Chapter 5). The central idea is simple: By assuming that cultural styles tend to change gradually, archaeologists can chart the relative popularity of a style, such as pottery decoration, through time and across space. By fitting the various short-term assemblages into master curves, Ford developed a series of regional ceramic chronologies. Although sometimes overly simplistic, Ford's seriation technique was sufficient to establish the baseline prehistoric chronology still used in the American Southeast.

Ford then synthesized his ceramic chronologies into patterns of regional history. When C. B. Moore was excavating the hundreds of prehistoric mounds throughout the Southeast, he lacked a system for adequately dating his finds. Using seriation along with other methods, Ford helped bring temporal order to

his excavations, and he rapidly moved to synthesize these local sequences across the greater Southeast. He proposed the basic division between the earlier Burial Mound Period and the subsequent Temple Mound Period, a distinction that remains in use today.

Americanist Archaeology at Mid-Twentieth Century

The biographies of these forebears provide a sense of how Americanist archaeology developed during the first half of the twentieth century. You have no doubt noted that none of them are women. Nonetheless, women such as Madeline Kneberg (1903–1996), Frederica de Laguna (1906–2004), H. Marie Wormington (1914–1994; see Figure 1-4), and Florence Hawley Ellis (1906–1991) were, in fact, contributing—but because they were commonly excluded from traditional communication networks, their contributions are more difficult to find. Today, this is no longer true—in fact, half of all American archaeologists are women.

American archaeology began as a pastime of the genteel rich such as C. B. Moore, but through the years, it developed into a professional scientific discipline. As trained practitioners, most archaeologists after Moore's time have been affiliated with major museums and universities; others have joined the private sector, working to protect and conserve America's cultural

© Denver Museum of Nature and Science

Figure 1-4 Marie Wormington was a female pioneer in American archaeology.

heritage. This institutional support not only encouraged a sense of professionalism and fostered public funding, but also mandated that public repositories would care for the archaeological artifacts recovered. The twentieth-century Americanist archaeologist is not a collector of personal treasure; all finds belong in the public domain, available for exhibit and study.

We can also see a distinct progression toward specialization in our target archaeologists. Scholars knew virtually nothing about American prehistory in the early nineteenth century. But by the end of that century, so much archaeological information had already accumulated that no single scholar could know everything relevant to Americanist archaeology. Although C. B. Moore became the leading authority on southeastern archaeology, he knew little about the finds being made by his contemporaries in Peru, Central America, and the American Southwest. By the mid-twentieth century, archaeologists like Ford were forced to specialize in specific localities within limited cultural areas. Today, it is rare to find archaeologists with extensive experience in more than a couple of specialized fields.

Possibly the greatest change, however, has been the quality of archaeologists' training. Although Harvard-educated, Moore was untrained in archaeology; his fieldwork methods were based on personal trial and error. Nelson and Kidder were members of the first generation of professionally trained Americanist archaeologists, and they studied under America's most prominent anthropologists. From then on, Americanist archaeologists were, almost without exception, well versed in anthropology.

Although archaeologists by mid-century wished to transcend mere cultural chronology, in truth classifying artifacts and sorting out their patterns in space and time left little time for more anthropological objectives, such as reconstructing society. Most archaeologists by mid-century were involved in what is called **culture history.** Their main goal was to track the migrations and development of particular prehistoric cultures by documenting how material culture changed over time and space. Differences in artifact frequencies between sites were attributed to the presence of different cultures; changes in artifact frequencies over time, such as the types of pottery found in different layers of earth at a site, were attributed to the diffusion of ideas from other cultures or the replacement of one culture by another. Some archaeologists did try to explain changes by relating them to climatic change, for example, or to vague ideas about cultural development. But for the most part, artifact changes were "explained" by the diffusion of ideas or the influx of a new people.

However, by the 1950s, the basic prehistory of North America was sufficiently well understood that some archaeologists were ready to move beyond simple documentation to more in-depth reconstructions of prehistory and even to efforts at explaining prehistory.

Revolution in Archaeology: An Advancing Science

Beginning in the 1940s, a succession of scholars challenged orthodox archaeological thinking, urging explosive change and demanding instantaneous results. Two such crusaders were particularly influential in shaping modern archaeological thought.

Walter W. Taylor: Moses in the Wilderness

Educated first at Yale and then at Harvard, Walter W. Taylor (1913–1997), shown in Figure 1-5, completed his doctoral dissertation late in 1942. After returning from overseas military service, he published in 1948 an expanded version of his dissertation as *A Study of Archeology.* It was a bombshell. Greeted with alarm and consternation by the archaeological community, the book was no less than a public call for revolution. Taylor blasted the archaeological establishment of the day. Few liked Taylor's book, but everybody read it.

Taylor launched a frontal attack on the elders of Americanist archaeology. This assault was particularly plucky, as Taylor was himself a wet-behind-the-ears newcomer, having published little to establish his credentials as an archaeologist, much less a critic.

culture history The kind of archaeology practiced mainly in the early to mid-twentieth century; it "explains" differences or changes over time in artifact frequencies by positing the diffusion of ideas between neighboring cultures or the migration of a people who had different mental templates for artifact styles.

Courtesy of Walter W. Taylor

Figure 1-5 Walter W. Taylor in Coahula, Mexico, in 1937. Taylor advocated that archaeologists focus less on grand temples and more on the lives of common people.

A Study of Archeology blasted A. V. Kidder, among others. Kidder repeatedly maintained that he was an anthropologist who had specialized in archaeology. But Taylor probed Kidder's publications to determine how well his deeds conformed to his stated anthropological objectives and boldly concluded that they did not. He could find in Kidder's research no cultural synthesis, no picture of life at any site, no consideration of cultural processes, no derivation of cultural laws—no anthropology at all, in Taylor's opinion.

These were serious charges, considered blasphemous by most archaeologists of the time. But Taylor supported his case with a line-by-line dissection of Kidder's published record. Kidder's research at Pecos and elsewhere in the American Southwest was said to be full of "apparent contradictions," merely "description for its own sake." Taylor claimed that Kidder was incapable of preparing a proper site report (a charge that was a bit over the top), much less of writing the anthropology of the prehistoric Southwest.

Taylor turned to Kidder's prestigious research into the archaeology of the Maya and, once again, accused him of failing to live up to his own goals. Granting that Kidder began his investigations with anthropology in mind, Taylor concluded that "the road to Hell and the field of Maya archeology are paved with good intentions." Taylor deduced that the Carnegie Institution, under Kidder's direction, "has sought and found the hierarchical, the grandiose. It has neglected the com-

mon, the everyday." Kidder, Taylor declared, had been blinded by the "pomp and circumstance" of Classic Maya archaeology, the grand temples and ceremonial centers. According to Taylor, Kidder merely skimmed off the sensational, the spectacular, the grandiose—and forgot all about the Maya people themselves: How did they live? What did they do? What did they believe?

In 1948, Taylor was indeed archaeology's angriest young man. Kidder and other luminaries were accused of compiling **trait lists,** an account of the presence or absence of particular kinds of artifacts at different sites to no real purpose; of classifying artifacts and describing them, but for the mere sake of classification and description. Taylor pointed out that whereas Kidder and his generation claimed to be anthropologists, they failed to do anthropology (at least according to Taylor). Though careful not to deny the initial usefulness of their strategies, Taylor urged archaeologists to get on with the proper business of anthropology: finding out something about ancient people. Chronology, to Taylor, was merely a stepping stone, a foundation for more anthropologically relevant studies of human behavior and cultural dynamics.

Taylor's prescription was his so-called **conjunctive approach** to archaeology. By this, Taylor meant combining ("conjoining") a variety of lines of evidence to create a picture of what the past was like and to discuss the functions of artifacts, features, and sites. From his critique, we can see that Taylor would have scrutinized the artifacts and features of a single Maya center, inferred their functions, and then written a comprehensive description of the people who once lived there.

Taylor urged archaeologists to forsake the temples for the garbage dumps, for it was there that the lives of everyday people were recorded.

Taylor proposed that archaeologists quantify their data, rather than merely create trait lists, and that they

trait list A simple listing of a culture's material and behavioral characteristics, for example, house and pottery styles, foods, degree of nomadism, particular rituals, or ornaments. Trait lists were used primarily to trace the movement of cultures across a landscape and through time.

conjunctive approach As defined by Walter W. Taylor, using functional interpretations of artifacts and their contexts to reconstruct daily life of the past.

test hypotheses that would progressively refine their impressions (too often, Taylor asserted, initial observations were taken as gospel). He also argued that archaeologists must excavate less extensively and more intensively to detect patterning *within* sites. Archaeologists must recover and decode the meaning of unremarkable food remains—bones and plant parts—and embrace specialties in the analysis of these finds. Taylor also argued that we should write more effective and detailed site reports, illustrating more than just the glamorous finds, and include precise proveniences.

In perusing Taylor's propositions nearly six decades after he wrote them, we are struck by how unremarkable they now seem. Where is the revolution? Today's archaeologists do quantify their results; they do test hypotheses; they do excavate intensively; they do save food remains; they do involve specialists in analysis; and they do write detailed site reports.

But archaeologists did not do these things routinely in 1940, and this is what Taylor was sputtering about. Oddly, though, Taylor himself never carried through and implemented the conjunctive approach. Maybe the time just wasn't right. Nonetheless, Taylor's suggestions of 1948 embody few surprises for today's student—testimony to just how far archaeological doctrine and execution have matured since Taylor wrote *A Study of Archeology*.

Lewis R. Binford: Visionary with a Message

Americanist archaeology's second angry young man is Lewis R. Binford (1930–) (Figure 1-6). After a period of military service, Binford enrolled in 1954 at the University of North Carolina, wanting to become an ethnographer. By the time he moved on for graduate education at the University of Michigan, however, Binford was a confirmed archaeologist.

As a young professional, Binford was a man on the move—literally. He taught a year at the University of

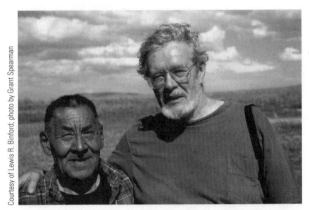

Courtesy of Lewis R. Binford; photo by Grant Spearman

Figure 1-6 Lewis R. Binford (right) poses with a Nunamiut friend, Johnny Rulland, at Tulugak Lake, Alaska, in 1999. Binford helped develop the "new archaeology" of the 1960s.

Michigan, then moved on to the University of Chicago, to the University of California at Santa Barbara, down the coast to UCLA, on to the University of New Mexico, and then to Southern Methodist University (in Dallas).

The mid-1960s was a hectic time for archaeology. Baby Boom demographics and the GI Bill inflated university enrollments. Campuses were the focal point of waves of social and political confrontation that rolled across the nation. Clashing opinions over the war in Vietnam and civil rights created a revolutionary atmosphere.

Archaeology was firmly embedded in this intellectual climate. Everyone, including archaeologists, was primed for change.

Binford fit into this cultural climate. He could lecture, sometimes for hours, with the force and enthusiasm of an old-time southern preacher, and he rapidly assumed the role of archaeological messiah. His students became disciples, spreading the word throughout the land: as the study of cultural change, archaeology has obvious relevance to modern problems. To fulfill this role, archaeology must transcend potsherds to address larger issues, such as cultural evolution, ecology, and social organization. Archaeology must take full advantage of modern technology by using scientific methods and sophisticated, quantitative techniques. Archaeology must be concerned with the few remaining preindustrial peoples in order to scrutinize firsthand the operation of disappearing cultural adaptations. And archaeology must be concerned with the methods we use to reconstruct the past. In the 1960s, this became known as the **new archaeology** (see "In

new archaeology An approach to archaeology that arose in the 1960s, emphasizing the understanding of underlying cultural processes and the use of the scientific method; today's version of the "new archaeology" is sometimes called *processual archaeology*.

IN HIS OWN WORDS
The Challenge of Archaeology

By Lewis R. Binford

As I was riding on the bus not long ago, an elderly gentleman asked me what I did. I told him I was an archaeologist. He replied: "That must be wonderful, for the only thing you have to be to succeed is lucky." It took some time to convince him that his view of archaeology was not quite mine. He had the idea that the archaeologist "digs up the past," that the successful archaeologist is one who discovers something not seen before, that all archaeologists spend their lives running about trying to make discoveries of this kind. This is a conception of science perhaps appropriate to the nineteenth century, but, at least in the terms which I myself view archaeology, it does not describe the nature of archaeology as it is practiced today. I believe archaeologists are more than simply discoverers. . . .

Archaeology cannot grow without striking a balance between theoretical and practical concerns. Archaeologists need to be continuously self-critical: that is why the field is such a lively one and why archaeologists are forever arguing among themselves about who is right on certain issues. Self-criticism leads to change, but is itself a challenge—one which archaeology perhaps shares only with palaeontology and a few other fields whose ultimate concern is making inferences about the past on the basis of contemporary things. So archaeology is not a field that can study the past directly, nor can it be one that merely involves discovery, as the man on the bus suggested. On the contrary, it is a field wholly dependent upon inference to the past from things found in the contemporary world. Archaeological data, unfortunately, do not carry self-evident meanings. How much easier our work would be if they did!

From *In Pursuit of the Past: Decoding the Archaeological Record*, pp. 19, 23.

His Own Words: The Challenge of Archaeology" by Lewis R. Binford).

The new archaeology (an odd term, since it is now quite old to all of us—and especially to today's student) became associated with a new way of studying the past and doing archaeology. The plan for it was set forth in a series of articles published through the 1960s and early 1970s, many by Binford and his students.

Binford asked why archaeology had contributed so little to general anthropological theory. His answer was that, in past studies, material culture had been simplistically interpreted. Too much attention had been lavished on artifacts as passive traits that "blend," "influence," or "stimulate" one another. Echoing Taylor, Binford proposed that artifacts be examined in terms of their cultural contexts and interpreted in their roles as reflections of technology, society, and belief systems.

Binford also underscored the importance of precise, unambiguous scientific methods. Archaeologists, he argued, should stop waiting for artifacts to speak up. They must formulate hypotheses and test these on the remains of the past. Binford argued that, because archaeologists always work from samples, they should acquire data that make the samples more representative of the populations from which they were drawn. He urged archaeologists to stretch their horizons beyond the individual site to the scale of the region; in this way, an entire cultural system could be reconstructed (as we discuss in Chapter 3). Such regional samples must be generated from research designs based on the principles of probability sampling. Such procedures are commonplace in other social sciences, and Binford insisted that archaeologists apply them to their research problems.

Binford's mostly methodological contributions were gradually amplified by projects designed to demonstrate how the approach fosters the comprehension of patterning of African Acheulian (500,000 years old) assemblages. He proposed new ideas, rooted in the field of human ecology, to explain the origins of plant domestication. These investigations were critical because they embroiled Binford in factual, substantive debate. Not only did he advocate different goals and new methods, but he also gained credibility among field archaeologists through these substantive controversies—he argued about specifics, not just theory. And Binford conducted his own ethnographic fieldwork among the Nunamiut Eskimo, the Navajo, and the Australian aborigines, testing the utility of archaeological concepts and methods on the trash of living peoples.

In Taylor-like fashion, Binford lambasted archaeology's principals, accusing them of retarding progress in the discipline. And yet his reception was quite different from Taylor's. Whereas Taylor's *A Study of Archeology* languished on the shelf, Binford was hailed as "the father of the new archaeology." Taylor was the unwelcome harbinger of impending change, but Binford was the architect.

Binford and his students set off a firestorm that quickly spread throughout the archaeological community. A 1970s generation of graduate students and young professionals was greeted with the inquisition "Are you a new archaeologist, an old archaeologist, or what? Make up your mind!" Today, the new archaeology of the 1960s has transformed into what is termed *processual archaeology*. In Chapter 2, we explore the tenets of this position and also examine how yet another wave of archaeological criticism—*postprocessual archaeology*—finds fault with Binford's approach and suggests some alternative directions.

Archaeology in the Twenty-First Century

So, what about today? Who is a mover and shaker of the twenty-first century?

Perhaps in another 50 years or so, hindsight will suggest one person who truly captures the spirit of these times. But right now, we do not detect a single, defining trend that dominates Americanist archaeology; instead, the discipline has several branches, each growing and intersecting in interesting ways. Many of these diverse approaches result from new techniques and perspectives; others arise from the nature of employment in archaeology. Some archaeologists still work in museums and universities, but many more are employed in federal agencies and private archaeology firms (companies that arose as a response to federal legislation passed in the 1960s designed to protect the nation's archaeological resources—more about these in Chapter 13).

Prior to the 1970s, most American archaeologists were white and male. Today, the archaeological profession comprises equal numbers of men and women, and more minorities, including Native Americans, are actively involved in the field. Throughout these pages, we meet some archaeologists who exemplify those trends (in boxes labeled "Profile of an Archaeologist"). For now, we wish to present one more archaeologist as a way to introduce modern archaeology.

Kathleen Deagan: Archaeology Comes of Age

Born the year that Walter Taylor published his harangue of American archaeology, Kathleen Deagan (1948–) represents in many ways the fulfillment of

Taylor's call. Pictured in Figure 1-7, Deagan received her doctorate in anthropology from the University of Florida in 1974. Former chair and currently a curator at the Florida Museum of Natural History, she specializes in Spanish colonial studies. She is pushing the frontiers of historical archaeology (see Chapter 12), pioneering the archaeological investigation of disenfranchised groups and actively involved in bringing archaeology to the public. She is concerned with the people and culture behind the artifact and with explaining the social and cultural behaviors that she reconstructs from archaeology. Taylor would have approved of all this (but so would have Kidder).

Deagan is well known for her long-term excavations at St. Augustine (Florida), continuously occupied since its founding by Pedro Menéndez in 1565. St. Augustine is the oldest European enclave in the United States (complete with the "oldest pharmacy," "oldest house," "oldest church," and so on). Deagan's research here dates back to her graduate student days, her doctoral dissertation neatly encompassing the traditionally separate studies of historical archaeology, ethnohistory, and anthropology (see "In Her Own Words: The Potential of Historical Archaeology" by Kathleen Deagan).

Deagan addressed the processes and results of Spanish–Indian intermarriage and descent, a topic dear to the hearts of many anthropologists and ethnohistorians. The fact that people of such mixed descent (**mestizos**) constitute nearly the entire population of Latin America brought this issue to the forefront long ago. Similar processes took place in Spanish Florida, but the Hispanic occupation left no apparent mestizo population in La Florida, what Deagan calls "America's first melting pot." Accordingly, when she began her doctoral research, we knew virtually nothing about such early race relations in North America.

Deagan hypothesized how the mestizo population fit into this colonial setting. Given the nature of the unfortunate interactions that characterized eighteenth-century Florida, she expected the burdens of acculturation to have fallen most heavily on the Indian women living in Spanish or mestizo households. Because no mestizo people survive here, the tests for her hypothesis were necessarily archaeological. If her hypothesis is true, then acculturation should affect mostly the Native American women's activities visible in archaeological sites (food preparation techniques, equipment, household activities, basic food resources, child-related activ-

© Kathleen Deagan

Figure 1-7 Kathleen Deagan, a contemporary archaeologist, excavates at St. Augustine, Florida.

ities, and primarily female crafts such as pottery manufacture). Moreover, male-related activities (house construction technology and design, military and political affairs, and hunting weapons) should show less evidence of Indian infusion.

To explore these processes, Deagan began in 1973 a series of archaeological field schools at St. Augustine. This long-term, diversified enterprise excavated sites whose inhabitants represented a broad range of incomes, occupations, and ethnic affiliations. Hundreds of students have learned their first archaeology at St. Augustine, where a saloon long sported an aging placard celebrating the years of "Digging with Deagan."

It was not long before her explorations into Hispanic–Native American interactions led Deagan to the Caribbean, where she headed interdisciplinary excavations at Puerto Real, the fourth-oldest European New World city (established in 1503). As she steadily moved back in time, Deagan's research eventually led her literally to the doorstep of Christopher Columbus.

In northern Haiti, Deagan discovered La Navidad, the earliest well-documented point of contact between Spanish and Native American people. On Christmas Eve, 1492—following two nights of partying with local Taino Arawak Indians—Columbus's flagship *Santa*

mestizos Spanish term referring to people of mixed European and Native American ancestry.

IN HER OWN WORDS

The Potential of Historical Archaeology

By Kathleen Deagan

From its emergence as a recognized area of research in the 1930s, historical archaeology has advanced from providing supplemental data for other disciplines, through an anthropological tool for the reconstruction of past lifeways, to a means of discovering predictable relationships between human adaptive strategies, ideology, and patterned variability in the archaeological record.

Because it can compare written accounts about what people said they did, what observers said people did, and what the archaeological record said people did, historical archaeology can make contributions not possible through any other discipline. Inconsistencies and inaccuracies in the written records may be detected and ultimately predicted. Insights into conditions provided by such written sources may be compared to the more objective archaeological record of actual conditions in the past in order to provide insight into cognitive processes.

The simultaneous access to varied sources of information allows the historical archaeologist to match the archaeological patterning of a given site against the documented social, economic, and ideological attributes of the same site to arrive at a better understanding of how the archaeological record reflects human behavior. The unique potential of historical archaeology lies not only in its ability to answer questions of archaeological and anthropological interest, but also in its ability to provide historical data not available through documentation or any other source. Correcting the inadequate treatment of disenfranchised groups in America's past, excluded from historical sources because of race, religion, isolation, or poverty, is an important function of contemporary historical archaeology and one that cannot be ignored.

From *Avenues of Inquiry in Historical Archaeology,* 1982, pp. 170–171.

Maria ran aground. He abandoned ship, moved to the *Niña,* and appealed to the local Native Americans for help. This disaster left the explorers one boat short. When Columbus sailed home with his world-shattering news, he left 39 unfortunate compatriots behind, protected by a small stockade built from the timbers of the wrecked *Santa Maria.* Returning a year later, Columbus found the settlement burned, his men killed and mutilated.

Columbus soon established the more permanent settlements of La Isabela and Puerto Real—sites of the first sustained contact between Europeans and Native Americans—and Deagan has also conducted important field excavations there. Having a population of nearly 1500 people, La Isabela was home to soldiers, priests, stonecutters, masons, carpenters, nobles, and warriors. Although this first Columbian town lasted only four years, several critical events took place here: the first intentional introduction of European plants and animals; the first expedition into the interior; and the first Hispanic installation of urban necessities, such as canals, mills, streets, gardens, plazas, ports, ramparts, roads, and hospitals.

The biological effects of the Columbian exchange soon overtook La Isabela. European and Native American alike suffered from dietary deficiencies, an excessive workload, and contagious disease. Influenza struck during the first week, affecting one-third of the population. When Columbus ordered the settlement abandoned in 1496, fewer than 300 inhabitants were left. Deagan extended her research to investigate daily life in the initial colonial period, including the ways in which European colonists coped with their new and largely unknown New World environment.

Beyond new directions in historical archaeology, Deagan's research demonstrates the degree to which contemporary Americanist archaeology is played out in the public arena; she creates headlines wherever she works. Newspapers around the world chronicle her success, and her research was featured in consecutive years in the pages of *National Geographic* magazine. Most recently, she published, with Venezuelan archaeologist José María Cruxent, two books on La Isabela, one a data-laden professional monograph, the other a readable volume for the public.

Deagan shows skill and patience with the onslaught of well-meaning reporters because she knows that archaeologists cannot afford to isolate themselves in ivory towers or archaeology labs. One way or another—whether through federal grants, state-supported projects, tax laws, or private benefaction—archaeology depends on public support for its livelihood, and consequently it owes something back to that public. Decades ago, Margaret Mead (1901–1978), one of the nation's first anthropologists, recognized the importance of taking the work of anthropologists to the public, and she spent considerable effort keeping anthropology alive in the print and electronic media. Today, archaeology enjoys unprecedented press coverage, and archaeologists like Deagan know that without such publicity, Americanist archaeology has no future.

Deagan's research and publications have also helped establish historical archaeology as an anthropologically relevant specialty of archaeology. Although awash in time-specific details and artifacts, she is ultimately addressing the general processes behind the particulars: the sexual and social consequences of Spanish–Indian intermarriage, the demographic collapse and biological imbalance resulting from Old World–New World interchange, and the processes behind the disintegration of traditional cultural patterns. Although her data are documentary and archaeological, Deagan is confronting issues of anthropological relevance.

Conclusion: Archaeology's Future

Archaeology has a vibrant, lively future. The field enjoys enormous public interest, as shown by the popularity of places such as Mesa Verde National Park, television programming, and related college courses. This level of public support suggests that more, not less, archaeology will be needed in the future.

Americanist archaeology has evolved from a pastime of the wealthy to an established scientific discipline. But with these changes have come the realization that studying the human past raises numerous ethical issues. Nobody can practice archaeology in a political or cultural vacuum. As we learn more about how archaeologists go about studying the past, we also confront, in several of the following chapters, some of the ethical issues facing archaeology today.

Summary

- Archaeology today is a lively field that contributes enormously to an understanding of the human condition and as such confronts serious ethical dilemmas.

- The beginnings of an interest in the past can be traced back to the sixth-century BC Babylonian king Nabonidus, who looked at the physical residues of antiquity to answer questions about the past.

- In North America, archaeology began as the pastime of antiquarians, the curious and the wealthy, most of whom lacked formal training.

- Archaeology as a formal discipline dates to the late nineteenth century and was characterized by a scientific approach and rigorous methods of excavation and data collection.

- Early on, archaeology was necessarily concerned with description and with culture history, constructing chronologies of material culture and relating these to the diffusion of ideas and the movements of cultures; but it also drew upon a variety of fields, especially the natural sciences, to help recover and reconstruct the past.

- By the 1950s, archaeology began to move beyond description and chronology to more focus on the reconstruction of past lifeways.

- This trend continued in the 1960s, with the addition of efforts to employ a scientific approach aimed at discovering universal laws and to develop theories to explain the human history uncovered by archaeology.

- Today, archaeology is a diverse field that covers both prehistoric and historic archaeology. The number of archaeologists has grown dramatically since the 1960s, and the field today is diverse, representing many different theoretical perspectives and acknowledging the need to communicate results to the public.

Media Resources

Doing Fieldwork: Archaeological Demonstrations CD-ROM

This CD gives you a vivid glimpse of what it is like to be involved in an archaeological dig . . . without leaving your chair. With this CD, you will see archaeologists involved in actual excavations—many of which are referenced in your Thomas/Kelly text—using a number of the field techniques covered in this chapter. Organized according to the various stages of a live excavation, the CD presents hands-on interactive activities, live-action demonstration videos, and quizzes to help you better understand the processes and techniques that are important to an excavation.

The Companion Website for Archaeology: **Down to Earth,** *Third Edition*

http://anthropology.wadsworth.com/thomas _kelly3e_down/

Supplement your review of this chapter by going to the companion website to take one of the practice quizzes, use the flash cards to master key terms, and check out the many other study aids that are designed to help you succeed in your introductory archaeology course.

2

The Structure of Archaeological Inquiry

Outline

Hayonim Cave in Israel, where archaeologists have made important discoveries in human evolution.

Preview

I N THIS CHAPTER we consider how archaeologists relate to the broader approaches of anthropology, science, and the humanities. Central to this discussion is the concept of *culture;* as you will see, the anthropological use of the term takes on quite a different meaning from its everyday use. We also explore the adaptive and ideational perspectives, two rather different ways of studying culture. These contrasting perspectives also condition the contrast between scientific and humanistic approaches. These opposing, yet complementary, research strategies are each important to understanding diversity and universals among humanity.

Here, we set out the theoretical baseline for the rest of the book:
- Low-level theory is required to make basic observations on archaeological sites and objects.
- Theory at the middle level is what links these archaeological data to human behavior.
- Sometimes archaeologists generate these links by conducting controlled experiments, sometimes by observing living peoples to see how behavior is translated into the archaeological record.
- High-level (or "general") theory aims to answer larger "why" questions.
- Paradigms (particularly cultural materialism and postmodernism) provide the overarching frameworks for understanding the human condition.

We understand that many students are put off by obscure discussions of various "-ologies" and "-isms," but it's important that you understand these basic theoretical points. We'll try to minimize the jargon; in the coming chapters, we think you'll recognize the importance of understanding these basic theoretical concepts.

 Doing Fieldwork CD-ROM: Archaeological Demonstrations
See the "What Is the Question?" and "Reconstructing the Past" sections of the CD-ROM to learn more about topics covered in this chapter.

Introduction

Some 50 years ago, archaeologist Philip Phillips declared, "Archaeology is anthropology or it is nothing." Today, Americanist archaeology remains a subfield of anthropology. Both of us have earned multiple degrees in anthropology, and we both work in departments of anthropology.

In this chapter, we examine the broader anthropological context of archaeology. We also explore how scientific and humanistic perspectives condition archaeological approaches to the past. Although we draw a dichotomy between science and humanism, you should know that most archaeologists are a bit of both; many archaeologists, for example, receive funding for their research from the National Science Foundation and the National Endowment for the Humanities.

So, What's an Anthropological Approach?

Everyone thinks they know what anthropologists do: they study native people and fossils and chimpanzees. They grin from the pages of *National Geographic* mag-

Figure 2-1 The four subfields of anthropology and their areas of study.

azine, make chit-chat on late-night talk shows, and show up on the Discovery Channel. They are Richard Leakey, Jane Goodall, and Don Johanson. Some people think that the late Stephen Jay Gould was an anthropologist (actually, he was a paleontologist and a brilliant historian of science).

But this is a limited vision of anthropology. The truth is that few people seem to know what anthropologists actually do, what anthropologists share, what makes them anthropologists at all. **Anthropology** is tough to pin down because anthropologists do so many different things.

What holds anthropology together is its dogmatic insistence that every aspect of every human society, extant or extinct, counts. For a century, anthropologists have tried to arrive at the fullest possible understanding of human similarities and diversity. Because of this broad-brush approach, anthropology is uniquely qualified to understand what makes humankind distinct from the rest of the animal world. This is not to say that all anthropologists study everything: Margaret Mead never excavated an archaeological site, and Richard Leakey never interviewed a native Lakota speaker. Nobody can hope to do everything well, so anthropologists specialize; archaeologists are anthropologists who specialize in the deceased. But archaeologists still draw upon each of the other subfields of anthropology (not

to mention several other sciences). Before examining how modern archaeology goes about its business, we first must see how anthropologists have carved up the pie of human existence (Figure 2-1).

Biological anthropologists study humans as biological organisms. They study the biological evolution of humans, how *Homo sapiens* came into being, by examining fossil evidence and living primates. Biological anthropologists also study human biological variability, and the field of bioarchaeology studies the past through human skeletal remains (see Chapter 9). Each year, roughly 12 percent of the 250–300 anthropology PhD degrees granted in the United States are awarded in biological anthropology.

anthropology The study of all aspects of humankind—biological, cultural, and linguistic; extant and extinct—employing an all-encompassing holistic approach.

biological anthropology A subdiscipline of anthropology that views humans as biological organisms; also known as physical anthropology.

Cultural anthropologists describe and analyze the culture of living human groups. They do so by personally questioning and observing people while living in their society. Anthropologists study rituals, kinship, religion, politics, art, oral histories, medical practices—everything that people in contemporary societies do, say, or think. They may focus on particular aspects of a society, for example, religious rituals, or they may produce *ethnographies,* comprehensive descriptions of other societies. Archaeologists often make use of these documents to reconstruct the past from its material remains. About 60 percent of the PhDs in anthropology are awarded to cultural anthropologists.

Anthropological linguists study how sounds are made, how sounds create languages, the relationship between language and thought, how linguistic systems change through time, the basic structure of language, and the role of language in the development of culture. They also use language to chart historical relationships and track ancient migrations between now-separate, but linguistically related, populations. Today, linguistic anthropology accounts for only 1 percent of all PhDs in anthropology.

Archaeology accounts for about a quarter of the doctoral degrees awarded in anthropology. Archaeologists also attempt to understand human culture, but their technology and field methods differ radically from those of ethnologists and linguists. Lacking living, breathing informants, archaeologists have formulated a powerful array of techniques for gleaning relevant information from the material remains of the past.

The future of archaeology is bright indeed. Archaeology is a strong element of many graduate programs in anthropology, and undergraduates often find archaeology to be the most lively and exciting program within anthropology. This excitement is due, in part, to the dazzling assortment of new ways to explore the past that we discuss in this text. Archaeology is also the subfield of anthropology most capable of delivering jobs to undergraduates.

The Culture Concept in Anthropology

We have already said that a global, comparative, and holistic perspective tends to unite the diversity within anthropology. But even more than that, it is the concept of **culture** that brings together the subfields of anthropology.

Many disciplines purport to study culture: economics, sociology, linguistics, political science, history, art history, cultural geography, psychology, and so forth. What sets anthropology apart from these fields is a concern with *culture* and not just *cultures.* This overarching investigation into culture traditionally melds many diversified (and sometimes conflicting) concerns into the anthropological perspective. Nearly 50 years ago, Alfred Kroeber and Clyde Kluckhohn compiled more than 200 distinct definitions of culture. But Sir Edward Burnett Tylor's definition of culture appeared in 1871 on the first page of anthropology's first textbook and remains one of the clearest:

> Culture . . . taken in its wide ethnographic sense is that complex whole which includes knowledge, belief, art, morals, law, custom, and any other capabilities and habits acquired by man as a member of society.

Culture in Tylor's sense is *learned*—from parents, peers, teachers, leaders, and others. It is neither biological nor genetic. And under the anthropological definition, all peoples have the same amount of culture. Someone who can recite Shakespeare and who listens to Beethoven's *Moonlight Sonata* is no more (or less) cultural than someone who reads *Reader's Digest* and prefers Flatt and Scruggs's *Foggy Mountain Breakdown.*

Culture creates very different conceptions of life, of what is proper and what is not. Tribal people in New Guinea think it laughable that American women wear earrings, but they think it normal to wear bone or shell nose ornaments for ceremonies. Material factors (such as nutrition) and historical factors (such as contact

cultural anthropology A subdiscipline of anthropology that emphasizes nonbiological aspects: the learned social, linguistic, technological, and familial behaviors of humans.

anthropological linguistics A subdiscipline of anthropology that focuses on human language: its diversity in grammar, syntax, and lexicon; its historical development; and its relation to a culture's perception of the world.

archaeology The study of the past through the systematic recovery and analysis of material remains.

culture An integrated system of beliefs, traditions, and customs that govern or influence a person's behavior. Culture is learned, shared by members of a group, and based on the ability to think in terms of symbols.

with other peoples) help create and affect these differences. Given that archaeology is concerned with how cultures change over time, the concept of learned culture is essential to archaeology.

Culture is also *shared*. By this, we mean that although each person is an individual with their own values and understandings, human groups share some basic ideas about the world and their place in it. Shared ideas, rather than individual variations on them, are the traditional focus of anthropology.

Finally, culture is *symbolic*. Consider the symbolism involved in language: there is no reason that the word *dog* in English means "a household pet," anymore than do *chien, perro,* or *alika* (French, Spanish, and Malagasy). And there is no reason that dogs are necessarily pets. Indeed, in many places in the world, such as Micronesia and Southeast Asia, dogs are feast foods. Many Americans consider this disgusting, but neither the idea of "pet" nor "food" is inherent in a dog—they are symbolic meanings that cultures give to dogs.

So, culture is learned, shared, and symbolic; it provides you with a way to interpret human behavior and the world around you; and it plays a key role in structuring the material record of human behavior—which archaeologists recover.

Anthropologists study culture in two basic ways. An **ideational perspective** focuses on ideas, symbols, and mental structures as driving forces in shaping human behavior. It takes as its lead the idea that culture is a complex set of conceptual designs and shared understandings that underlie the way people act. Culture, in this sense, is principally what humans think, not what they do. This perspective emphasizes ideas, thoughts, and shared knowledge and sees symbols and their meanings as crucial to shaping human behavior. It encompasses material culture insofar as material things reflect symbolic ideas.

The ideational theorist insists on "getting inside a person's head" to seek out the shared meanings of a society. According to the ideational view of culture, one cannot comprehend human behavior without understanding the symbolic code for that behavior. Moreover, according to this view, our interpretation and, in fact, the symbolic meanings that we give to things heavily influence our perception of the world around us.

Alternatively, an **adaptive perspective** isolates technology, ecology, demography, and economics as the key factors driving human behavior, often conceptualizing "culture as a system." Social and cultural differences are viewed not as reflections of symbolic meanings, but rather as responses to the material parameters of life, such as food, shelter, and reproduction. Human behaviors are seen as linked together systemically, such that change in one area, say technology, will result in change in another area, such as social organization. And it is this cultural system—technology, modes of economic organization, settlement patterns, forms of social grouping, and political institutions—that articulates the material needs of human communities with their ecological settings.

Scientific and Humanistic Approaches in Archaeology

Anthropologists also distinguish between scientific and humanistic approaches. This struggle is between two incompatible views of the world (culture again!) and consequently is a disagreement about which tools are best for any particular task.

What's a Scientific Approach?

Science (from the Latin "to know") refers in its broadest sense to a systematic body of knowledge about any field. Although the era of modern science is generally considered to have begun in the Renaissance, the origins of scientific thought extend far back in human history. The **archaeological record**—the documentation of artifacts and their contexts recovered from archaeological sites—has preserved examples of early scientific reasoning: astronomical observations, treatment of disease, calendrical systems, recipes for food and drink. Cave paintings and carvings in bone or stone are often cited as early instances of systematizing knowledge.

ideational perspective The research perspective that defines ideas, symbols, and mental structures as driving forces in shaping human behavior.

adaptive perspective A research perspective that emphasizes technology, ecology, demography, and economics in the definition of human behavior.

science The search for universals by means of established scientific methods of inquiry.

archaeological record The documentation of artifacts and other material remains, along with their contexts recovered from archaeological sites.

So, what exactly is science? A good definition is hard to pin down; perhaps it is easiest to simply list some key characteristics. Lawrence Kuznar (Indiana-Purdue University at Fort Wayne) provides several:

- *Science is empirical, or objective.* Science is concerned with the observable, measurable world. Questions are scientific (1) if they are concerned with detectable properties of things and (2) if the result of observations designed to answer a question cannot be predetermined by the biases of the observer.
- *Science is systematic and explicit.* Scientists gather information in such a way that they collect all data that are relevant to a problem, and they do this in such a way that any trained observer under the same conditions would make the same observations.
- *Science is logical.* It works not only with data, but with ideas that link data with interpretations and with ideas that link other ideas themselves together. These linkages must be based on previously demonstrated principles; otherwise; an argument is a house of cards.
- *Science is explanatory and, consequently, predictive.* Science is concerned with causes. It seeks theories—explanatory statements that allow one not only to predict what will happen under a specified set of conditions, but also to explain why it will happen. The goal of science is to develop theories that can be criticized, evaluated, and eventually modified or replaced by other theories that explain the data better.
- *Science is self-critical and based on testing.* Many people think that science requires white lab coats, supercomputers, and complex equations. Although science might entail these things, it is really about honesty. Scientists always ask themselves, How do I know that I know something? They are professional skeptics, look for biases in their data, and test their methods and ideas against competing ones.
- *Science is public.* A scientist's methods and observations are explicit and available for scrutiny by the public. The source or political implications of ideas are unimportant; what matters in science is that the ideas can be tested by objective methods.

Archaeologists have been doing scientific research for a long time. Consider, for example, how scientific methods were used to solve the "mystery" of the Moundbuilders.

How Science Explains Things: The Moundbuilder Myth

When Europeans arrived on the North American continent in the sixteenth century, they of course met Indians. And in so doing, they confronted a serious issue: Who were these people? This was an important question, for in its answer lay the answer to another question: Did Europeans have the right to take the land?

Later, as colonial Americans began to expand westward through Indian lands, they discovered thousands of mounds and earthworks, especially in the Ohio River and Mississippi River valleys. Some of these mounds were modest in size, but others were enormous: Monk's Mound at the site of Cahokia, in Illinois, just across the Mississippi River from St. Louis, stands nearly 70 feet high and covers as many acres as the largest pyramid in Egypt. Some were conically shaped; others were truncated pyramids. Some were "effigy mounds," fashioned in the shape of animals such as serpents and birds; still others were precise geometric embankments that enclosed many acres.

Today, we know that mounds were constructed as early as 3500 BC in the southern Mississippi River valley and that the practice was fairly widespread in the eastern United States by 1000 BC. But the colonists lacked this knowledge, so they devised a variety of hypotheses to account for the mounds. Some argued that the Moundbuilders were the ancestors of living Indians, but the "race" had degenerated. Others believed that the Moundbuilders had migrated to Mexico, where they became the Toltecs and Aztecs.

But the favored interpretation was that the Moundbuilders were a superior race that had been wiped out by the Indians. Some scholars claimed that this earlier race was Viking; others said the Moundbuilders were Egyptians, Israelites, Chinese, Greeks, Polynesians, Phoenicians, Norwegians, Belgians, Tartars, Saxons, Hindus, Africans, Welsh, and Atlanteans from the lost continent of Atlantis. Anyone, it seemed, could have been the Moundbuilders—except the ancestors of American Indians. More important, it provided colonists with a justification for taking Indian land.

From its beginning, the Moundbuilder myth attracted scrutiny at the highest levels of American society. One of the most notable was Thomas Jefferson (1743–1826), author of the Declaration of Independence, third president of the United States—and the first scientific archaeologist in America.

Jefferson's contribution to Americanist archaeology was presented in his only book, a response to questions sent to him by French scholars. First appearing in 1784, *Notes on the State of Virginia* dealt, in part, with the origin of the aborigines of Virginia and the question of the mounds. Jefferson listed the various Virginian tribes, relating their histories since the settlement of Jamestown in 1607 and incorporating a census of Virginia's current Native American population. Jefferson argued that Native Americans were in no way mentally or physically inferior to the white race, and he rejected all current racist doctrines used to explain Indians' origins. He reasoned that Native Americans were wholly capable of having constructed the prehistoric earthworks of the United States.

Then Jefferson took a critical step: he proceeded to excavate a burial mound located on his property. Today, such a step seems obvious, but Jefferson's contemporaries would have rummaged through libraries and archives rather than dirty their hands with bones, stones, and dirt to answer intellectual issues. This is why Jefferson is often said to be the founder of American archaeology.

Jefferson's account described his method of excavation, the different layers of earth, and the artifacts and the human bones that he encountered. He then tested the **hypothesis** that the bones resulted from warfare. Noting the absence of traumatic wounds and the interments of children, Jefferson rejected the idea that the bones were those of soldiers who had fallen in battle. Noting that some remains were scattered, he surmised that the burials had accumulated through repeated use. Although Jefferson did not come out strongly on either side of the Moundbuilder debate, in 1799 (as president of the American Philosophical Society), he distributed a pamphlet calling for the systematic collection of information on the mounds. A few scholars did dig into mounds, but it was not until 1848 that the systematic compilation that Jefferson desired finally appeared.

Ephraim Squier (1821–1888), a Connecticut civil engineer, surveyor, journalist, and later in life, a politician, teamed up with Edwin Davis (1811–1888), an Ohio physician, to study the mounds. In their 1848 monograph, *Ancient Monuments of the Mississippi Valley,* the first publication of the newly formed Smithsonian Institution, they provided a thorough description of mounds throughout the eastern United States.

Squier and Davis claimed that they did not seek to "sustain" any particular hypothesis about the Moundbuilders, but in the monograph's final pages they suggested that the Moundbuilders were related to the "semi-civilized" nations of Central America (such as the Aztecs), thus providing fodder for supporters of the Moundbuilder hypothesis. By 1873, the president of the Chicago Academy of Sciences thought it "preposterous" that Indians could have built the mounds. And in his 1872 book, *Ancient America,* J. D. Baldwin considered any relationship between the Moundbuilders and Indians to be "absurd."

Because the Moundbuilder issue was of such public interest, Congress insisted that the new Bureau of Ethnology spend $5000 a year—*one-fifth the Bureau's budget*—on mound exploration. Cyrus Thomas (1825–1910), a lawyer, merchant, and entomologist, was selected to lead the inquiry.

Through the Bureau of Ethnology, Cyrus Thomas began his own program of survey and excavation. Over the next 12 years, and with the aid of local affiliates, he compiled data on some 2000 sites in 21 states, finally publishing a 700-page report in 1894. In the beginning, Thomas was a proponent of the Moundbuilder hypothesis, but he nonetheless collected the empirical data to test the hypothesis that the mounds were built by someone other than Native Americans.

Concluding his thorough investigation, Thomas quietly but definitively concluded that "the author believes the theory which attributes these works to the Indians to be the correct one." There was no lost race of Moundbuilders. They had not been overrun by Native Americans. The myth that had helped perpetuate a racist attitude toward Native Americans was simply that—a myth. Sadly, by 1894, the truth about the Moundbuilders had come too late. The Indian Wars were officially over, virtually all Native Americans were confined to reservations, and a change in racist attitudes toward Native Americans was still decades away.

 hypothesis A proposition proposed as an explanation of some phenomena.

The Scientific Method

This brief description of the Moundbuilder myth provides a example of some characteristics of the **scientific method,** which we can reduce to six simple steps:

1. Define a relevant problem.
2. Establish one or more hypotheses.
3. Determine the empirical implications of the hypotheses.
4. Collect appropriate data through observation and/or experimentation.
5. Test the hypothesis by comparing these data with the expected implications.
6. Reject, revise, and/or retest hypotheses as necessary.

We admit that this is an ideal process only, and, in hindsight, we can see that scientific research often does not proceed neatly through each of these steps, although that remains the goal of scientists today.

The Role of Inductive Reasoning

Steps 1 and 2 define a relevant question and translate it into an appropriate hypothesis. The idea is to get beyond a simple description of the known facts and create a hypothesis to account for them. Such hypotheses are generated through **inductive reasoning,** or working from specific facts or observations to general conclusions. The facts as known serve as premises in this case; the hypothesis should not only account for the known facts but should also predict properties of as yet unobserved phenomena. No rules exist for induction. It does not matter from where or how one derives

a hypothesis. What matters is how well the hypothesis accounts for unobserved phenomena.

Jefferson, Squier, and Davis worked in the inductive phase (Steps 1 and 2) of Moundbuilder research. Because no one knew much about the mounds, the first order of business was to gather some facts: How many mounds were there? What was in them? How old were they? What were they made of? From these data, Squier and Davis inductively derived a conclusion: The living Indians of the United States were not descendants of the Moundbuilders.

Science Is Self-Correcting

Squier and Davis, as it turned out, were completely wrong; but the beauty of the scientific method is that it is self-correcting. Science insists that we always ask, Do we really know what we think we know? Squier and Davis thought they were at Step 6 in the process, but in hindsight we can see that they had only inductively formulated a hypothesis. It was left to others to test this idea, to take their conclusion and treat it as a hypothesis.

How does one accomplish Steps 4 and 5—that is, test a hypothesis? Once a hypothesis is defined, the scientific method requires its translation into testable form. Hypotheses *can never be tested directly* because they are abstract statements. Instead, what you verify are the logical material consequences of hypotheses (the empirical implications established in Step 3).

Deductive reasoning is required to uncover these logical outcomes. A deductive argument is one for which the conclusions must be true, given that the premises are true. Such deductive arguments generally take the form of *if . . . then* statements: *if* the hypothesis is true, *then* we expect to observe the following outcomes. Bridging the gap from *if* to *then* is a tricky step.

In the "harder" sciences, these bridging arguments derive from known mathematical or physical properties. In astronomy, for instance, the position of "unknown" stars can be predicted using a chain of mathematical arguments grounded in physics. The classic deductive method begins with an untested hypothesis and converts the generalities into specific predictions based on established mathematical and/or physical theory.

These are sometimes called **bridging arguments.** But how do archaeologists bridge this gap? Where is the well-established body of theory that allows us to transform abstract hypotheses into observable predictions?

scientific method Accepted principles and procedures for the systematic pursuit of secure knowledge. Established scientific procedures involve the following steps: define a relevant problem; establish one or more hypotheses; determine the empirical implications of the hypotheses; collect appropriate data through observation and/or experimentation; compare these data with the expected implications; and revise and/or retest hypotheses as necessary.

inductive reasoning Working from specific observations to more general hypotheses.

deductive reasoning Reasoning from theory to account for specific observational or experimental results.

bridging arguments Logical statements linking observations on the static archaeological record to the dynamic behavior or natural processes that produced it.

Although Cyrus Thomas was never explicit about this, we can see in his reasoning the simple bridging arguments he employed for his version of Step 5. For example, *if* American Indians did not know about mound building, *then* there should be no explorer accounts of mound building by Indians. Or, *if* the mounds were built by a long-vanished race, *then* they should be considerably older than the known age of Indian culture. And, *if* metal artifacts in mounds were signs of a "superior" Moundbuilder culture, *then* the manufacturing technology associated with them should be absent from later Indian culture. In doing this, Thomas laid out the criteria whereby he could falsify the Moundbuilder hypothesis. (We return to bridging arguments when we discuss middle-range research in Chapter 7.)

For Thomas, "testing" meant collecting data, analyzing it, publishing it, and openly evaluating it against the competing hypotheses. The **testability** of a hypothesis is critical. An idea is testable if the hypothesis' implications can be measured in some fashion *with the same results by different observers*. That is, the observation has to be independent of whoever is doing the observing. We have to know that you would make the same observations that we would make.

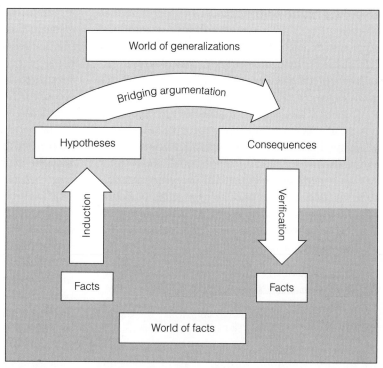

Figure 2-2 The scientific cycle. *After Kemeny (1959), 86.*

Science Is Reiterative

The scientific method is actually more of a cycle because it is repetitive, as shown in Figure 2-2. Step 6 (testing, rejecting, or revising the hypothesis) normally leads back to Step 1 (redefining the problem at hand). Figure 2-2 shows the same process with more emphasis on the kinds of reasoning that researchers use to move through the steps.

Scientific cycles commence in the world of facts—in the Moundbuilder example, the amassed data from hundreds of excavations and maps plus contemporary accounts plus bogus artifacts. Through the process of induction, these facts are probed, and hypotheses are devised to account for what is already known. But because hypotheses are general declarations, they cannot be tested against further facts until they are trans-

lated into their logical consequences, through the judicious use of bridging arguments.

The scientific cycle thus begins and ends with facts. But these newly discovered facts themselves will suggest new hypotheses, and, once again, inductive reasoning will lead from the world of facts to the world of abstraction, initiating a new cycle of investigation. As a method, science implies a continual spiral in knowledge.

Science Is Not Infallible

Philosophers of science generally agree that (1) there is no single right way to do science and (2) a scientific approach cannot guarantee right answers.

It is clear, for instance, that the Moundbuilder hypothesis was not drawn directly and inductively from sterile archaeological facts. This idea was widespread well before anyone knew much about the mounds because the myth facilitated and justified what colonists wanted—seizure of Indian land. Science is

testability The degree to which one's observations and experiments can be reproduced.

embedded in the scientist's culture and so it is not free of cultural biases. The social, cultural, and political context of archaeology influences its theories.

Because of these biases, some archaeologists reject scientific methods in archaeology. The argument often goes like this: Because archaeology is not precise in the same sense as are the physical sciences, then the methods of science are inappropriate (or even harmful) when applied to the study of humans. Although these claims contain some truth, most blatant attacks on the scientific methods are directed at exaggerated caricatures that depict science as claiming infallibility, a claim rejected by even the most "scientific" of archaeologists. But this sense still leads some archaeologists to adopt a different approach.

What's a Humanistic Approach?

In general, **humanism** tends to emphasize the dignity and worth of the individual. Humanistic-style inquiry begins with the premise that all people possess a capacity for self-realization through reason. Unlike the purely scientific approach, which stresses objectivity and independent testing, humanists believe that their scholarship should proceed in precisely the opposite direction: By stressing the intuitive and subjective, humanists seek strength and understanding in the very biases that science seeks to circumvent.

Virtually all modern archaeologists, whether "humanist" or "scientific," believe in careful scholarship, in generalizations backed by firm data, in honesty, and in giving full consideration to data that run contrary to one's favored ideas. But archaeologists are not emotionally or politically neutral data-gathering machines. Archaeologists will always make moral or ethical judgments about the past because archaeologists are "historically situated," meaning simply that they are products of the times in which they live. This is why many archaeologists bring a humanistic perspective to their understanding of the past, and, in this section, we see why most archaeologists are both scientists and humanists.

The primary distinction between scientific and humanistic approaches occurs over the issue of **objectivity.** If you believe that archaeology is "mostly objective," then you probably lean more toward the scientific side. You probably see a clear-cut separation between the observer and what is observed—the "facts" of archaeology. And you probably search for an inherent regularity to cultural behavior (which you might term "laws"). You probably believe that the world out there can be known in a manner more or less independent of your ability to perceive and engage it. Finally, you likely are more inclined to take an adaptive perspective on human cultural behavior, looking for explanations in factors that are "outside" the culture—that is, in the environment, in biology, in technology, or in demography.

But if you think that archaeology is "mostly subjective," then you are likely more comfortable with humanistic perspectives, which emphasize that the observer and the observed can never really be separated, that our knowledge of the past mostly depends on who is doing the observing. You probably mistrust conventional science and feel more comfortable with an ideational perspective. You may be more interested in approaches that focus on what people think rather than on what they do. You are probably more intrigued by human languages, cultural values, and artistic achievements of other cultures.

Levels of Archaeological Theory

Now it's time to address the notion of **theory,** a common term used in several different ways. In the more casual, popular usage, a theory is simply an idea. Sometimes the word *theory* is used as a put-down, referring to an untested explanation that the speaker believes clearly to be false. For example, some might speak of Erich von Däniken's goofy *Chariots of the Gods* "theory," in which he argues that major accomplish-

---

humanism A doctrine, attitude, or way of life that focuses on human interests and values. In general, a humanistic approach tends to reject a search for universals and stress instead the importance of the individual's lived experience.

objectivity The attempt to observe things as they actually are, without prejudging or falsifying observations in light of some preconceived view of the world—reducing subjective factors to a minimum.

theory An explanation for observed, empirical phenomena. It is empirical and seeks to explain the relationships between variables; it is an answer to a "why" question.

ments in prehistory, such as construction of the pyramids, were directed by extraterrestrial beings.

A theory may also be a set of untested principles or propositions—in other words, theory as opposed to practice. Thus a new invention to harness solar energy might work "in theory" (that is, on paper), but would require extensive field testing before one could decide whether it was a successful design. If the solar device functioned as expected, the theory would be valid; if the device failed, scientists would consider the theory behind it invalid.

Although both usages are common, neither has much to do with scientific theories, which are statements that purport to explain observed, empirical phenomena. Theories are answers to "why" questions. These questions occur at different levels; we will call them low level, middle level, and high level. We distinguish the different levels not by complexity or difficulty, but by their functions in the process of archaeological inquiry.

Low-Level Theory

Low-level theories help make the observations that emerge from hands-on archaeological fieldwork. Although you may be accustomed to thinking of such observations as self-evident data or facts, we will see why even the baseline facts of archaeology are themselves really the results of theories. But what, exactly, are those baseline facts? What, in effect, are archaeological data? To answer this question, we introduce an archaeological site that crops up later in this text.

Gatecliff Shelter is a prehistoric **rockshelter** in Nevada where people camped now and again beneath a shallow overhang over a period of some 7000 years (Figure 2-3). David Thomas found Gatecliff in 1970, and he worked there with an interdisciplinary team that, throughout the 1970s, excavated the deposits in the shelter.

DOING FIELDWORK: ARCHAEOLOGICAL DEMONSTRATIONS CD-ROM

Go to the Live-Action Demonstration in the "What Is the Question?" section of the CD-ROM to view a video on Gatecliff Shelter, as well as Butler Cave.

Gatecliff was discovered by old-fashioned, dogged fieldwork (see Chapter 3 to find out how). The excavation was "vertical"—in some places nearly 40 feet deep, with cultural deposits stacked up within a floor area of about 300 square feet. Buried within Gatecliff Shelter were thousands of artifacts: projectile points, bone awls, basketry made of willow splints, grinding stones, small pieces of slate incised with enigmatic geometric designs, woven sagebrush bark mats, stone scrapers, shells and turquoise used as ornaments. Gatecliff also contained objects not made by humans—**ecofacts**—which are items relating to the natural environment, such as bighorn sheep bones, charcoal, piñon nut hulls, and pollen. We also encountered **features**—pits, hearths, rodent burrows—which are cultural and noncultural things that archaeologists measure, draw, photograph, and sample, but that they cannot take home in a bag.

The point here is simple but important: After nearly a decade of excavating at Gatecliff, Thomas excavated no data at all. Why would any archaeologist waste a decade digging holes that produce no data?

Thomas found no data at Gatecliff because archaeologists do not excavate data. Rather, they excavate objects. **Data** are *observations made on those objects.* Those observations are critical to making *interpretations* of the objects. Observations answer one or more questions that permit the archaeologists to make interpretations; data, therefore, are observations that allow us to make interpretations. They tell us *why* something is what we think it is. And this means that the observations we make on objects, as well as the interpretations of those observations, *are all theory driven.* This

low-level theories The observations and interpretations that emerge from hands-on archaeological field and lab work.

rockshelter A common type of archaeological site, consisting of a rock overhang that is deep enough to provide shelter but not deep enough to be called a cave (technically speaking, a cave must have an area of perpetual darkness).

ecofact Plant or animal remains found in an archaeological site.

feature The nonportable evidence of technology; usually fire hearths, architectural elements, artifact clusters, garbage pits, soil stains, and so on.

data Relevant observations made on objects that then serve as the basis for study and discussion.

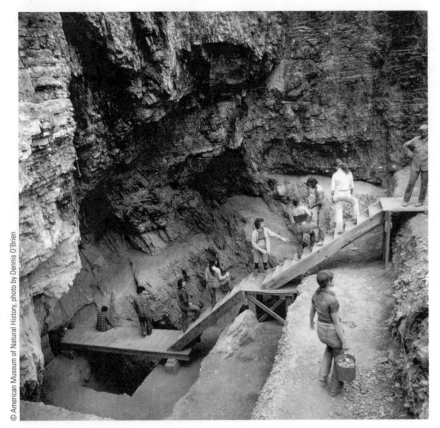

© American Museum of Natural History, photo by Dennis O'Brien

Figure 2-3 Gatecliff Shelter, late in the excavation: removing deposits through a bucket brigade method.

unit B-5, 56 cm below the surface." Why are these theoretical statements? Because each of them is actually based on a "why" question: Why do we know that something is obsidian? Because the stone has certain characteristics that fit a definition of obsidian (a dark volcanic glass) and that clearly differentiate it from other stone types, such as chert or quartzite. Why do we know the length, weight, and provenience? Because these measurements were made using digital instruments whose ability to measure things reliably is based on theories from the field of electronics.

Low-level theory is critical because it allows archaeologists to know that their data are comparable. However, these basic observations can become the focus of scrutiny if, for instance, archaeologists try to determine when humans began to use fire intentionally (perhaps some hundreds of thousands of years ago). In this case, what constitutes an *intentional* hearth becomes of more than passing interest. The same is true when archaeologists try to determine whether some chipped stones are tools or simply rocks that Mother Nature has broken in fortuitous ways (more than one archaeologist has been fooled). When archaeologists give this sort of attention to inferences made from observations, they move into the realm of middle-level theory.

is why it is important to understand the different levels of theory in archaeology. Knowing this, we can return to theory building.

Low-level theory in archaeology concerns generating facts or data about objects. Some data consist of physical observations. For example, "Artifact 20.2/4683 is (a) made of obsidian, (b) 21.5 mm long, and (c) weighs 2.1 grams." This statement contains three pieces of data—observations made on an archaeological object (the number 20.2/4683 is the item's unique catalog number for identification). Other observations might be contextual: "Artifact 20.2/4683 was found in

Middle-Level Theory

Middle-level theory (or, more commonly, "middle-range theory") links archaeological data with the relevant aspects of human behavior or natural processes (for example, the actions of water or animals) that produced them. This is the unique realm of archaeology because it moves from the archaeologically observable (the "facts")

middle-level (or middle-range) theory Hypothesis that links archaeological observations with the human behavior or natural processes that produced them.

Figure 2-4 Kelly (in middle) conducts ethnoarchaeological research in Madagascar.

their own stone tools in order to see how stoneworking techniques (which are not directly visible archaeologically) are translated into archaeologically observable evidence (such as flaking scars, breakage patterns, and by-products). Others conduct middle-level research as **ethnoarchaeology,** in which they observe present-day societies (as shown in Figure 2-4) to see how behavior, such butchering techniques translates into the archaeological record. **Taphonomy** studies the role that natural processes, such as soil formation or animal behavior, play in the formation of an archaeological site. This helps archaeologists distinguish between the effects of human behavior and natural factors.

to the archaeologically invisible (human behavior, cultural beliefs, or natural processes of the past). Here the archaeologist answers questions such as "*Why* do we think that this stone tool was used for scraping wood (and not hides)?" or "*Why* do we know that these bones came from an animal hunted and butchered by humans, and not killed and eaten by lions?"

The archaeological record is the *contemporary* evidence left by people of the past. As such, the archaeological record is composed only of static objects—the artifacts, ecofacts, and features that have survived the passage of time. Those objects are the products of two things: human behavior and natural processes. Our job is to infer the long-gone behavior and processes from the static results—the objects we recover from archaeological sites.

Archaeologists conducting research at the middle level seek situations in which they can observe (1) ongoing human behavior or natural processes and (2) the material results of that behavior or those processes. There are three areas of middle-level research (which we discuss in more detail in Chapter 7). In **experimental archaeology,** we use controlled experiments to determine the effect of one archaeologically invisible variable on an archaeologically observable one. For example, archaeologists conduct controlled experiments in which they manufacture

High-Level Theory

Then there is **high-level (or general) theory,** which seeks answers to larger "why" questions. *Why* did hunter-gatherers become agriculturalists? *Why* do some societies fight whereas others cooperate? *Why* did some societies evolve stratified social and political systems whereas others remained egalitarian? This is archaeology's ultimate objective; low- and middle-level research is necessary to attain this goal. High-level theory goes beyond the archaeological specifics to address

experimental archaeology Experiments designed to determine the archaeological correlates of ancient behavior; may overlap with both ethnoarchaeology and taphonomy.

ethnoarchaeology The study of contemporary peoples to determine how human behavior is translated into the archaeological record.

taphonomy The study of how organisms become part of the fossil record; in archaeology it primarily refers to the study of how natural processes produce patterning in archaeological data.

high-level (or general) theory Theory that seeks to answer large "why" questions.

the "big questions" of concern to many social and historical sciences. High-level theory applies to all intellectual inquiry about the human condition.

Some general theories stress environmental adaptation, some emphasize biological factors, and some involve only cultural causality; others try to combine these.

Paradigms in Archaeology

We now turn to the concept of **paradigm**. A paradigm provides the overarching framework for understanding some research problem. Paradigms are not specific to archaeology, but apply to intellectual inquiry in general. A paradigm is a lot like "culture" because just as culture provides you with some idea about what is (or is not) acceptable behavior, a paradigm also guides a researcher's path of inquiry. Your paradigm defines your questions and data by drawing our attention to some facts and blinding us to others.

Just as all humans participate in a culture, all archaeologists operate within a paradigm, whether they are aware of it or not. Without a paradigm, nothing would make sense. So, although a paradigm can give you an inaccurate bias, our goal cannot be to free ourselves of any paradigm. Instead, we simply must be aware of the paradigm we are using and always ask ourselves if that paradigm is the most useful for the kind of theory we are trying to construct or for the problem we are trying to solve.

We can characterize Americanist archaeology in terms of two paradigms: the processual and the postprocessual. Processual archaeology is embedded within cultural materialism, and postprocessual archaeology is embedded within postmodernism. We present the basics of cultural materialism and sketch its importance to archaeology's processual paradigm. We then look at the premises of postmodernism to see how it gave rise to archaeology's postprocessual paradigm.

Cultural Materialism

Although its roots extend back at least a century, modern cultural materialism is largely associated with Marvin Harris (1927–2001), a cultural anthropologist, who gave it its name.

Cultural materialism posits that environmental, technological, and economic factors—the *material* conditions of existence—are the most powerful and pervasive determinants of human behavior. By explicitly (and exclusively) embracing a scientific framework to examine the effects of material factors on human societies, cultural materialists reject humanist, ideational approaches and advocate the adaptive view of culture discussed earlier.

Cultural materialism focuses on behavioral events, which must be distinguished from mental events because they are observed in different ways. Modern human behavior is available to the scientific community in a form that can be observed, measured, photographed, and objectively described. We observe human thought, the events of the mind, only indirectly. Although distinct relationships exist between behavior and thought, we must demonstrate these associations, not assume them. This is obviously true for archaeology—given that the people who left the objects behind are long dead—and it is also true for cultural anthropology, because we must still infer ideas from speech and other behaviors.

Although behavior is symbolic—actions carry meaning to the one doing the action and to those observing it—cultural materialists concentrate on the observable behavioral outcomes: warfare, marriage, dietary patterns and food taboos, settlement and demographic trends, and gender roles. It contains within it a wide variety of sub-paradigms—some that take an explicitly evolutionary approach and others that are more ecological.

Cultural materialists use three concepts in their approach: infrastructure, structure, and superstructure. **Infrastructure** denotes those elements considered most important to satisfying basic human needs:

paradigm The overarching framework, often unstated, for understanding a research problem. It is a researcher's "culture."

cultural materialism A research paradigm that takes a scientific approach and that emphasizes the importance of material factors—such as environment, population density, subsistence, and technology—in understanding change and diversity in human societies.

infrastructure In cultural materialism, the elements most important to satisfying basic human survival and well-being—food, shelter, reproduction, health—which are assumed to lie at the causal heart of every sociocultural system.

food, shelter, reproduction, and health. These demographic, technological, economic, and ecological processes are assumed to lie at the causal heart of every sociocultural system. The infrastructure mediates a culture's interactions with the natural and social environment through the following two mechanisms.

At the next level, the sociocultural system's **structure** includes behaviors that are less directly related to the acquisition of food and other basic necessities of life, such as family structure, division of labor, enculturation, age and sex roles, hierarchies, and sanctions. It also includes political organizations, factions, clubs, associations, corporations, division of labor, taxation, tribute, political socialization and education, social divisions and hierarchies, discipline, police/military control, and warfare.

Finally, **superstructure** refers to a society's values, aesthetics, rules, beliefs, religions, and symbols, which can be behaviorally manifested as art, music, dance, literature, advertising, religious rituals, sports, games, hobbies, and even science.

Distinguishing cultural materialism from other approaches is the **principle of infrastructural determinism,** which holds (1) that human society strives to meet those needs most important to the survival and well-being of human individuals (primarily sex, sleep, nutrition, and shelter); responses to these needs occur directly in the realm of infrastructure; and (2) that the infrastructure determines the rest of the sociocultural system. To cultural materialists, social change is largely a product of change in the infrastructure. Though clearly interrelated, the infrastructure, structure, and superstructure influence one another differentially, and cultural materialists assign causal priority to the modes of production and reproduction. Cultural materialists argue that their paradigm is better than alternatives in conforming to the canons of acceptable scientific explanation.

Processual Archaeology: Materialism at Work in Archaeology

The **processual paradigm** is cultural materialism applied to the study of the past. It includes the new archaeology we described in Chapter 1, as well as the brands of evolutionary archaeology practiced by many Americanist archaeologists today. For now, it is only important that you understand the basics of the

processual paradigm and how they differ from those of postprocessual archaeology.

Remember from Chapter 1 that processual archaeology grew out of dissatisfaction with the increasingly sterile cultural-historical and largely descriptive archaeology of the 1950s. Processual archaeologists correctly noted that culture history, as a paradigm, was inadequate for the description of ancient lives, as well as for the explanation of how cultures operate and change. Thus, the processual paradigm has several key characteristics:

1. *Processual archaeology emphasizes evolutionary generalizations, not historical specifics, and it downplays the importance of the individual.* The processual agenda is scientific rather than historical, emphasizing regularities and correlations. Processual archaeology explicitly associates itself with the generalizing social sciences, such as economics, political science, sociology, and ethnology. This evolutionary perspective holds that specific human decisions and specific historical sequences were not of particular interest or significance in their own right.

2. *Processual archaeology views culture from a systemic perspective and defines culture as humanity's extrasomatic means of adaptation.* The ultimate goal of processual archaeology is to produce law-like generalizations that could be useful for understanding modern society.

structure The behavior that supports choices made at the level of the infrastructure, including the organization of reproduction, production, exchange, family structure, division of labor, age and sex roles, political units, social organization, and warfare.

superstructure A group's values, aesthetics, rules, beliefs, religions, and symbols, which can be behaviorally manifested as art, music, dance, literature, advertising, religious rituals, sports, games, hobbies, and even science.

principle of infrastructural determinism Argument that the infrastructure lies at the causal heart of every sociocultural system, that human society responds to factors that directly affect survival and well-being, and that such responses determine the rest of the sociocultural system.

processual paradigm The paradigm that explains social, economic, and cultural change as primarily the result of adaptation to material conditions; these conditions (for example, the environment) are assumed to take causal priority over ideational factors in explaining change.

ARCHAEOLOGICAL ETHICS
Does Archaeology Put Native Americans on Trial?

We've mentioned that many American Indians do not trust anthropologists, including archaeologists. This is especially odd because anthropologists have long been the champions of Native American legal and cultural rights; many anthropologists, for example, testified on behalf of tribes in the 1950s and 1960s when Indian land claims were decided in courts, and many work to maintain Indian rights and languages today.

One problem is that anthropologists often take a scientific perspective toward American Indian culture, while Native Americans more commonly express humanistic views. Many Native Americans see a "scientific" approach to understanding their history as denigrating their own indigenous versions of history. This disconnect is particularly evident in the research regarding American Indian origins. Biological and linguistic data demonstrate without a doubt that the ancestors of Native Americans migrated from Asia at least 13,500 years ago. This position stands in stark contrast to most Native American origin stories; none of the various religions of Native North Americans explicitly state that "people came from Asia," and many Native Americans consider saying so to be an affront to their reli-gious beliefs (just as the idea of evolution is insulting to fundamentalist Christians). Some scholars agree, suggesting that archaeologists have no right to ask questions that put Native American religion on trial.

We disagree with this implied censorship and, more to the point, think that asking questions about Native American origins does not challenge American Indian (or any other) religion. Science evaluates claims about the *material* world, and religion is fundamentally about the *nonmaterial* world. When religions make claims about the material world, these can be evaluated with scientific methods. If proven false, does this mean that the religion is also false? If scientific archaeology holds that the ancestors of Native American people came from Asia, does this prove that Native American religions are wrong?

Absolutely not. We can neither prove nor disprove claims of the nonmaterial world using a method that evaluates claims about the material world. Science merely encourages one to look deeper into religious beliefs, to find a significance that goes beyond mere space and time. In this way, scientific and humanistic perspectives can be compatible

---

3. *Explanation in processual archaeology is explicitly scientific.* Initially, the processual agenda depended on deductive models grounded in the hard sciences and emphasized the importance of absolute objectivity. More recent formulations stress the interplay between induction and deduction and the relative objectivity of observations.

4. *Processual archaeology attempts to remain ethically neutral and claims to be explicitly nonpolitical.* Processual archaeology tries to provide positive evidence about the past. Politics of the present have nothing to do with the ancient past and processual archaeologists avoid sub-jectivity. The processual agenda avoids passing moral judgments on people of the present or the past.

At least half of Americanist archaeologists today pursue the processual paradigm in one form or another. This paradigm appeals to many archaeologists because cultural materialism emphasizes technology, economy, environment, and demography—those aspects of human existence that leave the clearest traces in the archaeological record. But cultural materialism may also be popular because it suggests that the world and cultural change result from orderly processes—an idea that is attractive to many but that the postmodern paradigm challenges.

Postmodernism

Although *postmodernism* is more often used to describe literary and artistic styles, it helped structure the late twentieth-century format of the social sciences as well. Just as cultural materialism informs processual archaeology, postmodernism underlies the post-processual paradigm of Americanist archaeology.

To understand **postmodernism** you need to know that it was a response to European philosophical ideas that reigned from the seventeenth through nineteenth centuries—an exciting period known as the **Enlightenment.** The Enlightenment, or "Age of Reason," marked a shift in Western thought when thinkers began to develop objective sciences and universal standards for morality and law. The Enlightenment worldview held that rational thought was the key to progress, and that technology would free people from the control of nature and permit the development of moral and spiritual virtues.

Enlightenment scholars saw the world as knowable through science. They argued that scientific thought would always produce truth, and truth was always right (and good). This was a period of great optimism, when scholars threw off the fetters of religious dogma and made scientific discoveries that helped humanity control the perversities of nature. Enlightenment thinkers appealed to the ideas of linear progress, absolute truth, planning of ideal social orders, and the standardization of knowledge. Thomas Jefferson was an Enlightenment scholar; Sigmund Freud, Karl Marx, and Charles Darwin, all of whom saw society as improving (although for different reasons), were scholars of the late Enlightenment—a period that sociologists refer to as "modern." This gives us the "modern" in the term *postmodern.*

Serious cracks began to appear in this system of thought in the early twentieth century, especially after World War I. The "Great War" showed many people that the science and rational thought, which was supposed to produce a better society, could also produce the horrors of tank and gas warfare. Many young intellectuals felt betrayed, for the world was not as they thought it was.

Postmodernism arose in the latter half of the twentieth century, especially after the 1960s. Andy Warhol was a postmodern artist, and Jorge Luis Borges and Thomas Pynchon were postmodern writers. Modernists believed that art, literature, and science could help people find moral unity and coherence in the world. But postmodernism sees no forward movement to history, no "grand narrative," and no promise of a brighter future made possible by science. Indeed, postmodernism argues that there really is no truth and no coherence *except* that all understanding and meaning is "historically situated," only a product of the time in which we live.

Deconstruction and the Maya

Just as science was the primary tool of the Enlightenment, **deconstruction** is the primary tool of postmodernism. Coined by French philosopher Jacques Derrida (1930–2004) in the 1960s, the term refers to efforts to expose the assumptions behind the allegedly scientific (objective and systematic) search for knowledge.

Here's an archaeological example. The Maya civilization flourished in portions of Central America and Mexico, reaching a zenith about AD 700. The Maya constructed magnificent centers with stone pyramids, surrounded by thousands of households. These complexes were the center of a rich ceremonial life, places where kings recorded their exploits in hieroglyphics on stone monuments called **stelae** (Figure 2-5). The society ran according to a set of complex calendars and supported its agriculture with water storage systems.

postmodernism A paradigm that rejects grand historical schemes in favor of humanistic approaches that appreciate the multiple voices of history. It seeks to see how colonialism created our vision of the world we occupy today; it eschews science and argues against the existence of objective truth.

Enlightenment A Western philosophy that advocated ideas of linear progress, absolute truth, science, rational planning of ideal social orders, and the standardization of knowledge. It held that rational thought was the key to progress; that science and technology would free people from the oppression of historical traditions of myth, religion, and superstition; and that the control of nature through technology would permit the development of moral and spiritual virtues.

deconstruction Efforts to expose the assumptions behind the alleged objective and systematic search for knowledge. A primary tool of postmodernism.

stelae Stone monuments erected by Maya rulers to record their history in rich images and hieroglyphic symbols. These symbols can be read and dated.

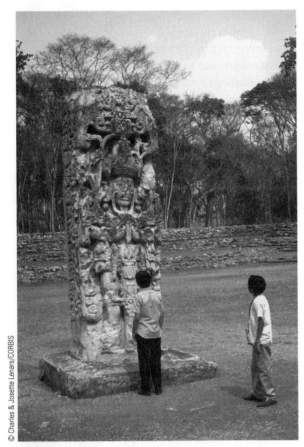

© Charles & Josette Lenars/CORBIS

Figure 2-5 Stela B at Copán, Honduras; erected AD 731. It depicts the ruler, 18-Rabbit.

By AD 900, however, people had abandoned the centers, which were gradually consumed by the jungle. Although the Maya remained (they are still there today), Maya civilization had collapsed. Why?

Processual archaeologists proposed many explanations. These fell into three areas: war, environmental degradation, and the abuse of power by political elites. Anthropologist Richard Wilk (Indiana University) showed that these three explanations waxed and waned in popularity, as indicated by articles published in pro-

fessional journals, in relation to major U.S. political events. Warfare as an explanation began in 1962, the beginning of the Vietnam War, and grew in popularity until the end of that war. During the ecology movement of the mid-1970s, explanations that focused on environmental degradation became prominent. And after 1976, in the aftermath of the Watergate fiasco and historic resignation of Richard Nixon, abuse of government power was the favored explanation.

Wilk argues that by deconstructing archaeological thinking about the Maya collapse, we can see the degree to which modern political events affected the views of archaeologists working on this problem. There is nothing new in suggesting that archaeologists are products of their own culture: people who consider themselves scientists (like Wilk) have always tried to discover biases, remove their effects, and move on. What is new in postmodernism is that deconstruction is often the *goal* of research. Postmodernism is the foundation of archaeology's postprocessual paradigm.

Postprocessual Archaeology: Postmodernism at Work in Archaeology

Although it had forerunners in the United States and elsewhere, the formal **postprocessual paradigm** arose largely in Great Britain and Europe, nurtured by archaeologists such as Ian Hodder (Stanford University). Adherents today can be found on both sides of the Atlantic. We can perhaps best characterize postprocessual archaeology by contrasting it with processual archaeology. We list some of these characteristics following; but note that postprocessual archaeologists, like their processual colleagues, have ameliorated the initial, extreme position in recent years.

1. *Postprocessual archaeology rejects the processual search for universal laws.* Consistent with postmodern interpretivism, the postprocessual critique holds that such universals of human behavior simply do not exist.

2. *Postprocessual archaeology rejects the systemic view of culture and focuses on an ideational perspective.* Postprocessual archaeologists ridiculed the "systems" approach of the processual paradigm as "the robotic view of the human past." To postprocessualists, a society is comprised of

postprocessual paradigm A paradigm that focuses on humanistic approaches and rejects scientific objectivity; it sees archaeology as inherently political and is more concerned with interpreting the past than with testing hypotheses. It sees change as arising largely from interactions between individuals operating within a symbolic and/or competitive system.

RAPID REVIEW — Some Contrasts between Processual and Postprocessual Archaeology

Processual Archaeology	Postprocessual Archaeology
Emphasizes evolutionary generalizations and regularities, not historical specifics; prefers materialist approaches	Rejects the search for universal laws and regularities; prefers ideational approaches
Views culture from a systemic perspective and defines culture as adaptation	Rejects the systemic view of culture; focuses on the individual's actions and their role in creating social change
Explanation is explicitly scientific and objective	Rejects scientific methods and objectivity as too limiting
Attempts to remain ethically neutral; claims to be explicitly nonpolitical	Argues that all archaeology is unavoidably political; takes political positions and concerns itself with analyzing the presentation of the past

individuals, groups, families, and classes, whose goals are not necessarily identical and whose interests and actions are commonly in conflict with the "adaptive" success and "functional" needs of the cultural system as a whole. This perspective allows for internal social dynamics as a significant engine of change, rather than merely a passive agent in systemic change instituted from the "outside."

3. *Postprocessual archaeology rejects objectivity and explicitly scientific methods.* Postprocessual critics point out that much of the early processual research rigidly adhered to rote rules of evidence and interpretation and in so doing shut themselves off to alternative interpretations. Consequently, many postprocessualists distrust science in any form.

4. *Postprocessual archaeology argues that all archaeology is political.* Postprocessual archaeologists place the political implications of their research front and center. For many, this means that the study of the *presentation* of the past, in museums, scientific publications, and popular media, is as critical as the study of the past itself, if not more so.

Processual-Plus?

Considerable tension still exists between those who call themselves processualists and those who prefer the postprocessual label. But much intellectual change occurs through the process of "thesis–antithesis–synthesis." An analogy to a pendulum clock is useful here. One paradigm pushes the clock's pendulum to one side. In response, another paradigm pulls it to the other. And in the end, the pendulum comes to rest in the middle. In recent years, many (perhaps the majority) of Americanist archaeologists have listened to debates between hard-core processual and postprocessual archaeologists and found a middle road that Michelle Hegmon (Arizona State University) calls "processual-plus" (see "Profile of an Archaeologist: An Academic Archaeologist").

Hegmon points out that many archaeologists adhere to some form of scientific inquiry as a way to evaluate ideas; few subscribe to the extreme postmodern idea that we cannot know anything true about the past. And many still feel that material factors such as technology, subsistence, and environment play critical roles in how human societies have changed. But few seek universals; instead, many seek generalities, patterns that point to

PROFILE OF AN ARCHAEOLOGIST
An Academic Archaeologist

Michelle Hegmon (pictured on left) is a professor of anthropology at Arizona State University.

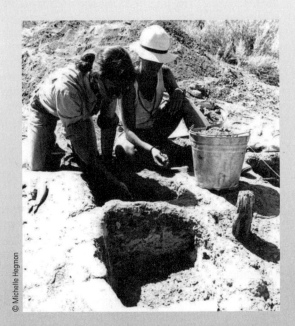

© Michelle Hegmon

Two tenets are key to my brand of archaeology, processual-plus. The first is open-mindedness, a willingness to set theoretical egos aside, and the second is recognition of the power of theory, words and labels to shape our understanding of the past.

I work in the Mimbres region of New Mexico, a place that is famous for its pottery. In my first archaeology class, Steve Plog described how ceramic designs could tell us about the social lives of people 1000 years ago. And that's what caught my interest: solving puzzles and learning from artifacts.

I began graduate school in 1981 at the University of Michigan—renowned for its processual approach—and in 1982, postprocessualism appeared. By the time I finished my dissertation, which returned me to my early interest in pottery design, I had developed much of what I now call processual-plus: a melding of postprocessual's interest in symbols and meaning with processual concerns regarding systematic generalizations.

At the conclusion of my PhD defense, my committee stood to congratulate me. I stood, and (I am only 5 foot 3) literally looked up at the tall men surrounding me. Until then, I had paid little attention to gender. My mother, a physicist and feminist, had fought those battles for me; her generation made it possible for women in mine to move ahead with relative ease. For me, Southwest archaeology was a supportive environment. At a seminar on engendering Southwest archaeology, I joined a group of colleagues who pushed the intellectual envelope. As my mother's daughter, I assumed prehistoric women's domestic labor (such as corn-grinding) was drudgery, but others assumed it was highly respected. This disagreement made clear the importance of labels and of prior experience. Gender research—a key component of processual-plus—also taught me that feminism still has much to do.

I've done most of my professional research as part of the Eastern Mimbres Archaeological Project (EMAP), which Peggy Nelson and I began in 1993. The rich floodplain of the Mimbres River of southwest New Mexico is known for its Classic Mimbres villages, many of which were depopulated at a time of low rainfall around AD 1130. EMAP is a collaboration, and becoming part of it is one of the best things I have ever done. Peggy Nelson's specialties include lithic technology and ecology, while mine are ceramic style and social theory, but rather than dividing these realms we have brought our perspectives together to delve into issues such as socioecology and the technology of style. As teachers, we are preparing the next generation of young scholars to move ahead in a world of both women and men.

With our colleagues at Arizona State University, we are also embarking on several interdisciplinary projects, that, by their very nature, draw on data and theory more vast than any of us can master single-handedly. As such, they must be collaborations in which we set our theoretical egos aside.

how material factors may constrain or channel, but not determine, cultural change.

These same archaeologists also recognize the importance of other factors. All archaeologists know that artifacts carried symbolic meanings for people in the past and that humans respond to their situations in terms of cultural understandings of the world. Likewise, few see the details of history (and prehistory) as minor matters whose effects can easily be subtracted to discover the evolutionary processes behind them. History is a product of evolutionary processes, but it is also the result of contingencies—such as environmental disasters, particular political decisions, or cultural views.

And most archaeologists recognize that all of history results from the actions of individuals. In one way or another, an understanding of individual actions and motivations for those actions is critical to understanding the cultural evolutionary processes at work. Especially important has been a trend to look at gender, at the roles that men and women played in ancient societies. And, finally, most archaeologists today recognize the links between politics and their research. Although few approach their research for purely political purposes, most archaeologists at least understand the political context of their research.

The Structure of Archaeological Inquiry

A century of archaeological practice has taught us a great deal about how archaeologists need to go about doing archaeology. So, what did we learn from this?

Figure 2-6 presents a model of the process of archaeological inquiry. This synthesis is similar to the model of the scientific cycle, presented earlier, but is presented in a format specific to archaeology.

The entire process of archaeological inquiry takes place within a box labeled "Social, Cultural, Political Context." This arrangement recognizes that no scientist can step outside his or her culture—should we try that, we would cease being human, and our ability to analyze and understand the world would disappear. By continually checking ourselves, over time, we should be able to distinguish between what is cultural bias and what is actually true.

The dotted line surrounding the "Paradigm" box in Figure 2-6 symbolizes this interplay between one's research agenda and cultural context. Both paradigm and culture provide (often vague) understandings of the world, and each point the researcher toward a question's answers. These biases are not necessarily wrong.

Paradigms provide specific guidelines for high-level theory. For example, a processual archaeologist might generate a hypothesis such as "Agriculture occurs when a human population grows to the point where it exceeds the natural carrying capacity of the local environment." In contrast, someone operating within a postprocessual paradigm might say, "Agriculture originated from the need to create goods to give away at competitive feasts." Both statements are linked to the overarching paradigm by directing researchers to measure some variables (such as demography or social competition) and to set other variables aside.

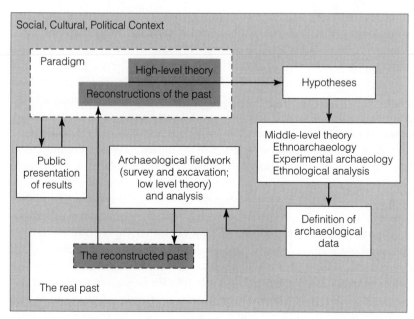

Figure 2-6 A model of archaeological inquiry.

Testing Ideas

The next step is to construct hypotheses designed to test the various propositions—to see if our ideas might actually be true. For each hypothesis, we would frame one (or more) if . . . then statements that build upon the research proposition and predict some presently unknown aspect of the archaeological record. This is how we test ideas. Figure 2-6 shows this as "Hypotheses" resulting from high-level theory.

Take, for example, the hypothesis relating population growth and agriculture. Suppose we already know that in our research area, an agricultural economy began by 2000 BC. We might hypothesize thus: If our proposition is true—that is, if population is the driving force behind agriculture—then signs of population growth and subsequent pressure on the food base should appear prior to 2000 BC.

The hypotheses then lead to a need for middle-level theory (as shown in Figure 2-6). Testing the proposition requires some way of inferring population numbers from archaeological data. We can't measure population directly, of course—the people in question died a long time ago—so we need a bridging argument to infer change in population over time from archaeological variables. To do so, we might have to survey existing ethnographic data or conduct our own ethnoarchaeological research to find correlates between population size and things that an archaeologist could record, for example, house or village size.

We also need a way to measure "stress" on the food base. Perhaps we may need to conduct experiments, such as gathering foods with aboriginal technologies and measuring the efficiency with which they are collected. Such research might tell us that very small seeds are less efficiently harvested than large seeds and therefore that their use might signal subsistence stress.

Once we have adequate middle-level theory, we can define what constitutes relevant archaeological data (shown at lower right in Figure 2-6). If we believe that house size is the best variable to measure population change, then we need to measure a sufficient number of houses from sites that date to various time periods before and after 2000 BC—to see if there is evidence of population growth *before* the appearance of an agricultural economy. If we decide that decreasing seed size is a good way to show that an ancient population was approaching an environment's carrying capacity, then we must recover and measure seeds from the appro-priate archaeological sites (in Chapter 8, we discuss how archaeologists do this).

This background work done, we can state the general hypothesis in a more specific way: If agriculture appears because population exceeds carrying capacity, then (1) house size should increase before 2000 BC, and (2) seeds found in trash associated with those houses should become smaller through time.

This brings us to the fun part, the archaeological fieldwork (shown in the center of Figure 2-6) to collect the data necessary to test our hypothesis. We must design such fieldwork to generate adequate samples of house floors and seeds from the right time periods. Low-level theory is required to identify house floors (through the presence of postholes, packed clay floors, hearths, and so forth) and to identify seeds. (We discuss fieldwork much more in the following chapters.)

Reconstructing the Past

Testing such hypotheses requires that we reconstruct the past, that we say something about what actually happened back in time (as shown at the lower left in Figure 2-6). Perhaps we will find that houses became larger over time (or maybe not); perhaps we learn that seeds became smaller through time (or maybe not). Notice that in Figure 2-6, the dotted line enclosing "The reconstructed past" is itself inside a larger box labeled "The real past." We did this for two reasons. First, we wish to emphasize that we cannot hope to reconstruct the complete past. There was, to be sure, a real past made up of real people who lived real lives and who died real deaths; but our reconstructed past will never be an exact duplicate.

Second, as the postprocessual critique makes clear, our experiences in the present heavily color our vision of the past. The hypothesis used here as an example looks to demography (rather than religion or social change) to explain a change in subsistence. The upshot of this hypothesis is that, to reconstruct the past, we focus on some issues and downplay others. Had we hypothesized a religious cause to agricultural origins, we would have sought very different data during our fieldwork. For example, we might have looked for evidence of how plants were used in different rituals, and that might have led us to excavate religious structures rather than houses.

Now we return to our original propositions to see whether we confirmed or falsified them. Did the field-

LOOKING CLOSER

Contrasting Views of Archaeology at Zuni Pueblo

By Roger Anyon and T. J. Ferguson

Roger Anyon is cultural resources coordinator for Pima County, Arizona, and T. J. Ferguson is proprietor of Anthropological Research, LLC, and an adjunct professor of anthropology, University of Arizona.

Cultural resource management in the U.S. is conducted under a patchwork of legal and regulatory mandates promulgated by people educated, working, and living in a Euroamerican cultural milieu—rather than being informed by Zuni values. The differing cultural views of archaeological sites and of human burials are instructive.

As viewed by archaeologists, and enshrined in federal regulatory language, archaeological sites are valued for their potential to inform about the past: sites are abandoned inanimate things from which information can be extracted.

As viewed by Zunis, archaeological sites are an essential link to the land, their ancestors, their culture and traditions: sites embody life forces. Religious offerings made when sites were established and lived in, and when they were left during the tribe's migrations, still have power and significance in present day Zuni religion. Zunis have no concept of sites having been abandoned. Ancestral spirits continue to reside in these places, the stewards of the land that provide a temporal link to present day Zuni.

Archaeologists view human remains as they do sites: things holding information about population structure, diet, disease, genetics, burial practices, and

so forth. To Zunis, human burials are on a journey: each person passes through four stages during their journey of existence, of which the life that we know is only the first. Each human burial is at some point along the latter three stages of that life journey, completed only when the skeletal remains have finally disintegrated into the earth. No human burial should be disturbed; disrupting the journey that each individual must complete has unimagined consequences for both the deceased and the living.

In general, the Euroamerican view of cultural resources is restrictive, limiting them to archaeological remains and to those places actively used today in a cultural tradition. These small "cultural islands" within the larger landscape have a fixed significance. For Zunis cultural resources are any tangible or intangible aspect of the world that has meaning, regardless of when it was last active in any ceremony. Cessation of ritual activities at a shrine or disused trail for hundreds of years does not diminish its present cultural significance. Nor are cultural resources bounded for Zunis. How can one bound and separate a spring at which a deer drinks from the ancestral archaeological sites this deer visits to pay its respect to the spirits inhabiting that site?

In the Zuni view the entire landscape is a cultural resource, with no fixed boundaries and no fixed significance. Temporal and spatial concepts define meaning and significance, and these may change—for example, by time of year, by virtue of the conduct of a particular ceremony, or depending upon the landscape scale within which it is viewed.

work and ensuing analyses find evidence of population growth and resource stress prior to 2000 BC, or did they not?

At this point, the archaeologist presents the results to a public audience. This presentation begins with scientific monographs or papers that other archaeologists scrutinize. But modern archaeologists also know that

results need to be conveyed to a broader public through books or magazine articles written in lay terms, public lectures, television presentations, museum exhibitions, or even novels. In this way, the public can learn from and comment upon the research. And, through this recursive process (shown at middle left in Figure 2-6), archaeologists may find such a lack of fit between their ideas and the empirical archaeological record that they may discard their paradigm for another.

In truth, few archaeologists can do every step in the process; instead, nearly everyone specializes. Some focus their careers on middle-level theory, doing experimental or ethnoarchaeological research. Others concentrate on the public side, presenting their research and that of others to a broader audience. Others work mostly with theory, and still others spend most of their time doing fieldwork. It's even more important, then, that archaeologists understand what role they play in the whole process.

Conclusion: Scientist or Humanist, Processualist or Postprocessualist?

So, should Americanist archaeology declare a preference for scientific or humanistic perspective? Archaeologist Steve Lekson (University of Colorado) sees it this way: "I divide scientific and humanistic approaches by method: scientific approaches build knowledge that is external and cumulative while humanist approaches seek knowledge that is internal and historical. The former depersonalizes, the latter is highly personal. The two are compatible and co-exist in each of us—think of Leonardo da Vinci, artist and scientist." When archaeologists wish to seek and understand patterns and regularities in prehistoric cultures, they are scientists. When they wish to understand the history and culture of particular past societies, they are humanists. So archaeologists will be more one than the other, at different times, depending on their objective.

But there is more. Where do we get new ideas, new thoughts, new insights? One place is through other cultures: by taking humanistic approaches that ask us to step into another culture's shoes and see the world differently, we discover new ideas, new insights, and new ways of understanding the past. This is why a humanistic approach is critical to a scientific approach. But at the same time, the scientific method is critical for checking whether the conclusions derived from humanistic approaches are correct. A humanistic approach is good at generating ideas, but it is less useful for testing those ideas; that's where science comes in. Good archaeologists know that they need a humanist in their hearts and a scientist in their hands.

With respect to competing paradigms in archaeology, we believe that Americanist archaeology works best when it sees paradigms as tools rather than as dogmatic religions. If you look at the field that way, then archaeologists should be able to draw what is useful from each paradigm rather than be forced to ally themselves unwaveringly with one way of viewing the world.

And indeed, one sees relatively few hard-core processualists or diehard postprocessualists these days. Most are processual-plus archaeologists, refusing to reduce the past to mechanical processes, but still believing in the power of scientifically tested ideas. Most contemporary archaeologists agree that multiple ways exist to learn about the past. And most would also agree that we can accept a certain amount of ambiguity and yet still learn something real about, and from, the past.

Summary

- Anthropologists believe that a true understanding of humankind arises from a comparative and holistic perspective.

- Culture unifies these diverse fields. Culture is a learned, shared, and symbolically based system of knowledge that includes traditions, kinship, language, religion, customs, and beliefs.

- Two major strategies of research characterize contemporary anthropological thinking: The ideational perspective sees culture as primarily an instrument to create meaning and order in one's world; the adaptive perspective emphasizes the environment, technology, and economics, and sees culture as the way that humans adapt.

- Archaeologists draw upon both ideational and adaptive perspectives, and no single anthropological school dominates contemporary archaeology.

- Archaeology is grounded in a scientific perspective, which allows us to understand the workings of the visible world. The goal of science is to develop ideas that can be criticized, evaluated, and eventually modified or replaced by ideas that explain the archaeological data better.

- Many archaeologists also believe in humanistic approaches—those that look for holistic syntheses of the cultural patterns of the past, for the role of the individual, for the feelings and thoughts of the long dead.

- For decades, archaeologists have prided themselves on their ability to straddle the fence between scientific and humanistic perspectives.

- Low-level theory involves the observations that emerge from archaeological fieldwork; this is how archaeologists get their "data," their "facts."

- Middle-level (middle-range) theory links archaeological data with human behavior or natural processes and is produced through experimental archaeology, taphonomy, and ethnoarchaeology.

- High-level ("general") theory provides answers to larger "why" questions.

- Paradigms are frameworks for thinking that interrelate concepts and provide research strategies. They apply to intellectual inquiry in general and are not specific to archaeology.

- Two major paradigms in modern Americanist archaeology are processual and postprocessual archaeology; they are derived, respectively, from cultural materialism and postmodernism. The former takes a scientific approach and focuses on the material factors of life; the latter emphasizes humanistic perspectives and symbolic meaning.

- A model of archaeological inquiry shows how the different levels of theory, paradigms, and the public presentation of results help to ensure that our understanding of the past continually improves over time and overcomes the biases presented by the archaeologist's particular cultural context.

Media Resources

Doing Fieldwork: Archaeological Demonstrations CD-ROM

This CD gives you a vivid glimpse of what it is like to be involved in an archaeological dig . . . without leaving your chair. With this CD, you will see archaeologists involved in actual excavations—many of which are referenced in your Thomas/Kelly text—using a number of the field techniques covered in this chapter. Organized according to the various stages of a live excavation, the CD presents hands-on interactive activities, live-action demonstration videos, and quizzes to help you better understand the processes and techniques that are important to an excavation.

The Companion Website for Archaeology: Down to Earth, *Third Edition*

http://anthropology.wadsworth.com/thomas_kelly3e_down/

Supplement your review of this chapter by going to the companion website to take one of the practice quizzes, use the flash cards to master key terms, and check out the many other study aids that are designed to help you succeed in your introductory archaeology course.

3 Doing Fieldwork: Surveying for Archaeological Sites

Outline

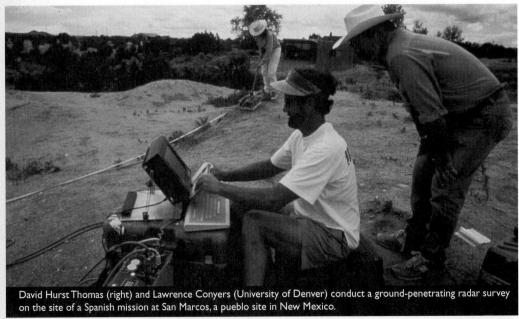

David Hurst Thomas (right) and Lawrence Conyers (University of Denver) conduct a ground-penetrating radar survey on the site of a Spanish mission at San Marcos, a pueblo site in New Mexico.

© American Museum of Natural History, photo by Samantha Williams

Preview

N OW THE FUN BEGINS. In the next few chapters, you will get a glimpse of what it's like to actually do archaeology. For many in the discipline—ourselves included—fieldwork is why we became archaeologists in the first place. That said, we must begin this introduction to archaeological field techniques with two important warnings:

- There is no one "right" way to look for and excavate sites (but there are plenty of wrong ones).
- Nobody ever learned how to do proper archaeological fieldwork from a book (including this one).

Despite recent advances, archaeological fieldwork remains as much art as science. All we can do here is examine some common techniques, list some archaeological standards and principles, and give you a sense of what it feels like to participate in an archaeological exploration.

 Doing Fieldwork CD-ROM: Archaeological Demonstrations

See the "Remote Sensing" and "Beginning to Excavate" sections of the CD-ROM to learn more about topics covered in this chapter.

Introduction

Every archaeologist addressing a general audience is eventually asked the same question: "How do you know where to dig?" There are many answers. We've known about some **archaeological sites,** such as Egypt's pyramids, for centuries—they were never lost. The locations of other sites have been handed down through the generations, preserved in oral and written traditions. Sites are also discovered in large-scale systematic surveys, during which large regions are scanned for the remains of previous habitation. And some of the most important archaeological sites in the world were found by accident, hard work, and luck.

Good Old Gumshoe Survey

In Chapter 2, we mentioned Gatecliff Shelter in Nevada, where both of us excavated in the 1970s. But before we could dig at Gatecliff, of course, the site had to be found. How did that happen?

Gatecliff was found by a fortunate combination of happenstance, hard work, and luck, a process that James O'Connell (University of Utah) calls old-fashioned "gumshoe survey."

In the summer of 1970, Thomas was in central Nevada's Reese River valley conducting systematic archaeological survey. Basically, this fieldwork entails mapping and collecting archaeological stuff found on the ground. The survey went well, but it could not answer all the questions. Thomas needed to know, for example, something about prehistoric subsistence and the chronology of different artifact types. Such information can only come from buried sites, where food

 archaeological site Any place where material evidence exists about the human past. Usually, *site* refers to a concentration of such evidence.

remains (bones and seeds) might be preserved and where artifacts can be dated. Rockshelters and caves often contain the necessary buried deposits but, despite the Reese River crew's best efforts, they could not locate one.

At the end of the first field session in Reese River, Thomas assembled the crew for steak dinners in the town of Austin, about an hour's dusty ride away. Austin is a pocket-sized Nevada mining town with fewer than 250 citizens. Writer Oscar Lewis described it as "the town that died laughing," and William Least Heat Moon called it "a living ghost town: 40 percent living, 50 percent ghost and 10 percent not yet decided." When two dozen grubby archaeologists come to such a town for steaks and beverages, word gets around quickly. Thomas soon found himself talking with the waitress's husband, Gale Peer, a mining geologist who had prospected central Nevada for 40 years. There are few places Gale Peer had not been, so Thomas asked if he knew of any caves or rockshelters.

Indeed, Mr. Peer did know of a cave—in Monitor Valley, about 20 kilometers east of Austin. He had not been there in years, but the details were fresh in his mind.

"You take the main dirt road south in Monitor Valley, then turn west, up one of the side canyons. I don't remember which one. As you drive along, oh, let's see, maybe 10 or 15 miles, there's a large black chert cliff. At the bottom of the cliff is a cave. Some time, a long time ago, the Indians painted the inside of the cave. There are pictures of people and animals, plus a lot of writing I don't understand. Top of the shelter's caved in. Maybe in an earthquake. There's not much of the cave left. Drive out there when you get a chance. I'd like to know what's in that cave." He sketched a map on his business card. This is the essence of gumshoe survey—hanging out in coffee shops, bars, and gas stations, listening to those who know more about the landscape than you do.

The next summer Thomas and his crew returned, hoping to find the cave that Mr. Peer had described. They knew that the rockshelter was several miles up a canyon, on the north side—but there were 15 such canyons.

Beginning at the southern end of Monitor Valley, the crew drove up and down each side canyon, working their way northward. They were hampered by spring snow and washed-out roads—typical fieldwork conditions in central Nevada. Each of the canyons had potential. The crew would see something, stop the truck, and skitter up the hillside. But each time, the "something" turned out to be a shadow, an abandoned mine shaft, or just a jumble of boulders.

After a week, Thomas came to Mill Canyon, just the next one on the list, with no greater potential than the ten canyons they had already combed. The road was a little worse than most and, even in four-wheel drive, the truck lurched down a steep ridge into the rocky canyon. Finally, as the crew moved up the flat canyon bottom, a black cliff loomed ahead, riddled with small caves and rockshelters.

As had happened many times before, the shelters were empty, unless you count coyote scats and pack rat nests. Finally, the crew spied a dim shadow where the black dolomite formation was swallowed up beneath the Mill Canyon bottomland.

The paintings were invisible until you stood right in the mouth of the shelter. But there they were, just as Mr. Peer had said: small human figures, painted in red and yellow. On the other wall were cryptic motifs in white and black. And, yes, the roof had caved in years before. One boulder dwarfed the pickup.

There was nothing "archaeological" on the surface, but a small test pit turned up telltale signs that people had once lived in the shelter: several pieces of broken bone, a few of them charred, and a dozen stone flakes (probably debris from resharpening stone knives or **projectile points**).

Across the campfire that night, the crew assayed the finds. The rock art was intriguing; only two similar sites were known in central Nevada. The stones and bones were suggestive, but the shelter seemed hardly the deep site they were seeking. Thomas named the site after the rock formation, Gatecliff, in which they found it.

On the strength of this meager evidence, they decided to dig some—a good decision, it turned out, because the deposits inside Gatecliff Shelter proved to be 12 meters deep, making it one of the deepest rockshelters in the Americas. And the strata were spectacularly layered, not jumbled up like most sites in the area. Flash floods had periodically inundated the shelter, the surging waters laying down thick layers of rock-hard

---

projectile points Arrowheads, dart points, or spear points.

silt. This flooding occurred at least a dozen times, separating the deposits into clean occupational "floors."

This meant that Gatecliff had what textbooks—including this one—describe as "layer-cake stratigraphy." Sandwiched between these sterile flash-flood deposits was a wonderful 7000-year record of human activity and environmental change in Monitor Valley. The University of California (Davis) began the research, followed by the American Museum of Natural History, which dispatched five major expeditions to Gatecliff Shelter. The National Geographic Society supported part of the fieldwork, shot an educational film, and wrote a book about the site. The *New York Times* and *The New Yorker* magazine published stories about Gatecliff. There was television and radio coverage. Even a U.S. congressman became involved in preserving the site.

Gatecliff Shelter was on the map—and all because a waitress's husband in Austin, Nevada, remembered an interesting place from years before. In fact, many important sites have been found by ranchers, cowboys, sheepherders, farmers, geologists, and amateur archaeologists—anyone who spends a lot of time wandering about outdoors.

Surface Archaeology in the Carson Desert

Archaeologists feel lucky to find sites like Gatecliff Shelter, which was a marvelous place to dig. But the goal of archaeological survey is not just to find deep sites full of interesting artifacts. Some surveys are designed to document the range of archaeological remains that occur across a landscape to avoid a biased image of the lives of ancient peoples.

We do this by looking at the distribution of sites across a region. Decades ago, archaeologists often ignored surface sites because they lacked the contextual relations necessary to establish solid cultural chronologies. But such sequences, although important, are only part of the puzzle. Surface sites provide unique

---

LOOKING CLOSER
How Do Archaeological Sites Get Their Names?

It's an archaeologist's prerogative to name new sites. Many are named after a prominent topographic feature, for example, the canyon in which the site is located, or a nearby mountain, river, town—or a rock formation, in the case of Gatecliff Shelter.

Sites on private land are commonly named after the landowners; some become the namesake of the amateur archaeologists who find them. And sometimes the archaeologist can have fun with a site's name. Robert Bettinger (University of California, Davis) named one California cave site Gimme Shelter (after the Rolling Stones' tune).

Some names have stories attached to them. Danger Cave, on the edge of Utah's Great Salt Lake, for example, was originally called Hands and Knees Caves by locals, to describe how it was entered. But during Elmer Smith's 1941 excavation, a huge piece of the lip broke off and crashed into the excavation, narrowly missing several of the crew members and, according to legend, landing right where some had just finished lunch. This incident resulted in a permanent name change. During Jesse Jennings's excavations there in the 1950s, several students elected to change the name to Lamus Cave, after Blair Lamus, a superintendent of the potash plant in nearby Wendover, to recognize the help he had given to the project (which apparently included small amounts of dynamite to help speed the digging). Jennings apparently nixed the suggestion.

So sites acquire their names in many different ways. There is, in fact, only one cultural rule to follow: The archaeologist can *never* name a site after him- or herself.

data regarding past human–land relationships, and Kelly's work in the Carson Desert of western Nevada illustrates how archaeologists can implement this regional perspective.

The Great Basin is best known for vast stretches of sagebrush and arid mountain ranges, and most of the available ethnographic information documents these upland adaptations. But the Great Basin also contains a number of substantial wetlands, and without much ethnographic data, archaeologists in the 1970s debated how the wetlands were incorporated into the seasonal round of the region's native peoples.

One hypothesis held that the wetlands provided an abundant, high-quality food source and assumed that people living would become sedentary (that is, stay in one location year-round) wherever food was abundant. An opposing hypothesis viewed wetland food resources as lower quality and more difficult to gather than others, such as piñon and large game, suggesting that the wetlands were only one element in a broader seasonal round. And, in contrast, this hypothesis assumed that hunter-gatherers became sedentary when the lack of food elsewhere *forced* them to do so. Expressed succinctly, the hypotheses were: Did prehistoric peoples settle down and focus on the wetlands, or did they incorporate the mountains' resources into a more diversified seasonal round?

One of the Great Basin's largest wetlands lies in the Carson Desert, about 100 kilometers east of Reno, Nevada. A large basin filled with sand dunes and alkali flats, the Carson Desert is also the terminus of several large rivers that create a vast, slightly alkaline wetland. This wetland is host to many species of plants and animals that provided ancient peoples with food and various kinds of raw material for clothing, houses, and tools: cattail, bulrush and other plants, fish, muskrats, and other small mammals. Piñon pine nuts are found in the forest of the Stillwater Mountains that form the eastern edge of the Carson Desert; foragers could find tubers, seeds, bighorn sheep, and other game there as well. Previous research suggested that people had lived in this region off and on for more than 9000 years.

To understand ancient life in the Carson Desert fully, we needed to explore the regional archaeological record: What kind of archaeological remains are found near the marsh, in the dunes, in the low foothills of the Stillwater Mountains, and, higher in the mountains, in the piñon-juniper forest? Put simply, we proposed that if the wetlands were exploited by a sedentary population, then we should find evidence of large, year-round populations living near the marsh. There should be little evidence of use of the mountains, except perhaps by hunting parties seeking bighorn sheep. People should have made far less use of the dunes and alkali flats, because their economic potentials are low compared with that of the wetland.

But on the other hand, if the wetlands were just one stop on a broad-scale seasonal round, then we should find evidence of more transient use of the wetlands and a more intensive use of the mountains.

With this in mind, we generated some archaeological expectations for each hypothesis. Because we would rely strictly on surface archaeology, where organic remains are not preserved, we focused on stone tools (pottery is rare in this region) and the waste flakes from their manufacture and resharpening. We talk more about these kinds of artifacts in Chapter 7.

The point is this: Long before we took to the field, we had a good idea of what we should find *if* one hypothesis was correct and the other was incorrect. For example, if a sedentary population had used the wetlands, then we expected to find dense scatters of waste flakes and broken tools (the remains of villages occupied for years at a time) in the wetland. In the uplands, we expected to find only evidence of hunting activities, in the form of small campsites containing broken projectile points. But if the second hypothesis was correct, then we expected to find smaller, less dense settlements on the valley floor and evidence of hunting, but also tuber, seed, and piñon gathering in the mountains, as shown by **manos** and **metates,** grinding stones used for processing seeds and nuts.

Some Sampling Considerations

So, you can see that the fieldwork needed to test our hypotheses required that we explore the character of archaeological evidence across the region. But what

mano A fist-sized, round, flat, hand-held stone used with a metate for grinding foods.

metate A large, flat stone used as a stationary surface upon which seeds, tubers, and nuts are ground with a mano.

should that region be? And did we need to search every square inch of it? Given the practicalities of desert archaeology, it was obvious that we could not look everywhere. We must *sample*, but capricious and biased sampling methods can lead the archaeologist astray. What if we looked only in places where we thought sites would be located? Not being Great Basin hunter-gatherers, we would surely not see the landscape as past foragers did. We would undoubtedly overestimate the importance of some places and overlook others, generating a biased image of the region's archaeology.

The best way to ensure unbiased results is through judicious use of **statistical sampling.** We cover only the basic principles of this large and complex subject here. (But note that any student contemplating a career in archaeology will need to take several statistics courses, because statistical analysis is as indispensable to archaeologists as their trowels.)

To acquire a statistical sample, you must first define the **statistical population** that you wish to characterize. Statisticians use the term "population" to refer not to physical objects but to data, which are, as you will recall, *observations made on objects.* The difference is subtle yet important. A defined group of people, such as Shoshone Indians or American males, could make up a biological or sociocultural population, but they are not a statistical population. Only measurements made on variables—such as stature, daily caloric intake, or religious beliefs—could constitute a statistical population. A statistical population consists of a defined set of observations of interest.

Statistical sampling also requires that we define a relevant **sample universe**, the archaeological sites that will provide the sample population. Because the research question concerned the relationships between sites on the valley floor—in particular, those in the wetland and those in the mountains—our sample universe had to contain both of these regions.

The result was a sample universe—a survey area—of some 1700 square kilometers (shown in Figure 3-1). Because soil formation in deserts is often slow and vegetation is sparse, many archaeological remains still lie on the surface, where people dropped or discarded them hundreds or even thousands of years ago. Doing surface archaeology in such places means that you simply spot an artifact, plot its location in your field notes, pick it up, and label it—no digging!

But who could survey all 1700 square kilometers? That would take lifetimes! This is where statistical sampling theory helps out, providing a set of methods that allows us to characterize a population without having to record data on every item in that population. We draw upon the same set of methods and theory that pollsters use to take the nation's political pulse by interviewing only a thousand people.

You begin by randomly selecting those sites that will be included in the sample. The word *random* here is critical, for it specifically means that *each site has an equal chance of being selected for the sample.* If there were 100 sites, say, then each site must have a $1/100 = 1$ percent chance of being included in the sample. If the sample is not selected in a random manner, then some sites may be overrepresented and others underrepresented in the sample. And that would bias the final results.

Random sampling provides the only way for archaeologists to collect meaningful negative evidence. This is important because, in addition to knowing what activities took place where, archaeologists want to know which activities did not occur in a particular area or biotic community. Randomly selecting the samples also permits us to analyze the results statistically.

Getting the Sample

Once we had decided on the sample universe, the next task was to select the sample. The first step is to determine the **sample fraction.** What portion of the sample population would be included—1 percent of the sites? 5 percent, 10 percent, 50 percent? After considering the possibilities, we decided in 1980 to begin with a 1 percent sample of the entire region and then to increase

statistical sampling The principles that underlie sampling strategies that provide accurate measures of a statistical population.

statistical population A set of counts, measurements, or characteristics about which relevant inquiries are to be made. Scientists use the term "statistical population" in a specialized way (quite different from "population" in the ordinary sense).

sample universe The region that contains the statistical population and that will be sampled. Its size and shape are determined by the research question and practical considerations.

sample fraction The percentage of the sample universe that is surveyed.

Figure 3-1 Map of the Carson Desert and Stillwater Mountains (Nevada), showing the locations of survey transects, quadrats, and spring surveys. *Robert Kelly, "Prehistory of the Carson Desert and Stillwater Mountains,"* University of Utah Anthropological Papers, No. 123, 2001. Used by permission.

meter squares (we called them *quadrats*) as the sample unit. We located these squares randomly using the **UTM grid** (Universal Transverse Mercator), a standardized 1 × 1 meter squares grid system plotted on the standard U.S. Geological Survey (USGS) topographic map. Then we randomly selected sets of north and east coordinates (by putting the UTM coordinates in a hat—nothing fancy here!). The set of north and east coordinates defined the northwest corner of a 500 × 500 meter sample square; for example, the coordinates of Quadrat 36 were 4416000 North, 407500 East.

We also drew 500-meter-radius circles around all the active springs in the northern mountains. Water is obviously critical for hunter-gatherers living in a desert environment. In the Stillwater Mountains, water is mostly present as springs that create a small seep or a short creek. Only one "stream" exists in the Stillwaters; jokingly labeled "Mississippi Canyon" on USGS maps, it trickles only a few hundred meters before disappearing beneath rock and sand.

On the valley floor, we used 100 meter-wide transects (instead of 500-meter squares) to sample the area. We chose this width because we had 10 to 12 students working on the project, and this meant that they could be spaced about 10 meters apart. We located the first transect by randomly selecting a UTM north coordinate from the northern end of the valley survey and used that line to define the middle of the 100-meter transect width. Then, to increase the sample to the desired fraction, we selected additional transects at 10-kilometer intervals south of the first. Later, additional transects were selected by placing them between these first ones.

the sample fraction in particular areas the following summer. Areas with a lot of variability in archaeological remains require larger sample fractions than do areas of low variability.

But how, actually, do you acquire such a sample? We decided to use randomly selected **sample units.** Sample units can be many different shapes, although squares, circles, and transects (long, narrow rectangles) are the most commonly used; all three were employed in this survey. The choice of which to use depends somewhat on the research questions, but also on practical considerations. In the mountains, we used 500 × 500

Doing the Work

We completed the Carson-Stillwater survey in two summers. In the first summer, we took a 1 percent

---

sample units Survey units of a standard size and shape, determined by the research question and practical considerations, used to obtain the sample.

UTM grid Universal Transverse Mercator, a grid system whereby north and east coordinates provide a location anywhere in the world, precise to 1 meter.

sample and found that archaeological remains were most dense and variable in the piñon-juniper forest of the mountains and in the dune area. Site density and variability was somewhat less in the wetland region of the valley floor and in the unforested portion of the mountains. So, during the second summer, we pursued a **stratified random sample,** which "stratifies" the sample universe into five strata: the wetland, the dune area to the west of the wetland, the south valley, the northern Stillwater Mountains, and the southern Stillwater Mountains. As a result of the first summer's survey sample, we sampled some of these areas more intensively than the others.

The first summer's survey team consisted of 10 to 12 student archaeologists and volunteers, walking at 8–10-meter intervals through the sagebrush and greasewood. A similar procedure was used on the quadrats but, because these units were 500 × 500 meters, we made five 100-meter-wide passes across them; we used the same procedure for the spring surveys, but with up to ten such passes.

When someone found a site, each crew member marked his or her place on the line (so they'd know where to resume surveying) and then gathered together. We located the site on a sketch map of the quadrat, drew a map of the site itself, and filled out a site form (that included information on location and topographic setting; distance to water; vegetation; erosion; potential for buried deposits; estimates of site age and size, and so on). We also gave each site a field number, but eventually each site was assigned a permanent **Smithsonian number**—a cataloging system that most states use to keep track of their sites. For example, one site found in our survey acquired the number 26CH798: The 26 stands for Nevada, because it is the twenty-sixth state alphabetically (excluding Alaska and Hawaii, which acquired statehood after this system was in place; they are now 49 and 50). The CH stands for Churchill County, and 798 means it was the 798th site recorded in that county.

After two summers, we had surveyed 57 quadrats, 8 springs, and 260 kilometers of transects—about 47 square kilometers, or a sample fraction of the total survey universe of about 3 percent. But some strata were sampled more intensively than others.

We recorded 160 sites and collected some 10,400 stone tools and more than 70,000 manufacturing and resharpening waste flakes. We analyzed these over the next several years.

What We Learned

Recall that the original research question concerned two different hypotheses about the role of wetlands in the ancient hunter-gatherer seasonal round. The first hypothesis held that wetlands had been the focus of a sedentary settlement system, predicting that the highest site density should be in the wetland. But our survey found that the highest site densities are found in the dunes, the south valley region, and the northern forested portion of the mountains.

The first hypothesis also predicted that sites in the wetlands should contain evidence of long-term habitation. But the archaeological survey recovered stone tools and evidence of stone tool manufacturing techniques suggesting that wetland sites were short-term camps. This evidence is more in line with the second hypothesis, which argued that the wetland was but one stop on a complex seasonal round (and the sites in the dune region contained tools and waste flakes that suggested even more transient stays than those in the wetland).

The second hypothesis, however, also suggested that the piñon forests should have been included in the seasonal round. But although we found evidence of hunting there, evidence for plant collecting, in the form of grinding stones, was almost nonexistent.

So, as it turned out, neither hypothesis seemed to provide an adequate reconstruction of ancient life in the Carson Desert and Stillwater Mountains. We have come full circle in the research cycle and are now back at the beginning, proposing new hypotheses that take into account what we learned.

What about Things That Lie below Ground?

In places like the Carson Desert, important archaeological remains have lain on a stable desert surface for millennia. But in many other places, artifacts may be washed away or deeply buried (as at Gatecliff Shelter).

stratified random sample A survey universe divided into several sub-universes that are then sampled at potentially different sample fractions.

Smithsonian number A unique catalog number given to sites; it consists of a number (the state's position alphabetically), a letter abbreviation of the county, and the site's sequential number within the county.

LOOKING CLOSER
The Surveyor's Toolkit

If you are thinking of doing archaeology, your first job will likely be survey. To prepare yourself, you'll need many of the following items in addition to the normal things you would carry on a long day hike (water, food bar, first aid kit, matches, rain gear, sunscreen, and so on):

- A GPS instrument (Garmin makes some good, inexpensive models)
- A two-way radio (with at least a 2-mile capacity)
- A good but cheap watch (we've crushed several climbing over rocks)
- A good compass (Brunton's pocket transit or Finland's Suunto)
- A K+E field notebook (college bookstores carry them)
- Mechanical or regular pencils

- Ziploc bags (of different sizes; these can be purchased inexpensively online)
- A black Sharpie marker
- A trowel (for quick test pits)
- A tape measure (metric only!)
- Graph paper (for site maps; crew chiefs often carry this and other paperwork in an aluminum clipboard box)
- A small flashlight (useful when investigating caves and rockshelters)
- In some places, a snake bite kit (although we have yet to use one), pepper spray in bear country (archaeologists in grizzly territory often carry guns), mosquito repellent, or shin guards to protect against snakes in more densely vegetated areas

This issue cropped up in the Carson Desert project. A few years after we finished our survey in 1981, torrential rains and heavy snows fell across the headwaters of the Humboldt River, which eventually drains into the Carson Desert. The heavy precipitation kept up until the Carson Desert—that barren basin of sand dunes and alkali flats—had become a 40-mile-wide lake.

During the summer of 1986, the floodwaters began to recede. As they did, they stripped away the tops of dunes and exposed hundreds of human burials and archaeological sites containing shallow houses, storage pits, bones, stone tools, beads, and grinding stones (we discuss these sites and burials in Chapters 8 and 9). When the U.S. Fish and Wildlife Service (the agency that manages the Carson Desert's wetland) plotted the newly exposed finds, their maps showed that our survey crews had literally walked right over some of these sites. We missed them because there was no surface indication of what lay buried below. However, the kinds of projectile points found in the wetland strata of the survey and in the newly exposed sites were the same: the survey had, in this regard, accurately characterized the wetland's archaeology.

Still, it is clear that surface archaeology documents only what lies on or near the ground surface. Surface and subsurface material often correlate, but you can never be absolutely certain about what lies below.

Archaeologists working in the eastern United States, Europe, and elsewhere confront this problem all the time, because these areas witness considerable soil buildup, and artifacts rarely lie on the undisturbed ground surface. In agricultural regions, archaeologists do **plow-zone** archaeology, walking through plowed fields after spring tilling (and especially after a rain), because the plow will turn up shallowly buried archaeological remains.

plow zone The upper portion of a soil profile that has been disturbed by repeated plowing or other agricultural activity.

In other areas, archaeologists use a procedure known as **shovel testing.** Survey crews carry shovels and sometimes small backpacked screens with them. As the crew moves across a survey unit, each member stops at a predetermined interval, digs a shallow hole and screens the dirt back into the hole, looking for evidence of buried archaeological remains. It is slow going, and it obviously cannot locate remains that are more than a foot or two deep.

Looking for more deeply buried remains, some archaeologists use backhoe trenches or hand or mechanical soil augers, but the former can be very expensive (as well as destructive) and the latter very slow. We normally use them in areas that previous research suggests are good places to prospect for buried remains. In other cases, archaeologists use natural exposures, such as arroyos or riverbanks that sometimes expose deeply buried deposits.

Later in this chapter, we discuss some high-tech ways to "see" below ground. Here, we consider a way in which surface survey was combined with a subsurface sampling strategy to find Mission Santa Catalina, a Spanish Franciscan mission lost in Georgia's Sea Islands for more than 300 years.

How to Find a Lost Spanish Mission

At its seventeenth-century zenith, Spanish Florida had three dozen Franciscan missions, each a satellite settlement heavily dependent on the colonial capital at St. Augustine. To the west lived the Timucuan, Apalachee, and Apalachicola Indians; to the north, toward St. Catherines Island, lay the province of Guale. Although a dozen sixteenth- and seventeenth-century missions once existed in the present state of Georgia, archaeologists and historians had not identified one such mission site when Thomas began his search for Santa Catalina.

Many historians and archaeologists felt that the lost mission of Santa Catalina lay along the western margin of St. Catherines Island, a 1400-acre tract 80 kilometers south of Savannah. Unlike the other so-called Golden Isles, St. Catherines Island has not been subdivided and suburbanized. The Georgia-based, not-for-profit St. Catherines Island Foundation owns the island and regulates a comprehensive program of research and con-

servation. This enlightened and progressive land management policy ensured that Mission Santa Catalina was not destroyed beneath the crush of condos and fast-food joints that typify the southern barrier islands.

The Transect Survey

In 1974, when we first visited St. Catherines Island, the combined French, English, and Spanish historic documentation supplied only vague geographic clues, and, although several first-rate archaeologists had previously worked on the island, none had successfully located this important mission site.

Virtually uninhabited, St. Catherines Island is today blanketed with dense forest, briar patches, and almost impenetrable palmetto thicket. When we began our search for Santa Catalina, we were overwhelmed by the vastness of the area involved. We knew so little about the landscape that we could not overlook any portion of St. Catherines Island.

By its nature, archaeological fieldwork is slow and tedious—and nobody could (or should) excavate an entire island—so we began by random sampling. Taking the island's size into consideration, Thomas figured that 30 east-west transects, each 100 meters wide, would provide a 20 percent sample of the island. This sample would allow us to characterize the island's archaeology and help search for the lost mission of Santa Catalina de Guale. But recall that sampling, even with a relatively large 20 percent sample, is not always good at finding rare sites—and there was only one Santa Catalina de Guale.

In surveying, the idea is to walk in the straightest line possible, climbing over rocks and deadfalls, walking along the sides of steep ridges—looking even in places where you really don't expect to find anything. In Nevada's wide-open spaces, it is fairly easy to keep your bearing even if you don't have a compass: just keep walking toward that peak, mesa, or other landmark in the distance. But on densely vegetated St. Catherines Island, it was impossible to see past the palmetto bush a meter in front of you (Figure 3-2). The

shovel testing A sample survey method used in regions where rapid soil buildup obscures buried archaeological remains; it entails digging shallow, systematic pits across the survey unit.

St. Catherines Island, Georgia

0   km   2   0   miles   2

Figure 3-2 Systematic archaeological survey on St. Catherines Island (Georgia).

entire crew was experienced in desert survey and carried compasses, but even then, some veered off their paths as they wound their way through bushes and briars. Palm-sized orb spiders hung down from Spanish

moss-draped oaks; an occasional scream told others that someone had taken one in the face. Fortunately, orb spiders are not dangerous. But the cottonmouths and canebrake rattlesnakes are, and the crew quickly learned about tides and alligators.

In the Great Basin, we can see sites on the ground—but on St. Catherines, most of the sites are buried. We searched for them partly by using probes: meter-long, sharpened steel rods. We would push the probe down into the ground every few steps and see if we hit something. This was effective because St. Catherines Island is one huge sand dune—there is no natural stone on the island. Eventually, we learned to tell the difference between the feel of a tree root and rock or shell—the last two suggesting a buried archaeological site. We recorded 135 sites, ranging from massive shell middens to isolated shell scatters. We investigated each site with several 1-meter-square test units; we excavated more than 400 such test pits.

The Power Auger Survey

The surface survey and testing told us that sixteenth- and seventeenth-century Spanish ceramics occurred only at 5 of the 135 archaeological sites, all but one along the western perimeter of the island. The ruins of Mission Santa Catalina almost certainly lay buried in a target area the size of 30 football fields along the southwestern margin of the island.

But 30 football fields is still a huge area to dig with dental pick and camel hair brush. Moreover, although our confidence was growing, we had to admit almost complete ignorance of what we were looking for. Did Santa Catalina survive merely as heaps of sixteenth- and seventeenth-century garbage? Or could we realistically hope to find buried evidence of buildings as well? Clearly, it was time to scratch the surface.

Looking around for better ways to find the needle hidden in this haystack, Thomas learned from Kathleen Deagan about her successful search for sixteenth-century St. Augustine. She and her students used a gasoline-powered posthole digger and excavated hundreds of round holes on a grid system. Following her lead, we did the same on St. Catherines Island for the area that the survey had identified as most likely to contain the mission. With the noisy, nasty auger, two people could dig a 3-foot-deep hole in less than a minute. The power auger threw up a neat doughnut of dirt that was hand-sifted for artifacts. Hundreds of such holes were dug.

Once the field testing was complete, we identified all materials recovered and plotted the distribution in a series of simple maps. Since then, a number of readily available computer programs have greatly assisted the data conversion process. But even using the hand-plotted maps, the power auger data allowed us to focus further field evaluation on a single 100 × 100 meter square in the overall sampling grid where diagnostic mission-period artifacts were found.

Although this area contained absolutely no surface evidence to distinguish it from the surroundings, judicious use of surface and subsurface sampling had narrowed the search from an entire island to a relatively small area. And this is indeed where we eventually discovered the remarkably well-preserved ruins of Mission Santa Catalina de Guale.

Next, we complete the Santa Catalina story by showing how remote sensing technology helped find the invisible mission site. By using a combination of proton magnetometers, ground-penetrating radar, and soil resistivity techniques, we pinpointed actual buildings inside the mission complex—before we ever excavated them.

GPS Technology and Modern Surveys

Surveys today are also assisted by **global positioning system (GPS)** technology. This system did not exist when we surveyed St. Catherines Island and the Carson Desert, but we certainly wish that it did. We had to use triangulation, pacing, and topography to locate sites on maps—and all that took time. Additionally, we've since discovered that, in the heat of the day, a lot of mistakes can be made.

GPS technology has changed all that. The GPS consists of 27 satellites (24 active ones and 3 spares) that circle the Earth in 12-hour, evenly distributed orbits at an altitude of about 14,000 kilometers. These orbits repeat the same ground track (because the Earth turns beneath them) twice each day. Each satellite carries a computer and very accurate atomic clocks.

Hand-held GPS units operate by picking up the continuously broadcast signals from at least four satellites. The GPS receiver triangulates a position fix using the interval between the transmission and reception of the satellite signal. In the 1980s, GPS units cost thousands of dollars, were bulky and heavy, and required a car battery for their power. And they were not terribly accurate. But today you can buy a cell-phone-sized GPS unit at discount stores for about $150. And a few years ago, the military turned off selective availability, so now the field archaeologist can get 5-meter accuracy within seconds with an easily portable and affordable unit. Most units give locations using the UTM coordinates mentioned previously (or latitude and longitude, but UTM coordinates are easy to use). Expensive devices can even give subcentimeter accuracy.

GPS technology has made fieldwork easier—calculating a location is as easy as pushing a button—and no archaeologist would undertake fieldwork today without one.

Remote Sensing: Data at a Distance

Generations of archaeologists have longed for some magical X-ray machine that would allow us to peer beneath the Earth's surface without digging. Today, that dream has almost come true.

Remote sensing refers to an array of photographic and geophysical techniques that rely on some form of electromagnetic energy—it might be raw electricity, light, heat, or radio waves—to detect and measure some characteristics of an archaeological target. This greatly enhances our ability to see, quite literally, because the naked eye detects less than 1 ten-millionth of the entire electromagnetic spectrum. Remote sensing technology comprises a battery of different geophysical methods that provide cost-effective ways of doing archaeology in a noninvasive, nondestructive manner. It's often possible to learn much about the

global positioning system (GPS) Hand-held devices that use triangulation from radio waves received from satellites to determine your current position in terms of either the UTM grid or latitude and longitude.

remote sensing The application of methods that employ some form of electromagnetic energy to detect and measure characteristics of an archaeological target.

LOOKING CLOSER
Anasazi or Ancestral Pueblo?

For more than 60 years, archaeologists have used the word *Anasazi* to denote the last prehistoric (about AD 200–1600) culture centered on the Four Corners area of northwestern New Mexico, northern Arizona, southwestern Colorado, and southern Utah.

Generally, archaeologists consider the Anasazi to be ancestors of modern Pueblo groups in New Mexico and the Hopi people of northwestern Arizona.

But over the past several years, some Pueblo people have expressed concern over use of this term. *Anasazi* comes from a Navajo word meaning "ancient enemy." Why, Puebloan peoples ask, should their ancestors be known by a non-Puebloan term, especially one that means "enemy"?

Although archaeologists have offered a number of substitutes, many today prefer the term "ancestral Pueblo" to "Anasazi."

extent and contents of a site before excavation; sometimes, these new techniques can even acquire the necessary information and obviate the need for any excavation at all.

High-Altitude Imagery

The first well-documented application of remote sensing methods in archaeology took place in 1891, when a British archaeologist tied a camera to a crewless balloon to get better pictures of the site he was digging in India. Since then, archaeologists have used an array of aerial techniques—at first balloons and airplanes, more recently the space shuttle and satellites—to sense their sites "remotely."

Perhaps the most famous early application of remote sensing methods was by Charles Lindbergh (1902–1974), the famous American aviator-explorer, who took some of the earliest archaeological aerial photographs. Two years after his 1927 nonstop transatlantic solo flight, Lindbergh undertook "goodwill tours" throughout Mexico, Central America, and the West Indies. Working closely with archaeologist A. V. Kidder, Lindbergh photographed important Maya archaeological ruins at Chichén Itzá (Mexico) and Tikal (Guatemala). He also did extensive photographic reconnaissance at Chaco Canyon, New Mexico. These photographic records have proven invaluable to archaeologists working in these areas today. Let's look at what they did for Chaco Canyon.

The Ancient Roads of Chaco Canyon

Chaco Canyon (New Mexico) was the center of a vast social and political network between AD 1050 and 1150. During this time, two distinct kinds of sites appeared in the region. Throughout the Four Corners area, numerous smaller pueblo sites dotted the landscape. But huge sites—the so-called Great Houses such as Pueblo Bonito—appeared in Chaco Canyon and a few other places on the Colorado Plateau. The Great Houses were centrally located amid a cluster of smaller sites, defining a "community." By AD 1100, the Great Houses had developed into large, formal ancestral Pueblo towns.

In 1970–1971, archaeologist R. Gwinn Vivian (Arizona State Museum) was mapping what he thought was a series of ancient canals in Chaco Canyon. As he began excavating, Vivian realized that the linear features were like no canals he'd ever seen. Instead of having a U-shaped cross-section, the Chaco "canal" appeared to be a deliberately flattened and carefully engineered *roadway*. Although some archaeologists working in Chaco had speculated about possible roads, they lacked the technology to trace these possibilities very far, and their ruminations were buried deep inside voluminous field notes, unavailable to Vivian.

Vivian described his curious find to Thomas Lyons, a geologist hired to experiment with remote sensing possibilities in Chaco Canyon. Together, Vivian and Lyons started looking at the available aerial photographs from the area. They compared one set taken in the 1960s with Lindbergh's 1930s series (before grazing was permitted at Chaco). The more they looked, the more they saw unmistakable traces of a prehistoric road network. They commissioned new flights, and road segments were field-checked against the aerial photographs. By 1973, Gwinn and Lyons had identified more than 300 kilometers of prehistoric roads (diagrammed in Figure 3-3). Amazingly, Lindbergh's photographs showed the famous Chacoan roads. But nobody recognized them as such until 1971, when archaeologists had a clue of what to look for (actually, Navajos living in Chaco Canyon had known about portions of the roads more than a century ago, although they, too, were unaware of their complete extent).

Aerial photography today is far more advanced than taking black-and-white photographs while hanging off the side of a biplane. Early photographic techniques were restricted to the visible portion of the electromagnetic spectrum, and cloud cover often hampered them. A variety of new photographic techniques allows film to capture portions of the electromagnetic spectrum that the naked eye cannot see and that are unaffected by cloud cover.

Figure 3-3 Schematic diagram of Chaco road system as it may have appeared by AD 1050.

One technique that NASA used at Chaco in the 1980s was **thermal infrared multispectral scanning,** or **TIMS.** TIMS measures infrared thermal radiation given off by the ground; it is sensitive to differences as little as 0.1° C. Although we've had the ability to make infrared photographs for some time, TIMS is an advance because of the quality of the photographs.

All photographs consist of pixels, and an instrument cannot record anything smaller than the size of a particular technique's pixel. In earlier satellite imagery (for example, Landsat photos), the pixels were 30 meters on a side, so these techniques could not record anything smaller than about 900 square meters. Such photos were of limited use to archaeology. The resolution of

thermal infrared multispectral scanner (TIMS) A remote sensing technique that uses equipment mounted in aircraft or satellite to measure infrared thermal radiation given off by the ground. Sensitive to differences as little as 0.1° C, it can locate subsurface structures by tracking how they affect surface thermal radiation.

TIMS images varies with altitude, but some projects have attained resolutions as small as 1–2 meters. These photographs can be quite useful to archaeology, and they are unaffected by cloud cover.

TIMS images are taken with a very complex kind of camera, and the data—the sensed infrared radiation—are transformed via a computer program into so-called false-color images. False-color images map the ground in terms of infrared radiation—rendering terrain in garish reds, blues, and purples. Because the Chacoan roads are more compacted than the surrounding soil (even if their compacted surface is buried), they should reflect more radiation than the surrounding sand.

And indeed they do. In false-color images, the roads appear as clear, tan lines against a backdrop of red sand. The Chaco experiment proved that TIMS can detect features such as buried road systems, even if they are invisible to an archaeologist standing on top of them.

Today, analysis of aerial and high-altitude photographs has revealed possibly as much as *600 kilometers* of ancient roadways around Chaco Canyon. These roads are only 5–10 centimeters deep and yet sometimes 7–10 meters wide. Often they turn suddenly in doglegs and are occasionally edged by low rock walls. Sometimes they are littered with potsherds. Sometimes they are cut into the earth, and sometimes they were made by simply clearing away the surface rock and vegetation.

The longest and best-defined roads, probably constructed between AD 1075 and 1140, extend some 50 kilometers outward from Chaco Canyon. Sometimes the roads are just short segments, and it is unclear if they were intended to be segments, if they were unfinished, or if portions of the road have disappeared through erosion. In places, the Chacoans constructed causeways, and elsewhere they cut stairways into sheer cliffs. The generally straight bearings suggest that the Ancestral Pueblo laid out the roads prior to construction, although archaeologists are unsure exactly how they did it.

Why did the Chaco people build these roads across the desert? This elaborate road system covered more than 250,000 square kilometers, and yet the Ancestral Pueblo had no wheeled vehicles or even beasts of burden. Why are the roads so wide and so straight? What were they used for?

Although we don't have answers to these questions yet, it is clear that archaeologists had unknowingly walked over the remains of the Chaco road system for decades. Their discovery had to come from data that were sensed remotely. Today, a battery of different, highly sophisticated photographic techniques helps archaeologists find buried remains. Other techniques, used on the ground rather than in airplanes or satellites, also help archaeologists see below the ground.

Remote Sensing at Mission Santa Catalina

Previously, we explained how transect survey and power auger testing helped us narrow down the location of Mission Santa Catalina to a 1-hectare (2.6-acre) area on St. Catherines Island, Georgia. One of the survey units in this area, Quad IV, was an undistinguished piece of real estate covered by scrub palmetto and live oak forest. The only evidence of human occupation was a little-used field road for island research vehicles. Although we could see aboriginal shell midden scatters here and there, Quad IV betrayed absolutely no surface clues as to what lay below.

At this point, we shifted our field strategy from preliminary subsurface testing to noninvasive, nondestructive remote sensing. Choosing the right method depends on what you expect to find. What, exactly, were we looking for? For more than a century, Santa Catalina had been the northernmost Spanish outpost on the eastern seaboard, and this historical fact implied considerable size and permanence. The seventeenth-century mission must have had a fortified church; some buildings to house soldiers and priests; plus enough granaries, storehouses, and dwellings for hundreds of Guale Indian neophytes.

We reasoned that the mission buildings were built by a *wattle-and-daub* technique. Freshly cut timbers were probably set vertically along the walls and reinforced with cane woven horizontally between the uprights. This sturdy wattlework was then plastered (daubed) with a mixture of marsh mud, sand, and plant fibers (probably Spanish moss). Roofs were thatched with palmetto.

So constructed, wattle-and-daub buildings are biodegradable. If the roof does not burn, then its thatch will eventually rot and blow away. And once directly exposed to the weather, mud and twig walls simply wash away. Archaeologists seeking such a dissolved mission would soon be out of business.

But thatched roofs often burn, and if that happened at Santa Catalina, the heat would have fired and hardened the daub walls, as happens with a pot baking in a kiln. Fired daub, nearly as indestructible as the ubiquitous potsherd, thus became a key in our search for the mission.

So, how do you find chunks of burned mud buried beneath a foot of sand without excavating thousands of square meters?

A Proton Magnetometer Approach

It turns out that the marsh mud used in daub plaster contains microscopic iron particles. Normally, these are randomly oriented to all points of the compass. But when intensely heated, the particles orient toward magnetic north—like a million tiny compass needles. To pinpoint these magnetically anomalous orientations, we relied upon a **proton precession magnetometer**. The theory behind this device is complicated, but the principle is simple: Magnetometers measure the strength of magnetism between the Earth's magnetic core and a sensor controlled by the archaeologist. If hundreds of these readings are taken across a systematic grid, a computer plotter can generate a magnetic contour map reflecting both the shape and the intensity of magnetic anomalies beneath the ground surface.

Many subsurface anomalies are archaeologically irrelevant magnetic "noise"—interference from underlying rocks, AC power lines, or hidden iron debris. The Earth's magnetic field fluctuates so wildly on some days that the readings are meaningless, and electrical storms can hopelessly scramble magnetometer readings. Even minor interference, such as the operator's wristwatch or eyeglasses, can drive a magnetometer crazy.

But when everything works just right, the magnetometer provides the equivalent of a CAT scan, telling archaeologists what is going on beneath the Earth's surface. Many archaeological features have characteristic magnetic signatures—telltale clues that hint at the size, shape, depth, and composition of the archaeological objects hidden far below. Shallow graves, for instance, have a magnetic profile vastly different from, say, a buried fire pit or a wattle-and-daub wall.

We worked with Ervan Garrison (University of Georgia) and a magnetometer team from Texas A&M University (Figure 3-4). As they were packing up their field equipment to work up the data in their lab, they

shared a couple of hunches, based strictly on their raw magnetometer readings: "If we were y'all, we'd dig in three places: here, over yonder, and especially right here." We took their advice, exploring each of the three magnetic anomalies in the few days remaining in our May field season. One anomaly—"especially right here"—turned out to be a large iron barrel ring. Excavating further, we came upon another ring, and more below that. At about 3 meters down, we hit the water table. Digging underwater, we encountered a well-preserved oak well casing.

Archaeologists love wells because, like privies, they can be magnificent artifact traps. After removing the bones of an unfortunate fawn (which had long ago drowned), we found an array of distinctive Hispanic and Guale Indian potsherds and a metal dinner plate dropped (or tossed) into the well. All artifacts were typical of the sixteenth and seventeenth centuries. We had indeed found Mission Santa Catalina, and we pressed on to see what else the magnetometer might have turned up.

Our second magnetic anomaly—the one "here"—was a small mound. We thought at first that it might be a grave or tomb. But after removing the overburden, we came across a burned daub wall that, as it fell, had crushed dozens of Spanish and Guale domestic artifacts: imported tin-enameled glazed cups, painted ceramic dishes, a kitchen knife, and at least two enormous pots for cooking or storage. Charred deer and chicken bones littered the floor, and dozens of tiny corncobs lay scattered about. This time, the magnetometer had led us to the kitchen (in Spanish, *cocina*) used by seventeenth-century Franciscan friars at Santa Catalina.

Finally, we began digging the "over yonder" anomaly, which proved to be a linear daub concentration more than 12 meters long—obviously the downed wall of yet another, much larger mission building. Here excavations turned up none of the everyday implements and debris so common in the scorched *cocina*. Instead, we found human graves.

proton precession magnetometer A remote sensing technique that measures the strength of magnetism between the Earth's magnetic core and a sensor controlled by the archaeologist. Magnetic anomalies can indicate the presence of buried walls or features.

© American Museum of Natural History, photo by Dennis O'Brien

Figure 3-4 Ervan Garrison and Deborah Mayer O'Brien look for Mission Santa Catalina (on St. Catherines Island, Georgia) using a proton magnetometer. She is holding the sensor, and he is recording magnetometer readings.

The search was over. We had discovered the church, the paramount house of worship at Santa Catalina de Guale. Our magnetometer survey had given us trustworthy directions to the buried daub walls and iron barrel hoops, and had taken us to the very heart of Mission Santa Catalina.

Since the discovery of Santa Catalina, we have spent a decade excavating the church ruins. The lateral church walls were constructed of wattle and daub that, when encountered archaeologically, consisted of a densely packed linear rubble scatter; this is what the magnetometer "saw" in Quad IV. Beneath the nave and sanctuary of the church, we discovered the cemetery, where the Franciscans had interred 400 to 450 Christianized Guale Indians.

A Soil Resistivity Approach

Proton magnetometry was just one of the techniques used to locate and define Santa Catalina de Guale. **Soil**

soil resistivity survey A remote sensing technique that monitors the electrical resistance of soils in a restricted volume near the surface of an archaeological site; buried walls or features can be detected by changes in the amount of resistance registered by the resistivity meter.

resistivity survey monitors the electrical resistance of soils in a restricted volume near the surface of an archaeological site. Perhaps partially because of its relatively low cost, soil resistivity survey has become a popular technique of geophysical prospecting over the past four decades.

The degree of soil resistivity depends on several factors, the most important of which is usually the amount of water retained in the soil—the less water, the greater the resistance to electrical currents. Compaction such as occurs in house floors, walls, paths, and roads tends to reduce pore sizes and hence the potential to retain water; this registers as high resistance. In effect, when electricity is sent through the soil, buried features can often be detected and defined by their differential resistance to electrical charge (caused by their differential retention of groundwater).

The aggregation of fill in pits, ditches, and middens will also alter resistivity. Foundations or walls, particularly those in historic period sites, generally have *greater* resistivity than surrounding soil, whereas the generation of humus by occupation activity increases the ion content of the soil, *reducing* resistivity.

After the initial discovery of the mission and a pilot resistivity survey, Mark Williams and the late Gary Shapiro returned to St. Catherines Island to work with Thomas to conduct a more comprehensive study. We measured soil resistance by setting four probes in line at 1-meter intervals, each probe inserted to a depth of 20 centimeters. We passed an electrical current between the probes and recorded the electrical conductivity between the two center probes.

We took readings on east-west grid lines at 1-meter intervals. The line was then advanced a meter north or south, and another set of readings were taken. This procedure resulted in a gridded array of resistance values, recorded in the field on graph paper and eventually transferred to a computer. We also charted the locations of trees, backdirt (the piles of dirt created by excavation), roads, and other features that might influence resistance.

We conducted one of the preliminary resistivity surveys in a 15 × 15 meter area that straddled a test excavation of Structure 2 at Santa Catalina, initially located by the proton magnetometer survey. From our test excavations, we suspected that this building was probably the kitchen, but we had no idea of the building's configuration. The resistivity diagram clearly identified the margins of the unexcavated building. Later, excavations confirmed the accuracy of the soil resistivity diagram.

In some circumstances, archaeologists opt to use conductivity meters, which measure the inverse of what a resistivity meter measures—that is, how well sediment *conducts* electricity. A conductivity instrument, which looks like a 1- to 3-meter-long carpenter's level, is easy to use. The archaeologist simply lays it on the ground along a grid line, pushes a button, and records the reading. Conductivity meters are useful when soil is completely dry, because resistivity meters require wet, but not saturated, soils. However, conductivity meters are expensive (about $17,000), and the data they generate are not as easily manipulated and analyzed as are resistivity data.

A Ground-Penetrating Radar Approach

Yet another method of geophysical prospecting is **ground-penetrating radar (GPR)**. Although this method tends to be expensive, its cost is offset to some degree by its speed. But neither operating the radar equipment nor interpreting the results is simple, and the assistance of trained specialists is required.

GPR was first developed in 1910, but a significant peak in relevant articles coincided with the *Apollo 17* lunar sounding experiment in the early 1970s. Today, engineering firms commonly employ GPR techniques to find buried rock or deep swamp deposits, or to search for caverns.

In GPR, radar pulses directed into the ground reflect back to the surface when they strike targets or interfaces within the ground (such as a change in the density of dirt, groundwater, buried objects, voids, or an interface between soil and rock). As these pulses are reflected, their speed to the target and the nature of their return are measured. The signal's reflection provides information about the depth and three-dimensional shape of buried objects.

With *transducers* (devices that convert electrical energy to electromagnetic waves) of various dimensions, a researcher applying GPR can direct the greatest degree of resolution to the depth of specific interest.

A pulsating electric current is passed through an antenna, inducing electromagnetic waves that radiate toward the target and return in a fraction of a microsecond to be recorded. The dimensions of the transducer influence the depth and detail that are desired in any specific archaeological application. As the antenna is dragged across the ground surface, a continuous profile of subsurface electromagnetic conditions is printed on a graphic recorder. The location and depth of subsurface targets can be inferred from, and tested against, this graphic record.

Why did we begin using GPR at Santa Catalina? Historical documents suggested that the Spanish had fortified the mission as a precaution against British attack, perhaps by building a stockade-and-moat complex to protect the buildings immediately adjacent to the central plaza. Yet, after 3 years of using magnetometer and resistivity surveys and limited test excavations, we had failed to locate any trace of defensive fortifications, such as palisades, bastions, or moats encircling the central mission zone. Given that these features might not have burned and because they could be as saturated with water as the surrounding sediment, they might have eluded the magnetometer and resistivity instruments. However, these features might have differed from the background sediment in terms of their compaction, and that suggested to us that GPR might help locate them.

We ran a number of systematic north-south transects at 20-meter intervals, locating significant anomalies on the ground by means of pin flags. We then ran a third set of transects at a 45° angle, to intercept buried anomalies at a different angle. Directed by these radar profiles, our test excavations led directly to the discovery of the palisade-and-bastion complex encircling the central buildings and plaza at Santa Catalina. Although this defensive network could surely have been located by extensive test trenching, the radar approach proved to be considerably more cost effective and less destructive than conventional archaeological exploration.

ground-penetrating radar (GPR) A remote sensing technique in which radar pulses directed into the ground reflect back to the surface when they strike features or interfaces within the ground, showing the presence and depth of possible buried features.

Cerén: The New World Pompeii?

Remote sensing studies work best when we can calibrate instrumentation and imagery to local conditions and when field verification is possible. Such a situation existed at the site of Cerén, located in the Zapotitán Valley of El Salvador.

A bulldozer operator discovered the Cerén site in 1976 as he attempted to level a platform on which to build some grain storage silos. When he noticed that his bulldozer blade had uncovered the corner of a deeply buried building, the curious workman stepped down and looked around. When he found some old-looking pottery buried in the building, he stopped work and notified the National Museum in San Salvador. Unfortunately, when a representative of the museum arrived 3 days later, he dismissed the find as very recent construction and gave the heavy equipment

operator his blessing to continue working. As a result, several other ancient buildings were also bulldozed.

Two years later, when Payson Sheets and his students from the University of Colorado arrived to conduct a survey of the Zapotitán Valley, townspeople told them of the unusual find and showed them where some of it remained. Sheets saw some adobe columns protruding from the disturbed area and expected to find bits of plastic and newspaper eroding out of the ruined building. Even when he found some Maya polychrome pottery (that Sheets knew dated to AD 500–800), he too thought that the building was modern—the thatch roof was almost perfectly preserved, even though it was buried beneath nearly 5 meters of volcanic ash (Figure 3-5).

But after a few hours of excavation, Sheets found lots of ancient Maya artifacts—without any sign of historic period material. Sheets worried: What if he announced these well-preserved buildings were prehistoric and they turned out to be recent? The whole issue turned, of

© Payson Sheets

Figure 3-5 Adobe columns and flooring of Structure 1 at the Cerén site (El Salvador). This Maya house was buried instantaneously in about AD 590 by nearly 5 meters of volcanic ash from the nearby Loma Caldera. When archaeologist Payson Sheets and his crew excavated this house, they found all artifacts left in place. Even the thatched roof had been preserved.

Figure 3-6 Ground-penetrating radar profile across three buried structures at the Cerén site.

course, on dating. Sheets collected some of the buried roof thatch for radiocarbon analysis (we discuss dating methods in Chapter 5). When the results of the tests came back, he no longer worried about embarrassing himself—all the thatch samples (and therefore the buried houses as well) were 1400 years old.

Large volcanoes and cinder cones, many of which are active, surround the Zapotitán Valley. The Cerén site, as it came to be known, was buried in about AD 590 by several meters of volcanic ash from the nearby Loma Caldera. Because the ash had cooled off considerably by the time it hit, nearly all the ancient agricultural features and cultural artifacts were miraculously preserved—crops still in the field, orchards, a central public plaza surrounded by adobe houses with artifacts left exactly as buried—even ancient Maya farmers' footprints!

But the ash that so preserved Cerén also completely obscured it. How could Sheets map a village buried beneath 5 meters of volcanic debris?

Sheets and his colleagues turned to GPR as a way to see what lay below the surface. The depositional conditions at Cerén were almost ideal for remote sensing. The overlying volcanic ash contained relatively little clay and there was only minimal soil formation. One of the radar antennas, using 300 MHz frequency radar energy, could penetrate 5 meters deep, and it could detect features as small as 45–50 centimeters (about 18–20 inches). The resulting readout is shown in Figure 3-6.

Sheets mapped and reconstructed the entire ancient landscape at Cerén from the GPR results and then ver-

ified the reconstruction with test pits and broad excavations. By carefully working out the various radar signatures from the excavated houses, Sheets was able to map these unexcavated pre-Columbian houses precisely using remote sensing and associated computer modeling techniques. The population density of the buried zone was surprisingly high. On the day it was buried, Cerén was a prosperous farming village with closely packed domestic, civic, and religious buildings constructed on elevated platforms, with all intervening space between them taken up by agricultural crops.

Because of its extraordinary Pompeii-like preservation, the Cerén site is one of the most important places in Central America for studying ancient land-use practices. And GPR mapping proved to be a cost-effective method for discovering buried houses—some of which were excavated, the rest preserved for the future.

Geographic Information Systems

Archaeological data are inherently spatial, and archaeologists map things all the time. Maps show where things are and, more important, how they relate to each other. Archaeologists use maps to plot the results of remote sensing, such as artifact distributions within a site and distributions of sites across a region, state, or even a continent.

But in their traditional form, maps are difficult to update with new information, and the resulting distributions are often unwieldy to analyze.

This all changed in the late 1980s with the advent of **geographic information systems (GIS),** computer programs designed to store, retrieve, analyze, and display cartographic data. GIS lets you view information—any geographically related information—visually. The

geographic information system (GIS) A computer program for storing, retrieving, analyzing, and displaying cartographic data.

RAPID REVIEW   Remote Sensing Methods

Method	What Does It Measure?	Where Does It Work Best?
Soil resistivity	Sediment's resistance to electrical current	In damp sediments; useful to locate compacted surfaces that retain less water and hence are more resistant to electrical current; also looser fill in pits that will retain water and increase conductivity
TIMS (a technique of aerial photography)	Thermal radiation given off by the Earth's surface	Where the archaeological features of interest are fairly large, 8–10 meters in size
Proton magnetometer	Magnetic anomalies	Burned buildings and hearths; significant subsurface disturbance such as buried ditches or pits
Ground-penetrating radar (GPR)	Strength and speed of radar pulses directed into the Earth	Buried surfaces that differ in their compaction from surrounding sediments

most common programs in use today are ArcView and ArcInfo.

Every GIS consists of three primary components: a powerful computer graphics program used to draw a map, one or more external databases that are linked to the objects shown on the map, and a set of analytical tools that can graphically interpret or statistically analyze the stored data. Most U.S. states are in the process of putting all their site records into a GIS. Clearly, GIS is a basic skill that any student contemplating a career in archaeology should learn.

In true GIS format, the Earth's various features are not depicted visually—as they would be on standard two-dimensional maps—but as digital information. Virtually every standard USGS topographic map is now available digitally (some high-end GPS units contain them already). Data stored digitally, of course, can be manipulated and displayed in numerous ways.

georeferenced Data that are input to a GIS database using a common mapping reference—for example, the UTM grid—so that all data can be spatially analyzed.

In GIS, a database is composed of several themes, or layers. Envision a base topographic map—that's one theme. Now envision laying a clear sheet of Mylar plastic over that map (this is how we used to do it!). You plot on the Mylar sheet all the archaeological sites you just found in a survey. This layer is another theme. Over the first Mylar sheet, we lay another on which we draw in all the water sources; this is a third theme. On yet another sheet, we draw the distribution of different vegetation communities. On another, we plot the results of high-altitude imagery. On still another, the region's different soils . . . you get the picture.

Mapping like this with physical sheets of paper or Mylar is unwieldy, and the resulting patterns are difficult to analyze statistically. However, by inputting all these different data digitally into a single **georeferenced** database, we can call up one or more of the layers and analyze the distributions. *Georeferenced* means that all the data are input using a common mapping reference, for example, the UTM grid system mentioned earlier. Because the data are digital, we can do spatial analyses in minutes that previously might have taken weeks or longer. Each of the data points are linked to a database, which can include complete information on that point. A site record, for example, might contain information on a site's artifacts—how many projectile points or potsherds were found there—plus other data such as its size, its slope, and the kind of architecture that was present.

GIS and the Chacoan Roads

GIS is a tool that opens up new ways to analyze spatial data. For example, a GIS can create viewsheds that show what portion of a landscape is visible from a particular site. With such a capability, we could test the proposition that a site on a ridge top is a hunting stand or lookout, since the view from a hunting stand should encompass land where we would expect to find grazing animals or migrating herds of game. GIS can also test hypotheses that otherwise might have required months if not years of fieldwork. To show how, let's return to the Chacoan roads that we mentioned above and ask the question "If the Chacoans had no wheeled vehicles or beasts of burden, what were these roads for?"

One hypothesis is that the Chaco roads functioned strictly economically, as a way to move foods and goods across the landscape. The roads radiate outward from Chaco Canyon, so perhaps they were a way to provision the inhabitants of the canyon's Great Houses with maize, timber, and other supplies.

But these roads also tend to cut straight across hills, rather than skirt around them, and some make inexplicable sharp turns in the middle of desert. These facts lead some to suggest that the roads were not economic at all, but instead served some ceremonial function with symbolic meanings.

The likely descendants of the people who inhabited Chaco Canyon are the Keres, the Puebloan peoples who live among the pueblos of the northern Rio

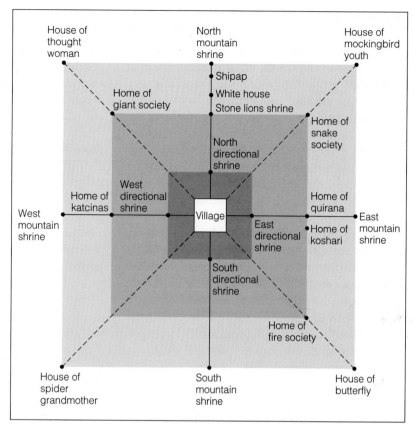

Figure 3-7 The symbolic structure of the Keres. *From J. Snead and R. Preucel, "The Ideology of Settlement: Ancestral Keres Landscapes in the Northern Rio Grande." In W. Ashmore and A. B. Knapp (Eds.),* Archaeologists of Landscape: Contemporary Perspectives *(pp. 169–197). Oxford: Blackwell Publishers. Used by permission.*

Grande in New Mexico. In traditional Pueblo theology, the world consists of several nested layers, surrounded at the edges by four sacred mountains. As James Snead (George Mason University) and Robert Preucel (University of Pennsylvania) describe them, these nested layers center on a village, and different directions are associated with different powers, societies, and supernatural beings, as well as with maleness and femaleness (Figure 3-7).

This symbolic landscape is physically manifested by different kinds of shrines. For example, the shrine on Mount Taylor, the west mountain shrine for Laguna Pueblo, is a shallow pit where people still come to pray. Directional shrines may be located closer to the villages and are often found in caves or near springs. One important directional shrine is two mountain lions carved from bedrock and surrounded by a circle of stones. Closer to villages are directional shrines that mark a village's boundaries. Located in the four cardinal directions, they are often keyhole-shaped stone structures with openings to the north or east. Other shrines are found within the village itself, especially in plazas where important dance rituals take place.

Clearly, in the Puebloan world the landscape has symbolic as well as economic meaning. Direction, in particular, seems to hold special symbolic significance in Pueblo religion. Although the ancient Chacoans probably did not share the Keres worldview exactly, they may have had a similar one, or at least one in which shrines marked significant places and directions on the landscape.

Working in a region just south of Chaco Canyon, John Kantner (Georgia State University) used a GIS to test whether the roads were linked to the economic or symbolic aspects of the desert landscape. He reasoned that if the roads were for purely economic purposes, then they should follow the path of least resistance between Pueblo villages; if they did not, then perhaps the roads fulfilled a religious purpose that was driven by the ancient peoples' symbolic interpretation of the landscape.

Using a digitized model of the area's topography (called a "digital elevation model"), Kantner asked the GIS to do a straightforward task: Find the easiest walking route between settlements that are connected by roads. Although it would take an archaeologist many days to walk out the possibilities in the field or even to trace them out on topographic maps, the GIS could quickly calculate the "path of least resistance" for someone walking from one settlement to another.

Interestingly, Kantner found that the GIS did *not* predict the locations of the roads. In fact, some of the roads cross terrain that is substantially different from that predicted by the GIS. The Chacoan roads do not follow the path of least resistance.

Kantner had assumed that anyone as familiar with their landscape as the Ancestral Pueblo people were would know the easiest way to walk from one settlement to another. But perhaps this assumption was wrong— perhaps people did *not* know or did *not* use the easiest paths between settlements. To test this hypothesis, Kantner asked whether there were any archaeological remains associated with the GIS-predicted paths.

In fact, he found that small stone shrines occur along the predicted footpaths; it appears that someone was using the predicted paths, and probably on a regular basis. In addition, large circular stone shrines, ones that required more effort to construct, were almost always found with the roads, not the predicted footpaths.

From this, Kantner concluded that although people may have moved food and goods along the roads, this was not the roads' primary purpose. Instead, people used the small trails for mundane economic purposes. The formal roads' association with large shrines suggests that they performed some other role. Perhaps they were religious paths; some, in fact, lead directly to places on the landscape that figure prominently in modern Puebloan religion. Or perhaps they helped to integrate the small far-flung pueblos with the Great Houses in Chaco Canyon. We still don't know the purpose of the roads for sure, but GIS clearly casts doubt on the "economic hypothesis."

Conclusion: The Potential and Limitations of Noninvasive Archaeology

We began this chapter with a discussion of "gumshoe survey," the process of looking around for a good site to excavate by talking with lots of people, none of whom may be archaeologists. This is a good way to find rare or spectacular sites because those are the kinds of places that nonarchaeologists remember. Few would note, or even notice, small scatters of potsherds or stone flakes.

But archaeologists aren't just interested in the big, eye-catching sites. They are interested in the whole range of human settlement, in everything from spectacular pueblos to the small scatter of a single broken pot. Sample surveys arose in the 1960s as a way not to find sites, but to adequately characterize a region's archaeology. Spectacular sites are always informative, but they are much more informative when we know something about their regional context. And sample survey provides that context.

GIS has likewise become an important tool for understanding context. One of archaeology's strengths is its ability to use spatial patterns to test hypotheses about ancient cultural behavior. GIS is extremely useful to federal and state agencies that must manage the archaeological sites on their properties. For these reasons, it is likely that GIS will become as indispensable to archaeologists as their Marshalltown trowels. However, these methods will never replace our trowels, or our need to excavate sites.

We have also provided examples of how remote sensing works in archaeology. Archaeology today is also pervaded by a new conservation ethic. Because only a finite number of sites exist in the world, we excavate only what we must to answer a particular research question, saving portions of sites, or entire sites, for future researchers. Remote sensing helps to target excavation and thus to conserve sites.

One drawback has been that remote sensing techniques are expensive, but the cost has been going down as the machinery becomes more widely available. And remote sensing can pay for itself, given that the cost of

the alternative—hand excavation—goes up each year. By targeting excavation efforts, remote sensing could actually reduce a project's cost.

But remote sensing cannot work everywhere—at least not yet. The different geophysical devices work best under certain conditions. In places where there is a lot of background noise—such as a high groundwater table, lots of background rock, or natural subsurface features—it is often difficult to pick out which anomalies in the magnetometer, resistivity, or GPR readings are worth investigating. And high-altitude imagery has to be ground-truthed (that is, verified with physical observation) to determine what the images are recording. But with increasing refinements to the technology, remote sensing has already proven itself to be an indispensable excavation tool.

Summary

- Archaeological sites are found in different ways, and there is no single formula. Luck and hard work are the major keys; other sites are found through systematic regional survey.

- Settlement pattern archaeology transcends the single site in order to determine the relationships among sites used by past societies.

- In some places, archaeological remains have lain on stable ground surfaces rather than becoming buried by sand, silt, and gravel. We can sample such areas using one or more probability-based pedestrian sampling designs.

- Judicious use of survey sampling can help locate a rare buried site whose existence, if not its exact location, is already known.

- Survey methods depend on the question the archaeologist seeks to answer, the time and resources available, the topography, and the specific character of

the archaeology (for example, ephemeral surface scatters of stone flakes or deeply buried sites with no surface indications).

- Archaeological sites are nonrenewable resources that we must use carefully so that future generations can bring better techniques and new questions to them. Important to carrying out this task are a variety of methods for doing noninvasive, and hence relatively nondestructive, archaeology. These include high-altitude imagery, proton magnetometry, soil resistivity, and ground-penetrating radar, each of which can detect certain kinds of buried features.

- Geographic information systems (GIS) allow archaeologists to construct georeferenced databases. These permit us to portray and analyze spatial relationships between archaeological and other kinds of data or to create powerful models to predict regional patterns in the spatial distribution of archaeological data.

Media Resources

Doing Fieldwork: Archaeological Demonstrations CD-ROM

This CD gives you a vivid glimpse of what it is like to be involved in an archaeological dig . . . without leaving your chair. With this CD, you will see archaeologists involved in actual excavations—many of which are referenced in your Thomas/Kelly text—using a number of the field techniques covered in this chapter. Organized according to the various stages of a live excavation, the CD presents hands-on interactive activities, live-action demonstration videos, and quizzes to help you better understand the processes and techniques that are important to an excavation.

The Companion Website for Archaeology: **Down to Earth,** *Third Edition*

http://anthropology.wadsworth.com/thomas_kelly3e_down/

Supplement your review of this chapter by going to the companion website to take one of the practice quizzes, use the flash cards to master key terms, and check out the many other study aids that are designed to help you succeed in your introductory archaeology course.

4

Doing Fieldwork: Why Archaeologists Dig Square Holes

Outline

Excavations at the *convento* (friars' housing) at Mission Santa Catalina (Georgia). Archaeologists in the foreground are mapping finds within a horizontal grid system. Those in the mid-ground use the shovel-skimming technique (a technique used to remove sandy deposits that contain few artifacts; skimming the surface of the excavation unit, the excavator removes only a fraction of an inch each time). All dirt is screened in gasoline-powered sifters evident in the background.

© American Museum of Natural History, photo by Deborah Mayer O'Brien

Preview

A SK MOST PEOPLE what archaeologists do, and they'll tell you this: "They dig." And that's true. Despite what we have seen in the preceding two chapters about archaeological survey techniques and remote sensing technology, digging up old stuff remains at the heart of archaeology—and probably always will.

But excavation is a more complex and sophisticated venture than throwing a shovel into a pickup and heading off for the mountains. Archaeologists are well aware of the fact that as they gather data from a site, they are also destroying that site, because once a site is excavated, it can never be excavated again. Therefore, it's essential that archaeologists record as much detail as possible, so that future archaeologists can reconstruct what earlier archaeologists did and use the records to answer new questions. This means that you dig slowly and take excruciatingly careful and detailed notes. Nonetheless, as Kent Flannery (University of Michigan) once said, "Archaeology is the most fun you can have with your pants on." And he's right, as anybody who has ever participated in a dig will tell you. Thomas joined his first archaeological expedition as a college junior; Kelly as a high school sophomore. We were both hooked from the start.

We warned earlier about the problems of learning archaeological field techniques from a book (even this one): you just can't do it. But in this chapter we describe common archaeological field methods, and we do hope to show you how fieldwork is done and what it really feels like.

Doing Fieldwork CD-ROM: Archaeological Demonstrations

See the "What Is the Question?" "Beginning to Excavate," "Excavation," and "Stratigraphy" sections of the CD-ROM to learn more about topics covered in this chapter.

Introduction

In Chapter 3, we talked about how archaeologists go about finding sites, such as Gatecliff Shelter. But locating sites is only the beginning; excavating these sites can be far more time consuming. Along with fields such as geology and paleontology, the science of

archaeology destroys data as it is gathered—for once we excavate a site, nobody can ever dig it again. This is why archaeologists are compulsive about field notes—recording, drawing, and photographing everything we can about an artifact or a feature before removing it. This is also why we usually try to leave a portion of a site unexcavated for the future.

This chapter can be reduced to one simple point: An artifact's **provenience,** its location and context within a site, is the most important thing about that artifact;

provenience An artifact's location relative to a system of spatial data collection.

some might even say it is more important than the artifact itself. Here's one account that demonstrates that fundamental principle.

The Folsom Site and Humanity's Antiquity in North America

In Chapter 2, we discussed how eighteenth-century scholars were preoccupied with the question of where Native Americans came from. A closely related question was, "How long have Native Americans been here?" As we saw in the Moundbuilder controversy, many scholars believed that American Indians arrived in the Western Hemisphere only shortly before European colonists. This matter was politically important because, if archaeology showed that American Indians were longtime inhabitants of the New World, then their claim to the land was strengthened. But if Indian people were only recent immigrants, their hold on the land could be minimized in favor of the Europeans.

And so, from the earliest colonial times, scholars debated the antiquity of humanity in the New World (and they still do). Some claimed that the discovery of apparently crude stone tools demonstrated that humans had been in the New World for thousands of years, since the last phase of the Ice Age, but others showed that these crude artifacts could be mere quarry rejects, unfinished pieces that the artisans deemed too flawed to complete. For some scholars (notably, most of them worked for the federal government), the lack of ancient tools similar to those that Boucher de Perthes had found in France (see Chapter 1) showed that Indians were recent arrivals in the New World.

Eventually, the argument over the antiquity of humanity in the New World came down to animals. This is not as odd as it sounds. Nineteenth- and early twentieth-century archaeologists had no way to date their sites absolutely. But they knew that the world had experienced a great Ice Age in the distant past. And they reasoned (quite accurately it turns out) that this Ice Age, more properly called the **Pleistocene,** had ended about 10,000 years ago. Scholars also knew that different kinds of animals lived in North America during the Pleistocene—mammoths, mastodons, a large species of bison, giant bears, ground sloths, horses, camels, and so on. Anybody who found artifacts in undisputed association with the bones of such extinct fauna would prove that humans had been in North America for at least 10,000 years. And thus, the quest relied heavily on context: seeking ancient artifacts in unquestionable association with the bones of extinct fauna.

In Chapter 3, we mentioned that some of the most important archaeological sites are found by non-archaeologists. A hard-rock miner found Gatecliff Shelter, and an ex-slave named George McJunkin (1851–1922) found the Folsom site—the place that proved the extent of human antiquity in the Americas (Figure 4-1).

The Black Cowboy

Born into slavery in 1851, McJunkin acquired his freedom at age 14. That year, he "borrowed" a mule that belonged to his former owner and left his home on a Texas plantation in search of work. By 1868, he was breaking horses for a Texas rancher and later held down a string of ranch jobs in Colorado and New Mexico. He became an expert cowboy and knew just about all there was to know about horses and cattle.

McJunkin also learned a lot about many other things. Although he never received a formal education, he taught himself to read and play the fiddle. He was curious about everything, especially natural history, and one of his prize possessions was a wooden box filled with rocks, bones, fossils, and arrowheads. McJunkin never married and lived most of his life as the only African American in his community.

Early in the 1890s, McJunkin's talents were recognized by the owner of the Crowfoot Ranch, in northwestern New Mexico near the town of Folsom. Soon, McJunkin was ranch foreman and proved himself an able leader of men, as well as cowpuncher and wrangler.

One day in August 1908, torrential rains fell on the Crowfoot Ranch, creating a flash flood that destroyed much of Folsom. (Many people were killed, but more would have died had not the local telephone operator, Sarah Rooke, remained at her post, calling people to warn them until the floodwaters claimed her life.) After helping to search for the dead, McJunkin began checking the Crowfoot's fences. Up Wild Horse Arroyo, he found a line that dangled across a now-deep, muddy

Pleistocene A geologic period from 2 million to 10 thousand years ago, which was characterized by multiple periods of extensive glaciation.

Figure 4-1 The Folsom site in 1997. Wild Horse Arroyo runs through the middle of the photo; site excavators David Meltzer and Lawrence Todd are at the lower left.

gully. Pondering how to fix it, he spotted bones protruding from the walls of the arroyo, some 15 feet down the embankment.

McJunkin had seen plenty of cow bones in his day, and these were definitely not cow. The bones even seemed too large for bison. McJunkin returned to the site over the years to collect bones that he then stacked on his mantle at home. He would talk to anyone who showed an interest in them and showed the site to several townsfolk.

A Spear Point between the Ribs

Eventually, the site was brought to the attention of Jesse Figgins, director of the Colorado Museum of Natural History (now the Denver Museum of Nature and Science), who was looking for skeletons of the extinct Pleistocene bison, *Bison antiquus,* for a museum display. Sadly, McJunkin had died a few years before Figgins's arrival, so he did not live to see the day that his site made archaeological history.

Some of the townsfolk who had visited the site with McJunkin had occasionally found an artifact or two among the bones (now identified as ancient bison), but they did not document their finds, meaning that the context of these artifacts was unknown. And in 1926, Figgins's crew also found a beautifully made spear point with a distinct central groove or channel (what we now call a "flute"). But, unfortunately, they could not tell whether the artifact was found with the bison skeletons or had fallen from a later, higher level—meaning that the newest find still lacked the necessary context.

Figgins telegrammed the crew to leave any artifacts exactly where they were discovered, so that he could personally observe them in place. And so, when excavators located similar spear points the following summer, they left the artifacts **in situ** (in place), so that

in situ From Latin, meaning "in position"; the place where an artifact, ecofact, or feature was found during excavation or survey.

their context could be recorded. One of these points lay between the ribs of a bison. Figgins sent telegrams to prominent members of the archaeological community, including the skeptical A. V. Kidder, who was excavating at Pecos only 100 miles away.

After joining other archaeologists at the excavation site, Kidder solemnly pronounced that the association between the spear points and the extinct bison remains was solid. There was no evidence that rodents had burrowed into the deposit, carrying later artifacts from higher in the ground down to the bison skeletons. There was no indication that streams had redeposited the artifacts on top of the remains. Everyone present saw undeniable evidence that the spear points had killed the extinct bison.

For the first time, the association between extinct fauna and human artifacts was confirmed: people had been in the Americas since at least the end of the Pleistocene, some 10,000 years ago. Today, we know McJunkin's site as the Folsom site, and the distinctive spear points found there are called "Folsom points"— both named after the nearby town that had nearly been destroyed by the deadly flood that first exposed the site.

As you can see, context was everything at the Folsom site. And this is true for any site. In fact, other than "When's lunch?" what you hear most frequently on any archaeological dig is, "Show me exactly where that came from."

Excavation: What Determines Preservation?

Excavation procedures depend on several factors, beginning with the kind of materials that have survived the passage of time. Some sites have wonderful preservation of organic materials, including basketry, leather, and wood; but in other sites, only ceramics, stones, and bones survive; and in the earliest archaeological sites, only stone tools remain. Here are some examples that demonstrate the various conditions under which organic remains are preserved.

The Duck Decoys of Lovelock Cave

Lovelock Cave (Nevada) sits on a barren hillside, just north of the Carson Desert (see Chapter 3). But thousands of years ago, anybody sitting in the cave's mouth would have looked out upon a vast wetland, just a few kilometers away. Lovelock Cave was first excavated in 1912 (by Lewellyn Loud, a museum security guard at the University of California, who was sent by anthropologist Alfred Kroeber to gather museum specimens), and again in 1924, by Mark Harrington of New York's Museum of the American Indian.

The dry and dusty interior of Lovelock Cave was better suited for storing things than for shelter, and Loud and Harrington found several caches of gear. One that Harrington found, Pit 11, held a buried basket that contained 11 duck decoys. Cleverly crafted from tule reeds twisted to simulate the body and head of a duck, some had plain tule reed bodies, and others were adorned with paint and feathers. As artifacts, the decoys are striking. Even *Sports Illustrated* has extolled the creativity and craftsmanship of these prehistoric duck hunters.

Someone buried this basket of decoys in Pit 11 (in fact, they were interred beneath the pit's false bottom), intending, evidently, to use them on a later duck hunt. Although the person who buried the decoys never retrieved them, it was wise to cache them inside Lovelock Cave because they were perfectly preserved; they are usable even today. We now know from radiocarbon dating (discussed in Chapter 5) that these decoys were made about 2000 years ago.

The Houses of Ozette

Equally remarkable, yet strikingly different, preservation is seen at the site of Ozette on Washington's Olympic Peninsula. Ozette was a major beachside village once occupied by the ancestors of the Makah people. In fact, some Makahs remained at Ozette into the 1920s, and their oral traditions helped lead Richard Daugherty (then at Washington State University) to the site in the first place.

Ozette was once a lively village stretching for a mile along the Pacific Coast, home to perhaps 800 people who lived in massive split-plank cedar houses. They hunted; gathered berries in the forest; collected shellfish along the coast; and fished for halibut, salmon, and other fish. They even hunted killer whales.

Part of the village lay along the bottom of a steep hill. Some 300 years ago, during an especially heavy rain (or possibly a tsunami), the hillside above the village became saturated and, with a roar, an enormous mudslide descended on the village, shearing the tops off five houses and burying their interiors. Some people escaped, but others were caught inside. Because the coast of Washington is so wet, the destroyed portion of Ozette remained waterlogged and was capped by a thick layer of clay by the mudslide.

The saturated dirt and the clay cap preserved entire houses with all their furnishings and gear. During the 1970s, Richard Daugherty excavated the houses, recovering some 42,000 artifacts, including baskets, mats, hats, halibut hooks, bowls, clubs, combs—even an entire cedar canoe. The archaeological team worked closely with the Makah people, and many of the artifacts from Ozette village are now on display at the Makah Cultural and Research Center in Neah Bay, Washington. These displays highlight the remarkable degree of preservation at this important waterlogged site.

The Ice Man of the Alps

Our third example demonstrates yet a different kind of archaeological preservation. In 1991, two skiers in the Alps came upon the body of a man lying in a pool of icy glacial water at 10,000 feet. The body was so well preserved that the authorities thought at first he was perhaps a mountaineer who had perished in a blizzard a few years earlier. But today, we know this man as Ötzi, the "Ice Man," who died some 5300 years ago. His body was remarkably well preserved—even tattoos are clearly visible on his skin—because he froze shortly after he died, and a small glacier then sealed his body in the shallow depression where it had come to rest. Here he freeze-dried and lay undisturbed until the warmth of recent decades caused the glacier to recede, exposing his remains (Figure 4-2).

Realizing the significance of the Ice Man, archaeologists scoured the site and recovered portions of his clothing—a belt to hold up a leather breechcloth and leggings, a coat of deerskin, a cape of woven grass, a leather fur-lined cap, and calfskin shoes, filled with grass. They also recovered tools, including a hafted copper axe, a bow and a quiver of arrows, bone points, extra bowstrings, a wooden pack frame, birch-bark containers, a stone scraper, a hafted knife, and a net.

By analyzing the contents of the Ice Man's stomach and intestine, scientists determined that he had not eaten for at least 8 hours before his death and that his final meal had been barley, wheat, deer, and wild goat.

Pollen analysis of the contents of his intestine suggests that he died in the spring.

Why did this 30-year-old man die at such a high elevation, far from any village or camp? An arrow point that penetrated past his shoulder blade suggests that he had been attacked shortly before his death. One of his hands also bears unhealed cuts, as though he warded off an assailant armed with a knife. One guess is that he was fleeing, stopped to rest in a depression away from the wind, and quietly passed away from his wounds.

The Preservation Equation

So, why were the Lovelock duck decoys, the houses of Ozette, and the Ice Man so well preserved?

Decomposition is carried out by microorganisms that require warmth, oxygen, and water to survive. In each case, one of these was lacking: Lovelock Cave lacked moisture, the wet deposits beneath the clay cap at Ozette were anaerobic (oxygenless), and the Ice Man's glacial environment lacked warmth. These different preservation conditions present the archaeologist with both opportunities and challenges. At Ozette, for example, the waterlogged archaeological deposits were a muddy gumbo that was almost impossible to trowel or shovel. And because the wooden artifacts were saturated with water, a misplaced shovel stroke could slice them like a knife through butter. To cope with these conditions, Daugherty assembled a complex system of pressurized hoses to wash the mud away. By adjusting the water pressure, they could use fire hoses to clean off the massive house posts and wall planks, switching to a fine misting spray when exposing delicate basketry.

Likewise, sites such as Lovelock Cave offer a wealth of artifacts not normally found, but such sites tend to be extremely complex. They are favorite places for rodents and carnivores, whose actions can move artifacts up and down, making it difficult to sort out what belongs with what. This means that they require especially slow excavation. And although the Ice Man contributed enormously to our knowledge of the past, his preservation now requires a sophisticated storage chamber (at Italy's South Tyrol Museum), where museum personnel control the temperature and humidity.

Preservation, of course, is only one factor conditioning how we excavate a site; other determinants ods. Archaeologists excavate ancient Pueblo sites in New Mexico that contain well-defined room clusters very differently from high-altitude caves in Peru. Peeling off sequential levels of a Maya temple in Guatemala differs radically from excavating through seemingly homogeneous shell midden deposits in Georgia. Submerged sites, such as ancient shipwrecks, require their own special brand of archaeology.

There are many ways to excavate a site, and each is appropriate if it allows the archaeologist to achieve the project's research goals within the constraints of time, funding, and technology. The only important thing is that *the excavation techniques must record an artifact's context as precisely as possible.*

© AP/Wide World Photos

© South Tyrol Museum of Archaeology/www.iceman.it

Figure 4-2 Ötzi, the "Ice Man" (top), and portions of some of his tools (bottom).

Principles of Archaeological Excavation

The key to maintaining information about an artifact's context is to record its provenience. *Provenience* means an artifact's location, but location is both hierarchical and relative.

include the site's depth, time and financial constraints, accessibility, and, perhaps most important, the research questions being pursued. We have excavated with backhoes, shovels, trowels, dental tools, and garden hoses (see "Looking Closer: The Excavator's Toolkit"). We even used a jackhammer once (to remove several massive blocks of stone that had fallen from the roof in Gatecliff Shelter).

Sometimes the archaeologist can rely on the latest technology; but other times, financial constraints or remote conditions require the use of less elegant meth-

Location is hierarchical because an artifact's provenience is simultaneously a particular country, a particular state in that country, a particular county in that state, a particular site in that county, a particular excavation unit in that site, a particular vertical level in that unit, and a particular position and orientation in that level. Obviously, the last levels in this hierarchy are more useful than the first levels. Figgins's excavators found some spear points at the Folsom site, but it was not until they were found in situ, lying between the bison's ribs, that their provenience became meaningful

LOOKING CLOSER
The Excavator's Toolkit

In Chapter 3, we presented a list of equipment that the modern archaeological surveyor should carry. Here we list things that the well-equipped excavator should carry in his or her excavation toolbox:

- A 5- to 4-inch trowel (Marshalltown brand only, accept no substitute! Sharpen the edges and cut a V-notch in one of the back edges—it's useful for cutting roots. It's also useful to have both a pointed and a square-ended kind—the latter is especially helpful when cleaning stratigraphic profiles.)
- A metal file (for sharpening that Marshalltown)
- A 2-meter and a 25-meter tape measure (metric only)
- Work gloves
- A builder's line level and string (nylon, yellow)
- A builder's angle finder (to take artifact inclinations)
- A compass (to take artifact orientations)
- Pencils (regular and mechanical), pencil sharpener, and Sharpie pens
- Spoon (a very useful excavation tool and handy at lunchtime)
- Jackknife (one with a serrated edge is useful against larger roots)

- Nails (of various sizes, for example, to hold a level string for drawing a stratigraphy)
- Straight-edge ruler with metric markings
- Torpedo level (to maintain good vertical profiles)
- Root clippers
- Small wire cutters (to cut root hairs to prepare a stratigraphic profile for photos)
- Empty film canisters (for various sorts of samples)
- A variety of small Ziploc bags (as in your survey kit)
- Toilet paper (for wrapping delicate artifacts)
- Dental tools (dentists throw them out after a limited number of uses)
- Brushes (whisk broom and 1- to 2-inch paint brushes)
- Bamboo slices (whittle the ends to a rounded tip; essential for excavating bone)
- Aluminum foil (for radiocarbon and other samples)
- Toothpicks (useful for temporarily marking artifact locations or strata in a profile)

---

to a particular question. Of course, we can make use of artifacts whose proveniences are imprecise to answer some types of research questions, but nonetheless *the excavator's first goal is to record context by recording provenience as accurately as possible.*

Location is relative because we measure an artifact's position relative to a spatial system. We could use the UTM grid (mentioned in Chapter 3), or we could use a site-specific format. The key is to find a procedure that will allow a future archaeologist to reconstruct, in great detail, where you found things in the site.

So, how do we go about excavating a site so that we recover an artifact's provenience? Let's return to Gatecliff Shelter to see how this is done.

Test Excavations

From day one, Thomas wanted to learn two things: how long people had used Gatecliff Shelter and whether the buried deposits could tell us about how human life had changed over time in this part of the Great Basin. The initial goal, then, was to decide if Gatecliff could help answer these questions. This meant that Thomas had to know what kind of historical record Gatecliff preserved. Was it a short or long record? Was it nicely stratified or a jumbled mess?

For this reason, the initial **test excavation** strategy was vertical, designed to supply, as expediently as pos-

test excavation A small initial excavation to determine a site's potential for answering a research question.

sible, a stratified sequence of artifacts and ecofacts associated with potentially datable materials. Consequently, Thomas "tested" Gatecliff with two test pits (the French call them *sondages*, or "soundings"). Like most archaeologists, we dig metrically, typically in 1-meter squares, for practical as well as scientific reasons: squares much smaller would squeeze out the archaeologist, and larger units might not allow sufficient accuracy and would remove more of the site than necessary to answer the initial questions.

Test pits are quick and dirty because we must excavate them "blind"—that is, without knowing exactly what lies below. But even when digging test pits, archaeologists maintain three-dimensional control of the finds, recording the X and Y axes (the horizontal coordinates) and the Z axis (the vertical coordinate) for each one. This is one reason why archaeologists dig square holes. Provided the pit sidewalls are kept sufficiently straight and perpendicular, excavators can use the dirt itself to maintain horizontal control on the X and Y axes by measuring directly from the sidewalls. Here the horizontal provenience is relative to the sidewalls of the pit. (In some sites, this can become problematic if one is not careful: as test pits deepen, their sidewalls slope inward, creating a "bathtub" effect that throws off the measurements.)

What about vertical control? At Gatecliff, Thomas dug the test pits in arbitrary, but consistent, 10-centimeter levels. Everything of interest—artifacts, ecofacts, soil samples, and so forth—was kept in separate level bags, one for each 10-centimeter level. The Z dimension for each level was usually designated according to distance below the ground surface: Level 1 (surface to 10 centimeters below), Level 2 (10–20 centimeters below), and so forth. This way, excavators measured vertical provenience relative to the ground surface. This also can be a problem, given that the ground surface can change over time and make it potentially difficult for future archaeologists to correlate their levels with those of a previous archaeologist. But every project requires trade-offs, and there is no point to investing much effort in a site before knowing if it will provide the necessary information. This is why test pits often record only minimal levels of provenience.

Expanding the Test Excavation

At Gatecliff, the test pits told Thomas that the site warranted a closer look, and he returned the next year to do just that. He first divided the site into a 1-meter grid system, oriented along the long axis of the shelter. The exact compass orientation of this grid was recorded (many archaeologists today routinely orient their grids to magnetic or true north, but sometimes pragmatics dictate otherwise). He assigned consecutive letters to each north-south division and numbered the east-west division (see Figure 4-3). By this method, each excavation square could be designated by a unique alphanumeric name (just like Bingo—A-7, B-5, and the ever-popular K-9). Other archaeologists use different systems, some numbering each unit according to the X and Y coordinates of the units' southwest corner. In this system, a unit with the designation North 34 East 45 (or N34 E45) means that its southwest corner is 34 meters north and 45 meters east of the site's N0 E0 point.

At Gatecliff, the east wall of the "7-trench" (so named because it contained units B-7 through I-7) defined a major profile that exposed the site's stratigraphy. Stratigraphy, you recall from Chapter 1, is the structure produced by the deposition of geological and/or cultural sediments into layers, or strata. The stratigraphy is a vertical section against which the archaeologist plots all artifacts, features, soil and pollen samples, and radiocarbon dates. (Some archaeologists use the term "stratification" to refer to the physical layers in a site, reserving "stratigraphy" only for the analytical interpretation of the temporal and depositional evidence.)

A vertical datum was established at the rear of the shelter. For all on-site operations, this **datum point** was arbitrarily assigned an elevation of zero. All site elevations from this point on were plotted as "x centimeters below datum," rather than below surface (given that the surface almost never has the same elevation across any given site). Using an altimeter and a U.S. Geological Survey topographic map, Thomas determined the elevation of this datum point to be 2319 meters (7607 feet) above sea level. All archaeological features—fire hearths, artifact concentrations, sleeping areas, and the like—were plotted on a master site map, and individual artifacts found in situ were plotted in three dimensions—their X and Y coordinates based on the map, and their Z coordinates

datum point The zero point, a fixed reference used to keep control on a dig; usually controls both the vertical and horizontal dimensions of provenience.

Figure 4-3 Plan view of the two grid systems used at Gatecliff Shelter. The alphanumeric system (consisting of letters and numbers) defined 1-meter excavation squares used in the first four seasons. Roman numerals designate the 2-meter squares used later, when large horizontal exposures were excavated. *After Thomas (1983), figure 8. Courtesy American Museum of Natural History.*

the site in an area that would remain undisturbed by construction, natural processes, or future excavation. The datum would be an aluminum or brass cap marked with the site's Smithsonian or other identifying number, set in concrete or on top of a long piece of concrete reinforcement bar driven into the ground. Today, we would also use a global positioning system (GPS) instrument to determine the datum's elevation and UTM (Universal Transverse Mercator) location. Once the datum is tied into the UTM grid, a future archaeologist could recreate its location even if the marker were destroyed.

How Archaeologists Dig

Despite what action-hero characters like Indiana Jones or Lara Croft might lead you to believe, archaeologists do not dash in, grab the goodies, and then run for their lives. We don't even mindlessly shovel dirt into a bucket. Instead, we excavate within horizontal excavation units in **natural levels** and **arbitrary levels.** Natural levels are the site's **strata** (singular, **stratum**), which are more or less homogeneous or gradational material, visually separable from other levels by a change in the texture, color, rock or organic content, or by a sharp break in depositional character (or any combination of these).

Excavators at Gatecliff, like archaeologists anywhere, excavated by natural levels wherever possible. Where these natural levels were thicker than 10 centimeters, they excavated in arbitrary levels no more than 10 centimeters in thickness within the natural levels. (Today, many archaeologists excavate in arbitrary levels only 5 centimeters deep to maintain even greater control over provenience.)

Excavators carefully troweled the deposit, then passed it outside the cave for screening (we say more about this later); artifacts and ecofacts found in the screen were bagged by level. Individual excavators kept

(that is, their elevation) based on the datum point. Incidentally, artifacts found in the test pit are brought into this system simply by determining the depth below datum of the ground surface at the test unit and plotting the test unit onto the master site grid.

This is how we did things in the 1970s. Today, however, we would have placed the datum many meters off

natural level A vertical subdivision of an excavation square that is based on natural breaks in the sediments (in terms of color, grain size, texture, hardness, or other characteristics).

arbitrary level The basic vertical subdivision of an excavation square; used only when easily recognizable "natural" strata are lacking and when natural strata are more than 10 centimeters thick.

strata (singular, **stratum**) More or less homogeneous or gradational material, visually separable from other levels by a discrete change in the character of the material—texture, compactness, color, rock, organic content—and/or by a sharp break in the nature of deposition.

field notes at this stage in bound, graph-paper notebooks. Good field notes record everything, whether or not it seems important at the time. Remember, the excavator's goal is to capture the detail that will allow a future archaeologist to "see" what the excavator saw as he or she was digging. Today, field notes employ standardized forms (unique to each excavation) so that excavators record the same detailed information for each level. Depending on how much he or she finds, it might take the excavator a week to complete this one form (but usually it is less than a day). This information includes the date, the excavator's name, a map of the unit showing where artifacts and features were found, and a detailed description of the sediments ("rock hard clay, grading from brown to reddish-orange" or "loose, and dusty, with a lot of packrat feces and cactus spines"). A geologist's Munsell soil color chart is often used to record sediment colors.

Excavators also record the level's beginning and ending elevations, observations on how this level was different from that above it ("There is more charcoal in this level"), whether any samples were taken (soil, carbon, plant materials), and so on. In addition, copious photographs (black and white, color slides, and digital) are taken of all unit profiles, all significant finds in situ, and all features. Nowadays, some archaeologists make a video recording of all excavation units at the end of each day, or during the excavation of important features and finds.

Figure 4-4 An exposure of the lower stratigraphy at Gatecliff Shelter.

American Museum of Natural History, photo by Susan L. Bierwith

Expanding Gatecliff's Excavation

The vertical excavation strategy at Gatecliff was a deliberately simplified scheme designed to clarify chronology. By the end of the fourth field season, Trench 7 had reached a depth of 9 meters below the ground surface. We had learned a good deal about the cultural sequence of Gatecliff Shelter, but our vertical excavation strategy had also left us with a series of extremely steep and hazardous sidewalls (Figure 4-4). Even though the excavation was stair-stepped to minimize the height of these sidewalls, they were still dangerous. Today, deep excavation trenches are heavily shored. Unshored walls higher than 4 feet are a violation of federal OSHA (Occupational Safety and Health Administration) regulations. And with good reason: more than one archaeologist has been nearly killed by collapsing profiles. Clearly, a change was in order for reasons of safety.

Change was required for conceptual reasons as well. The early excavations demonstrated that Gatecliff could contribute much more than mere chronology. The vertical excavation showed us that Gatecliff had witnessed something unique. Periodically, flash floods filled the shelter with thick beds of silt. Eventually, the shelter dried out, and people used it once again. The result was that layers of sterile silt neatly separated **living floors,** occupational surfaces, inside the overhang. This was a remarkable opportunity to study discrete living surfaces within a rockshelter environment.

Few archaeologists have such a chance, and so we shifted away from the initial chronological objectives to concentrate on recording the spatial distributions of artifacts and features on the living floors. The goal now was to reconstruct what activities took place in the shelter as indicated by the distribution of artifacts across the living floors sandwiched between the silt layers. With the stratigraphy suitably defined, extensive vertical sections were no longer necessary, and we concentrated on opening entire (horizontal) living surfaces.

We switched to 2 × 2 meter units, but excavated the living floors more slowly than in the previous vertical excavations, and excavators tried to recover and map all artifacts in situ. We excavated and screened features such as hearths separately, and soil samples were retained for laboratory processing. We plotted artifacts, scatters of waste flakes from stone tool manufacture, concentrations of bone—anything found in situ—on master living floor maps.

This horizontal strategy required significantly more control within contemporary layers. A single excavator carefully worked each 2-square-meter unit, attempting to find as many artifacts as possible in situ. All artifacts, features, and large ecofacts were plotted onto the large-scale living floor maps for each surface. The result was a set of living floor maps that are rare among rockshelter excavations in the world (Figure 4-5).

Precision Excavation

This description of the Gatecliff excavation provides a general sense of what goes on at archaeological sites. But excavation has become an even more exact science since Thomas excavated Gatecliff in the 1970s. Given the importance of an artifact's context, archaeologists continue to devise ways to record provenience for more objects with greater precision.

For example, at Gatecliff we first used string line levels tied to the datum and tape measures to determine an artifact's vertical provenience (its depth below datum); we later switched to a more precise builder's level and measuring rod. We recorded horizontal provenience by measuring distances from two of a unit's sidewalls. But today, many archaeologists, ourselves included, use *total stations* to record provenience (see Figure 4-6). New instruments cost a pricey $5000, but they are necessary for state-of-the-art excavation.

How do total stations work? The devices are set up on a tripod over the site's datum. After workers input the correct data, the total station "knows" where it is on the grid system and which direction it is pointing. When an artifact is found, a glass prism is held on the artifact's location, and the total station is turned and aimed at the prism. Push a button, and the station shoots a beam of infrared light at the prism. By measuring the time it takes the light to bounce back, the total station calculates and records the artifact's X, Y, and Z coordinates—its provenience. This information is later downloaded to a database for mapping and analysis. Total stations take only a second or two to make measurements that are accurate to $\pm$ 3 *millimeters.* And these instruments can be used at distances of hundreds of meters so that a site may need only one, rather than the several datums that other measurement systems may require.

Some archaeologists record the provenience of virtually every item found in situ (a practice sometimes called "piece plotting"). Others set a cutoff, recording provenience on everything found in situ that is larger than, say, 3 centimeters (about an inch) in any dimension. As we said before, there are always trade-offs. Recording the provenience of every item found in situ provides the archaeologist with a very accurate record of where you found things, but it takes much more time—meaning that less gets excavated (this is a special problem if the site is threatened with destruction). How much you piece-plot depends on how much time you have for the excavation and the questions you need the data to answer.

Is That All There Is to It?

No, there is more to recording provenience than simply location. Today, archaeologists sometimes record not only an artifact's X, Y, and Z coordinates, but also which side of the artifact was "up" when it was found (sometimes we mark the object's "up" side with a dot

living floors A distinct buried surface on which people lived.

Incised stone	Rough percussion blank	Scraper plane	Finished knife
Shouldered projectile point	Fine percussion blank	Mano	Sagebrush mat fragment
Unshouldered projectile point	Pressure flaked blank	Metate	Basketry fragment
Projectile point tip	Bone awl	Bone bead	Promontory peg
Shouldered projectile point base	Drill	Hammerstone	Utilized flake

330° magnetic

0   m   1

Figure 4-5 A living floor map showing the distribution of artifacts and hearths on Horizon 2 (deposited about AD 1300) at Gatecliff.

Figure 4-6 Harold Dibble (center) and Shannon McPherron (right) record data on site while excavating Pech de L'Azé IV in France; the student at the far left is using a total station.

in permanent ink), the compass orientation of its long axis, and its slope or inclination (recorded with a builder's angle finder or *clinometer*). We would also note whether the artifact is burned, has calcium carbonate or a particular kind of sediment adhering to it, or possesses other characteristics. Although this can make excavation mind numbing, the resulting information is critical to understanding how a site was formed and consequently for inferring what people did there.

Sifting the Evidence

Digging is just the beginning of excavation. No matter how carefully you excavate, it is impossible to see, map, and recover everything of archaeological interest; this is why we use sifters to find things that hand excavation misses. This is also the second reason why we excavate in square units—sometimes only .5 × .5 meter in size. If the excavator misses something, the sifting process can at least tie its provenience down to a particular level in a particular unit—a very small area of the site.

At Gatecliff, excavators removed deposit with a trowel and whisk broom or paint brush, carefully sweeping it into a dustpan. When an excavator found an artifact in situ, he or she recorded the artifact's provenience; sometimes it was photographed in place and a sketch drawn in the field notes before the artifact was placed in a separate bag and labeled with an identifying number.

The dustpan of dirt was then poured into a bucket and tagged with a label identifying the unit and level. When the bucket was full, the day's "gopher" took it to the screening area, outside the shelter in the hot sun (the gopher is the person whose daily assignment was to "go for" this and "go for" that). Here the bucket was poured onto a screen with 1/8-inch mesh (to give you some idea of the size, standard window screen is 1/16-inch mesh), where workers sifted and carefully checked

Figure 4-7 A few of the innumerable sifter designs used by archaeologists.

for any artifacts missed by the excavators, including stone tool manufacturing waste flakes, fragments of bone, and anything else of importance.

Although archaeologists agree that Marshalltown makes the only trowel worth owning, there are many opinions on screens. Many archaeologists manufacture their own, and the design and workmanship of screens varies from dig to dig (a few are shown in Figure 4-7). Some are suspended from tripods, some are mounted on rollers, and others are driven by gas engines to speed things up. When Thomas dug Alta Toquima, a village located at 12,000 feet in the mountains of central Nevada, he invented a "backpacker" design for the screens. At Gatecliff, we used the most common kind—a shaker screen mounted on two pivoting legs.

Exactly what kind of screen you use is far less important than the mesh. Many archaeologists prefer 1/8-inch hardware cloth, but the choice of mesh size varies with the circumstances. The important point is that *screen size affects what you recover and how fast you can recover it.* Use 1/4-inch mesh and you can process dirt faster, but you will lose a surprising number of important objects. Use 1/16-inch mesh and the recovery rate goes up—but so does the time to process the dirt.

Thomas did an experiment some years ago to see how different screen sizes might affect the recovery of animal bones in archaeological sites. He built a three-decker screen with superimposed layers of 1/4-inch over 1/8-inch over 1/16-inch mesh screens. He then ran a set of faunal remains recovered from a site through the screens.

As you might guess, he found that 1/4-inch mesh was adequate for recovering bones of large animals such as bighorn or bison. But he also found that significant numbers of bones of medium-sized animals, such as rabbits and rodents, were lost. The 1/8-inch mesh screen was better for recovering the bones of these small mammals. But, in fact, significant amounts of small mammal bones are even lost through 1/8-inch screens! One needs 1/16-inch mesh (or flotation, dis-

cussed later in this chapter) to recover the remains of animals the size of, say, pack rats, small birds, and especially fish.

Water Screening and Matrix Sorting

Archaeologists sometimes use **water screening,** especially when the artifacts and ecofacts are expected to be very small. As the name suggests, water screening requires that plenty of water be available. The dirt is simply poured onto a screen (usually 1/8- or 1/16-inch mesh) and sprayed with a garden hose until all the sediment is washed through. The screen will then be set aside and, once dry, searched. Kelly used water screening at a site in the Stillwater Marsh in the Carson Desert (Figure 4-8). Because the site was located on a clay dune that contained no natural rock, he simply water screened the deposits through 1/16-inch mesh, dried what was left, and bagged it all. He saved literally everything—flakes from the manufacture of stone

water screening A sieving process in which deposit is placed in a screen and the matrix washed away with hoses; essential where artifacts are expected to be small and/or difficult to find without washing.

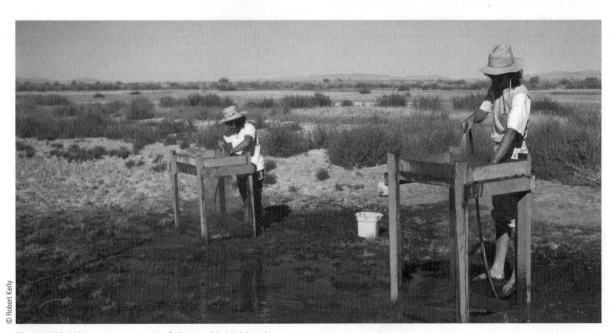

Figure 4-8 Water screening in the Stillwater Marsh, Nevada.

© Robert Kelly

tools, burned pieces of mud, fish and bird bones, and shell fragments—and sorted it later in the field camp.

You should always use the finest mesh screen possible. But sometimes this isn't possible, due to time constraints or the presence of sediments that can clog even a 1/4-inch screen quickly. For this reason, we sometimes use a larger screen mesh in the field, but take bulk sediment samples from each level. These samples are processed in the lab and provide a sample of those items missed by the screens. If the deposit has a low clay content, the sediment samples may simply be fine-screened. If they have a high clay content, they may be *deflocculated* (have the clay removed) by soaking the sediments in a solution of dishwasher detergent. After the clays are broken down, the slurry is poured through a fine screen (or often a set of screens), dried, and sorted by hand to separate stone from small stone tool waste flakes, shells, bits of ceramics, and bones. This is known as **matrix sorting,** and, along with writing catalog numbers on artifacts, it is often one of the first tasks a novice may be assigned in a lab.

Flotation

In some archaeological sites, like the upper parts of Gatecliff Shelter, the deposits are sufficiently protected from moisture that plant remains simply dry up and can be recovered by screening. But in other kinds of deposits, plant remains may be preserved only if they were burned and carbonized. These remains are often quite small and nearly impossible to collect by hand in the field.

The most common method of recovering such plant remains is **flotation.** Several procedures exist for floating archaeological samples, but all are based on the same principle: Dirt doesn't float, but carbonized plant (and some animal) remains do. By using water flotation, archaeologists can float most burned plant remains out of samples of archaeologically recovered dirt.

In one of the earliest applications, Stuart Struever (retired, former president of the Crow Canyon Archae-

ological Center) floated soil samples from 200 features attributable to the Middle Woodland component at Illinois' Apple Creek site. The samples were hauled to nearby Apple Creek, where they were placed in mesh-bottomed buckets and then water separated by students who worked midstream. More than 40,000 charred nutshell fragments, 2000 carbonized seeds, and some 15,000 identifiable fish bones were collected in this manner. Standard dry-screening techniques would have missed most of these.

While excavating at Salts Cave in Kentucky, Patty Jo Watson (Washington University) and her associates were not blessed with a nearby stream, so they improvised. Sediments were placed in double plastic bags and carried outside the cave. They first spread the samples (weighing a total of 1500 pounds) in the shade to dry. They then filled two 55-gallon drums with water, and placed the dry samples in metal buckets whose bottoms had been replaced with window screen. They submerged the buckets in the 55-gallon drums.

After a few seconds, the investigator skimmed off the charcoal and carbonized plant remains that had floated to the surface, using a small scoop made from a brass carburetor screen (cloth diapers work well, too). They spread the debris that floated to the top (called the "light fraction") and the stuff that sank (the "heavy fraction") on labeled newsprint to dry again. These flotation samples yielded carbonized remains of hickory nuts and acorns, seeds from berries, grains, sumpweed, chenopods, maygrass, and amaranth.

Today, flotation is not an expensive or even a particularly time-consuming process. Flotation techniques can (and should) be fitted to the local requirements. At Mission Santa Catalina, Thomas also used a converted 55-gallon drum, and one person could process dozens of samples each day. Some elaborate power-driven machines are equipped with aeration devices and use *deflocculants* or chemicals to remove sediment that might adhere to and sink carbonized plant remains. The technology is available to fit any budget.

But accuracy, not technology, is the issue. For a long time archaeologists saved only bone (and even then, just the large, identifiable pieces) but ignored plant remains. This frequently led archaeologists to overemphasize hunting and herding, thereby deemphasizing the plant component of the economy. Now that flotation techniques have come into their own, we are discovering new things about the past. For example, from

matrix sorting The hand sorting of processed bulk soil samples for minute artifacts and ecofacts.

flotation The use of fluid suspension to recover tiny burned plant remains and bone fragments from archaeological sites.

those seemingly innocuous burnt seeds of sumpweed, chenopods, maygrass, and amaranth that Patty Jo Watson and others collected through flotation, archaeologists made the important discovery that Native Americans had domesticated some indigenous plants of North America's eastern woodlands more than 4000 years ago—more than 1000 years before maize appeared on the scene. Those tiny bits of burnt plant material floating on the water turned out to be very important.

Cataloging the Finds

Excavating objects is just the beginning; in fact, excavation is only about 15 percent of a project—most of our time is spent in the lab analyzing the finds. And before the artifacts and field data can be analyzed, the objects must be cataloged. In many cases, the archaeologist assigns artifacts their catalog numbers in the field, as they are excavated. We do this by printing up sheets of sequential catalog numbers on peel-off return address forms (we've used the format 48BH3178/xxxx, where the 48BH3178 is the site's Smithsonian number and the xxxx is a sequential number, but others use more complex systems). When an artifact is found, it is piece-plotted and placed in a small Ziploc bag. The excavator peels a catalog number off the sheet (ensuring that there can be no duplicate numbers) and places it inside the bag (in case the label peels off, it will still be in the bag with the artifact). A crew member then records the number in the total station's data log and on the excavation level form.

Back in the lab, the archaeologist catalogs the artifacts. Most archaeologists are fanatical about cataloging their finds, because it's easy for one distracted lab worker to mess up an artifact's record of provenience. The catalogers work through the field bags, writing the catalog number onto the artifact itself with an archival pen, and sealing the number with clear fingernail polish; numbered tags are sometimes tied to some artifacts, such as small beads. Some archaeologists preprint the catalog numbers on minute labels and glue them to artifacts with archivally stable glue. Even those items that were not found in situ or otherwise assigned a catalog number in the field are given a number in the lab. The catalog number is what ties a particular artifact back to observations made in the field. Thus, although cataloging can often take hundreds of person-hours, it is necessary to ensure that an artifact's original provenience, and consequently its context, is never lost.

Lab workers then enter the cataloged artifacts' information into a computer database, usually including rudimentary observations (such as weight, condition, color), collection date, its provenience (for example, unit, level, X, Y, Z coordinates), and contextual data (for instance, stratum, inclination, orientation). A digital photo may be attached to the data record. Copies are then made of the database so that the artifacts' all-important contextual data will not be lost.

Site Formation Processes: How Good Sites Go Bad

Every archaeological site is unique. Some sites are remarkably well preserved; others are not. Some lie on the surface, some are deeply buried, and others lie underwater. Some are frozen, others are dry. The casual observer may think of an "archaeological site" as stable and unchanging, but every archaeologist knows better.

Sites are complex, and things can move around after they are buried. It's the job of the archaeologist to draw inferences about human behavior from sites, but to do that we have to know how a site formed over time.

To accomplish this important task, we must always bear in mind that *the archaeological record is only the contemporary evidence left over from past behavior.* Artifacts are the static remains of past dynamic behavior. However, because both natural and cultural factors impinge on these remains to such a degree, the archaeological record is rarely a *direct* reflection of past behavior.

The archaeological record is a contemporary phenomenon. Although the objects and their contexts might have existed for centuries or millennia, observations and knowledge about those objects and contexts are as contemporary as the archaeologists who do the observing. Archaeological strata are "leaky," and artifacts can move around quite a bit from where they were originally deposited.

To interpret the archaeological record more accurately, Michael Schiffer (University of Arizona) distinguishes between archaeological and systemic contexts. Artifacts, features, and residues were once part of an ongoing, dynamic behavioral system. Arrowheads were manufactured, used for specific tasks, broken, repaired, and then lost or deliberately discarded. Potsherds were once part of whole pots, which were manufactured and decorated according to prescribed cultural criteria. People used the pots for cooking or storage or ceremonial functions. The pots broke or were intentionally broken or discarded, perhaps as part of a ritual. Food bones and plant remains are the organic residues of a succession of activities—hunting or gathering, butchering or processing, cooking, and eating. While these materials are being manufactured and used, they exist in their **systemic context.** These items are part of the living behavioral system.

By the time such materials reach the archaeologist's hands, though, they have long since ceased to participate in this behavioral system. The artifacts, features, and residues encountered by archaeologists are recovered from their **archaeological context,** where they may continue to be affected by human action, but where they are also affected by the natural environment.

Formation Processes in the Systemic Context

Using Schiffer's distinction between systemic and archaeological context, we can discuss **formation processes,** how artifacts enter the archaeological record and how they are modified once they are there (Table 4-1). For our purposes, we distinguish among four distinctive processes in the systemic context that influence the creation of archaeological sites: cultural deposition, reclamation, disturbance, and reuse.

Cultural Depositional Processes

Cultural depositional processes constitute the dominant factor in forming the archaeological record. Artifacts enter the archaeological record in four primary ways:

1. *Discard.* Tools, clothing, structures—everything eventually breaks or wears out and is discarded. When this happens, the object ceases to function in the behavioral system and becomes part of the archaeological context. This is one way that things enter the archaeological record.
2. *Loss.* Other things are inadvertently lost, such as an arrow that misses its target or a necklace or pot left at an abandoned camp. In this case, the items are most likely small and still in usable condition.
3. *Caching.* Still others are intentionally cached. The Lovelock duck decoys we mentioned were intentionally buried. They remained part of the archaeological record because the person who cached them never returned.
4. *Ritual Interment.* Burials and their associated grave goods are the most obvious example of ritual interment, but other examples include offerings left at a shrine or, alternatively, deliberate destruction and burial of a shrine or religious site.

systemic context A living behavioral system wherein artifacts are part of the ongoing system of manufacture, use, reuse, and discard.

archaeological context Once artifacts enter the ground, they are part of the archaeological context, where they can continue to be affected by human action, but where they also are affected by natural processes.

formation processes The ways in which human behaviors and natural actions operate to produce the archaeological record.

TABLE 4-1 Site Formation Process Summary

SYSTEMIC CONTEXT	ARCHAEOLOGICAL CONTEXT
Cultural Deposition	Floralturbation (plants)
Discard	Faunalturbation (animals)
Loss	Cryoturbation (freezing)
Caching	Argilliturbation (wet-dry cycles)
Ritual interment	Graviturbation (hillslopes)
Reclamation	
Cultural Disturbance	
Reuse	

Reclamation Processes

Part of the archaeologist's job is to figure out whether the artifacts entered the archaeological record through discard, loss, caching, or ritual interment. This task is made difficult because artifacts can move back and forth between the systemic and archaeological contexts through **reclamation processes.** Archaeologists frequently find artifacts that were scavenged by later peoples. Pueblo peoples, for example, believed that ancient stone arrow and spear points contained power. If they happened to encounter a point while out working, they might keep it and later make a ritual offering of it. In this case, the arrowhead has moved from a context where it was (perhaps) unintentionally lost to one in which it was intentionally interred. It has also moved from the context of an earlier time period to one of a later time period, as well as from a context that records its original everyday function to one that records another culture's ritual.

Whenever a discarded projectile point is resharpened, a potsherd picked up and used to scrape hides, or an old brick reused in a new fireplace, reclamation has occurred.

Likewise, all archaeologists must cope with the fact that nonprofessionals (amateur archaeologists and looters) often collect artifacts from sites. If we ignore this fact, we run the risk of misinterpreting archaeological data. In the Carson Desert, for example, we knew that local people had collected projectile points from sites in the wetland for decades. One man had more than 25,000 in his collection. The walls of his dining room were covered with picture frames full of points, and he lined his driveway with large stone mortars and metates. The fact that our survey recovered relatively few projectile points from sites in the marsh probably reflected this reclamation process—otherwise known as looting—and not necessarily a lack of hunting.

Cultural Disturbance Processes

Reclamation processes are the transfer of materials from the archaeological to the systemic context. But the archaeological record is also heavily conditioned by transformations *within* the archaeological contexts through **cultural disturbance processes.** Disturbance changes the contexts of materials within the archaeological site itself. Examples include such diverse cultural mechanisms as dam building; farming; and construction of houses, pits, hearths, and so on.

Reuse Processes

In reuse process, an object moves through a series of **reuse processes** before it enters the archaeological record. This can entail the recycling of some objects. Potsherds, for example, are sometimes ground up and used as temper in manufacturing new vessels. Broken arrowheads are sometimes rechipped into drills and scrapers. Beams from one building are sometimes pulled out and reused in another. The point here is that an object can be created for one purpose, but it can be modified and deposited in an entirely different context than are similar objects that are not reused.

The difference between reuse and reclamation has to do with whether the archaeological context is involved. If beams are taken from a currently occupied building, it is an instance of reuse; if they are taken from a building long abandoned, then it is reclamation. The distinction seems trivial and yet it tells us something about the potential difference in the age of the items being reused. Items that are reclaimed are probably moving from an archaeological context considerably older than the systemic context they enter;

reclamation processes Human behaviors that result in artifacts moving from the archaeological context back to the systemic context, for example, scavenging beams from an abandoned structure to use them in a new one.

cultural disturbance processes Human behaviors that modify artifacts in their archaeological context, for instance, digging pits, hearths, canals, and houses.

reuse processes Human behaviors that recycle and reuse artifacts before the artifact enters an archaeological context.

reused items, on the other hand, are probably moving between systemic contexts that are much closer in age.

This review of cultural formation processes shows that archaeologists need to be aware that human activities frequently move things from their original depositional provenience to another. This can make archaeological sites very complicated and difficult to interpret. And natural processes can complicate matters even more.

Formation Processes in the Archaeological Context

Once an object enters an archaeological context, a host of natural as well as cultural formation processes takes place. These natural processes determine not only whether organic material will be preserved, but also where objects will be found. Following are a few major categories of natural site formation processes (summarized in Figure 4-9). This assortment of processes is only a brief introduction, and its purpose is to help you conceptualize just how complex an archaeological site can be. Additionally, this discussion shows that natural processes can both disrupt patterns that would otherwise tell us something about human behavior and, at the same time, create their own patterns, which could be misinterpreted as the result of human behavior. They warn us, then, that *there is no simple correspondence between the distribution of artifacts in a site and human behavior.* We give an example of how important an understanding of site formation processes can be when we revisit this important aspect of archaeology in Chapter 7.

Floralturbation

Anybody who has walked down a sidewalk knows what tree roots can do to concrete slabs. **Floralturbation** refers to all the things that plant growth does to archae-

DOING FIELDWORK: ARCHAEOLOGICAL DEMONSTRATIONS CD-ROM

Go to the Live-Action Demonstration in the "Excavation" section of the CD-ROM to view a video on chronology via stratigraphy at Mission San Marcos, New Mexico.

ological sites. Roots can tear buried ancient walls apart; and, by loosening soil, they also promote the downward movement of artifacts from their original stratigraphic context. But they can also move artifacts upward. When a large tree falls over, its roots pull up large amounts of sediment. We call this "tree throw" and, after hundreds or thousands of years, it can churn a site's sediments, pulling ancient materials up to more recent surfaces and creating holes that then fill with material of various ages.

Faunalturbation

Faunalturbation refers to all the things that animals can do to archaeological sites. Rodents and other animals often dig into sites, producing two major effects. First, burrowing rodents can push artifacts that were originally deposited in lower layers up to the surface. This can place old artifacts in a younger stratigraphic context. Second, burrowing can *size-sort* artifacts vertically, moving larger artifacts downward and smaller artifacts upward. For example, pocket gophers dig their burrows around objects larger than about 5 centimeters; anything smaller than this they push out of their burrows to the surface. The larger artifacts and rocks left behind might eventually tumble to the bottom of the burrows. Repeat this process over hundreds or thousands of years, and you end up with a site where the small artifacts and stones are near its top, and the large artifacts and stones are near its bottom. Someone applying the law of superposition blindly might conclude that people changed from using large to small tools over time. But you would be wrong: The pattern only tells us about pocket gophers, not people.

Sometimes these burrows are filled with rock and earth washed or blown in from above, forming a feature called a **krotovina** (pronounced "kro-toe-*vee*-na"; the term comes to us from Russian soil science and

floralturbation A natural formation process in which trees and other plants affect the distribution of artifacts within an archaeological site.

faunalturbation A natural formation process in which animals, from large game to earthworms, affect the distribution of material within an archaeological site.

krotovina A filled-in animal burrow.

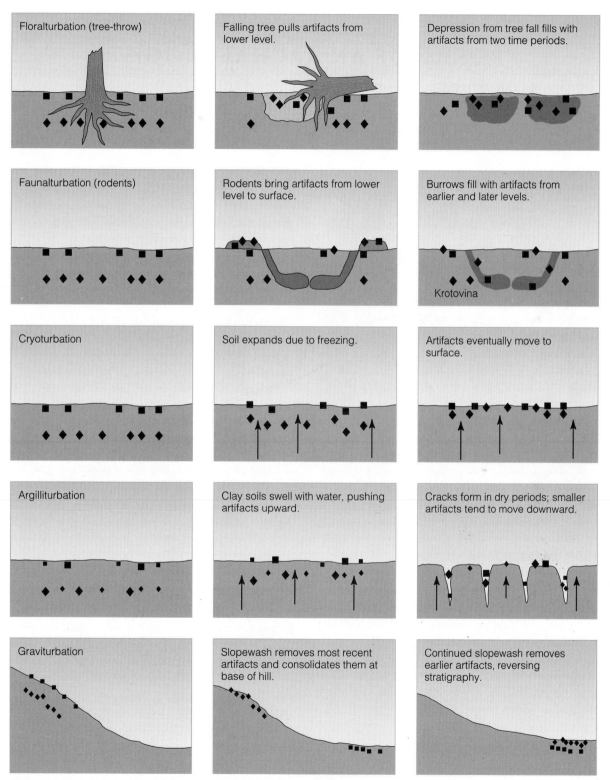

Figure 4-9 The effects of some natural formation processes on the distribution of artifacts in a hypothetical archaeological site.

PROFILE OF AN ARCHAEOLOGIST
An African Archaeologist

Chapurukha (Chap) M. Kusimba is curator of African archaeology and ethnology at the Field Museum of Natural History in Chicago.

I became interested in the natural history of East Africa when, as a youth, I learned of the discoveries of Louis and Mary Leakey in Olduvai Gorge in my native country of Kenya. I was intrigued by claims that East Africa was the cradle of humankind and fascinated by the idea that all humankind ultimately traced its beginnings to Africa. The fact that there was so much to discover in my own backyard shaped the way I viewed my heritage and encouraged my interest in becoming a scientist.

The study of social complexity has long been contentious in Africa. Assuming that Africans could not be innovative, previous scholars credited the origins of social complexity and "high culture" to immigrants from Southwest Asia. Today, African archaeologists have rejected diffusion as the initiator of cultural and technological transformations in Africa, and look instead to the specific processes of development.

My research focuses on the role of technology, economy, and interregional interaction in the development of chiefdoms and states in East Africa. In so doing, it evaluates the roles of Indian Ocean trade, iron working technology, and interregional interaction in the development of social complexity in East Africa. I have conducted regional archaeological surveys, defined settlement patterns, and augmented these with problem-oriented excavations in key

means "mole hole"). If so, then archaeologists can excavate the burrow separately from the surrounding sediments. But if the burrows simply collapse, they can be difficult or impossible to see.

And burrowing animals are only one culprit. Even the humble earthworm can obliterate the edges of features like burials, pits, and hearths, making them more difficult for the archaeologist to see and record.

cryoturbation A natural formation process in which freeze/thaw activity in a soil selectively pushes larger artifacts to the surface of a site.

Cryoturbation

In northern climates, freeze/thaw processes, or **cryoturbation,** can move artifacts up in a stratigraphic sequence. As the soil freezes, it expands, pushing artifacts upward. As the soil thaws, soil particles move down first, partially or completely filling the void below artifacts, ensuring that the artifacts cannot move back down. Thus, freeze/thaw cycles move large artifacts upward (sometimes at a rate of several centimeters per year). This can create a site in which artifacts are vertically size-sorted, with the smallest artifacts at the bottom of the sediment and larger ones near the top (the opposite effect of burrowing animals). Cryoturbation also tends to orient buried artifacts vertically—that is, with their long axis pointing up and down.

locales and sites in Southeastern Kenya. The results are published in a number of research articles and in my book, *The Rise and Fall of Swahili States,* a text on the archaeology of social complexity in Africa.

With a few exceptions, all thoroughly investigated sites on the Kenya coast are large urban centers with monumental structures composed of elite residences, chiefly courts, and mosques. The focus on large urban sites inevitably introduced significant biases in data collection and influenced the rendering of the regional history. But African archaeologists cannot ignore the relationship between urban areas and their trading partners in the hinterlands. And so, beginning in 1998, Dr. Sibel Barut Kusimba (Northern Illinois University) and I began to examine the role of trade in shaping East Africa's diverse ethnic identitie. We did this by surveying areas in the Tsavo National Park and surrounding area, 150 kilometers from Kenya's eastern coast. We described more than 200 sites, from the Early Stone Age into the historic era, including hunter-gatherer rockshelter camps and residences, pastoral, agropas-

toral, and agrarian villages and chiefdom-level settlements, fortified stockades, market centers, and iron production areas. So far, we have excavated twelve of these sites and conducted intensive interviews with local communities called the Wataita, Somali, and Waata.

An important pattern emerging from our research is the web of social interactions among peoples of diverse origins and languages practicing and inventing different ways of life. The Tsavo region was a mosaic of political and economic alliances, an example of regional systems that exist in many areas of the world but are not completely understood. Understanding the development of social complexity in Africa requires attention to such regional interactions. Indeed, the mosaic is important to us not just as grist for the archaeologist's mill, but as a reservoir for potentially understanding Africa's future, since Africa's modern dynamics of ethnicity, social, and political power are rooted in these earlier interactions.

Argilliturbation

A similar process, known as **argilliturbation,** happens in clay-rich soils that undergo wet/dry cycles. As these soils become wet, they expand and push larger artifacts upward for the same reason as cryoturbation. But as these soils dry, they form cracks—sometimes several meters in depth—down which artifacts can fall. Run this process over and over for hundreds or thousands of years, and a site's stratigraphy can become thoroughly churned.

Graviturbation

Archaeological materials deposited on hillsides eventually move downslope. **Graviturbation** is accomplished through slopewash, gravity, or the slow

movement of water-saturated sediments. In any case, the result is that archaeological materials originally deposited on a hillside move downslope and eventually come to rest in a context completely different from the one where they were originally lost, discarded, cached, or ritually interred.

argilliturbation A natural formation process in which wet/dry cycles push artifacts upward as the sediment swells and then moves them down as cracks form during dry cycles.

graviturbation A natural formation process in which artifacts are moved downslope through gravity, sometimes assisted by precipitation runoff.

Some sites (like Gatecliff) have a high degree of stratigraphic integrity—meaning that artifacts are found where they were lost, discarded, cached, or ritually interred. Other sites are complex, with little stratigraphic integrity. In these sites, a range of cultural and natural formation processes have moved artifacts from their initial archaeological context. But these processes do *not* make archaeology impossible. It does mean, though, that one of our first tasks is to establish just how the artifacts got to where the archaeologists found them. Although how we do this is different for each site, the objective is the same: understanding the effects of site formation processes is the first step in knowing what an archaeologist can realistically accomplish with the information from a site. Archaeologists need to keep in mind all the processes that affect how artifacts and ecofacts enter the ground—and everything that can happen to them once they are there. In so doing, the archaeologist has to think of the site not only as a record of human behavior, but as a record of natural processes also. He or she must think of the site as a geological record, as well as an archaeological record. Increasingly, archaeologists find that extremely careful and meticulous data, such as the orientation and inclination of plain old rocks as well as of artifacts, are needed to accomplish this goal. Thus, this realization of the importance of formation processes requires even greater precision and care in site excavation.

Conclusion: Archaeology's Conservation Ethic: Dig Only What You Must

Archaeologists have traditionally protected their excavations against vandals and pothunters. Excavation often draws unwanted attention, and vandals have been known to attack sites during field season even during the night. On Thomas's first job in archaeology, a 24-hour guard (armed, appropriately enough, with bow and arrow) was posted to protect the open excavation units from looters. At Gatecliff, we tediously backfilled the site by hand every year to protect the archaeology from the curious public, and the public from the dangers of open-pit archaeology.

On St. Catherines Island, the problem is somewhat different. The only visitors are scientists, who realize the research value of archaeological sites and leave the excavations untouched. It is thus possible to open a few test units on several sites, process the finds, and then return next year to the more promising sites for more intensive excavation.

On strictly research projects—like our work at Mission Santa Catalina—the sites are not threatened by outside incursions, and one must adopt a conservative excavation strategy. Archaeologists never excavate more of a site than is needed to answer their research questions; extensive excavations are undertaken only in the case of sites threatened by development or erosion. Most archaeologists leave as much of a site intact as possible for later investigators, who undoubtedly will have different questions and better techniques. And, as we have seen, remote sensing technology and archaeological survey techniques sometimes provide archaeologists with low-impact ways of learning without digging at all.

Regardless of whether we use high-tech instruments or old-fashioned elbow grease, our personal responsibility for site conservation remains unchanged and fundamental. Archaeology is a destructive science. We said it at the beginning of this chapter and it is worth repeating: Sites can be excavated only once, so it is imperative we do things right. Sometimes those sites have remarkable preservation and sometimes not. The degree of preservation affects what kind of excavation techniques we use and how quickly the excavation proceeds. But how much or how little we find does not change the fact that we must take any step necessary to ensure that provenience for virtually every artifact, ecofact, and feature is acquired during the excavation and recorded. We excavate in controlled units, sometimes as small as .5 × .5 meter, using a systematic grid system; we excavate in natural levels where possible, and, even if natural strata are present, in levels no more than 10 or even 5 centimeters thick; we record everything we can about an item before we pull it from the ground; and we assign catalog numbers to everything found so that each item can be related back to information gathered on its context. Once we have this information in hand, we are prepared to move on to the next chore of archaeology: making sense of everything we have found.

Summary

- The guiding rule in all excavation is to record context, and this means recording provenience of the artifacts, features, and ecofacts. Diverse excavation strategies respond to different preservation conditions, constraints, and objectives.

- Preservation is enhanced in continuously dry, continuously wet, and/or very cold environments—any place where conditions prevent the existence of microorganisms that promote decay.

- In a horizontal strategy, designed to explore the conditions of past lifeways, the contexts of artifacts and ecofacts within excavation strata become critical; excavation proceeds with the goal of finding all artifacts in situ. When an excavator misses an artifact—and it turns up in the screen—a significant piece of information has been lost because that artifact can then be located only within the excavation square and level.

- Archaeologists use screening, flotation, and bulk matrix processing to recover extremely small artifacts with some control on provenience.

- All recovered materials are cataloged so that each item is permanently linked to its excavation record.

- From test pit through full-scale excavation, archaeologists maintain exact records of the three-dimensional provenience of the objects being recovered and their context. The objective of archaeological records is to record the excavation in such a way that another archaeologist could "see" what the original excavator saw.

- You must understand the difference between an artifact's systemic and archaeological contexts in order to know how an artifact in the ground relates to the complex chain of human behavior and natural processes that brought it there.

- Artifacts can enter the archaeological record through a variety of cultural depositional processes, including loss, discard, caching, and ritual interment.

- Once in the archaeological context, artifacts can continue to be moved and altered by a variety of natural site formation processes, including landslides, burrowing animals, earthworms, tree throw, and the actions of water and climate.

- It's hard to overemphasize the importance of hands-on experience in archaeology. There is no substitute for personal field experience, and no textbook, computer simulation, or classroom exercise satisfactorily simulates the field situation.

Media Resources

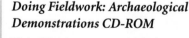 ***Doing Fieldwork: Archaeological Demonstrations CD-ROM***

This CD gives you a vivid glimpse of what it is like to be involved in an archaeological dig . . . without leaving your chair. With this CD, you will see archaeologists involved in actual excavations—many of which are referenced in your Thomas/Kelly text—using a number of the field techniques covered in this chapter. Organized according to the various stages of a live excavation, the CD presents hands-on interactive activities, live-action demonstration videos, and quizzes to help you better understand the processes and techniques that are important to an excavation.

 The Companion Website for Archaeology: Down to Earth, Third Edition

http://anthropology.wadsworth.com/thomas_kelly3e_down/

Supplement your review of this chapter by going to the companion website to take one of the practice quizzes, use the flash cards to master key terms, and check out the many other study aids that are designed to help you succeed in your introductory archaeology course.

5 Chronology Building: How to Get a Date

Outline

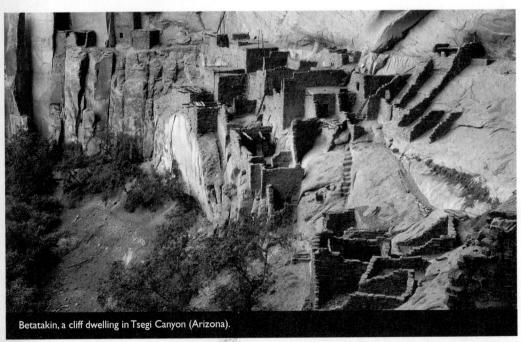

Betatakin, a cliff dwelling in Tsegi Canyon (Arizona).

© Jeffrey S. Dean and the Laboratory of Tree-Ring Research/University of Arizona

Preview

THIS CHAPTER IS about dating archaeological sites—how archaeologists get a grasp on time. Here, you'll find a broad range of dating techniques: tree-ring dating, radiocarbon dating, thermoluminescence dating, and others that allow us to date organic material, rocks—even dirt itself. The chemical and physical underpinnings of these techniques can be mind boggling, but you need to have at least a basic understanding of them in order to understand when you can and cannot use a particular technique.

You also need to understand the basis of these techniques in order to know just what the "date" is actually telling you, because dates in and of themselves mean nothing. Demonstrating the *validity of associations* between dates and human behavior is the key issue in archaeological dating.

Doing Fieldwork CD-ROM: Archaeological Demonstrations

See the "Dating" section of the CD-ROM to learn more about topics covered in this chapter.

Introduction

The Fourth Egyptian Dynasty lasted from 2680 to 2565 BC. The Roman Coliseum was constructed between AD 70 and 82. The Battle of the Little Big Horn took place on June 25, 1876. Each date represents the most familiar way of expressing chronological control: the **absolute date.** Such dates are expressed as specific units of scientific measurement—days, years, centuries, or millennia—but no matter what the measure, all such absolute determinations pinpoint a specific year or a specific range of years (the latter are sometimes referred to as "chronometric," rather than absolute, dates).

Absolute dating methods were not available in archaeology's early days. Prior to the 1950s, most dates were instead **relative dates.** As the name implies, relative dates are not specific segments of absolute time but, rather, express relationships or comparisons: the stepped pyramid at Saqqara in Egypt is *earlier* than

Khufu's pyramid; the historic settlement of Williamsburg is *later* than the pueblos of Chaco Canyon; Folsom spear points are *earlier* than Chupadero black-on-white pottery. Relative dates are obviously not as precise as absolute dates, but prior to the 1950s, they were the best that archaeology had.

absolute date A date expressed as specific units of scientific measurement, such as days, years, centuries, or millennia; absolute determinations attempting to pinpoint a discrete, known interval in time.

relative dates Dates expressed relative to one another (for instance, earlier, later, more recent, and so forth) instead of in absolute terms.

Relative Dating

The keys to relative dating are (1) the law of superposition and (2) the index fossil concept.

The Law of Superposition

Nicolaus Steno (1638–1686) is acknowledged as having formulated the **law of superposition,** which says that, in any pile of **sedimentary rocks** undisturbed by folding or overturning, the strata on the bottom were deposited first, those above them were deposited second, those above them third, and so on. This principle seems preposterously simple, but it was a critical observation in the seventeenth century. Why?

Steno, an anatomist, was dissecting a shark when he noticed that the teeth looked exactly like things that naturalists occasionally found in rocks, what his colleagues called "tongue stones." These tongue stones were, in fact, fossil shark teeth, but scholars of Steno's day commonly believed that fossils were stones that had fallen from the moon or had grown inside rocks; a contemporary of Steno attributed them to "lapidifying virtue diffused through the whole body of the geocosm," which isn't especially helpful.

But others, including Steno, held the then-radical notion that these odd "stones" were in fact ancient shark teeth. Left unsolved, however, was the perplexing question of how one solid, a shark's tooth, came to be inside another solid, a rock. In his *Preliminary Discourse to a Dissertation on a Solid Body Naturally Contained within a Solid* (1669), Steno pondered this question. He concluded that at some point in time, one of them must not have been solid. But which one? Believing that all rock began as liquid, Steno postulated

that rocks must have been laid down horizontally (a concept he termed "the principle of original horizontality"); any departure from the horizontal, Steno reasoned, must have resulted from later disturbance. He then argued that if a thing were already a solid when the liquid rock was laid down, it would force that liquid to mold itself around the existing solid. Thus, Steno argued that fossils came to be inside solid rock because the fossils were older, and because the rock was originally laid down as a liquid. Conversely, if a solid formed after the rock had hardened, it would conform to voids and fissures already in the rock (thus crystals and mineral-filled veins conform to voids in the rock that contains them).

Working from these observations, Steno postulated that if rock were originally deposited horizontally as a liquid, then the oldest layer should be the deepest and progressively younger layers should lie above it. Although formulated as an aside, Steno's law of superposition became the foundation of all stratigraphic interpretation—whether we are talking about the Grand Canyon or Kidder's excavations at Pecos Pueblo.

The Index Fossil Concept

Developed in the early nineteenth century, the **index fossil concept** is often attributed to British geologist William "Strata" Smith (1769–1839), a civil engineer who made the world's first geologic map. Geologists of Smith's day wrestled with the problem of how to correlate the ages of widely separated exposures of rock. Smith observed that forms of life changed over time, and so different fossils characterize different rock strata. Thus, widely separated strata could be correlated and assigned to the same time period if they contained the same fossils. It seems like a simple idea, but it allowed Smith and others to make geological maps, and these radically altered the way that geologists conceived of the landscape. Now they could see broad patterns that told a story of ancient seas, mountain building, and ice ages.

Archaeology faced a similar problem. The law of superposition could indicate which artifact types or styles were older than other forms in particular sites, but how could the individual site chronologies be chronologically related to one another? The index fossil concept provided the answer. In archaeology, however, artifacts replace fossils, and strata in widely

---

law of superposition The geological principle stating that, in any pile of sedimentary rocks that have not been disturbed by folding or overturning, each bed is older than the layers above and younger than the layers below; also known as Steno's law.

sedimentary rock Rock formed when the weathered products of preexisting rocks have been transported by and deposited in water and are turned once again to stone.

index fossil concept The idea that strata containing similar fossil assemblages are of similar age. This concept enables archaeologists to characterize and date strata within sites using distinctive artifact forms that research shows to be diagnostic of a particular period of time.

separated sites that contain the same distinctive artifact forms—called **time markers** in archaeology—are assumed to be of similar age.

The index fossil concept was introduced to archaeology by Swedish archaeologist Oscar Montelius (1843–1921). Trained in the natural sciences, Montelius switched to archaeology and became interested in Europe's Neolithic, Bronze, and Iron Ages. Working for the State Historical Museum in Stockholm, he traveled across Europe examining collections from various sites, paying special attention to objects in unmixed contexts, such as those from burials, hoards, and individual rooms.

Using hundreds of cases, Montelius divided the Bronze, Neolithic, and Iron Ages into chronological subdivisions, each with its own set of distinctive artifacts or artifact styles, such as particular kinds of axe heads, swords, or brooches. In some cases, Montelius had stratigraphic controls to help decide which artifact styles were earlier or later, and sometimes the artifacts appeared in contexts, such as Egyptian tombs, where documentary sources could provide the age. But he also employed assumptions about how styles change over time and arranged objects in sequences such that they formed, in his opinion, a "logical" progression from, say, small simple brooches to large, complex ones. Although this simple-to-complex assumption might work in paleontology because animal forms are linked through biological reproduction, it is tenuous in archaeology, because artifacts don't reproduce; their shapes come from their makers' minds and not directly from "ancestral" artifacts.

Nonetheless, Montelius advanced archaeology by developing a way to create a chronology of artifact time markers for Europe.

Time Markers in the American Southwest

What Montelius could have really used, however, was a *master sequence*—a site with a deep stratigraphic profile that would permit the law of superposition to demonstrate the changing sequence of artifact types and styles. Nels Nelson, who was aware of European archaeology (and even helped excavate a cave in Spain), searched for just such a master sequence for the American Southwest during his excavation at Pueblo San Cristobal (New Mexico). Nelson knew that

there were deep deposits at San Cristobal, and he hoped that a carefully controlled excavation into them would show whether certain artifacts could act as time markers (Figure 5-1).

Selecting an area with minimal disturbance, Nelson isolated a block of debris measuring 3 feet by 6 feet wide and nearly 10 feet deep. Clearly, the midden had accumulated over a long interval, and several distinctive kinds of pottery were buried there. Because the dusty black midden lacked sharp stratigraphic divisions, Nelson personally excavated the block in 1-foot arbitrary levels, cataloging the potsherds recovered by level. Imposing arbitrary levels on an undifferentiated stratigraphy seems almost pedestrian today but, in 1914, Nelson's stratigraphic method was revolutionary and immediately seized upon by New World archaeologists as a fundamental of excavation (for the record, however, Nelson got the idea of stratigraphic excavation from his European colleagues).

Nelson then applied the law of superposition to look for culture change within the midden column. All else being equal, the oldest trash should lie at the bottom, capped by more recent accumulations. Even though the dense midden lacked tangible stratigraphy, Nelson searched for time markers in the form of distinctive pottery types.

Nelson thus applied the index fossil concept to the prehistoric ceramics of San Cristobal. Just as geologists learned to distinguish certain extinct life forms as characteristic of various rock strata, so too could archaeologists use distinctive artifact forms to characterize and correlate strata between archaeological sites. Pottery was a natural choice, given that potsherds were common cultural debris and Nelson knew that ceramic styles varied considerably across the American Southwest.

More than 2000 potsherds turned up in the 10-foot test section at San Cristobal. Nelson first grouped the potsherds into obvious types and then plotted their distribution according to depth below the surface (we discuss the principles of creating types in Chapter 6). Table 5-1 summarizes his results: Column 1 contains the frequency of corrugated pottery, the most common everyday cooking ware. Because the relative frequency

time markers Similar to index fossils in geology; artifact forms that research shows to be diagnostic of a particular period of time.

Figure 5-1 General view across Nels Nelson's excavations at San Cristobal (New Mexico). The 700-year-old walls of this huge pueblo are clearly evident. Note also that no screens appear anywhere; sifting of archaeological deposits did not become standard practice until nearly 50 years after this picture was taken.

traded into San Cristobal from elsewhere. But these frequencies did not change markedly throughout the stratigraphic column either, and he also rejected biscuit ware as a potential time marker.

Nelson then turned to the three remaining kinds of pottery—which he termed Types I, II, and III—and discovered, just as the Europeans had with their fossils, that certain forms were associated with specific stratigraphic levels (Figure 5-2). The most ancient levels at San Cristobal contained a predominance of Type I painted pottery, black designs on a white background. Type I potsherds were most numerous at and below the 8-foot mark and only rarely recovered above 7 feet. Type II pottery—red, yellow, and gray potsherds ornamented with a dark glaze—occurred most commonly at and above the 7-foot mark. In other words, Type I potsherds characterized the lower strata, and the Type II potsherds characterized the upper deposits.

The Type III pottery, three-colored glazed ware, was rare at San Cristobal and appeared only in the uppermost levels of Nelson's column. This made sense, given

of corrugated potsherds remained more or less constant throughout the occupation of San Cristobal, Nelson rejected Column 1 as a potential time marker. Column 2 tabulates the frequencies of biscuit ware, a dull whitish-yellow pottery that Nelson thought was

TABLE 5-1 Potsherds at San Cristobol						
DEPTH BELOW SURFACE	**CORRUGATED WARE**	**BISCUIT WARE**	**TYPE I: BLACK-ON-WHITE GLAZE**	**TYPE II: TWO-COLOR GLAZE**	**TYPE III: THREE-COLOR GLAZE**	**TOTAL**
	1	2	3	4	5	
1st foot	57 (36.7)	10 (6.5)	2 (1.3)	81 (52.2)	5 (3.2)	155
2nd foot	116 (31.3)	17 (4.6)	2 (.01)	230 (62)	6 (1.6)	371
3rd foot	27 (15.3)	2 (1.1)	10 (5.7)	134 (76.1)	3 (1.7)	176
4th foot	28 (21.3)	4 (3)	6 (4.5)	93 (70.9)	0 (0)	131
5th foot	60 (17.3)	15 (4.3)	2 (.01)	268 (77.6)	0 (0)	345
6th foot	75 (18.6)	21 (5.2)	8 (1.9)	297 (73.8)	1? (.01)	402
7th foot	53 (23.1)	10 (4.3)	40 (17.5)	126 (55)	0 (0)	229
8th foot	56 (24.6)	2 (.01)	118 (51.9)	51 (22.4)	0 (0)	227
9th foot	93 (45.4)	1? (.01)	107 (52.5)	3 (1.4)	0 (0)	204
10th foot	84 (54.4)	1? (.01)	69 (44.8)	0 (0)	0 (0)	154
Total	649	83	364	1,283	15	2,394

Source: Nelson 1916.

Figures in parentheses are row-wise percentages.

Figure 5-2 Examples of Nels Nelson's Types I (bottom), II (middle), and III (top) pottery from San Cristobal Pueblo.

that Pueblo peoples were making three-colored wares when the Spaniards arrived in New Mexico in the sixteenth century.

Nelson's arbitrary levels made possible the definition of three important ceramic time-markers. Not only did he document the specific ceramic changes at San Cristobal, but more important, his controlled stratigraphic excavation provided a master sequence with which to place other sites, strata, or features in the region into a relative chronological sequence. Alfred Kidder later applied Nelson's observations to Pecos Pueblo, using the presence of black-on-white ware to locate the original settlement.

The Next Step: Seriation

The index fossil concept was essential to archaeology in the early twentieth century. The law of superposition permitted archaeologists to produce a chronology of cultural change at a particular site, and the index fossil concept allowed archaeologists to date sites *relative* to one another. Given this discovery, archaeologists could date other Southwestern Pueblo sites based on the type of pottery found in them. A site with predominantly black-on-white pottery would be older than one that contained red glazed pottery. The archaeologist did not know *how much* older the first site was than the second, but he or she could nonetheless still place sites into a relative chronological sequence based on their ceramics. This was a tremendous advance for the time.

And this advance became the basis of **seriation,** a relative dating technique that was crucial to archaeology in the mid-twentieth century. First developed by European archaeologists in the late nineteenth century, the technique was introduced to the New World by Alfred Kroeber (1876–1960). Seriation is grounded in the same commonsense observation that guided Oscar Montelius: Styles change and new technologies arise over time. In ancient times just as now, most new ideas are slow to catch on, with only a few pioneers participating in the fad. Eventually, a new idea may become chic and replace earlier vogues, only to fall gradually into disuse and be replaced by the next "new thing." The index fossil concept relied primarily on the presence or absence of distinctive kinds of artifacts. Seriation refined this by using changes in the *frequencies* of artifacts or styles to date sites relative to one another (paleontologists, by the way, do the same thing with fossils).

To get a sense of how seriation works, look at Figure 5-3, which shows changes in lighting technologies in late nineteenth-century Pennsylvania. At mid-century, most houses were illuminated by candles and oil lamps; only a few households had gas lamps. But over

seriation A relative dating method that orders artifacts based on the assumption that one cultural style slowly replaces an earlier style over time; with a master seriation diagram, sites can be dated based on their frequency of several artifact (for instance, ceramic) styles.

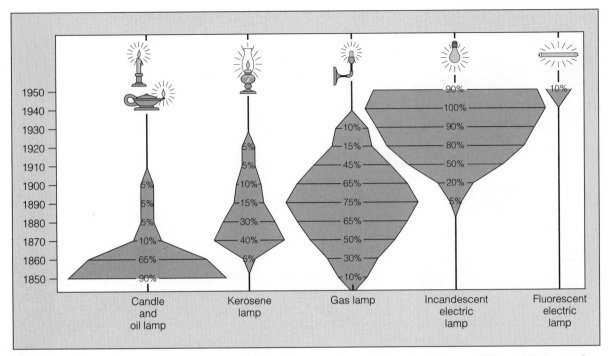

Figure 5-3 Seriation diagram showing how methods of artificial illumination changed in Pennsylvania between 1850 and 1950. *Redrawn from Mayer-Oakes (1955), figure 15.*

the next 50 years, more and more families switched to gaslights. Those who could not afford such installations used kerosene lamps (made possible by the growing petroleum industry in Pennsylvania and elsewhere). By 1900, however, electric lights were replacing gaslights and, by 1940, gaslights had all but disappeared. By that year, virtually everyone used incandescent light bulbs—which by 1950 were already being replaced by fluorescent lamps.

The shape of such popularity curves, which James Ford termed "battleship curves" because they often look like a battleship's silhouette from above, is the basis for seriation. By arranging the proportions of temporal types into lozenge-shaped curves, one can determine a relative chronological sequence.

This phenomenon is evident in Nelson's potsherd counts from San Cristobal Pueblo (Figure 5-4 translates the frequencies from Table 5-1 into a seriation diagram). As we've already noted, when San Cristobal was first built, ceramics were most commonly decorated with black designs painted on a white background; corrugated ware was also fairly common. Moving up Nelson's stratigraphic column, however, two-color glaze rapidly takes over in popularity, with

black-on-white pottery fading out. In the top half of the column, three-color pottery comes into use. The town dump at San Cristobal faithfully preserved these changes in ceramic "fashion."

This sequence can help archaeologists date other archaeological sites in the American Southwest. Instead of just using the presence or absence of a particular artifact type, we use frequencies of those different artifacts to place sites into a finer chronological sequence. For example, sites with high percentages of black-on-white ceramics would be older than sites with high percentages of two-color glaze and small percentages of black-on-white pottery. These sites, in turn, would be older than sites with high percentages of two-color glaze, small percentages of corrugated ware, and only trace amounts of black-on-white pottery. And these sites would be older than sites dominated by two-color glaze with trace amounts of three-color glaze.

We can use the seriation method based on a single master stratigraphy, or we can compile one analytically by linking several overlapping stratigraphies at different stratified sites. Thus, seriation takes the index fossil concept and refines it to permit a more fine-grained relative sequence. Nonetheless, seriation still cannot

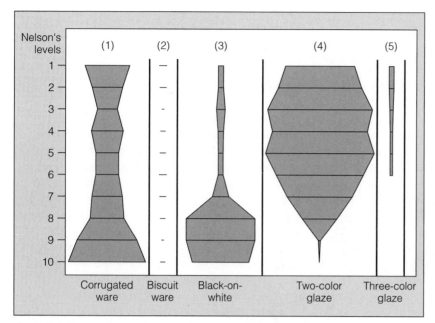

Figure 5-4 Seriation diagram based on Nelson's San Cristobal potsherd frequencies.

dating as a way to demonstrate the issues that archaeologists must consider when determining what a date actually means.

Tree-Ring Dating

Tree-ring dating, also called **dendrochronology,** was developed by Andrew E. Douglass (1867–1962), an astronomer interested in the effect of sunspots on the Earth's climate. Douglass knew that trees growing in temperate and arctic areas remain dormant during the winter and then burst into activity in the spring. This results in the formation of the familiar concentric growth rings. Because each ring represents a single year, it's a simple matter to determine the age of a newly felled tree: just count the rings. Trees have alternating dark and light rings. The light rings are a year's spring/summer growth, and the dark rings are that year's late summer/fall growth (the darkness comes from the cell walls; when they do not grow quickly, the cell walls crowd together and take up a greater proportion of the ring's space).

For many tree species, the widths of the rings vary, and Douglass reasoned that the rings might preserve information about past climatic change. Because environmental patterning affects all the trees maturing in a given region, Douglass reasoned, year-by-year patterns of tree growth manifested as variable ring widths should fit into a long-term chronological sequence.

Douglass began his research on living trees, mostly yellow pines in central Arizona. He examined recent stumps and cores taken from still-living trees, counted the rings, and recorded the pattern of light and dark ring widths. He then extended this chronology backward in time by searching for an overlap between the early portion of young trees with the final years of

tell us *how old* a site or stratum is, only whether it is older or younger than another.

Seriation was a common technique in the mid-twentieth century, but today it is used mostly where absolute dating methods cannot be employed or are not sufficiently specific. And archaeologists still use the index fossil concept, but only as a rough guide. For example, excavations have shown that Folsom spear points, like those found at the Folsom site mentioned in Chapter 4, date to around 10,300 to 10,900 radiocarbon years ago (we explain what we mean by "radiocarbon years" later in the chapter). If we excavated a site with Folsom points in it, we would gleefully tell our colleagues that "we had a Folsom site," and they would know how old the site is. But we would *always* try to refine that estimate by using one of the absolute dating techniques discussed next.

Absolute Dating

Absolute dating gave archaeology an incredibly powerful tool and helped shape it into the science that it is today. In this chapter, we only highlight the most commonly used methods among the many techniques available. And we give special attention to radiocarbon

tree-ring dating (dendrochronology) The use of annual growth rings in trees to assign calendar ages to ancient wood samples

ARCHAEOLOGICAL ETHICS
What's Wrong with Buying Antiquities? (Part I)

There is, unfortunately, a lively market in ancient artifacts, and it is the greatest threat to archaeology today. Across the country, folks get together at artifact "fairs" to swap stories and buy and sell artifacts. Often, these are things that Grandpa found on the farm when he was a little boy and that were passed down through the family. Sometimes, they are objects that people find while out walking. They picked them up out of curiosity and placed them on their mantle or mounted them in a picture frame in the den. It seems harmless enough.

Sometimes these artifacts appear on e-Bay or other online sales venues. Some of these auction houses have policies that prohibit the sale of unethically or illegally obtained materials. For example, e-Bay's policy states that Native American human remains, gravesite-related items, and burial items may not be listed on e-Bay.

Native American masks and "prayer sticks" from all southwestern tribes are also prohibited. This prohibition includes Native Hawaiian human remains, gravesite-related items, and burial items.

E-Bay's policy also states that artifacts taken from any federal, state, public Department of Interior Agencies (NPS, BLM, USFWS) and Department of Agriculture Agencies (USFS), Native American land, or battlefield are prohibited for sale.

Nonetheless, on the day we wrote this, e-Bay was auctioning 11 Mimbres black-on-white pots. The total value of these pots was estimated at about $78,000.

Mimbres pottery is special. It was manufactured only between AD 1000 and 1150 in southern New Mexico's Mimbres Valley. The bowls are especially noteworthy because they contain naturalistic designs that are rare in southwestern pottery: depictions of rabbits, bighorn sheep, birds, and people.

Even more important, these bowls are disproportionately found in graves. They usually were ritually "killed" by punching a small hole in the bowl's center and then were placed over the deceased's head. Of the 11 bowls on auction at e-Bay, 8 were ritually killed. Most if not all of these bowls had probably been taken from graves—a violation of e-Bay's policy.

The selling of artifacts promotes their unauthorized and destructive collection. *There is not a single Mimbres pueblo that has not been looted;* some were flattened by bulldozers in a search for the graves that lie beneath the pueblos' floors. Others were scooped up at night by a front loader and dumped into trucks, the dirt later sorted in secret. Looters are arrested when they can be caught—two men were convicted in 2001 of looting a Mimbres site, sentenced to a year in prison, and ordered to pay nearly $20,000 in restitution. But no amount of money can replace what they destroyed. And for every looter arrested, a dozen evade the law.

And Mimbres sites are not the only ones hit hard: Dry caves that preserve organic remains such as baskets are targets, as are Maya, Inka, and Egyptian sites—almost any site, in fact.

You can be sure that in the gathering of Mimbres bowls, plenty of other artifacts were disturbed and destroyed, to say nothing of the human remains. We will never know what information was lost from looted sites, but we can be sure that it was volumes, because not only does the artifact disappear into the marketplace, but its contextual information is also obliterated.

Buying artifacts is like buying drugs: The buyer is the only reason the business exists. And the business is the reason that we are losing irreplaceable artifacts and information about the past every day.

And that's what's wrong with buying artifacts.

Figure 5-5 How a tree-ring chronology is built up by matching portions of tree-ring sequences from known-age living trees (lower left) to older archaeological samples; the diamonds indicate the portions of the sequences that overlap.

growth of an old tree or stump. In doing so, he created a master sequence of tree rings extending back in time. But, altogether, the stumps and living trees went back only about 500 years.

Douglass worked in the American Southwest, where arid conditions enhance preservation. Sampling ancient beams in pueblo sites, he slowly constructed a prehistoric "floating chronology," which spanned several centuries but was not tied into the sequence based on modern samples (Figure 5-5). Eventually, Douglass bridged this gap between the sequences of ancient and modern trees and gave southwestern archaeology a reliable, year-by-year dating tool.

Methodology of Tree-Ring Dating

In practice, tree-ring dating works like this: the archaeologist digs up a sample of charcoal or wood of the appropriate species and that bears at least 20 rings. He or she then sends it to the appropriate lab—there are several around the world (such as the University of Arizona's Laboratory of Tree-Ring Research)—with appropriate contextual data. There, an analyst cuts or sands the sample down so that the rings are easily visible, and the widths are then measured individually.

Now the hard work begins. Normally, the archaeologist has some idea of how old the site is—perhaps less

than 500 years old, or between 750 and 1000 years old. A lab analyst tries to match the sample to the appropriate portion of the regional sequence. This can be a slow, laborious process, because the analyst is looking for a segment of the master sequence that has the same order of variable-width rings as the archaeological sample—say, a pattern of four thick summer rings, followed by three thin ones, then three thick rings, two thin rings, and finally four not-quite-so-thick rings. Computer programs can assist in this task, but the matching often requires visual comparison because some samples have oddities, such as missing rings or partial rings, that only a trained technician can detect.

For tree-ring dating to work, the analyst has to make several adjustments and consider several factors. For example, trees grow more quickly when they are young than when they are old. Thus, absolute tree-ring width is a function of climate and a tree's age. But by using the estimated curvature of the ring on a sample, dendrochronologists solve this problem through a mathematical function that converts a tree's rings into a standardized index that takes the tree's age into account.

Additionally, a sample's age is the age of the last (outermost) ring present on the piece. But if that ring is not present—if the outer portion of the sample was adzed off or burnt away—we still won't know what year the tree died. However, by looking for markings that are diagnostic of the outer edge of a tree—such as signs of bark or beetle activity—a trained analyst can determine whether the outermost ring on the sample was the tree's final ring. If so, then you have what is known as a *cutting date;* if not, then your date is only a maximum age (that is, we could say that a specimen was cut down after, say, AD 1225, but we would not be able to say *how many* years after).

Finally, the sample sent to the lab must also have at least 20 rings visible on it in order to increase the chance that the sample will match one and only one segment of the master sequence. A sample with few rings might match to several segments, leaving the archaeologist guessing which match is the correct one.

We can apply tree-ring dating to many species of trees as long as the species reflects climatic change. The most commonly used are piñon pine, ponderosa pine, Douglas fir, juniper, and white fir. Limber pine, bristlecone pine, oak, red cedar, and the giant sequoia are also useful. But some species are not suitable. Cottonwood, for example, grows only near water sources and taps into a more continuous supply of groundwater. As a result, its rings do not reflect local climate very well and, without climatically induced variation in ring width, we cannot link individual samples and build a chronology.

Additionally, because climate varies between regions, a tree-ring sequence is useful only for the region whose climate the tree rings reflect. A tree-ring sequence from northern New Mexico, for example, is not useful in the Mediterranean, or even in southern New Mexico.

Dendrochronological sequences have been developed in many areas, including the American Southwest, the Arctic, the Great Plains, the American Midwest, Germany, Great Britain, Ireland, New Zealand, Turkey, Japan, and Russia. In the American Southwest alone, more than 60,000 tree-ring dates have been established for some 5000 sites. Here the logs used to make pueblo rooms and pithouses allow the tree-ring sequence to extend back to 322 BC; using oaks preserved in ancient bogs, one sequence in Germany extends back to 8000 BC.

Tree-ring dating has tremendous potential to provide absolute dates—to the year, in many cases—for archaeological sites, subject to the one important limitation of all dating methods: there must always be a clear-cut association between the datable specimen (the tree) and cultural behavior (say, the construction of the building). In the American Southwest, archaeologists determined that beams were scavenged from old rooms and incorporated into new rooms. In Alaska, archaeologists found that the driftwood used in some structures had apparently lain on the shore for a century before being used. In both cases, the tree-ring dates would be older (perhaps much older) than the cultural behavior of interest.

Tree Rings and Climate

Dendrochronology also provides climatic data. Because tree-ring width is controlled by precipitation as well as temperature, trees preserve a record of past environmental conditions. Although tree metabolism is complex, analysts have made great progress in such ecological reconstructions. In the American Southwest, for instance, detailed models can tell us how much rain fell in, say, northwestern New Mexico, year by year, even season by season. For example, these data demonstrate that catastrophic floods occurred there in AD 1358. These detailed climatic reconstructions can provide archaeologists with fine-grained paleoenvironmental chronologies—provided the research focuses on an area with a dendrochronological sequence.

Radiocarbon Dating: Archaeology's Workhorse

In 1949, physical chemist Willard F. Libby (1908–1980) announced to the world that he had discovered a revolutionary new dating technique: radiocarbon dating. For his efforts, Libby deservedly received the Nobel Prize in chemistry in 1960. Although dendrochronology is a more precise technique, radiocarbon dating is more widely applicable and is the workhorse in archaeology's stable of dating methods.

How It Works

There are three principal isotopes of carbon: ^{12}C, ^{13}C, and ^{14}C. The isotope ^{14}C (read this as "carbon-14") is of interest here, even though it is the rarest: only one ^{14}C atom exists for every trillion atoms of ^{12}C in living material. ^{14}C is produced in the upper atmosphere, where cosmic radiation creates neutrons that replace one of nitrogen's (^{14}N) protons to create ^{14}C. This ^{14}C is oxidated to form carbon dioxide, which is dispersed throughout the atmosphere by stratospheric winds. About 98 percent of all ^{14}C enters the oceans; plants take up much of the rest through photosynthesis. From plants, it enters herbivores, and then carnivores. So all organic life (including you) contains radioactive carbon.

All radioactive isotopes are unstable and break down, or "decay," over time. ^{14}C breaks down through beta emissions (the emission of a negatively charged electron) into ^{14}N. The amount a living organism loses through decay is replaced from the environment, so as long as an organism is alive, the amount of ^{14}C in it remains in equilibrium with the atmosphere. But once the organism dies, it ceases to take ^{14}C in, and hence the amount of ^{14}C in its body begins to decrease through decay.

But not very quickly. Libby calculated that after 5568 years, half of the ^{14}C available in a sample will have converted to ^{14}N; this is termed the **Libby half-life** of ^{14}C. (We have since learned that the actual half-life of ^{14}C is 5730 years—the so-called Cambridge half-life. To convert a date using the Libby half-life to one using the Cambridge half-life, simply multiply the Libby date by 1.029.)

What do we mean by "half-life"? Imagine a sample of charcoal that contains 100 atoms of ^{14}C (actually, it would contain much more, but let's keep it simple). After 5730 years, 50 of these atoms would have decayed into ^{14}N. After another 5730 years, half of the remaining 50 ^{14}C atoms (that is, 25 atoms) would have converted to ^{14}N, leaving us with only 25 ^{14}C atoms. After another 5730 years (a total of 17,190 years), this amount would be halved again to about 12 ^{14}C atoms. As you can see, after a long time very few ^{14}C atoms remain. Theoretically, radiocarbon dating should extend far back in time, but current technology places a practical limit on it: Radiocarbon dating is good only for organic remains that are no more than about 45,000 years old.

Radiocarbon dating can be used on any organic material, although some are better sources of dates than others. Carbon, or charcoal, is perhaps the most common material dated in archaeology. After being collected in the field, the sample is sent to one of the world's 130 radiocarbon labs with appropriate contextual data. The archaeologist first examines the sample microscopically for intruding root hairs or other organic contaminants; he or she also tries to identify the wood species (see "Are All Organics Created Equal?" following).

The lab pretreats the carbon with one of several protocols, depending on its characteristics. The sample might, for instance, be physically crushed and dispersed in de-ionized water, then washed with hot hydrochloric acid to remove carbonates and then with an alkali wash (NaOH) to remove organic acids (these could make the date younger or older if not removed). Such pretreatment is important because even a small amount of contamination can greatly alter the measured date of a sample.

Once the sample has been pretreated, the lab counts the amount of ^{14}C in the sample by using a scintillation or ionization detector (devices akin to very sophisticated Geiger counters), which counts the number of beta emissions over a measured interval of time. The rate of emissions will be high if the sample is young and low if the sample is very old. By using an established equation, the lab converts the measured rate of beta emissions to an age.

What the Lab Can Tell You

The archaeologist who submits a sample will eventually receive a detailed report from the radiocarbon lab.

Here's one date we received on a carbon sample from the Pine Spring site in southwestern Wyoming:

Beta-122584 6510 ± 70 BP

The alphanumeric string records the laboratory and sample number: Beta Analytic (a radiocarbon lab in Florida) and sample number 122584 (in our reports, we always publish this number with the date so that another archaeologist could consult data in the lab's sample logbook). The second part estimates the age of the sample in radiocarbon years BP (before present—*present* being defined as 1950). Therefore, the radiocarbon lab told us this about the Pine Spring sample: A plant died and burned about 6510 radiocarbon years before AD 1950.

Why 1950? In radiocarbon dating, the present is defined as the year AD 1950—the year Libby invented the method. The reason for this is that "the present" keeps becoming the past, so we need a standard that keeps still. This means that a date of, say, 1000 BP obtained in the year 1960 is actually about 1054 years old in the year 2004 (add 54 years because 2004 is 54 years after AD 1950).

Why "radiocarbon years"? Labs measure samples in radiocarbon years, not calendar years. As we will see, radiocarbon dating has certain biases, and the

Libby half-life The time required for half of the carbon-14 available in an organic sample to decay; the standard is 5568 years, although it is known that the half-life is closer to 5730 years.

laboratory date must be corrected to reflect actual calendar years. We return to this later.

Can You Handle the Uncertainty?

So far, so good. But remember that the lab report attached ± 70 to the age estimate. The decay process of ^{14}C is a statistical process, and the number of beta emissions is not constant over short periods (but the rate does average out over the half-life). For this reason, the lab measures the amount of beta emissions over several lengths of time and then averages those emissions to get an age. In Beta-122584, the number 6510 estimates the actual age of the sample; it is the mean of a number of measurements made by the lab.

That counting process also produces a standard deviation, read as "plus or minus," which estimates the degree of consistency among the counting runs. The standard deviation expresses the range within which the true date falls. We know from statistical theory that there is a 68 percent chance that the true date falls within one standard deviation on either side of the mean date. By both adding and subtracting 70 years from the age estimate, we know that there is a 68 percent chance that the true age of the carbon falls between 6440 (6510 − 70) and 6580 (6510 + 70) radiocarbon years BP. If you want to be even more certain, statistical theory tells us that there is a 95 percent chance that the actual age falls within *two* standard deviations of the mean date, which in this case means between 6370 and 6650 radiocarbon years BP.

The standard deviation must never be omitted from the radiocarbon date, because without it one has no idea how precise a date is. When archaeologists get a date back from a lab, they first look at the mean date, but they evaluate that date's utility by looking at the standard deviation. If it is very large, the date may be worthless (although it depends on the specific research question).

photosynthetic pathways The specific chemical process through which plants metabolize carbon; the three major pathways discriminate against carbon-13 in different ways, therefore similarly aged plants that use different pathways can produce different radiocarbon ages.

Are All Organics Created Equal?

The simple answer is no.

Bone, for example—and especially very old bone (> 5000 years)—can create problems. Bone is very complex chemically and contains nonorganic as well as organic components. In addition, it can be easily contaminated by younger carbon percolating in from the surrounding sediments. For these reasons, bones can give dates that are quite a bit older or younger than their actual ages. One way around this problem is to extract the amino acids chemically and date the carbon that is part of those organic molecules.

We also have to take care with plant remains. All plants take in carbon through the process of photosynthesis, but different plant species do it through one of three **photosynthetic pathways.** The first such pathway (discovered in experiments with algae, spinach, and barley) converts atmospheric carbon dioxide into a compound with three carbon atoms. This so-called C_3 pathway is characteristic of sugar beets, radishes, peas, wheat, and many hardwood trees. A second pathway converts carbon dioxide from the air into a complex compound with four carbon atoms. This C_4 pathway is used by plants from arid and semiarid regions, such as maize, sorghum, millet, yucca, and prickly pear. A third, the CAM pathway ("crassulacean acid metabolism"), is found in succulents, such as cactus.

The importance of these different photosynthetic pathways is that C_4 plants end up taking in *more* ^{14}C relative to the other isotopes of carbon than do C_3 and CAM plants. Because Libby developed radiocarbon dating before this diversity in photosynthesis was known, his system uses the photosynthetic process of C_3 plants as the standard. This can create problems.

Imagine a maize plant growing next to an oak; the maize, being a C_4 plant, will take in more ^{14}C than the oak, a C_3 plant. If both die at the same time, and both are later dated by an archaeologist, the maize sample will appear to be *younger* than the oak tree by 200–300 years, because the maize began the decay process with more radiocarbon than did the oak.

Fortunately, radiocarbon labs can correct this problem by measuring the ratio of ^{13}C to ^{12}C and using that value to normalize the resulting date on the sample. And this is why archaeologists should always try to identify the kind of plant that they are dating.

The Reservoir Effect

A second problem concerns the **reservoir effect.** Libby's method was based on the abundance of ^{14}C in the atmosphere, but some organisms obtain their carbon from sources whose carbon content may be significantly different from that of the atmosphere. Snails that live in lakes in areas of limestone will incorporate "dead" carbon (meaning that the carbon source is so old that no discernible ^{14}C remains) by incorporating the limestone's carbonate into their shells. If dated, a snail that died yesterday in such a situation can appear to be hundreds, or even thousands, of years old.

Similarly, this affects the dating of the remains of marine organisms that archaeologists find in coastal sites. Fish and shellfish take in carbon from the water, not the atmosphere. The ocean is another reservoir of carbon containing more "old" carbon than the atmosphere at any given time. Given that the radiocarbon method is based on an atmospheric standard, marine organisms also tend to date somewhat older than they actually are—by about 400 years. This creates an ancillary problem in dating skeletal remains of humans or animals who relied heavily on seafood, for their skeletons will reflect the isotopic composition of the foods they consumed—and hence they also appear to be older than they actually are. Again, labs can correct this problem if they have background information on the sample.

Tree Rings Refine Radiocarbon Dating

In order to test the radiocarbon method, Libby had to calculate radiocarbon dates on material of known ages. He chose wood from the tombs of Egyptian pharaohs, because those burials were dated through documents. Although Egyptologists warned that the radiocarbon dates did not quite square with the historically derived dynastic chronology, Libby attributed this disparity to experimental error. But we now know that the effect is due to differential production of atmospheric ^{14}C over time.

The first investigator to find fault with the atmospheric assumption was Hessel de Vries of the Netherlands. In the 1950s, de Vries cut several beams from historic buildings and determined the age of the wood by counting the rings. When he dated the known-age specimens by radiocarbon assay, he found the ^{14}C dates to be 2 percent older than expected for the known-age wood. Scientists at the time generally dismissed the work, because the errors de Vries discovered were relatively small—just barely outside the limits of expected error.

But the specter of larger errors finally inspired several radiocarbon labs to look more closely into the problem. In one landmark study, Hans Suess (University of California, San Diego) analyzed wood from bristlecone pine trees. Native to the western United States, bristlecones are the world's oldest living organisms (some living specimens are 4600 years old). Working from live trees to ancient stumps, investigators had already extended the bristlecone tree-ring sequence back nearly 8200 years (by the tree-ring technique discussed above). Suess radiocarbon-dated dozens of known-age samples and compared the results obtained by each method. When he did so, it became clear that significant fluctuations, now known as **de Vries effects,** occurred in the atmospheric ^{14}C concentrations. There were at least 17 such fluctuations over the past 10,000 years, produced, we believe, by pulses in sunspot activity.

This tree-ring research led to the discovery that the production of ^{14}C has not remained constant over time as Libby assumed. This is generally not a big problem for dates younger than about 3500 years; but it becomes progressively worse as we move farther back in time. In fact, a piece of carbon that gives a radiocarbon date of around 10,000 years is actually closer to 12,000 years old.

So the bad news is that *radiocarbon years are not the same as calendar years.* The good news is that we can fix the problem.

The fluctuations in ^{14}C are worldwide because the Earth's atmosphere is so well mixed; studies made during aboveground testing of atomic bombs show that material released into the atmosphere is more or less evenly distributed throughout the atmosphere in a few

reservoir effect When organisms take in carbon from a source that is depleted of or enriched in ^{14}C relative to the atmosphere; such samples may return ages that are considerably older or younger than they actually are.

de Vries effects Fluctuations in the calibration curve produced by variations in the atmosphere's carbon-14 content; these can cause radiocarbon dates to calibrate to more than one calendar age.

LOOKING CLOSER
How Old Is Egyptian Agriculture?

In 1978, archaeologists Fred Wendorf (Southern Methodist University) made a remarkable discovery in southern Egypt, just west of the Nile River, in Wadi Kubbaniya (a *wadi* is a dry stream drainage). The wadi contained many sites with stone tools, mostly blades fashioned from flint, large grinding stones, and the bones of fish and eel, along with waterfowl, wild cattle, hartebeest, and gazelle bones. Wendorf also found several hearths and from these they took some 30 charcoal samples that dated the sites to between 17,000 and 18,300 years old.

None of the food remains were surprising in a site of this age. The evidence pointed to a foraging population that fished, hunted, and gathered plants along what was then a sluggish stream.

What was surprising, however, were four grains of domesticated barley and one grain of wheat. At the time, all evidence suggested that agriculture began about 10,000 years ago, far to the east in places such as Iran and Iraq. The evidence from Wadi Kubbaniya, however, suggested that agriculture in Egypt was 7000–8000 years *older*. This was indeed an important find.

But note that the few grains of wheat and barley were not themselves dated; instead, their age was based on their *association* with hearths that contained charcoal that was dated. You've learned that small objects like seeds can move around quite a bit in archaeological sites. So the question was: Were the seeds deposited at the same time that the hearths were used?

Wendorf saw no obvious evidence that the seeds had moved from a later level. But he knew that such evidence is often hard to see and that the best thing would be to date the wheat and barley themselves. But these small seeds, even if lumped together, would be too small for the conventional radiocarbon method.

Wendorf is a cautious archaeologist, so he wanted to check his claim. In 1978, AMS dating was just under development, but Wendorf knew that it could test the conventional radiocarbon dates. He submitted four barley seeds for analysis, along with some charcoal from the hearths as a control. As before, the charcoal yielded dates from 17,500 to 19,000 BP, but the barley seeds were *less than 5000 years old*. The barley seeds (and presumably the lone wheat seed as well) were contaminants, seeds that had worked their way down from a later level into an ancient site. Admirably, Wendorf quickly published a retraction of his earlier claim. Were it not for AMS dating, our understanding of the origins of agriculture in the Near East might be quite different—and wrong.

years. We say "more or less" because Southern Hemisphere radiocarbon dates are 24–40 years too old compared with Northern Hemisphere dates (that is, a sample of carbon from South Africa will give a radiocarbon age that is 24–40 years older than a sample from Germany that is the same age). The land-to-ocean ratio is smaller in the Southern than in the Northern Hemisphere, and this means that the oceans deplete the Southern Hemisphere's atmosphere of ^{14}C relative to the Northern Hemisphere. But 24–40 years is minor, and we can correct for it before calibration.

Using tree-ring chronologies from several places in the world, researchers have extended the calibration curve to 11,800 calendar years. Other methods push the calibration curve back even farther, but these are still controversial. We can now convert radiocarbon dates into calendar dates through easy-to-use programs that are available online. And radiocarbon labs routinely provide the calibrated date along with the conventional radiocarbon age.

Accelerator Dating: Taking Radiocarbon to the Limit

Some scholars see archaeology as an odd science because it progresses through unique and unrepeatable experiments. Digging remains our primary "experimental" method, and all archaeologists know that, as they dig, they are destroying data that no one has even yet thought of collecting. Before 1950, for example, archaeologists rarely saved charcoal—how could they have anticipated radiocarbon dating? This is why, today, we slowly excavate only that portion of a site necessary to answer a question, and it's why we compulsively save at least a sample of everything we find. We know that future technologies will allow us to learn things that we cannot even imagine now. New methods of radiocarbon dating demonstrate this fact.

Recall that labs obtain conventional radiocarbon dates by counting beta emissions. To do this effectively, you need to submit a fairly large sample of carbon. Back in the 1970s, in fact, archaeologists sometimes said you needed a good "double handful" of carbon for a decent date. But often all we find are small, isolated bits of carbon; we can't simply combine them because we'd then risk combining carbon of vastly different ages—which would produce a standard deviation so large that the date may be useless.

The development of **accelerator mass spectrometry (AMS)** for radiocarbon dating in the 1980s changed this by drastically reducing the quantity of datable material required. Accelerator technology does not count beta emissions as conventional technology does. Instead, it uses an electrostatic tandem accelerator and a technique known as mass spectrometry to count the *proportion* of carbon isotopes in a sample. Given that a single gram of modern organic material contains some 59 *billion* atoms of ^{14}C, a much smaller amount of material is required by AMS. In fact, it requires only a few milligrams of carbon—a sample about the size of a sesame seed.

This new radiocarbon method allows archaeologists to test old ideas by allowing sites or objects to be dated that previously defied adequate dating. In some cases, AMS dating has corrected some significant errors (see "Looking Closer: How Old Is Egyptian Agriculture?").

Trapped Charge Dating

Radiocarbon dating is limited to objects that are less than about 45,000 years old. But other techniques allow us to date sites that are even older. One class of these are jointly known as **trapped charge dating,** which consists of three methods: thermoluminescence, optically stimulated luminescence, and electron spin

resonance. Rare a decade ago, these techniques are increasingly common in archaeology today. Their age ranges are unknown, but they extend back to at least 300,000 years. Their geochemical basis is complex, but we will keep the explanations simple. Working archaeologists need to understand both the potential and the limitations of these dating tools.

The same principle underlies all three techniques: Over time, background gamma radiation in sediment causes some electrons of the atoms of certain minerals, notably quartz and feldspar, to move to a different energy state. When this happens, some electrons are "trapped" in atomic imperfections in the minerals' crystal lattices (Figure 5-6). As time passes, an increasing number of electrons are trapped in this way.

Assuming that the radiation dose is constant over time, electrons become trapped at a constant rate. If we could somehow measure the number of electrons trapped in the crystal lattice, we would have an estimate of the *total* radiation dose the specimen has received over time. If we then knew the *annual* background radiation dose, we could calculate a specimen's age simply by dividing the first measure by the second. How do we calculate these values?

We figure the annual dose by burying a radiation-measuring device, called a **dosimeter,** in an archaeological site and retrieving it a year later. The device records how much radiation it was exposed to in a year's time.

To determine a specimen's total radiation dose, we need to measure the number of trapped electrons in that specimen. Obviously, you can't just count them. But several methods accomplish this task, and the three techniques are partially distinguished by the methods

accelerator mass spectrometry (AMS) A method of radiocarbon dating that counts the proportion of carbon isotopes directly (rather than using the indirect Geiger counter method), thereby dramatically reducing the quantity of datable material required.

trapped charge dating Forms of dating that rely upon the fact that electrons become trapped in minerals' crystal lattices as a function of background radiation; the age of the specimen is the total radiation received divided by the annual dose of radiation.

dosimeter A device to meaure the amount of gamma radiation emitted by sediments. It is normally buried in a stratum for a year to record the annual dose of radiation. Dosimeters are often a short length of pure copper tubing filled with calcium sulfate.

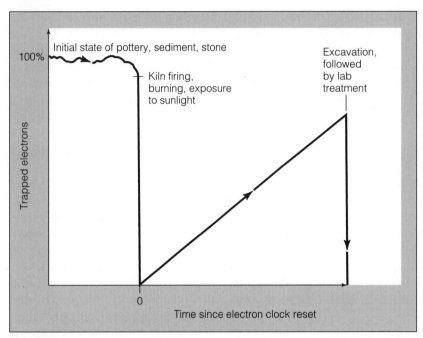

Figure 5-6 The process of setting an object's clock to zero in trapped charge dating. An object begins with some number of trapped electrons that are "reset" when the object is heated or exposed to sunlight. The object then gathers more trapped electrons through time due to background radiation; its clock is then reset in the lab, where the number of trapped electrons are estimated to calculate the object's age.

used to determine the total radiation dose, as well as the kinds of material that they date. To understand *how* we can measure the total radiation dose, you must first understand *what* it is that trapped charge techniques measure.

The important thing to know is that electrons that are moved *out* of their orbits (that is, trapped) by background radiation are *returned* to their orbits by sufficient heat (500° C) or by exposure to even a few minutes of sunlight. Through the application of heat or light, the specimen has its clock reset to zero, so to speak, and the slow trapping process will begin again. So, strictly speaking, *trapped charge dating identifies the last time a specimen had its electron traps emptied.* Knowing this tells us how to apply the different techniques.

Thermoluminescence (TL) measures the total radiation dose by heating a specimen rapidly to 500° C.

Trapped electrons in quartz and feldspar crystals slip free and move back to their orbits. When they do, they release energy in the form of light. Using special equipment, the lab measures the amount of light released as the specimen is heated; this gives us the needed measure of the total radiation dose. Like radiocarbon dating, trapped charge dating produces a mean date with a standard deviation. *TL dates the last time an artifact was heated.*

Archaeologists have used TL to date ceramics. Imagine a ceramic pot, consisting of clay with some sand added to give the pot strength. The sand contains quartz and feldspar that have been slowly accumulating trapped electrons. When that pot is fired, however, those traps are emptied, and the pot's clock is reset. Eventually, the pot breaks and its sherds are discarded. Once those sherds become buried, the quartz and feldspars are exposed to gamma radiation and begin to collect trapped charges again. When the sample is reheated under laboratory conditions (a small portion of the specimen has to be destroyed for analysis), the intensity of the light emission measures the number of electrons that were trapped between the two episodes of heating—in the original fire and in the lab. The method is also used to date burned stone artifacts, because heat resets the TL clock of the minerals in the stone. (And museums use the method to detect ceramic forgeries, because TL can quickly distinguish between an ancient clay figurine and a twentieth-century fake.)

The artifact's context is therefore especially important, because what interests the archaeologist is the age of the artifact, which may or may not coincide with the events that trapped charge methods date. For instance, if a stone tool was accidentally burned 1000 years after its manufacture, TL will date the age of the burning, not the age of the artifact's manufacture—and it is usually the latter that interests archaeologists. None-

thermoluminescence (TL) A trapped charge dating technique used on ceramics and burnt stone artifacts—anything mineral that has been heated to more than 500° C.

theless, by paying attention to context, trapped charge dating has the potential to rewrite prehistory, because it can date objects that radiocarbon cannot and because it can date objects that are beyond the range of radiocarbon.

For example, archaeologists Ofer Bar-Yosef (Harvard University) and Bernard Vandermeersch (University of Bordeaux) employed this technique to challenge our understanding of human evolution. The transition between **Neanderthals** and modern *Homo sapiens* was for many years based on the chronology of western Europe. There, *Homo sapiens* replaced Neanderthals about 40,000 years ago. But for various reasons, Bar-Yosef suspected that "archaic *Homo sapiens*" (called such because their skulls appear to be transitional between earlier hominids and biologically modern humans) appeared earlier in the Near East. Excavating the site of Qafzeh in Israel, Bar-Yosef and Vandermeersch found strata containing skeletal remains of archaic *Homo sapiens* along with stone tools, some of which had burned in hearths. These strata were beyond the range of radiocarbon dating and hence must be at least 45,000 years old—older than the western European counterparts.

But how much older? TL dating provided the answer. Dating a series of the burnt stone tools, Bar-Yosef found that the artifacts had burned some 92,000 ± 5000 years ago, much earlier than the European chronology. Although the date's standard deviation might seem large, note that it is only about 5 percent of the mean date. And even allowing for the large standard error, the TL date on the tools suggests that modern humans might have first appeared in the Near East rather than in Europe.

Another trapped charge dating technique, **optically stimulated luminescence (OSL)**, is finding many uses in archaeology because it can date the most common material in archaeological sites: dirt. This technique relies on the fact that some of the trapped electrons are sensitive to sunlight as well as to heat.

Sand grains of quartz and feldspar have their clocks reset (referred to as bleaching) in a matter of minutes as they blow through the air and are exposed to sunlight; once buried, they begin accumulating trapped electrons again. *OSL therefore dates the time when the sands were buried.* Although OSL can be used on a variety of sediments, eolian sands are the best because they are more likely to have been sufficiently bleached by

sunlight (and thus have their clocks reset) than alluvial sands.

Instead of measuring luminescence through the application of heat, OSL measures it by passing light of a particular wavelength over the specimen. This causes light-sensitive electrons to emit their own light as they return to orbit; the intensity of that light is a measure of the total radiation dose. Incidentally, when we take sediment samples for OSL dating, we must be sure not to expose them to sunlight.

Our final trapped charge dating method is **electron spin resonance (ESR)**, which is primarily used to date tooth enamel. Ninety-six percent of tooth enamel consists of the mineral hydroxyapatite, which contains no trapped charges when formed. Once the tooth is deposited in the ground, however, it accumulates charges from the background radiation. To measure those trapped charges, a portion of the specimen is exposed to electromagnetic radiation, which resets the electrons. In this case, the total radiation dose is proportional to the amount of microwave energy absorbed by the specimen.

ESR dating has also challenged our understanding of human evolution. As we noted previously, the European chronology showed that modern humans rapidly replaced Neanderthals about 40,000 years ago. But when ESR was applied to tooth enamel of animals found in strata containing evidence of *Homo sapiens* and Neanderthals at Qafzeh in Israel, as well as at three nearby cave sites (Tabun, Skhul, and Kebara), the dates suggested that *Homo sapiens* existed as early as 120,000 years ago, and Neanderthals as late as 60,000 years ago. This means that for a long period of time, perhaps as much as 60,000 years, modern humans and Neanderthals existed side by side—a different scenario than

Neanderthals (or **Neandertals**) An early form of humans who lived in Europe and the Near East about 300,000 to 30,000 years ago; biological anthropologists debate whether Neanderthals were in the direct evolutionary line leading to *Homo sapiens*.

optically stimulated luminescence (OSL) A trapped charge dating technique used to date sediments; the age is the time elapsed between the last time a few moments' exposure to sunlight reset the clock to zero and the present.

electron spin resonance (ESR) A trapped charge technique used to date tooth enamel and burnt stone tools; it can date teeth that are beyond the range of radiocarbon dating.

in western Europe, where they may have overlapped for much less time.

Trapped charge dating techniques can date objects that are beyond the range of radiocarbon dating. But we must remember that what we are dating is *the last time that the clock was reset*—by light in the case of OSL and by heat in the case of TL (neither seem to affect ESR measurements). Like radiocarbon dating, these techniques date accurately to a range of years, not a single year.

Potassium-Argon and Argon-Argon

Archaeologists have a variety of other radiometric dating techniques that, like radiocarbon dating, are based on the fact that radioactive isotopes decay at known rates. These include **potassium-argon dating,** and its variant, **argon-argon dating.** *These techniques are useful for dating the age of the formation of a particular layer of volcanic rock itself.*

Because these radioactive isotopes have extremely long half-lives, they are useful for dating materials that are hundreds of thousands or millions of years old—they cannot be used on rock that is less than 200,000 years old. For this reason, these are important dating methods for archaeologists who work in Africa and Asia where early human remains are found.

Many rocks, including volcanic minerals, contain traces of potassium, which, like carbon, occurs naturally in several isotopic forms. One of these, potassium-40 or ^{40}K, decays slowly, with a half-life of 1.31 *billion* years, into argon-40 (^{40}Ar), an inert, stable gas—hence the name potassium-argon dating. By comparing the relative proportions of these potassium and argon isotopes in a sample, we can determine its age. As with radiocarbon dating, the principle is simple: The more ^{40}Ar in a sample relative to ^{40}K, the older that sample is.

potassium-argon dating An absolute dating technique that monitors the decay of potassium (K-40) into argon gas (Ar-40).

argon-argon dating A high-precision method for estimating the relative quantities of argon-39 to argon-40 gas; used to date volcanic ashes that are between 500,000 and several million years old.

Homo erectus A hominid who lived in Africa, Asia, and Europe between 2 million and 500,000 years ago. These hominids walked upright, made simple stone tools, and may have used fire.

For potassium-argon dating to work, there must have been no argon trapped at the time of rock formation. Like trapped charge dating methods, a rock's argon-accumulating clock must have been reset to zero such that all argon is the result of potassium decay. Fortunately, volcanic rock provides a comparable method for "zeroing out" the potassium-argon clock. During all major volcanic eruptions, high temperatures drive all gases—including ^{40}Ar—out of the microscopic rock crystals. Such episodes set the potassium-argon clock to zero, and all ^{40}Ar present in the ash today therefore accumulated since the ash was ejected from the volcano. In addition, all argon must be retained in the rock structure without loss to the atmosphere. Some rocks "leak" argon, and so care must be exercised in deciding which rock types to subject to potassium-argon dating.

This is why volcanic ash deposits are so useful. If an archaeologist finds human fossils or stone tools just *below* a layer of volcanic ash, the law of superposition tells us that the potassium-argon method will provide a *minimum* age estimate for the tools and fossils contained in the archaeological stratum below. Find fossils between two layers of volcanic ash deposits, and you bracket the age of the archaeological material (although you can't date the archaeological material itself).

The maximum age range of potassium-argon dating is theoretically the age of the Earth. Although this method is not as precise as radiocarbon dating, its results are close enough, and it provides dates for some critically important early sites in Africa and elsewhere.

For example, potassium-argon dating was used to estimate the age of **Homo erectus,** an early hominid, in Asia (see Figure 5-7). For decades, investigators believed that *Homo erectus* evolved exclusively in Africa, the earliest fossils being slightly less than 2 million years old. Then, sometime after 1.5 million years ago, *Homo erectus* expanded out of Africa, colonizing other parts of the Old World.

Thus, human paleontologists were shocked in 1971, when Garniss Curtis (University of California, Berkeley) used potassium-argon to date the sediments associated with an infant *Homo erectus* skull from Mojokerto, Java. Because Java is a long way from Africa, most investigators thought that the Mojokerto skull should be much younger than a million years. But Curtis estimated that it was nearly twice that age: 1.9 million

Figure 5-7 A 1.8 million-year-old *Homo erectus* skull (KNM-ER 3733) from Koobi Fora, Africa.

years old. Most paleontologists rejected this extraordinarily ancient age because they were convinced that the only hominids in the world prior to 1 million years ago lived in Africa.

Both these early dates and the technique itself came under criticism. Although potassium-argon dating had been around for decades, the laboratory methods were cumbersome, and the process required a large sample that increased the chance for contamination.

So Curtis teamed up with Carl Swisher (Arizona State University) to develop a new dating method. The argon-argon method simplifies the lab process and avoids the contamination problem by using small samples. The method works by irradiating the volcanic crystals. When a neutron penetrates the potassium nucleus, it displaces a proton, converting the potassium into ^{39}Ar, an "artificial" isotope not found in nature. The minute quantities of artificially created argon and naturally occurring ^{40}Ar are then measured to estimate the ratio of potassium to ^{40}Ar. This high-precision method, which is replacing potassium-argon dating, also allows investigators to focus on single volcanic crystals, which can be dated one by one; thus any older contaminants can be discarded.

In 1992, Curtis and Swisher used the argon-argon method to date some white volcanic pumice obtained from the matrix inside the braincase of the Mojokerto fossil. The result was virtually the same as the "old fashioned" K-Ar date: 1.8 million ± 40,000 years. These dates remain controversial, but received some support with the discovery of 1.75-million-year-old *Homo erec-*

tus (some classify it as *Homo ergaster*) at the site of Dmanisi, in the country of Georgia. More to the point, dating techniques such as the argon-argon method will be increasingly important in evaluating fossil evidence in the years to come.

What Do Dates Mean?

These are just some of the ways that archaeologists can date sites—there are many others. It is important to keep in mind what materials the different techniques date, how far back in time they can extend, and what events the techniques actually date (summarized in Rapid Review), because these factors are necessary to answering the most important question of all: What do the dates mean?

We can never date archaeological sites by simple equivalences. The radiocarbon lab, for instance, takes a chunk of charcoal and tells you how long ago that tree died. By itself, this date says nothing important about your site. However, if we can show that the charcoal came from a tree used as a roof beam in a pueblo, then we have a date that matters.

In every case, you have to show that the dated event is contemporaneous with a behavioral event of interest—such as building a house, cooking a meal, killing a deer, or making a pot. We can drive this point home by examining a common issue of radiocarbon dating: the **old wood problem.**

How Old Are the Pyramids?

When most people hear the word *archaeology,* they think about Egypt's pyramids (Figure 5-8). And with good reason: they are impressive structures, especially the three that stand watch over modern Cairo on the Giza Plateau. One of these, the pyramid of Khnumkhuf ("the god Khnum is his protection"; often abbreviated to Khufu, or, in Greek, Cheops) is the

old wood problem A potential problem with radiocarbon (or tree ring) dating in which old wood has been scavenged and reused in a later archaeological site; the resulting date is not a true age of the associated human activity.

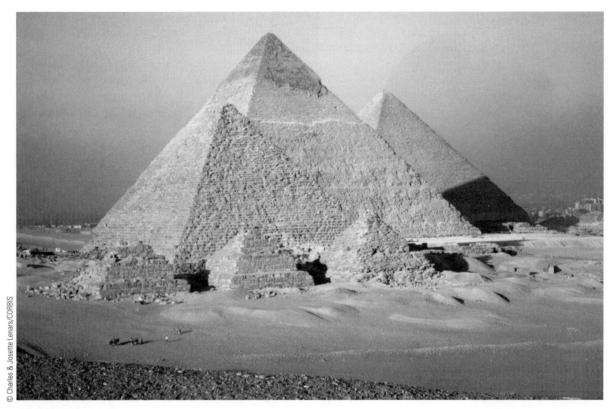

Figure 5-8 The pyramids at Giza.

largest in Egypt. Khufu began building his tomb soon after his reign began in 2551 BC. Made of some 2,300,000 blocks of stone, each weighing an average of 21.2 tons, the pyramid measures 230 meters (756 feet) on a side and is oriented only 3 minutes 6 seconds off true north. It contains several interior passageways and three chambers—one at the end of a tunnel cut into the bedrock deep below the structure. The burial chamber, in the center of the pyramid, has several roofs above it; the Egyptians specifically engineered this roof to distribute the weight of the overlying rock outward and prevent the chamber from being crushed. The pyramid's exterior was originally covered in polished white limestone—making it a landmark that would have shone above the horizon for miles around (the limestone was scavenged by later rulers). At 146 meters (481 feet), Khufu's pyramid remained the world's tallest building for 4440 years—until the Eiffel Tower was built in 1889! It is a remarkable piece of architectural engineering.

How old is it? The ages of the pyramids are based on historical documents—the hieroglyphs that cover the insides of tombs and temples (and that are found on papyrus used to stuff the bulls, crocodiles, ibexes, and other animals that were mummified and buried in the pyramids and other structures). The hieroglyphs give us the dates of the reigns of kings and document their accomplishments. The Egyptian civilization is probably one of the best dated in the world, and the pyramids on the Giza Plateau outside Cairo are among the oldest in Egypt.

But some speculate that the pyramids are actually thousands of years older, built by a civilization some 10,000 years ago. To check the ages based on historical documents, a consortium of archaeologists in 1984, led by Shawki Nakhla and Zahi Hawass (the Egyptian Supreme Council of Antiquities), decided to date the pyramids through radiocarbon dating. But what could they date? The pyramids are made of stone, and the organic remains buried in them were often treated with tar and chemicals that make them unreliable for radiocarbon dates.

But Nakhla and Hawass knew of another source of carbon. Contrary to popular belief, the pyramids were

RAPID REVIEW   Summary of Absolute Dating Methods

Technique	Target Material	Range	Comments
Carbon-14	Any organic material; carbon is the most common	45,000 BP	Requires calibration; calibration curves reliable only to 11,000 years. Accelerator mass spectrometry (AMS) permits dating of minute samples
Thermoluminescence (TL)	Ceramics, burnt stone	Unknown, but perhaps to 300,000 BP	Dates the last time an object was heated to 500° C
Optically stimulated luminescence (OSL)	Quartz, feldspar in eolian sands	Unknown, but perhaps to 300,000 BP	Dates the last time sand was exposed to sunlight sufficient to empty the electron traps; samples must avoid sunlight; lab must date individual grains
Electron spin resonance (ESR)	Tooth enamel, burnt stone tools, corals, shell	10,000 to 300,000 years or more	Dates when a tooth was buried; electron traps reset by exposure to electromagnetic radiation in lab
Argon-Argon	Volcanic ash	200,000 to several million years	Dates the eruption that produced the ash; Argon-Argon requires minute ample

put together with mortar. Workmen made this mortar by burning gypsum, apparently on the work platforms that were erected around the pyramid as it was being constructed. They mixed the resulting ash with water and sand and then slopped the mortar into the cracks between the massive blocks of stone. Inadvertently, pieces of carbon from the fires were caught in the mortar, trapped there for eternity.

In 1984 and 1985, the Egyptian archaeological teams scrambled over the pyramids like ants on an anthill, looking for fingernail-sized bits of carbon. They found quite a few pieces, dated them using the AMS method, and then calibrated the dates. They found not a shred of evidence that the pyramids were thousands of years older than the documentary sources indicate. But what they found still surprised them.

The radiocarbon dates on Old Kingdom (2575–2134 BC) pyramids were from 100 to 400 years *older* than the documentary dates suggested. And yet dates on later Middle Kingdom pyramids (2040–1640 BC) were not far off from their accepted ages. Why were the Old Kingdom dates "too old"?

The first explanation was the "old wood" problem: In desert (or high-altitude or arctic) environments, wood can lie around without decaying for a long time. In California's White Mountains, you can make a fire today from bristlecone wood, send a piece of the charcoal to a lab, and be told that your fire was 2000 years old. The wood is 2000 years old—but the fire that made the charcoal is not.

Egyptian archaeologists thought this "old wood" problem was unlikely. By Old Kingdom times, the Nile

River valley had been occupied for millennia, and by a large population. Excavations near the pyramids reveal a community of stoneworkers, builders of the pyramids, which housed 20,000 people. All the Nile's people cooked over wood and used wood in house construction. And there is not much wood to begin with along the Nile; the floodplain is rich, but it's a narrow strip of green in a vast, treeless desert. For these reasons, the archaeologists postulated that there could have been no old wood lying along the Nile.

But perhaps Egyptians found another source of old wood. The Old Kingdom's construction projects at Giza were massive: three huge and several small pyramids, associated temples, boat docks on the Nile, the Sphinx, and the workers' quarters. These projects required massive amounts of wood—for construction; for ovens to bake bread for the workers; for levers, wedges, and sledges to move the stone blocks; for scaffolding; and for firewood to produce the mortar.

To get all the wood needed, it is likely that Khufu and other pharaohs scavenged older settlements or looted their predecessor's temples and tombs for wood—which Egypt's dry climate would preserve for hundreds, even thousands, of years. We know that pharaohs raided earlier temples and tombs for construction material and jewelry. Perhaps for these Old Kingdom projects, they also sought out firewood. This may account for the early dates on Old Kingdom pyramids.

But then, why were the Middle Kingdom radiocarbon dates not "too old"? By Middle Kingdom times, Nakhla and Hawass reasoned, earlier construction projects had depleted the sources of old wood, and Middle Kingdom builders had to make do with the wood at hand—which would not have been very old.

The point here is that every absolute dating technique dates a particular event, but it is up to the archaeologist to decide how the age of that particular event is meaningful in terms of human behavior.

The Check, Please

How an archaeologist excavates a site depends on several factors, one of these being cost. None of these dating methods is cheap. Right now, a standard radiocarbon date runs about $300 (including the $^{13}C/^{12}C$ calculation); an AMS date costs about $600. Bone dates can run as high as $850 per sample. Tree-ring dates are cheaper—the University of Arizona's Tree-Ring Lab charges about $25 per sample. TL and OSL dates may cost $800 a shot. There are no commercial rates for the other trapped charge and radiometric dating methods, but they have hidden costs. Because so much background data is required for their successful implementation, it is often necessary to finance a visit to the site by the specialist and cover additional sediment and dosimetry studies.

Archaeologists try to get as many dates as they can for a site, but they always have to do so within budget limitations.

Conclusion: How Dating Changed Archaeology

In Chapter 1 we pointed out that archaeology underwent a revolution of sorts in the 1960s. Walter Taylor's generation began that revolution in the 1940s and 1950s, but it was Lewis Binford's generation who brought about the transformation of archaeology. Binford, however, claimed it was the widespread availability of absolute dating methods in the 1960s, notably radiocarbon dating that brought the change in how we do archaeology.

As you have seen, relative dating techniques helped to lift the fog of time that obscures the past. They were a significant advance because they helped to place objects and cultures into a historical sequence. Absolute dating techniques were an even more significant advance, because they could assign artifacts to a particular year or a specific range of years. Absolute dating techniques allow us to see not only the order of events, but the rate of change as well. Why did this permit Binford's generation to change archaeology?

One reason is that absolute dating techniques freed archaeologists to do other things with their data. Instead of spending time on seriation diagrams, an archaeologist could simply send a piece of carbon to a lab for a radiocarbon date.

But a more significant reason is that absolute dating techniques allowed archaeologists to control a major dimension of their data—age—in a more rigorous and absolute manner. Seriation was grounded in an often-unspoken theory of culture change—material items appear, grow in popularity, then disappear. No one knew, or really seemed to care, why this happened; all that mattered was that the technique provided a way to build a chronology. But for archaeologists to transcend chronology, they needed to know more. They needed to know how rapidly an item became prevalent, or how rapidly another replaced it. They needed to know how long a piece of material culture was used—50 years, 500 years, 5000 years? They needed to know whether an item first appeared in a particular region and then spread to others, or whether it had multiple centers of origin.

Relative dating methods could not answer these questions very precisely, and, in fact, relative dating methods tended to carry their own answers to them. Archaeologists relying on seriation, for instance, tended to see innovations as having only one center and then spreading outward from there. They saw cul-

tural change as gradual, rather than abrupt. Absolute dating methods permitted archaeologists to know when styles appeared, how quickly they spread, and whether there were multiple centers of innovation. These methods opened the door to questions about past lifeways instead of focusing simply on chronology. This is why absolute dating techniques had a large effect on archaeological paradigms.

In recent years, technology has afforded us increasingly sophisticated ways to date artifacts, sites, and strata, and they show no sign of stopping. We can expect, then, that continual advances in dating methods will not only permit a greater understanding of the chronology of the past, but will also help create new paradigms, new ways of understanding the past.

Summary

- Contemporary archaeologists have a battery of techniques that can date objects of the past; these are divided into relative and absolute methods.

- Relative dating methods include use of the law of superposition, the index fossil concept, and seriation. Called time-markers in archaeology, index fossils are artifacts with known dating orders that allow strata in different sites to be correlated; seriation refines this approach, placing sites or strata into a relative sequence based on changing frequencies of material culture. These techniques help understand the chronological order of culture change, but not the actual age.

- The advent of absolute dating methods helped usher in a new age of archaeology.

- Tree-ring dating (dendrochronology) enables archaeologists to establish the precise year of death for many species of trees commonly found in archaeological sites. This technique is limited to relatively small regions and, in the American Southwest, where it is an important technique, only dates sites of the past 2000 years.

- Radiocarbon dating is a major radiometric technique that uses the known rate of decay of ^{14}C to determine the age of organics. It is useful for archaeological sites that are less than 45,000 years old.

- The atmospheric level of radiocarbon has changed over time. Using correlations between tree rings and radiocarbon levels, archaeologists can calibrate dates—that is, convert radiocarbon years into calendar years—of the past 10,000 years.

- The accelerator (AMS) technique allows us to radiocarbon-date minute amounts of carbon.

- Trapped charge dating methods—thermoluminescence, optically stimulated luminescence, and electron spin resonance—date ceramics or burnt stone tools, eolian sediments, and tooth enamel, respectively. They date an object by calculating the amount of radiation an object was subjected to since the object's electron "clock" was last reset by heat (TL) or sunlight (OSL). These techniques date items tens of thousands of years old—beyond the range of radiocarbon dating.

- Potassium-argon dating and argon-argon dating are radiometric techniques used to date volcanic rock, especially ashes. These techniques are useful in places where archaeological sites are too old to use radiocarbon and trapped charge dating.

- Keep in mind that, by themselves, dating techniques tell us nothing about cultural activities. Radiocarbon dating, for example, tells us only when a plant or an animal died. In each case, the event being dated must be related to a behavioral (cultural) event of interest.

Media Resources

Doing Fieldwork: Archaeological Demonstrations CD-ROM

This CD gives you a vivid glimpse of what it is like to be involved in an archaeological dig . . . without leaving your chair. With this CD, you will see archaeologists involved in actual excavations—many of which are referenced in your Thomas/Kelly text—using a number of the field techniques covered in this chapter. Organized according to the various stages of a live excavation, the CD presents hands-on interactive activities, live-action demonstration videos, and quizzes to help you better understand the processes and techniques that are important to an excavation.

The Companion Website for Archaeology: **Down to Earth,** *Third Edition*

http://anthropology.wadsworth.com/thomas_kelly3e_down/

Supplement your review of this chapter by going to the companion website to take one of the practice quizzes, use the flash cards to master key terms, and check out the many other study aids that are designed to help you succeed in your introductory archaeology course.

6

The Dimensions of Archaeology: Time, Space, and Form

Outline

A collection of artifacts that can provide key time-markers in archaeology.

From left: © Archivo Iconografico, S.A./CORBIS; Bettmann/CORBIS; George H. H. Huey/CORBIS

Preview

I N THE NINETEENTH CENTURY, archaeological sites were viewed as little more than mines in which to prospect for artifacts. But trained archaeologists, such as Nels Nelson and A. V. Kidder, shifted their objectives to focus more on understanding the person behind the artifact rather than the artifact itself. And in the 1960s, archaeology further refined that focus, attempting not only to reconstruct what happened in the past, but to explain that past as well.

To achieve these objectives, archaeology analyzes how artifacts and features fall into changing patterns over space and time; this chapter shows how archaeologists identify those patterns. We first consider classification—the ways that archaeologists divide the many kinds of objects found into reasonable and useful artifact types. We then discuss the concepts of archaeological cultures, periods, phases, assemblages, and components—all of which are used to organize archaeological data into space-time systematics.

Introduction

The title of this chapter comes from an article by archaeologist Albert Spaulding (1914–1990), who pointed out that archaeology is about patterns in artifacts and features through time and across space. For example, the kinds of houses found in much of the American Southwest in 200 BC were semi-subterranean pithouses, usually round, and covered with heavy log roofs and a layer of sod. They were warm in the winter and cool in the summer. At the same time (200 BC), but in a different place—farther north toward the Great Basin—houses were more ephemeral, consisting of simple windbreaks or shade structures for summer houses and conical log structures for the winter. Returning to the Southwest, we see a dramatic change in house form around AD 700. At that time, many people made and lived in square, above-ground masonry homes—the familiar masonry

pueblos—rather than pithouses. Back in the Great Basin, however, people continued to live in the same sort of houses that they occupied in 200 BC. Archaeologists have spent the greater part of the previous century documenting such patterns in how material culture changes through time and across space; these patterns are what archaeologists seek to explain. How we go about organizing data into meaningful spatial and temporal patterns is the subject of this chapter.

This organization is vital to the field, because archaeology's major strength is its access to tremendous quantities of time and space. Although many ethnologists study cultural evolution and culture change, they are restricted to short-term study if they deal exclusively with ethnographic evidence. And even if they include oral history or historical documents, ethnologists cannot go back in time more than a century or two. Archaeology, on the other hand, can address the entire complex history of humanity based on the things that people left behind, from 2.5-million-year-old stone tools in Africa to World War II destroyers on the bottom of Pacific lagoons. No other social science has so much time at its disposal.

Archaeologists also deal with worlds of "space." Many ethnologists study entire societies for years on end, but none can realistically employ the tools of ethnography to study an entire region, such as the American Southwest, to say nothing of continents or hemispheres. So what archaeology loses in detail it makes up for by recording what the ethnologist cannot: patterns of human behavior as they were manifested over vast reaches of space, far beyond the confines of a single community.

The goal of archaeology is to reconstruct and explain the past: What did people do, and why did they do it? But to reach this goal, we must first gain a firm grasp on artifact patterning in time and space. You must know the *when* and the *where* in broader terms before contemplating the *how*, the *who*, the *what*, and especially the *why*. Defining a spatial and temporal framework requires that archaeologists date the physical remains, classify archaeological objects into useful categories, and explore their distribution across time and space. In previous chapters we've discussed the fieldwork of archaeology. In this and succeeding chapters, we move into the other half of archaeology: the part that goes on after the excavation.

After the Excavation: Conservation and Cataloging

Suppose that you've just completed a regional survey and have excavated a sample of the sites discovered. You did the survey and excavations by the book, dated the sites, studied the sites' formation processes, and so on. You've returned home with many, carefully labeled bags full of bones, stone tools, ceramics, beads, and figurines. What happens to all the stuff now that the fieldwork is over?

The first step is to conserve the recovered materials. Once this meant little more than washing the artifacts off with water (but not things that water would obviously damage, such as basketry). But today, many archaeologists hesitate to wash some artifacts because even this simple operation might destroy some information. Stone and ceramic artifacts, for example, can contain pollen or residues of blood, plants, or other materials that can be identified and used to reconstruct tool use and diet (see Chapter 8)—but not if a scrupulous lab worker has thoroughly scrubbed the piece. In general, though, a simple cleaning is in order.

Other artifacts may require more attention, especially organic or metal artifacts recovered from wet deposits. Conservation on wooden artifacts recovered from the Ozette site (see Chapter 4) began as soon as excavators removed them from the muddy matrix, because wet wooden artifacts quickly crumble as they dry out. Richard Daugherty preserved Ozette's wooden artifacts by soaking them in vats of Carbowax—polyethylene glycol—melted and diluted with water. He needed huge vats to soak the houses' cedar timbers. Some of the artifacts, especially those made of hardwoods (which have small pores and soak up liquid slowly), had to soak for years.

And during an excavation near New York's Wall Street, archaeologists found several Revolutionary War–era cannons lying on the bottom of what was once the East River. The first task in preserving these artifacts was to replace the brackish water that had impregnated the metal with fresh water. Looking for watertight containers large enough to hold the bulky cannons, project directors Roselle Henn (U.S. Army Corps of Engineers) and Diana diZerega Wall (City College of New York) finally settled on metal coffins! The conservation of artifacts has become a significant specialty within archaeology (see "Looking Closer: Preserving the *Hunley*").

It may also be necessary to reconstruct broken pieces. This is frequently done with pottery, because ceramics are often found in pieces, and reconstruction obviously tells us more about vessel shape, size, and decoration. Piecing together a broken pot is like trying to put together a three-dimensional jigsaw puzzle where every piece is a different shape and there is no picture on the box. It requires a particular personality—somebody who can stay put for long hours—and a sculptor's eye. Some people can do this with ease; others are lucky if they get two pieces to fit.

LOOKING CLOSER
Preserving the Hunley

In 1864, the Confederacy was losing the Civil War, and it took desperate measures to destroy the Union Navy, whose blockades were strangling the South. The Confederacy then unveiled their secret weapon: a small submarine designed to destroy Union vessels from beneath the waves.

Funded by Horace Hunley, whose name would grace the third design, the sub was a bold and ingenious design. Early versions of the *Hunley* capsized, killing most of the crew (including Hunley himself), but a new crew always stepped forward. Crammed into a space 18 feet long and 4 feet wide, seven men turned a crankshaft while the captain guided the *Hunley* and controlled depth with ballast tanks. Two manholes fore and aft, 15 inches in diameter, were the only escape routes; a single candle lit the captain's depth gauge.

On February 17, 1864, the *Hunley* met the USS *Housatonic*. The sub immediately dove and rammed the enemy's hull with a long, barbed spar with a 90-pound explosive charge attached to it. As the sub backed away, a rope played out. At 150 feet, the rope tightened and detonated the charge, sinking the Union's largest ship within minutes. The *Hunley* surfaced, signaled shore, and started home. But for reasons still unknown, she sank before reaching port, killing all eight men aboard.

Her location remained a mystery until 1995, when author Clive Cussler and archaeologists Ralph Wilbanks, Wes Hall, and Harry Pecorelli found the *Hunley* using a magnetometer towed behind a research vessel. Lying only 30 feet below the surface, the submarine's hatches were unopened (only one viewport was broken) and the hull unbreached, still enclosing the remains of the crew members and their personal effects. Three feet of silt protected the sub from the saltwater currents that normally destroy iron ships.

Once removed from the sea, the iron ship would have quickly corroded. To prevent this, the hull was sprayed with water from the moment it was raised until it was placed into a specially designed water-filled tank. A lab now keeps the tank's fresh water at 10° C to prevent the growth of fungus and algae and to reduce the rate of corrosion. The inside was systematically excavated, and the human remains were reburied in April 2004 in Charleston, South Carolina.

Over the years, the sub had developed a carbonate coating that reduced the amount of oxygen that reached the actual metallic surface. Keeping this carbonate layer intact is a critical step in preserving the *Hunley*. But the challenge is immense, and conservators are still wrestling with how to preserve this unique piece of American history for posterity.

The cataloging procedure that actually starts at the excavation (and that we discussed in Chapter 4) continues in the lab after the field season is over. Every single item must be accounted for and its provenience retained through a catalog. And the novice's first job in a lab is almost guaranteed to be cataloging: writing all those minute numbers on artifacts or labels and entering the information into a database. This can take a great deal of time. In fact, as a rule of thumb, for every week spent excavating, archaeologists spend 3–5 weeks or more cleaning, conserving, and cataloging the finds. Sometimes it seems mindless, but cataloging is essential because, without the catalog, provenience is lost, and without provenience an artifact's value to future researchers is greatly reduced.

Archaeological Classification

Cataloging and conservation are just the beginning because, at the end of those tasks, you are faced with thousands of artifacts that differ in terms of function, style, raw material, provenience, and condition. This is where the really time-consuming part of archaeology begins. Archaeologists spend far more time analyzing their finds than they do excavating them.

Archaeologists begin to get a handle on variability in artifacts through **typology,** the classification of artifacts into types. Even before cataloging and conservation begins, an archaeologist has begun to classify the objects. When things turn up in the sifter, the screener sorts the finds into simple categories of stone, bone, shell, ceramic, organic, brick, cloth, wood, metal, or some other category, depending on the nature of the site. Sometimes, objects can't be identified and sorted in the field, so the on-site rule is always "When in doubt, sent it to the lab." In the lab, the cataloged artifacts are usually then further separated into even finer categories. The stone tool analyst might sort the stone artifacts into waste flakes and retouched pieces (flakes that have been chipped into tools) and then sort each of those into even narrower categories. Ceramics may be sorted into decorated and undecorated sherds, or into rim sherds (those that preserve a bit of the vessel's rim or mouth) and body sherds. And so forth.

But then what? How should you deal with all this stuff?

Here's a clue: The archaeologist's first responsibility is to simplify. Generations of archaeologists have found it unrealistic, even preposterous, to cope simultaneously with all the variability that turns up in even the simplest batch of archaeological objects. You could write a detailed paragraph on each artifact that you found. But although that might produce a wonderful descriptive catalog, it would teach us little. Meaning lies not in endless data, but in patterns *within* those data. And patterns appear only when you isolate some aspect of the variation and ignore the rest (for the time being).

So you simplify to reveal meaningful patterns. Because archaeology's twin strengths are time and space, we first develop the categories necessary to reveal patterns in material culture through time and space. Such patterning is known in archaeology as **space-time systematics.** And our first step in that direction is identifying types of artifacts.

artifacts, say, a workshop of woodworking tools. Carpenters classify their tools by function—hammers, saws, planes, files, drills, and spokeshaves. But when insuring a carpenter's workshop, the insurance agent uses another classification, sorting these same tools into new categories, such as flammable and nonflammable, or perhaps according to replacement value: "Under $10," "Between $10 and $25," and so on. Should the carpenter relocate, the furniture movers will group these same tools into another set of divisions such as heavy or light, bulky or compact, or perhaps fragile or unbreakable. While storing the tools, the carpenter may classify them into "Things my kids can touch" and "Things my kids should not touch." This discussion serves to make two important points.

First, *types are abstractions* imposed by the archaeologist on a variable batch of artifacts. We saw in Chapter 2 how cultures classify the world differently. Dogs are considered food in some cultures, pets in others. There is nothing inherent in dogs that makes them "really" food or "really" pets. And there is nothing inherent in an artifact that makes it belong to one and only one type.

As we've said before, your analysis (and the types you create) will depend on your research question. Suppose, for instance, we wanted to learn whether everyone in an ancient society made pots, or if pots were made only by specialized potters. To do this, we might develop a way to classify pots into those made by novices and those made by experts, maybe by classifying pots according to the quality of their construction or painting. On the other hand, if we were interested in the household functions carried on in different rooms, then we might classify a site's ceramics into cooking vessels, water jars, serving vessels, and storage containers. We can classify the same object in many different ways.

Do *not* think that our goal is always to classify things the way ancient peoples would have classified them. Archaeologists may divide stone scrapers into many

Types of Types

Archaeology's basic unit of classification is termed a **type.** Be careful here, because *type*, like *culture*, is an everyday word appropriated by anthropology and reassigned a very specific, nonintuitive meaning.

Archaeologists can classify the same object in many different ways. Think about a familiar set of modern

typology The systematic arrangement of material culture into types.

space-time systematics The delineation of patterns in material culture through time and over space. These patterns are what the archaeologist eventually tries to explain or account for.

type A class of archaeological artifacts defined by a consistent clustering of attributes.

different types based on their shape (to see if any could be useful time markers), but ancient peoples may have recognized only two kinds: ones that were still useful and ones that were used up. Both classifications have their purpose, and both are valid.

And this brings us to our second point: We formulate a classification with a specific purpose in mind. Archaeology has no general, all-purpose classification. As Irving Rouse (Yale University) puts it, "Classification—for what?"

In Chapter 5, you saw one answer to this question: to create time markers. At San Cristobal, Nelson sought distinctive types of pottery that he could use to assign strata or sites to a relative chronology. We began that discussion with some pottery types, such as biscuit ware and three-color glaze pottery. Nelson was not concerned with the pots' functions, or quality, or anything else; he simply wanted to know if some types were earlier or later than other types. Another researcher might have a different purpose and create a different typology.

But where do such types come from? To answer this question, let's first consider three major types of types.

Morphological Types

Modern observers exploring the range of material remains left by an extinct group will encounter many unfamiliar artifacts. To make sense of the past using these remains, the first analytical step is to describe the artifacts carefully and accurately by grouping them into **morphological types.**

Emil Haury (1904–1992), an eminent southwestern archaeologist, drafted one such description of some enigmatic stone disks (Figure 6-1) he recovered while digging at Ventana Cave, in Arizona:

> Discs—Of the twenty-four stone discs, twenty-two are centrally perforated. They were all made of schist, from 36 to 75 mm. in diameter and averaging 8 mm. in thickness. The customary way of producing them was by breaking and then smoothing the rough corners by abrasion. . . . Only one was well

Figure 6-1 Two prehistoric stone disks excavated from Ventana Cave (Arizona). *After Haury (1950), 29; American Museum of Natural History.*

made. . . . Drill holes are bi-conical and not always centrally placed. Two were painted red. Next to nothing is known about these discs.

Note that Haury did not speculate on how people used the discs; he simply illustrated and described the discs in enough detail so that other archaeologists could visualize the artifacts without having to view them firsthand. Such bald description is the primary function of a morphological type (sometimes termed a "class" in archaeological literature).

Morphological types have a second, basic property: they are abstract. Types are not the artifacts per se; they are the composite descriptions of many similar artifacts. This means that every morphological type must encompass a certain range of variability: several colors may have been applied; the quality of manufacture might vary; absolute size may fluctuate; and so forth.

Morphological types are purely descriptive. We ascribe no function to them at this point, and they don't necessarily have any chronological significance. No set rules exist for creating morphological types, although basic raw material (pottery, stone, shell, bone, and so on) is normally the first criterion, followed by shape. Morphological types help communicate what the archaeologist found without describing every single specimen.

---

morphological type A descriptive and abstract grouping of individual artifacts whose focus is on *overall* similarity rather than function or chronological significance.

Temporal Types

Temporal types are morphological types that have specific chronological meaning for a particular region. In other words, they are time-markers. If morphological Type B, for instance, occurs only in strata dating between AD 500 and 1000, then it can be elevated to the status of a temporal type. This promotion is important because, when artifacts belonging to temporal Type B turn up in undated contexts, the time span from AD 500 to 1000 becomes the most plausible hypothesis for their age.

Functional Types

Functional types reflect how objects were used in the past. Functional types can crosscut morphological types. A set of stone scrapers, for instance, might have all been used to prepare hides (that is, they all had the same function), so they are a functional type. But some are big and others are small; some are thin and others are thick; some are made of chert, but others are of quartzite and obsidian; some are sharpened on the ends of stone flakes, others along their sides. But all these objects are the same with regard to their function. The remaining variability is (for now) irrelevant.

Functional types can also crosscut temporal types. Sometimes, pots are painted with distinctive designs for a limited period (like some of the pottery types that Nelson defined at San Cristobal). These distinctive styles of finish make the ceramics a temporal type. But all the differently decorated pots may be of the same functional type—they may all be cooking vessels, water jars, or seed storage pots.

Doing Typology

A good typology possesses two crucial characteristics:

1. Regardless of its final purpose, *a typology must minimize the differences within each created type and maximize the differences between each type.* If a lot of overlap and ambiguity occurs in the types, then they will not reveal any significant or meaningful patterning.
2. The typology must be *objective and explicit.* This means that the result should be replicable by any trained observer. If it is not replicable, then your methods cannot be duplicated (and your work is therefore not scientific).

Once you've created your typology, you can focus on placing it in time and across space. Here's an example.

Projectile Point Typology at Gatecliff

To show you how typology works, we're going to take you step by step through Thomas's classification of the Gatecliff projectile points. And by now, you know that the first question to ask is this: What was the goal of Thomas's classification?

When Thomas began excavating Gatecliff Shelter, he was searching for a useful way to classify projectile points to create temporal types (time-markers) that could be tested against the radiocarbon dates available at Gatecliff. Once defined, these temporal types could estimate the age of surface assemblages (where radiocarbon dates could not be processed). That was the goal—the research question—of the Gatecliff typology.

Choosing Criteria

Great Basin archaeologists knew that projectile points were made out of different types of stone, such as chert, quartzite, obsidian, or rhyolite. But experience showed that raw material did not change over time in a systematic way; in fact, it mostly told archaeologists what kind of material was locally available. A typology based on raw material would not help construct temporal types.

But archaeologists who worked in the Great Basin also knew that projectile point *shape* changed over time. Small points, for example, tended to occur in upper (later) strata; larger points occurred in lower (earlier) strata. And small points that were notched from the side seemed to occur stratigraphically above small points notched from the corners. These observations suggested that a typology based on shape and size could be used to construct temporal types.

The first step in applying your criteria can be informal, sometimes just separating superficially similar artifacts into piles on the laboratory table. We can

temporal type A morphological type that has temporal significance; also known as a time-marker or index fossil.

functional type A class of artifacts that performed the same function; these may or may not be temporal and/or morphological types.

ignore variables like stratigraphy, time depth, cultural affiliation, and even provenience because (for now) the primary concern is to reduce the complexity to our primary criteria—shape and size.

Look at the projectile points in Figure 6-2. These are just a few of the 400 points recovered from Gatecliff Shelter. If you are any kind of observer at all, you will distinguish some important similarities and differences among them. The points at the top of the figure, for instance, are smaller than those at the bottom. Another difference is in how the points are notched for hafting. Some are notched from the side (for example, 7, 8, and 9), and others from the base (for instance, 14 and 15); some are notched from the corner (16 and 24), and some are not notched at all (1 and 3).

Defining Attributes

Differences like size and notch position are **attributes,** which are measurable or observable qualities of an object. We could make an infinite number of observations and take an infinite number of measurements on a projectile point, a few of which are shown in Figure 6-3. There are no rules governing the number of attributes to record; in general, we try to use as few as seem necessary to accomplish the purpose of the typology.

The two attributes of size and notching are sufficient to create workable morphological types. But it is insufficient simply to say "size" and "notch position." To define adequate attributes, we must explain precisely what we mean by the terms, so that another observer could make identical observations.

Take size. We all know what size means, but it can be recorded in several ways. Measure the length of a projectile point and you know something about its size. The width also reflects size. Or you can weigh something to find its size. So, what size are we talking about?

Weight provides a good way to measure the size of a projectile point (although it is necessary to estimate the original weight of broken specimens). Other attributes that measure size (such as length, width, and thickness) all correlate with weight: as a point gets longer, wider, and/or thicker, it also becomes heavier.

© American Museum of Natural History

Figure 6-2 An unsorted batch of stone projectile points recovered at Gatecliff Shelter (Nevada).

attribute An individual characteristic that distinguishes one artifact from another on the basis of its size, surface texture, form, material, method of manufacture, and design pattern.

But weight is the easiest to measure, and so it was one of the first attributes Thomas used to define morphological types. The lightest point in the Gatecliff sample weighs only 0.4 gram (about the weight of a common paper clip) and the heaviest, more than 5 grams (about the same as a nickel). The weights for the 25 Gatecliff points in Figure 6-2 are presented in Table 6-1.

Notice that the weights are patterned, with certain natural breaks in the distributions, defining three projectile point sizes in this collection (this is even clearer when you look at the data on all 400-plus points):

Small points: Weight less than 1.0 gram
Medium points: Weight between 1.0 and 2.5 grams
Large points: Weight over 2.5 grams

Some variability arises naturally among projectile points because flintknappers cannot fix their mistakes;

TABLE 6-1 Attributes for Gatecliff Shelter Projectile Points		
SPECIMEN NUMBER	WEIGHT IN GRAMS	PROXIMAL SHOULDER ANGLE
1	(0.9)	—
2	0.8	—
3	0.9	—
4	0.4	—
5	(0.9)	—
6	(0.4)	200
7	0.8	180
8	(0.6)	180
9	0.7	180
10	(0.8)	190
11	2.3	100
12	(1.5)	100
13	(1.4)	95
14	1.5	85
15	2.5	80
16	4.1	110
17	3.5	120
18	3.9	130
19	3.5	120
20	(4.2)	150
21	(2.8)	80
22	(3.4)	85
23	(5.5)	80
24	2.7	100
25	(5.5)	60

Note: Weights in parentheses are estimates on broken points.

they must work around errors, creating some variability in the finished product. In addition, points break when they are used. If they are not too severely broken, they can be reshaped into usable points—but this too makes them smaller than the maker initially intended (this can have an effect on typology; see "Looking Closer: The Frison Effect"). But for each of the three weight categories, the point's maker had a mental template of what the "proper" point's size should be. By and large, the three size categories reflect natural breaks in the distribution of weights.

The second attribute is notch position. Among the small points (Points 1 to 10 in Figure 6-2), some have notches and others do not. Two categories are hence apparent: small, unnotched points and small, side-notched points. Thomas was hardly the first archaeol-

ogist to note this distinction, and the literature of Great Basin archaeology refers to these two morphological types in this way:

Cottonwood Triangular (Points 1–5)
    Weight: Less than 1.0 gram
    Notching: Absent
Desert Side-notched (Points 6–10)
    Weight: Less than 1.0 gram
    Notching: Present (from the side)

So the smallest points—Points 1 through 10—belong to already-recognized morphological types.

Points 11 through 15 are medium-sized (weighing between 1.0 and 2.5 grams) and have notches creating a small base (or stem). Thomas described them as follows:

Rosegate Series (Points 11–15)
    Weight: Between 1.0 and 2.5 grams
    Notching: Present

Point types are named by the archaeologists who create them. The first name generally refers to the site or region where they were first distinguished. The last name describes some morphological characteristic. Thomas's term "Rosegate" is a combination of "Rose Spring," a site in southeastern California, and "Eastgate," a small overhang near Eastgate, Nevada. Originally, two different point types were defined, one named after each site, but Thomas could find no significant difference between the two, and so he combined them. (In this case, he modified the naming convention somewhat: the first term still denotes the places of discovery, but because "Rosegate" combines two former types, it is termed a series—a higher-order category.) Points 11 through 15 have now been "typed."

The larger points are more complicated. Numbers 16 through 25 weigh more than 2.5 grams. Some have expanding bases (that is, the neck is narrower than the base), and others have contracting bases. But "expanding" and "contracting" are ambiguous terms, and on given points, archaeologists often disagree about just which stems expand and which contract. Look at Point 24: we call this stem contracting, but you might think that it is expanding. Who's right? Neither, because we have yet to define the attribute—a necessary step toward replicability.

The stem is created by the notches—the two slits added so that the point can be tied more securely to a shaft. The lower edge of this notch forms an angle with

LOOKING CLOSER
The Frison Effect

Stone tools are ubiquitous in prehistoric archaeological sites. As stone tools are resharpened, they become smaller and change shape. This can have an effect on tool typologies.

François Bordes (1919–1981) was a well-known French archaeologist whose groundbreaking research on stone tools influenced many archaeologists. He was especially intrigued by stone tools found in Neanderthal cave sites. These assemblages, dating from 130,000 to 35,000 years ago, are called **Mousterian** (after Le Moustier, the site where they were first found). Bordes's experiments showed how the tools were produced, and taking into account the shape and inferred function, he divided Mousterian tools into 63 types, including a variety of points, scrapers, knives, handaxes, and denticulates (flakes with crenulated edges). Using the procedures of the day, Bordes created this seat-of-the-pants typology simply by laying assemblages out and then sorting them into morphological categories.

Looking at the Mousterian sites, Bordes found that the 63 tool types co-occurred in four fundamental patterns. The Mousterian of Acheulean Tradition, for instance, contained many handaxes, denticulates, and backed knives, but only moderate numbers of scrapers; the Typical Mousterian contained few handaxes and backed knives. But none of the four assemblages was restricted in time; instead, they seemed to alternate with one another throughout a site's strata. Bordes argued that the four assemblages reflected four different cultural groups of Neanderthals, just as different car and architecture styles reflected different groups of Europeans.

Bordes's typology exposed an unexplained, higher level of patterning, and his interpretation assumed that the stone tools were in their final intended form. Scrapers, for example, looked that way because their makers had different ideas about what a "proper" scraper should look like.

But as scrapers wear out, they are rejuvenated by removing a few flakes along their edges. In the 1960s, George Frison (University of Wyoming) pointed out that resharpening stone tools can change their shape considerably. Harold Dibble (University of Pennsylvania) decided to investigate whether the "Frison effect" could account for some of the variation Bordes saw. After experimental and archaeological studies, Dibble concluded that resharpening could create some of Bordes's scraper types. Single-edge scrapers, for instance, turn into "transverse scrapers" when resharpened.

This does not mean that Bordes's typology was wrong. By categorizing the visible morphological variation, Bordes saw a higher level of patterning. We now understand that his interpretation of this patterning may be wrong (or at least incomplete), because some differences in tool form reflect how tools were used (rather than cultural differences). Strata with many transverse scrapers, for example, probably saw heavier use by Neanderthals than strata dominated by single-edge scrapers. Archaeologists proceed in exactly this way—sorting through variability, removing those parts that are explained by humdrum factors to focus on the more intriguing parts. Classification is an important first step in that process.

Mousterian A culture from the Middle Paleolithic ("Middle Old Stone Age") period that appeared throughout Europe after 250,000 and before 30,000 years ago. Mousterian artifacts are frequently associated with Neanderthal human remains

the major longitudinal axis of the point, and angles are useful because they can be measured.

To measure the angle, draw an imaginary line along the long axis of the point (Line A in Figure 6-3). Now draw another line (Line B) along the bottom of the

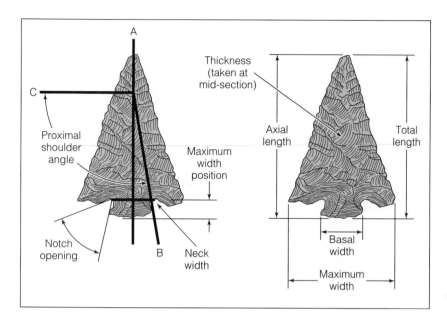

Figure 6-3 A Great Basin projectile point and some of the data that can be recorded from it. These observations are only a few of all that could be made on a projectile point.

point's notch, extending it to where it intersects the line you drew down the axis. Finally, draw a line perpendicular to that point of intersection on the opposite side of the point (Line C) and measure the angle between Line C and Line B.

Thomas called this attribute the "proximal shoulder angle" (PSA), because this side of the notch is nearest ("proximal to") the point shaft. Table 6-1 lists the proximal shoulder angles for the ten large points (Points 16 through 25) from Gatecliff Shelter. Now the difference between expanding and contracting stems is apparent: points 16 through 20 have PSAs greater than 110°, and Points 21 through 25 have PSAs smaller than that. On this basis, Thomas separated them into the following morphological types:

Elko Corner-notched (Points 16–20)
  Weight: Greater than 2.5 grams
  PSA: ≥ 110° and ≤ 150°
Gatecliff Contracting Stem (Points 21–25)
  Weight: Greater than 2.5 grams
  PSA: < 100°

Elko points were initially recognized at sites in Elko County, Nevada, and Thomas first defined Gatecliff points from data recovered at Gatecliff Shelter. As morphological types, they differ only in basal form, as described by the PSA measurements.

We have now classified all 25 points. This example is purposely simplified, but it demonstrates the first step

in projectile point classification. Although a number of additional attributes were necessary to deal with the more than 400 points found at Gatecliff, the fundamental procedures are the same.

Memorizing endless type names may seem meaningless, but dealing with these five descriptive names is many times better than coping with 25 individual artifacts—to say nothing of the 400 individual points at Gatecliff, or the thousands found throughout the Great Basin. And that is the function of morphological types.

What Did the Typology Do?

Our typology has now organized the jumble of projectile points into groups based on measurable characteristics. But before we use the typology to think in broader terms—those crucial dimensions of time and space—we must first ask if it has fulfilled the two necessary characteristics of a typology.

Consider the first characteristic: *minimize the differences within and maximize the differences between each type.*

In the past, archaeologists accomplished this goal simply by placing artifacts on a table and sorting them into piles. However, most typologies today make use of statistical analyses (with names like *cluster* and *discriminant analysis*) that are designed to take a set of attributes and provide an objective measure of how well a typology accomplishes this goal. We've avoided statistical detail of the Gatecliff typology because it is beyond the scope of this book, but you can get a sense of where such an analysis might go by looking at Figure 6-4. In this figure, we plotted the 20 notched points in terms of their weight and PSA. The Desert Side-notched, Elko Corner-notched, and Rosegate points are clearly different from the others in terms of both weight and notching—the differences within each group are minimized and the differences among them maximized. Rosegate and Gatecliff Contracting Stem points are less easily distinguished. They are similar in terms of PSA, and their difference in weight is less clear. However, Gatecliff points are more frequently resharpened than are Rosegate points—making them smaller than they were originally. The difference is subtle here, but a larger sample would separate these two point types more clearly in terms of weight. Therefore, the typology meets the first criterion: it minimizes the differences within groups and maximizes the differences between groups.

The second characteristic was that *the typology must be objective and explicit.* Thomas's typology actually made use of many more attributes than simply weight and proximal shoulder angle, and he defined more than the four projectile point types we've discussed here. By examining patterning in attributes, Thomas

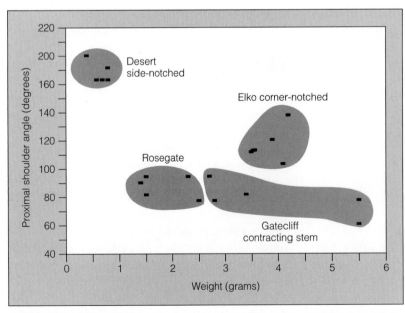

Figure 6-4 The relationship between the attributes of weight and proximal shoulder angle for the 25 Great Basin projectile points in Figure 6-2.

was able to organize the resulting Great Basic projectile point types into a flowchart, shown in Figure 6-5.

To see how this typology is objective and explicit, let's take an "unknown" projectile point and classify it according to the Gatecliff criteria. Figure 6-3 illustrates Artifact 20.4/2010, a projectile point recovered during Kelly's survey of the Carson Desert.

Projectile point 20.4/2010 has the following attributes:

Total length: 37.5 mm
Axial length: 37.5 mm
Basal indentation ratio: 1
Maximum width: 18 mm
Length to maximum width position: 4 mm
Basal width: 7 mm
Neck width: 7 mm
Proximal shoulder angle: 100°
Notch opening: 40°
Weight: 1.6 grams

To type this point, a few definitions of Thomas's other attributes are needed.

Total length is obvious; axial length, however, is the length from the point's tip to the basal concavity. For Artifact 20.4/2010, there is no basal concavity, so the axial length equals the total length. (If this point had a concave base, the axial length would be somewhat shorter than the total length.) The utility of this measurement is that, by dividing the axial length by the total length, we have a measure of how concave is the base, what Thomas called the "basal indentation ratio." A high ratio means a relatively shallow concavity; a low ratio means a relatively deep concavity.

The maximum width position is simply the distance from the point's base to the point's greatest width. By dividing the maximum width position by the total length, we have one measure of a point's shape. A high ratio indicates a more triangular point (like 20.4/2010); a lower ratio indicates a more leaf-shaped point.

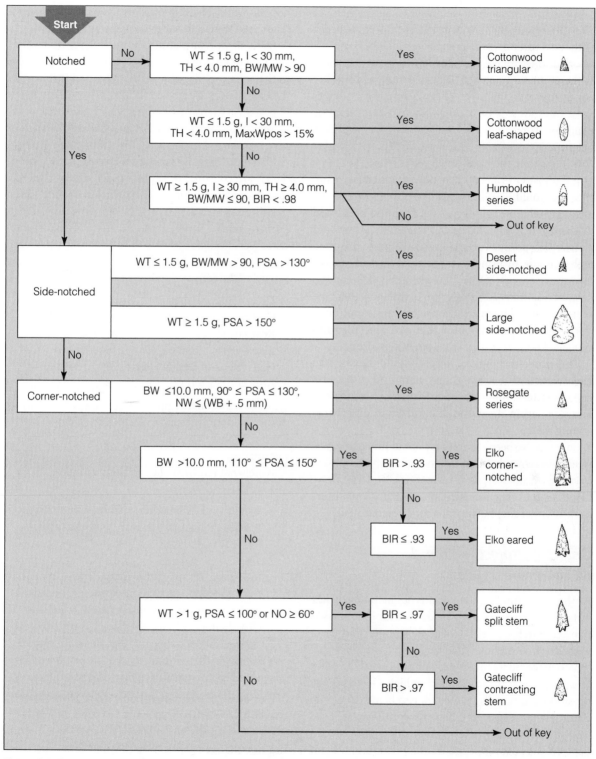

Figure 6-5 The Central Great Basin projectile point key. *From Thomas, 1981,* Journal of California and Great Basin Anthropology *3:7–43, p. 25, a Malki Museum Press Publication. Used by permission. The Journal is available by subscription. Malki Museum, 11–795 Fields Road, P.O. Box 578, Banning, CA 92220, www.malkimuseum.org.*

With these attributes, we can now classify Artifact 20.4/2010 using the flowchart in Figure 6-5. We begin with the question: Is the point notched? The answer is yes, and so we follow the arrow down to the next box. Is the point side-notched? No, so we move on to the corner-notched box. We are now faced with a set of three questions: Is its basal width (BW) less than or equal to 10 millimeters (mm)? Yes, it is. Is its PSA between 90° and 130°? Also, yes. Is the neck width (NW) less than the basal width plus .5 mm? Yes.

If the answer to any of these three questions were no, then we would have moved to the box below. But the answer to all these questions is yes, so the point is typed as a Rosegate. With this key, any trained student would classify this point as accurately as the most seasoned archaeologist. By using an explicit and objective typology, archaeologists know that, when they talk about a "Desert side-notched" or "Rosegate" or some other type of point, each of them are talking about the same thing. We have created attributes that are objective and explicit. And that is what "replicability" is all about.

Therefore, the typology fulfills both of the essential characteristics: it sorts things using objective and explicit criteria into categories that minimize the differences within them and maximize the differences among them.

So far, we've been talking only about morphological types, but remember that the goal of this typology was to create temporal types, time-markers. Now that we've identified the types occurring at Gatecliff, we can determine whether they have any temporal significance.

Gatecliff Projectile Points as Temporal Types

As the name implies, temporal types help archaeologists monitor time; they provide us with index fossils that allow archaeologists to date surface sites and strata within buried sites.

We can compare the stratigraphy of Gatecliff Shelter to a giant layer cake stacked 40 feet high. Geology's law of superposition tells us that, all else being equal, the oldest artifacts lie at the bottom, with later artifacts showing up in progressively higher strata. The Gatecliff deposits thus provide extraordinary temporal control over the past 7000 years, so when we plot the vertical distribution of the more than 400 classifiable projectile points from Gatecliff Shelter, we arrive at the distribu-

tion shown in Figure 6-6. (This figure includes all the types used to classify the entire Gatecliff collection.)

Look at the sharp stratigraphic differences (which, you should note, exhibit the battleship curves like those in the seriation diagrams of Chapter 5; note also that the living floors are labeled "horizons"—a different use of that term than as we define it later). Note that all the Desert Side-notched and Cottonwood Triangular points occurred in the very uppermost part of Gatecliff Shelter. These had replaced Rosegate series points, which are confined to slightly older strata. These, in turn, had replaced Elko points, which are found lower, in still-older strata. Elko points had replaced Gatecliff points, which are older still. Because 47 radiocarbon dates were available to date the geological sequence at Gatecliff, it was possible to assign the following time ranges to the projectile point types discussed:

Desert Side-notched	post–AD 1300
Cottonwood Triangular	post–AD 1300
Rosegate series	AD 500–AD 1300
Elko Corner-notched	1500 BC–AD 500
Gatecliff Contracting Stem	2500 BC–1500 BC

With this critical step, several of our morphological types have become temporal types. Each time similar points are found in undated contexts, we now have a clue (a hypothesis, really) about their time of manufacture.

Note what has happened in this example:

1. Individual artifacts were initially grouped strictly on formal criteria; all that mattered for morphological types was that the artifacts looked alike.
2. These morphological categories were then tested against independent evidence—specifically, the layer-cake stratigraphy and the chain of 47 radiocarbon dates available from Gatecliff Shelter.
3. All five morphological categories were significantly restricted in time, and so they were elevated to the status of temporal types.

Not every morphological point type from Gatecliff made the grade. The frequencies of some morphological types (especially the larger, concave-base points) did not change significantly through time, and these types flunked the test for graduating to the level of temporal type. Maybe somebody, eventually, will demonstrate that concave-base points are indeed time-

Figure 6-6 Relative proportions of selected projectile point types across the stratigraphic units of Gatecliff Shelter. Note how one or two extremely abundant temporal types seem to dominate most strata. *After Thomas (1983), figure 66; Courtesy American Museum of Natural History.*

markers in the Great Basin; but until that demonstration, these types remain merely "morphological," without temporal significance.

We began with the simplifying assumption that change through time reflects shifts in ancient peoples' "mental templates" for an idealized projectile point shape. Never mind what the artifacts meant to the makers, whether they were spear or arrow points, or how they were made. For now, we care only about whether some cluster of measurable attributes (which we call "types") changed through time. This is why and how we created some projectile point time-markers at Gatecliff Shelter.

This is also why we must recognize that time-markers have distinct limitations. The seriation-like diagram for Gatecliff projectile points shows us what changes over time and what does not, which permits us to pose more interesting questions. For instance, although we now know that Desert Side-notched and Cottonwood Triangular points postdate AD 1300, we do not know *why* two morphological types existed simultaneously. Are two social groups living at Gatecliff after AD 1300? Are Desert Side-notched points designed for hunting bighorn, whereas Cottonwood points are for rabbits? Are Cottonwood points for "war arrows"—left unnotched so that they remain embedded in a body

even if the shaft is pulled out? Or perhaps the difference is technological: could the Cottonwood Triangular points be unfinished, intended to be later notched (and thereby becoming Desert Side-notched points)? Notching is often the last thing done to a point, and if done incorrectly, it can ruin hours of work. Were Cottonwood Triangular points made by novices who were not adept at notching points? All these guesses are hypotheses at present untested—and they would have been impossible without first creating projectile point temporal types.

Space-Time Systematics

So far we have been talking only about the temporal dimension of archaeology, change in artifacts over time. We now shift and consider the spatial dimension of these temporal changes.

Americanist archaeology has adopted a relatively standardized framework for integrating the kind of chronological information just discussed into a regional framework. Gordon Willey (1913–2002) and Philip Phillips (1900–1993) initially set out this regional infrastructure in their influential book *Method and Theory in American Archaeology* (1958).

Since then, the nomenclature has varied somewhat from region to region, some terms have been discarded because they reflect outdated theoretical paradigms, and others do not have quite the significance that they once carried. Nonetheless, the 50-year-old Willey-Phillips framework remains the most generally accepted system in the Americas.

Archaeological Cultures: Dividing Space

To begin, however, we must go back to before Willey and Phillips's day, to the early twentieth-century concept of *culture areas.* Long before anthropology existed as a discipline in America, scholars recognized that not all Native American societies were alike. Some people were nomadic, others lived in large pueblos. Some hunted bison, others were maize farmers. Those in California relied heavily on acorns for their food; northwest coast peoples fished and hunted sea mammals. By the late nineteenth century, American anthropology had formalized these observations into culture areas, large regions defined primarily in terms of what people ate (which of course had a lot to do with the environment). The theory that attempted to explain these geographic patterns is no longer important to anthropology, but the culture areas left a legacy in that archaeologists who study the prehistory of North America tend to focus on one of these culture areas. They work on the Plains, or in the southeastern United States, California, or the Southwest.

Working with the prehistory of one of these regions, archaeologists quickly saw "subculture areas"—regions within a culture area whose material culture (such as house styles, settlement patterns, ceramics, or subsistence) differed from one another. These subdivisions of culture areas are called "traditions" or *archaeological cultures.* Figure 6-7 shows the location of the three major archaeological cultures of the Southwest culture area: the Hohokam, Mogollon (*muh-gee-own*), and Anasazi. These three regions are distinguished from one another in terms of pottery and architectural styles.

However, these archaeological cultures are *not* the same as ethnographic cultures. If we could go back in time in, say, the Mogollon region and travel around,

we would probably encounter several different languages, as well as different customs in different villages. In all likelihood, people in a village at the southern end of the Mogollon region considered themselves different from those who lived at the northern end. By drawing lines around areas on a map and labeling them archaeological cultures, we are simply drawing attention to spatial differences in the kinds of artifacts that are found in those regions. The *meaning* of these differences is another matter.

Periods: Dividing Time

As archaeologists began to investigate the prehistory of regions, they also discovered that the Native American culture that ethnographers documented (and that formed the basis for maps of culture areas) had not always been there. The people who lived in the American Southwest some 5000 years ago, for example, were nomadic hunter-gatherers who never knew maize or built pueblos. As the chronologies of different culture areas were worked out, prehistory was organized into slices of time that were given different names.

Archaeologists divided prehistory into **periods** based on gross changes in easily observable archaeological remains, such as subsistence or house forms. These were sometimes labeled "stages," although that term is rarely used today. But the concept of periods is still used to organize archaeological thinking about time. For example, pick up a text on southwestern archaeology, and an early chapter will be on the "Paleo-Indian Period" (from 9000 to 5500 BC), a period of time in which the distinctive Pueblo archaeological cultures, such as the Mogollon, did not exist, and people were nomadic hunters of large game and gatherers of some plant foods.

The next chapter might be on the "Archaic Period" (from 5500 BC to AD 100). This is a time when people made heavier use of plant resources, began to develop distinctive region traditions in material culture, and experimented with agricultural crops, most notably maize. This may be followed by chapters that describe "Early Village" and "Pueblo" periods.

Major cultural transitions, such as the appearance of ceramics, settled life, or agriculture, were labeled *horizons.* These are analogous to (but should not be confused with) soil horizons and marker beds in that they form cultural "fault lines" that can crosscut archaeological cultures and culture areas. This kind of

period A length of time distinguished by particular items of material culture, such as house form, pottery, or subsistence.

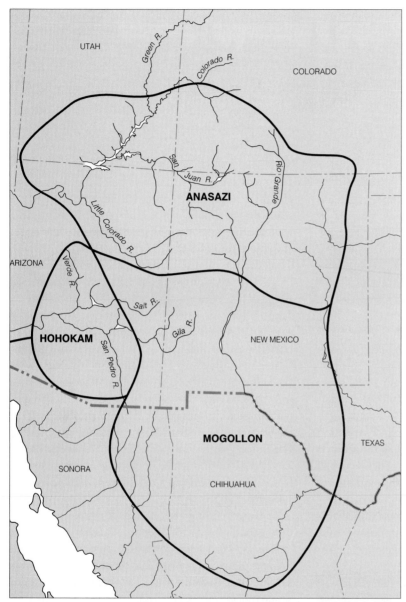

Figure 6-7 Southwestern archaeological cultures, or traditions. The theory that lay behind these areas is outdated today, but the patterns that stand behind these traditions still demand explanation. *From L. Cordell,* Prehistory of the Southwest, *p. 15. Reprinted by permission of Elsevier.*

association with an outdated evolutionary paradigm and because we now know that many transitions, including that from hunting and gathering to agriculture, were not as quick as the horizon concept assumed.

Nonetheless, like archaeological cultures, the concepts of periods and horizons helped to map out major spatial and temporal patterns in material culture. Periods and horizons record change over time, archaeological cultures record change over space. Knowing *how* and *when* material culture changed over time and space is an obvious first step toward explaining *why* those changes occurred.

Phases: Combining Space and Time

As archaeologists became increasingly familiar with the time markers of a region, they observed that different regions in a culture area did not all change in lockstep with one another. Pottery, for example, may first appear at different times in different areas (forming a ceramic horizon that crosscuts different culture areas); likewise, from a common base, pottery styles may differentiate over time at different rates and in different ways in different regions. In other words, there are temporal and spatial changes in material culture of which periods and horizons were just first approximations.

A **phase** is a block of time that is characterized by one or more distinctive artifact types, a particular kind of pottery, housing style, and/or projectile point, for

cultural horizon might have different ages in different regions. Maize, for example, was first domesticated in southern Mexico; over time people farther to the north adopted it, and it gradually spread to other people living still farther to the north. Thus, the agriculture horizon appears progressively later in time as we move from southern Mexico to the Great Lakes region (the northern limit of maize horticulture). This concept is not heavily used in archaeology today because of its

phase An archaeological construct possessing traits sufficiently characteristic to distinguish it from other units similarly conceived; spatially limited to roughly a locality or region and chronologically limited to the briefest interval of time possible.

RAPID REVIEW   Principles of Archaeological Classification

- Decide what the purpose of the typology is.
- Choose attributes that will achieve this purpose.
- Define the attributes objectively so that they can be replicated by others.
- Construct types that minimize differences within types and maximize differences between types.

example. The phase has become the practicable and intelligible unit of archaeological study, defined by Willey and Phillips as "an archaeological unit possessing traits sufficiently characteristic to distinguish it from all other units similarly conceived . . . [and] spatially limited to the order of magnitude of a locality or region and chronologically limited to a relatively brief interval of time."

How do we construct phases?

Phases are defined by temporal types (like our Gatecliff points), items of material culture that show patterned changes over time. We have already seen how to derive temporal types: you group individual artifacts into morphological types, then test them against independent data (such as site stratigraphy, correlation with other known sites, or direct dating of the artifacts themselves). We recognize those types of artifacts that change systematically and observably through time as time-markers.

The next analytical step is to see how the time markers themselves cluster to reflect site chronology. Here we have to define a few other terms that archaeologists commonly use.

Archaeological sites consist of **assemblages,** collections of artifacts recovered from some unit of provenience. We could talk about a site's stone tool or ceramic or projectile point assemblage. In this case, the provenience might be the site itself. We could also talk

about the assemblage of a particular stratum, say, the stone tool assemblage of Stratum 22 at Gatecliff. In a well-stratified and carefully excavated site like Gatecliff, there could be many assemblages.

We might then analytically cluster these assemblages into **components.** A component is considered a culturally homogeneous unit within a single site. By "culturally homogeneous" we mean that, although the assemblages that go into a component might have been deposited during different years and by different individuals, they were deposited by people who were the same culturally. Some small archaeological sites may contain only one assemblage representing a single component; some could contain multiple assemblages that nonetheless still represent one component. Others may contain multiple assemblages representing several components. And some sites may be too badly mixed to sort out assemblages and define components at all.

Because defining archaeological components rests on the intangible factor of cultural homogeneity, there can be no firm rules for their construction, but it helps if the strata are obvious from the stratigraphic profile, as at Gatecliff. Gatecliff's numerous strata of nonartifact-bearing silts separated the deposits into discrete living floors. During analysis, we could keep the floors distinct (as individual assemblages) or group them together on the basis of shared similarities. Although Gatecliff contained many living surfaces, Thomas decided that it contained only five distinct cultural components, each incorporating the assemblages from one to six living surfaces. Components are thus site-specific: a given component is, by definition, from a single site.

Each component at Gatecliff is defined by its associated array of dates and its particular set of characteristic artifacts, including our much-analyzed projectile

assemblage A collection of artifacts of one or several classes of materials (stone tools, ceramics, bones) that comes from a defined context, such as a site, feature, or stratum.

component An archaeological construct consisting of a stratum or set of strata that are presumed to be culturally homogeneous; a set of components from various sites in a region will make up a phase.

PROFILE OF AN ARCHAEOLOGIST
A Cultural Resource Management Archaeologist

William Doelle is the president of Desert Archaeology, Inc., a cultural resource management firm in Tucson, Arizona, and the Center for Desert Archaeology, a nonprofit corporation that promotes the study and preservation of archaeological sites in the American Southwest.

© William Doelle

"Holy <expletive deleted>!" It was the only appropriate response to the cream-colored stone tool that had just caught my eye.

I was walking the centerline of a half-built road. Representatives from the Tohono O'odham Nation in southern Arizona had protested when they observed road machinery cutting through a buried Hohokam village ("Hohokam" means "those who have gone" in the O'odham language and refers to village sites dating after AD 700). Work was halted, and the slow legal process of compliance begun. A competitive bid process awarded an archaeological contract to my young firm.

Our work on the Valencia Site on Tucson's south side began in 1983 when despite the construction, we found some 25 intact Hohokam pithouses. Over the past two decades, I have conducted six additional projects at this site, each one expanding our knowledge of the Valencia community between AD 400 and 1200. An overview of that work provides a cross-section of the diversity in modern *cultural resource management,* or CRM—the professional area where I have made a living since 1974.

Our 1983 fieldwork was constrained to a narrow strip less than 20 meters wide and some 500 meters long because we had a great deal to accomplish in a very brief time—the bulldozers were waiting for us to finish.

In 1991, the local community college planned a new campus in the area. Our surface collection and testing program discovered an earlier, more subtle pithouse site, almost certainly the ancestral village for Valencia. We helped planners situate the new two-story buildings off the main occupation area. Later, we documented over 100 early pithouses and projected a total of around 400. The arrangement of houses around a large central plaza provided the excavators with information to develop a refined model of early village life.

My company had grown from one fulltime employee in 1983 to 35 in 1997. I am now largely an observer in the research process. I keep watch over the rapid development of Tucson and work with various groups—such as the community college, the city, the Tohono O'odham, the archaeological community, park planners, and landscape architects—to develop plans to preserve archaeological sites.

These opportunities are further enhanced through the nonprofit Center for Desert Archaeology. Through grants, endowment building, and a membership program, this institution pursues a mission of preservation archaeology. We balance research, public outreach, and stewardship in our programs in the American Southwest and Mexican Northwest. Archaeology in the private sector presents unique challenges, but I have found it to offer great rewards.

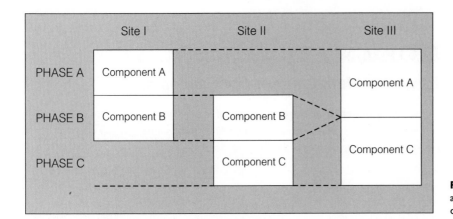

Figure 6-8 Relationship of archaeological sites to the analytical concepts of component and phase.

points and artifacts such as incised slates and carved wooden pegs (used to construct snares to trap small mammals).

How do these observations help create phases? By comparing Gatecliff's components with those of other nearby sites, we define the spatial and temporal range of particular artifact types and from this comparison a regional chronology of phases is constructed. Briefly, assemblages (all items of one kind from one stratum or location) are grouped into site-specific components (differentiated in culture and in time). Components from nearby sites are grouped into phases. These building blocks therefore identify similarities across space and time.

To see how this works, consider the three hypothetical archaeological sites in Figure 6-8. These three hypothetical sites are located in the same geographic region—say, Montana. They have been carefully excavated and analyzed and, as is often the case, no single site contains the complete cultural sequence. The first site has Components A and B; the second site contains Component B plus a new component called C; and the third site has Components A and C but lacks Component B. By analyzing the temporal types shared among the components and comparing the absolute dates, a regional sequence of phases can be constructed from evidence at these three sites.

To give a more concrete example, archaeologists working in the central Great Basin divide the post-3550 BC era into five phases, each defined by one or more temporal projectile point types. You can see these in Figure 6-6, which showed how different morphological point types at Gatecliff sort out in time. These phases were defined on the basis of the analysis of assemblages from many stratified sites and the consistent association of particular morphological artifact types with particular spans of time.

For instance, the latest of these, the Yankee Blade Phase (named after a nineteenth-century silver mine in the town of Austin) is typified by Desert Side-notched and Cottonwood Triangular points, as well as simple pottery. This phase began about AD 1300 and lasted until Euro-American contact, about 1850 in central Nevada. The other phases were similarly defined, each composed of different kinds of artifacts (primarily projectile points) and spanning other episodes of time.

Phases: The Basic Units of Space-Time Systematics

Phases are defined by time, but also by space. There is no Yankee Blade Phase in Georgia, or New Mexico, or even Utah, because the nature and tempo of change in material culture in these areas was not the same as in the central Great Basin. Even within the Great Basin, phases are not synchronous and different phase names are used in the western and central Great Basin, each defined by particular artifact types that have particular temporal ranges in their particular regions.

While it's relatively easy to define the temporal boundaries of say, the Yankee Blade Phase, you might be wondering where the geographic "edge" of the central Great Basin chronology is. At the town of Austin, in central Nevada? Or 100 miles east, at Fallon in the Carson Desert? It's hard to say. Think of phases as analogous to pieces of a three-dimensional puzzle with very fuzzy edges. Neighboring regions do not neces-

ARCHAEOLOGICAL ETHICS
What's Wrong with Buying Antiquities? (Part II)

Like most archaeologists, we don't have a problem with the weekend collector who picks up arrowheads. Frankly, we'd prefer that they didn't do it, but we know that most of these people are well intentioned and are not responsible for the massive loss of data that professional looting causes. We also understand that professional archaeologists don't "own" the past.

But there is another side to this. The serious collectors, the ones willing to shell out thousands of dollars for Mimbres pots or Etruscan statues, argue that if it were not for the collectors, many of the world's treasures would never be recovered at all. Why let wonderful pieces of ancient art lie beneath the ground, waiting until an archaeologist gets the time and funding to recover them? Given that archaeologists have to dig so slowly, that will take centuries! And in the meantime, aren't those undiscovered pieces in harm's way, because of the ravages of time and other countries' lax antiquities laws?

Wouldn't it be preferable, some collectors ask, to recover artifacts now, quickly, and get them out where they can be enjoyed by people? Indeed, some proponents of this view point out that the world's major museums own objects that were originally gathered by private collectors, at the collectors' own expense. And they are right (look at the Parthenon marbles in the British Museum). Thus, collectors argue that any archaeologist who is proud of a museum but who criticizes collecting is a hypocrite.

We disagree. Had there been professional archaeologists around when Lord Elgin was removing the marble statues from the Parthenon, we'd like to think they would have raised hell about it. And remember that, for archaeologists today, an artifact's provenience is as important as, if not more important than, the artifact itself. Looters don't record context, so there is a big difference between nineteenth-century collecting and twenty-first-century looting.

This point was driven home on April 11, 2003, a few days after the U.S. military entered Baghdad, Iraq. Although the Pentagon had assured several professional organizations that Iraqi cultural institutions would be protected, they left the Baghdad Museum unguarded, and it was looted. Some artifacts were wantonly smashed, and the computer and paper records were partially destroyed.

An investigation headed by Colonel Matthew Bogdanos, USMC, concluded that 40 items were stolen from the main galleries, including the 4300-year-old Bassetki statue and the heads of Roman era statues, as well as 3138 items from the old storage rooms and 10,337 items from a basement storage room. The investigation also showed the presence of thieves with intimate knowledge of the museum. And they had inside help, given that some locked storage areas were opened with keys. These thieves were selective in what they took from the galleries, foregoing beautiful replicas for the most valuable genuine pieces. Many believe that, although the looting was carried out by Iraqis, it was orchestrated by wealthy, unscrupulous buyers in Europe, Japan, or the United States.

Other Iraqi museums were also hit, and archaeological sites were attacked by armed looters. Although some called for a "Shoot first, ask questions later" approach to looters, one can hardly blame a poverty-stricken Iraqi farmer for exploiting an opportunity to make ten years worth of wages in a night of digging. Instead, it's the wealthy buyers in developed nations who are to blame. They are the ones who drive this destruction, who encourage a country to rob itself of its cultural patrimony and to destroy irreplaceable records of human history.

Iraq is a stark reminder of what is wrong with buying antiquities. If collectors truly wish to see the world's heritage protected (and do not simply want to add to their personal collections), then they should turn their financial resources to aiding those countries that need assistance in discovering, protecting, and displaying their cultural heritages.

sarily have the same phases, because they did not see the same progression of change in material culture.

The construction of phases allows archaeologists to synthesize reams of data into a series of (admittedly simplistic) time-slices which, in turn, can be compared and contrasted with similar schemes from neighboring areas. They allow us to see, in a rough way, differences and similarities in the spatial and temporal scale of artifact change over time. Because we presume that artifacts reflect behavior, phases are ultimately ways to track spatial and temporal change in human cultural behavior. Phases are the first step toward developing ideas about regional patterns and trends—ideas that can be tested, refined, and expanded.

Phases can be as short as a few generations or thousands of years long. The length depends in part on the kind of archaeological remains involved and upon our contemporary knowledge of those remains. If pottery styles changed rapidly, then we can, with sufficient study of tightly controlled and well-dated stratigraphic excavations, develop short phases using seriation. Chronological control tends to be better for younger material, and so young phases tend to be shorter than old phases. One of the phases preceding the 550-year-long Yankee Blade Phase is the Reveille Phase, from 1300 BC to AD 700—some 2000 years. The Reveille Phase is longer simply because the material remains used for its definition (including Elko series projectile points) continued to appear over a longer span of time than the remains used to define the Yankee Blade Phase (Desert Side-notched points, Cottonwood Triangular points, and pottery). Phases covering the most recent prehistory of the American Southwest may be only 25 to 50 years long.

The phase concept is vague, and deliberately so. Archaeology needs to impose a set of minimal units on time. The phase is that minimal unit. They allow archaeologists provisionally to define time, which is actually a continuous variable, as if it were a discrete set of temporally ordered points. When we discuss the Yankee Blade Phase, we are treating the time span from AD 1300 to AD 1850 as if it were an instant. By definition, two components of the Yankee Blade Phase are simultaneous, provided that "simultaneous" is understood to last 550 years.

But bear in mind that phases are always defined *provisionally*. As knowledge of the Yankee Blade Phase expands, we may be able to recognize divisions within

the phase—for instance, to distinguish an early Yankee Blade component from a late Yankee Blade component. When this happens, the initial phase is divided into *subphases*. This increasing subdivision reflects the amount of research accomplished on each phase and underscores the degree to which our knowledge of the archaeological record is a contemporary phenomenon. This is why we leave the concept of phase vague, so that it can accommodate new findings and help us learn more, rather than place blinders on our ability to see new patterns in prehistory.

Conclusion: Space-Time Systematics and Archaeological Objectives

We began this chapter by pointing out that this search for patterning falls along three dimensions: space, time, and form (of artifacts). And this search leads to the construction of space-time systematics, a simplification of the enormous variation in material culture over time and space into some meaningful patterns. You now have some sense of how we go about doing that. But the construction of space-time systematics is not the goal of archaeology; it is the means to an end. The goals of archaeology are to reconstruct and explain the past. How do space-time systematics help accomplish these goals?

Let us look at the case of Shoshone pottery to answer this question. Shoshone ceramics appear suddenly in many parts of the Desert West about AD 1300 (forming a ceramic horizon), and the Shoshone people made similar pottery until about 1860. Shoshone pottery thus implies certain limits: time (AD 1300–1860, the Yankee Blade Phase in the central Great Basin) and space (the Desert West).

With its temporal parameters estimated, Shoshone pottery becomes a useful time-marker. Sites containing these potsherds in the Desert West can be provisionally assigned to the AD 1300–1860 interval.

But we are nowhere near finished. In fact, we have just begun, for Shoshone pottery, taken as a time-marker, leaves many more questions unanswered. Was this pottery introduced by migrating Shoshone-speaking peoples? Or did the idea of pottery simply spread across the Desert West? Did the various peoples of the Desert West independently invent the idea of pottery? Or were the vessels traded in from neighboring ceramic manufacturing areas?

Each is a research question that could inspire years of investigation: Is it possible to document a population movement across the Desert West at AD 1300? If so, where did these newcomers come from? And what happened to the pre–AD 1300 inhabitants of the Desert West? Are there signs of trading activity or warfare in AD 1300?

Questions like this can pile up without end. Although we cannot reconstruct what happened in the past by looking only at time-markers, we also don't even know the relevant questions to ask or hypotheses to test until we know something about the when and the where of the past.

And reconstructing *what* happened in the past is itself but one step in the process. As we pointed out in Chapter 1, archaeologists today are equally interested in *why* prehistory took the particular courses that it did; we are interested in explaining the past as well as in reconstructing it. The time-marker Shoshone pottery tells us that distinctive potsherds occur in archaeological deposits dating from AD 1300 to 1860 across the Desert West. But viewed as a time-marker, Shoshone pottery tells us nothing about *why* pottery was introduced in AD 1300. For some reason, one segment of the Desert West cultural system changed, and people began manufacturing pottery. This complex issue can be studied only by pursuing related shifts in the lifeway, drawing evidence from the settlement pattern and demography, cultural ecology, social organization, and religion.

For example, let's say that we eventually conclude through research that the pottery was introduced through a migrating Shoshone population. The next question would be, Why did this population migrate in? What gave it the ability to replace the existing (pre–AD 1300) population? Did climate change render the pre–AD 1300 adaptation untenable, thereby enabling the Shoshone to invade the Desert West? Did the ecological adaptation change to make ceramic vessels more efficient after AD 1300? Could it be that a ceramic-using population moved into the Desert West and intermarried with the previous inhabitants? Did population growth drive the migration, or was it warfare, or some environmental calamity?

By definition, we base our time-markers on selected aspects of shared culture; time-markers deliberately ignore much cultural behavior. Obviously, questions such as diffusion, migration, invention, and adaptation are complex, reflecting changes in the underlying cultural systems. Time-markers, grounded only in shared behavior, are patently inadequate for unraveling the mechanics of cultural systems.

In many respects, the space-time systematics of archaeology have been worked out, especially for North American archaeology, and they no longer preoccupy archaeology the way they did in the first half of the twentieth century. Nonetheless, space-time systematics were and are a crucial first step in the archaeological process. It is only after documenting temporal and spatial change in selected artifacts that we can set about reconstructing what people actually did in the past. And in the following chapters, we discuss how archaeologists go about doing exactly that.

Summary

■ Archaeology's major contribution to anthropological knowledge is found in large-scale patterns in space and time. Although archaeology cannot recover the detail that ethnography can, it contributes to anthropology by studying the long-term temporal processes and vast spatial patterning that ethnology cannot record.

■ After the excavation, archaeologists catalog and conserve the artifacts recovered. This can be time consuming and can require the help of trained specialists.

■ The next task is to classify the artifacts in order to construct space-time systematics. This involves typology, the construction of a process to place artifacts into types. This process begins during the excavation, where artifacts may be sorted according to their raw material for the sake of convenience. Classification becomes more rigorous in the lab.

■ Archaeologists create morphological types by relying on the shared aspect of culture. We assume that people made an item of material culture in a particular way because they shared a common idea of what a tool or object "ought" to look like. At this point, whether the final form was important to the maker or meaningful in any way is not significant to our analysis.

■ The type is the basic unit of artifact analysis. It is an idealized construct that allows archaeologists to transcend individual artifacts so that they can consider more generalized categories.

■ Morphological types are descriptive and emphasize broad similarities. Temporal types monitor how artifacts change through time. And functional types group artifacts in terms of their function, regardless of their morphology.

■ A typology groups artifacts in such a way that the differences within groups are minimized and the differences between groups are maximized.

■ Types are based on criteria that are objective, explicit, and replicable.

■ Spatial patterning in material culture helps define archaeological cultures or traditions, but these are not the same as ethnographic cultures.

■ By seeking out clusters of temporal types we construct site components, which are culturally homogeneous units within a single site and can be synthesized into phases—archaeological units of cultural homogeneity that are limited in both time and space. Phases are the basic archaeological building blocks for regional synthesis.

■ Space-time systematics is but one step toward the larger goals of reconstructing and explaining the past.

Media Resources

The Companion Website for **Archaeology: Down to Earth,** *Third Edition*

http://anthropology.wadsworth.com/thomas_kelly3e_down/

Supplement your review of this chapter by going to the companion website to take one of the practice quizzes, use the flash cards to master key terms, and check out the many other study aids that are designed to help you succeed in your introductory archaeology course.

7 Taphonomy, Experimental Archaeology, and Ethnoarchaeology

Outline

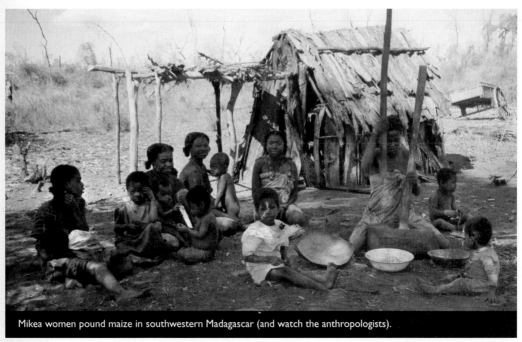

Mikea women pound maize in southwestern Madagascar (and watch the anthropologists).

© Robert Kelly

Preview

W E HAVE EXPLORED how archaeologists locate and excavate sites, how they date those sites, and how they construct cultural chronologies. Now it is time to move a step up the theoretical ladder and examine the role of middle-range research in modern archaeology. We have already discussed the various natural and cultural processes that combine to create the archaeological record. Low-level theory enables us to generate data from this record. Now, we can apply theory developed in middle-range research to relate these data to past human behaviors. If you flip back to the model of archaeological inquiry in Figure 2-6, you'll recall that archaeologists sometimes put down their trowels, climb out of their trenches, and conduct research designed to give them the tools they need to interpret the data they have generated. That is what this chapter is about.

Here, we concentrate on three areas of middle-range research that we introduced in Chapter 2:

1. Taphonomy studies the role that natural processes play in creating the archaeological record.

2. Experimental archaeology uses controlled experiments to replicate the past under different conditions to look for links between human behavior and its archaeological consequences.

3. Ethnoarchaeology studies living societies to see how behavior is translated into the archaeological record.

Introduction

Archaeologists are often compared to detectives, and this comparison is both appropriate and instructive. Both are concerned with what happened in the past, and both make inferences about the past based on recovered material remains. But, ideally, detectives deal with crime scenes that are found and sealed off as soon after the crime as possible. Imagine detectives confronted by a crime scene that is several thousand years old, in which nothing organic survives and burrowing rodents have jumbled the evidence. Even Sherlock Holmes would have a hard time making his conclu-

sions stand up in court. And yet, this is what archaeologists deal with all the time.

Archaeologists also deal with the complication that, unlike detectives, they often recover objects whose function and meaning are unknown. Imagine if our detectives first had to figure out that the metallic cylinder lying on the floor was a spent cartridge (and not a piece of jewelry, child's toy, or the ever-popular ritual object). Detectives routinely use "common sense"—knowledge of their own culture, actually—to decide if something "doesn't look right" at a crime scene. Imagine how much more slowly investigations would proceed if those detectives first had to decide if the distribution of furniture in the room—a chair lying on its side, dishes strewn about the floor—was culturally normal or an aberration.

A complex suite of natural and cultural processes interacts to create archaeological sites, and they make each site unique. And this means that archaeological interpretation is *never* straightforward; the low-level facts of archaeology cannot explain themselves. Middle-range research aims to provide archaeology with the tools needed to infer behavior from the contemporary archaeological record.

Middle-Range Research: What Is It?

To develop such tools, archaeologists must observe behavior and its material correlates simultaneously, but independent of one another. In an archaeological site, we have only the material remains. Behavior must be inferred from those remains, and thus it cannot be observed independent of them. Where, then, do archaeologists get the means to make these inferences?

Let's consider how archaeology's sibling discipline, geology, solved this problem. Like the archaeological record, the geological record consists of two things: objects and the relationships among them. A *geological fact* is a contemporary observation made by a geologist on objects from the geological record. Rocks do not speak, so how do geologists go from contemporary observations to meaningful inferences of the remote geological past?

Geologists addressed this question in the eighteenth century. A Scottish doctor and farmer, James Hutton (1726–1797), was also intrigued by geology. He formulated a simple principle that provides one of the cornerstones of modern geology. What became known as the **principle of uniformitarianism** asserts that the processes now operating to modify the Earth's surface are the same as those of the geological past. It's that simple: geological processes in the past and the present are assumed to be *identical*.

We know from modern observations, for instance, that as glaciers move, their massive weight leaves *striations*—that is, scratches—on bedrock deposits. They also deposit rock and earth at their fronts and sides,

often in distinctive formations called *moraines*. Study of modern glaciers shows that moraines and striations are formed only through glacial action.

Now suppose a geologist finds moraines and striated rocks in New England, where no glaciers exist today. Armed with knowledge of contemporary glacial processes, a geologist can confidently interpret those features as evidence of past glaciers.

The same logic applies to archaeology. Archaeologists recover the material remains of past human behavior. And, like geologists, archaeologists must also look to the contemporary world to provide them with hypotheses that account for the formation and deposition of these physical remains. This is an important point: observation of the contemporary world provides the information necessary to infer past human behavior and natural processes from observations on archaeological objects.

Some Bones of Contention

Perhaps you are thinking that, sure, this makes sense—but shouldn't the meaning of remains still be relatively obvious?

To address this question, consider a simple problem in the interpretation of animal bones (also known as **faunal** remains) from archaeological sites. As we discuss in Chapter 8, archaeologists study animal bones to learn about past diets, hunting and butchering practices, how animals were domesticated, the season in which the hunt occurred, and other related issues.

Most of these faunal studies begin by considering the relative frequencies of animal bones in a site. When analyzing the bones from Suberde, a seventh-millennium BC Neolithic village in Turkey, Dexter Perkins and Patricia Daly observed that the upper limb bones of wild oxen were usually missing. Perkins and Daly suggested that the frequencies of the different bones resulted from how people had butchered the oxen. They must have first skinned the animals, then stripped the meat from

principle of uniformitarianism The principle asserting that the processes now operating to modify the Earth's surface are the same processes that operated long ago in the geological past.

faunal In archaeology, animal bones in archaeological sites.

the forequarters and hindquarters, and then thrown away the defleshed upper limb bones. Perkins and Daly presumed that the meat was piled on the skin and that the lower limb bones were used to drag the hide bearing the meat back home. Calling this the "schlepp effect," they believed their interpretation explained why only lower limb bones were discarded at the habitation site.

Now jump across Europe to England, where R. E. Chaplin analyzed the bones recovered from a late ninth-century AD Saxon farm. The facts in this case also included a shortage of the limb bones of sheep and cattle, but Chaplin suggested that these bones disappeared because the carcasses were dressed and exported to market.

Across the Atlantic, archaeologists working on American Plains Indian sites also discovered that the upper limb bones of food animals were often missing. Theodore White decided that the bones were destroyed during the manufacture of bone grease. Relying on ethnographies of Plains Indians, White argued that the limb bones were pulverized and boiled to render their grease to make pemmican (a mixture of dried meat, fat, and berries), which was stored for the winter.

We could cite other examples, but the point should be clear: three different teams made three different inferences from exactly the same archaeological facts—the lack of upper limb bones in habitation sites.

Archaeologists face such problems daily: several competing hypotheses accounting for the same body of facts. And all the hypotheses are reasonable.

Scientific protocol stipulates how to select among the competing hypotheses (and for the present, we restrict our attention to the three target hypotheses). Each one is a generalized statement about human behavior. But a contemporary archaeologist can never observe a Neolithic villager butchering a wild ox, and none of us will ever watch nineteenth-century American Plains Indians making bone grease. Archaeologists must therefore concentrate on finding the material *consequences* of activities like butchering Neolithic oxen or making bison bone grease.

We do this by constructing a series of logical *if . . . then* statements: *If* bone grease were manufactured from bison bones, *then* we should find artifacts X, Y, and Z and physical residues M, N, and O; bones should be distributed in patterns C, D, and E; and bone elements J, K, and L should be missing. Similarly, to test the second hypothesis, we must generate some *if . . . then* statements regarding the trading of meat and bones. Before we can

do that, we need answers to some very specific questions: Which are the best cuts to trade? How far can meat be transported before it spoils? Is meat marketed only in the winter months? Are carcasses butchered in special ways so that certain cuts can be traded? Then we can create arguments like "*If* these carcasses were being dressed for market, *then* we should see marks A and B on bones X and Y, and the site should include features G or H and implements K and L."

These *if . . . then* statements become *bridging arguments,* a concept we first mentioned in Chapter 2 (page 30) that translate hypotheses into specific expectations that can be tested using archaeological evidence. These bridging arguments are essential to testing ideas with archaeological evidence, and their construction is one of the most difficult things that archaeologists do.

But—we hope you are wondering—how do we know these things? Why do archaeologists surmise that making bone grease requires artifacts X, Y, and Z? And how do we know which bone elements are destroyed in the process? Hypothesis testing is only as robust as these *if . . . then* bridging arguments. If we generate incorrect implications, then our hypothesis testing will be worse than useless, because it will lead us to specious or erroneous conclusions. For instance, if we assume that the lack of limb bones *always* means that people were rendering grease from bones, we would make a completely incorrect inference if the lack of limb bones in a particular site was really the result of the schlepp effect.

Here is where the notion of middle-range research comes into play. Because the facts cannot speak for themselves, archaeologists must provide bridging arguments that breathe behavioral life into the objects of the past. Properly formulated, middle-range theory links human behavior to empirical data that are archaeologically observable. Although it has been an important aspect of archaeological inquiry for more than a century, Lewis Binford's call for middle-range research served to focus additional attention on this neglected area of archaeology.

To create relevant bridging arguments, archaeologists must observe the workings of a culture in its systemic context, much as geologists defined their processes through observation of the contemporary world—such as streams carrying silt to a delta or the wind blowing sand across dunes. Geologists interested in glacial processes cannot study firsthand the massive

ARCHAEOLOGICAL ETHICS
The Ethics of Doing Ethnoarchaeology

Archaeologists are more accustomed to dealing with the dead than with the living. We are used to thinking about whether our crews are well fed, happy, and satisfied—but not about whether the site feels the same way.

But doing ethnoarchaeology means thinking about the ethics of working with members of another culture. Cultural anthropologists have thought about this quite a bit—in fact, the first line of the American Anthropological Association's Statement on Ethics reads, "Anthropologists' paramount responsibility is to those they study."

Anthropologists involve the host population in the project, seek the approval of those who participate, and avoid harm. For every house he measured, every settlement that he mapped, every photo that he took in Madagascar, Kelly explained his goals and asked permission. If the individual declined, he moved on.

Often, however, conflict arises between research goals and human decency. One cannot stand idly by while people are harmed, but an anthropologist also has a responsibility to the research and to the organization that sponsored it. Bram Tucker (University of Georgia) confronted such a problem during his research with the Mikea:

In July 1998, I was living in Behisatse, a hamlet of six houses in the Mikea Forest. I was studying how the Mikea make a living in an unpredictable environment. Rainfall, the main source of water for wild and domestic plants and animals, varies unpredictably from 100 mm to 1500 mm each year. Mikea cope with this unpredictability by diversifying their economy, combining foraging with farming, herding, and producing hard goods for market. They forage in different microenvironments. They plant a mix of crops that do well in rainy years and those that do well in dry years.

Some years, even the best economic strategies are ineffective, and the food supply is inadequate. This was the case in 1998. The maize crop germinated late because of insufficient rainfall, and then grasshoppers ate the withered stalks. Thieves ransacked manioc fields in the night. By March, the families at Behisatse were relying almost entirely on wild ovy tubers. Ovy is an excellent food, but is prone to overharvesting. As the ovy patches near camp were depleted, foragers traveled increasing distances to find food, returning to camp each evening with barely enough to see them through the night.

I was faced with an ethical dilemma. The curious scientist in me wanted to know how Mikea households cope with food shortage. But as their friend and honorary kinsman, I couldn't just watch them go hungry!

My field assistant and I informed the camp elder that we planned to do something to help. The next day we visited a farmer friend in a distant village. I purchased 100 kg of manioc, enough to feed everyone in Behisatse for a month and a half, for 40,000 Malagasy francs, about $7. The farmer said it would take a week to finish drying the manioc. During the following week at Behisatse, the adults continued to forage for ovy all day, leaving the children back at camp hungry. So, at each meal we prepared twice as much food as normal and invited the children to join us. Eventually our manioc gift arrived. Our friends continued to work hard and forage frequently, but they could now afford to rest a little without worry.

I still learned a lot about how Mikea cope with food shortage. By the time our gift arrived, people were starting several alternative strategies, including planned movements to other locations and recalling debts from more prosperous acquaintances. But as field researchers, we become part of the communities we study. As such, we have a responsibility to help out when we can.

continental glaciers that once covered portions of the Northern Hemisphere. But they can examine the effects that mountain glaciers today have on the landscape and use those observations to infer the past from geological traces.

Archaeologists do the same: they study modern analogies in order to understand the processes that created the archaeological record.

Analogy versus Middle-Range Theory

We used the term *analogies* in the previous paragraph, and you may be asking yourself if there is a difference between analogy and middle-range theory. The answer is that *middle-range theory is a particularly rigorous analogy.*

To see what we mean by this, let's first consider what a simple analogy is. An **analogy** notes similarities between two entities—for example, an archaeological feature and an ethnographic description of a similar feature—and infers from those facts that an *additional* attribute of one (the ethnographic feature) is also true of the other (the archaeological feature). Following Nicholas David (University of Calgary) and Carol Kramer (1943–2002), simple analogies take the following form:

- An archaeological object is characterized by attributes A, B, C, and D.
- The ethnographic analogy is characterized by A, B, C, and D and has the function or property E.
- Therefore, the archaeological object also has the function or property E.

For example, the first archaeologists to excavate ancient pueblo ruins in the American Southwest dis-

analogy Noting similarities between two entities and inferring from that similarity that an *additional* attribute of one (the ethnographic case) is also true of the other (the archaeological case).

kiva A Pueblo ceremonial structure that is usually round (but may be square or rectangular) and semi-subterranean. They appear in early Pueblo sites and perhaps even in the earlier (pre-AD 700) pithouse villages.

sipapu A Hopi word that loosely translates as "place of emergence." The original sipapu is the place where the Hopi are said to have emerged into this world from the underworld. Sipapus are also small pits in kivas through which communication with the supernatural world takes place.

covered many **kivas** in the settlements. Kivas are religious structures where native peoples of the American Southwest held various rituals. They are usually round and semi-subterranean, with massive log roofs that were covered by dirt. They were entered via a ladder placed in a central opening in the roof that also served as a smokehole.

Many kivas share certain features: an exterior, stone-lined vertical shaft that opens near the kiva floor, a central fireplace, and an upright stone slab (or a small masonry wall) between the fireplace and the shaft's opening. These features (shown in Figure 7-1) are probably functional. The fireplace provided light and warmth. The shaft provided ventilation, and the upright stone deflected wind blowing down the shaft and prevented smoke and embers from annoying the ritual's participants.

Along the wall opposite the ventilator shaft, archaeologists usually find a very small pit or simply a depression called the **sipapu** (a Hopi term meaning "place of emergence"). Unlike the fireplace, ventilator shaft, and deflector stone, the sipapu has no apparent material function. To interpret this recurrent feature, archaeologists turned to living Pueblo societies, such as the Hopi, who use kivas today for rituals.

Hopi kivas also contain this small, innocuous pit, and its size belies its cultural significance, for the sipapu symbolizes the place where the Hopi emerged from the underworld. In traditional Pueblo theology, the world consists of several levels, and oral histories recount stories of people moving from one level to the next by crawling through a small opening. The current world, the Hopi say, is the fourth world, with more worlds above it. The kiva's sipapu is a reminder of these stories, providing a portal through which the natural and supernatural worlds communicate. Archaeologists infer that sipapus in archaeological kivas had the same function as they do in modern kivas.

Does this inference fit the definition of an analogy? Let's put it into the David and Kramer definition:

- Archaeological kivas are semi-subterranean with entry through the smokehole; they have a central fireplace, a ventilator shaft, a deflector stone, and a small pit opposite the ventilator shaft.
- Hopi kivas are semi-subterranean with entry through the smokehole; they have a central fireplace, a ventilator shaft, a deflector stone, and a

small pit (the sipapu) opposite the ventilator shaft. The sipapu represents the hole where the Hopi emerged into the current world; it allows communication between the natural and supernatural worlds.

- Therefore, the sipapus in archaeological kivas also represented the place where ancient peoples say they emerged from a previous underworld, and they also allowed communication between the natural and supernatural worlds.

Such analogies must be used cautiously. Why? Because just as we enumerated the similarities between the Hopi and the archaeological kivas, we can also list the *differences* between them: Hopi kivas are often square, not round; they are often placed in open plazas or streets between room blocks, rather than incorporated into blocks of residential rooms as they were at many prehistoric pueblos. We could list the similarities between Hopi and archaeological kivas and stack those up against the differences. But how similar do ethnographic and archaeological cases have to be for the analogy to hold true?

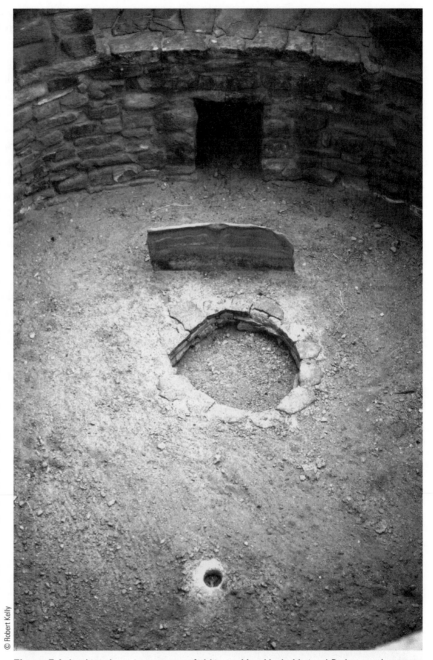
© Robert Kelly

Figure 7-1 Looking down into an unroofed kiva at Mesa Verde National Park; note the square opening for the ventilation shaft (at the top of the photo), the upright stone between the ventilation shaft and the central hearth, and the sipapu—the small hole near the bottom of the photo.

Formal and Relational Analogies

To answer this question, we introduce you to two major kinds of analogy, which Alison Wylie (University of Washington) terms **formal** and **relational analogies.** Formal analogies rely on similarities in *form*—hence "formal" attributes—between the archaeological and

formal analogies Analogies justified by similarities in the formal attributes of archaeological and ethnographic objects and features.

relational analogies Analogies justified on the basis of close cultural continuity between the archaeological and ethnographic cases or similarity in general cultural form.

ethnographic cases, regardless of whether the analogies come from the same culture. For example, we infer that stone projectile points, such as those you saw in Chapter 6, are in fact projectile points because they are so similar to the stone tips found on the projectiles of many ethnographically known peoples the world over. Formal analogies are, of course, strengthened (1) if many ethnographic cases demonstrate the same pattern and (2) if the archaeological and ethnographic cases have many attributes in common. But no rules exist to tell us *how many* ethnographic cases make a strong analogy, or *how many* similarities between the archaeological and ethnographic cases are needed to justify the analogy.

Relational analogies entail formal similarities, but the archaeological and ethnographic cases are related in some fashion. By "related," we mean that they both come from societies with similar settlement systems, economies, or environments—for instance, they may both be desert-adapted hunting-and-gathering societies or the ethnographic society that serves as an analogy may be a cultural descendant of the archaeological case.

In addition, relational analogies may entail "natural" relations, that is, a causal and hence necessary link between the attributes of an object or a feature and

their interpretation. We come back to this aspect of relational analogies in a moment.

Our kiva example entails elements of both formal and relational analogies. There are formal similarities between the archaeological and Hopi kivas, and modern Hopi culture is clearly related to ancient Puebloan culture. Analogies such as this have been and always will be important to archaeological inference.

However, analogy entails certain risks. Suppose, for instance, you are studying a prehistoric horticultural and pastoral society in the deserts of Kenya. In your site you've excavated many stone scrapers. You are interested in inferring who used these tools, men or women. As we see in Chapter 10, inferring the activities of different genders from archaeological data is an extremely difficult task. Analogy is one option for making the inference.

Knowing that analogies are safer the closer they are in time and space to the archaeological case, you look around Africa for a contemporary society that is roughly comparable to the archaeological one—one that lives in a similar environment with a similar economy and a similar culture. Doing so, you encounter the ethnographic research of Steven Brandt (University of Florida) and Kathryn Weedman (University of South Florida) with several Ethiopian peoples. Among these people today are individuals who work cattle skins to manufacture bedding and bags (see Figure 7-2). About a third of those who work hides use stone tools.

These seem to be wonderful sources for building an analogy, but which Ethiopian group should you use? If you pick the Gamo, you'll find that men do all the hide working and tool manufacture. The Gamo-based analogy would imply that men also did the hide working in your archaeological society. But among the Konso, *women* do virtually all the stone tool manufacture and hide working, so the Konso analogy would obviously lead to a very different conclusion.

Figure 7-2 Sokati Chirayo, a Konso woman in Ethiopia, works a hide with a stone scraper mounted in a wooden handle.

Like dynamite and backhoes, analogies are part of the archaeologist's toolkit, but they must be used with caution.

One way out of this problem is to determine the relative strength of the analogy. By increasing the number of formal similarities between an ethnographic and archaeological case, we increase the probability that the formal analogy is correct. Still, though, we wouldn't know if an analogy that relies on ten attributes is twice as good as one that relies on only five. Even the best analogy is no more than a probability—and retains the chance that it could be wrong.

Drawing the analogy from an ethnographic case that is culturally related to the archaeological one improves the analogy, but what if recent events caused cultural discontinuity between the past and the present? And what happens with archaeological cases that have no clear ethnographic referent, such as the 10,000-year-old Folsom site we mentioned in Chapter 4?

Middle-Range Theory as Powerful Analogy

As we noted earlier, relational analogies can rely not just on cultural continuity but also on "natural" relationships, by which Wylie means causal linkages between attributes of a thing and the inference to be made from it.

We refer to analogies based on such causal linkages as "middle-range theory." Middle-range theory is a special kind of analogy simply because it *is* theory. As you recall from Chapter 2, theories explain things; they answer *why* questions. Middle-range theory tries to make an analogy more certain by explaining why there is a *necessary* relationship between an object's or feature's attributes and an inference made from those attributes. Relying on the principle of uniformitarianism, middle-range theory attempts to explain *why* an inference should necessarily be true.

This is hardly an easy task. In fact, this may be an archaeologist's most difficult chore. Consider the hypothetical example in which the archaeologist wished to know if men or women used stone scrapers. What theory would *necessarily* link some observable attribute of a scraper—such as length, width, thickness, raw material, or context—to the gender of its user? It's hard to imagine.

Certainty may forever elude archaeological inference, but archaeologists have been able to make new and more secure inferences from archaeological remains by constructing their middle-range theories through taphonomy, experimental archaeology, and ethnoarchaeology.

Taphonomy

The word *taphonomy* (from the Greek term *tapho*, meaning "death" or "tomb") was coined by the Russian paleontologist I. A. Efremov; it refers to the study of how organisms become part of the fossil record. Archaeologists use the term to refer to the study of how natural processes contribute to the formation of archaeological sites. In Chapter 4, we discussed site formation processes—how human behavior and natural processes affect the creation of the archaeological record. Taphonomy is an important aspect of the study of site formation processes because it considers how human behavior and natural processes incorporate bones and plants into sites.

Taphonomists study some bizarre stuff. One might record how large animal carcasses decompose on an African savanna (Figure 7-3). How long does it take the carcass to disarticulate? Which bones separate first? Which ones are carried away by carnivores? And how far? Is decomposition in the rainy season the same as in the dry season? Others might examine lion kills and ask what telltale markings lions leave behind. How do these differ from the evidence that human hunters leave behind?

Another might find raptor nests along a cliff and collect their feces or vomit (many raptors eat prey whole and then regurgitate the bones and hair). What do rodent bones look like after they have passed through a raptor? Or what do fish bones look like that have passed through a dog? How about through a human? Depending on your perspective, taphonomic research is either gross or really cool.

In archaeology, taphonomy has expanded from paleontology's traditional concern with bones to include plant remains. What are the various ways that seeds, leaves, twigs, and pollen enter archaeological sites? Here you might study the feces of various herbivores, the plant-collecting behavior of pack rats, or the way that wind or water carries leaves, pollen, and sediments.

Recall that taphonomy aims primarily at understanding how natural processes contribute to a site's formation. Although it's not easy, it's easier to infer natural processes from artifacts and ecofacts rather than

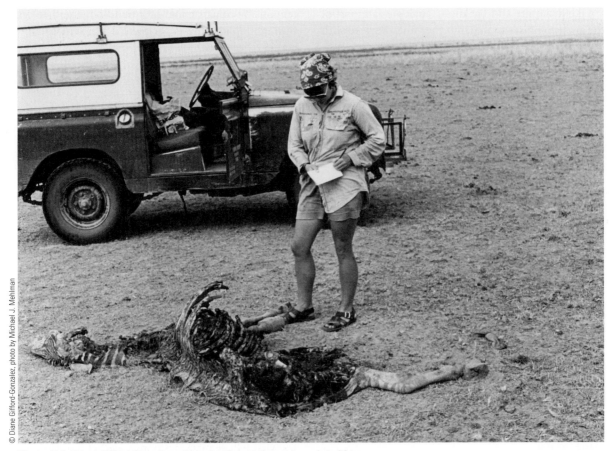

© Diane Gifford-Gonzalez, photo by Michael J. Mehlman

Figure 7-3 Diane Gifford-Gonzales collects data for a taphonomic study in Africa.

human behavior because natural processes are more mechanistic and hence more predictable than human behavior. This observation is useful to archaeology for two reasons: first, recall that data are *observations* on objects, and that archaeologists seek *patterns* in their data. Therefore, one strategy for understanding an archaeological site is first to *remove all the patterns that are the result of natural processes.* Once we do this, we know that the remaining patterns are the ones that need to be explained in terms of human behavior.

Second, understanding how a site formed is crucial to understanding not only the human behavior that occurred at the site but also the *environmental context* of that behavior. It can tell us if the climate was tem-

perate or tropical, if a landscape was eroding away or aggrading, if streams were running or were dry, if forest fires were prevalent, and so on.

In taphonomic research, archaeologists develop bridging arguments by simultaneously yet independently observing natural processes in action and their material results. By trying to explain *why* those natural processes produce the particular material results that they do, you move from simple analogies into middle-range theory. The Hudson-Meng bison **bonebed** provides an example of what taphonomic research can do for archaeology.

Taphonomy at the Hudson-Meng Bison Bonebed

The Hudson-Meng site lies in a low swale in windswept northwest Nebraska, where the remains of at least 500 bison are crowded into an area of about 1000 meters square (Figure 7-4). Twenty-one spear points (or point

bonebed Archaeological and paleontological sites consisting of the remains of a large number of animals, often of the same species, and often representing a single moment in time—a mass kill or mass death.

Figure 7-4 Students excavate a small portion of the Hudson-Meng site, Nebraska. A weatherport covers this excavation.

fragments) were found among the remains. Accelerator mass spectrometry (AMS) dates indicate that the site is about 9500 radiocarbon years old.

Paleontologist Larry Agenbroad (Northern Arizona University) was the first to dig at Hudson-Meng, in the 1970s. Using the standard conventions of the day, he inferred human behavior from *patterns* he observed in the faunal remains. One clear pattern was that the tops of the crania were missing. Mandibles were present along with some cranial fragments, but the top of nearly every single skull was missing. Agenbroad knew that modern Plains Indians often broke bison skulls open to remove the brains and use them in tanning hides. Using this as an analogy, he reasoned that the skull tops at Hudson-Meng were missing for the same reason and therefore that humans must have killed the animals.

Agenbroad then made several more inferences. How could people on foot, armed only with spears, have killed 500 bison? People without horses, Agenbroad decided, could not control a herd of 500 bison. So he inferred that there must be a low cliff nearby that is now buried beneath the sand that blows daily across

western Nebraska. The hunters drove the bison over the cliff and then dragged some 500 of them to a processing area. And, calculating that 500 bison could produce nearly 10,000 kilograms of dried meat, Agenbroad inferred that the ancient hunters were a large group and that they had a sophisticated storage system.

So Agenbroad inferred (1) the presence of humans, (2) hunting strategy, (3) group size, and (4) food storage from patterning—the missing skull tops—evident in the skeletal assemblage. These inferences were based on an analogy with historically known Plains Indians, one that had elements of both formal and relational analogies:

It was a formal analogy because it relied on the similarity in bison skull form (the missing top of the cranium), and similarities between the site and ethnographically documented butchering practices. It was also a relational analogy because it took a known practice of Plains Indians and extrapolated back in time to the ancestors of Plains Indians.

However, this is not middle-range theory because Agenbroad did not try to explain the character of the skulls he found in light of what might happen to bison crania butchered by known Plains Indian practices. The necessary bridging argument was assumed, not demonstrated.

From a taphonomic perspective, modern archaeologists look at the foundation of Agenbroad's inferences (the missing crania) and wonder: Could a natural process create the same pattern?

Hudson-Meng has always presented some troubling facts. For example, comparing it with similar bison kill sites, we might expect something closer to 150 points and point fragments, not just 21.

And why are there no cut marks on the bones? In the process of butchering 500 bison, it seems likely that a stone knife would occasionally have cut to bone as it sliced through tendons and meat. Archaeologists have encountered thousands of such telltale nicks at other kill/butchery sites, but only carnivore tooth marks appear on the bones at Hudson-Meng.

Finally, many of the skeletal remains are in anatomical position, lying in the ground as if the bison had simply died there and were buried undisturbed. If ancient hunters had butchered these animals, we'd expect them to have removed at least some of the meaty portions of the body, such as the upper rear leg (containing the femur).

Lawrence Todd (Colorado State University) and David Rapson (independent scholar) were bothered by these facts, and so they excavated a portion of the Hudson-Meng site using a battery of high-precision excavation techniques. They also applied the perspective of taphonomy, and began by asking this simple question:

How Do Bison Fall Apart?

For years, taphonomists had studied the carcasses of large animals as they lay decomposing on North America's high plains, Africa's Serengeti, and elsewhere. Some of these animals had been shot; others had frozen to death or simply died of old age. Some were ravaged by carnivores, others were undisturbed. Some died on hillsides, others in gullies. Some died in the winter or wet season, others in the summer or dry season. Sometimes the hide dried to form an armor-like case, holding the bones together years after death, sometimes the rotting carcass burst from the maggots within. In other words, taphonomists had documented what actually happens to large animal carcasses under a variety of circumstances.

Are there any patterns in how these large animal skeletons fall apart? Absolutely. Andrew Hill (Yale University) and Anna Behrensmeyer (Smithsonian Institution) found that the first joint to disarticulate is where the scapula attaches to the vertebral column, allowing the entire front limb to drop away. Then the caudal (tail) vertebrae-to-sacrum joint goes, followed by the scapula-humerus joint, and then the "elbow," where the humerus articulates with the radius and ulna. The last joints to disarticulate tend to be those of the vertebrae. Such documented sequences of natural disarticulation provide a baseline against which to judge the distinctiveness of human butchering practices.

Through time, the decomposing bison carcass eventually collapses into a flat pile of bones (Figure 7-5). The skull often ends up resting on its mandibles (the lower jaw). Carnivores may drag some limb bones away and, eventually, the entire skeleton lies flat on the ground—with the skull poking up above all the other bones.

Then what happens? The bones become a sediment trap, catching blowing dust and sand. It takes 10–15 centimeters of sediment to cover the now-collapsed limb bones and rib cage, but 30–40 centimeters to cover the skull. This means that much of the skull is left sticking up above the ground surface after the rest of the bones are buried. And once leg bones, vertebrae, and ribs are buried—thus covering most of the irregular surface that traps blowing sand—sediment accumulates less quickly, leaving the top of the skull exposed for a longer period of time than the rest of the skeleton.

Then the sun does its work. Sunlight is quite destructive of bone, and the exposed top of the skull quickly flakes away. Eventually, the top of the skull is destroyed and the rest is buried.

Taphonomy and Uniformitarianism

So the incomplete crania, the basis of Agenbroad's analogy, are readily explained by natural processes, not human behavior. This is more than simple analogy—it is middle-range theory, because we understand *why* bison bones disarticulate, become buried, and weather the way that they do. But this understanding is based on observations of modern animals. Can we trust these observations to explain archaeological remains?

The principle of uniformitarianism applies here, because ancient animals, like the bison that died at

Hudson-Meng, had the same anatomy as the animals observed in taphonomic studies. Bison disarticulation is governed by the amount of cartilage and tendons holding bones together and the amount of muscle tissue around them. The more cartilage, tendon, and muscle in a joint, the more resistant is the joint to disarticulation. If skeletal disarticulation is largely a product of anatomy, and if bison anatomy has not changed over the past 10,000 years (and it hasn't), then modern observations are relevant to the interpretation of archaeological data.

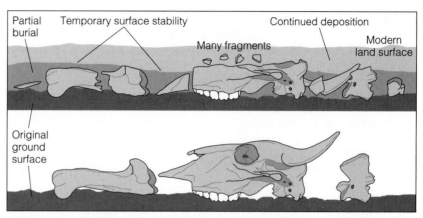

Figure 7-5 Todd and Rapson's reconstruction of how taphonomic processes, rather than human butchering, created the pattern of incomplete crania at the Hudson-Meng site. The animal dies and decomposes; as the body collapses into a pile of bone (*bottom*), it continues to trap sediment until it is mostly buried, although the skull's top remains exposed. The cranium weathers (*top*), and the small bone fragments that flake off are blown away by the wind.

Likewise, the effect of sunlight on bone is a product of the nature of bone and the nature of sunlight. And given that neither sunlight nor bone composition has changed over time, we have gone beyond analogy to explain *why* particular natural factors have particular predictable effects on bone. This is what qualifies work as middle-range theory.

And, it suggests that humans played little role, if any, in the deaths of the 500 bison at Hudson-Meng. But if humans did not dispatch the bison—what happened? Todd and Rapson hypothesize that a summer storm sparked a massive prairie fire that drove the bison herd into the swale for protection (many of the bison lie with their heads to the southeast, which, using analogy with modern bison behavior, suggests that they were responding to a northwest wind). None of the bones are burned, so these animals were not burned to death. But the fire could have jumped the swale and asphyxiated the bison by sucking up all the oxygen for a few critical minutes. This hy-pothesis remains to be tested.

And what of the 21 projectile points found there? As you have seen in previous chapters, archaeological sites are often reoccupied. In their careful excavations, Todd and Rapson found several thin soils containing a few archaeological remains *above* the bison. In fact, Agenbroad found fewer than ten points *among* the bones. The spear points, then, were probably discarded or lost long after the bison had died, decomposed, and become buried, and a few points moved downward through

rodent burrowing and sediment processes into the bonebed.

Experimental Archaeology

Taphonomy uses observations of modern processes to help make inferences from archaeological data. But what if this is impossible? What if we want to know the material effects of behaviors that *no longer exist*? This is especially relevant to human behaviors, because people did things in the past that they no longer do today. Understanding the material remains of these behaviors requires experimental archaeology.

Experimental archaeology is by no means new. Nearly 100 years ago, for example, Saxton Pope, a surgeon at the University of California Medical Center (San Francisco) began experimenting with archery methods. The poignant story began in 1911, when a starving, defeated Indian was found crouching in a slaughterhouse corral near Oroville, California. His family may have been murdered, or perhaps they starved to death. Ishi (circa 1860–1916) himself may have lost his will to live. He could neither speak nor understand English. The local sheriff locked him in the jail, because "wild" Indians were not allowed to roam about freely in those days.

Alfred Kroeber, a young anthropologist at the University of California, heard the story and recognized the Indian's language as Yahi, a native language of

RAPID REVIEW   Characteristics of Middle-Range Theory

- Middle-range theory creates bridging arguments that link material remains to human behavior or natural processes.

- It uses the structure of analogy, but adds the element of the principle of uniformitarianism.

- The principle of uniformitarianism argues that relationships observed in the present were true of the past because they are inherent to the objects or actions being observed.

- The principle of uniformitarianism is essential to giving middle-range theory its power of inference.

California. Kroeber named the man Ishi ("human" in Yahi) and brought him to San Francisco, where he stayed at the university museum, worked as an assistant janitor, and demonstrated arrow-making and fire-starting for museum visitors. Kroeber and his staff taught Ishi their culture, and the Indian revealed many secrets of his survival.

But Ishi soon developed a tubercular cough—which later cost him his life—and he was treated daily by Dr. Pope. Over their short association, Pope and Ishi found a common interest in archery. An odd combination: Pope, the urbane scholar paired with the Yahi Indian, hair singed in tribal custom, together shooting arrows through the parks of downtown San Francisco. Pope was a good student and, after Ishi's death, the doctor continued his research, studying bows and arrows in museum collections and often test-shooting the ancient specimens.

Pope wrote *Hunting with the Bow and Arrow* in 1923, describing his experiments in archery. The book provided baseline information for interpreting ancient finds and quickly became the bible of the bow-hunting fraternity (in fact, it is credited with reviving the sport of bow hunting in America).

heat treatment A process whereby the flintknapping properties of stone tool raw material are improved by subjecting the material to heat.

flake A thin, sharp sliver of stone removed from a core during the knapping process.

core A piece of stone that is worked ("knapped"). Cores sometimes serve merely as sources for raw materials; they also can serve as functional tools.

From early studies such as Pope's, experimental archaeology expanded dramatically and has become an important way for archaeologists to reconstruct the past.

How Were Stone Tools Made?

Many prehistoric techniques died with their practitioners, and experimental archaeologists have been forced to rediscover them. Making stone tools is one such technique, and many archaeologists have experimented by manufacturing their own stone tools.

To make a stone tool, you must first locate and collect the appropriate raw materials—rocks that break with a glassy fracture such as obsidian, quartzite, or chert. This may require excavating into bedrock, because frost fracturing and sunlight can ruin surface specimens. Some ancient peoples excavated major quarries into bedrock using only fire, wooden wedges, and stone mallets.

If the stone is chert or quartzite, you might improve it by **heat treatment**—burying large **flakes** or small **cores** in about 5 centimeters of sand, then burning a fire on top for a day or so. Ancient flintknappers learned that they could more easily chip and shape stone treated in this way. The problem is that, over the millennia, plenty has been forgotten about the detailed technology required to make good stone tools from a pile of rocks.

Fortunately, a school of experimentalists—many of them dedicated amateur archaeologists—has rediscovered some of this technology. One of the best known, Don Crabtree (1912–1980) spent a lifetime experimenting with stone tool manufacturing methods.

One of his projects was to rediscover the techniques used to fabricate Folsom spear points. Remember from Chapter 4 that Folsom points, such as those found at the Folsom site in New Mexico, date to 10,200–10,900 radiocarbon years ago. These exquisite points turn up in many sites on the Great Plains and in the Rocky Mountains where, mounted on spears or darts, they brought down game, including bison. Although the points are often only about 6–8 centimeters (2–3 inches) long, Crabtree counted more than 150 minute sharpening flakes removed from their surface.

The most distinctive property of Folsom artifacts are the **flutes**—wide, shallow, longitudinal grooves on each face of the point (Figure 7-6). Flutes are made by removing **channel flakes** from the point's base on both sides. Nobody is sure why these artifacts were thinned in this fashion, but everybody agrees that fluting is an extraordinary feat of flintknapping.

The technical quality of Folsom points intrigued Crabtree. With enough practice, one can learn to quickly fashion many projectile points. But making Folsom points must have required hours, assuming that one understood how to do it in the first place. And in the twentieth century, nobody did.

Archaeologists speculated for years how ancient peoples removed the channel flakes. And for 40 years, Crabtree tried every way he could think of to manufacture Folsom replicas. He described 11 different methods he had tried to remove channel flakes. Most simply didn't work: either the method was impossible with primitive tools or the resulting flute was different from those on the Folsom points. One method succeeded only in driving a copper punch through his left hand.

© American Museum of Natural History

Figure 7-6 Folsom-style spear points manufactured by Don Crabtree. Note the two large "fluting" flakes that were removed from the points at the bottom of the photograph.

Crabtree eventually concluded that channel flakes could be removed in only two ways. In one experiment, he placed an antler shaft, known as a "punch," on the bottom of the unfinished artifact and then struck the

flute Distinctive channel on the faces of Folsom and Clovis projectile points formed by removal of one or more flakes from the point's base.

channel flake The longitudinal flake removed from the faces of Folsom and Clovis projectile points to create the flute.

punch with a sharp upward blow. Because placement of the antler punch was critical, this technique required two workers. A second technique was based on the seventeenth-century observations of Juan de Torquemada, a Spanish Franciscan friar who traveled through the Central American jungles in 1615. This method used a chest crutch, with padding at one end and an antler tine hafted to the other, to drive flakes off a core. So, Crabtree manufactured one following Torquemada's description. He then tied an unfinished experimental Folsom point into a wood-and-thong vise, which he gripped between his feet. Bracing the crutch against his chest and pressing downward, he successfully detached channel flakes, time after time. The resulting artifacts were almost identical to prehistoric Folsom points.

Crabtree's research unleashed an avalanche of experimentation in the fluting problem. These efforts show that some ten different methods can successfully remove channel flakes and produce the distinctive flutes of Folsom points.

Experimental Archaeology and Uniformitarianism

Archaeologists have used replicative experiments in many different areas of archaeology. They have experimented with ways of moving enormous blocks of stone, such as the huge statues on Easter Island in the Pacific Ocean. They have experimented with ways to manufacture just about everything that is found in archaeological sites—stone tools, pottery, basketry, metal tools, houses, and so on. They've even built structures and then burned them down to see how destruction translates into archaeology.

But what do these experiments prove? Researchers found many ways to remove channel flakes from Folsom points, but which method was actually used in Folsom times? Where's the element of uniformitarianism?

Obviously, a variety of methods work. Crabtree demonstrated that it was *not impossible* to use a chest crutch to replicate Folsom points. But experiments show that other methods were also possible. None of the experimental flintknappers demonstrated conclusively how Folsom points were *actually made*. Replicative experiments often only demonstrate that a given technique could have been used in the past—that it was *not impossible*.

To determine which method or methods were used by Folsom flintknappers, further research is required to compare the characteristics of ancient Folsom points and the waste flakes from their manufacture with experimentally produced Folsom points and waste flakes. Because we know that stone breaks according to certain principles of fracture mechanics, we know that the characteristics of flakes produced today in experiments can help us infer what techniques were used in the past.

But even lacking this element, experimental archaeology can still teach us something about the past. For example, experimental archaeology has taught us three important things about Folsom spear point manufacture. First, regardless of which technique is used, it's difficult to flute points; it takes years of practice. Second, fluting results in a rather high breakage rate near the end of the manufacturing sequence, regardless of the technique. And third, fluting appears to have no specific function. In fact, after Folsom times, similar but unfluted spear points were made for another thousand years. Presumably, these were as effective as Folsom points.

This last point adds a new dimension to our understanding of Folsom spear points. Bruce Bradley, one of the world's premier flintknappers, suggests that fluting was part of a prehunt ritual. We don't know if Bradley is right, but the fluting experiments tell us that we need to consider other hypotheses to not only explain *how* people fluted their points, but also *why*.

Furthermore, the uniformitarian element of experimental archaeology often comes in the guise of telling us what *could* or *could not* have happened in the past. Although this may not pinpoint the precise technique that was actually used, it can provide powerful tests of hypotheses.

Here's another example.

Building the Pyramids

Swiss author Erich von Däniken has long argued that aliens from outer space built the world's prehistoric wonders, including the pyramids. Von Däniken looked at those engineering marvels (see Chapter 5) and asked, How is it possible that a primitive people working with the simplest of tools could have built structures of such astounding size and sophistication? In fact, he asked, how could the Egyptians have even moved the large stones and statues without the aid of advanced technology? Of course, they must have had help from outer space!

This hypothesis can be tested using experimental archaeology: Can stones that weigh several tons be moved using only the tools and materials that the ancient Egyptians had available to them? If not, then perhaps von Däniken's hypothesis has some merit. But if such stones *can* be moved with Egyptian technology, then his hypothesis is undermined.

Had von Däniken actually bothered to learn anything about Egyptian archaeology, he would have quickly discovered paintings within tombs that depict men hauling stones and statues. One shows 172 men pulling a statue of Djehutihotep (a Middle Kingdom noble) estimated to weigh some 58 tons (thus, each man is pulling about 650 pounds). The statue rides on a wooden sledge accompanied by a man who pours a liquid onto the runway in front of the sledge—no doubt to ease the workmen's burden.

But does this method really work? Can it haul stone up ramps hundreds of feet long? Maybe the Egyptian tomb painters just made it up.

More than a decade ago, experimental archaeology answered this question. Archaeologist Mark Lehner (Oriental Institute of the University of Chicago and Harvard Semetic Museum) and stonemason Roger Hopkins staged an experiment to see whether they could really move large blocks of stone in this manner. Working with Egyptian quarrymen and masons, they built a pyramid 20 feet high using ancient Egyptian technology. A TV crew from the series *NOVA* filmed the experiment, and so Lehner and Hopkins had to complete the pyramid on a tight schedule—3 weeks.

Lehner experimented with several possible techniques to move and lift stone. One entailed the method depicted in Djehutihotep's tomb, but with the loaded sledge resting on wooden rollers. As the sledge was pulled, workmen would pick up the rollers behind the sledge and move them to the front. Although this idea seemed sound, Lehner's experiment showed that, if the rollers were not placed perfectly, the sledge would veer off course. The same error happened if the rollers were not perfectly lathed. Lehner concluded that moving large stones over long distances with this method might have been more trouble than it was worth.

Another idea was that wooden levers helped to lift the stones up high. In this method, one side of the block is levered up, and planks are placed beneath it.

Then the block's opposite side is levered up, and planks are placed below that side. The workers then repeated the process until they raised the stone to the desired height. This idea worked for small rises but, as the block rose higher, levering became difficult and the stone's balance became precarious.

So Lehner then turned to ramps. Archaeologists have found remnants of ramps at several Egyptian sites, including the stone quarry beside the Giza Plateau. These ramps consist of two parallel retaining walls, the area between them filled with rubble and topped with a coat of sand or crushed gypsum. In this top layer, the Egyptians set planed logs, perpendicular to the retaining walls, about 50 centimeters apart.

Egyptologists speculate on the kinds of ramps used by the ancient Egyptians. Some suggest a straight ramp—although, by the time the pyramid reached its peak, the ramp would have been hundreds of meters long. Other suggestions include ramps that formed a spiral up the sides of the pyramid or multiple ramps built at different levels during construction.

Lehner built his ramp with an incline of about 7 percent. He found that a 2-ton stone resting on a sledge could easily be hauled up by 20 men. Once the stone was on top of the pyramid, 4 or 5 men using levers could roll it. With this method, Lehner built his pyramid within the 3 weeks allotted for the task.

As in the Folsom fluting experiments, researchers found many ways to build a ramp, and perhaps the Egyptians used all of them. But the precise technique does not matter in this case. The principles involved in simple machines like levers and wedges have not changed from the days of the pharaohs; their capabilities today are the same as they were in the past. This is the important element of uniformitarianism that allows Lehner's experiments to test von Däniken's outlandish hypothesis. With no more than dirt ramps, wooden sledges, rope, and plenty of strong backs, the ancient Egyptians were well equipped to move the stones necessary to build their pyramids and temples. Aliens from outer space were not required.

Ethnoarchaeology

What if we wanted to know about ancient kinship, social, or political organizations that no longer exist? These questions were the sort that archaeology in the

1960s wished to answer, and they required the sorts of behavioral inferences that Walter Taylor and Lewis Binford sought.

Binford Takes Off for Points North

In the 1960s, the ways to infer social behavior from archaeological remains were little more than simple rules of thumb that were often culturally biased. Archaeologists began to test them through ethnoarchaeology, with the understanding that if generalizations cannot cover *contemporary* behavior, then they cannot be used to interpret the evidence of *ancient* behavior.

Binford was concerned with this inferential problem and, to help solve it, he conducted ethnoarchaeological research in the 1970s among the Nunamiut Eskimo of Alaska. Binford's real interest lay in the Middle Paleolithic archaeology of Europe, especially France. Why would he study living Eskimos in Alaska if he were interested in the Middle Paleolithic archaeology of France?

Recall from Chapter 6 (see "The Frison Effect" on page 132) that the French archaeologist François Bordes argued that different stone tool Mousterian assemblages were a product of different Neanderthal cultures. These assemblages often alternated throughout the strata of some key French sites, and Bordes argued that this meant that the caves were used alternately by different "tribes" of Neanderthals.

Binford saw things differently. He suspected that the different assemblages were the by-products of different activities, not different tribes. He argued that Bordes's inference (different tool assemblages = different Neanderthal tribes) needed to be evaluated. But we cannot evaluate an inferential argument using archaeological data, because the systemic context (the behavior) cannot be observed independently of the archaeological data. Binford had to find a place where he could observe living hunting peoples and see what residues their activities left behind. The Nunamiut's Arctic environment was somewhat analogous to the French Middle Paleolithic environment, and the Nunamiut hunted large game (caribou and sheep), as had the Neanderthals. But Binford was not as interested in animal bones or the Nunamiut as he was in evaluating the concepts that archaeologists of the time employed to understand the past.

Binford accompanied Nunamiut hunters on their hunting trips, recording what they did at each locality and what debris was left behind. In so doing, he demonstrated that the same people—the same individuals, in fact—leave different kinds of tools and bones at different locations on a landscape. What Nunamiut hunters left behind was not just a product of their culture, but also of tasks being performed, the season of the year, the distance back to camp, the availability of transportation, the amount of food already in camp, the weather, and other factors. Although culture plays a significant role in determining what kinds of artifacts are left behind, Binford demonstrated that archaeologists couldn't uncritically *assume* that a difference in artifacts reflects *only* a difference in culture. Other hypotheses, such as site function, have to be tested and discarded before inferring that different tool assemblages in a site's strata indicate use of the site by different cultures.

Ethnoarchaeology has frequently provided such cautionary tales. But ethnoarchaeology can also be a powerful tool for creating middle-range theory. It can do so (1) if it focuses on aspects of ethnographic data that are archaeologically observable, and (2) if it attempts to explain why a relationship between behavior and archaeologically observable remains should necessarily hold true. As we will see, however, the principle of uniformitarianism is harder to implement in ethnoarchaeology than in taphonomy or experimental archaeology.

Ethnoarchaeologists have researched pottery and stone tool production, hunting and butchering, plant gathering, architecture, trash disposal, trade, and burial rituals in many kinds of societies all over the world. All these studies help archaeologists create better ways of inferring human behavior from archaeological remains.

Here we describe one such project conducted by Kelly in Madagascar.

Ethnoarchaeology in Madagascar

Kelly was trained as an archaeologist, with interests in the archaeology of western North America. He was particularly interested in how nomadism factored into people's lives. In some cultures, especially hunting-and-gathering societies, people are highly nomadic, moving as often as every week. In others, especially part-time farming cultures, people change their residence less frequently, perhaps only once or twice a year.

IN HIS OWN WORDS
Why I Began Doing Ethnoarchaeology

By Lewis R. Binford

In 1967 I received funds to go to Europe for a year to work more closely with François Bordes in Bordeaux. My program for research was the following. If we could not study the chipped stone directly, perhaps we could study faunal remains and the horizontal distributions, on excavated archaeological floors, of both fauna and chipped stone. Then it might be possible to relate variability in the lithics to these other properties of the archaeological sites in question. I worked for a year in France, identifying and plotting all the stone tools and animal bones by anatomical part and by breakage pattern.

Thus began a series of disillusionments. I performed one correlation study after another—so many, in fact, that I needed a great steel trunk in order to carry all the papers back to the United States. I could tell you cross-correlations between any pair of Mousterian tool-types, between tools and bones, between bones and the drip-lines in cave sites, between almost any type of data you care to name. What I found, of course, was many new facts that nobody had seen before. But none of these new facts spoke for themselves.

My metal trunk was so big and heavy that I decided to return home by boat and that 5-day trip from Le Havre to New York gave me an opportunity for some disconsolate self-reflection. The whole project was obviously a total failure. What had I done wrong? What had I not done that I should have done? Could it really be that archaeologists simply cannot learn anything about the past? Where was I missing the real problem?

By the time we steamed into New York City, just before the New Year of 1969, some of the answers to these problems were suggested, at least in my thoughts. I prepared a research proposal to go to the Arctic in the spring of 1969 to live with a group of Eskimo hunters. My reasons for going there were little more specific at that stage than that it could hardly fail to be a good educational experience. If I was ever to be able to make accurate inferences from archaeological facts, I was convinced that I had to understand the dynamics of living systems and study their static consequences.

Some people return seasonally to a settlement for several years in a row, and some stay year-round in sedentary villages.

Kelly was concerned with archaeology's ability to discern different levels of nomadism archaeologically, so he looked for an ethnographic situation in which he could see variation in nomadism and study its material consequences. He finally learned of the Mikea, a little-known society in the forest of southwestern Madagascar who grow maize and manioc, raise cattle, and do some hunting and gathering.

If you know anything about Madagascar, it probably has to do with lemurs leaping through a tropical forest, but such forests actually make up only a small part of Madagascar. The southwest part of the island, where the Mikea live, is drier and more open. It has distinct wet and dry seasons, and the wet season is blisteringly hot. The forest contains dense vine-covered thickets, stands of 5-meter-high cacti, and baobab trees. There are no rivers in the Mikea Forest and only a few wells. Bordering the forest on one side is the Mozambique Channel and on the other, a vast savanna.

Mikea live in four major kinds of settlements that differ in how long they are occupied (Figure 7-7). Many have houses in large, permanent villages of 1000 people or more located on the edge of the forest. Here they grow manioc and other crops and raise cattle, pigs, and chickens. These villages frequently host weekly markets that people attend from many miles around.

Some Mikea live most of the year in forest hamlets, in kin-related groups of about 40 people. Most people who live in these hamlets also maintain a house in the

© Robert Kelly

Figure 7-7 Mikea habitations. *Clockwise from upper left:* A family sits around a hearth outside a lean-to in a temporary forest camp; a wattle-and-daub house in a permanent village (note the lack of trash); a house with shade structure in a forest hamlet; and a set of houses lacking shade structures in a seasonal hamlet.

larger villages. Around these forest hamlets are **slash-and-burn** maize fields. As the arable land around the settlement becomes exhausted, the hamlet is moved, about every 3 to 10 years.

Some Mikea who live in the villages also occupy seasonal hamlets in the forest during the growing season so that they can tend to their maize fields. These are much like forest hamlets, but they differ in that they are mostly occupied for a much shorter period of time—during the growing season.

Finally, Mikea in the forest hamlets and some who live in the villages move away from their homes and into the forest during the dry season. These foraging camps are smaller and are occupied for up to 2 weeks. While in these camps, people collect tubers and honey and search tree hollows for estivating hedgehogs. Kelly focused on the question "Are the different lengths of stay reflected in the material remains left behind at these sites?"

Mikea Settlements from an Archaeological Perspective

Recall that ethnoarchaeology's first objective is to relate behavior to archaeologically observable phenomena. Over time, the only thing that might remain of the Mikea settlements are features, such as postholes, hearths, and pits, as well as scattered trash, such as burnt maize, bone fragments, and broken tools.

Accordingly, Kelly and his associates collected data on houses, features, and the distribution of trash in some 30 settlements; for some they recorded data over a 3-year period (see "Looking Closer: Doing Ethnoarchaeology in Madagascar"). They also counted the number

slash-and-burn A horticultural method used frequently in the tropics wherein a section of forest is cut, dried, and then burned, thus returning nutrients to the ground. This permits a plot of land to be farmed for a limited number of years.

LOOKING CLOSER
Doing Ethnoarchaeology in Madagascar

By Robert Kelly

I conducted ethnographic work in Madagascar with my wife, Lin Poyer, a cultural anthropologist. On our first trip we flew to Washington, D.C., then to Paris, Cairo, Nairobi, and finally to the capital of Madagascar, Antananarivo. The entire trip took nearly 48 hours. After meeting officials and finalizing permits, we flew to the provincial capital of Toliara, where we met our Malagasy colleagues, Jean-François Rabedimy and Jaovola Tombo.

You do archaeology with a trowel and ethnography with a pencil and notebook, but that's just the beginning of the differences. In Madagascar, all educated people speak French, and few speak English. And the Mikea spoke only their dialect of Malagasy. So our daily language was a mixture of French, Malagasy (as we learned the dialect), and English.

There's also no schedule—an ethnographer is always "on the job." One time we arranged to leave "early in the morning." Our guide arrived at 3 a.m., and so we got up, packed, and left. Another time, the men in the village, armed with spears, went after cattle rustlers—at midnight. So, we stayed up all night to learn the result.

We spent several weeks, on and off, living in Mikea hamlets and foraging camps. It was the dry season, and we joined the Mikea in walking many kilometers to the nearest well or digging up *babo* (a wonderful water-engorged tuber) and eating it. Meals were tubers, white rice with a dollop of peanut butter, and the occasional scrawny chicken or dried fish.

The Mikea wanted virtually everything that we owned, especially clothing (which is hard for them to come by). We avoided such dunning by carrying no spare clothing. But we freely handed out tobacco and occasionally offered gifts of food, money, and clothing; and, when possible, medical assistance.

The Mikea were curious and a little suspicious about why we were there. They couldn't believe that foreigners would travel so far just to measure house posts, draw maps, and weigh tubers. They were remarkably patient with us.

An ethnographer tries to immerse him- or herself in another culture and to participate in it as much as possible. We witnessed trance dances, spirit possession ceremonies, and a goat sacrifice. Like the Mikea, we traveled on foot or by oxcart, often in the cool of the night. We dug tubers, hunted hedgehogs, ate honey from a hive while bees buzzed about, and slept on the ground around a fire.

Ethnoarchaeology is the best way for archaeologists to learn firsthand how difficult it is to interpret human behavior from static material remains. But even more, it is an extreme growth experience: you learn as much about your own limits and prejudices as you do about another culture.

of posts in houses and measured their diameter—an activity that amused their Mikea hosts (and once sparked an accusation of witchcraft). They mapped the settlements, showed the locations of houses and features, as well as the placement of trash deposits. Through interviews, Mikea told the history of each settlement, how they were used, why they were abandoned, as well as other information. What did Kelly find out?

Trash Disposal

Ethnoarchaeologists often begin by observing what people do with their trash. In foraging camps, people unceremoniously toss ash from fires and other trash into bushes, only 1–2 meters away from the family hearth. In the forest and seasonal hamlets, trash is disposed in an arc some 3–9 meters in front of the house door. Unlike the foraging camps, hamlets were periodically swept clean. This meant that larger items would end up in the trash arc, whereas smaller pieces missed by the broom were trampled into the sand.

And as people occupied their hamlets for longer periods of time, they deposited their trash farther away from their house's door. For example, Kelly visited one settlement the year it was established and found that trash was deposited some 3–4 meters from houses. A year later, trash was deposited some 8 meters away. Why? Early in a settlement's life, bushes grow near the house, and they are a convenient place to toss trash. Eventually, however, the bushes are destroyed (for firewood, by children playing, and by goats and cattle foraging). As bushes disappear, trash is swept into bushes farther from the house. In hamlets occupied for several years, in fact, periodic cleanings create a second trash deposit, this time as a ring around the entire settlement.

The permanent villages exhibit a major change in the disposal of trash. Here one cannot simply sweep trash to the side of one's household, because this would mean sweeping trash into a neighbor's space. Consequently, people throw trash into pits next to the houses (the pits were excavated to make mud for the wattle-and-daub houses), or they collect trash in baskets inside the houses and periodically dump it at the edge of the settlement, as much as 30 or 40 meters away.

By the way, this discussion doesn't imply that Mikea settlements are filthy or reeking of rotting garbage. Much of the trash, in fact, is maize husks and other dry plant material. Any wet garbage—including almost all bones—is eaten by ever-hungry dogs and pigs.

House Posts

After trash, the next thing an ethnoarchaeologist might notice are houses. Other ethnoarchaeological studies have found, not surprisingly, that people invest more labor and care in houses that they expect to inhabit for a long time, and the Mikea are no different. But how is that investment reflected archaeologically?

In the villages, Mikea often build wattle-and-daub houses about 10 square meters in size. They first set posts upright in the ground, 75 centimeters deep, and then weave smaller saplings horizontally between these posts. They pack this lattice with coarse mud, smoothing the surface. The house has a door made of planks, usually with a lock, and one or two windows, with wooden shutters. The floors are packed clay. Most of these houses have thatch roofs that extend beyond the walls, forming a narrow veranda around the house. A wattle-and-daub house takes a month or more to build but, if the owner maintains the roof, the house should last 25 years or more.

In the forest hamlets, Mikea have more modest homes. About half the size of village houses, they are made of thinner posts not so deeply set and have roofs of baobab bark slabs and walls of bark, grass, or reeds. A cold wind blows nightly in the dry season, so the door is on the north wall, and the south wall is woven tightly. There is a hearth just inside and to one side of the door. Two to three meters outside the door is another hearth, covered by a shade structure, the top of which serves to store dried corn and tools. These forest hamlet houses can be built in a week and need repair every year or so. Some are used for only a year.

The houses in seasonal hamlets look similar to those in forest hamlets, but they appear to a Westerner's eye to be shabbier. They are often shorter and have fewer shade structures outside the front door.

Because foraging camps are used in the dry season and it rarely rains at that time of the year, houses are rare in foraging camps; when they are present, they are no more than lean-tos or simple boxlike structures, fashioned from whatever wood is handy, and built in an hour or two.

As you might expect, the longer people intend to live in a house, the more time they invest in it. Foraging camps are the most transient of the four settlement types and contain the most ephemeral of shelters (when present at all—most families simply sleep by the fire), whereas the permanent villages contain the largest houses with the most substantial walls and roofs.

The amount of labor involved in each of these houses is reflected in a house's roof and walls, but these things disappear. However, the amount of labor is also reflected in the postholes. And these features are familiar to most archaeologists, because they are often all that remain of ancient houses. What can they tell us?

Plenty, and all of it is pretty commonsense. Although some of the wattle-and-daub houses are large, many of the reed or grass houses are about the same size. Nonetheless, the long wall of village houses contained *twice* as many posts as did the same wall in houses in seasonal hamlets; houses in forest hamlets fell between these two. In addition, the posts used in seasonal hamlets had more variable diameters than the posts used in the more permanent settlements—especially the wattle-

TABLE 7-1 Summary of Differences in Mikea Settlements

SETTLEMENT TYPE	HOUSE SIZE	POST VARIABILITY	SECONDARY POSTS	DISTANCE TO TRASH (METERS)	FEATURE DIVERSITY
Villages	Various, but can be large	Low	Many, closely spaced	10–40+	High
Forest Hamlets	Small	Low-Medium	Fewer, farther apart	4–9	Medium
Seasonal Hamlets	Small	High	Fewer, farther apart	3–4	Medium-Low
Foraging Camps	Lean-tos or "boxes," if present at all	N.A.	N.A.	1–2	Low

N.A. = not applicable.

and-daub houses. In seasonal hamlets, people used whatever wood was handy, often scavenging poles from abandoned houses. Post diameters as well as consistency in post diameters reflect the fact that people are more selective about the wood they use when building houses that are more permanent.

Features outside Houses

Recall from Chapter 2 that features are artifacts that can't be removed from a site—things like hearths, houses, pits, and postholes. In Mikea settlements, these outdoor features include different kinds of houses, fenced compounds, animal corrals, wash areas, cook houses, public troughs, drying racks, stores, wells, ceremonial enclosures, maize threshers, bellows, and storage bins and racks. The particular kinds of features found in a settlement are linked to the particular kinds of activities that take place in Mikea settlements and are not so useful to the development of universal middle-range theory. But differences in the range of diversity of features among the different settlement types are useful.

The more permanent a Mikea settlement is, the greater the range of features it contains. When people intend to stay in one place for years or plan to return to a settlement seasonally for several years, they invest more time in features that have a single purpose, rather than "making do" with temporary facilities. Washhouses, for example, are never found in foraging camps or seasonal hamlets: people are basically "camping" at both, and water is a rare commodity in dry season forest camps. People bathe back at the forest hamlet or village. Washhouses are also rarely found in forest hamlets—where the small, related community means that people can expect privacy without bothering to

build a separate facility. However, washhouses are common in the densely populated villages, where privacy is more difficult, and where investment in a facility is worthwhile.

Table 7-1 summarizes these differences among Mikea settlements. In this table we related some archaeologically recoverable variables (trash distribution, postholes, features) to human behavior (the length of occupation). Simply by recording the way trash is distributed, the range of features present, the number of postholes per house, and the variation in posthole diameter, we could place a new settlement into one of the four categories with a high degree of accuracy. This fulfills the first criterion of a middle-range study—it focuses on aspects of ethnographic data that are archaeologically observable. But does it explain why the relationship between behavior and archaeologically observable remains is necessarily true? What do such ethnoarchaeological studies do for archaeology?

Ethnoarchaeology and Uniformitarianism

As we have pointed out, middle-range theory tries to *explain* patterning between behavior and material remains. Such explanations depend on the principle of uniformitarianism. It is relatively easy to see how this principle applies in both taphonomy and experimental archaeology, because both study natural processes and mechanical relationships.

But the principle of uniformitarianism is tougher to apply in ethnoarchaeology, because human behavior is anything but mechanical. We conducted our study of the Mikea within the materialist paradigm (explained in Chapter 2); more specifically, it relied upon a theoretical framework known as "human behavioral ecology." One of the tenets of this framework is that, because people have many demands on their time, they make choices that maximize the utility of their decisions. Choices about what kind of house to build reflect this fact. Why would someone in a forest hamlet invest more than a month in building a wattle-and-daub house when one built in less than a week would suffice for the time that the hamlet would be occupied? The "extra" 3 weeks can then be put toward clearing another maize field, building a ceremonial enclosure, or some other important task. Similarly, why take time to select just the right poles for a house in a seasonal hamlet that will be occupied for only a few months of the year? From a materialist perspective, the time would be better spent in clearing more fields, planting, weeding, or preparing for a celebration. In fact, the Mikea themselves said that the longer they intended to remain in a settlement, the more care they put into constructing houses and facilities such as maize-threshing bins and outhouses. They also said they would be more selective in their building material, choosing poles of a particular diameter for posts and even searching out certain species of wood, such as ones known for their ability to resist destruction by insects.

These seem like logical choices, and several ethnoarchaeological studies have found similar patterns in trash disposal, house form, and feature diversity in other societies in the world. Combined with these other studies, the Mikea research helps form a strong formal analogy; combined with the theoretical framework of human behavioral ecology, it also contains elements that make it middle-range theory.

What about Culture?

But the issue of culture can make ethnographic analogies, even ones strong enough to qualify as middle-range theory, problematic. We have discussed, for instance, the disposal of trash among the Mikea as being simply a function of how long a settlement is occupied. The longer it is occupied, the farther away from a house trash is removed. But cultural ideas about trash may come into play.

Ian Hodder, a postprocessual archaeologist, conducted ethnoarchaeological research with the Moro and Mesakin in Sudan. Both groups raise various grains, as well as pigs, cattle, and goats. In both, families live in household compounds. But the Moro's compounds are relatively free of trash, whereas the Mesakin's are messier; in particular, the Moro keep pig bones out of the compounds.

Hodder argues that some of the difference between the two societies and the way they deal with trash lies in different ideas about women. Moro men see contact with women as potentially "polluting" their strength and authority. And, because Moro women take care of pigs, they are associated with these animals; men are associated with cattle. As a result, Moro men consider pig remains to be foul, and Moro women take care to remove pig bones from the trash and dispose of them separately. The Mesakin do not share the Moro's beliefs about women, and they treat pig bones the same as any other animal remains. Thus, Hodder argues that archaeologists need to consider the symbolic meanings of material culture in order to appreciate how it will be treated as trash.

But the "cultural" component is very difficult to study archaeologically. And this means that the principle of uniformitarianism remains difficult to implement in ethnoarchaeology. For some archaeologists, this means that ethnoarchaeology can provide us only with strong analogies, not middle-range theory.

For others, ethnoarchaeological studies conducted across a spectrum of societies provide archaeology with analogies that, taken together, suggest some important principles of human behavior. These principles could *provisionally* be taken as uniform for the purpose of creating and testing hypotheses; this approach can permit ethnoarchaeology to act as middle-range theory to support archaeological inferences.

Conclusion: The Importance of Middle-Range Theory

Archaeology is all about making inferences from artifacts, ecofacts, features, and their contexts. Middle-range theory is what allows archaeologists to know that they really do know something about the past. It lies at the heart of archaeology, because archaeology is the study of the past based on material remains. As you have seen in this chapter, archaeologists go about constructing all-important middle-range theory through taphonomy, experimental archaeology, and ethnoarchaeology.

It requires that archaeologists step out of their excavation trenches and conduct a different kind of research. Some archaeologists, in fact, have permanently hung up their trowels and devoted their careers to the development of middle-range theory. And this is good, because without middle-range theory, our inferences from archaeology would be little more than just-so stories, with no more credence behind them than silly ideas like aliens building pyramids. In the following chapters, we see how archaeologists have put studies in taphonomy, experimental archaeology, and ethnoarchaeology to use in reconstructing the past.

Summary

- Because the "facts" of archaeology are incapable of speaking for themselves, archaeologists must follow geology's principle of uniformitarianism and study ongoing processes and their material remains.

- Analogy is one way to reconstruct the past but is limited in its utility to societies that have very close geographic and cultural counterparts (preferably ones with a historical connection) or to fairly low-level inferences.

- Middle-range research allows archaeologists to make better inferences from archaeological data by clarifying the basis for the inference; it is research designed to create bridging arguments that link human behavior and/or natural processes to their material remains.

- The principle of uniformitarianism is critical in the development of middle-range theory because it is what allows confidence in a middle-range theory's ability to infer human behavior or natural processes from archaeological remains.

- Analogies can be formal, relational, or a mixture of both. Formal analogies rely on similarities in form, and relational analogies rely on cultural continuity or causal linkages to justify their use in archaeological inference.

- Middle-range theory is a particular kind of analogy in that it attempts to demonstrate *why* a particular

pattern in archaeological data can be unambiguously interpreted in a particular way.

- Taphonomy studies how natural processes help create the archaeological record; it helps weed out patterns that result from natural processes and thus helps define patterns that need to be interpreted in human behavioral terms. It also helps the archaeologist understand the environmental context of past human behavior.

- Experimental archaeology (such as replicating stone tools) studies things that can no longer be observed in action today, such as ancient technologies that are no longer practiced.

- Replicative experiments are one class of experimental archaeology. They can help show what techniques could or could not have been used in the past.

- Experimental archaeology, such as stone tool use-wear studies, can also link human behavior and material signatures.

- Ethnoarchaeologists study living societies, observing artifacts, features, and material remains while they still exist in their systemic, behavioral contexts. Ethnoarchaeology links human behavior with archaeologically observable material remains.

- Of the three ways to develop middle-range theory, the principle of uniformitarianism is most difficult to implement in ethnoarchaeology.

Media Resources

 The Companion Website for **Archaeology: Down to Earth,** *Third Edition*

http://anthropology.wadsworth.com/thomas kelly3e_down/

Supplement your review of this chapter by going to the companion website to take one of the practice quizzes, use the flash cards to master key terms, and check out the many other study aids that are designed to help you succeed in your introductory archaeology course.

8 People, Plants, and Animals in the Past

Outline

The remains of a partially butchered bison at the Agate Basin site, Wyoming.

© University of Wyoming, Frison Institute

Preview

ARCHAEOLOGISTS HAVE PLENTY of methods and techniques for reconstructing how people made a living in the past, and in this chapter, we discuss a few of them. We begin with faunal analysis, the identification and interpretation of animal remains recovered in an archaeological context. Animal bones not only enable the archaeologist to study ancient hunting methods and diet, they also assist in reconstructing past environments.

Of course, getting at the meaning behind bones is neither easy nor straightforward. This chapter provides you with the basics for understanding what we can do with a bunch of animal bones.

Plant remains are also valuable to archaeology. We have already seen how the study of tree rings provides archaeologists with a trustworthy way of dating specific events of the past and past climates. Archaeological plant remains—pollen, seeds, charcoal, and phytoliths—also tell us what wild plants people collected, the crops they grew, the fuels they burned, and even the roles played by plants in rituals. Plant and animal remains can also tell us in what season of the year people occupied a site.

 Doing Fieldwork CD-ROM: Archaeological Demonstrations
See the "Reconstructing the Past" section of the CD-ROM to learn more about topics covered in this chapter.

Introduction

So far, we have talked mostly about artifacts and features—objects created by humans. Archaeological sites also contain ecofacts—plant and animal remains; some of these are food refuse, left by humans, but sometimes ecofacts enter sites through natural processes (as when plants and animals die on a site). As you recall, taphonomic studies figure out how plant and animal remains accumulate in archaeological sites. In this chapter, we are more concerned with what plant parts and animal bones tell us about human behavior.

Archaeologists use many methods to recover and interpret animal and plant remains. So many, in fact, that we can present only a few here. Rather than blanket the field, we introduce some of the major categories of data and provide a sense of how archaeologists go about interpreting them. We begin with archaeofaunas.

What's an Archaeofauna?

An **archaeofauna** consists of the animal bones recovered from an archaeological site. Archaeofaunas differ from paleontological assemblages because humans

archaeofauna The animal bones found in an archaeological site.

IN HER OWN WORDS

Zooarchaeology and Biological Conservation

By Virginia Butler

Virginia Butler is associate professor of anthropology at Portland State University.

Habitats and species around the world are being lost with increasing speed in the face of human population growth and habitat destruction. Under legislation such as the Endangered Species Act (1973), recovery plans are being developed to save or reestablish species and environments. Drawing from recent records, decisions are made on which species should be targeted for recovery, and which should be disregarded. In stark terms, these decisions determine which organisms "belong on the ark." But with access to faunal records dating back hundreds and thousands of years, zooarchaeology brings a much-needed historical perspective to wildlife management policy.

Zooarchaeological research demonstrates the ways past human predation and landscape alteration affected animal populations, and this has important implications for wildlife management. Environments that early European explorers encountered were not free of human influence—they were occupied by Native Americans. Contemporary policy that creates preserves without considering past human actions is trying to recreate environments that never existed. Management of wapiti (elk) in Yellowstone National Park provides a case in point. In the 1990s, over 60,000 wapiti lived in the greater Yellowstone area, yet wapiti remains are rare in archaeological sites. The rarity of wapiti remains suggests that humans kept this animal's populations low through hunting. Charles Kay (Utah State University) argues that this means the "hands off" management policy in Yellowstone, which allows wapiti populations to increase unchecked, does not duplicate pre-AD 1900 conditions, and has led to serious overgrazing of the park.

My own research in California's Owens Valley helps understand the effects of habitat loss and exotic (introduced) species on the loss of native fish species in the American west. Owens Valley contains four indigenous species of fish: pupfish, chub, a minnow, and the Owens sucker, the first three of which are in severe decline. Analyzing an 8000-year zooarchaeological record, Michael Delacourt (California State University, Sacramento) and I found that both the size and abundance of the different species changed over time in response to changes in climate that affected the size of the valley's lakes. But none of them was in danger of extinction. The only thing that changed in the last 100 years was the introduction of exotic species, predatory fish against which the indigenous species cannot compete. With this information, managers can make informed decisions about how to save the indigenous species from extinction.

Zooarchaeological research is aiding conservation measures in many other ways. For example, when wildlife biologists reestablish a species, they try to do so with animals from a source population that is closely related to the original native stock. Since new techniques allow genetic data to be extracted from skeletal remains, genetic analysis of zooarchaeological remains can provide the genetic signature of the locally extinct native stock. In Oregon, for example, biologists wanting to re-introduce the sea otter turned to archaeological remains to determine whether Alaskan or southern California sea otters are the closest genetic match to the population that formerly inhabited Oregon's waters.

Through these and other approaches, zooarchaeology promises to help us understand long-term animal population dynamics so we can take the necessary steps to stop the loss of species diversity and conserve environments for future generations to enjoy.

may have had a hand in their formation. Animal bones turn up in two major archaeological contexts:

1. At a **kill** or butchering **site,** bones may lie more or less the way they were when the hunters left, affected by carnivore scavenging, weathering, and other natural factors.
2. In camps and villages, we find bones where hunted animals were brought back or domesticated animals were butchered.

Sometimes a site's faunal remains number in the tens of thousands and may include those of animals killed on the site, those transported from kill sites elsewhere, and those of animals that simply died in the site or that carnivores or raptors carried in.

After recovering an archaeofauna, archaeologists commonly perform a **faunal analysis;** the person who does this is a **zooarchaeologist** (also known as a *faunal analyst*). To show you how this is done, let's look at how one zooarchaeologist went about analyzing the archaeofauna of the Folsom component at Wyoming's Agate Basin site.

The Agate Basin Site

Sometime around 1916, rancher William Spencer was riding across the broken terrain of his ranch in eastern Wyoming. Visiting a spring, he noticed some large bones protruding from the edge of an arroyo (just as George McJunkin did at the Folsom site in New Mexico). His curiosity piqued, he returned to the spring several times, eventually collecting a number of large, beautiful spear points as well as bison bones from the site.

Years later, after more bison bones and spear points had turned up, Frank H. H. Roberts (Smithsonian

Institution) started excavating at the "Agate Basin site." Eventually, William Bass (then at the University of Kansas), George Frison (University of Wyoming), and Dennis Stanford (Smithsonian Institution) all excavated there. And more recently, Matt Hill (Iowa State University) took a close look at the archaeofauna contained in the site's Folsom component.

Let's begin with Hill's conclusions. About 10,780 radiocarbon years ago, a small group of Folsom hunters camped at the Agate Basin site in late March or early April. They killed at least 11 bison (*Bison antiquus*) and 5 pronghorn antelope (*Antilocapra americana*), probably not too far from their camp. They partially butchered the bison at the kill site and, for the most part, brought entire limbs back to camp. They field-dressed the antelope at the kill site and brought the nearly intact carcasses back to the camp. Despite their success, the hunters may have had a hard time making ends meet: unlike later hunter-gatherers on the Plains, these Folsom hunters seem not to have relied heavily on meat storage.

These are remarkable conclusions. How did Hill extract all this information from a bunch of broken bones?

Identifying Bones

Hill began by identifying the bones from the Folsom component, working through the cataloged collection, piece by piece, and assigning each bone or bone fragment to a species, if possible.

"Identifying the bones" is more complicated than it might sound. Field archaeologists know, at least in a rough way, what mammal, bird, reptile, and fish bones look like, but far more detailed information is needed in faunal analysis. The first step is to assign each specimen to **element** (the anatomical part of the body). Is this bone a rib splinter, part of the pelvis, or a skull fragment? A femur, tibia, or calcaneus (the heel bone)? Identifying elements requires a solid working knowledge of comparative anatomy (Figure 8-1).

But conventional comparative anatomy classes are insufficient because they deal with whole bones—not the dirty fragments that archaeologists confront. Classroom experience helps, but you really learn faunal analysis by handling a lot of bones yourself.

The next step is to identify the specimens to **taxon** (kind of animal). One's success here depends on the

kill sites Places where animals were killed in the past.

faunal analysis Identification and interpretation of animal remains from an archaeological site.

zooarchaeologist (also **faunal analyst**) An individual who studies the faunal (animal) remains recovered from archaeological sites.

element In faunal analysis, a specific skeletal part of the body—for example, humerus or sternum.

taxon In faunal analysis, the classification of a skeletal element to a taxonomic category—species, genus, family, or order.

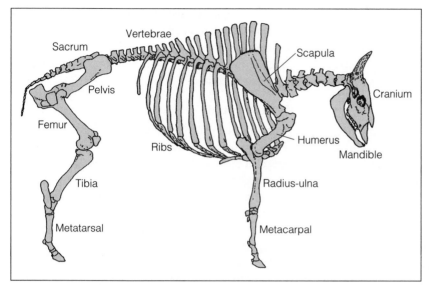

Figure 8-1 Bison skeleton showing major elements.

these identifications using a **comparative collection.** The standard zooarchaeology lab contains box after box of modern animal skeletons—everything from elephants to deer mice. Each box is labeled with the species, the individual's approximate age at death, its sex, and where and when it was collected. A comparative collection contains examples of young and old, as well as male and female, members of a species. These collections are put together by hunting or trapping the animals, picking up road kills (you need a license to do these things in most states), or acquiring carcasses from a state fish and game office (sometimes confiscated from poachers).

Once collected, the specimens are manually defleshed and cleaned. Sometimes the remains are buried and nature is allowed to take its course. Other methods include simmering the bones in a solution of detergent or placing the greasy bones in a colony of dermestid beetles, which, over a few weeks' time, will literally pick the bones clean of all tissue.

Using such a comparative collection, Hill identified the archaeological bones to taxon. Measurements taken on some adult bones helped determine if the bone was from a male or female.

Hill eventually assigned all the Agate Basin bones to element and taxon (or size class). Most bones were bison (1033) or pronghorn (297), but other species included wolf, striped skunk, and frogs. But because there were only a few bones from these species, Hill focused on the bison and pronghorn.

condition of the specimen and the expertise of the analyst. The aim is to identify each bone to species, but sometimes the bones are so fragmentary that you can only identify them to higher-order groups, such as family or class. For instance, one can rarely determine whether a long bone fragment (that is, a small piece of one of the long limb bones, such as a femur shaft fragment) came from a deer or a bighorn sheep—but anyone can tell that it's not a mouse bone. In this case, the analyst might only be able to identify the fragment to the order *Artiodactyla* (because deer and sheep are in different families, the next-broader level of classification is used). Identification to taxon, therefore, often means "narrowing down the possibilities," rather than identifying the exact species—although that is always preferred.

In other cases, the specimen might be so difficult to identify that you can only assign it to one of five standard animal **size classes.** Rodent- and rabbit-sized animals are in size class 1; wolf- and pronghorn antelope–sized animals are class 2; animals the size of mule deer and bighorn sheep are in size class 3; bison- and elk-sized animals are in class 4; and in class 5 are large animals such as giraffes and elephants.

So, how did Hill know whether a scrap of bone was from a bison femur, a pronghorn radius, a peccary tibia, or a skunk skull? The zooarchaeologist makes

size classes A categorization of faunal remains, not to taxon, but to one of five categories based on body size.

comparative collection A skeletal collection of modern fauna of both sexes and different ages used to make identifications of archaeofaunas.

Natural or Cultural?

Recalling the discussion of taphonomy in Chapter 7, you should be wondering how Hill could be certain (1) that the bison and pronghorn remains were deposited by humans and (2) that they were deposited during the same occupation of the site.

For one thing, the bones bore some stone tool cut marks (which we know how to distinguish from carnivore tooth marks), some were burned, and some of the larger ones had impact fractures—distinctive breaks that resulted when the Folsom people smashed the bones open to retrieve the fatty, calorie-rich marrow. Frison and Stanford also found a cluster of antelope bones, some of them burned, around a hearth.

A few of the bones did show evidence of carnivore gnawing. But tooth marks appeared on only a few bison humeri and femora, and on only three antelope specimens. So, the evidence pointed to humans as the agents responsible for the antelope and bison bones at Agate Basin.

Hill also thinks that the antelope and bison bones were deposited during the same occupation of the site. The Folsom assemblage is not large, nor is it widely dispersed; some of the remains, in fact, still lie in anatomical position. This is what we would expect to see in a one-shot use of the site. Also, we might expect all the bones to be equally weathered, just as we saw at the Hudson-Meng site in Chapter 7—an "instantaneous" herd death, where nearly all the skulls were weathered in the same way.

To reach this conclusion, Hill took bone size into account. Because antelope bones are smaller than bison bones, they are more easily broken (by carnivores and also by hunters, who broke the bones for their marrow). Because they're smaller, sediment will cover antelope bones more quickly than the larger bison bones. So, even if all the faunal remains were deposited at about the same time, the bison bones should be slightly more weathered than the antelope bones. This was the case at Agate Basin, and Hill concluded that the bison and antelope bones in the Folsom component were animals killed by the same people during the same occupation.

What to Count?

To reconstruct human behavior at Agate Basin, Hill needed to search for meaningful patterns in the bone data, and this required that he count the bones.

Zooarchaeologists count bones in two ways, depending upon their objectives. One method involves the **number of identified specimens,** or **NISP.** This count is simply the total number of bone specimens that are identified to a particular taxon. Table 8-1 shows the NISP for the Folsom component at the Agate Basin site. NISP is useful for comparing large numbers of collections from different sites, but it has a severe limitation in reconstructing human behavior at a single site.

Table 8-1 suggests that bison were more important than pronghorn at Agate Basin. But what if the 1033 bison specimens came from a single highly fragmented skeleton, whereas each of the 297 antelope bones came from 297 different individuals? If so, then antelope would be many times more important than bison.

Problems like this have led archaeologists to another way of counting bones, called the **minimum number of individuals,** or **MNI.** Developed by paleontologists, MNI is the *minimum* number of individuals that are necessary to account for all the skeletal elements of a particular species found in the site. Suppose, for instance, that you excavated 100 fragments of bison bone from a site. The NISP equals 100, but what is the MNI? That is, what is the minimum number of individual bison required to account for those 100 bone fragments?

To figure this out, you must tabulate bone frequency by element (left femur, right tibia, hyoid, and so on) to determine the most *abundant* skeletal element. This process requires that you not only assign the specimens their correct *element,* but for those bones that come in pairs, to their correct *side* as well. If four right femurs show up in the 100 bone fragments, then you know that *at least* four bison account for the fragments. But MNI has some limitations as well. When bones are fragmented, it is possible that the "four right femurs"

number of identified specimens (NISP) The raw number of identified bones (specimens) per species; a largely outmoded way of comparing archaeological bone frequencies.

minimum number of individuals (MNI) The smallest number of individuals necessary to account for all identified bones.

TABLE 8-1 NISP Counts for the Folsom Component at the Agate Basin Site

COMMON NAME	SCIENTIFIC NAME	NISP
Bison	Bison antiquus	1033
Pronghorn antelope	Antilocapra americana	297
Wolf	Canis lupus	7
Coyote	Canis latrans	3
Red fox	Vulpes vulpes	1
Striped skunk	Mephitis mephitis	1
Flat-headed peccary	Platygonus compressus	1
Dog	Canis sp. (possibly domestication)	5
Jackrabbit	Lepus cf. townsendii or californicus	10
Rabbit	Sylvilagus cf. mutallii or audubonii	4
Grouse	Centrocercus urophasianus	2
Frog	Rana pipiens	Few
Elk	Cervus elaphus (antler only)	2
Camel	Camelops sp. (possible tool)	1

Source: Hill (2001). The "sp." in some scientific names means that while the genus is certain, the species is not. The "cf." in other cases means that the specimen compares very well with one or two species within a genus, but that the researcher is not certain of the identification. Camel became extinct about 11,200 radiocarbon years ago, and there is no good evidence that humans ever hunted them; the specimen here might be a piece that a Folsom hunter picked up someplace.

are really fragments from the same upper leg bone. To eliminate this problem, you must compare the bone fragments, one by one, to see whether two fragments could have come from the same bone. In our hypothetical example, if we found that two of the four right femur fragments could have come from the same femur, then the MNI would only be three.

Calculating MNI also depends on how you divide your site. Agate Basin was probably occupied once by Folsom hunters for a few weeks. But what if the assemblage is the result of many different occupations, covering decades, or even longer? In that case, we could compute the minimum number of individuals, but this might have the unfortunate consequence of reducing hundreds of bone fragments to a possibly misleadingly very few MNI. Ultimately, the decision depends on the site's specific characteristics. In general, MNI is most useful and accurate when fine stratigraphic divisions are used and when bones are not overly fragmented. And the Folsom component at Agate Basin meets these criteria.

Where did Hill go from here? Of the 1033 bison bones, Hill could identify 843 to element; likewise, he could identify 198 of the 297 antelope bone fragments to element. Although the antelope specimens were fragmented, Hill identified four right and one left

humeri (upper arm bones). This might suggest an MNI of four (given that the single left humerus could be a match to one of the right humeri). But the single left humerus was not the same size as any of the right humeri, and so Hill concluded that *at least* five antelope were brought to the site.

Because they are larger and heavier, the bison bones were more intact. Taking the humeri, radii, femora, and tibiae, Hill assigned each to a side and then decided, using a comparative collection, whether they were male or female (or indeterminate; young animals don't exhibit characteristics that allow assigning to a sex). He then compared their sizes to see if the rights and lefts of each sex could possibly have come from the same animal, or whether the femora and tibiae, and the humeri and radii could *anatomically refit* (that is, would they fit together in their usual anatomical positions; femora and tibiae, for example, articulate at the patella, the knee cap). If they did refit, then they could have come from the same animal (Figure 8-2).

From this comparison, Hill determined that there were *at least* four males, four females, and three immature bison brought to the site.

So now we know the minimum number of animals that Folsom hunters killed at the Agate Basin site: 11 bison and 5 pronghorn antelope.

Figure 8-2 Anatomically refit calf bison humeri (*top*) and radii (*bottom*). Carnivore gnawing has removed the proximal (upper) end of the humerus on the right.

axial skeleton The head, mandibles, vertebrae, ribs, sacrum, and tail of an animal skeleton.

appendicular skeleton All parts of an animal excluding the axial skeleton.

Reconstructing Human Behavior at Agate Basin

By looking at which specific elements were present, Hill found that elements of the **axial skeleton** (the head, mandibles, vertebrae, ribs, sacrum, tail) for both bison and pronghorn were rare compared with bones from the **appendicular skeleton** (everything else). Bison limb bones were also more common relative to the other bison bones, and antelope lower leg bones (especially for the front legs) and toes were rare.

What accounts for these patterns?

Viewed as food, bones function two ways: as a support for meat and as a container of marrow. Experimental research can quantify how much food value a bone represents in terms of these two entities. Bison long bones, for instance, rank high in both meat and marrow content, suggesting that hunters brought back only the high-utility portions of the bison and left the axial skeleton at the kill site.

The pronghorn skeletons at the Agate Basin site were more complete than the bison skeletons. Apparently, the antelope were gutted and field-dressed by removing the feet and lower limb bones, which contain little marrow and have little meat wrapped about them. The hunters then carried the more or less complete carcasses back to camp. The ribs and vertebrae may have been crushed for bone grease or eaten by dogs and carnivores, as suggested by taphonomic research.

Ethnoarchaeological studies suggest some other possibilities. Hunters consider several factors when deciding which parts of an animal to transport home: the distance back to camp, the number of hunters present, weather, terrain, and food needs of the household. If the animal is killed near camp, women and children might come out to help carry the entire carcass of a large animal back. If so, then the entire skeleton might end up in the camp rather than at the kill site. If an animal is killed far from camp, the hunters might eat some of it immediately and then butcher the animal, bringing only meat and a very few bones back to camp. In this case, most of the skeleton would remain at the kill site (see "Looking Closer: Hunter-Gatherers as Optimal Foragers" for other thoughts on how foragers decide which foods to harvest).

Based on these ethnoarchaeological observations, Hill suggested that the Agate Basin hunters killed the animals individually, relatively close to camp. The smaller antelope were carried back with minimal field

LOOKING CLOSER
Hunter-Gatherers as Optimal Foragers

Figure 8-3 An Aché man hunts.

Optimal foraging theory helps to predict which foods foragers will harvest based on some principles borrowed from evolutionary ecology. In its most widely applied version, the diet-breadth model, optimal foraging asks, Which foods should a forager harvest from all those available if he or she wishes to maximize their *rate* of return? This model requires ethnoarchaeological and/or experimental research to determine the return rates of potential food resources.

Steven Simms (Utah State University), for instance, wanted to know the return rate of Indian ricegrass (*Oryzopsis hymenoides*) in the Great Basin. Because nobody collects ricegrass today, Simms did it himself, using a woven "seed beater" as Shoshone women had done a century before: After knocking the seeds into a basket, he ground them into flour using a stone mano and metate. In one such experiment, Simms processed 98 grams of ricegrass flour in 41 minutes; knowing that ricegrass contains 2.74 calories per gram, he calculated the return rate as follows: (2.74 calories/gram × 98 grams) / 41 minutes = 6.55 calories/minute, or 393 calories/hour.

Factoring in the necessary search time, the diet-breadth model predicts which resources a forager should use. Large game animals take a long time to find, but they have high return rates; plant foods are easier to find, but they require considerable processing. The diet-breadth model predicts that as high return rate resources become rare, the diet should expand to include lower return rate resources.

Kim Hill (University of New Mexico) and Kristen Hawkes (University of Utah) demonstrated this principle among the Aché, seasonal hunter-gatherers of Paraguay's tropical forest. Aché hunters take a range of animals while hunting with bows and arrows, including peccaries (65,000 calories/hour), deer (27,300 calories/hour), birds (4700 calories/hour), and monkeys (1200 calories/hour). But when the Aché began using shotguns, they could avoid lengthy periods of stalking (because firearms don't require the line of sight necessary for bow hunting). The optimal foraging model predicted that when shotguns were used, diet breadth should contract (as small birds and monkeys were ignored). When the Aché went back to using bows and arrows, the diet expanded to include the smaller game.

Optimal foraging models cannot account for foods that are eaten or shunned for cultural reasons: the model predicts only which foods should be taken *if maximization of the return rate is the only foraging goal*. But with such predictions as a backdrop to an analysis of archaeofaunas and botanical remains, optimal foraging models can help determine which foods were or were not eaten for purely cultural reasons.

butchery. However, because the bison could not be carried whole, it is likely that the Agate Basin hunters (and perhaps their wives and children) ate some of the meat attached to the vertebrae and ribs at the kill site and then transported the legs—with their large meat packages and high marrow content—to camp, using the lower limbs as convenient handles.

What Do Broken Toes Mean?

Although relatively rare there, some bison metapodials (portions of the foot) at Agate Basin, as well as bison and antelope phalanges (toe bones) were broken open, presumably to extract the marrow. But foot bones contain little marrow, and there is no meat attached to them. Why did the hunters bother with toes, when they apparently had bison haunches and antelope tenderloin roasting on the fire?

Hill interprets the foot bones as evidence that, despite the 11 bison and 5 antelope, the Agate Basin Folsom hunters were experiencing some hard times. From paleoclimatic data, we know that the average annual temperature was some 11° C colder during Folsom times. Perhaps late winter or early spring storms—which can strike with a vengeance on the high plains—made that day's hunt impossible. Or perhaps the meat stored in camp was frozen, leaving the camp's inhabitants with no choice but to extract marrow from low-utility elements, such as metapodials and phalanges.

Hill also concluded that these Folsom hunters were living more hand to mouth than did later hunter-gatherers on the high plains. The late winter and early spring is a tough season for hunter-gatherers, because game animals are lean (and lean meat is difficult to digest) and plants are not yet ripe. Many foragers survive the spring by relying on food stored from a previous fall hunt. But these Folsom hunters probably lacked stored food, because they were hunting on a weekly or even daily basis during the spring that they occupied the site.

This interpretation depends on knowing that the Folsom hunters camped at Agate Basin in the spring. How did Hill know this?

In What Season Was Agate Basin Occupied?

Recall from the discussion of seasonal rounds in Chapter 7 that hunter-gatherers do not spend the entire year in a single camp or village. Folsom hunters moved across the landscape; so did the nineteenth-century Shoshone in Nevada, and so do Mikea forager-horticulturalists. To understand what life was like in the past, we must pay attention to **seasonality,** the time of year that a site was used.

Hill determined the seasonality of Agate Basin by knowing that modern bison give birth during the last two weeks of April and the first two weeks of May. Hill assumed that bison in the past did likewise. This uniformitarian assumption seems justified because giving birth in the early spring allows calves the maximum time to mature before the next winter arrives. Even considering climate change, it is likely that the birthing season of modern bison approximates that of their ancient cousins.

Bone development and tooth eruption in modern bison also follow quite predictable schedules (as they do for all animals, including humans). Young animals are important here; indeed, once all their teeth have erupted, adults lose their value as seasonal indicators. The teeth of the youngest bison at Agate Basin showed that it was about 11 months old when it died. A second young bison had teeth that suggested an age of about 23 months. In other words, these two animals were just one month shy of their first and second birthdays, respectively. Assuming that these two bison were born in late April–early May, then they probably died in late March or early April. The presence of some fetal bison bones (either a late-term fetus or a newborn) supports this inference. With this information, Hill concluded that Folsom hunters occupied Agate Basin at the tail end of winter or the beginning of spring.

The Zooarchaeology of a Peruvian Civilization

Now that we know something about the basics of faunal analysis, let's jump to Peru, to see how these techniques work in a very different context.

The site of Chavín de Huántar (pronounced "cha-veen day whantar") is one of the most celebrated ceremonial centers in the Andes. It flourished from 850 to 200 BC, making it one of the earliest civilizations in

seasonality An estimate of the part of the year a particular archaeological site was occupied.

South America. Located at an elevation of nearly 3150 meters (10,000 feet) above sea level, Chavín de Huántar is ringed by snow-covered mountains (with peaks rising more than 5500 meters [18,000 feet]).

The initial settlement was a small ceremonial center surrounded by domestic structures that made up a vigorous highland community. Its location on a key trade route midway between the Peruvian coast and the lowland tropical forest to the east made Chavín de Huántar a natural trade center.

The site has given its name to the famous Chavín art style, which contains a range of fantastical and representational figures, usually combining the features of humans, snakes, jaguars, caymans (alligators), and birds with intricate geometrical and curvilinear motifs. The most elegant expression of the Chavín style is in the 150 stone carvings of the huge Chavín de Huántar temple complex (we discuss these images in Chapter 11).

The site's ceremonial buildings are honeycombed with rooms, passageways, stairways, vents, and drains (Figure 8-4). Inside the largest structure is a knife-shaped monolith 15 feet tall, set into a narrow, interior gallery. The top of the elaborately carved sculpture reached through the ceiling, into a gallery above, where the priests of Chavín de Huántar, acting as the voice of an oracle, may have spoken to the worshipers below.

Chavín's art and temple architecture attracts the attention of Andean archaeologists, but we also need to know something about the more mundane aspects of the Chavín lifeway.

What, for instance, did the Chavín people eat? We could look to the stone iconography expressed in their sculpture, but it is unlikely that people living at 10,000 feet in the Andes dined on alligator and jaguar. Religious iconography is not a very accurate reflection of everyday diet.

George Miller (California State University, Hayward) and Richard Burger (Yale University) took a more direct approach to the problem by looking at the trash of the center's several thousand inhabitants.

Figure 8-4 The main temple at Chavín de Huántar.

© Robert Kelly

When Burger excavated at Chavín de Huántar, he encountered subsistence remains in the domestic structures and refuse heaps around the ceremonial center, including some 12,000 fragments of discarded food bone.

These bones were identified, first to body part and then to taxon. Next, Burger computed the MNI for each of the three major cultural phases. He then estimated the "usable meat values" for each phase by multiplying the MNI figures per phase by the average animal's butchered weight for each taxon.

Early Patterns at Chavín de Huántar

Four kinds of camelids (animals of the family *Camelidae*) live today in the Andes. The llama was used mostly as a pack animal, and secondarily for its coarse hair. The alpaca was valued mostly for its fine and abundant fleece. Both of these domesticated species played important roles in religious rituals. *Guanacos* (wild llamas) were hunted as a source of meat. Finally, the vicuña, also a wild species, was hunted mostly for its extremely fine hair.

During the earliest or Urabarriu phase (900–500 BC), more than half the meat came from camelids (see Figure 8-5), and most of these were llamas. Stable isotope analysis (a technique we discuss in Chapter 9) of their bones suggests that these early llama herds consumed considerable quantities of maize and therefore were

probably domesticated. The other camelids were mostly vicuña.

White-tailed deer came in second (31 percent of the available meat). Skunk, large cats (either jaguar or puma), fox (or dog), and guinea pig bones also turned up in small numbers. The bones of some of these rarer animals may have been used for tools, rather than for food (although guinea pigs are today considered a delicacy in highland Peru). In other words, the Urabarriu phase bones strongly suggest a transitional pattern of mixed hunting and herding.

The Later Fauna at Chavín de Huántar

Things changed markedly during the subsequent Chakinani phase (500–400 BC). Deer frequencies drop off dramatically, and camelid frequencies jump to 83 percent, with llama bones becoming considerably more common than those of vicuña.

The large faunal sample from the terminal Janabarriu phase (400–200 BC) continues this trend: camelid bones constitute 93 percent of the assemblage. During this phase, the rapidly expanding population had virtually abandoned hunting in favor of domesticated llamas. This much seems clear.

But recall that Miller and Burger identified the bones from Chavín de Huántar to both taxon and element. The taxonomic changes through time indicated that subsistence activities changed markedly at Chavín de Huántar. But by looking at differential representation

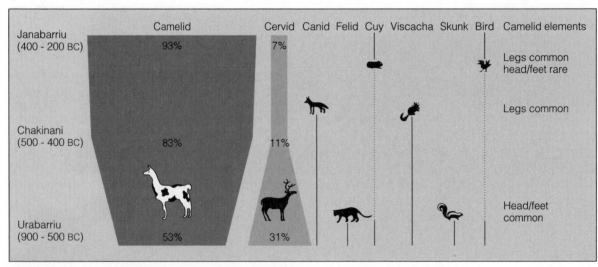

Figure 8-5 Changing relative abundance of the major animal groups in faunal remains at Chavín de Huántar. *After Miller and Burger (1995), Figure 4; courtesy of the authors and the Society for American Archaeology.*

of elements (that is, body parts), Miller and Burger explored the way in which the various animal products entered the community.

They found a curious pattern: the early Urabarriu camelid assemblage consisted mostly of head and foot bones. During the two subsequent phases, however, leg bones become considerably more frequent, with cranial and foot bones becoming rare. What does this pattern mean?

Camelid Taphonomy

As we pointed out in Chapter 7, interpretation requires middle-range theory, and one source of such theory is ethnoarchaeology. George Miller had conducted ethnoarchaeological research on contemporary South American pastoralists in the **puna,** the high grassy plateau of southern Peru. This experience helped him to analyze the remains excavated by Burger. Interestingly, Miller found that the bone refuse in modern herding communities mirrored almost exactly the early pattern from Chavín de Huántar: plenty of head and foot bones, and not many leg bones. Why?

Miller first considered the matter of bone survival. He conducted experiments on camelid bones to see which ones survive and which ones disappear. Not surprisingly, he found that the dense foot bones and enamel-covered teeth lasted much longer than the hollow leg bones and the relatively porous vertebrae.

Miller then looked at how butchering patterns might create a different representation of skeletal parts. Put simply, the process of modern camelid butchering accelerates the skewing effects already suggested from the bone density studies. Because people commonly break up leg bones to get at the marrow inside, such long bones often enter the archaeological record fragmented, and hence are more difficult to identify to element and taxon. Like other taphonomists, Miller discovered that when dogs gnaw on camelid remains, they consume spongy bones (such as vertebrae) almost entirely, but repeated gnawing leaves dense teeth and foot bones marked, but intact. In other words, the processes involved in differential preservation—bone density, butchering patterns, and carnivore gnawing—all operated to bias the modern faunal assemblage in precisely the manner observed from the early deposits at Chavín de Huántar.

But another factor is at work here, what Miller calls the "ch'arki effect." Today, herders of the puna preserve

llama and alpaca meat by alternately drying it out in the intense Andean sun, then freezing it during the cold, high-altitude nights. The product of this freeze-drying process—called **ch'arki** in the native Quechua language—has made its way into English as "jerky." But unlike the overpriced beef jerky peddled in gas stations throughout the United States, Peruvian ch'arki consists of meat dried on the bone. In general, the head and feet are cut off in the ch'arki-making process and eaten at home by the local herding communities. Ch'arki is a major trade item between the highland puna herders and those living in the intermontane valleys and along the Pacific coast today.

So, what is the archaeological evidence of ch'arki making?

The pattern depends entirely on whether you are making or receiving the ch'arki. If you're in the puna, where llama are herded and ch'arki is made, you will find lots of cranial and foot bones. These are the heavy, dense bones (without much meat attached) that nobody wants to drag around the Andes. So they are cut off and discarded, entering the archaeological record of the puna. But if you are on the receiving end of the ch'arki trade network—in the downhill intermontane valleys and along the coast—then the pattern is the opposite. The camelid bones you receive from the uplands are those still left adhering to the ch'arki chunks. So, your garbage will contain lots of leg bones and vertebrae, but not many skull parts or foot bones.

Given this simple taphonomic patterning based on behavior of modern camelid-herding communities, we can return to the bone assemblages from Chavín de Huántar and look at the bones in a more informed manner.

The Behavior behind the Bones

Remember that the faunal remains from the Chakinani (500–400 BC) and Janabarriu (400–200 BC) phases contained mostly camelid bones—llama and some vicuña, with deer frequencies dropping off markedly from earlier times. The rapidly expanding population

puna Native American (Quechua) term for the treeless, windswept tablelands and basins of the higher Andes.

ch'arki Native South American (Quechua) term for freeze-dried llama and alpaca meat.

LOOKING CLOSER

Palynology of Shanidar Cave: Why Formation Processes Matter

Whether Neanderthals intentionally buried their dead remains a hotly contested issue, and the palynology of Shanidar Cave has played an important role in this debate.

Shanidar Cave (Iraq) was occupied sporadically over the past 100,000 years. Ralph Solecki (then of Columbia University) discovered several Neanderthal skeletons (one of which was the inspiration for the shaman in Jean Auel's novel *The Clan of the Cave Bear*). One of these, Shanidar IV, was very fragile, and the entire block was removed in a plaster jacket and shipped to an Iraqi museum, where it sat for two years. Investigators eventually found that Shanidar IV contained three adults and an infant.

French palynologist Arlette Leroi-Gourhan (Musée de l'Homme, Paris) tested the Shanidar IV samples for pollen and—to everyone's surprise—found large amounts of well-preserved pollen near the feet, the shoulders, and the base of the spine of one individual. The ancient pollen concentrations came from at least seven species of brightly colored wildflowers, including grape hyacinth, bachelor's button, and hollyhock. Leroi-Gourhan suggested that the fresh flowers (which bloom in late May through early July) had been woven into the branches of a pinelike shrub. The pollen data suggested that this Neanderthal burial was a formal interment, with a degree of "humanness" that few were willing to grant Neanderthals at the time.

Some asked whether the pollen grains could have blown into the cave, and are merely "background pollen rain." If so, then flower pollen should have been typical of all of the cave's deposits, not just the grave. But it was not: the sediments outside the grave not only contained far *less* flower pollen than the burial pit, but the pollen grains in the burial fill were clumped (as if they had fallen from flowers laid into the grave). Some pollen even lay in the form of the flowers' anthers, suggesting that the entire flower

---

the Lehner site 11,000 years ago was only slightly wetter and cooler than today, followed by a rapid shift toward drier conditions. As many palynology studies have found, only a small shift in temperature and/or precipitation was required to produce dramatic differences in the environment at the Lehner Ranch site. And it may have been that slight change in rainfall and temperature that caused mammoths, horses, and a range of other animals to disappear from the southern Arizona landscape forever.

The main contribution of pollen analysis to archaeology is the reconstruction of environmental change. But properly applied, pollen studies can also help archaeologists understand past human behavior (see "Looking Closer: Palynology of Shanidar Cave: Why Formation Processes Matter"). And pollen also can play a role in figuring out what plants were important in prehistoric diet. An example from Nevada's Stillwater Marsh shows how and introduces other sources of paleoethnobotanical information.

What Plants Did People Eat in the Stillwater Marsh?

You recall from Chapter 3 that floods exposed dozens of archaeological sites and human burials in the Stillwater Marsh of Nevada's Carson Desert. We discuss the burials in the next chapter; here we focus on the plant remains recovered from one site.

Site 26CH1062 sits on a low clay dune and contains pits, postholes, and at least two ephemeral houses.

was once present. None of these patterns should exist if the pollen had simply blown into the cave.

But archaeology is never simple. Perhaps the pollen came into the site on flowers, but does this mean that the flowers were laid in the grave by the hands of a grieving Neanderthal?

Solecki noted that all the burials at Shanidar were riddled with rodent burrows, sometimes complete with dead rodents, identifiable as *Meriones persicus*, the Persian jird. This rodent hoards flower heads, neatly clipped from their stems, including those of the species that Leroi-Gourhan had identified. Jeffrey Sommer (University of Michigan) believes that such rodents could be responsible for assembling the Shanidar burial "bouquets," stored in chambers that just happened to be near the buried Neanderthals.

And so the search for convincing evidence of ritual and religion among Neanderthals continues—and we see why formation processes are so critical.

Figure 8-7 Neanderthal skull as it was being exposed at Shanidar Cave (Iraq). This person was probably killed by rooffall inside the cave.

People lived there at least twice, about 1400 and 1000 radiocarbon years ago.

We water screened all the sediments, and recovered a large number of stone tools, manufacturing waste flakes, shells, and faunal remains. We also floated sediment samples from several of the features and retrieved many carbonized macrobotanical remains. These we sent to paleoethnobotanist David Rhode (Desert Research Institute). Looking at the samples under a microscope, Rhode identified the carbonized seeds and charcoal using a comparative collection; most of the charcoal was reed (*Phragmites australis*), greasewood (*Sarcobatus* sp.), and willow (*Salix* sp.). These plants are found today in the Carson Desert, and they could have been firewood, or used in housing or tools.

Rhode also found the carbonized seeds of cattail, dock, seepweed, chenopods, pickleweed, silverscale, heliotrope, saltbush, and goosefoot. The site's inhabitants could have gathered any of these as food, and all, again, occur in the area today.

The most abundant seed was that of bulrush (*Scirpus* sp.), one of the many plants that the Paiute Indians gathered and ate in the nineteenth century. Experimental data show that bulrush seeds are an efficiently gathered and nutritious resource.

But *did* people collect bulrush for food? Maybe the seeds were attached to bulrush plants that were used to build shelter or baskets, and were accidentally burned. Were bulrush plants, and not just their seeds, present on the site? To answer this question we looked at another source of plant data in archaeological sites.

Phytoliths

Phytoliths, literally "plant stones," are microscopic plant opals. As plants take in water, they also take in silica and deposit it between cells, within cell walls, or in the cells themselves. Phytoliths occur in various grasses, as well as in rushes, sedges, palms, conifers, and deciduous trees. When plant material decays, the almost indestructible phytoliths are left behind.

Phytoliths take the shape of the cells in which they were deposited, and since different grasses have different cell shapes, their phytoliths also have different shapes. This means that we can identify the presence of certain kinds of plants long after those plants have decayed and disappeared. Phytolith analysis, therefore, is similar to pollen analysis, although phytoliths are not quite as identifiable to species as pollen.

Nonetheless, phytoliths were very useful in the Stillwater Marsh. Our sediment samples contained abundant well-preserved phytoliths. Most of these were from *Phragmites,* a common marsh grass. What was most intriguing, however, was the *absence* of sedge phytoliths (phytoliths produced by plants such as bulrush). This means that no bulrush plants decayed on the site.

Perhaps, then, there was no bulrush in the Stillwater Marsh 1000 years ago. Perhaps the seeds came in as seed cakes from another wetland, such as Walker Lake to the south. This is a question about the *regional* vegetative environment, and it is best answered through pollen data. So, we also took pollen samples from several of the site's features. Analysis showed these to contain pollen that is little different from the modern pollen rain; in fact, bulrush pollen was abundant.

So, now we know (1) that burnt bulrush seeds were present on the site, (2) that bulrush plants were not on the site, but (3) that bulrush was abundant in the wetland. We concluded that bulrush seeds were brought to the site to be eaten.

The macrobotanical remains told us that a range of wetland plants were harvested. But what was missing from the flotation samples was also intriguing: the seeds of upland plants such as ricegrass (*Oryzopsis hymenoides*) or piñon (*Pinus monophylla*) pine nut

hulls, both important food sources to the nineteenth-century Paiute. This suggests that when people lived in the Stillwater Marsh, they got their plant food exclusively from the wetland. They did not travel even a few kilometers into the low foothills to gather ricegrass, nor did they hike another 20 kilometers into the hills to gather piñon.

Site Seasonality

The seasonality of the Agate Basin site was determined using faunal remains, but at 26CH1062 we used the macrobotanical remains. Establishing seasonality from plant remains is a matter of determining the plant foods' seasons of availability. Recall that we found seeds of bulrush, cattail, seepweed, dock, chenopods, pickleweed, heliotrope, silverscale, saltbush, and goosefoot. We know that most of these seeds ripen in the mid- to late summer and into the early winter, although dock and heliotrope are gathered throughout the summer only. All of these resources, therefore, are only available in the late summer, and that is probably the best estimate of when the site was occupied, although an occupation from mid-summer into the late fall cannot be ruled out.

Coprolites of Hidden Cave

Human coprolites are another source of information on prehistoric diet. Paleontologists first used the term *coprolite* (from the Greek *kopros,* "dung," and *lithikos,* "stone") about 1830 to describe fossilized dinosaur feces. Archaeologists use the term, but the feces we analyze are desiccated, not fossilized. Although not commonly found, human coprolites are, for obvious reasons, an excellent source of information on human diet.

David Rhode studied the human coprolites found in Hidden Cave, which overlooks the Stillwater Marsh. This cave's opening was very small, barely large enough to crawl into; and even though the cave itself is a spacious chamber, it was a lousy place even to spend the night. The cave is dark and dusty and, if you made a fire, the chamber would soon fill with smoke. Thus, we were not surprised to find no hearths, stone tool waste flakes, or bones left over from meals. People did not live in Hidden Cave; instead, they used it as a place to cache various kinds of gear in pits.

But there were also many *quids*—expectorated pieces of plants (such as cattail and bulrush) that people

---

phytoliths Tiny silica particles contained in plants.

had chewed for their juices. And found nearby were bits of cordage, made from strips of bark rolled together. This suggests that people also used the cave as a place where they could escape the summer afternoon's heat, passing the afternoon by chewing succulent stalks of bulrush and cattail in the cave's cool interior while rolling bark together to make cords to tie together bundles, repair sagebrush bark sandals, or repair torn baskets.

Many of the artifacts found in Hidden Cave were projectile points; these might suggest that men were the primary visitors to the cave (we deal with such gender assumptions in Chapter 10). Rhode investigated the coprolites to see what the men who used the shelter were eating. He was surprised by what he found.

Rhode prepared the 19 coprolites by first soaking them in a solution of trisodium phosphate to reconstitute them. He then washed each specimen through fine mesh screens and dried the residue. Next, he examined and sorted this material under a microscope.

Rhode had a small macrobotanical remain from each coprolite radiocarbon-dated using accelerator mass spectrometry (AMS), and found that the coprolites fell into two time periods: one batch dated between 3800 and 3400 BP, the other from 1900 to 1500 BP. All of the coprolites contained abundant evidence of plants, fish, and bird remains (people may also have eaten large mammals, but obviously their bones would not appear in coprolites).

Bulrush seeds were common, as was cattail pollen. Rhode also found small waterfowl feathers, as well as the bones of tui chub, a minnow that lives in the Stillwater Marsh. In fact, fish cranial (head) and caudal (tail) bones tell us that these small fish were eaten whole. Insects showed up too, as well as snails.

Only one coprolite contained a piñon pine nut hull. Curiously, this coprolite, Number 167, also contained cattail seeds and pollen. This is interesting, because piñon nuts ripen in late September or early October, but cattail pollen is collected in July. Clearly, one of these resources must have been stored, and it was most likely the piñon, held over from the previous fall's harvest.

All this was interesting, but then came the surprise. We can determine if a man or woman voided a coprolite depending on the abundance of the sex hormones estradiol, progesterone, and testosterone. This is done using a complex technique known as *high-pressure liq-uid chromatographic analysis*. After applying this technique, Rhode found that the coprolites' levels of sex hormones indicated that *women* had voided the coprolites. We don't know if it was also women who cached the projectile points, spit out the quids, and spun the cordage. But coprolite analysis clearly opens up new approaches to diet as well as new approaches to reconstructing the ancient lives of men and women.

The Symbolic Meaning of Plants: The Upper Mantaro Valley Project

So far, we have talked about plants, animals, and people from a strictly economic perspective: What did people eat, and when did they eat it? But more can be done with archaeofaunas and macrobotanical remains. They can tell us not only how people interacted materially with their environment, but how they interacted with it symbolically as well. The Upper Mantaro Valley Project in Peru is one example.

The Upper Mantaro Valley sits at 3300 meters (about 10,800 feet) above sea level in the central Andes of Peru. The intensively settled and cultivated valley floors are surrounded by rocky hillsides, supporting a few rocky fields, but mostly grasses, a few shrubs, and small trees. And it has probably been that way since humans first moved in, several thousand years ago.

The Upper Mantaro Archaeological Project excavated numerous house compounds from six archaeological sites spanning the period AD 500–1500 (divided into six phases: Pancán 1 through 4, and Wanka II and III). During the Wanka II phase, the population of the Upper Mantaro aggregated into large, walled towns located on protected knolls just above the plains. This was a time of fighting between villages, and land use was restricted to areas close to the walled settlements. After the Inka conquest during Wanka III times, the population was relocated into villages on the valley floor.

As part of the excavations, researchers collected more than 900 6-liter sediment samples from the floors, middens, pits, and hearths encountered in each excavation unit. These contained thousands of pieces of charcoal and plant fragments, recovered by both dry screening and flotation. The recovered plant remains

LOOKING CLOSER

What Did Sixteenth-Century Colonists Eat in Spanish Florida?

Elizabeth Reitz (University of Georgia) and C. Margaret Scarry (University of North Carolina) have used historical documentation to chronicle subsistence practices in sixteenth-century Spanish Florida. Accounts from St. Augustine and elsewhere emphasize the chronic shortages of traditional Iberian foods and the substitution of less-valued New World resources. Why, then, would faunal analysis be useful to historical archaeology if documentary sources are available?

One reason is that significant biases and gaps often exist in documentary sources (see Chapter 12). Many important records were lost; letters often exaggerated (or falsified) the situation to elicit greater support from the Spanish crown. Contradictions in eyewitness accounts are common.

The main problem, however, is that the historic record for Spanish Florida rarely contains the mundane details that archaeologists need. Even though the contemporary accounts show that the Spanish were displeased with their new diet, there is no substitute for the physical evidence obtained through archaeological excavation. Reitz and Scarry synthesized the subsistence data recovered in excavations at St. Augustine and Santa Elena (South Carolina). Their results demonstrate the importance of dietary reconstruction in historical archaeology.

Many colonists found that their traditional Old World subsistence practices did not work in the New World. Key Iberian food crops failed miserably in coastal Florida, and the Spanish were forced to alter their husbandry techniques.

Lacking any sophisticated ecological knowledge, the settlers had to pass through a period of adjustment and experimentation. The Spanish tried to cater to the traditional preference for mutton, but sheep could not defend themselves against wild dogs and wolves and would not reproduce freely. Several species, especially marine fishes, first filled the gap left by mutton; however, the meat supply of Spanish Florida eventually shifted to beef and especially pork.

The colonists of Spanish Florida tried to raise their favorite Old World crops, particularly wheat and grapes. But they noted how successfully the Native Americans grew their own indigenous crops, and soon the Spaniards were supplementing their harvests with maize, beans, and squash (the native peoples, in turn, adopted the Spanish peach).

In effect, the Spanish strategy shifted toward an essentially aboriginal subsistence pattern, complemented by those European domesticates that could survive and prosper. Considerably more than half of the meat consumed in St. Augustine and Santa Elena by both Spanish settlers and aborigines derived from wild species, especially deer, shark, sea catfish, drum, and mullet. Spaniards also ate small mammals—such as opossums, squirrels, and raccoons—which they disparagingly termed "the scum and vermin."

The subsistence pattern that emerged at St. Augustine was a fusion of the various elements available to the Spanish colonists. Despite adopting many aboriginal items, the St. Augustine diet remained distinctly Spanish, processed through the unmistakably Spanish institutions of the slaughterhouse and the marketplace. Occasionally, the rare supply ship from home would provide European delicacies, such as olives, walnuts, and hazelnuts.

St. Augustine was established 70 years after the Spaniards began colonizing the New World, and some valuable lessons had been learned in this interval. Nevertheless, Reitz and Scarry found that significant dietary adaptations were still necessary to cope with the conditions of coastal Florida. And once established, the balance remained virtually unchanged for the next two centuries.

RAPID REVIEW   Classes of Data from Plant and Animal Remains in Archaeological Sites

Faunal Remains

- NISP (number of identifiable specimens), provides measure of abundance and diversity of animals

- MNI (minimum number of individuals), another measure of abundance, most useful where stratigraphic associations are very clear

- Butchering patterns, based on cut marks and breakage; reconstruct diet and trade

- Seasonality, using ages of animals based on tooth eruptions

Plant Remains

- Macrobotanical remains, provide measures of abundance and diversity of plant remains; usually retrieved as burnt remains, or in coprolites

- Phytoliths, used to reconstruct the presence of particular plants on a site

- Palynology, used to reconstruct past environments from pollen

- Seasonality, based on plants' schedules of growth and maturation

---

were classified into three simple categories: grass, stem (small-diameter twig fragments), and wood (pieces of mature wood). The wood category was further subdivided if the tree species could be identified.

Paleoethnobotanists Christine Hastorf (University of California, Berkeley) and Sissel Johannessen (U.S. Army Corps of Engineers) examined these flotation samples to analyze the changing patterns of fuel use. People can burn many different things to cook food and to heat their homes. Grass, tied in tight bundles, small twigs, dung from herbivores, and, of course, mature wood can all be used. What does it mean if people use one source rather than another?

Hastorf and Johannessen found that grass, twigs, and mature wood were all used for fuel, and that mature wood was always the dominant fuel source. But it is the relative frequencies, rather than the absolute figures, that matter. Figure 8-8 graphs the ratio of wood to stems and wood to other (stems and grass) fuel sources for the six phases that cover the 1000-year-long sequence of the Upper Mantaro Valley. Prior to AD 1300 (during the Pancán phases), the relative proportion of mature wood fragments dropped, meaning that over time people used more grass and

stems as fuel, rather than mature wood. Then, during Wanka II and III times, this trend reversed, with stems and grass remains decreasing.

Hastorf and Johannessen also noted that the species composition of the mature wood shifted through time. Up to 40 different kinds of wood are present in the Upper Mantaro Valley samples, with no particular taxa being especially dominant. But the most common taxa did change in relative frequency through time. The five most popular wood types during the early Pancán phases (from yet-unidentified trees) dropped out entirely by Wanka II times. And beginning around AD 1300, new wood types appeared. One notable example is *Buddleia* sp. (known as *quishuar* in Quechua), a high-elevation tree that became the most popular fuel source during Inka (Wanka III) times.

What Explains Wood Use?

Let's work through the analysis step by step, following the arguments developed by Hastorf and Johannessen. First, we must consider whether the charcoal distributions on the diagram in Figure 8-8 can be attributed to factors other than fuel use; to changes, for instance,

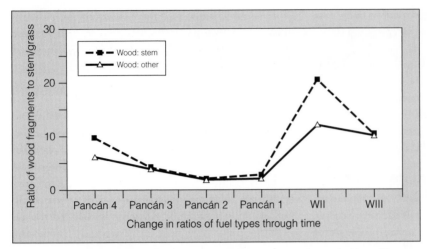

Figure 8-8 The changing ratios of wood to other fuel types through time in the Upper Mantaro area of Peru. *After Hastorf and Johannessen (1991); courtesy Christine Hastorf.*

in house construction materials, subsistence, or differential plant preservation through time.

Hastorf and Johannessen rejected all these possibilities. They noted that most of the charcoal comes from fire refuse accumulated over a span of several months or years. Although some of the charcoal may have come from inadvertent fires (such as accidental burning of thatch roofs), the investigators assume that the majority of the charcoal reflects intentional fuel use for heating and cooking. They also note that the composition of the house compounds (mud and stone), the general subsistence remains, and the depositional contents are basically constant throughout the 1000-year sequence. And there is little reason to believe that rates of preservation changed significantly through time.

Hastorf and Johannessen then moved to interpret the charcoal distributions strictly in terms of changing fuel-use patterns. Beginning their paleoethnobotanical analysis in standard fashion, they first determined whether the archaeological patterning of fuel use revealed long-term shifts in the relationship between these highland people and their environment.

From this strictly economic perspective, the increased reliance through time on twigs and grasses during the Pancán sequence is just what one might expect in a relatively treeless landscape. Through time, the growing human population and more intensive agricultural land-use patterns made fuel wood scarce. It makes sense that, as people denuded their landscape of trees, they turned to less-desirable fuels, such as small

shrubby plants, twigs, and grasses.

But if this is so, then why would this trend reverse during later Wanka times? Contrary to strictly ecological expectations, the archaeologically recovered plant remains show that the use of high-quality fuels actually *increased* after AD 1300.

Perhaps the evidence from settlement pattern archaeology provides a clue. Beginning in Wanka II times, an elite class began social and political consolidation of the area. Maybe this elite class mandated some sort of fuel management program, perhaps in the form of tree cultivating, resulting in a greater availability of mature wood sources. This scenario is certainly possible, because we know that tree cultivation was practiced during Inka times.

Fuel, of course, has an important economic role in Andean life, especially at an elevation in excess of 3300 meters where the days, to say nothing of the nights, are cold. The increased fuel management/tree cultivation explanation provides a workable, rational answer in economic terms, but leaves several questions unanswered:

- Why does the change take place in Wanka II times? Why not earlier (when the population first increased) or later (when the Inka took over and restructured the location of the production system)?
- Why would cultivation be chosen to alleviate the fuel shortage? Why not simply go farther afield to gather fuel? Or why not just shift to lower-quality fuels?
- And why do certain tree taxa show up during Inka times, when they were absent before?

At this point, Hastorf and Johannessen decided to explore explanations that went beyond conventional economic and ecological factors. They delved into the ethnographic and ethnohistoric records to document the relationships among Andean people, the upland forest, and traditional fuel sources. In so doing, Hastorf and Johannessen found that wood is more than simply fuel in the Andes. It also has an important symbolic dimension.

Collecting fuel was an important aspect of Inka life, consuming up to 4 hours each day for some segments of the population. We know from documentary accounts that logs, kindling, and straw were also important tribute items in the Inka state.

But trees also had important, symbolic connotations in Andean cosmology. Certain sacred trees were planted at administrative sites. Others were symbolically linked with deities. In fact, the Inka burned *quishuar,* the wood that appeared during Wanka III times, in large quantities at festivals and ritually burned human figures carved of *quishuar* as sacrifices to the divine ancestor of the Inka dynasty. Trees were also symbolically associated with water, as well as with women, clouds, winter, and the moon.

From these and other ethnohistoric and ethnographic examples, Hastorf and Johannessen concluded that wood had strong symbolic as well as economic roles in Inka life, being used to cement social relations (perhaps because it was so important and so rare). Brothers-in-law, for instance, sometimes provided wood and straw to relatives at a wake.

Relating Ideology to the Past

Hastorf and Johannessen supplemented their ecological perspective with a new appreciation of the cultural relationship between ancient Andean people and their environment. But why did the change take place in Wanka II times?

Hastorf and Johannessen argue that the ideology associated with the planting of certain trees could have been a factor in establishing the local political consolidation occurring at the time: the tree symbolized family continuity on the land, with the roots symbolizing ancestors and the fruits, the children. In fact, a ritual step in contemporary marriage ceremonies is termed "to bring the branch" and involves the bringing forth of ritual offspring. The dramatic increase in the use of *quishuar* might thus be attributed to its ritual significance of bringing social groups together into larger entities, rather than simply its mundane use as firewood.

These investigators believe that the act of planting trees—which could be interpreted as a purely economic response to a fuel shortage—was chosen from the other available alternatives because of cultural values concerning the ways in which cultivation and trees functioned as symbols of life and lineage, socially and politically.

Conclusion: Economic and Non-economic Explanations

This chapter has illustrated how archaeologists go about investigating the relationships among people, plants, and animals. From these remains we can determine what plants and animals people ate, what seasons of the year they were taken, and what sorts of tactics were used to hunt or gather them. They can help reconstruct trade relations. Often, archaeologists view information from plant and animal remains as evidence of ancient peoples' purely materialistic and mundane relations with their environment. And often, that is correct.

But the final example from Peru suggests that our interpretations of the past may often be layered, and that material interactions with the environment may have symbolic importance as well.

Summary

- Plant and animal remains aid in the reconstruction of past diet and environments. Dietary reconstructions mean little without their environmental context.

- Faunal analysis—the study of animal remains in archaeological sites—can provide direct evidence of which species were hunted (or collected) for food, how many animals were killed, how they were captured, and what butchering methods were employed.

- Faunal remains can help establish the season of the year when a site was occupied using animal birthing and tooth eruption schedules.

- Plant remains are also powerful sources of data regarding ancient life. Flotation is the most commonly used method for recovering carbonized plant remains from archaeological sites.

- Palynology—the study of pollen—is most useful in reconstructing past *regional* environments. Pollen diagrams enable us to document how local and regional vegetation has changed through time.

- Plant remains are important to paleoenvironmental reconstruction but are also direct evidence of which plant species were exploited, the season of site occupation, and plant processing technology.

- Phytoliths, small grains of silica that form inside plant stems, are less sensitive indicators of plants on a site, but can demonstrate which plant stems (as opposed to seeds) were present on a site.

- Coprolites (desiccated feces) provide evidence of what people ate. They are especially useful indicators of plants (because some seeds pass through undigested) and small animals (because their bones, feathers, or fur may also pass through). Coprolites also tell us what people ate in a single day and hence can point to food storage practices.

- People's interaction with the environment has an economic basis, but culture may frequently place layers of symbolic meaning on top of that interaction.

Media Resources

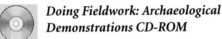

Doing Fieldwork: Archaeological Demonstrations CD-ROM

This CD gives you a vivid glimpse of what it is like to be involved in an archaeological dig . . . without leaving your chair. With this CD, you will see archaeologists involved in actual excavations—many of which are referenced in your Thomas/Kelly text—using a number of the field techniques covered in this chapter. Organized according to the various stages of a live excavation, the CD presents hands-on interactive activities, live-action demonstration videos, and quizzes to help you better understand the processes and techniques that are important to an excavation.

The Companion Website for Archaeology: Down to Earth, *Third Edition*

http://anthropology.wadsworth.com/thomas_kelly3e_down/

Supplement your review of this chapter by going to the companion website to take one of the practice quizzes, use the flash cards to master key terms, and check out the many other study aids that are designed to help you succeed in your introductory archaeology course.

9 Bioarchaeological Approaches to the Past

Outline

Exhumation of an unknown post–Civil War Era white settler at the Bordeaux Trading Post in Wyoming. The man was shot in the hip and between the eyes with a large-caliber weapon. His hat covers his face, a typical burial ritual in the late nineteenth-century West.

© George Gill

Preview

THIS CHAPTER EXAMINES bioarchaeology, a specialty that straddles the fields of archaeology and biological anthropology. Bioarchaeologists study the human biological component of the archaeological record. Some bioarchaeologists study the origin and distribution of ancient diseases; others reconstruct human diets, analyze the evidence for biological stress in archaeological populations, and reconstruct past demographic patterns—all of this by exploring human bone, bone chemistry, and the DNA preserved in human tissues. Although this chapter is a bit heavy on chemistry and biology, the archaeological payoff is worth the effort.

The analysis of human remains today is a sensitive subject in many parts of the world. Handling, photographing, and sampling the physical remains of a once-living, breathing human being is upsetting to many Native Americans (and, really, to plenty of other Americans as well). These concerns surfaced in the Kennewick case that we introduced in Chapter 1. Here, we discuss the astonishing amount of information that science can learn from human skeletal remains (and this chapter merely scratches the surface). In the process, we demonstrate how scientists can conduct such studies in a respectful and sensitive manner. No skeletal remains of Native Americans are portrayed in this or any other chapter.

Introduction

In Chapter 4, we described Kelly's archaeological survey project in the Carson Desert of western Nevada. We mentioned that the survey had failed to find many archaeological sites in the marsh because they were obscured by sand and vegetation. However, in the mid-1980s, the greatest floods to strike the Carson Desert in a millennium exposed many sites in the marsh.

But more was exposed than arrowheads and faunal remains. Kelly visited the marsh in the summer of 1986, while the Nevada State Museum was recording the new archaeological sites for the U.S. Fish and Wildlife Service (on whose lands most of the new sites were located). Many of the newly exposed sites were accessible only by airboat. Jetting up to the shore of one site, Kelly saw several human skulls rolling about in the wake. The flood had exposed not only many new sites, but dozens of human burials as well.

In 1987, after the floodwaters had receded, Kelly returned to the Stillwater Marsh to excavate one of the habitation sites (Site 26CH1062, mentioned in Chapter 8) and to survey the marsh for burials and human bone. By this point, Clark Spencer Larsen (Ohio State

University), a noted **bioarchaeologist,** had joined the team. Bioarchaeologists like Larsen study the human biological component of the archaeological record. Larsen received graduate training in biological anthropology, with a focus on the human skeleton as a record of past human activity. But because he worked with skeletal remains recovered from archaeological sites, Larsen was fully aware of the complex nature of archaeological data as well.

A well-trained field archaeologist can tell the difference between human and animal bones. But few archaeologists are trained to go beyond such simple identification. When modern archaeologists expect to encounter human remains—as did Kelly when he approached the Stillwater Marsh—they involve a bioarchaeologist from day one. And if those remains are Native American, as they were at Stillwater Marsh, archaeologists likewise involve the appropriate American Indian community (or communities). And so, before proceeding further, we'd like you to know that all the data collection discussed in this chapter was approved beforehand by the local Native American community (see "Looking Closer: Native Americans and the Stillwater Burials").

In 1987, we surveyed the previously flooded portions of the wetland, looking for new archaeological sites and human remains. Along with the Nevada State Museum, we recovered the remains of more than 500 individuals. This was significant because the Stillwater finds *tripled* the number of human burials known from the entire state of Nevada. These remains were studied by Larsen and a team of bioarchaeologists he assembled to handle specific analyses.

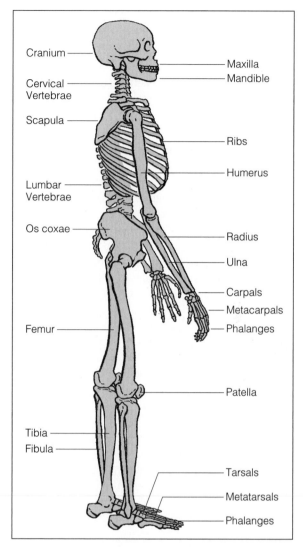

Figure 9-1 Some major bones of the human skeleton.

Skeletal Analysis: The Basics

Larsen first had to confirm that all the bones collected by the survey team were in fact human. After all, the flood had washed out plenty of archaeological midden, scattering ancient and recent animal bone among the human remains. Although human bone is distinctive, archaeological skeletal remains are often fragmented and weathered, making them difficult to identify. We have seen surgeons who were unable to identify a bone scrap as a piece of a human femur. But archaeologists are accustomed to seeing things in their broken, dirty, smashed forms. Larsen learned how to

identify bone through classes in human anatomy and **osteology,** but his real skill was acquired simply by handling thousands of human bone fragments. Figure 9-1 shows some of the major bones of the human skeleton, including ones mentioned in this chapter.

Bioarchaeologists working with bones from grave sites are accustomed to working with well-defined sets

bioarchaeology The study of the human biological component evident in the archaeological record.

osteology The study of bone.

LOOKING CLOSER
Native Americans and the Stillwater Burials

Looters first found the Stillwater burials, looking for skulls to decorate their fireplace mantels. But dedicated amateur archaeologists raised a cry, and soon the local Fallon Paiute-Shoshone Tribe asked that the U.S. Fish and Wildlife Service (USFWS) protect their heritage. The USFWS increased patrols of the marsh, began a public education campaign to reduce looting, and with the Nevada State Museum, collected and recorded more than 4000 human remains and 140 burials exposed by the flooding.

Although no legislation at the time protected American Indian burials, in the 1980s archaeologists were sensitive to the issue, and everyone felt the need to do the right thing. But what would that be?

The first right thing was to involve the local Fallon Paiute and Shoshone Indian community. Local solutions always work better than those imposed by a distant government, and it helps if those involved are genuinely respectful of the other side. USFWS archaeologist Anan Raymond was the right person for this task, and he consulted with the tribe immediately. At first, the tribe wanted the remains to stay where they were found. But knowing about the looters, the tribe agreed that endangered burials should be excavated, and less threatened burials would be covered over (with their location plotted on a USFWS map, so they could be monitored). The chair of the Fallon tribe, Richard Hicks, inspected every burial located during our archaeological survey, and we excavated only those for which he gave permission.

Although the tribe consented to nondestructive analysis, they were hesitant to allow radiocarbon dating, stable isotope analysis, or the cutting of long bones to obtain cross sections. But because tribal members were interested in what these analyses might tell them, they permitted destructive analyses provided that (1) the tribe approve the studies, (2) such analyses be kept to a minimum, and (3) we use already broken bones.

Although the tribe requested that all remains be reburied, Raymond wanted the remains preserved for the future. Working together, they eventually decided on a novel approach: a subterranean crypt that satisfied the tribe's wish to reinter the remains, but that would safely store the burials for future analyses. Today, the Stillwater burials rest in small, individual redwood coffins in a large, ventilated concrete vault buried on USFWS land. The vault's door has two locks; the USFWS has one key, and the tribe has the other.

Although the tribe had the power to shut off any analysis, it elected not to and, as a result, some good scientific research was completed. This is because (1) the tribe was involved from the start (rather than as an afterthought), (2) the scientific issues were described in terms that everyone could understand, and (3) most important, the tribe had a seat at the table—one of genuine authority, respect, and power.

of remains, each from a single individual; this is why, unlike zooarchaeologists, bioarchaeologists are rarely concerned with issues of minimum number of individuals (MNI) or number of identified specimens (NISP).

burial population A set of human burials that come from a limited region and a limited time period. The more limited the region and the time period, the more accurate will be inferences drawn from analysis of the burials.

Instead, bioarchaeologists are concerned with whether the human remains constitute a **burial population,** individuals who came from a specific area and who died over a relatively short period of time (as might be found in a historic period cemetery). The Stillwater burials, however, came from a 16-square-kilometer area of marsh, not a single, well-defined cemetery. Few of the burials contained any grave goods (meaning that we could not use temporal types to place the burials within archaeological phases). And only a few of the burials were dated by accelerator mass spectrometry (AMS) radiocarbon determinations. But these dates, as well as those from nearby sites, however, suggested that most of the burials dated to the Underdown phase, AD 500–1300.

Good preservation conditions provide the bioarchaeologist with a nearly complete human skeleton. But sometimes, only the hardest bones survive—parts of the skull, the central portions of the limb bones, and—the hardest portion of the human skeleton—the teeth. We've seen burials where nothing remained except for an eerie smile in the sand.

Ancient cultural practices can also mix human skeletal remains together and make it difficult to group skeletal remains by individual. Many eastern Native American tribes, for example, laid bodies out in a **charnel house,** where the body was allowed to decompose in the open. Eventually, the bones were cleaned of remaining flesh, bundled together, and ritually placed into a communal grave (these are known as **bundle burials**). Over time, the bones of various individuals would commingle. Careful excavation might be able to regroup bones by individual, but sometimes this is impossible. In other cases, as at the Stillwater Marsh, post-depositional processes scatter the once-intact burials. In fact, of the 500 individuals recovered, only 54 were encountered as intact burials. In this chapter, we focus on the analysis of those remains.

Determining Sex

After removing any nonhuman bones from the collection, Larsen assigned sex and age to the intact burials. How can we determine sex from bones? One obvious place where men and women differ is the pelvic area. Evolution designed women's hips (the hips are technically composed of two halves, the right and left *os coxae* or *innominates*) to birth children; as a result, the **sciatic** (pronounced "sy-*a*-tik") **notch,** a U-shaped indentation in each os coxa's posterior (rear) portion, is wider in women than in men. There is variation among the world's population in *how much* wider, but within a burial population, one can usually see a clear difference between those os coxae with wide and those with narrow sciatic notches.

Unfortunately, the os coxae are porous, making them some of the first bones to decompose. So, if preservation is not excellent, the bioarchaeologist must look elsewhere.

The human skull also provides clues to a deceased individual's sex. Adult male skulls tend to be more robust than female skulls, with heavier brow ridges over the eyes, larger mastoid processes (two protrusions of bone on the bottom of the skull, one beneath each ear), and more rugged muscle attachments. Male skulls also tend to have squarer chins and eye orbits. A skilled bioarchaeologist can often "sex" a skull simply by its feel. Again, the world's populations vary in how robust or how gracile male and female skulls are; but within a burial population, bioarchaeologists can usually detect discernible differences between *adult* male and female skulls. The sex of a child, however, is difficult to determine because the sexually distinctive characteristics of bone do not develop until young adulthood.

Larsen found that the Stillwater collection contained almost twice as many males as females, but sex could not be assigned to a large number of the burials (because some of the adult burials were poorly preserved or were missing key elements; others were the skeletons of children).

Determining Age

Age at death is next. Here, like a zooarchaeologist, Larsen used osteological standards based on comparative collections. Because the pattern and timing of crown formation and tooth eruption is consistent among human populations, teeth are extremely useful for telling the age of younger individuals. Larsen determined age by recording which teeth had formed their crowns and/or erupted through the mandible or maxilla (the lower and upper jaw bones, respectively).

charnel house A structure used by eastern North Americans to lay out the dead where the body would decompose. The bones would later be gathered and buried or cremated.

bundle burial Burial of a person's bones, bundled together, after the flesh has been removed or allowed to decay off the bones.

sciatic notch The angled edge of both halves of the posterior (rear) side of the pelvis; measurement of this angle is used to determine sex in human skeletons. Although its width varies among populations, narrow notches indicate a male and wider notches indicate a female.

Patterns of bone fusion are also useful for determining age in skeletons of youths and young adults. At birth, many bones are actually several different pieces. The long bones, such as the femora or humeri, are made up of the central shaft and the two **epiphyses**—the ends that articulate with other bones. The epiphyses fuse to the shaft at known rates. For example, the proximal epiphysis of the radius (*proximal* refers to the end of a long bone that is closest to the body's center, in this case, the end of the radius closest to the elbow; *distal* refers to the end of the long bone farthest from the body) completely fuses by about age 19, whereas portions of the scapula do not fuse until age 23. Noting to what extent various bones are fused can estimate an individual's age at the time of their death.

But most bones are fully fused by age 25 and, by that same age, most teeth have erupted. Therefore, other methods are required to age the skeletons of mature adults, and these are more difficult to implement. The first of these is bone wear. After age 30, bones begin to wear down. Much of the wear is related to a person's activity level (as well as diet). But some bones tend to wear no matter what. One particularly sensitive area is the **pubic symphysis,** the place where the right and left os coxae meet in a person's groin area. As the cartilage between the two halves erodes with age, the symphysis undergoes distinct changes. At age 20, for example, the symphysis has a distinct set of surface ridges that look like ocean waves. By age 35, these ridges have disappeared, and a rim has formed along the edge of the symphysis. By age 50, the rim has disappeared, and the symphysis looks like a shriveled prune. But because the os coxae are among the first bones to decay, this useful method of determining skeletal age is not applicable to many archaeological skeletons.

Another method to age a skeleton uses the degree of tooth wear and loss. Because teeth wear down continually with age, bioarchaeologists have generated standardized tables (from nonindustrial populations) to estimate age from the extent of tooth wear. But cau-

tion is required here too, because the rate of tooth wear and loss is strongly related to diet. People dependent on food processed on grinding stones will have higher rates of wear because of the grit in their diet. And if their food is high in carbohydrates, people may also experience a higher rate of tooth loss from cavities (see "Cavities" later in the chapter).

Using these different methods, Larsen determined that the Stillwater burials ranged in age from fetuses to individuals of more than 50 years old—but these estimates have some limitations. Rarely can bioarchaeologists assign a specific age to a skeleton; instead, because of the different indicators of age and slight error factors in the various methods, skeletons are placed into five-year age classes (0–5 years, 6–10 years, 11–15 years, and so on). It's also difficult to pin down the age of individuals older than about 50 years.

How Well Did the Stillwater People Live?

Eventually, Larsen derived the basics of the Stillwater population: he knew how many males and females there were, and he knew these individuals' approximate ages. Now he could turn to questions he wanted to ask of this population. One of these was, How well did the people of Stillwater Marsh live? He did not ask this question out of idle curiosity. Instead, he wanted to use the Stillwater population to shed light on a major dilemma of anthropology.

Prior to the 1960s, many anthropologists assumed that the lives of ancient hunter-gatherers were, to use the words of seventeenth-century philosopher Thomas Hobbes (1588–1679), "nasty, brutish, and short." In this view, hunter-gatherers had to work excessively hard, lived hand-to-mouth with barely enough food, suffered high rates of infant mortality, and lived short lives. But research with the Ju/'hoansi of southern Africa's Kalahari Desert and other foragers in the 1960s suggested that hunter-gatherers actually had plenty of leisure time, an adequate diet, and low levels of disease. Anthropologist Marshall Sahlins (University of Chicago) went so far as to label hunter-gatherers the "original affluent society." In the 1960s, this image of prehistoric peoples resonated with those seeking an alternative to the perceived excesses of modern industrial life.

epiphyses The ends of bones that fuse to the main shaft or portion of bone at various ages; most bones are fused by age 25. This fact can be used to age skeletons of younger individuals.

pubic symphysis Where the two halves of the pelvis meet in the groin area; the appearance of its articulating surface can be used to age skeletons.

Is one of these characterizations more accurate than the other? Both were based on ethnographic data, but the observers might have been predisposed to see hunter-gatherers in one way rather than the other. Larsen thought that the skeletal data of an archaeological population could provide an objective assessment of the nature of the foraging lifeway. He wanted to see whether the Stillwater foragers of 1000 years ago were closer to the "nasty, brutish, and short" or the "original affluent society" image of hunter-gatherers.

To do this, Larsen turned to **paleopathology,** the study of ancient disease. This specialization includes the identification of specific diseases, but few specific diseases can be identified from bones (syphilis, tuberculosis, and leprosy are the major ones that leave distinctive lesions and other characteristics on bone). Broken bones, even if healed, are also easy to identify; unhealed breaks are usually evidence of trauma that was the immediate cause of death.

But bioarchaeologists can glean more from human skeletons if they look at human bone as being formed by complex interrelationships among the environment, behavior, physiology, and cultural behavior. Larsen used this perspective to look for *nonspecific* indicators of stress, particularly those caused by nutritional deficiencies and/or nonspecific infectious disease in the Stillwater burial population. Though challenging, the study of biological stress has become an important area of bioarchaeology.

Disease and Trauma at Stillwater

Larsen found little trace of specific diseases among the skeletal remains from Stillwater Marsh—no evidence of syphilis, tuberculosis, or leprosy. He did, however, find some signs of iron deficiency anemia.

Iron is essential for adequate transport of oxygen by red blood cells. But sometimes iron is limited, perhaps by the lack of red meat in the diet (a primary source of easily absorbed iron), chronic diarrhea, or parasites (such as hookworm, which can cause internal bleeding and the loss of a body's iron stores). Regardless of the specific cause, whenever iron is limited, the body tries to produce more red blood cells. Because these cells are produced in the marrow cavities of bone, these cavities enlarge. When this happens in the cranium, the surface of the skull takes on a spongy appearance, a characteristic known as **porotic hyperostosis.** The same phenomenon can happen to bone in the eye

sockets (where it is known as **cribra orbitalia**). Larsen documented evidence of iron deficiency in only 4 of the 54 burials from the Stillwater Marsh.

The Stillwater group showed little evidence of physical trauma. Sheilagh Brooks (retired, University of Nevada, Las Vegas), who also studied the Stillwater materials, found only 18 individuals with bone breaks (all healed); 6 of these (5 males and 1 female) had broken noses. In general, then, the Stillwater population seemed to have been relatively healthy, suffering from a few broken bones (and perhaps the occasional fistfight).

These observations were made largely on adult skeletons, but many anthropologists will tell you that, to understand overall quality of life, you must look at the children. Because they are fragile, children's skeletons (especially those of the very young) are rarely well preserved, making it more difficult to find appropriate samples to study. But human bone has a "memory," and some childhood events leave a telltale record on the adolescent and adult skeleton.

Growth Arrest Features

Childhood growth may be periodically arrested because of disease, trauma, or malnutrition. Whenever this happens, the bones record the cessation of growth. In long bones, such as the tibia and femur, this growth arrest appears as a thin line of bone, known as **Harris lines,** perpendicular to the bone's long axis. These lines are not visible on the outside of the bone, but they do appear in X-rays. These lines form in childhood, but disappear later in life, as the bone is remodeled as it grows.

Teeth likewise register the cessation of growth. Adult teeth form, of course, in the mandible and maxilla during childhood. When a child becomes severely ill or is malnourished, tooth growth stops. If the child recovers,

paleopathology The study of ancient patterns of disease and disorders.

porotic hyperostosis A symptom of iron deficiency anemia in which the skull takes on a porous appearance.

cribra orbitalia A symptom of iron deficiency anemia in which the bone of the upper eye sockets takes on a spongy appearance.

Harris lines Horizontal lines near the ends of long bones indicating episodes of physiological stress.

© Clark Larsen, photo by Barry Stark

Figure 9-2 Enamel hypoplasias.

growth starts up again, but the episode of growth arrest is forever encoded as shallow grooves, known as **enamel hypoplasias,** across the front of the teeth (Figure 9-2). Because teeth grow at known rates, bioarchaeologists can measure the distance from the hypoplasia to the tip of the root to estimate at what age the growth arrest event took place. Likewise, the width of a hypoplasia indicates the duration of the period of stress.

Since enamel hypoplasias are more permanent than Harris lines, Larsen focused on them. (He could also analyze them without the cost of X-rays and with minimal disturbance to the bone.) Working with Dale Hutchinson (University of North Carolina), Larsen found that two-thirds of the individuals had hypoplasias, and that most of these occurred between the ages of 3 and 4. But the number of hypoplasias per tooth, and the average width of the grooves, was less than for other Native American populations. Larsen and Hutchinson concluded that the children of Still-

water Marsh had seen some hard times, but conditions were by no means as bad as they might have been.

The specific cause of the Stillwater hypoplasias, however, is more difficult to determine. They could have resulted from physical trauma to the face, parasitic infection, or malnutrition. We know that trauma was relatively rare (and restricted to adults), and the evidence for extensive infections was limited. Larsen and Hutchinson concluded that fluctuations in the food supply from the marsh—subject to the vagaries of local climate—most likely caused periods of malnutrition for young children.

In fact, the young population might be especially hard hit by a fluctuating food supply. Among hunter-gatherers, children are often not fully weaned until they are 3, 4, or even 5 or 6 years old. This means that, if the 3- or 4-year-olds at Stillwater Marsh were in the process of being weaned during a severe winter or a lean spring, the child might very well have suffered a limited period of malnutrition.

That the individual survived to adulthood, however, demonstrates that this hard time was not insurmountable.

Workload

To this point, Larsen had discovered that the people who lived in the Stillwater Marsh enjoyed a relatively healthy life. But other skeletal data show that this life came at a cost.

As we said before, bones have a memory—they are a lifetime diary that records whether you lived life as a hotshot fighting forest fires or as a couch potato. Bones can be hard to read, but they do not lie.

Bioarchaeologists use a variety of ways to determine how much physical labor a person saw in his or her lifetime. When working with the Stillwater collection, Larsen relied on patterns of osteoarthritis and the study of bone biomechanics.

Osteoarthritis

Osteoarthritis is a joint disorder created by the loss of cartilage, often caused by mechanical stress. This condition appears as a bony growth (known as an **osteophyte**) that forms a lip around the edge of an articular surface of a long bone's epiphysis (for example, at the elbow or knee) or between vertebrae, as shown in Figure 9-3. When the cartilage disappears completely, the articular surfaces rub against one another, creating a

enamel hypoplasias Horizontal linear defects in tooth enamel indicating episodes of physiological stress.

osteoarthritis A disorder in which the cartilage between joints wears away, often because of overuse of the joint, resulting in osteophytes and eburnation.

osteophyte A sign of osteoarthritis in which bones develop a distinct "lipping" of bone at the point of articulation.

Figure 9-3 A vertebra with osteoarthritis.

© Clark Larsen

polish known as **eburnation.** Eburnated joints are extremely painful to move.

Larsen found that *every single adult* skeleton in the Stillwater collection had osteoarthritis in at least one joint. In fact, this was the most severe osteoarthritis that Larsen had ever seen in any skeletal population. The people of Stillwater Marsh may have lived a healthy life, but they apparently had to work—and suffer aches and pains—for it.

Males were slightly more osteoarthritic than females, and not in all the same places. Men suffered from osteoarthritis more in the hip, ankle, and foot; women, more in their lumbar vertebrae—their lower back. Larsen suggested that the males in the Stillwater population probably did more walking—and more difficult walking—than did women. This makes sense, because women probably foraged for plants, fish, and small game within a short distance of camps within the marsh itself, while the men probably traveled farther, into the rougher terrain of the Stillwater Mountains, in search of large game. The women were hardly taking it easy, though. They, too, had osteoarthritis that indicated they did a great deal of difficult walking, no doubt carrying children and gear when they moved camp. But men evidently did even more walking.

Why the high incidence of osteoarthritis in the lower backs of women? Larsen pointed to two likely factors: child rearing and food processing. Because hunter-gatherer children breastfeed until they are several years

old, children must stay with their mothers. And if the Stillwater women were to complete their daily foraging tasks, they probably had to carry the children with them (just as many hunter-gatherer women do). If so, then the Stillwater women probably carried children throughout most of their adult lives—with resulting strain on the lower back.

In addition, the seeds and tubers that women collected in the marsh were ground on metates. A lifetime of such seed grinding could have led women to overuse their lower vertebrae and given them a higher incidence of osteoarthritis there.

Biomechanics

Larsen also worked with Christopher Ruff (Johns Hopkins University) to transfer knowledge from civil engineering to the analysis of **long bone cross-sections.** Civil engineers know that the type of supports used in a building is a function of how much stress the building will place on the beams (which is largely a function of the building's height). Bones are the same, except that, unlike a building's support beams, bones change their cross-section over time as they respond to stress. Although the specifics are complex, the principle is simple: when femora are placed under heavy mechanical stress (for example, by routine walking over difficult terrain while carrying a heavy load), they tend to develop a more oval cross-section. The cross-sections of the femora of a couch potato, on the other hand, are more rounded.

Larsen and Ruff obtained cross-sections of the femora through CAT scans at the Veteran's Administration hospital in Reno, Nevada. Although the overall bone mass was relatively low in the Stillwater femora, bone strength was among the highest that Larsen and Ruff had ever seen. And, as was true for osteoarthritis, the femur cross sections indicated that men did more—and more strenuous—walking than did women. This could be because the Stillwater folk, especially the

eburnation A sign of osteoarthritis in which the epiphyses of long bones are worn smooth, causing them to take on a varnish-like appearance.

long bone cross-sections Cross-sections of the body's long bones (arms and legs) used to analyze bone shape and reconstruct the mechanical stresses placed on that bone—and hence activity patterns.

men, were generally robust, with large, heavy bones. But when Larsen and Ruff looked at the cross sections of the humeri (the upper arm), they found no difference between men and women, and no real difference between the Stillwater and other populations of native North Americans. This suggests that the difference in men's and women's femoral cross sections was produced by a difference in men's and women's behavior and not simply by differences in the size of men and women.

In sum, the femur cross-sections and the patterns in osteoarthritis indicated that the people living at Stillwater Marsh walked a great deal to make a successful living. And men did more walking than women. Neither of these conclusions was particularly striking, but it was conclusive proof that the people who lived at Stillwater were nomadic, and it gave Larsen clearer ideas about differences in men's and women's lives.

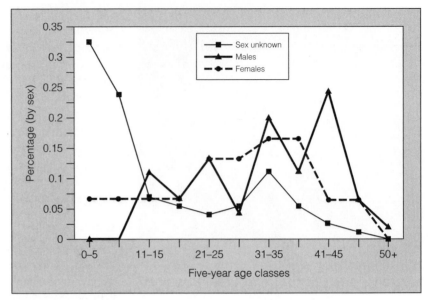

Figure 9-4 The Stillwater mortality profile. *From data in Brooks et al. (1988).*

Paleodemography

Still another way to judge quality of life is to examine patterns of mortality. **Paleodemography** reconstructs parameters such as life expectancy at birth, the age profile of a population, and patterns in the ages of death. Bioarchaeologists do this by constructing various sorts of **mortality profiles** for a prehistoric population based on the age and sex data of burials. Mortality profiles show at what age adult males, adult females, and children died.

Paleodemography works best with well-defined cemetery populations (that is, for a skeletal sample derived from the same biological population over a few years or decades). Although radiocarbon dates suggested that the Stillwater burials dated to the Underdown phase, this phase covers 600 years. For this reason, the Stillwater population is not an ideal candidate for a paleodemographic study.

Still, bioarchaeologist Sheilagh Brooks was able to derive some useful data from mortality profiles for the Stillwater burials. One of these profiles (Figure 9-4) shows the burial data sorted into 5-year age classes by sex. Note first that the 0–5 age category is composed mostly of "unknowns"; as we mentioned earlier, it is almost impossible to determine the sex of very young children.

Why did so many children die so young? Ethnographic data show that the mortality of newborns and toddlers is very high among hunting and gathering populations—50–60 percent of all children born in a foraging population do not survive to 5 years of age. The Stillwater mortality profile reflects this sad fact.

Notice also that there are no strong peaks in female age at death. Girls may have had a slightly higher chance of dying at a young age compared with boys, and men may have had a slightly greater chance of surviving into their forties than women. The female mortality profile shows an increase in deaths beginning at age 21, the early child-bearing years; this is also similar

paleodemography The study of ancient demographic patterns and trends.

mortality profiles Charts that depict the various ages at death of a burial population.

RAPID REVIEW   Classes of Basic Data from Human Skeletons

Information	Based on:
Age	Teeth, bone fusion, pubic symphysis
Sex	Skull, pelvis observations
Life expectancy	Analysis of age distributions in burial populations
Stature	Femur measurements
Disease	Manifested in different bones depending on specific type
Growth arrest	Dental hypoplasias, Harris lines in long bones
Workload	Bone joint osteoarthritis records which joints were heavily used; long bone cross-sections

to other foraging populations. Finally, notice that few individuals are assigned to the 46–50 and 50+ age categories; this reflects a shorter overall life expectancy. Although we might regard the late forties as the prime of life, a 48-year-old person in Stillwater was an elder.

Stature

Measuring stature is yet another way to assess quality of life. Bioarchaeologists estimate stature with equations that relate the length of certain long bones to an individual's height. These equations were created, incidentally, from measurements on cadavers (individuals who donated their bodies to science).

The femur is the best bone for computing stature (because tall people tend to have long femora and short people tend to have short femora). But because the relationship between height and femur length varies from population to population, it is important that the bioarchaeologist apply the appropriate equation. Here, for instance, is the stature formula, which has an error factor of ± 3.5 centimeters, for ancient populations in central Mexico:

$$\text{living height} = (2.26 \times \text{femur length}) + 66.38$$

This equation tells us that, if a femur excavated in central Mexico measures 40 centimeters in length, it likely belonged to an individual who stood about 157 centimeters tall (5 feet 2 inches) give or take 3.5 centimeters. Different formulae are available for skeletons recovered from other parts of the world.

Height provides a useful measure of overall health, because it is closely related to diet. However, because different populations have different genetic capacities for height, it is best to use this variable as a measure of health when looking at data for one burial population across time. Larsen did not use height estimates for the Stillwater burials, because most of the burials dated to the same phase, and no good comparative population data were available.

However, Larsen did use height estimates to track health changes in another project that examined individuals who lived on St. Catherines Island and elsewhere along the coast of Georgia. Here he was interested in testing hypotheses about the effect of maize agriculture on a human population's health. He estimated the heights from skeletons of the hunting-and-gathering population (pre-AD 1150) and those of the agricultural population (post-AD 1150). Contrary to what you might expect, he found that the average agricultural male was 1 percent, and the average female agriculturalist 3 percent *shorter* than their foraging ancestors. In this case, agriculture was a poorer diet than the hunting-and-gathering one, and it hit women harder than men.

Reconstructing Diet from Human Bone

The people who lived at Stillwater were hunter-gatherers. But can we go beyond this general statement to talk more specifically about what people ate? Following the old adage "You are what you eat," diet can be reconstructed from human bone in several ways. We discuss two of these methods here.

PROFILE OF AN ARCHAEOLOGIST
A Native American Archaeologist

Dorothy Lippert is a Native American archaeologist who works at the Smithsonian Institution.

Deciding to become an archaeologist was the easy part. Although I had no fixed ideas about what such a career would involve, I wanted to participate in the scientific process of understanding our human past. I was unaware of the role that my own Native American heritage would play. My career choice centered around a love of history and science, although I had little patience for a simple series of dates and sterile sets of data. Archaeology, for me, must be a humanistic endeavor in which we come to know and respect people of the past.

I find that archaeologists who are also Native American seem to have similar views of the discipline. These people are our ancestors and, as archaeologists, it becomes our privilege and our responsibility to care for them and to speak about their lives. A common thread within indigenous cultures is a respect for our elders and this permeates archaeology as it is practiced by Native Americans.

In 2003, there were 11 Native Americans with doctorates in archaeology. I suspect this is because few Native Americans hold doctorates in any subject, and because archaeology holds particular hazards, emotional and scholarly, for us. Many tribal people feel that archaeology is something done to Native peoples by outsiders. Those of us who practice archaeology from a Native perspective understand this impression; in the eyes of some, we have become outsiders ourselves. I have been told by tribal people that I must not be truly Native if I practice archaeology. I have an added burden because I study human osteology. Frequently, when I meet other Native people, I don't mention that I'm an

Cavities

Dental **caries** (cavities) can help differentiate between agriculturalists and hunter-gatherer populations. Caries result when simple carbohydrates, especially refined sugar but also starchy foods like maize or tubers, remain on your teeth. Bacteria that feed on the carbohydrates produce an acid as a by-product that dissolves tooth enamel. If you ate mostly meat, you would have few caries—regardless of whether you brushed your teeth.

The prevalence of caries, then, serves as an indicator of starchy diets (which, in ancient North America, generally means the consumption of maize). A skilled bioarchaeologist, in fact, can glance at a subject's teeth and make a good guess as to whether the person was an agriculturalist or hunter-gatherer—just by looking for caries.

The people at Stillwater Marsh were strictly hunter-gatherers; they did not grow or eat maize. Because their diet was low in simple carbohydrates (and obviously

caries Cavities.

archaeologist until late in the conversation, in hopes of forestalling a negative response.

Other Natives are more supportive, saying that it's about time that we (indigenous people) have started doing this work. Many understand just how difficult a career this can be and encourage me to continue. In their minds, as in my own, archaeology is a way to work for Native Americans, both the ancestors and present-day communities.

Many non-Native archaeologists are unaware of these reactions. Some think that archaeology done from a Native perspective will be somehow less scientific (as if their cultural heritage plays no role in their own studies). While I believe in scientific rigor, I also think we must illuminate our studies with the cultural legacy that was maintained, sometimes at horrendous cost, by our ancestors. As Natives participate more fully in archaeology, the discipline will become broader in approach and more open to other knowledge bases that inform our understanding of a more human past.

In speaking with other Native Americans about the practice of archaeology, I find that we are trying to answer questions that are influenced by our cultural background. In my own studies of health and medical theory, for instance, I want to understand the experience of those living in a small community whose inhabitants lived and died some 400 years ago. I never saw my research as simply collecting data; instead, I felt that I was communicating with these ancient ones. Their cold, white bones used my breath and mind to tell this world their long forgotten story. Through science, I became their voice.

Even when looking through pages of dry archaeological text, I feel myself searching for the humanity of those whose remains or material objects are being studied. I realize that this perspective is not limited to indigenous archaeologists. A number of non-Natives also intuitively approach our science with a very humanistic flair, and see our discipline as dealing with fellow beings.

Shakespeare summed it up well. "You are not stones, nor bones, but men." While archaeology frequently encounters both stones and bones, we must keep in mind that what we are really encountering are human beings.

did not include refined sugar at all), only 3 percent of the Stillwater skeletons had dental caries—a remarkably low figure.

This is not to say that they were free of dental problems. The Stillwater folks lost many of their teeth by middle age, generally due to excessive tooth wear—a product of the grit in their diet from seeds and tubers ground on metates. They also suffered from abscesses, which appear as large voids in the mandibles and maxillas. In fact, some teeth had shallow grooves worn into their sides, where a person had habitually twirled a toothpick-sized twig to overstimulate the nerves and alleviate the pain of an abscess.

Bone and Stable Isotopes

Ancient diets can also be reconstructed by analyzing the carbon and nitrogen stable isotopes preserved in human bone.

We already encountered the concept of isotopes when discussing radiocarbon dating (in Chapter 5). Carbon, you remember, has both stable and unstable isotopes. One stable form, ^{12}C, makes up about 99 percent of the world's carbon; ^{13}C is also stable but accounts for only about 1 percent. The unstable isotope, ^{14}C, most familiar to archaeologists because of its importance for dating, is extremely rare.

As we pointed out in Chapter 5, plants take carbon in through one of three photosynthetic pathways: C3, C4, and CAM. You will recall that the C4 plants (such as maize) take in more ^{13}C and ^{14}C isotopes than do C3 and CAM plants. Because human bone reflects the isotopic ratios of plants ingested during life, bioarchaeologists can reconstruct the dietary importance of certain classes of plants by measuring the ratio of carbon isotopes contained in bone **collagen,** the organic component of bone. A diet rich in C4 plants (such as maize), for example, can produce bones with a significantly higher ratio of ^{13}C to ^{12}C than diets low in C4 plants.

Nitrogen also has two stable isotopes, ^{14}N and ^{15}N. Some plants obtain their nitrogen from the air and others absorb nitrogen from the soil. These diverse mechanisms result in different ratios of ^{15}N to ^{14}N in various plants. Using this information, bioarchaeologists analyze a bone's stable isotope composition to determine which plants were eaten and which were not. In addition, we know that carnivores tend to lose ^{14}N through their urine, but they retain ^{15}N. This means that humans who consume large amounts of meat have a higher ratio of ^{15}N to ^{14}N than those who eat mostly plants. To complicate things further, marine plants tend to have ^{15}N to ^{14}N ratios that are 4 percent higher than terrestrial plants. These differences are passed up the food chain, and so marine mammals also tend to have higher ratios of ^{15}N to ^{14}N than do terrestrial mammals. You can't interpret the values blindly, however, because of environmental differences. For example, hot desert soils tend to have higher nitrogen ratios than cool forest soils; so much so, in fact, that bones of desert-dwelling individuals with purely terrestrial diets can produce nitrogen values that, in another part of the world, would suggest a marine diet.

Control for these environmental factors, however, and differences in nitrogen values tell us whether people relied more heavily on marine than terrestrial foods or had more or less meat in their diets. Carbon and nitrogen values are measured relative to a known international standard. Larsen submitted samples of human bone from 39 of the individuals recovered at Stillwater Marsh to Margaret Schoeninger (University of California, San Diego), one of the world's premier analysts of bone chemistry. With the human bone samples, Larsen also submitted several modern plant specimens and animal bones (identified to species) to act as controls.

The actual measurement of a bone's carbon and nitrogen isotope ratios is a complex process involving a mass spectrometer and need not concern us here. But Schoeninger's findings are not difficult to understand. To make her point, Schoeninger compared the results of the analysis of the Stillwater materials to two very different populations (Figure 9-5): the skeletal remains from Pecos Pueblo in New Mexico, a maize-dependent population, and the skeletal remains of a foraging population from Ontario, Canada, which was heavily dependent on meat. In Figure 9-5, the horizontal axis plots the ratio of ^{13}C to ^{12}C—higher ratios are farther to the right (indicating more C4 plants like maize in the diet), and lower ratios to the left (meaning fewer C4 plants in the diet). Don't let the negative numbers confuse you. To make measurements comparable, Schoeninger reports the stable isotope values calibrated as deviations from an agreed-upon standard (the fossil *belemnitella,* in the Pee Dee limestone formation of South Carolina). The vertical axis plots the ratio of ^{15}N to ^{14}N; higher ratios are at the top (more carnivorous diet) and lower ratios are at the bottom (less carnivorous diet).

As Figure 9-5 shows, the Pecos population has a high ratio of ^{13}C to ^{12}C and a low ratio of ^{15}N to ^{14}N. This means that the Pecos population ate plenty of maize and very little meat. At the upper left part of the graph, the Ontario hunting population has a high ratio of ^{15}N to ^{14}N, with virtually no C4 plants in its diet; this makes sense, because the Ontario foragers lived in an environment unsuitable for horticulture and relied primarily on fish, moose, and caribou (rather than plants) for food. The Stillwater ("Carson Desert") population lies between these two extremes, with very few C4 plants in its diet, but a diet that was a mixture of plant and animal foods.

Schoeninger took her results even further. Remember that she also analyzed some modern plant samples; one of these was piñon pine. It turns out that piñon has a very low ratio of ^{15}N to ^{14}N. Schoeninger figured that if piñon was important to the Stillwater diet, then the bones of this population should have a much lower nitrogen ratio than the graph indicates. Because they do not, Schoeninger concluded that piñon could not have been an important component of the Stillwater diet. Instead, by looking at the values for the other plant and animal control samples, Schoeninger concluded that a strictly marsh-based diet could readily account for the observed carbon and nitrogen isotope ratios in the Stillwater remains.

Note in Figure 9-5 that the Stillwater population has a greater *range* of nitrogen values than either the Ontario or Pecos populations. Schoeninger looked to see if this range was associated with an individual's age or sex. For example, if men spent time hunting large game, then perhaps they ate more meat than women; or maybe children ate less meat than adults. However, there was no association between nitrogen values and age or sex. She also found no clear association between nitrogen values and the radiocarbon ages on the burials.

Consequently, Schoeninger suggested that the range of nitrogen values might be a product of dietary variability. Although bone chemistry is a lifelong average of one's diet, the period of youth and adolescence is particularly important because this is when bone collagen forms. If the foods available in the wetlands varied from decade to decade because of flooding, fires, climate change, or other factors, then perhaps people ate different suites of food over the years. In some years, perhaps jackrabbits were commonly roasted over the fire; in other years, bulrush seed cakes might have been the daily fare. If this dietary variability accounts for the differential nitrogen ratios, then it suggests that the Pecos farmers and Ontario foragers had far more monotonous diets than did the people living at Stillwater Marsh.

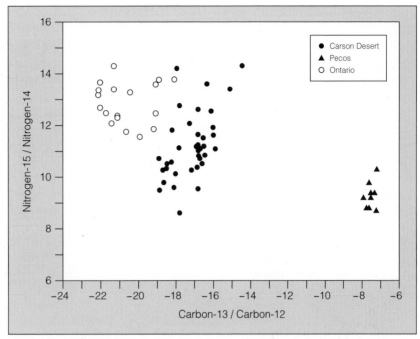

Figure 9-5 Stable carbon and nitrogen isotopes for the Stillwater burial population compared with those of Archaic Ontario hunter-gatherers and of Pecos Pueblo maize horticulturalists.

Lives of Affluence? or Nasty, Brutish, and Short?

We can now return to Larsen's original research question: Does the Stillwater burial population reflect human lives that were "nasty, brutish, and short" or those of an "affluent society"?

The answer, evident from these analyses, is "Both" and "Neither." The people of Stillwater Marsh consumed a varied diet that probably went beyond their minimal nutritional needs. They were relatively healthy, generally free of serious disease, disorders, broken bones, and infections. This part seems to fit the "original affluent society" image.

But the Stillwater people also worked hard, and some had good reason to complain about aching knees and backs. Some youngsters suffered periods of malnutrition, and a large proportion of the Stillwater children did not live to their fifth birthday. Nobody lived much beyond 50 years. These data conform more to the "nasty, brutish, and short" model.

Our objective, of course, is not to pigeonhole the Stillwater burial population; it is to learn what life was

ARCHAEOLOGICAL ETHICS
Should We Excavate and Analyze Human Remains?

In many places in the world, archaeologists have no qualms about excavating human skeletal remains. But many archaeologists who do field research in the United States excavate human remains only if they are in the way of a construction project that cannot be rerouted. And no archaeologist would excavate a burial without consulting at least the nearest tribe; such consultation, in fact, is today mandated by law if the excavation is on federal land. Bioarchaeologists also find it increasingly difficult to work with skeletal collections in museums; the scientists involved with the Kennewick case had to file a very public lawsuit to get access to that skeleton.

All of this raises major ethical questions. Some modern archaeologists believe that we should cease studying human skeletons out of respect and sensitivity to Native Americans who find the excavation and analysis of ancestral remains disrespectful.

Archaeologists have long curated Native American remains in museum collections, in case new techniques enable us to learn more about the past. And such breakthroughs do occur: who, in 1965, would have thought that within two decades we could extract genetic material from 7000-year-old human skeletons? There is so much more to learn.

But in many museums, the proportion of Native American skeletons often outweighs the non-Indian remains—reflecting, in large measure, the historical interest of American archaeology in excavating American Indian burial sites. But when archaeologists found the *Hunley*, the Confederate submarine that sank on its first mission (see "Looking Closer: Preserving the *Hunley*," page 126), they immediately agreed to rebury the remains of the Civil War dead—it was the obvious, and respectful, thing to do. Such differential attitudes toward the dead still condition the practice of archaeology in America.

Scientists will always want to learn more about the past, to increase our understanding of the history of humanity. This is a good thing. And Native Americans will always want to see their ancestors (and themselves) treated with respect; this is also a good thing.

How do we balance these differing views? Should science trump every other concern? Does one group of people have the right to shut out scientific inquiry about themselves and their ancestors?

What is knowledge worth? What is knowledge *for*? Every archaeologist, especially those who study human skeletal remains, must carefully consider these questions today.

---

like for people in the past. We seek to understand the various factors that influenced their diet, their rates of infection and bone breakage, their workloads and their dental health. In some ways, the Stillwater people had a good life; in other ways, it was not so easy. The past can almost never be characterized in simple black-and-white terms.

Most of the time, bioarchaeologists analyze human skeletons to answer questions about human behavior and quality of life. But recently developed technology now allows us to analyze the biology of ancient human populations in order to answer some old questions in new ways. The rest of this chapter explores the developing frontiers of archaeology at the molecular level.

Archaeology and DNA: Tracing Human Migration

How was the world colonized? Are modern humans related to Neanderthals? When did Native Americans arrive in the New World?

In the past, archaeologists used artifacts alone to talk about ancient migrations and the historical relationships among the world's populations. But modern genetic technology provides another avenue to reconstructing the past. By using genetic material—DNA from human skeletal remains and living peoples—geneticists and archaeologists have joined forces to create a new approach to reconstructing the past known as **molecular archaeology.** As is so often true, this new approach raises as many questions as it attempts to answer.

A Little Background on DNA

Most of our genetic information exists as 46 chromosomes inside the nucleus of each cell in our bodies; this stuff, called **nuclear DNA** (deoxyribonucleic acid), makes each of us unique and is inherited from our biological parents. Your DNA contains the recipe for your biological composition, telling your body to create blue or green eyes, to be short or tall, to have straight or curly hair. A **gene** is a segment of a chromosome, one small piece of the recipe that codes for particular biological attributes; your body has about 50,000 genes.

Nuclear DNA is extraordinarily useful to the genetics of living populations, but it is not so useful to archaeology. Nuclear DNA degrades fairly quickly, and, by the time the human body decomposes, nuclear DNA is no longer intact (although sections of about 200 nucleotide base pairs can survive for thousands of years).

But another form of DNA, known as **mitochondrial DNA (mtDNA),** is found in the cells' mitochondria (organelles responsible for the cell's energy metabolism)—outside the nucleus. mtDNA contains only about 0.0006 percent of the genetic material of nuclear DNA, which would seem to limit its use, but mtDNA has three interesting properties. First, although it contains only a limited segment of the total genetic recipe, each cell contains thousands of copies of it (in contrast to just the two in the nucleus). This translates to a greater probability of retrieving mtDNA than nuclear DNA. But don't think that there are gobs of mtDNA just lying in archaeological sites: its recovery is made possible through the technique of *polymerase chain reaction* (PCR), which enables researchers to create billions of copies of a very small sample of mtDNA, so that this genetic material can be more readily studied.

The second intriguing property of mtDNA is that you inherit yours *only* from your mother. Although

mtDNA is present in the tail of sperm, after fertilization occurs the tail breaks off. This means that your mtDNA comes entirely from the ovum. If you are female, you pass along your mtDNA to your children. If you are male, none of the mtDNA that you inherited from your mother is passed on to your biological offspring. This makes it possible to define molecular "family trees" and to trace the movement of female lineages.

Finally, mtDNA is thought to change in a particular way and at a particular rate that makes it potentially useful to archaeology. Briefly, although mtDNA is probably not completely free from the pressures of natural selection, it appears to be under less selective pressure than nuclear DNA. And because it is transferred from mother to offspring as a chunk, it does not recombine (as does nuclear DNA). Instead, mtDNA appears to change over time largely as a result of random mutations. Nuclear DNA can also change as a result of random mutation (this is, in fact, how new genetic material appears in a species). But compared with nuclear DNA, mtDNA mutates rapidly, 2–4 percent every million years. Although this may seem awfully slow, it is *nearly 10 times* faster than nuclear DNA's mutation rate. *If* one assumes that this rate of change has been constant through time, then differences in the mutations between related mtDNA samples can be used to estimate how much time has elapsed since the branches of the family tree diverged. For this reason, mtDNA is sometimes used as a "clock" to date the timing of human population movements in the remote past.

Prospecting for Ancient DNA

In 1984, Allan Wilson (1943–1991) and his student Vince Sarich (University of California, Berkeley) were the first to identify genetic materials from old tissue.

molecular archaeology The use of genetic information in ancient human remains to reconstruct the past.

nuclear DNA Genetic material found in a cell's nucleus; this material is primarily responsible for an individual's inherited traits.

gene A unit of the chromosomes that controls inheritance of particular traits.

mitochondrial DNA (mtDNA) Genetic material found in the mitochondria of cells; it is inherited only from the mother and appears to mutate at a rate of 2–4 percent per 1 million years.

When they cloned DNA from the 140-year-old skin of quagga—a recently extinct, zebra-like African beast—the Berkeley team showed the world that DNA could indeed survive after the death of an organism.

The next year, Swedish researcher Svante Pääbo (Max Planck Institute of Evolutionary Anthropology, Germany) cloned DNA from a 4400-year-old Egyptian mummy. This was the first time that anyone had applied PCR techniques to ancient humans. Not long after, Pääbo pushed the barrier back another 2600 years by extracting ancient DNA from human brains preserved at the Windover site in Florida.

Some 7000–8000 years ago, ancient Native Americans at Windover buried their dead in a spring that flowed through an ancient limestone sinkhole. Water levels fluctuated seasonally, with a maximum depth of less than 4 feet. At the bottom were several strata of peat—compact, dark brown organic material built up from the partial decay and carbonization of vegetation. The team of archaeologists, headed by Glen Doran (Florida State University), dug into these peat levels while pumps bailed out the encroaching water. Because peat deposits are anaerobic, Doran found many well-preserved skeletons, some still held in place by large stakes, probably placed there at the time of burial to keep the bodies from floating to the surface.

The low oxygen level and neutral pH of the peat bog were also perfect for preserving soft tissue. More than 60 well-preserved human brains turned up at Windover, including the one used by Pääbo in his pioneering extraction of ancient DNA. Geneticists were particularly excited about the number of burials, because it provided the first chance to examine gene frequencies across a prehistoric burial population.

Microbiologists were surprised to find how little the genetic makeup of the Windover population had changed during the thousand years that the burial ground was used, possibly a sign of ancient inbreeding. If this trend held for other early Native American populations, it would suggest that early Indian groups tended to stay put, perhaps explaining the remarkable linguistic diversity among the New World's indigenous peoples.

Skulls and DNA: Tracking the First Americans

The most consequential, if least dramatic, event in the history of the Americas came when that first human footprint appeared in the New World. Nobody knows exactly when or where this happened. We do not know what these initial colonists of the New World wore, spoke, looked like, or thought. We do not know when they left their Asian homeland or what conditions they experienced along the way.

And yet there remains no reasonable doubt that the first Americans did indeed travel across a land bridge from Asia during the late Pleistocene; it is the timing and conditions surrounding their arrival (or arrivals) that remain incompletely known.

Clovis points, which we mentioned in Chapter 8, appeared in North America about 13,500 calendar years ago (about 11,500 radiocarbon years). Not so long ago the standard textbook account was that Clovis was the first and only migration, and all native peoples of the New World descended from it. In this account, small numbers of people migrated from Asia via the Bering land bridge that formed between Russia and Alaska during the height of the last glacial age, between 25,000 and 10,000 years ago. These arctic hunters walked from Asia into Alaska, migrating down the so-called ice-free corridor between the continental ice sheets that covered the Canadian Rockies on the west and much of Canada to the east.

A number of problems have risen with this scenario. First, it doesn't appear that the ice-free corridor was open until about 13,000 years ago—a little too late to allow Clovis through in order to be in the continental United States by 13,500 years ago. And current studies suggest that, even when the corridor was open, it may have been uninhabitable—a vast wasteland of rock, sand, and lakes so laden with silt washing out from glaciers that they could support no fish or plant life.

Even more important, South America contains a number of sites that appear to be as old as, if not older than, Clovis. The best-known and best-documented of these is the site of Monte Verde, in southern Chile. Like the Windover sites, Monte Verde is located in a wet peat bog, and so the preservation is remarkable. The excavator, Tom Dillehay (Vanderbilt University), found the remains of wooden structures, stone projectile points, hearths, pegs driven into the ground with leather straps still tied on, slabs of organic material identified as mammoth (or mastodon) meat, footprints, and other definitive evidence of human occupation.

Although the site's preservation is phenomenal, what makes it really special is that it appears to be 1000 years *older* than Clovis. If people came to the New World from Asia via Alaska and reached southern Chile by 14,500 years ago, then they had to pass through North America prior to this date. A handful of sites exist that *might* provide evidence of a pre-Clovis occupation of North America—sites such as Meadowcroft Rockshelter in Pennsylvania and some mammoth kill sites in Wisconsin. But none of these are as well demonstrated as Monte Verde, and some archaeologists still wonder why it is that, although Clovis appears in virtually all 48 contiguous states, evidence for a pre-Clovis occupation is almost impossible to find—despite the dogged efforts of many archaeologists.

Possibly the first migrants bypassed the interior of North America by migrating along the western coast. At first, this may have been to avoid the massive glaciers that covered much of northern North America. Once south of the ice sheets, however, they may have simply kept their maritime economy and continued to move along the coast all the way to Tierra del Fuego. Clovis people may have been a later migration from Asia or a population that eventually left the western coast and adapted to terrestrial hunting.

Testing the early coastal migration hypothesis means looking for early sites along the western coast. But this is quite difficult, for when the Pleistocene ended about 10,000 years ago, and the massive continental glaciers melted, sea levels rose and flooded the coastlines. Any sites left behind on the New World's western coast 14,000 or more years ago are now under water—150 meters of it in places—and layers of silt. Some archaeologists have tried dredging likely places on the sea bottom for artifacts, but they are looking for the proverbial needle in a haystack, and most have come up empty-handed.

Bioarchaeology and the Colonization

Frustrated with the difficulties of finding early archaeological sites, some have turned to bioarchaeological evidence. Christy Turner (Arizona State University) has conducted extensive studies of variability in human teeth. He knows what he is talking about: he's looked at some 200,000 teeth from 9000 individuals.

Focusing on the crown and root areas, Turner discovered that modern and pre-contact American Indian teeth are most similar to those of northern Asians. For example, individuals in both groups tend to have shovel-shaped incisors (incisors whose lateral edges curve to give the incisors a shovel shape) and three-rooted lower first molars. Examining geographic patterns in the frequency of different dental traits, Turner found three major groups. One included all Native Americans from southern Canada to Tierra del Fuego (a group labeled "Amerind," for American Indians), a second was the Na-Dene (Athapaskan) speakers of northern Canada and central Alaska, and a third, the Eskimo and Aleut.

Turner postulates an initial migration out of northeast Asia at the end of the Ice Age followed by two later migrations (oddly, he sees the Na-Dene arriving after the Eskimo-Aleut). Turner could not, however, place a date on these migrations.

The Skulls' Story

Recently, a new twist has been added to the story, this time using skulls rather than teeth. We have very few human remains that date to the New World's colonization era. In fact, for the entire New World, we only have about 40 skeletons that are 10,000 or more calendar years old; only a handful of these are Clovis-aged.

Given two spacious continents and a period of 2000–3000 years, these 40 burials are not a good burial population. But some archaeologists and biological anthropologists still find it curious that a large number of these early skeletons have skulls whose shapes are distinctly different from those of later Native Americans. Kennewick, the case study that began this book (see Chapter 1), is one of those skeletons; another comes from Spirit Cave, a site in the Carson Desert, in Nevada.

The early skulls, such as those of Kennewick and Spirit Cave (see Figure 9-6), are different from other Native American skulls because they are long and narrow, rather than round; they have a high-bridged nose and a gracile mandible, but prominent and square chins. Several studies conclude that, in a biological sense, the earliest Native Americans (including Kennewick) are more closely related to groups such as the Ainu, the native peoples of Japan, than to living Native Americans. (Some skulls from South America, in fact, appear to be more like those of Africans or Australians than later Native Americans.) Because skull shape largely reflects genes, the implication is that the earliest colonists of the New World came from a different Asian population than later migrants (who must have then genetically "swamped" the people who were already here).

Figure 9-6 Facial reconstruction of Spirit Cave man by Sharon Long.

mtDNA's Story

So, teeth and skull shape suggest that more than one migration occurred—perhaps even three or more. But when did these migrations begin? Here the geneticists jump in. They argue that the initial population moving out of northeastern Asia ran into a severe geographic bottleneck as they passed across the Bering Strait into the New World, limiting the genetic diversity in the newly arrived population. This explains why Native Americans from Canada to southern South America are genetically similar. It also means that the differences between Asian and Native American populations must *postdate* the time when they separated at the Bering Strait. Thus, measurement of the genetic distance

haplogroup Genetic lineages defined by similar genes at a locus on a chromosome.

between New World and Asian populations should estimate the time elapsed since these two groups separated, the age when someone first set foot in the New World.

Now we return to mtDNA. Recall that you inherit your mtDNA only from your mother. Using blood samples of living Native Americans from all over the New World, several studies have found that there are only five mtDNA lineages in the Americas, referred to as **haplogroups.** These are labeled A, B, C, D, and X. Three of these—A, C, and D—are found in northern Asia. Along with other evidence, such as Turner's dental records, this fact points to an Asian origin for Native Americans. And the fact that so few haplogroups are present among Native Americans suggests that the migration(s) entailed only small groups who brought a limited sample of their original population's genetic diversity with them. In fact, it is possible that 95 percent of all Native Americans came from a small number of Asian founding families.

What about the other two haplogroups? Haplogroup B appears today in south central China and coastal southern Asia. It is possible that it has simply disappeared in northern Asia. It's also possible, as some geneticists argue, that it points to a separate migratory wave from Asia. This could support the argument from the skulls—an early migration from southern China—but geneticists think that haplogroup B came in a later, not earlier, migration.

Haplogroup X is more enigmatic. It is very rare among living Native Americans as well as Native American skeletal remains; it is most common among speakers of Algonkian languages, in northeastern North America, but it is also found in the 8000-year-old Windover burials. It's present in Asia (though very rare), as well as in Europe (where it is only slightly more common).

Some geneticists and archaeologists suggest that haplogroup X points to an ancient migration from *Europe,* in addition to ones from Asia. This seems implausible, because it would require a transatlantic voyage more than 8000 years ago; no land bridge ever connected North America and Europe. On the other hand, some geneticists ask, If haplogroup X points to an ancient migration from Europe, then shouldn't the more common European haplogroups (such as H) be present among modern Native Americans? Because the European haplogroups do not appear among Native Americans, these geneticists suggest that haplogroup

X is indicative of an extremely ancient (tens of thousands of years) shared genetic heritage between Native Americans and Europeans—perhaps dating back to the time when all human ancestors lived in Africa. We simply don't know.

Can mtDNA Tell Us When the Colonization Occurred?

Recall that the molecular clock uses the number of differences due to random mutations between two geographically separated haplogroups to determine when they split apart. Using this principle, one study suggests that differences in the mtDNA of Native Americans and Asians point to a migration somewhere between 21,000 and 42,000 BP. Another study at Emory University arrived at a migration time of between 22,000 and 29,000 years ago.

Archaeological data cannot support even the more conservative of these claims; possible pre-Clovis sites in North America range in age from 14,000 to 18,000 years old; and Monte Verde is at most 14,500 years old. Could the geneticists be wrong? Can the mtDNA clock be used to date human migrations? Much can happen between the time one population splits off from another and goes its merry way.

Some critics, fellow geneticists among them, point out that the mtDNA studies depend on the critical, but unconfirmed, assumption that all the observed genetic diversity among New World populations began after these tribes crossed the Bering land bridge into the New World. But suppose the tribes had split up someplace in Asia, prior to arriving in America. If that happened, then the biological clock would have begun ticking before, and perhaps long before, colonization of the New World. Perhaps the population split between those people (or rather, their descendants) who would migrate to the New World and those who would remain in Asia did occur 21,000 or 29,000 or 42,000 years ago—but the actual migration occurred much, much later. In sum, mtDNA differences may record when populations *diverged,* but not necessarily when populations *migrated.*

Some researchers also suggest that we really don't know the rate at which mtDNA mutates. Wilson's original research calculated the molecular clock's rate by dividing the difference between human and chimpanzee mtDNA by 5 million years, the assumed date of separation between the human and chimpanzee

lines. But we now suspect that the split between the human and chimpanzee lines is older—perhaps by as much as 2 million years ago. If so, then the mtDNA clock might run *slower* than Wilson originally thought.

On the other hand, a recent study in Europe used the standard mtDNA clock to predict that haplogroup V (a haplogroup that appears in Europe but not in the New World) should appear in the Basque region of Spain about 10,000 years ago. However, analysis of nearly 100 human skeletal remains could not find that haplogroup in any individual that was more than 4000 years old. So, perhaps the clock runs *faster* than we think. Maybe we've got the mtDNA molecular clock ticking too slowly or too quickly, or maybe the clock can speed up and slow down—given that we really don't know, it's best if mtDNA studies are verified by other methods.

The Guys Have Their Say

Recently, molecular archaeological studies have turned to the Y chromosome—genetic material that, unlike mtDNA, is inherited only through the male line. Like mtDNA, the Y chromosome also carries DNA that we don't think is under much pressure from natural selection and that mutates at a constant rate (at least, that's the assumption). Only a few Y chromosome haplogroups are known for Native Americans. One of these, haplogroup 10, also occurs in northern Asia. Both Asian and New World Y chromosomes contain a particular mutation (known as M242), suggesting that the mutation occurred before the migration. But the Native American haplogroup also contains another mutation, called M3, which does not appear in Asia. Using the hypothesized rate of mutation in the DNA of the Y chromosome, Mark Seielstad (Harvard School of Public Health) and his team propose that the split between the Asian and what would become the New World population occurred *no more* than 18,000 years ago. The colonization of the New World, then, had to occur sometime *after* this date. Although this date is more consistent with the available archaeological data, we cannot accept an estimate simply because it fits existing knowledge. If we did that, we would never learn anything new.

We lack any kind of final, definitive word about the peopling of the New World based on genetic data. But the preliminary results are sufficiently intriguing to suggest that, whatever the answer may be, molecular archaeology provides a major new source of data regarding the first Americans, as well as ancient migrations and population movements in general. If nothing else, these data force archaeologists to reconsider whether they really know what they think they know. And that, as we have said before, is what science is all about.

Conclusion: The Importance of Human Skeletons

The study of human skeletal remains is about as close as archaeologists can get to studying the people of the past. Where burial populations are available, our knowledge of the past can grow by leaps and bounds. Through analyses of skeletal morphology and bone chemistry, we can learn a great deal about men's and women's workloads, diets, patterns of disease, trauma, and quality of life. And the field of bioarchaeology is really in its infancy: it's producing new ways of analyzing bone every year and promises to expand our knowledge of the past considerably.

One of these areas is molecular archaeology, which promises to help reconstruct human migrations, if we can figure out how genes can be used as clocks. This is an area of middle-range theory that will require considerable attention in the future.

Bioarchaeology deals with the material effects of people's lives on their bones and genes. Although the links between behavior and bones are by no means direct or simple, in the following two chapters we move into elements of past human lives that are even more difficult to reconstruct: the realms of social and political behavior and the meaning of symbols.

Summary

- Bioarchaeology is the study of the human biological component evident in the archaeological record; it examines the health and workload of ancient populations. This specialty requires expertise in the method and theory of both biological anthropology and field archaeology.

- We use characteristics of several bones, notably the pelvis and skull, to determine an individual's sex.

- An individual's age can be determined by tooth eruption and patterns of bone fusion; tooth and bone wear are used to age individuals over the age of 25.

- Paleopathology is the study of those ancient diseases that leave skeletal traces. Iron deficiency, for example, leaves a distinctive spongy appearance on the skull and the interior of the eye orbits. In addition, growth arrest features, such as Harris lines and enamel hypoplasias, indicate childhood periods of severe disease or malnutrition.

- Bones respond to the routine mechanical stresses placed upon them; patterns of osteoarthritis and long bone cross-sections can point to different patterns of workload between the sexes or to changes through time.

- Paleodemography looks at patterns of death in a population, determining life expectancy, child mortality, and peaks in the age of death for men and women.

- Stature estimates can track changes in the quality of diet.

- Bioarchaeologists can also reconstruct diet: high frequency of dental caries indicates a diet high in simple carbohydrates and sugars. The ratios of carbon and nitrogen isotopes in bone can reconstruct the dietary importance of various kinds of plants and animals.

■ Molecular archaeology uses data from living and ancient peoples to reconstruct population migrations. Especially useful is mtDNA and the genetic material in Y chromosomes. Although we still have much to learn about the rates at which DNA mutates, current studies suggest that DNA studies will someday be important to reconstructing the past.

Media Resources

 The Companion Website for **Archaeology: Down to Earth,** *Third Edition*

http://anthropology.wadsworth.com/thomas _kelly3e_down/

Supplement your review of this chapter by going to the companion website to take one of the practice quizzes, use the flash cards to master key terms, and check out the many other study aids that are designed to help you succeed in your introductory archaeology course

10

Reconstructing Social and Political Systems of the Past

Outline

The Inka site of Machu Picchu (Peru).

Preview

W E NOW TURN to some aspects of past human society that are more difficult to infer from archaeological data than the diet, activities, seasonality, and settlement patterns already discussed. In this chapter, we explore ancient social and political organizations—what they were and how archaeologists find out about them.

This chapter explores three key components of human society—gender, kinship, and social status—each of which entails its own interpretive problems and middle-range difficulties. What men and women did in the past is essential to understanding how a society operates, yet assigning specific artifacts to men and women is difficult. Kinship is a major structuring principle of human social organization, but it leaves ambiguous traces. The archaeological record reflects social status a bit more clearly, but many ancient societies may have been organized politically in ways that have no straightforward ethnographic analogies today. We also discuss trade—its role in political and social systems and how archaeologists track trade relations. Although we are entering a more difficult realm of archaeology, we show that reconstructing past social and political systems is not impossible.

Introduction

Recall from Chapter 2 that Americanist archaeology is firmly situated within the broader field of anthropology. Right now, we must return to archaeology's roots in anthropology to define some terms and concepts.

Social Vocabulary

Social organization refers to the rules and structures that govern relationships between individuals within a group of interacting people. These relationships are never simple, because people belong to groups on many different levels; some of these crosscut one another, and others are hierarchically organized.

You, for example, simultaneously belong to one or more families (as a son or daughter, husband or wife, brother or sister) and to a town, a state, and a country. You are biologically male or female, and you may be a member of a sports club, political party, or community organization. Perhaps you hold formal positions in some of these groups. In other words, you play various roles in a variety of social groups. Which identity is currently operating depends upon the situation.

Some social groups are residential, consisting of domestic families or households, territorial bands, or community-level villages. Residential groups tend to be physical agglomerations of people; they are

social organization The rules and structures that govern relations within a group of interacting people. Societies are divided into social units (groups) within which are recognized social positions (statuses), with appropriate behavior patterns prescribed for these positions (roles).

face-to-face associations. Residential groups appear in the archaeological record as households and villages.

Other groups are nonresidential—associations of people that regulate some aspect of society. Nonresidential groups are groups in the abstract sense; in fact, some may never convene. Nonresidential groups are usually manifested archaeologically through the use of symbols, ceremonies, mythologies, or insignias of membership that appear as particular styles of material culture, such as ceramics, architecture, rock art, or burials. In a sense, the residential group functions to regulate discrete spatial matters, whereas the nonresidential group binds these territorial units together.

A related concept is **political organization,** the formal and informal institutions that regulate a society's collective acts. Sometimes, control will rest primarily at the level of the residential group, but in other cases, the nonresidential group exerts a powerful influence. The nineteenth-century Great Basin Shoshone and Paiute, for example, lived in nuclear families, three or four of which lived together in a residential group called a *band*. Such groups were ephemeral, and families would come and go in an ever-changing set of associations. Clusters of families would sometimes come together for a communal jackrabbit or antelope drive. When they did, one individual, recognized for his hunting ability, would take charge, but his authority would disappear when the drive was over. Shoshone families did not "do as they pleased," but neither did they participate in a formalized, permanent level of political integration above the family. This means that although behaviors such as murder and theft were considered antisocial, punishment varied depending on the particular circumstances and families involved.

Contrast this with nineteenth-century Tahitian society. At the time of European contact, Tahiti—an island in the South Pacific with a population of some 100,000—had a horticultural economy of taro, breadfruit, yams, and coconuts. People also raised pigs and

chickens, caught fish, and collected shellfish. Families lived in small villages along the coast and in the island's interior.

Unlike Shoshone bands, the membership of Tahitian villages was more or less permanent, with several strong and overarching levels of control. Tahitian villages were organized into about 20 competing **chiefdoms.** A sacred chief (*arii rahi*) ruled each of these chiefdoms. Below the sacred chiefs were "small chiefs" (*arii rii*), and under the small chiefs were subchiefs (*raatira*). Below the subchiefs were the commoners (*manahune*). Sacred chiefs claimed to be descended directly from the gods, whereas commoners were said to exist only to provide for the needs of chiefs. A person from one of these four classes could not marry someone from a different class. Chiefs owned the land in their respective villages, and they had larger houses and canoes than commoners, as well as distinctive clothing. Some chiefs had craft specialists in their employ, and chiefs controlled communal fishing gear and village production.

The sacred chief also controlled the distribution of food and goods between villages. Periodically, he demanded tribute for special feasts and demonstrated his authority by redistributing food and goods to all who attended. The chief always retained some portion of the tribute for use by his household; chiefs also handed out punishments for social transgressions.

Clearly, the Great Basin and Tahiti provide extreme examples of social and political organizations. To understand such differences, we restrict the present discussion to three broad areas of human social and political behavior: gender, kinship, and social status.

From Artifact to Symbol

Before doing so, however, we must emphasize an important issue in middle-range theory. As you have seen, archaeologists use the physical residues of human behavior to reconstruct past human activities. People butcher an animal and leave behind stone tools and some of the bones. They make, use, and break a pot, leaving the sherds behind in a trash midden. Natural processes then act on those remains. Discarded artifacts are sometimes reclaimed or recycled, meaning that they remain part of the cultural system long after fulfilling their original function. Archaeologists consider all these dimensions of artifact use and reuse when interpreting the archaeological record.

political organization A society's formal and informal institutions that regulate a population's collective acts.

chiefdom A regional polity in which two or more local groups are organized under a single chief (who is the head of a ranked social hierarchy). Unlike autonomous bands and villages, chiefdoms consist of several more or less permanently aligned communities or settlements.

Now we add another dimension to our consideration of artifacts, an aspect that is especially important to understanding social and political organization. It may seem that archaeologists act as though artifacts only reflect human behavior. But it is important to remember that artifacts are not just things, they are also *symbols*. Important life transitions, for instance, are often marked by material culture. In American society of the 1950s and 1960s, getting your first car was not simply acquiring a mode of transportation; the car you drove carried a symbolic meaning—it said something about your position in life. Similarly, thousands of years ago, a bow was a weapon for hunting, and it may also have been a powerful symbol of adulthood.

How an artifact enters the archaeological record is a product of how it was used. But because material culture carries symbolic meanings, people sometimes actively manipulate material culture to send culturally specific symbolic messages. Bringing flowers or a bottle of wine to dinner is a standard American way to thank a host. But such a gesture would be meaningless to the Mikea (the forager-horticulturalists we discussed in Chapter 7), who instead expect guests to bring tobacco.

This fact—that *material culture reflects symbolic meanings as well as functional behaviors*—means that artifacts can be exceedingly difficult to understand. But archaeologists are making progress in using artifacts to infer ancient social and political organization, and this chapter provides several examples of how this works.

Archaeology and Gender

Anthropologists distinguish between sex and gender, and between gender roles and gender ideology. *Sex* refers to inherited, biological differences between males and females. *Gender,* on the other hand, refers to culturally constructed ideas about sex differences. Humans have only two sexes, male and female—but there can be more than two genders. Some societies recognize men who choose to live as women or women who choose to live as men as a third gender. In some Plains Indian tribes, for example, **berdaches** (also known as "two-spirits") were men who chose to live as women, performing women's traditional roles, and even marrying men (although marriage in this case did not imply a sexual relationship).

This leads us to the difference between gender *role* and gender *ideology*. **Gender role** refers to the different participation of males and females in the various social, economic, political, and religious institutions of a cultural group. These roles describe culturally appropriate behavior for men and women. In some societies, women can play very public roles, for example, in politics; in others, women's public participation may be limited (though their private participation may still be influential). **Gender ideology** refers to the culturally specific meaning assigned to terms such as "male," "female," "sex," and "reproduction." In some societies, men and women have a generally equal footing; in others, men are considered of greater importance; and in others, the activities of men and women are so differently valued that adult men and women interact very little. In traditional New Guinean societies, for example, men spend much of their leisure time in a communal men's house rather than in their separate family homes.

These facts are important to understanding other societies, and they are important to understanding archaeological inference. Some years ago, recognition of gender ideology led Margaret Conkey (University of California, Berkeley) and Janet Spector (retired, formerly University of Minnesota) to argue that archaeology had a strong **androcentric** bias. Archaeologists at the time were mostly male, and they viewed the world largely in terms of men's activities and perceptions (and, in fact, in terms of white, middle-class, European male understandings of the world). Conkey and Spector saw this as a product of the reigning American gender ideology, in which women's contributions were downplayed and women were supposed to stay home and not participate in the "important" activities of the public sphere. They documented several cases in which this gender ideology was projected onto the past, with

berdaches Among Plains Indian societies, men who elected to live life as women; they were recognized by their group as a third gender.

gender role The culturally prescribed behavior associated with men and women; roles can vary from society to society.

gender ideology The culturally prescribed values assigned to the task and status of men and women; values can vary from society to society.

androcentric A perspective that focuses on what men do in a society, to the exclusion of women.

males portrayed as stronger, more active, and more important than women, who were portrayed as weak, passive, and dependent. According to the archaeological interpretations of the day, men made things happen and women went along for the ride.

Conkey and Spector argued that archaeologists saw specific artifact forms as associated with one gender or the other: Hunting weaponry was always male, plant-collecting gear was always female. Men made projectile points and other stone tools; women made pottery and baskets. Archaeologists blithely assumed that a woman buried with a grinding stone *used* this artifact in life. But they assumed that a man buried with the same grinding stone had *manufactured* it.

Conkey and Spector found that most archaeologists failed to identify the sources for their assumptions and rarely tried to confirm or validate them. In other words, *the only middle-range theory operating here was the archaeologists' culturally biased view of gender roles.*

As an example, consider the site of Indian Knoll in western Kentucky, a 2-acre, 8-foot-deep shell midden along the Green River (Figure 10-1). This midden accumulated over a long period, from about 6100 to 4500 years ago. Indian Knoll was first excavated in 1916 by C. B. Moore and then in the 1930s and 1940s by William Webb (1882–1964). (Formally trained as a physicist, Webb was almost certainly the only archaeologist to help develop the atomic bomb.)

Indian Knoll is a **shell midden**—the remains of tens of thousands of shellfish meals are preserved there—but it was also a burial place. Between the two of them, Moore and Webb excavated some 1200 burials at the site. Men were generally buried with axes, fishhooks, and other tools; women were buried with beads, mortars, and pestles.

Also in some burials were beautifully polished stones, a few inches long, and somewhat triangular in cross-section, with the sides slightly convex. A hole was drilled neatly lengthwise down the middle of the stone. With these stones were often found pieces of whittled, slightly curved antler, with a neat hook at one end.

shell midden The remnants of shellfish collecting; some shellfish middens can become many meters thick.

Moore was puzzled by these enigmatic objects. He thought the stones might have served to hold cords the appropriate distance apart when weaving fishing nets; the antlers he thought might be netting needles.

But having seen well-preserved examples from dry caves in Texas and Arizona, Webb recognized these artifacts as parts of *atlatls,* or spearthrowers. A wooden atlatl arm, perhaps 2 feet long, fit into one end of the drilled stone and the antler hook into the other; both were held in place by pitch or tree resin. The hook on the tapered end of the antler held the atlatl dart in place as the hunter took aim, and the stone weight increased the centrifugal force of the weapon as the hunter swung the atlatl overhead, launching the dart. The wooden atlatl arm and accompanying darts would have long since decayed in the Indian Knoll midden, but the stone and antler remained.

Webb was curious about the distribution of these atlatls. Of the 76 burials that held atlatl weights, 31 were adult males, 13 were adult females, and 18 were those of children (sex could not be identified on the remaining 14 individuals).Why, Webb wondered, did people place hunting weapons in the graves of women and children? In 1946, he wrote "it is hardly to be supposed that infants, children, *and women* would have any practical use in life for an atlatl" (emphasis added).

Trying to explain this apparent conundrum, Webb noted that the people of Indian Knoll often buried these beautifully made atlatls intact; but they also sometimes intentionally broke the spearthrowers at the time of burial, as evidenced by the presence of all the fragments of an atlatl weight in grave fill. Adding this to the fact that the atlatls were buried with children and women, Webb argued that the artifacts reflected an intentional burial ritual, rather than grave goods for use in the afterlife. We know that in some Native American societies, people cut their hair as a symbol of mourning. Perhaps thousands of years ago at Indian Knoll, the destruction and burial of atlatls carried a similar symbolic meaning—a way for men to express their grief for a deceased child, wife, sister, or mother in a culturally appropriate way.

Notice how Webb's argument is grounded in the assumption—by no means illogical—that atlatls were interred with adult males because they were tools used by men during their lifetime (hence they would need them in the afterlife). By this reasoning, of course, one must likewise assume that some of the women at Indian

Figure 10-1 The site of Indian Knoll (Kentucky). In the days of Works Progress Administration (WPA) archaeology, a huge portion of the site was excavated, and hundreds of human burials uncovered.

Knoll also hunted. But because Webb could not conceive of women as hunters, he searched for another explanation for the inclusion of atlatls in women's graves. Although his final explanation could still be right—why, otherwise, did people bury atlatls with children?— Webb's underlying logic demonstrates the importance of using caution to detect our own cultural biases, especially when it comes to matters of gender roles.

Before we look at how archaeologists reconstruct what men and women did in the past, let us pause to consider whether this difficult task is even necessary. Do we really need to know whether men or women did the hunting, or plant gathering, or other tasks? Isn't this concern with gender simply an imposition of the *current* American culture of political correctness? We don't think so; and the following ethnographic example demonstrates the importance of knowing what men and women did in the past.

Hunting in Africa's Rain Forest

Popularly known as "Pygmies," the BaMbuti are hunter-gatherers who live in the Ituri Rain Forest of central Africa. There, a number of different cultural groups such as the Efe, Aka, and Mbuti live in small temporary camps. They hunt a variety of animals and gather wild plants and honey in the forest. Nearly all these groups exchange meat for agricultural produce with their neighbors, Bantu horticulturalists. They also sometimes work for them in their fields.

Years ago, Colin Turnbull (1924–1994) initiated a long-running debate in anthropology when he observed that some BaMbuti hunt individually with bows and arrows whereas other groups hunt communally with nets. Among net-hunters, women and children drive game (such as the duiker, a small antelope) through the forest into nets, where men club the animals (though in some groups women kill the netted game). Archers shoot monkeys and other prey that seek refuge in treetops, but they, too, hunt the duiker. Archers sometimes hunt communally, but they also hunt alone.

From an archaeological perspective, these two kinds of BaMbuti societies would differ in their hunting technology—one would leave behind nets and evidence of their manufacture; the other, projectile points, bows, and arrows. Such differences in technology are precisely the sort of patterning that archaeologists seek to document and explain.

Why do the BaMbuti use different hunting methods? Turnbull attributed the difference to simple cultural preference; some groups, Turnbull argued, chose to use nets and other groups preferred the bow. But other anthropologists saw it differently. Some argued that Bantu horticulturalists introduced net hunting to the forest and that it had spread because it was more efficient than bow hunting; those who lived close to the Bantu had already benefited from this technology, whereas those living farther away had yet to acquire it. Others suggested that net hunting was a response to the crowding created by Bantu emigration; nets were a way to extract more food from limited portions of the forest. The bow hunters, on the other hand, worked in Bantu fields, receiving produce through their labor rather than by trading meat, and so they eschewed net hunting.

Others argued the inverse: that net hunting was *less* efficient than bow hunting and net hunters sacrificed efficiency for volume, using nets to harvest a surplus of meat for trade. Another explanation was that the thick undergrowth of the net hunters' environment made archery an impractical hunting technique there.

Anthropologists Robert Bailey (University of Illinois, Chicago) and Robert Aunger (University College, London) decided to test these competing hypotheses. Drawing upon ethnographic and environmental records, they found that (1) no significant differences exist between the environments of net hunters and those of archers, (2) net hunting is no more or less efficient than bow hunting, and (3) bow hunters did not live nearer to or trade more with Bantu peoples than net hunters. In other words, the evidence contradicted every available hypothesis.

Then Bailey and Aunger observed that whereas women participate in net hunts, they rarely hunt in the archer groups. So the question, perhaps, is not why some BaMbuti hunt with nets and others with bows and arrows, but rather *how women decide whether to participate in hunts.*

Recall that many BaMbuti trade meat with Bantu horticulturalists for produce; in fact, they can acquire up to three calories worth of agricultural food for every calorie of meat they trade. Some women also work as laborers for horticulturalists, and they receive some of the produce as payment. Bailey and Aunger argued that women decide to hunt or to work in fields depending on which activity gives them the greatest return for their effort. Testing this hypothesis, Bailey and Aunger found that net hunters live near Bantu with *small* gardens whereas bow hunters live near Bantu with *large* gardens.

In areas where gardens are small, Bantu women do not need BaMbuti women as laborers and, because they cannot work for produce, BaMbuti women help with the hunting. Presumably, as long as many people are available, net hunting is a better way to utilize this extra labor. Where gardens are large, Bantu women need assistance. They hire BaMbuti women, who apparently make a greater return as workers than as hunters. Without the extra labor, men hunt individually, with bows and arrows. The key to BaMbuti hunting choices, then, depended not merely on the hunting technology or environment alone, but also on women's choices.

This example demonstrates that options, decisions, and activities by both men and women condition the larger patterns in material culture that archaeology excels in revealing.

Reconstructing Male and Female Activities from Archaeology

One reason for archaeology's androcentric bias was the fact that for decades, the field was male-dominated. Another was that archaeologists were simply unaware of the extent to which their own culture affected the way they viewed and understood the world. We believed that, as true scientists, we could be objective about the past.

This attitude has changed significantly in recent years. Half of all professional archaeologists in the United States today are women, and few modern archaeologists would blithely make such simplistic correlations as atlatl = male or pottery = female. We recognize the biases of past archaeological research and understand that knowing what men and women did in the past is not just politically correct; it is important to understanding prehistory.

Some feminist archaeologists believe that it is unnecessary to ascribe particular tasks to men or women in order to take a gendered perspective on prehistory. But others argue that we can't answer important anthropological questions unless we know, for a particular archaeological case, whether men or women used this or that artifact.

Can we reconstruct what men and women did in the past? If so, how? These questions raise some difficult problems of middle-range theory. In Chapter 9, we explored one approach. Skeletal analysis can tell us something about the different mechanical stresses placed on men and women, but the cause of these stresses still requires some guesswork.

Stable isotope analysis can also point to differences in men's and women's diets. Following up Christine Hastorf's and Sissel Johannessen's research in the Upper Mantaro Valley (see Chapter 8), Michael DeNiro (University of California, Santa Barbara) analyzed bone samples from human skeletons dating to the different phases for carbon and nitrogen stable isotopes. He found no significant differences between men and women during the Wanka II phase, during which men and women apparently ate much the same foods. But analysis of human remains from the Wanka III phase (after the Inka had expanded into the Mantaro Valley) showed that half of the men had a considerably higher maize intake. DeNiro sees this as evidence that men participated in rituals (where maize beer was consumed) more often. If so, then not only did men participate in the public sphere of life more than women, but some men participated more than other men. This interpretation thus points out differences between men and women, as well as among men.

But human skeletal evidence can take us only so far. What about everything else found in archaeological sites? How would we know if a man or woman made or used a particular stone tool, pot, or basket? Because archaeologists lack an established method for objectively deriving this sort of information from material remains, most investigators are forced to rely on ethnographic analogy, with all its inherent limitations.

Were Ceramics Made by Men or Women?

Ceramic technology provides a case in point. There are two basic ways to make a pot. In the first method the potter constructs the vessel by hand, either by molding the clay or by rolling it into a long "snake" and then coiling it up to build the pot's base and walls; the pot's walls are then smoothed by hand.

The other technique is to throw a lump of clay onto a wheel that is rotated manually by the potter (and today by a powered device). The potter then uses the spinning clay's centrifugal force to shape it by hand. The method used on a given pot is relatively easy to determine from characteristics of potsherds.

Working from this simple baseline, Prudence Rice (Southern Illinois University) surveyed ethnographic data from a variety of societies around the world and discovered that, when pottery is fashioned by hand, it is usually manufactured by women. In contrast, men usually manufacture pottery made on a wheel. Archaeologists can draw on this kind of strong analogy to infer past behavior with a high (but not absolute) degree of certainty: If archaeological evidence shows that pottery was made by hand, then we infer that the pottery was *probably* made by women. In contrast, if we find evidence that pottery was made on the wheel, then we say that the potter was *probably* male.

As we cautioned in Chapter 7, this sort of analogy can be made stronger if we can actually *explain* the inferred pattern; but in this case, this explanation is not easy. There is, of course, no inherent reason why women could not have used the wheel to produce pottery (and, indeed, many female potters do so today). The uniformitarian assumption that we discussed in Chapter 7 fails in this case.

Perhaps the reason lies in the *purpose* of pottery made on the wheel versus that made by hand. Archaeologists know that the wheel is associated with craft specialization and the marketing of pottery. Thus, it appears that when pottery moves from production for the residential group to production for the nonresidential group, the task shifts from women to men. *Why* this should happen, however, is much harder to say.

An alternative approach is to use an ethnographic analogy that is historically linked to the archaeological population being studied. Rosemary Joyce used this approach to create some deeper understanding of Maya men and women.

Gender in Maya Iconography

The Maya often depicted themselves on stone stelae, on polychrome (multicolored) pottery, in paintings and carvings on lintels inside temples and tombs, and in books called **codices,** which were long strips of paper, many meters in length when unfolded, made of pounded inner tree bark. (The Spanish considered them heretical and destroyed all they could find; only four survive today.)

The images commonly depict Maya wearing intricate, complex costumes (Figure 10-2), which to us appear flamboyant, even outlandish. But the Maya mode of dress encoded considerable cultural information.

© Peabody Museum, Harvard University

Figure 10-2 A Mayan drawing from the site of Yachilan, Lintel 1. The figure at the right wears a *huipil* and carries a textile bundle.

These figures rarely have overt sexual characteristics, in large part because of the elaborate costuming. Women are sometimes identified with a particular glyph, but not always.

Because archaeologists can today read Maya hieroglyphic writing, we know a considerable amount about the meaning of these images. Rosemary Joyce and others have found that Maya iconography displays women wearing three distinctive dress styles: a simple wrapped garment that covers the breasts, body, and legs, but leaves the arms bare; a woven *huipil,* a housecoat-like garment that covers the entire body; and, more rarely, a jade-bead skirt, often with a fish-monster-and-shell belt.

Joyce used these clothing styles to identify women on the carved stelae, despite the lack of overt sexual characteristics. Women are seen holding and offering ceramic vessels, bundles of cloth, or paper and bloodletting instruments (which the Maya used to cut their tongues, in symbolic communication with the gods). The remaining figures, the male ones, often hold weapons, shields, or scepters that represent double-headed axes—the instruments of war. Although the women in the images might be dismissed as servants, Joyce looked for a deeper meaning in the ethnographic data gleaned from the codices, early Spanish observations, and modern ethnography.

The modern Maya participate in a **cargo system,** in which a responsible, married man is selected annually to direct the ceremonial system (today a combination of Catholicism and the indigenous religion), with men and women occupying complementary roles. This man

codices Maya texts, long strips of paper, many meters in length when unfolded, made of the pounded inner bark of certain trees; these texts helped analysts interpret Maya hieroglyphics on stelae.

cargo system Part of the social organization found in many Central American communities in which a wealthy individual is named to carry out and bear the cost of important religious ceremonies throughout the year.

holds a number of feasts to accompany rituals and his wife, who acts as an assistant, takes on the title of "Mother of" the man's named position. Other elderly women are responsible for preparing food, tending to incense for purification ceremonies, and enforcing appropriate manners and protocol during the feasts.

Joyce suggests that women depicted in the Classic Maya stelae may have occupied similar complementary (rather than subservient) roles. She points out that the stelae pair male and female figures in culturally appropriate ways, perhaps symbolizing a ruler's political aims of combining male and female elements—perhaps a claim to male/female prerogatives and powers and maybe as a way to extend the right of male rulers to claim the products of female labor (such as weaving).

Such interpretations are impossible without adequate ethnographic analogy, for better and for worse (as discussed in Chapter 7). Others might question the use of the cargo system as an analogy for interpreting Maya stelae. After all, many of the women shown on stelae are partners in marriages between royal families (marriages that created key military alliances, as they did in Europe). Thus, the purpose of women in these images is starkly different from that entailed in the cargo system.

One way to assess an analogy's strength is explore additional formal similarities between the analogy and the archaeological case. Joyce found that whereas male figures generally occupy the "public" side of the stela, women were often paired with men on the "backs" of stelae, facing away from the primary public area, and were sometimes rendered in a lower position than their male counterparts. Joyce also found that, when the stelae are viewed from prominent vantage points in a ceremonial center, women are more frequently depicted to the left of male images. Ethnographic evidence corresponds with such placements, with Maya women commonly relegated to left-hand and lower elevations, whereas men are associated with the right-hand and upper elevations. If this ethnographic pattern holds true for Maya stelae, then the analogy would be strengthened.

Nevertheless, modern archaeologists have little to say with certainty about gender roles and ideologies in the past. But when historically linked analogies are available, we at least have a way to frame some appropriate hypotheses.

Archaeology and Kinship

Kinship refers to the socially recognized network of relationships through which individuals are related to one another by ties of descent (real or imagined) and marriage. A kinship system blends the facts of biological descent and relatedness with cultural rules that define some people as close kin and others as distant kin, or not kin at all. These groupings are important because they condition, and sometimes dictate, the nature of relationships between individuals.

Kinship may not seem very significant to you. We don't mean that you don't care about your family, but on a day-to-day basis, most of the people you interact with are not kin. Instead, they are friends, teachers, representatives of the government, bosses, subordinates, and so on. But in the nonindustrial world, most people interact on a daily basis with people who are kin. The same was true of much of the ancient world.

So, if you fail to understand a society's kinship pattern, you might misread a lot of their behavior. For example, a woman from the island of Pingelap in Micronesia once casually listed the members of her household to Kelly: "That child there is my son, and that girl is my daughter. The young woman over there is my sister and the man next to her is her husband. Of course, my father over there is my mother's brother." If her last statement brings images of incest to mind, we assure you that you are wrong, and understanding the kinship system shows why.

Forms of Kinship

The world of kinship is incredibly complex; we simplify matters here by concentrating on three basic forms of kinship. Anthropologists depict kin relations in standard diagrams. In Figure 10-3, the triangles stand for males and the circles for females. The equal sign (=) stands for marriage, the solid horizontal lines connect siblings, and the vertical lines indicate offspring. The square (indicating either sex) places you within the kinship diagram.

kinship Socially recognized network of relationships through which individuals are related to one another by ties of descent (real or imagined) and marriage.

Bilateral descent should be familiar because it is the standard kinship in North America, as well as in many other industrialized nations. In bilateral descent, an individual traces his or her relatives *equally* on the mother's and father's sides. Although you might be closer to your mother's or father's side (because of geography, divorce, or personalities), neither side of the family is a priori more important than the other. Evidence of this is the fact that names applied to relatives on either side of the family are the same. Father's brother and mother's brother, for example, are both "uncles" (in English).

Kinship in cultures with bilateral descent tend to lack "depth"—meaning that few individuals know who their great or great-great-grandparents are, much less their great-great-grandparents' siblings' offsprings' offspring. This is because *in bilateral descent, the nuclear family is the important economic unit.*

The next two kinds of kinship systems are strikingly different from bilateral descent because they privilege one side of the family over the other; these are *unilineal* descent systems. In **patrilineal descent,** the nuclear family may constitute the residential unit, but the most important group is the **patrilineage,** people to whom you are related *through the male line.* Figure 10-3 shows two hypothetical kin diagrams, one of which represents patrilineal descent, in which the shaded individuals belong to "your" patrilineage. These are all the people that are biologically related to you through a male—your father and his siblings, your father's father and his siblings, your father's brothers' children, and your father's father's brothers' children; we could extend the same to your great-grandfather's and great-great-grandfather's generation, and so on. These individuals are members of one patrilineage.

In patrilineal descent, you acquire your patrilineage from your father. The other people in the diagram belong to other patrilineages (societies with unilineal descent commonly forbid marriage between men and

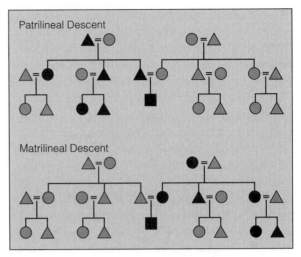

Figure 10-3 Patrilineal and matrilineal descent. The dark colored circles (females) and triangles (males) show who belongs to one patrilineage (*top*) and matrilineage (*bottom*).

women of the same lineage). So, your mother belongs to a different patrilineage than your father and, consequently, a different patrilineage than you.

Patrilineal societies make up about 60 percent of the world's known societies. They are associated with a wide range of conditions, including hunting-and-gathering, agricultural, and pastoral societies. They are also associated with internal warfare—that is, war with close neighbors.

Keep in mind that patrilineages contain both males and females—because anyone biologically linked to you through a male is a member of your lineage (such as your father's brother's daughters). Your father's sister is included, but not her offspring. And don't think that members of patrilineal societies are confused about matters of human reproduction. They understand the biological facts of life completely, and they do not ignore "kin" on their mother's side. But in patrilineal descent, your mother's side is simply less important. This is because the lineage normally owns or controls land and other resources, not the nuclear family. The lineage makes decisions about whether to move a village, go to war, or dig irrigation ditches. Thus, although the nuclear family matters, it is secondary to the interests and concerns of the patrilineage.

This difference is reflected in kin terms. Men call their biological father by a term meaning "father," but they may also call their father's brother "father," and

bilateral descent A kinship system in which relatives are traced equally on both the mother's and father's sides.

patrilineal descent A unilineal descent system in which ancestry is traced through the male line.

patrilineage Individuals who share a line of patrilineal descent.

consequently, they may call their father's brother's off-spring "brother" and "sister," rather than "cousins." In patrilineal descent your mother's brother's children belong to another lineage (*their* father's lineage), and so they are called by a term that we might translate as "cousin," but not "brother" or "sister." Your father's and mother's siblings are the same *kind* of relative in a bilateral descent system, but not in a patrilineal descent system.

The bottom chart in Figure 10-3 contains the same biological facts as the top one, but they are now organized into **matrilineal descent.** Here, you trace relatives through the female line, forming **matrilineages.** In matrilineal societies you get your lineage from your mother. Your lineage includes you, your mother, her siblings and her sisters' offspring, your mother's mother, her siblings and her sisters' offspring, and so on. As in patrilineal societies, nuclear families exist, but the primary unit is the matrilineage.

By now, you can probably guess why the Pingelapese woman said that her mother's brother was her father: in matrilineal societies, the mother's brother is a "fictive" father. The biological father, in fact, may have little to do with his biological offspring. Instead, he spends his time with his sister's children—because they are members of his lineage, and so it is they, not his biological offspring, who will inherit whatever resources, knowledge, or privileges he possesses.

Matrilineal societies are rare, composing only about 10 percent of the world's societies. They appear to be associated with horticulture, long-distance hunting, and/or warfare with distant enemies. In many instances, these different kinship groupings are reflected in archaeological remains (see "Looking Closer: Kinship and Residence among the Mikea").

Finally, to complicate things even more, we need to note that lineages are sometimes clustered into **clans,** which is a set of lineages that claim to share a distant, often mythical, ancestor (Figure 10-5, page 236). Clans, in turn, may be clustered into **moieties** (pronounced "*moy*-i-tees"; from the French word meaning "half"; in any society with moieties, there are only two). Moieties often perform reciprocal ceremonial obligations for each other, such as burying the dead of the other or holding feasts for one another. We come back to these terms later when we examine how kinship is reflected in the archaeology of the site of Moundville.

Archaeology and Social Status

Status consists of the rights, duties, privileges, and powers that accrue to a recognized and named social position. In our own society, the status of "mother" is determined by both the duties she owes to her son or daughter and the responsibilities she can legitimately demand of her children. Similarly, a child owes certain obligations to a parent and can expect certain privileges in return. As you will see, gender and age play important roles in status.

Two major ways of assigning status are through *ascription* and *achievement*. An **ascribed status** is assigned to individuals at birth, without regard to innate differences or abilities. Prince Charles, for example, has high status and expects to become king of England—not because of anything he has done, but simply because his mother is Queen Elizabeth II. His status and rights were ensured at birth.

Alternatively, many statuses are **achieved** and require that an individual possess certain admirable qualities or have accomplished certain tasks (the importance of these qualities and tasks being culturally defined). Rather than being assigned at birth, achieved statuses are earned through individual effort. A Shoshone man who proved to be a good hunter might achieve status as a leader in hunts but, upon his death, no one would automatically fill his former position.

---

matrilineal descent A unilineal descent system in which ancestry is traced through the female line.

matrilineage Individuals who share a line of matrilineal descent.

clans A group of matri- or patrilineages who see themselves as descended from a (sometimes mythical) common ancestor.

moieties Two groups of clans that perform reciprocal ceremonial obligations for one another; moieties often intermarry.

status The rights, duties, privileges, powers, liabilities, and immunities that accrue to a recognized and named social position.

ascribed status Rights, duties, and obligations that accrue to a person by virtue of their parentage; ascribed status is inherited.

achieved status Rights, duties, and obligations that accrue to a person by virtue of what they accomplished in their life.

LOOKING CLOSER
Kinship and Residence among the Mikea

To see whether descent systems can be detected archaeologically, we return to the Mikea of Madagascar, a patrilineal society that also practices **patrilocal residence** (in which a wife lives with her husband in his original village). Figure 10-4 is a kinship chart and map showing where people live in one particular Mikea forest hamlet; sometimes, young children and single, elderly individuals lived in small, separate houses. (The lines drawn through some of the kinship symbols indicate deceased individuals.)

Several trends emerge about Mikea kinship and settlement. Note that the houses are arranged in a linear, north-to-south scatter, with doors facing north. The hamlet contains two primary house clusters, marked by trampled areas of vegetation around the houses, and an untrampled belt of vegetation and trash (mostly maize husks) between the two. A path (shown with broken lines) connects the two clusters.

The kin diagram likewise demarcates two patrilineages at this hamlet, each with an older man and his wife, with their sons and their wives, and their unmarried children and grandchildren. These two patrilineages are linked by virtue of several marriages between the sons of one of the elder couples and the daughters of the other.

This arrangement is typical of Mikea forest hamlets, where members of two patrilineages live together, united by marriage ties or a link through a woman. There is usually some tension between these two clusters, and the sharing of tools and labor typically occurred *within* each of these clusters, but is rarer *between* the two.

Notice how the patrilineages map onto the ground: the northern cluster of houses contains men (and unmarried sisters) who belong to the same lineage along with their wives and children; similarly, the southern cluster contains brothers who belong to another lineage, with their wives and offspring. The same social relationships mapped out in virtually every settlement we visited: The closer a social relationship is between two people or two groups, the closer they live to one another.

Archaeologically, of course, the Mikea hamlets appear simply as two clusters of houses. Although we might infer that each cluster represents a social grouping, we'd be hard pressed to say whether it was a patrilineage, matrilineage, or some other grouping, such as a clan or moiety. As with gender, we must fall back on ethnographic analogy to understand kinship systems of the past.

Egalitarian Societies

The concept of status allows us to bridge from the level of the individual to that of the entire society. A society is termed **egalitarian** when there is no fixed number of positions of status; instead, the number of valued statuses is equal to the number of persons with the ability to fill them. No one individual wields complete authority over another. The important feature, then, is that *members of egalitarian societies generally have equal access to critical, life-sustaining resources.*

The social system of the nineteenth-century Great Basin Shoshone people was generally egalitarian, with leadership by those individuals believed to be the most capable of supervising others. Anthropologists call

patrilocal residence A cultural practice in which a newly married couple live in the groom's village of origin; it is often associated with patrilineal descent.

egalitarian societies Social systems that contain roughly as many valued positions as there are persons capable of filling them; in egalitarian societies, all people have nearly equal access to the critical resources needed to live.

Figure 10-4 Mikea hamlet map with kinship chart; notice how the patrilineages are linked by marriage and yet are separated on the ground.

such small-scale egalitarian societies **bands.** Authority was restricted to particular, short-term circumstances. A good hunter, for instance, might assume a temporary position of leadership when a group decided to hunt bighorn. An accomplished dancer might take charge of communal gatherings. Or the opinion of a gifted naturalist might convince others of the medicinal attributes of particular plants. But these individuals would have no authority outside their area of expertise. The key to leadership here is experience and social standing; such a social position is *not* inherited in an egalitarian society. Gender and age are the primary dimensions of status in egalitarian communities.

Ranked Societies

Ranked societies limit the positions of valued status so that not everyone of sufficient talent can actually achieve them. Such a social structure entails a hierarchy

band A residential group composed of a few nuclear families, but whose membership is neither permanent nor binding.

ranked societies Social systems in which a hierarchy of social status has been established, with a restricted number of valued positions available; in ranked societies, not everyone has the same access to the critical resources of life.

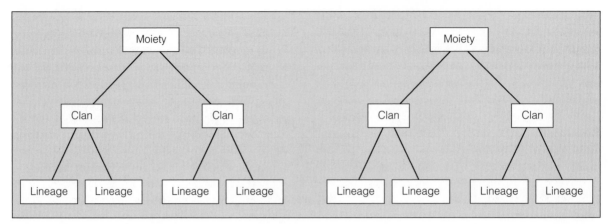

Figure 10-5 The relationships among lineages, clans, and moieties.

in which relatively permanent social stations are maintained, *with people having unequal access to life-sustaining resources.* Gender and age still play a role in the division of labor in ranked societies. But ranked societies tend to have economies that redistribute goods and services throughout the community, with those doing the redistributing keeping some portion for themselves. This creates one or more ranked social tiers to the society. Tahitian society, mentioned earlier, was a ranked society. Localized residential kin groups (such as a patrilineage) control resources, and major economic goods flow in and out of a regional center.

Death and Social Status

The categories "egalitarian" and "ranked" define a social spectrum of statuses that can be inferred from analyses of material culture. Mortuary remains are one important source of information on extinct political systems. For the past three decades, many archaeologists have used ethnographic data to show that *societies that have important social distinctions among living individuals will have material distinctions among the dead.*

Mississippian A widespread cultural tradition across much of the eastern United States from AD 800 to 1500. Mississippian societies engaged in intensive village-based maize horticulture and constructed large, earthen platform mounds that served as substructures for temples, residences, and council buildings.

Death, in a sense, is a period of separation and reintegration for both the deceased and those they leave behind. The deceased are separated from the living and must be properly integrated into the world of the dead. Social ties existed between the living and the once-living, and the ceremonial connections at death reflect these social relations. Mortuary rituals reflect who people were and the relationships they had with others when they were alive. Therefore, they should reflect the person's degree of social status in a society.

Rank and Status at Moundville

We can examine the ranking of social status at Moundville, one of the best-known and most intensively investigated ceremonial centers in the United States. Sprawling across 300 acres, Moundville overlooks Alabama's Black Warrior River. Three thousand people once lived here, and for centuries, Moundville was the largest center in the American Southeast.

This complex of about 30 earthen mounds was a bustling ritual center between about AD 1050 and 1450. Like most **Mississippian** political units, this maize-based society engaged in extensive trade, and their skilled artists worked in stone, ceramics, bone, and copper. Moundville contains 20 major ceremonial mounds—large, flat-topped earthen structures designed to function both as artificial mountains (elevating elite residences and possibly temples above the landscape) and as mortuary areas. A stout bastioned palisade protected Moundville's large central plaza.

This suggests that warfare was probably a recurring feature of life at Moundville (Figure 10-6).

Moundville was a major participant in the "Mississippian tradition," a term referring to the hundreds of societies that thrived between about AD 800 and 1500 throughout the southeastern United States. In their heyday, the Mississippian elite presided over breathtaking ceremonial centers (as at Moundville) that were invested with power by the thousands of people who lived in smaller nearby farmsteads.

The ubiquitous C. B. Moore conducted archaeological investigations at Moundville in 1905 and 1906, digging into both platform mounds and village areas. The Alabama Museum of Natural History then excavated at Moundville from 1930 through 1941. Over a half-million square feet of the village areas at Moundville were uncovered during this 11-year period, in part by workers in the Civilian Conservation Corps. The more than 3000 excavated burials from Moundville provide a unique database for studying Mississippian social structure.

The Symbolism of Grave Goods at Moundville

Christopher Peebles (Indiana University) and Susan Kus (Rhodes College) took advantage of this database and analyzed Moundville's burials with an eye toward reconstructing Moundville's political organization. They

Figure 10-6 A map of the site of Moundville; the letters designate mounds mentioned in the text. From Archaeology of the Moundville Chiefdom, edited by Vernon James Knight, Jr., and Vincas P. Steponaitis, published by the Smithsonian Institute Press, Washington, D.C.; copyright © 1998 by the Smithsonian Institution. Used by permission of the publisher.

LOOKING CLOSER

Help Find Moundville's Stolen Ceramics

The site of Moundville is now a state archaeological park managed by the University of Alabama. In 1939, the Jones Archaeological Museum opened there, built by the Civilian Conservation Corps. The museum long displayed human burials, but out of deference to Native American sensibilities, all remains were removed from public display in 1989.

There is something else that is not on display either: the 264 ceramic vessels and artifacts stolen from Moundville's archaeological repository in 1980. So far, the FBI has been unable to recover a single pot. These vessels amounted to one-fifth of the entire Moundville collection and were some of the finest specimens. The thieves knew exactly what they were looking for, and given that the pots have not turned up on the art market, it is likely that the theft was carried out on behalf of a well-heeled and unscrupulous collector.

You might be able to help recover these priceless pieces of Native American heritage. The Moundville website (http://moundville.ua.edu/home.html) contains photos of all the stolen vessels. If you see any of these for sale on the Web, in auctions, art houses, or flea markets, report it to the contacts listed on the website.

began with the grave goods, many of which display the distinctive symbols characteristic of what archaeologists call the **Southeastern Ceremonial Complex.**

During the Mississippian period, artifacts that bore striking stylistic similarities appear in a number of sites and several large centers, including Moundville, across the southeastern United States from Oklahoma to Florida. These artifacts include cups, copper plates, ceremonial axes and batons, effigy pipes, and flint knives—many decorated with one or more of a set of symbols, such as the "forked eye," the cross, the sun circle, the hand and eye, and the bi-lobed arrow (Figure 10-7). The distribution of these items parallels a trade network of exotic items, as well as basics such as food and salt. But the similarities in the motifs imply more than simple trade; a higher degree of social interaction was at work.

Whatever the Southeastern Ceremonial Complex really was—and archaeologists still debate it—it cross-cut the boundaries of many widely separate residential groups. At each major site are artifacts that bear local symbols. At Moundville, these artifacts are specially constructed animal effigy vessels or parts of animals (such as canine teeth, claws, and shells). The local symbols probably functioned as status items within Moundville, whereas the ceremonial complex symbols designated the rank of individuals in the overall region.

Each burial mound at Moundville contained a few high-status adults as indicated by their grave goods. These included copper axes, copper gorgets, stone disks, various paints, and assorted exotic minerals—such as galena (cubes of natural lead), mica (paper-thin sheets of translucent silicate minerals), and sheet copper. Copper and mica items often depict scalloped circles, swastikas, and the "hand-eye" motif (an open hand with an eye in the palm). Presumably, individuals buried with these artifacts had statuses and reputations recognized throughout the entire Moundville cultural system. Each mound also contained some presumably lower-status individuals who were buried with only a few ceramic vessels. Other commoners were buried in cemeteries away from the mounds with no burial goods (or, at least, none that preserved).

By correlating the presence of higher- and lower-status symbols, Peebles and Kus could infer that social

Southeastern Ceremonial Complex An assortment of ceremonial objects that occurs in the graves of high-status Mississippian individuals. Ritual exchange of these artifacts cross-cut the boundaries of many distinctive local cultures.

Figure 10-7 An image in the Southeastern Ceremonial Complex style, pounded in copper. Note particularly the forked eye motif around the eye, which probably represents a symbolic association with peregrine falcons, known for their keen vision and skill as hunters (from Spiro, Oklahoma).

status was ascribed at Moundville. Some infants and children—clearly too young to have accomplished anything noteworthy in life—were buried with lavish grave goods.

These children must have been important because of who they were at birth, not because of what they had done in their short lives. This is clear evidence of a ranked society.

Two Axes of Social Patterning

On the basis of ethnographic evidence, Peebles and Kus predicted that the Moundville population may have been subdivided along two major social axes, which they termed the "superordinate" and "subordinate." The subordinate division recognizes that certain symbols and the energy expended on mortuary ritual reflect the statuses of age and sex. With respect to age, the older the individual, the greater the opportunity for lifetime achievement, and hence the higher the deathbed rank can be. This means that at Moundville (along the subordinate axis, at least), adult burials should be more lavish than those of children, and children should be accompanied by more grave goods than infants. And because the subordinate division is also graded by gender, men and women should not be expected to have equivalent grave goods.

The superordinate division at Moundville is a partially hereditary ordering based on criteria other than age and sex. Among the elite—people whose status was assigned at birth—some individuals will be infants, some children, and the rest adults.

Peebles and Kus predicted that the statuses should form a pyramid-shaped distribution. At the base of the pyramid are the commoners, whose statuses are determined strictly by sex and age. The next step up the social ladder, the next rank, consists of those few individuals with ascribed status. Finally, at the top will be the paramount individuals, those who enjoy all the emblems of status and rank available in the society.

Quantitative Distribution of Moundville Grave Goods

This model was tested by performing a statistical analysis of the grave goods of 2053 of the best-documented burials from Moundville. This analysis uncovered three distinct clusters and subclusters, represented by burials that contained similar kinds of grave goods (and diagrammed in Figure 10-8). The seven burials of Cluster IA—the supreme division—are presumably chiefs, those individuals enjoying the highest of statuses and the ultimate political authority. All males (we think; these are based on Moore's field assessments), the elite were buried in Mounds C and D, small mortuary mounds in a secluded area to the north of the plaza, and were accompanied by a lavish array of material culture, including numerous ceremonial complex–adorned artifacts. Infants and human skulls (of individuals presumably sacrificed for the occasion) were buried as part of the Cluster IA ritual. Distinctive artifacts in these graves were large axes of copper—a metal too soft to have allowed the implements to function as chopping tools. These, then, must have served primarily as symbols, a culturally meaningful way to communicate an individual's high status and a visual reminder of the reasons for differences in people's ranks.

Cluster IB burials, both children and adult males, were interred in the mounds surrounding the plaza and in cemeteries near mounds. They also had a number of ceremonial complex artifacts plus mineral-based paints included in their grave goods. Cluster II, the final cluster of the superordinate division, included adults and children buried in cemeteries near the mounds and beneath what were charnel houses near

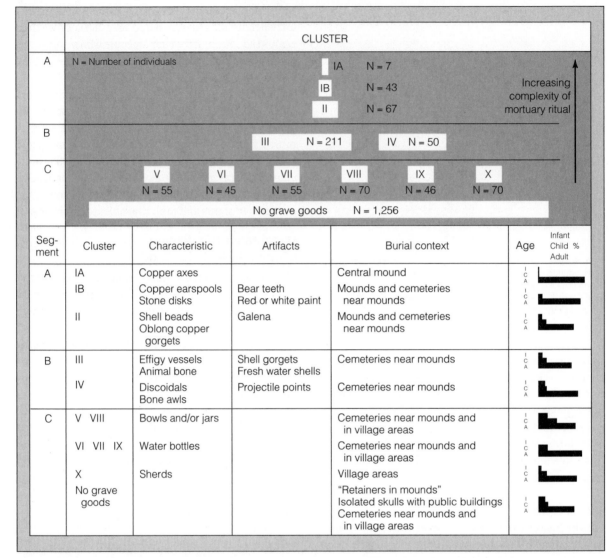

Figure 10-8 The hierarchical social clusters represented in burials at Moundville. *After Peebles and Kus (1977), Figure 3.*

the main plaza; their grave goods included chest beads, copper gorgets, and galena cubes.

Hierarchically below the Level A elite are those of subordinate Levels B and C (who enjoyed status largely on the basis of sex and age differences). In Cluster III, for instance, stone ceremonial axes are found only with adult males, whereas infants and children have "toy" vessels, clay "playthings," and unworked freshwater shells. Unworked bird claws and deer and turtle bones were found only with adults. The individuals in the lowest segment, Level C, were mostly buried away from the mounds and major ceremonial areas at Moundville. But some of the burials in this cluster were individuals

buried as retainers and isolated skulls placed at the bases of large posts.

Burial context appears to clarify the nature of ranking in the Moundville society. The most elite were buried in a sacred area and were accompanied by symbols of their exalted status. The Moundville elite also apparently lived in larger, more complex dwellings than did the commoners. Elite membership was conditioned by genealogy and, because social position was inherited within the elite, even children occupied such social positions.

Farther down the ladder, the villagers' graves also reflected their social status in life at this level, positions conditioned largely by sex and age distinctions rather than by inheritance. Their less glamorous grave goods were distributed in a different way. Graves contained pottery vessels, bone awls, flint projectile points, and stone pipes, all of which were distributed mostly to older adults. Peebles and Kus infer that these individuals were required to achieve—rather than inherit—their social status. Over half of the Moundville graves contained commoners buried with no grave goods at all.

Peebles and Kus suggested that Moundville conformed to a chiefdom model, a society similar to that of Tahiti and characterized by a status framework with fewer valued positions, although they saw no direct evidence for a redistributive economy.

Kinship at Moundville

Despite the differences in rank, Moundville was still an integrated society. And it may have been bonds of kinship that provided the integrating factor and that prevented extreme differences between the elite and the commoners. Indeed, although chiefdoms are internally ranked, their members commonly understand that everyone is ultimately, albeit sometimes distantly, a relative of the chief, who might even use kinship terms to refer to his followers.

To help reconstruct Moundville's social organization, Vernon Knight (University of Alabama) employed an ethnographic analogy with the nineteenth-century Chickasaw, the Native Americans who lived in the vicinity of Moundville at the time of European contact. Knight noted that there are two major classes of mounds at Moundville. Some of the mounds contain burials; others were residential mounds, with evidence for wattle-and-daub or thatch structures on their flat tops.

These mounds alternate around the square Moundville plaza so that each residential mound is paired with one and sometimes two burial mounds, forming eight burial/residential mound groups. Knight saw in this pattern a parallel to Chickasaw society.

The ethnographic data are limited, and Chickasaw society had undergone profound changes because of European contact, but Knight found that the ideal Chickasaw village had sets of houses arranged around a square plaza, just as the mounds at Moundville form a square plaza. In Chickasaw society, each set of houses belonged to a matrilocal clan that was the political and land-owning unit. In addition, the clans were grouped into moieties, and each moiety lived on opposite sides

of the square village layout. The highest ranking clan of each moiety was located on opposite sides of the north end of the square plan, with lower ranking clans to the south. Thus, Chickasaw villages spatially mirrored the kinship structure.

Knight wondered if this kinship pattern extended back to the inhabitants of Moundville. Perhaps, he suggested, each of the eight residential/burial mound units represents the high-ranking home of the leader of eight clans. Knight pointed out that the Moundville plaza can be neatly bifurcated by a line passing through Mound B at the north end of the plaza, through the central Mound A, and then between smaller burial mounds K and J (refer to Figure 10-6). Extrapolating from the Chickasaw analogy, the resulting halves might represent two moieties, each comprising four clans. Note also that the most elite burials were recovered in Mounds C and D; although these are not the largest mounds, they are located at either side of the north edge of the plaza.

But Moundville and Chickasaw villages exhibit crucial differences:

- In the Chickasaw camp layout, a large fire hearth in the center of the village structurally and symbolically united the two moieties. There was, however, no central mound or ceremonial structure.
- Knight points out that nineteenth-century Chickasaw society was not a chiefdom and did not possess a central individual who was the uniting focus of the social and political organization. In Moundville, the large Mound B, at the north end of the site, might have been the home of the chief—the highest-ranking individual—and evidence of a tier in the social organization that was not present among the Chickasaw.

In sum, Knight's analysis of the layout of Moundville's mounds supports a conclusion that Moundville was a chiefdom.

Trade and Political Organization

In our discussion of Moundville, we mentioned the Southeastern Ceremonial Complex, a social phenomenon that included an extensive trade network. All societies—from egalitarian bands to chiefdoms to modern states—exchange goods, ideas, and services. The geographic scale of trade tells us something about the nature of the nonresidential group that a population participated in and about how far-flung were their political, economic, and kinship connections.

In archaeological sites in the Great Basin, for example, archaeologists frequently find beads made of the shells of *Olivella, Haliotis,* and *Dentalia*—marine organisms that live along the coasts of California and Oregon. Obviously, they point to some sort of interaction between people on either side of California's Sierra Nevada.

The California shell beads in Great Basin sites are not numerous. They appear as personal ornaments in some burials, but they are not exclusively associated with men or women, the old or the young. Many are found in residential sites where, because they are small, they were probably lost as they fell off clothing or a necklace. It is more difficult to say if the beads indicate exchange of goods between the peoples of the Great Basin and California or were simply the personal belongings of people (wives or husbands? emigrants?) who moved from California to the Great Basin.

Anthropologists have found that, as societies change from egalitarian bands (like the Great Basin Shoshone) to ranked societies (such as those of Tahiti or Moundville), the formal trade of **exotics** becomes an integral part of the economy. Exotics are artifacts made of raw material or in a style that indicates contact with the people of a distant region. Members of the elite trade or give away exotics at competitive feasts as a way to communicate and maintain the social order. Exotic artifacts, therefore, can be symbols of status and prestige—visual reminders of an individual's social, political, or religious connections to a larger world. As such, they can be signs of power and, consequently, of social and political organization as well.

exotics Material culture that was not produced locally and/or whose raw material is not found locally.

direct acquisition A form of trade in which a person or group goes to the source area of an item to procure the raw material directly or to trade for it or finished products.

down-the-line trade An exchange system in which goods are traded outward from a source area from group to group, resulting in a steady decline in the item's abundance in archaeological sites farther from the source.

Tracing Exotics

Archaeologists have several methods to determine which objects are locally produced and which are non-local. In some cases, it is fairly easy to determine which objects are *not* locally produced or acquired. Recall that at Moundville, for example, some of the elite burials contained copper axes. This copper is not smelted, for smelting technology did not exist in North America prior to European contact. Instead, the copper was extracted in its raw form. We know that this kind of copper deposit, known as native copper, is not found around Moundville. In fact, native copper occurs only in the southern Appalachian Mountains and near the Great Lakes. The copper artifacts at Moundville have been traced to a geologic deposit in the southern Appalachian source. Likewise, the galena cubes have been traced to geologic sources in Missouri and Wisconsin.

Human societies create many different kinds of trade systems, but they tend to be of two major types. The first is **direct acquisition,** wherein you go to the natural source of a raw material and extract the material yourself, exchange goods or services for it or for a finished artifact, or receive an artifact or raw material as a gift. Direct acquisition might entail a special trip, or it may be embedded into a foraging excursion or a visit to relatives.

The second major type is **down-the-line trade,** in which people acquire a particular raw material or an artifact fashioned from that raw material from their neighbors, who have immediate access to the raw material. These people then trade it to others who live still farther away from the source, who may in turn trade it to people living still farther away. Down-the-line trade usually exhibits a steady decline in the frequency of artifacts made of a particular material in sites farther and farther away from the raw material's source. Occasionally, an unexpectedly high density of the raw material at a site distant from the source may signal that the site is a secondary trading center.

Down-the-line trade can move raw materials long distances. For example, archaeologists have found incised Gulf Coast shells in sites along the Missouri River in Montana.

Nobody knows how the copper axes made their way to Moundville—perhaps they were gifts sent between ranking elites—but they clearly signal that only a few people had the authority and power to acquire them or to merit receiving them as gifts. Although the copper axes had no material function—they would have made poor cutting implements—they were powerful symbols of the "connections" an elite individual had and perhaps of his ability to draw upon social, economic, military, or religious sanctions should anyone contest his hold on power.

Earlier we mentioned that the copper axes at Moundville were traced to geological sources in the southern Appalachian Mountains. Archaeologists do this primarily by "fingerprinting" an object and comparing it with similar fingerprints of known geologic sources of the raw material. Several different methods can do this; we focus on three here—one used to trace obsidian and two used to trace ceramics to their sources.

Fingerprinting Obsidian

Obsidian—the volcanic glass that makes such impressively sharp implements—occurs naturally only in geologic deposits of the western United States. So, why do obsidian artifacts appear in **Hopewell** burial mounds and sites in Ohio and Illinois?

You recall from Chapter 2 that Squier and Davis mapped and studied the earthworks of the eastern United States, especially along the Ohio River valley and its tributaries. We now know that some of the flat-topped pyramid mounds—such as those at Moundville—belong to the Mississippian period. But other mounds—geometric earthworks and some effigy mounds—are earlier, belonging to the Hopewell culture. "Hopewell" refers to a particular archaeological culture found in the Midwest, especially the Ohio River valley, between 200 BC and AD 400. Hopewell peoples were predominately hunter-gatherers, although they also cultivated indigenous plants and small amounts of maize. They lived in small, sedentary villages.

Hopewell culture is best known for its elaborate mortuary rituals, which suggest the beginnings of a ranked society. Many goods appear in elite Hopewell graves, including copper ornaments, incised pottery, carved mica, ceramics, and obsidian. The fact that obsidian is found almost exclusively in burials of Ohio Hopewell sites, rather than in middens, suggests that obsidian played something other than a purely functional role in Hopewell society.

Squier and Davis recorded small numbers of obsidian spear points in five Hopewell mounds, and more have since turned up in Tennessee, Illinois, and else-

where. At the time, Squier and Davis thought that the obsidian probably came from Mexico or perhaps the American Southwest. But this was simply a guess. Early in the twentieth century, several archaeologists proposed the Rocky Mountains as the source of the Hopewell obsidian—specifically the obsidian outcrops in Yellowstone National Park, some 2400 kilometers away. Richard Hughes (Geochemical Research Laboratory, California)—one of the world's leading authorities on obsidian sourcing—used the method of **energy dispersive X-ray fluorescence (XRF)** to test this idea.

How can XRF trace obsidian artifacts to their geologic source? Many geological deposits form slowly—over years, decades, thousands, or even tens of thousands of years. But obsidian deposits are produced during a single lava flow, and hence they are created in a geologic instant. A volcano could produce multiple flows, but because each flow forms quickly, it usually has a unique chemical "fingerprint." This fingerprint appears as particular amounts of trace elements—like zinc, rubidium, strontium, and barium. Different flows contain different amounts of these elements. If we can fingerprint samples from all geologic sources of obsidian—a formidable but not impossible task—and then fingerprint obsidian artifacts, we should be able to match up an artifact with its source.

XRF allows us to accomplish this goal. The analyst shoots an X-ray beam onto a piece of obsidian, causing the electrons to become excited and emit fluorescent X-ray energies. Because different trace elements emit different levels of energy, the analyst can measure the spectra of energy emitted from the piece of obsidian and, from this, determine the proportion of each trace element present—defining the sample's distinctive trace element fingerprint. Comparing the sample's trace element composition statistically with all known

Hopewell A cultural tradition found primarily in the Ohio River valley and its tributaries, dating from 200 BC to AD 400. Hopewell societies engaged in hunting and gathering and in some horticulture of indigenous plants. They are known for their mortuary rituals, which included charnel houses and burial mounds; some central tombs contained exotics. They also constructed geometric earthworks as ceremonial enclosures and effigy mounds.

energy dispersive X-ray fluorescence (XRF) An analytical technique that uses obsidian's trace elements to "fingerprint" an artifact and trace it to its geologic source.

sources allows the analyst to find the best match and, presumably, the geologic source of an artifact. XRF is a very useful technique because it is nondestructive, works well on very small samples (down to 1 millimeter in diameter), takes only minutes to complete, and is relatively inexpensive.

Hughes's analysis confirmed that most Hopewell obsidian came from Obsidian Cliff in Yellowstone National Park. But he also discovered that some obsidian, especially that found in Illinois and Indiana Hopewell sites, came from Bear Gulch in southeast Idaho. Moreover, we now know that obsidian from the Yellowstone region appears in small quantities on other Hopewell-age sites in Wisconsin, Iowa, Illinois, and Indiana. This suggests that high-ranking Hopewell individuals might have acquired obsidian through down-the-line trade rather than direct acquisition— its shiny black surfaces serving to remind people not of vacations to Yellowstone, but of the important social ties some individuals had to other high-ranking persons in distant Hopewell communities.

Fingerprinting Ceramics

To understand how archaeologists can fingerprint ceramics and trace them to their point of origin, we must expand upon our earlier discussion of pottery manufacture.

The first step in making a pot, of course, is to acquire the clay. Clays occur as geologic deposits, usually waterlaid, and different sources have different grain sizes and mineral composition. The mineral composition of the clay determines to some extent the kind of pottery that you can make from it. Potters use clay that is nearly pure kaolinite, for example, to manufacture fine porcelains.

After it is acquired, the clay is dried and pounded to remove any impurities. The potter then mixes in water and kneads the mixture to remove air bubbles. Clay's most important characteristic is that it is plastic; it can be modeled into shape. But as clay dries, it shrinks and then, when fired, it expands. Both processes can potentially crack the vessel.

Thousands of years ago, potters found that these problems could be alleviated by adding **temper** to the clay. Temper can be one of many kinds of materials: plant fiber, seed chaff, ash, ground-up shell or rock, sand, or even ground-up bits of old broken pots (sometimes called "grog"). The temper acts to hold the clay in place, gives the vessel strength, and prevents excessive shrinkage or expansion. After the temper is added, the potter shapes the pot and then fires it in an oven or an open-air fire, at temperatures in excess of 1000° C if possible.

If we could characterize the mineral composition of clays and tempers for both pots and likely geologic sources—as XRF does for obsidian artifacts and geologic sources—then we could fingerprint a pot (and, if sand or crushed rock were used, its temper) and trace both to their geologic sources. Archaeologists do this with several techniques, including **instrumental neutron activation analysis.** Likewise, minerals in the clay and in the pot's temper can also be identified through **petrographic analysis.**

Neutron activation analysis identifies a sherd's trace elements, those in the temper and the clay combined, by bombarding a potsherd with neutrons generated by a nuclear reactor. This produces radioactive isotopes of the elements. These isotopes immediately begin to decay (some have *very* short half-lives) and emit gamma radiation of different energy levels. By measuring the spectrum of gamma radiation, an analyst can identify the concentrations of 30 or more isotopes and obtain a sherd's "fingerprint."

To conduct petrographic analysis, you cut a thin section of the pottery and grind it to about 30 microns in thickness so that the minerals are translucent. This section is mounted on a slide and the various minerals identified beneath a polarizing microscope at 25–400X. To make source identifications, the analyst must also take samples of the temper and identify its mineral composition. Sometimes a temper is distinguished by the presence or absence of key minerals, but normally

temper Material added to clay to give a ceramic item strength through the firing process.

instrumental neutron activation analysis An analytical technique that determines the trace element composition of the clay used to make a pot and trace the clay to its geological source.

petrographic analysis An analytical technique that identifies the mineral composition of a pot's temper and clay through microscopic observation of thin sections.

the fingerprint consists of a particular combination of a standard range of minerals (feldspars, hornblendes, and so on) and different kinds of sand (for example, calcareous beach or volcanic sands).

Using these two methods, archaeologists have been able to trace the source of clay and temper in many places in the world and, in so doing, to reconstruct trading networks.

Conclusion: Reconstructing Past Social and Political Systems

In reconstructing social and political organizations, archaeologists remember that artifacts were not just utilitarian items, but also carried symbolic meanings—meanings that could be manipulated and that played a role in how those artifacts eventually ended up in an archaeological context. Sometimes these symbolic meanings reflect elements of social and political organization—such as gender roles, kinship systems, trade networks, and political connections. However, it's hard to construct middle-range theory that allows us to infer social and political organization from archaeological remains, and it may forever require well-supported ethnographic analogy. However, new techniques—analysis of physical and chemical properties of artifacts—give archaeology ways to test various hypotheses and continue to improve its reconstruction of the past.

In the following chapter, we go into an even more difficult area of archaeology: the analysis of symbols, concepts, and abstract thought. As you will see, reconstructing social and political organization is a walk in the park compared with trying to draw inferences from symbolic systems.

Summary

- This chapter dealt with social and political systems of the human past; the basic social unit is the *group*, both residential and nonresidential; how that group operates is a matter of gender, kinship, and status.

- We distinguished sex, which is a matter of biology, from gender, which is a cultural interpretation of biology.

- Inferring what men and women did in the past is difficult. Bioarchaeological analyses provide some clues, but strong empirical generalizations or historically linked ethnographic analogies are often needed.

- Kinship is the socially recognized network of relationships through which individuals are related to one another by ties of descent (real or imagined) and marriage. Like gender, kinship too plays a role in understanding the choices that people made in the distant past.

- Status refers to the rights, duties, and privileges that define the nature of interpersonal relations. Social statuses are apportioned according to culturally determined criteria.

- A key element of political organization is the difference between *ascribed statuses,* which are parceled out to individuals at birth without regard to the characteristics of those receiving status, and *achieved status,* which comes from what one accomplishes in life.

- Societies are *egalitarian* or *ranked,* depending on whether people have equal or unequal access to basic resources.

- Egalitarian and ranked societies are often studied through patterning in mortuary remains on the assumption that treatment in death reflects status in life.

- Trade networks reflect the geographic scale of non-residential groups, economic patterns, and political authority. Trade is established by determining whether artifacts were made locally and by determining the source of raw materials for artifact manufacture.

Media Resources

 The Companion Website for Archaeology: **Down to Earth,** *Third Edition*

http://anthropology.wadsworth.com/thomas_kelly3e_down/

Supplement your review of this chapter by going to the companion website to take one of the practice quizzes, use the flash cards to master key terms, and check out the many other study aids that are designed to help you succeed in your introductory archaeology course.

11 The Archaeology of the Mind

Outline

These animals were painted on the ceiling of Lascaux, in France, some 17,000 years ago.

Preview

AS CULTURAL BEINGS, humans construct the world in which they live. By "construct" we mean that they physically alter the world—through farming, construction, trash disposal, logging, mining, and so forth. But we also mean that human cultures interpret their world symbolically, which leads to different approaches to the physical world. In this chapter, we concentrate on these symbolic meanings. Some archaeologists have attempted to infer the symbolic meanings of specific artifact forms, and others have tried to reconstruct concepts and perceptions about how the ancients viewed the world and the place of humans in it.

As you might guess, symbolic approaches in archaeology raise some difficult issues, with both scientific and humanistic perspectives being applied. Although a huge range of human behavior falls under the category of "symbolic," we focus on investigations of ritual and religion, iconography, and the interpretation of prehistoric rock art.

Introduction

When processual archaeology gained prominence in the 1960s, it generated numerous studies of prehistoric demography, settlement patterns, subsistence, technology, and the human use of landscapes, plants, and animals. These important approaches relied heavily on rigorous scientific methods. The focus was heavily materialistic, because processual archaeologists believed that subsistence behavior provided the infrastructure for the rest of the cultural system (see Chapter 2).

At the outset, processual archaeologists were optimistic that they could study *all aspects* of the human

condition from archaeological data. But most processual archaeologists remained lukewarm toward **cognitive archaeology** throughout the 1970s and 1980s. For many, the archaeological record relating to "ideas" seemed too shaky and ambiguous to be approached in an explicitly scientific, objective manner. And cultural materialists assumed that the cognitive aspects of culture—including religion—were "epiphenomena," mere dependent variables deriving from the more critical technological and economic basics; as such, they were unimportant to understanding the past.

The appeal of cultural materialism to Americanist archaeology is fairly easy to understand. This is a research strategy that places priority on just those things that archaeologists are most confident in recovering from their sites—evidence about past environments, technologies, and economies.

But some archaeologists felt that such heavy-handed materialism dehumanized the past. They argued for an

cognitive archaeology The study of all those aspects of ancient culture that are the product of the human mind: the perception, description, and classification of the universe; the nature of the supernatural; the principles, philosophies, ethics, and values by which human societies are governed; and the ways in which aspects of the world, the supernatural, or human values are conveyed in art.

"archaeology of the mind" that emphasizes the values, ideas, and beliefs that make us all human. To be sure, any archaeology of the mind will have a more post-processual than processual flavor, because such an approach will necessarily be concerned with recovering *meanings* (rather than law-like statements or generalizations about human behavior). Today, much of cognitive archaeology remains interpretive, but as we demonstrate, such symbolic approaches can indeed lend themselves to scientific testing as well—if appropriate linkages can be made between the interpretations of ancient symbols and those human behaviors that can be more directly inferred from the archaeological record.

All humans interact with their world through their cultural perception of it, and modern archaeologists can ill afford to overlook the power of symbols. Take food, for example. Economic decisions might appear to be rather straightforward: eat this food because it is nutritious and efficiently gathered, harvested, or hunted, and avoid that food because it is not. Although such decisions do heavily condition subsistence practices, we also face an ever-changing background of cultural information about what is/is not edible. As we pointed out in Chapter 2, some societies consider dogs to be food, even prestigious feast foods. Yet people in other cultures are repulsed by the idea of eating their "pets." And some animals may be highly valued in particular cultures, not because of their nutritional content, but because of their symbolic meaning. Native peoples of New Guinea hunted cassowary birds not for food, but because their feathers were highly valued gifts that were given away at feasts (see "Looking Closer: Food Taboos in the Near East").

Symbolism goes beyond food to permeate all arenas of human life. We saw in Chapter 8, for example, that even something as apparently mundane and utilitarian as firewood was symbolically loaded for the Inka. And Chapter 10 explained how kinship involves the differential imposition of symbolic ideas about kin onto biological relationships. Male and female tasks also differ among societies, depending on what symbolic value a culture gives to different tasks. In industrial societies, advertising tells us that clothing, houses, cars, hairstyles, tattoos, beer—virtually everything, in fact—carries symbolic meaning.

Humans live in a material world, and nobody can avoid the realities of survival. But people also live in a culturally constructed world, and material decisions are always made against a backdrop of symbolic meanings. This is why a number of archaeologists have turned to an ideational emphasis in their research, examining the active role of symbols in shaping the economic, social, and even technological structure of societies.

What's a Symbol?

The ability to use symbols goes to the essence of what it means to be human. Language is made possible by symbols; so are stories, art, and poetry. Symbols shape the way that people see, understand, and feel about the world. We discussed the symbolic element of human culture in Chapter 2; now we consider symbols in more detail.

A **symbol** is an object or act (verbal or nonverbal) that by cultural convention stands for something else *with which it has no necessary connection.* Consider a simple symbol that is familiar to many Americans: a red circle with a red line running diagonally through it. With a capital *P* in the center of the circle, the symbol tells us "No parking"; with a cigarette in the middle, it means "No smoking." (The *P* and the cigarette, by the way, are not symbols but signs, because they are connected to what they signify.) Virtually all Americans understand that a red circle with a diagonal line through it forbids whatever is in the circle.

But is there any *necessary* connection between a red circle with a line through it and prohibition of a certain behavior? No. In fact, this symbol might just as easily mean the opposite: Parking *is* allowed here, smoking *is* permitted here. If you were not enculturated into the meaning of the symbol, you would have no way of deducing the symbol's meaning merely from the symbol itself—*because there is no necessary connection between a symbol and the thing it stands for.* Some anthropologists suggest that a few basic symbols might have an inherent meaning genetically programmed into our consciousness; the color red, for example,

symbol An object or act (verbal or nonverbal) that, by cultural convention, stands for something else *with which it has no necessary connection.*

LOOKING CLOSER
Food Taboos in the Near East

Many members of the Jewish and Islamic faiths eschew pork, a prohibition that dates back to the Near Eastern roots of both religions. Many other peoples eat pork; it's a perfectly nutritious food, and pigs can be raised quite efficiently. Why not Near Easterners? Here we contrast two different explanations for this food taboo—one materialist, the other symbolic.

Marvin Harris, the preeminent cultural materialist (see Chapter 2), argued that pigs were prohibited because they are forest dwellers, ill suited to the Near Eastern desert. Harris suggested that any food, even a formerly useful food, will be tabooed when the cost of producing it outweighs its value (in calories or nutrients). In the desert, the cost of trying to keep pigs alive would indeed be high.

But Harris's materialist explanation suffers from two problems. First, why is a taboo with supernatural sanctions necessary for a food clearly inefficient to produce or procure? Certainly, anybody trying to raise or harvest particular food could see it's not worth the effort. Second, pork is only one of many foods tabooed in the books of Leviticus and Deuteronomy. In those passages, God prohibited the followers of Moses from eating shellfish, pigs, rabbits, camels, insects, and a variety of birds. Many of these, such as camels, are perfectly suited for life in the desert.

Mary Douglas (University College, London), a symbolic anthropologist, argues that any explanation of tabooed foods must include them all. She reminds us that Near Eastern cultural ideas (as expressed in Leviticus) declared prohibited animals to be "unclean," a term that often means "disorderly." You might say that your house is "not clean," when you mean only that clothing is lying on the floor. Or you might refer to the "dirty" dishes in the sink when just moments before, you were eating off of them. The dishes aren't "dirty," they're simply not "in their place" (cleaned, dried, and in the cupboard).

Douglas found that virtually all prohibited animals were seen as violating cultural ideas about the order of creation. "Animals" were things that walk, hop, or jump on all four feet. Thus, insects that "swarm upon the land" are unclean because they are outside the cultural order of life. Similarly, edible animals were supposed to have cloven hooves and chew their cud. Herd animals of the Near East—cattle, sheep, and goats—are like this, but pigs are not (they have cloven hooves, but don't chew their cud). So pigs are "unclean," an anomaly in the natural order of animals. Avoiding certain animals, then, was not about food, but rather about culturally affirming God's order in the world.

Which explanation is right? Both? Neither? Archaeologists are continually confronted with competing hypotheses drawn from different paradigms. Often, the truth lies somewhere in between. And, usually one answer raises a new question: If pork was prohibited because it fell outside the natural order, what gave rise to that particular view of the world?

might carry the meaning of danger. But the vast majority of the symbols we use have no such "natural" meaning. (And if you think they do, rent a car in Paris and figure out the "natural" meaning of French road signs.)

This is why symbols are so powerful. A simple symbolic act can be made to carry enormous amounts of information. And, in fact, the same symbol can carry different meanings under different situations. Consider a simple wink of the eye. In one situation, it can signal a playful conspiracy between two people against a third; in another, the same gesture is flirting (or harassment). But in another culture, a wink might mean nothing more than that a person has something irritating his or her eye.

Because symbols have no necessary connection to their culturally assigned meaning, they can be used in different ways. Much of the humor, pathos, and poignancy in literature and the arts come from the playful or artful use of symbols (such as the use of the red prohibition circle in the film *Ghostbusters*). This is another way in which symbols are powerful.

But their essential qualities make symbols difficult to study archaeologically. If there is no necessary connection between a symbol and what it stands for, then how can an outsider know the meaning of a particular symbol? How would you know that a red circle with a line through it *prohibits* rather than *permits* a behavior? Deciphering these messages is difficult enough in an ethnographic context, where one has ready access to language, informants, and observable behavior. But it is manifestly more difficult—and

Figure 11-1 A panel of art from a rockshelter at La María, in southern Argentina. The central figure is a guanaco, a wild camelid.

some would say impossible—to understand symbolic behavior in an archaeological context, where the physical symbol survives, but its meaning does not.

Consider, for example, the rock art shown in Figure 11-1. This is one of the thousands of images found at La María, a complex of rockshelters in Patagonia (a region of southern Argentina). The central figure is a guanaco, a wild camelid once hunted by native peoples of the region. Along the guanaco's back and haunches is a series of white dots, and other white dots are on the body. In the upper right is a hand silhouette, created when the artisan placed his or her right hand on the wall and then blew paint over it (a similar image appears on the cover of this book). Between the hand and the guanaco runs a red, white, and black line, immediately below is a line of red dots.

What do these images mean? Was the hand painted as part of ritual? Or is it little more than graffiti "tagging"? Are the lines and dots representations of a hunting fence or drive line? Are they counters? Is this a map? Does the guanaco "mean" guanaco? Or is it a symbol that stands for something else, like a lineage? What about the dots on the guanaco? Is this hunting or fertility magic? There are no easy answers to these questions.

To interpret symbols, anthropologists might look at the various ways a particular symbol is used and its (possibly varied) contexts. They might see which symbols are consciously manipulated and which are not,

which can be used for humor (and who finds them funny). They might see if some symbols are exclusively used by or associated with women or men. By viewing a symbol's use in a variety of circumstances, we can construct an understanding of what the symbol means. This approach, however, requires the living context of the symbol, which archaeologists do not have.

This means that ancient symbolic systems may remain forever silent as to their specific, detailed meanings. But many contemporary archaeologists think it's worthwhile to examine human behavior as a system of meanings rather than simply as acts that meet material needs. Recall, for example, our discussion in Chapter 7 of the different treatment of pig bones in African societies. In the following two examples, we explore some of the potential and limitations involved with an archaeology of the mind.

The Peace Pipe as Ritual Weapon

Writing in the late 1970s, archaeologist Robert L. Hall (University of Illinois, Chicago) used the calumet —the peace pipe—to demonstrate how a cognitive approach could broaden the horizons of archaeological investigations.

Hall focused on the Hopewell "culture," which probably included many different peoples speaking different

RAPID REVIEW   Characteristics of Symbols and Their Archaeological Study

- All objects are symbolic to one extent or another.
- There is no necessary link between an object and its symbolic meaning.
- Symbols can be manipulated, and used in different ways for different purposes in different contexts.
- These characteristics make the archaeological study of symbols difficult.
- Specific meanings of ancient symbols may be forever lost to archaeology, but the effect of a system of meanings may not be.

languages and living in various ways, from the lower Mississippi to Minnesota, and from Nebraska to Virginia. But during Hopewell times (between 200 BC and AD 400) these diverse people apparently shared a unifying set of symbols that may indicate a common set of religious beliefs. Archaeologists referred to this common set of symbols found over a wide area as the **Hopewell Interaction Sphere.**

To understand what was going on, let's first consider whether the Hopewell people shared a common religion. Broadly speaking, anthropologists consider **religion** to be a specific set of beliefs about one's relation to the supernatural. Religion is a society's mechanism for relating supernatural phenomena to the everyday world—a set of rituals that enlists supernatural powers for the purpose of achieving or preventing transformations of state in humans and nature—in other words, to make sure that good things happen and bad things do not. In some religions, individuals use rituals to influence the course of events; in others, they help novices find their path in a world that they see as beyond their control. All living cultures have some form of religion, and we suppose that was true of past societies as well.

Religious beliefs are manifested in everyday life as **ritual,** a succession of discrete behaviors that must be performed in a particular order under particular circumstances—such as saying prayers at certain times of the day accompanied by particular acts or gestures. Rituals are fundamentally religious acts because they are the mechanisms by which individuals attempt to intercede with the supernatural.

This definition of religion is especially relevant to archaeology because rituals are behavioral acts that often entail material culture and therefore can be represented in the archaeological record. The analysis of past ritual behavior is thus archaeology's major contribution to the study of religion.

Some of the highly standardized Hopewell artifacts are perhaps indicative of rituals. One particularly intriguing artifact is the stone platform pipe, some examples of which are shown in Figure 11-2. Hopewell artists fashioned these from pipestone, often ornamenting them with carved mammals, birds, or reptiles that rest on a straight or curved base. The pipes were probably used to smoke tobacco (which is indigenous to the New World; the earliest evidence of tobacco in the eastern United States dates to about AD 100).

The effort taken to carve these pipes suggests that whatever rituals the pipes were involved in were a critical aspect of Hopewell ceremonial life. Hundreds of pipes were found in the so-called Mound of the Pipes at Mound City, near Chillicothe, Ohio. Some think that this mound was a monument to a master carver of sacred pipes.

What were the pipes used for? What did they signal to their users? To try to explain these pipes, Hall looked to historical and ethnographic data. He was especially

Hopewell Interaction Sphere The common set of symbols found in the midwestern United States between 200 BC and AD 400.

religion A specific set of beliefs about one's relation to the supernatural; a society's mechanism for relating supernatural phenomena to the everyday world.

ritual A succession of discrete behaviors that must be performed in a particular order under particular circumstances.

Figure 11-2 Hopewell effigy pipes. The bowl for tobacco is on the animals' backs. These would have been placed on the end of a wooden stem and may represent the hook on the end of an atlatl.

intrigued by the fact that the "peace pipe," used historically to establish friendly contact, almost always took the form of a weapon. He then reasoned that all cultures engage in certain culturally dictated customs whose exact meaning and origin may be lost in time. For example, the rite of toasting with drinks in Western culture originally was the sloshing and spilling together of two persons' drinks to reduce the possibility that one planned to poison the other. But how many of us who have toasted friends realize the origin of the custom? Or saluting, a custom that stems from the act of raising visors on armored helmets in order to expose the faces of the two persons encountering each other? Hall suggested that, although the original functions of the gestures lost their practical significance, the acts survive as elements of etiquette or protocol.

Hall applied similar reasoning to the Hopewell platform pipes by calling upon ethnographic data. Throughout historic times in the eastern United States, Indian tribes observed the custom of smoking a sacred tribal pipe. When the pipe was present, violence was ruled out. Moreover, the peace pipe usually was made in the shape of an atlatl (like those that appear in Figure 11-3)—a weapon that was a forerunner to the bow and arrow used in historic times. The Pawnee peace pipe, for instance, looked like an arrow, and the Osage word for *calumet* translated as "arrowshaft." Hall suggested

that the weaponlike appearance resulted from a specific ceremonial custom. Could it be that, at least during the period of European contact, the peace pipe symbolized a ritual weapon?

Hall then projected his idea back into ancient Hopewell times. Suppose that the distinctive Hopewell platform pipes were also ritual weapons—but made before these people knew of the bow and arrow. At the time, the most common Hopewell weapon was the atlatl (the spearthrower—discussed in Chapter 10).

Hall suggested that the distinctive Hopewell platform pipe symbolically represented a flat atlatl, decorated with an effigy spur. Hall observed that the animal on the bowl was almost always carved precisely where an atlatl spur would be. And the curvature of the platform seemed to correspond to the curvature of the atlatl.

These correspondences led Hall to conclude, "I see the Hopewell platform pipe as the archaeologically visible part of a transformed ritual atlatl, a symbolic weapon which in Middle Woodland times probably had some of the same functions as the calumet of historic times, itself a ritual arrow."

Hall went on to propose that the importance of the Hopewell pipe might well extend beyond mere symbolism—that the platform pipe was not merely one of many items exchanged between groups, but that "it

Figure 11-3 Some representations of atlatls in aboriginal North American art.

perhaps linked to some common religious ideas—the Hopewell Interaction Sphere tended to reduce regional differences and promote contact and communication between discrete groups.

We pointed out that interpretations of the symbolic meanings of artifacts are difficult to test *directly*. But it would be possible to test the *implications* of Hall's conclusions by assessing whether the archaeology of the Hopewell Interaction Sphere supports the social and political ramifications of Hall's interpretation of the stone pipes. For example, is there evidence of conflict in Hopewell sites? If it is present, how does it relate to the distribution of stone pipes and their source areas? Or how does the distribution of pipes across the Hopewell Interaction Sphere relate to evidence for subsistence stress (from faunal, macrobotanical, and human skeletal remains)? In other words, *if we treat symbolic interpretations as hypotheses, it is possible to test them by linking them to phenomena that are more archaeologically accessible.* To see how this might work, let's return to an example that we have used before, the Chavín culture of Peru.

may have been part of the very mechanism of exchange." Adaptively oriented research on eastern United States prehistory has conventionally defined the Hopewell Interaction Sphere primarily in economic and environmental terms. Perhaps, by maintaining relationships between large-scale networks of ritual trading partners, far-flung Hopewell communities joined economic forces, looking to one another for support in lean years.

Hall suggested that a shift away from strictly materialistic thinking—toward a more cognitive approach—could generate a deeper understanding of the Hopewell lifeway. Reasoning from Native American ethnographic analogies, Hall contended that peace pipe rituals served to mediate interaction over a vast area of eastern North America. By promoting a common set of symbols—

Exploring Ancient Chavín Cosmology

In Chapter 8, we discussed the Chavín culture of the central Andes. Specifically, we looked at the faunal remains recovered from Chavín de Huántar and learned what these finds could tell us about subsistence and trade.

But to most archaeologists, the term "Chavín" conjures up much more than llama bones. Archaeologists commonly consider Chavín to be Peru's first highland civilization because of its stratified social and political organization and its achievements in metallurgy, weaving, monumental architecture, irrigation systems, and stone sculpture.

Chavín also left a lasting legacy in Andean **cosmology**. By *cosmology* we mean a culture's understanding of how the world works, how it originated and developed, how the various parts fit together, what laws they obey, and, especially, the place of humans in the natural and supernatural worlds. A glimpse of a culture's cosmology can often be found in its **iconography**—its art forms or writing systems (such as Egyptian or Maya hieroglyphics) that symbolically represent ideas about religion or cosmology.

The iconography at Chavín de Huántar established the tone of subsequent central Andean cosmology. All deities of the succeeding generations in the central Andes looked more or less like the gods in the temple at Chavín de Huántar. Archaeologists Richard Burger and George Miller (whose faunal analysis of Chavín de Huántar we discussed in Chapter 8) have explored the nature of Chavín cosmology, looking in particular at the distinctive Chavín iconography that appeared over a wide area of the central Andes nearly 2500 years ago.

Animal Symbolism in Chavín Iconography

Chavín de Huántar has given its name to one of the Americas' most famous art styles: Chavín. Chavín iconography is derived from stone sculptures at Chavín de Huántar, an example of which appears in Figure 11-4. This art style was reproduced in many villages in the central Andes on locally made ceramics, textiles, goldwork, and stone.

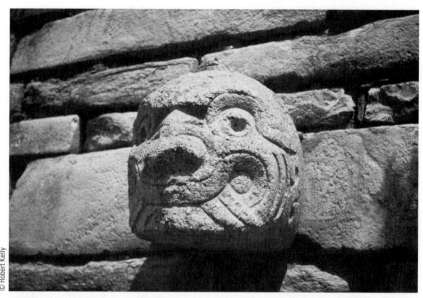

Figure 11-4 One of the carved stone heads on the temple at Chavín de Huántar, which represent a shaman's transition from human to jaguar.

You recall from Chapter 8 that the community of Chavín de Huántar depended on a range of animals for food, including wild deer, vicuña, llama, and guinea pigs. These were local beasts, probably encountered by local residents on a daily basis.

But the local highland animals of Chavín de Huántar are conspicuously absent from the thousands of known temple sculptures, ceramics, and textiles that display the widespread Chavín style. Instead, the Chavín style drew inspiration for its stylized fangs and talons, feathers and scales from the jaguar, crested eagle, monkey, serpent, and cayman (alligator). These creatures are native to the cloud forests and rain forests of the *eastern* Andean slope, if not the floodplains of Amazonia itself—located several hundred miles to the east, on the other side of the Andes. These same animals play a prominent role in the mythology and

cosmology The study of the origin, large-scale structure, and future of the universe. A cosmological explanation demonstrates how the universe developed—both the totality and its constituent parts—and also describes what principles keep it together.

iconography Art forms or writing systems (such as Egyptian or Maya hieroglyphics) that symbolically represent ideas about religion or cosmology.

religious symbolism of modern people of Amazonia, but they were utterly foreign to the inhabitants of Chavín de Huántar.

Why were the major animals of Chavín religious art drawn from outside the local highland environment?

Where Did Chavín Cosmology Come From?

Archaeologists have proposed several hypotheses to explain this puzzling aspect of Chavín cosmology. The first is that the climate was radically warmer and more humid during Chavín times. If so, then maybe the lowland complex of animals—the jaguar, the cayman, the crested eagle, and so forth—could have once lived in the highlands around Chavín de Huántar.

But this hypothesis is not correct. Several lines of evidence demonstrate that the climate was similar to the modern pattern during the Chavín time period (900–200 BC), and remember from Chapter 8 that the animal bones recovered from Chavín de Huántar belong to the same species as modern highland animals—camelids, deer, and so forth. Paleoenvironmental change cannot explain the nature of Chavín iconography.

Another hypothesis was championed by Peruvian archaeologist Julio Tello (1880–1947), discoverer of Chavín civilization and first excavator at Chavín de Huántar (in the 1930s), and later by American archaeologist Donald Lathrap (1927–1990). Plants indigenous to Amazonia—including manioc, bottle gourd, hot peppers, and possibly peanuts—all appear at Chavín de Huántar. Tello suggested that immigrants from the tropical forest introduced the lowland plants and animals to Chavín de Huántar. Lathrap attributed the migration to population pressure in the lowland Amazonian or Orinoco basins that forced the early Chavín folk into the Andean highlands. According to Lathrap, the heavy Amazonian component of Chavín religious art displayed homage and deference to the ancient homeland and subsistence regime that was responsible for the initial success of the Chavín elite.

But this hypothesis also seems to be incorrect. In the first place, the lowland crops are impossible to grow in the Andean environment. Their presence suggests trade or some other kind of contact between Chavín de Huántar and Amazonia, but they could not have been plants brought with and grown by an immigrant population. Burger also hypothesizes that, if a tropical for-

est people had moved wholesale into the Andes, their ceramic traditions should show a direct relationship to the Amazonian homeland. But the earliest ceramics at Chavín de Huántar show a conspicuous lack of Amazonian characteristics; the pottery looks local rather than imported. It also is clear that the basic high-altitude mixed agricultural subsistence pattern practiced by the pioneer population at Chavín de Huántar was not Amazonian at all; it had developed in place—in the highlands—at least a thousand years earlier. The ceramic and subsistence evidence make it unlikely that a tropical forest group was responsible for the lowland iconography evident on the earliest buildings at Chavín de Huántar.

For these reasons, Burger advocates a third hypothesis to explain the Amazonian elements of Chavín cosmology. Chavín de Huántar occupies a strategic gateway position, in a corridor that extends from the Pacific coast, to the highland Andes, and down to the lowland rain forest to the east. Burger argues that Chavín's religious leaders deliberately imported Amazonian symbolism, perhaps in the belief that the exotic lowland people had especially powerful esoteric knowledge. This interpretation, supported by ethnographic and ethnohistoric documentation, suggests that shamans and healers may have made pilgrimages to the distant lowlands—viewed as the powerful source of sacred knowledge, medicinal plants, and other ritual necessities. In fact, in many parts of the world anthropologists have found that people who live outside dense forests often ascribe magical powers or sacred knowledge to their neighbors who live in the forests. Burger argues that the Chavín people imported religious knowledge from the remote, exotic tropics to the Andean highlands.

Analysis of Chavín iconography provides some of the details, explaining the cult's remarkable success. Early sculptural evidence suggests that Chavín ideology held that priests had the ability to turn themselves into mythical beasts, in order to intervene with supernatural forces. Temple sculptures clearly demonstrate that, employing hallucinogenic snuff and beverages, Chavín shamans could transform themselves into jaguars or crested eagles. Specially designed drug paraphernalia—stone mortars, bone trays, spatulas, miniature spoons, and tubes—all seem to be part of the Chavín ritual toolkit. Use of similar artifacts can be documented among modern South American people.

Burger believes that this analogy—based on sixteenth-century ethnohistoric sources—may explain the singular success of the Chavín cult in uniting previously unrelated cultures throughout the Andean highlands and along the Peruvian coast.

The historical documents also provide a hypothesis for how this religious network might have operated 2000 years earlier. At the center of the religion was a large ritual complex featuring an **oracle,** accessible only to certain cult specialists. Based on the oracle's secret projections, cult members were able to provide "insider information," offering favorable intervention with the natural elements, protection against disease, and specialized knowledge concerning auspicious times for planting and harvesting.

Under this regional religious system, local communities could establish "branch shrines" by pledging support for the religion. If the pledge was accepted, a local priest was assigned, but in return, local communities allotted agricultural lands to produce tribute and promised public labor for farming and herding. In effect, these local branches supported the religion's headquarters with large quantities of cotton, corn, dried fish, llamas, guinea pigs, raw materials (such as gold and obsidian), and manufactured goods (such as fine cloth).

Burger suggests that this ethnohistoric cult provides a workable model of the distinctive regional organization that characterized Chavín civilization. He hypothesizes that the oracle cult center was located at the archaeological site of Karwa, which unfortunately was looted during the 1970s. Iconographic elements—particularly stylized felines and raptorial birds—woven into textile fragments recovered from tombs at Karwa show unmistakable ties to the sculptures at Chavín de Huántar. Despite the nearly 400 miles separating the two sites, the complex elements of Chavín cosmology seem to have been transported intact, without simplification or misrepresentation.

The Role of Cosmology in Andean Civilization

This model suggests that Chavín iconography was a widespread religion subdivided into a number of localized branches, each sharing in the major elements of Chavín iconography—probably reflecting major deities—but complemented by distinctive localized elements. According to this view, the Chavín religion maintained its characteristic regional flavor, but also demonstrated a willingness to incorporate motifs and symbols significant to local constituencies.

Burger emphasizes that the long-standing interest of archaeologists in Chavín iconography has led to a deep understanding of how this distinctive civilization came to be. Had this research taken place within a strictly materialistic framework, Burger suggests, the direction would have been much different and considerably more restricted. He stresses that interregional exchange and tribute in the form of gifts to the religious center, rather than local agricultural production, contributed to the development of Chavín civilization.

The spread of Chavín elements (500–250 BC) across the central Andes happened at a turbulent time, following the collapse of many early coastal political systems. An unprecedented amount of contact occurred between distant and unrelated groups, producing a previously unknown degree of sharing of ideology and technology, reinforced by the actual movement of goods and people. For Burger, Chavín culture was a forerunner of the many later attempts in Andean history to create single social entities out of a diversity of local cultures.

So, why did Chavín succeed where earlier attempts failed?

Relying on historical evidence from the sixteenth-century regional ceremonial complex, Burger argues that Chavín was a large-scale religion, transcending political and ethnic boundaries. Chavín ideology and rituals were sufficiently powerful to support a hierarchical organization, with officials overseeing local cult activities and monitoring deviation among local congregations. Although regional diversity was evident throughout the reach of the Chavín cult, a central authority exerted its power and extracted tribute from smaller communities. Thus, Chavín religion spread not because of political expansion, but because of the extension of a powerful shared cosmology, rendered visible in ritual objects and manifested through the growth of complex interregional exchange networks.

According to Burger, by 400 BC the centers of the Chavín horizon rivaled the classic Greek cities in size and beauty, with massive public structures of finely cut

oracle A shrine in which a deity reveals hidden knowledge or divine purpose.

and polished masonry, and the settlements were home to a complex society, differentiated by both social status and economic activities.

Burger argues that this power came from the original priests of Chavín de Huántar, who focused the growing Chavín mythology on the mysterious rather than the mundane. It was the mysterious animals of the lowlands that ultimately determined the long-term success of Chavín society and economy.

One message of Chavín art may have been that the prosperity and well-being of the community depended on maintaining the favor of forces alien to the local habitat and daily experience—forces redolent of the powers of the distant and mysterious tropical forest. The mediation of this relationship required the services of ritual specialists. This explanation suggests that Chavín ideology—heavily emphasizing the exotic tropical forest fauna—ritually reinforced the wealth and power of Chavín de Huántar society.

Current evidence suggests that social stratification may have first appeared in the highlands in association with long-distance exchange—offering local leaders an unparalleled opportunity to control and manipulate the existing socioeconomic system. Burger argues that tribute supplied to regional ceremonial centers by travelers and pilgrims could have been a major source of wealth and power for newly emerging elites.

Religious ideology seems to have played a central role in promoting and legitimizing these profound sociopolitical transformations, suggesting that many of the key ingredients for social complexity existed in the central Andes prior to the Chavín horizon. Although it remains a hypothesis to be tested, it was perhaps the power of Chavín's symbols—rather than a change in food resources, climate, or population density—that played a key role in the development of the Andes' first civilization.

Blueprints for an Archaeology of the Mind

Note that the two examples we have discussed so far share a couple of things. First, neither tries to interpret the exact meaning of the various symbols involved. Hall does not tell us what the raptors or other animals carved in stone on Hopewell pipes "mean." Neither do Burger and Miller attempt to explain what the jaguars,

caymans, or crested eagles symbolized to those who participated in the religion and iconography of the central Andes of some 2500 years ago.

Archaeologists simply cannot make the inferential leap from an ancient symbol to its past meaning based strictly on the symbol itself. Instead, we can only speak in general terms about what the symbols imply about a level of human interaction that is different from a purely material interaction with their environment.

Second, both examples rely upon solid ethnographic and ethnohistoric data. Hall's idea that Hopewell pipes were part of a peace pipe ritual was based on copious ethnographic data on such rituals among many eastern North American peoples. Likewise, Burger and Miller would have been hard pressed to generate a viable hypothesis to account for Chavín iconography without access to a rich historical and ethnographic record of the Andes Mountains.

Good researchers will always need to draw upon imagination to propose testable hypotheses. But ancient symbolic systems always pose the danger that imaginations can run amuck. Without some solid means to check the results of symbolic studies, archaeologists will always be in danger of what Kent Flannery and Joyce Marcus (University of Michigan) call "a bungee jump into the Land of Fantasy."

Likewise, Colin Renfrew (Cambridge University) warns of the pitfalls inherent in "new-age archaeology," insisting that cognitive archaeology proceed within the framework of acceptable scientific method. One must recognize that, at best, archaeology can capture only certain, limited aspects of ancient ideas. Renfrew discourages attempts to reconstruct "worldviews" or "totalities of thought"—emphasizing the notable lack of success among ethnographers who have tried to do this (and they work with living people, whose totality of thought is very much intact).

Marcus and Flannery also suggest that cognitive archaeology can follow relatively rigorous methods, *provided ample historical and ethnographic documentation is available.* In fact, they warn that if such data are lacking, "far less success should be anticipated." So, what do we do with truly ancient symbolic systems that have no such historically linked ethnographic data? Do we simply shrug our shoulders and turn to some other problem? To answer this question, let's examine how archaeologists have studied one of the earliest symbolic systems, the Upper Paleolithic cave art of western Europe.

Upper Paleolithic Cave Art

You will recall from Chapter 9 that the lineage that would eventually become *Homo sapiens* split from the rest of the primate lineage more than 5 million years ago. But the earliest evidence for artistic expression appears only in the last 90,000 years and does not become widespread until the last 40,000 years.

The **Upper Paleolithic** (40,000–10,000 BC) in Europe is distinguished by the appearance of a complex technology of stone, bone, and antler as well as wall art, portable art objects, and decorated tools—an example of which appears in Figure 11-5. Archaeologists sometimes call this an artistic "explosion," and the metaphor is appropriate. Only a handful of objects from the preceding 5 million years can be called art (and many of these may not be artifacts at all). But many, many Upper Paleolithic sites contain engraved, carved, or sculpted objects, and caves occupied by Upper Paleolithic peoples often contain wall paintings.

Cave paintings occur in some 200 French caves, and still more are found in Spain. Much of the painting dates to the **Magdalenian** phase (16,000–10,000 BC). However, a new site, Grotte Chauvet, was discovered in France in 1994, and AMS radiocarbon dates on the paintings themselves (the black paint is charcoal, and fat or blood is sometimes used as a binder) and some torch marks on the walls date to 30,000–24,000 BC.

Upper Paleolithic wall paintings have intrigued archaeologists for more than a century. More than simple line drawings, these are masterworks created by talented artisans who knew animal anatomy and behavior well. Careful shading shows the contours of animals' shoulders and haunches. Stags lower their heads to bugle in the rutting season. Some animals may be pregnant. Many of the images were painted with brushes, and hand silhouettes by the hundreds cover some cave walls.

The paintings are deliberately dramatic. The artists understood the principles of perspective, and they sometimes employed the natural topography of cave

Figure 11-5 Carved from reindeer antler, this bison probably served as the end of an atlatl and is an example of the artistic work that typifies the European Upper Paleolithic.

© American Museum of Natural History

walls to bring the animals to life. As you walk down one dark, narrow passage in the French cave of Lascaux, for example, two bulls appear to be running toward and to either side of you—a trick made possible by clever use of the cave's contours.

Upper Paleolithic paintings sometimes turn up in the most obscure of places, difficult to locate even with modern equipment. The art is often found in the deepest recesses of caves, some at the very ends of long passages. Imagine entering one of these caves with only a reed torch or stone lamp burning tallow as your source of light. There are pits, pools, and rivers to avoid, narrow passageways to crawl through, and jutting rocks to duck under; and, remember, you have to find your way out. At Lascaux, cave art even appears at the base of a deep pit. Not only does the descent into the

Upper Paleolithic The last major division of the Old World Paleolithic, beginning about 40,000 years ago and lasting until the end of the Pleistocene (about 10,000 BC).

Magdalenian The last major culture of the European Upper Paleolithic period (about 16,000–10,000 BC); named after the rockshelter La Madeleine, in southwestern France. Magdalenian artisans crafted intricately carved tools of reindeer bone and antler; this was also the period during which Upper Paleolithic cave art in France and Spain reached its zenith.

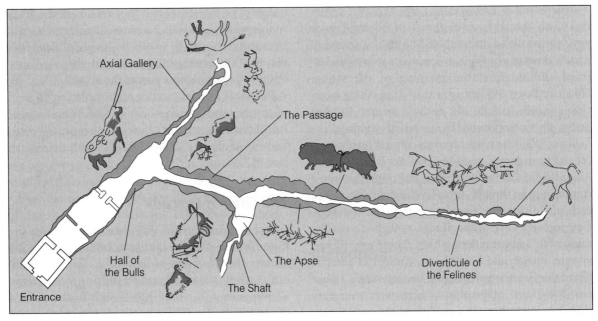

Figure 11-6 Map of Lascaux

Moving straight ahead, you enter the narrow Axial Gallery, which slopes more deeply into the earth. Many horses are on the walls here, with some aurochs and stags. Two of the horses have what appear to be spears or darts shooting toward them. A long line of black dots appear beneath a large stag in a bellowing posture; a horse faces the stag. Lewis-Williams sees these dots as evidence of the merging of abstract and representational images that occurs in trance.

Near the end of the Axial Gallery is one of the most intriguing images in Lascaux. Painted on a jutting piece of rock is a life-sized image of a horse, upside-down and apparently falling through the air. This image is not entirely visible until you walk around the bulge in the wall, single file. Several flint blades, covered in ochre and jammed into a crack, were found near this horse image. Walking around the "falling" horse, you encounter another horse, this one upright, and then the end of the passage.

Retracing your steps, you move back through the Hall of the Bulls and to the left. Passing through a low opening, you enter the Passage—this one longer than the Axial Gallery. The original opening was even smaller than it is today, and Upper Paleolithic artisans had to crawl through it.

In the Passage, the walls bear no calcite and the stone is softer. More horses and bulls are painted and engraved on the walls, although they are not as well preserved as in other parts of the cave. Images are piled up on top of one another, and the art here seems to be less "composed" than in the Axial Gallery and the Hall of the Bulls.

About 15 meters down the Passage, you encounter the Apse on your right, a small domed chamber with walls covered in engravings and a few paintings. Many different species are present—horses, bison, aurochs, ibex, deer, and perhaps even a wolf and lion. These images also overlay one another, producing a confusing jumble. Many engraved lines cut through the images.

Behind the Apse is the "Shaft" or "Well," a 5-meter-deep pit. Stone lamps were found at the bottom—turned upside down, as if the users meant to extinguish them. At the bottom of the pit is one of the oddest images of Upper Paleolithic art, which we show in Figure 11-7: a bison, his head lowered in defensive posture, appears to have a spear through the body. Some interpret the lines emanating from its belly to be entrails. In front of the bison is a stick figure of a man, his penis apparently erect, who appears to be falling backward from the bison's blow. The figure has only four fingers, however, and his head looks more like that of a bird. Beneath the man is a long vertical line, with what appears to be a bird perched on its top. The meaning of this image is the source of endless speculation.

Figure 11-7 Bison and "falling man" in Lascaux. It is not known if these images were painted at the same time (as a "scene") or at different times.

Something significant obviously transpired in these dark places. The aurochs, bison, and horses painted on Lascaux's walls and ceilings were not the fleeting whimsy of a Paleolithic artist. The same images appear in many caves and were used over thousands of years.

We do not know the specific meanings of these world-famous images (and, in truth, we probably never will). Lewis-Williams thinks that this art is somehow related to altered states of consciousness, but the images themselves could not, of course, have been produced while the artist was in a trance state, because one would need to be fully conscious to mix the paints, negotiate the cave's twists and turns with a stone lamp, and build scaffolding where needed. But Lewis-Williams thinks that the paintings at Lascaux and elsewhere provide firm evidence of Upper Paleolithic people trying to come to terms with understanding the meaning of altered states of consciousness—dreams and trances.

He sees the larger chambers, like the Hall of the Bulls, as places where communal rituals may have taken place, with people seeking assistance from a spirit world that existed belowground. Although the floor of Lascaux was damaged before it was investigated, the floors at Grotte Chauvet contain many human footprints, some 25,000 or more years old. Some of the prints are big and some are small, telling us that people of all ages visited even more remote portions of this cave.

Lewis-Williams also suggests that the distribution of art within a cave may parallel the stages of trances. In the front chamber are animals that figured in the lives of Upper Paleolithic people. Here, too, we find some abstract signs—the rectangles, wavy lines, and rows of dots that are apparent in early stages of trance. Deeper inside the cave, the narrowing passageway mimics the movement into the deeper states of trance. Lewis-Williams suggests that the falling horse at the end of the Axial Gallery is not falling at all, but it is instead an

Climbing out of the Shaft (which today is covered by a grid and accessed by a ladder), you return to the Passage and continue moving down its length. The walls contain more images for the next 15 meters or so, and then the images cease as the passage narrows and the ceiling drops. You encounter the two charging bison that we mentioned earlier—the ones that appear to be running toward and around you. After dropping to your knees and crawling along the cave floor, you encounter the Diverticule of the Felines, with its soft clay walls. If you are a small person, you are crouching; a larger person might be lying on his stomach.

Here there are aurochs and horses and bison, but also large cats—panthers or cave lions. Spears appear to pierce some of them, others are cut by lines or geometric markings or have lines emanating from their mouths and anuses. The images are well composed but seem to have been more hastily engraved than others in the cave. This section of the cave was rarely visited, because otherwise its soft clay walls would not have survived so well.

What Does All This Mean?

Leaving Lascaux, you might turn to look at the Hall of the Bulls one last time, trying to imagine how the scene would appear in the flickering light of a stone lamp.

LOOKING CLOSER
The Discovery of Lascaux

Like many major archaeological discoveries, Lascaux was found by accident . . . in this case, by a dog.

Lascaux is located in France's beautiful Dordogne region, a hilly landscape riddled with ancient caves and rockshelters. In 1940, several boys, led by Marcel Ravidat, were hiking those hills, looking for treasure. Marcel's dog, Robot, strayed and the boys eventually found him in a shallow pit. Bending down to scoop up his dog, Ravidat felt cold air rising from a small hole.

Thinking they had found a legendary tunnel leading to treasure, the boys explored further. Using improvised tools and paraffin lanterns, they dug, and eventually crawled down a long pile of rubble, arriving at a pool of water surrounded by gleaming white walls. They were startled to see a vividly painted horse in their flickering lights. Looking closer, they saw that the entire ceiling was painted. Bulls circled the ceiling.

The boys informed a local schoolteacher, who told Abbé Henri Breuil (1877–1961), a priest and scholar of Upper Paleolithic cave art (called by some "the Pope of Prehistory"). Breuil would eventually explore and document the art in Lascaux, which he called the "Sistine Chapel of Prehistory." But with World War II on, little could be done immediately.

Breuil asked the boys to camp near the mouth of the cave and protect it. To their credit, the boys faithfully guarded the cave through the long winter of 1940–41. Each boy eventually became involved in the war effort, and each survived, as did Lascaux.

In 1948, the cave was opened to visitors, with Ravidat serving as a guide. Although a ventilation system was installed ten years later, the steady stream of visitors brought with them humidity and microorganisms, and a green fungus began to cover the paintings. The government closed the cave to the public, and it remains closed today. Only a select few are allowed inside each week and the waiting list is several years long. But the French government built an astonishingly precise replica, Lascaux II, only 200 meters from the real cave.

Lascaux will always figure prominently in analyses of Upper Paleolithic cave art, and its magnificence is evident to the tens of thousands who visit Lascaux II each year. And it all began with a lost dog.

---

artist's representation of the vortex that one senses in the deeper stages of trance.

Farther into the cave, we see "confused" images, such as those in the Apse and the Diverticule of the Felines. These, Lewis-Williams suggests, may represent the merging of abstract and natural images in the deeper stages of trance or efforts by one shaman to bond with the power of another by drawing an image over that drawn by another shaman. Although rare in Upper Paleolithic art (and absent at Lascaux), occasional animal images take on human characteristics. They walk on two feet, sometimes hold their front legs in a human way, or turn to stare at the observer with an eerily human gaze. These might record instances where observers entered the deepest stages of trance and were unable to see the difference between themselves and animals.

Lewis-Williams suggests that vision quests may have been held in the deepest cave recesses. Without food or water, the total darkness and silence of a cave is a perfect medium for the production of visions. Perhaps people of the Upper Paleolithic saw caves as one place to access the spirit world.

Recall that some images make use of the bumps and contours of a cave's wall; Lewis-Williams believes this is more than a clever artistic trick. Shamans in hunting and gathering cultures often speak of a strong yet permeable membrane between themselves and the spirit world. Lewis-Williams suggests that the nature of trance would have suggested that portions of the spirit world lie belowground. By mimicking the vortex of trance, caves are the closest a person could come to the spirit world; the rest of the journey had to be made through trance. If the cave wall is the membrane between this world and the spirit world, then paintings and engravings were perhaps ways to access that spirit world. By using the cave's contours, the artist makes the painting more a part of the cave wall itself and, in so doing, increases its power. The flints, teeth, and bones left shoved into cracks may also have been similar efforts to break through the membrane and contact the spirit world.

In sum, Lewis-Williams argues that Upper Paleolithic art is not art for art's sake; nor is it fertility or hunting magic. Instead, he argues that the art reflects humanity's effort to come to grips with the perception that their quotidian life was not all that made up existence, to answer the question "What is the meaning of life?" And that fact gives us, the denizens of the twenty-first century, a strong link to the artisans who painted bulls on the ceilings of caves by torch light thousands of years ago.

Conclusion: The Archaeology of Symbols

An archaeology of the mind attempts to move beyond the more easily accessible matters of diet and settlement patterns to religion, ritual, and cosmology. People respond to their world through culture, an integrated set of symbolic meanings that are communicated through material culture. But given that there is no necessary link between symbols and their meanings, the development of reliable middle-range theory is almost impossible, and so this crucial area of human behavior often eludes archaeologists. Successful efforts rely upon historically linked ethnographic analogies, but these are limited to the more recent prehistory of regions with good ethnographic data. More ancient symbolic systems must be studied in ways that make use of uniformitarian elements of human neurology or perhaps a few symbolic universals (though these remain to be demonstrated).

Summary

- Deviating from the concerns of processual archaeology, cognitive archaeology aims to study the perception, description, and classification of the universe; the nature of the supernatural; the principles, philosophies, and values by which human societies are governed; and the ways in which aspects of the world, the supernatural, or human values are conveyed in art.

- Studying these ancient modes of thought requires the interpretation of symbols, objects, or acts (verbal and nonverbal) that by cultural convention stands for something else *with which it has no necessary connection.* This means that, without some ethnographic context, there is no easy way to connect a symbol to its meaning.

- Archaeologists attempt to understand past religions—the specific set of beliefs based on one's ultimate relation to the supernatural. Such religious beliefs are manifested in everyday life through rituals—behaviors such as prayer, music, feasting, sacrifice, and taboos. As such, ritual is a material manifestation of the abstract idea of religion and archaeology's easiest portal to the study of ancient religions.

- Archaeologists also attempt to understand cosmology. This encompasses how past cultures explain their universe—how it originated and developed; how the various parts fit together and what laws they obey—and express their concern with what the future of the universe holds.

- Where archaeologists have some ethnographic data available that are closely related to the archaeological case, they may be able to extrapolate backward from the present to the past. Even these cases, however, harbor the chance that a symbol meant something different in the past than it does in the present.

- Iconography, a culture's expression of abstract ideas in art and writing systems, can also be used to reconstruct the religious and other ideas that stand behind the art.

- The study of ancient symbols runs the risk of becoming a free-for-all, with any interpretation being as valid as another. It is perhaps important, then, that the study of ancient symbolic systems adhere to the canons of scientific analysis.

- In instances where ethnographic data are not available, the archaeologist must be more restrained in his or her interpretations and focus not on the specific meaning of particular symbols, but on the more general character of thought itself.

Media Resources

 The Companion Website for **Archaeology: Down to Earth,** *Third Edition*

http://anthropology.wadsworth.com/thomas_kelly3e_down/

Supplement your review of this chapter by going to the companion website to take one of the practice quizzes, use the flash cards to master key terms, and check out the many other study aids that are designed to help you succeed in your introductory archaeology course.

12 Historical Archaeology: Insights on American History

Outline

Custer's Last Stand (1899) by Edgar Samuel Paxson (1852–1919). Historical archaeology asks, Is this how it happened?

© Buffalo Bill Historical Center, Cody, Wyoming

Preview

Historical Archaeology is currently one of the most important directions in Americanist archaeology, but to this point, we have only briefly glimpsed what historical archaeologists actually do (for example, in discussing Thomas's excavations at Santa Catalina on St. Catherines Island, Georgia). In this chapter, we look at historical archaeology in more depth.

Historical archaeology is fundamentally similar to the prehistoric archaeology that we've discussed. Both fields maintain high standards of excavation, dating, and interpretation, but, because of its close relationship with the discipline of history, historical archaeology has its own distinctive flavor. Commonly less concerned with grand explanation, historical archaeologists often shed light on those lesser-known aspects of the historical past (such as the daily life of slaves), correct mistaken assumptions about history, and use the archaeological record to create views of the past that sometimes contrast with the picture derived from documentary evidence alone.

Introduction

Archaeologists have been investigating historic-period sites for a very long time. In fact, the first bona fide historical archaeology in America took place about 150 years ago. James Hall, a trained civil engineer, was a direct descendant of Miles Standish, who arrived with the Pilgrims aboard the *Mayflower* in 1620 and eventually became a leader in Plimouth Colony. Wanting to learn more about his celebrated ancestor, Hall located the foundations of the Standish homestead in Duxbury, Massachusetts, and, in 1853, he conducted detailed excavations there.

For more than a century, Hall's field notes and artifact collection from the Standish house remained unknown to anybody but immediate family members. In the 1960s, however, they surfaced in Mexico and were brought to the attention of James Deetz (1930–2000), a historical archaeologist working at Plimouth Plantation. As he looked over the surviving materials, Deetz was impressed at the high quality of Hall's 1853 excavation.

After carefully gridding the site and establishing datum points to maintain vertical control, Hall made a meticulous site map. He tried to recover artifacts in situ, plotting their locations onto this master site map. He even recorded stratigraphic relationships within the house ruin. After the excavation, Hall cataloged each artifact, carefully numbering each find. In short, Hall's 1853 excavation technique comports nicely with today's standards of acceptable archaeological practice.

Almost simultaneously, a second pioneering exploration in historical archaeology took place in Canada, under very different circumstances. In 1855, the Canadian government commissioned Father Félix Martin, a Jesuit priest from Montreal, to explore and excavate the site of Sainte Marie, Georgian Bay (near Midland, Ontario).

Sainte Marie was a tiny mission outpost founded in 1639 to bring Christianity to the local Huron Indians. Although they were 800 miles west of their supply base in Quebec, the missionaries enjoyed some success, and several left the mission proper to work with surrounding Huron communities. But during the winter of 1648–49, the Huron villages in this area came under attack from raiding Iroquois war parties. The resident Jesuit priests refused to flee, and several died martyrs' deaths. In March, the surviving priests abandoned Mission Sainte Marie. Although it had lasted only a decade, Sainte Marie became a sacred place in Christian history, what archaeologist Kenneth Kidd would later describe as "the pulsating heart of French missionary effort in America." Father Martin had this heritage in mind when he went to Sainte Marie in 1855. Seeking to establish a personal link to his own Jesuit past, Martin identified the site's location, mapped and described the ruins, painted several watercolors, and conducted limited excavations. Years later, the Jesuit order purchased the site to encourage its preservation and make it available for religious pilgrimages. Today, the Martyrs Shrine Church stands nearby, honoring both the Jesuit missionaries and the Christian Huron people who once lived there.

These two mid-nineteenth-century digs illustrate two important themes that eventually came to distinguish the field of historical archaeology. For one thing, both excavators were motivated by a dynamic and personal connection to their own past—Hall to his Pilgrim heritage and Father Martin to the legacy of his martyred Jesuit brothers. For both men, the past had a special relevance to the present.

Both excavators also were familiar with the documentary sources relating to their excavations. This meant that, before looking to the archaeology of their respective sites, they had some knowledge of what to expect: where to dig, what to look for, and generally what kind of material record they should encounter—expectations derived from basic historical sources. By themselves, however, these historical sources were incomplete and not entirely satisfying. Encountering the archaeological record itself—the physical remains of the past—induced Martin and Hall to undertake their own excavations.

So, what constitutes modern **historical archaeology**? Kathleen Deagan, the historical archaeologist profiled in Chapter 1, defines the field as "the study of human behavior through material remains, for which written history in some way affects its interpretation." Although this simple definition certainly captures the field, others point out that, because historical archaeology encompasses the past 500 years, historical archaeology also inherently must address the history of colonialism and capitalism. Next we show you how historical archaeology takes on different flavors depending on which of these definitions you choose.

Why Do Historical Archaeology?

At this point, you might be asking yourself, Why bother with the archaeology of historical sites if they are already described in documentary sources? Won't archaeology, with its problems of context, preservation, and interpretation, always prove inferior to the written sources?

Documentary sources can indeed be superior to archaeology. But they can also be quite selective and biased. Slave owners wrote little about the day-to-day life of slaves because they did not think it important, and slaves only rarely wrote letters or diaries, because most were illiterate (and often forbidden from learning). Most authors of documentary sources were biased toward the interests of their particular cultural, political, or ethnic group, and sometimes the documentary sources are simply wrong. Today, archaeologists look at archaeological and documentary records as *equally valid yet independent* lines of evidence. Rather than discard differences between the two as "exceptions" or "noise," we sometimes look for "ambiguities" between the historical and archaeological evidence, recognizing that *differences between the two are as important as each piece of information alone.* We demonstrate in this chapter that historical archaeology is an essential component to our understanding of the relatively recent past.

Historical Archaeology: Just a "Handmaiden to History"?

In the early days, excavations in historic period sites merely supplemented the "known," documentary view of the past. In the words of Ivor Noël Hume (former

historical archaeology The study of human behavior through material remains, for which written history in some way affects its interpretation.

director of the archaeological program at Colonial Williamsburg, Virginia), the proper role of historical archaeology was to serve as a "handmaiden to history"; the historical archaeologist was "a historian with a pen in one hand and a trowel in the other."

This perspective was particularly evident in projects closely linked to historical reconstruction and restoration. Archaeologists, for instance, recovered most of the architectural detail necessary to restore and interpret public sites such as Plimouth Plantation (Massachusetts), Jamestown and Colonial Williamsburg (Virginia), and Fort Michilimackinac (Michigan). Such projects in historical archaeology began in America in the 1940s and 1950s, concentrating on a very few selected sites—particularly houses of the rich and famous, forts, and other military sites.

Colonial Williamsburg served as a model for this early stage of historical archaeology. Architectural historians concentrated most of their early excavations at Williamsburg, their goal being little more than exposing historic-period building foundations. They did not dig very carefully and showed little interest in the trash middens and smaller structures that would eventually captivate archaeological interest. Only later did historical archaeologists follow the example of their colleagues in prehistoric archaeology and develop independent, artifact-based methods for dating sites and components.

Historical Archaeology Comes of Age

Things changed markedly in the 1960s, partly because of the growing impact of cultural resource management. Federal legislation from the 1960s requires that archaeology be done in advance of construction projects (we discuss this further in Chapter 13). This "applied" version of archaeology proved to be a boon for both prehistoric and historical archaeology. In the beginning, most historical archaeologists received their training on prehistoric sites. But today, the field of historical archaeology is highly specialized, with its own journals and professional societies—and not just in the United States, but around the globe. Historical archaeologists today study everything from the earliest colonial settlements to early nineteenth-century mining camps to World War II battlefields (Figure 12-1).

Early on, Lewis Binford (whom you first met in Chapter 1) clearly saw that historical archaeology readily fit beneath the umbrella of processual archaeology. Binford himself excavated at Fort Michilimackinac, an eighteenth-century French-British frontier site on Mackinac Island, Michigan. Binford believed that archaeologists could pursue processual objectives on historic-period sites only if historical archaeologists would recognize the importance of transcending their own particularistic objectives.

Stanley South (University of South Carolina) helped the transition along. In his influential book *Method and Theory in Historical Archeology* (1977), South argued that historical archaeologists should work within an explicitly evolutionary framework, employ logically grounded scientific methods, apply quantitative methods to data analysis, and formulate the findings of historical archaeology as timeless, spaceless generalizations about the human condition.

Characteristics of Historical Archaeology

Contemporary historical archaeology is every bit as diverse as the rest of Americanist archaeology, but three key factors provide historical archaeology with a slightly different flavor from its prehistoric counterpart.

For one thing, modern historical archaeology often has a *postprocessual* slant to it. Because historical archaeologists commonly have access to texts, ethnohistoric data, and oral traditions, they can often learn something about the meanings of symbols, ethnic affiliation, income, religion, occupation, family composition, economic network, and political restrictions—even before putting a trowel into the ground. It is not surprising, then, that a preeminent historian of archaeology, Bruce Trigger (McGill University), has argued that the most successful symbolic studies lie in the field of historical rather than prehistoric archaeology. The availability of textual information has also made possible many humanistic inquiries, and while historical archaeologists are hardly wed to a postprocessual agenda, the field is certainly amenable to it.

In addition, it is true that historical archaeology, especially as practiced in the United States, deals with time periods that are considerably shorter than are those of prehistoric archaeology. Documentary sources can often provide the precise years that a structure (or site) was used, along with detailed information on how its use changed over time. Prehistoric archaeologists

© Lin Poyer

Figure 12-1 A World War II plane in the Marshall Islands. Today, historical archaeologists study everything from the colonial past to World War II–related sites.

may consider themselves lucky if they date an assemblage to a span of a few hundred years. Historical archaeology tends not to study large-scale processes; instead, the high degree of temporal resolution of historical archaeology leads historical archaeologists to focus on the specific individuals and events that were part of those larger processes—for example, how a nineteenth-century frontier fort's trash reflects the development of the world trade system.

Finally, we must recognize that historical archaeology is often very close to us—not just temporally (the past 500 years in the United States), but also emotionally—whether one is of European, Hispanic, African, Native American, or Asian descent. The archaeology of the past five centuries records the time that all these different peoples came together and created the modern world. And discussion of this recent history is embedded in the continuing discussion of the modern world, with all its cultural, political, and ethical challenges. Because relatively few members of minority

groups are professional archaeologists today, such discussions of the recent past can sometimes become emotionally charged.

Themes in Historical Archaeology

These characteristics suggest three major themes of research in historical archaeology today. Although these directions hardly capture all of historical archaeology—and each theme exists within prehistoric archaeology as well—they seem to define the dominant research domains within historical archaeology today.

First, modern historical archaeology has shied away from a focus on the "oldest," "largest," and "most historically significant" sites, favoring instead the study of historically disenfranchised groups. Many historical archaeologists are working to uncover the history of African American and Asian American cultures, Native Americans during the historic period, and Hispanic

ARCHAEOLOGICAL ETHICS
Who Should Control and Own Sacred Sites?

Many places around the United States, as well as in other countries, are considered sacred sites. The Wailing Wall in Jerusalem is sacred to members of the Jewish faith. The Kabbah in Mecca is sacred to Moslems, and Mount Calvary is sacred to Christians. Devil's Tower in Wyoming is sacred to about 30 tribes, and South Dakota's Black Hills are sacred to the Lakota.

Sacred sites are sensitive because they embody religious ideas and history. And (particularly important for this discussion) sacred sites often include archaeological remains. Who should own and control these places?

This issue arose when the Church of Jesus Christ and Latter-Day Saints (LDS) sought to purchase about 900 acres of land in Wyoming that belonged to the federal Bureau of Land Management (BLM). Although the LDS Church originated in upstate New York in 1830, members eventually founded Salt Lake City, the religion's world center today. Some of the faithful moved westward in wagons; others put their belongings in handcarts that they literally pushed across the prairies. In 1856, 150 people in one of these handcart parties perished in an early winter blizzard along Wyoming's Sweetwater River, in a place now known as Martin's Cove.

The LDS Church considers Martin's Cove, located on BLM land, to be sacred. After leasing the land for years, the church sought to obtain the land permanently in 2001. When difficulties arose, Representative James Hansen (R-Utah) introduced a bill that would require the BLM to sell the land to the LDS Church.

Many organizations opposed the sale, pointing out that several groups had a stake in this land. The alleged site of the handcart party's suffering (some historians place Martin's Cove at another place on the river) also contains Native American archaeological sites and portions of the California trail, which many nonchurch members traveled. Should these groups surrender their interests in the land?

Some fear that Hansen's bill would set a dangerous precedent. If the church was allowed to buy Martin's Cove, then shouldn't any organization be allowed to buy any piece of federal land considered sacred? Jack Trope, executive director of the Association of American Indian Affairs, thinks that the Martin's Cove bill would open the door for tribes to purchase sacred sites such as Devil's Tower and the Black Hills.

Who should own America's sacred sites? And who should care for the site and control access? Right now, sacred lands on public lands are the subject of intense discussions between potential stakeholders. Take Devil's Tower, for example. This nearly 1300-foot-tall basalt tower (made famous in Steven Spielberg's movie *Close Encounters of the Third Kind*) is climbed by some 5000 people each year. Some tribes wish the climbing to cease, because climbing Bear's Lodge (as Devil's Tower is known to some tribes) is akin to scaling a cathedral or mosque for recreation. The monument currently has only a voluntary ban in effect for June, when Sun Dances are held nearby. Many climbers obey the ban out of respect for the tribes, although some professional guides disregard it. Should Devil's Tower be owned and controlled by the tribes?

What's the right thing to do? Should we privilege those who consider the land sacred? Or will we spiral into endless debates about dividing up the landscape into "your" sacred land and "my" sacred land? How do we balance the special interests of the diverse religions and cultures that comprise American democracy?

This concern is reflected in the position taken by the U.S. government with respect to Martin's Cove. In the fall of 2003, after legislative efforts failed, the LDS Church agreed to an offer of a 25-year extension to its current lease and, for the time being, has dropped efforts to purchase the property.

Americans—peoples whose histories are still sometimes ignored, only partially recorded, or related in a biased manner. There is a distinct parallel here to W. W. Taylor's call of a half-century ago, when he urged archaeologists to transcend the grandiose and to get on with the anthropology of "real" people (see Chapter 1).

Second, historical archaeology commonly tackles questions about the recent past that history books answer unsatisfactorily. In this regard, some historical archaeologists are more like forensic archaeologists (which we discuss in Chapter 13), collecting data like crime scene detectives to resolve disputes over the nature of key historical events.

Third, we see many historical archaeologists researching the nature of European colonialism (the developing capitalism of that time) and its effects on indigenous peoples. The postprocessual emphasis on power, for instance, meshes easily with historical archaeology's ample record of developing capitalist society of the last several centuries. Some use this research to challenge standard public presentations of mainstream history, calling into question, for example, the melting pot interpretation of America's past. This approach challenges citizens to think more critically of their history.

Let's look at some examples of each of these themes in historical archaeology.

Hidden History: The Archaeology of African Americans

African American history is inextricably linked to slavery, and especially slavery on plantations. Plantation archaeology began in 1931 at Mount Vernon (Virginia), George Washington's home. In his role as director of research and restoration at Mount Vernon, Morley Jeffers Williams—a landscape architect—wanted to locate the various structural remains on the property, so he conducted extensive and systematic archaeological testing. Although hardly up to contemporary standards, these excavations did permit the reconstruction of the first president's garden and outbuildings and kicked off the study of plantation archaeology as we now know it.

Most early plantation archaeology was aimed at architectural reconstruction, and, prior to the 1980s,

few restored plantations addressed the issue of slavery explicitly. Instead, the restorations usually emphasized the "big house" and the grandeur of the elite who lived there; guides commonly referred to slaves as "servants." This often-melancholy, *Gone with the Wind* perspective focused on the passing of an antebellum way of life (one that many white people saw as genteel, although descendants of slaves hold a different opinion).

Slave archaeology began in earnest in the late 1960s—doubtless connected to, or inspired by, the social upheavals of the time—when Charles Fairbanks (1913–1984) began exploring coastal plantations in Georgia and Florida. Fairbanks was the first to study the institution of slavery from the archaeological record and, when he emphasized the richness and diversity of the southern heritage, he was clearly departing from the traditional "melting pot" theme in America. Fairbanks and his students set out to dispel myths concerning the biological and cultural inferiority of African Americans—myths that were used to legitimize segregation and discrimination.

Today, the field of African American archaeology is a growth industry, helping to uncover information about aspects of slave life on which the documentary sources are often silent. We demonstrate this by looking at the slave archaeology of Monticello, the home of Thomas Jefferson.

Slave Archaeology at Monticello

Visitors motoring up the serpentine driveway to Thomas Jefferson's Monticello, shown in Figure 12-2, are first struck by the world-famous architecture, the vast gardens, and glimpses of mountains in the sprawling Virginia countryside. Walking through Monticello, polite guides provide the visitor with ample details about the life of Thomas Jefferson.

But only recently have we heard much about Thomas Jefferson the slave owner. In the days when Jefferson lived at Monticello, the approach to the main house was called Mulberry Row, and it was lined by 19 buildings—the houses and workshops of Jefferson's slaves, hired laborers, artisans, and indentured servants. The mansion at Monticello still stands, attracting tourists by the thousands, yet today aboveground traces of all but four of the structures along Mulberry Row have vanished.

Figure 12-2 Low-level aerial photograph showing Monticello (at the upper right) and Mulberry Row (the line of trees running horizontally through the middle of the photo).

Historical archaeologists working at Monticello have brought Mulberry Row back to life. Work here was begun by William Kelso (currently director of archaeology for the Association for the Preservation of Virginia Antiquities "Jamestown Rediscovery" project), and it continues under Monticello's archaeology program, directed by Fraser Neiman.

Jefferson had mixed feelings about slavery. He had a slave force numbering 200 people at times and knew that, without slave labor, the agrarian economy of the day would collapse. Yet he regarded the institution of slavery as preeminently brutal and immoral—and he personally favored its abolition. Recognizing this dilemma, Jefferson once said that slavery is like holding a wolf by the ears: "We can neither hold him nor safely let him go. Justice is in one scale, self-preservation in the other."

Jefferson reportedly did not mistreat his slaves, but he doubted whether Caucasians and Africans could successfully create a biracial society (despite the fact that he probably fathered six children with Sally Hemings [1773–1835], one of his house slaves). Instead, he favored a plan to transport free blacks back to Africa or elsewhere.

How Well Did Jefferson's Slaves Live?

Research at Mulberry Row is aimed at learning more about the living and working conditions of Jefferson's slaves. Although few ruins were visible, Kelso soon found by exploratory excavation that the subsurface record of Mulberry Row was relatively undisturbed

(Figure 12-3). The residents of Mulberry Row were probably the house servants and artisans who may have enjoyed a better standard of living than the field hands, who lived in settlements farther down the mountain.

Homes along Mulberry Row contained pig, cow, and deer bones; some of these bones were ground up, suggesting the use of meat in stews. Houses also contained ceramic assemblages, dating to AD 1770–1800, that were probably the remnants of table settings from Jefferson's home. No longer usable in the mansion (perhaps having lost a few key pieces), they were given to slave families. These hand-me-downs reflect the growing consumer revolution of the late eighteenth century and the availability of houseware replacements.

Social Life in Slave Houses

Neiman points out that the archaeology of Mulberry Row helps to answer a question posed by the historical documents. About 1776, Jefferson mapped his plan for buildings along Mulberry Row and included a building, some 17 × 34 feet in dimension, which he labeled the "Negro Quarter." By 1790, this building had burned and, in 1792–1793, Jefferson built several smaller homes on the site; these he labeled structures r, s, and t on a map made in 1796. He intended these structures to be slave homes; they were only 12 × 14 feet in dimension and were made of split logs, with dirt floors and chimneys of wood and mud.

In 1793, Jefferson served as President Washington's secretary of state, but he still minded the details of his plantation. Jefferson wrote to his overseer, instructing him to move Critta Hemings (the sister of Sally Hemings) and her family to the new House r. Hemings had been living in Building e—a stone house still standing today along Mulberry Row—and she was part of the house staff. According to Jefferson's description, Building e had two rooms, each about 290 square feet in size. It had a brick floor, a stone fireplace, and a single entry door decorated with a pedimented portico supported by columns.

Figure 12-3 Excavating slave dwellings built during Jefferson's lifetime at Monticello. Evident in this picture are the remains of Building l, the storehouse (foreground); Building m, the smokehouse-dairy (center); and the rebuilt walls of an 1809 stone slave house (background).

These houses contained what historical archaeologists call "subfloor pits," or cellars. These are rectangular holes, some $3\frac{1}{2} \times 4$ feet, and 1–3 feet deep. The early houses at Monticello contain up to four of these pits.

These early houses at Monticello are fairly typical of slave dwellings throughout the Chesapeake Bay area in the eighteenth century (although at other plantations, early slave houses usually contain four to ten subfloor pits). The function of the subfloor pits is not clear, but they probably served as places for families to store important belongings. If so, then they suggest that multiple families occupied the early slave dwellings. Neiman points out that theft is a real concern in situations where you have little choice over your housemates. The subfloor pits may have helped maintain a semblance of privacy and security in an otherwise open structure, because it would have been difficult to steal something if first it had to be exhumed from a pit.

Beginning about 1790, however, a transition in housing occurs at Monticello and at other plantations in the region (Figure 12-4). Houses became smaller—about 140 square feet (although they then became larger in the early nineteenth century)—and were extremely modest, consisting usually of a single room. But they had only one subfloor pit, not multiple pits, and these pits are smaller. This suggests that only one family lived there, and they did not have much need to stash possessions out of sight. And even where structures had two rooms, the rooms were separated by a solid wall, and a separate door opened into each room, permitting privacy. In fact, no subfloor pits have been found in slave houses that date after AD 1800 at Monticello.

So, when Jefferson asked that Critta Hemings and her family be moved to House r, perhaps this was not a demotion. Instead, Hemings would now live in her

Taken at face value, Hemings appears to have been demoted—she had to move to a smaller house with dirt floors and no architectural embellishments. Yet, she continued as a house servant—normally a favored status. In fact, Jefferson instructed the overseer to place her and her family in House r because "she is wanted around the house." How do we explain this apparent paradox?

The answer comes from the archaeology. The excavations at Monticello retrieved data on nine of the slave houses located on Mulberry Row. Three of the houses date to the 1770s (based on documentary and archaeological evidence). According to Jefferson's maps, the "Negro Quarter" house contained two large rooms, but only a single entryway. The two rooms had separate fireplaces that shared a single flue. A second building originally had a plan similar to that of the "Negro Quarter." A third structure was a single large room, some 250 square feet in size, with a single entryway and a wood and clay fireplace.

Figure 12-4 Artist's reconstruction of post-1790 slave housing at Monticello. This figure shows a view of a typical slave cabin and its foundation (with a single subfloor pit in front of the fireplace) superimposed over the archaeological plan (servant's House o) at Monticello.

own house, with her immediate family, where she could control her own household. A home of her own must have seemed quite a step up in her world. But it must have been a small consolation. After all, she and her family were still slaves.

New York City's African Burial Ground

When most people think of slavery, they think of the Old South and a cotton-based economy. How many people know that slavery was deeply ingrained in the economy north of the Mason-Dixon Line as well?

But we were all reminded of this forgotten past when, in 1991, the bones of 427 enslaved Africans, interred by their own community and forgotten for centuries, were discovered beneath a parking lot in downtown New York City at a place now known as the African Burial Ground.

Slavery in Old New York?

The story begins in 1626, when the Dutch West India Company unloaded its first shipment of enslaved Africans in New Amsterdam (today's New York City): 11 young men from what today is the Congo-Angola region of southwestern Africa. Two years later, the Dutch imported three African women "for the comfort of the company's Negro men." The Dutch at the time were experiencing a labor shortage in their colonies, and they found slave labor to be the answer to building and maintaining the colony.

Some scholars argue that the Dutch treated slaves better. They point out that some slaves had more rights than New Amsterdam's Jews, who were forbidden from owning land or serving in the militia. Under the Dutch, the Africans were permitted to intermarry with whites, attend white churches, own property, and enjoy the same status as whites in court.

According to this view, the Dutch practiced half-freedom; true slavery was introduced in 1664, when the Dutch ceded Manhattan to the British. At that time, enslaved Africans made up about *40 percent* of New Amsterdam's total population. Everywhere one looked in colonial New York, there were toiling slaves—loading and unloading ships on the waterfront, building the streets, and erecting the buildings to house the people and businesses of this bustling port city crowded onto the southern tip of Manhattan Island.

On the eve of the American Revolution, New York City had the largest number of enslaved Africans of any English colonial city except for Charleston, South Carolina. In fact, New York City had the highest proportion of slaves to Europeans of any northern settlement. Despite what is found in most American history books, it is clear that the African population had a significant hand in the building of colonial New York.

Eighteenth-century New York law prohibited the burial of Africans in Manhattan's churchyards. Left without a place to bury their dead, New York's African population eventually established a cemetery on a deserted tract of land lying just outside the city's protective wooden palisade (the "wall" of modern "Wall Street" fame). There, from roughly 1712 to 1790, the community buried somewhere between 10,000 and 20,000 people (mostly black, but also a few lower-class whites). A 1755 map of downtown New York clearly shows the "Negro Burial Ground" covering perhaps five city blocks.

In 1827, New York abolished slavery altogether. In the meantime, African American populations abandoned the downtown area, moving northward in New York City. Over the subsequent decades, the Negro Burial Ground was slowly swallowed up by urban expansion. By the late twentieth century, Manhattan's forgotten cemetery lay buried beneath 20 feet of fill, a scant two blocks north of New York's City Hall.

Archaeology Can Be Contentious

But the Negro Burial Ground was not destined to lie undisturbed. In 1990, the city of New York sold the property to the General Services Administration (GSA), the arm of the federal government responsible for constructing and maintaining federal buildings. The GSA planned to build a 34-story office tower at 290 Broadway, with a four-story pavilion on the parking lot area to house the U.S. attorney's office, a regional office of the Environmental Protection Agency, and a district office of the Internal Revenue Service. Although administrators knew that the pavilion was slated to rise directly above a colonial cemetery, they seriously underestimated its extent and the extraordinary degree of preservation.

As we discuss in Chapter 13, the United States has a legal framework to protect its archaeological resources—particularly those on public land. Part of this legislation requires that an environmental impact statement be filed before any construction can begin. Archaeologists and historians routinely participate in preparing such impact statements. The archaeological firm retained for the 290 Broadway historical inventory correctly noted that the "Negro Burial Ground" appeared on historical maps of the area and probably lay nearby. But, recognizing the long-standing construction history of the site, the impact statement concluded that the digging of nineteenth- and twentieth-century basements had probably obliterated any human remains within the historical boundaries of the cemetery. Although the researchers did note that a portion of the old cemetery might have survived beneath an old alleyway, nobody expected much in the way of human remains to surface when construction began at 290 Broadway.

Still, because there remained a possibility of finding significant archaeological deposits in the construction zone, federal law required that exploratory archaeological excavations be undertaken. Those excavations began in September 1991 and, right away, human bone was found—and not just a few scattered remains, but dozens (then hundreds) of intact human burials (Figure 12-5).

The excavations at 290 Broadway began interfering with construction schedules. Worried that the archaeology might delay the $276 million project, the GSA insisted that the archaeologists work faster, excavating skeletons 10 and 12 hours a day, 7 days a week. Laboratory crew members were reassigned to field excavation duty—anything to speed things up. The cost of the excavation skyrocketed, and the African American community was upset about the way the project was being handled.

Eventually, a working consensus was forged. A 5-year research program was planned, headed by Dr. Michael L. Blakey, a bioarchaeologist and, at the time, director of the Cobb Biological Anthropology Laboratory at Howard University, the nation's premier black research university (he is now at the College of William and Mary). Blakey had already conducted research at the First African Baptist Cemetery in Philadelphia, and so he was more than qualified to conduct the scientific research at the African Burial Ground (see "In His Own Words: Balancing Interests at the African Burial Ground" by Michael L. Blakey).

Blakey's analysis of some 400 individuals from the burial ground is a chilling statement on human brutality. Blakey found that half of the population died before reaching the age of 12, with another peak in mortality occurring between the ages of 15 and 20. Some of this was probably due to diseases for which Africans had not developed immunity, complicated by

Courtesy of African Burial Ground and U.S. General Services Administration

Figure 12-5 A 35- to 40-year-old woman with her child, interred at the African Burial Ground. Both probably died during childbirth or shortly thereafter.

This hard life must have contrasted dramatically with their lives in Africa, for the teeth show little evidence of hypoplasias (see Chapter 9), showing that as children these African men and women had lives relatively free of malnutrition and severe disease. It also contrasted sharply with the life of the other citizens of New York. For example, Blakey found that English settlers were eight times more likely to live past the age of 55 than African slaves.

The African Burial Ground Today

Visitors flock to the African Burial Ground center from around the world, and it has become a point of connection for Africans and Americans, white or black. Guided tours and videotapes of the African Burial Ground project are available through the Office of Public Education and Interpretation of the African Burial Ground, which is actively engaged in bringing the findings to a broader public through newsletters, workshops, and lectures. Finally, all the human remains were reburied in October 2003.

The African Burial Ground is a prime example of how archaeology can recover "lost" history. But the African Burial Ground is also a story about how a descendant community can be empowered through archaeology.

A final note: the artifacts and excavation documents from the African Burial Ground were stored in a basement of one of the buildings at the World Trade Center, along with those from the Five Points Project, another large historical archaeology dig in downtown New York. Most of the African Burial Ground material was recovered after the building's collapse on September 11, 2001; fortunately, the human remains were still stored in laboratories at Howard University. But virtually everything from the Five Points Project (the neighborhood that was the setting for Martin Scorsese's film *Gangs of New York*) was lost.

Beyond Slavery

We have focused on slavery—on and off plantations—because it was a dramatic and key element of African American history whose full impact is often not communicated in standard documentary sources. But African American history is much more than slave history, and a number of historical archaeologists have

the cold weather. But some people were clearly worked to death. Both men and women had enlarged muscle attachments, demonstrating continual demands on their physical labor, and some had lesions from torn muscle attachments. The bones also showed cranial and spinal fractures—a result of carrying excessive loads on the head and shoulders.

IN HIS OWN WORDS

Balancing Interests at the African Burial Ground

By Michael L. Blakey

Michael L. Blakey is professor at the College of William and Mary.

The African Burial Ground in New York City is the earliest and largest African cemetery in North America. Public and scientific controversy began when part of the site was uncovered in 1991. African Americans sought to stop archaeological excavation and building construction. They wanted to establish a fitting memorial and to determine for themselves whether research should be conducted. Rising protests, town meetings, and lobbying efforts were mounted by the African American "descendant community" in order to ensure proper treatment of their ancestors.

I organized a research team consisting of anthropologists, historians, geneticists, and other scientists who had previous experience in the study of both African American and African archaeology and biology. Based at Howard University, the research group includes African American and African scholars who shared many of the descendant community's concerns. Following partly from the African American tradition of "scholar activism" and partly from anthropological approaches to "public engagement," Howard anthropologists and their consultants involved the community in drafting their research design. They assumed that descendant or culturally affiliated persons should have the right to determine whether research was sufficiently worthwhile as to amount to something more than desecration of the cemetery.

Through public meetings, researchers described their methods for restoring the lost history of the enslaved Africans who were buried there. The community introduced their own research questions and thoughts about how the site should be interpreted. This community feedback was incorporated into the research design so long as the integrity of the scientific method remained intact. The result was a better and more meaningful research project that was not only acceptable to the descendant community, but which they had become part of.

The New York African Burial Ground tells us that archaeology, physical anthropology, and history are important to everyday people. Whether as a basis for defining national and group identity, the elucidation of processes leading to current social conditions, or as a guide to the future, disciplines that construct the past do so within the context of broader cultural and political meanings. Indigenous people in many parts of the world are advocating control of their cultural patrimony, including sacred archaeological sites and skeletal remains held by museums. Legislation has begun to protect those rights for Native Americans.

Working with the remains of the dead has an impact on living communities that are affiliated with the dead. Archaeologists and skeletal biologists who work with archaeological populations are well served when they have had "holistic" training in the history, ethnography, ethics, and even the political issues of living communities. These issues mark the terrain often entered when digging for the past.

turned their attention to the archaeology of early free black communities (see "Looking Closer: Fort Mose: Colonial America's Black Fortress of Freedom") in the South and African American settlements in the West.

Still other American historical archaeologists work to recover the history of other peoples by excavating the immigrant communities of early nineteenth-century mining towns, Chinese railroad labor camps, and early Mormon communities.

Correcting Inaccuracies

Historical archaeologists also attempt to correct inaccuracies in the public view of history. Sometimes these inaccuracies are simple mistakes or unintentional omissions and are often innocuous and trivial. But other historical inaccuracies are vastly more significant.

What Happened at the Battle of the Little Bighorn?

In the 1850s, American settlers were moving west through land that was the traditional territory of several tribes, including, on the northern high plains, the Lakota. When the settlers were simply moving through, relations were not so violent, but once settlers opted to remain and forts were constructed, hostilities ensued. By the late 1860s, the Lakota had gained the upper hand, and they were prepared to discuss terms of peace.

By signing the Laramie Treaty of 1868, Red Cloud and other Lakota leaders agreed to cease hostilities, and the United States created the Great Sioux Reservation, which included the Black Hills in eastern South Dakota; the treaty agreed that whites would make no settlements or unauthorized incursions into this territory. Still, some Indian leaders refused to sign (among them Gall, Sitting Bull, and Crazy Horse), and they were granted permanent hunting rights in the Powder River region of Wyoming and Montana.

But the legal details of the treaty were difficult to understand (and some are still in dispute). Apparently, the treaty allowed for railroad surveys in the Black Hills, which were conducted in 1872 and 1873. But an 1874 military expedition to the Black Hills to locate a military post may not have been allowed in the treaty. Regardless, what matters is that this expedition discovered gold, and the federal government only half-heartedly tried to stop the ensuing rush of miners. By 1875, the government wished to reduce the size of the Sioux reservation and also ordered that the nontreaty bands relocate to the reservation. In 1876, the government sent General George Armstrong Custer to find these Lakota and move them to the reservation.

On June 25, with the aid of Crow and Arikara scouts, Custer tracked a large band of Lakota, Northern Cheyenne, and Arapaho to the Little Bighorn River in Montana. Despite his scouts' warnings, he decided to attack. He broke his men into three battalions. One, headed by Captain Frederick Benteen, went to the south to cut off an escape route. Major Marcus Reno led another into the valley to attack the village from the southeast. Custer himself led the third over the river bluffs, eventually reaching a position north of the village. Reno encountered heavy resistance that brought him to a standstill, but his efforts did succeed in creating an exodus from the village. Custer apparently then moved through the low hills northeast of the river, pursuing the women, children, and elderly as they fled down the valley.

Images of the Battle

No U.S. soldier survived to describe what happened or what Custer's final moments were like. Nonetheless, sensationalist newspaper accounts quickly formed an image of the battle and Custer's gallant "last stand." Years later, that vivid image was immortalized in several paintings. In 1895, Adolphus Busch (the brewery magnate) commissioned Otto Becker to paint *Custer's Last Fight*. The image shows Custer, his men bravely circled around him, almost calmly fighting a huge band of Lakota and Cheyenne. Busch sent lithographs of the image to 150,000 saloons around the country. In 1900, Frederic Remington also painted an image of the battle's final moments where, again, a cool and collected Custer commands the men clustered around him.

Perhaps the most famous image is that by Edgar Samuel Paxson (see the chapter's opening photo), completed in 1899, which includes 200 individuals (some are recognizable individuals, as Paxson studied all the available photographs of Custer's men as well as those of Cheyenne and Lakota warriors). Here we see Custer calmly standing in a whirlwind of activity, revolvers at the ready, his chest thrust out defiantly. The men of the Seventh Cavalry are gathered around him, disciplined to the end.

Images like these helped to create a fatalistic attitude toward the country's push to the west: some would have to die in expanding the country westward, but they would die proud, knowing that what they were doing—bringing civilization to the wilderness (or massacring Indians and dispossessing them of their land, depending on your perspective)—was their God-given destiny. And Indians who stood in the way of this destiny should be punished.

LOOKING CLOSER
Fort Mose: Colonial America's Black Fortress of Freedom

African American archaeology is not exclusively focused on slavery. Yet another perspective on African American history was achieved through the discovery of Fort Mose, 50 miles south of the Georgia-Florida border. Here, archaeologist Kathleen Deagan and her colleagues at the University of Florida found concrete evidence of the first legally sanctioned, free African American community in the country.

Beginning with the founding of Charles Towne by the British in 1670, Spain employed free Africans to further its colonial objectives by having them populate and hold territories vulnerable to foreign encroachment. Both free and slave Africans were also used in military operations, a black militia having been established in St. Augustine. By 1673, the Spanish crown declared that all escaped fugitives from British plantations were to be granted sanctuary and, eventually, freedom in Spanish Florida "so that by their example and by my liberality, others

will do the same." Like so many episodes in African American history, the story of Fort Mose is incompletely known, a forgotten footnote to mainstream American history.

Deagan found the lost site of Fort Mose in 1986, and her excavations have provided an opportunity to reexamine the role of African Americans in colonial history. She is particularly interested in the effect of freedom on the blacks of Fort Mose. How much did they adapt to Spanish ways? Did they attempt to revive their African heritage?

Recognizing the relevance of the Fort Mose research, the state of Florida was quick to help out. State Representative Bill Clark, who sponsored the bill helping to finance the archaeology, has called Deagan's discovery of Fort Mose "a major historical find for black people." To Clark, himself an African American, the excavations demonstrate that "blacks were never content to be slaves. . . . These are America's first freedom fighters."

But there were other images of the battle. Although none of Custer's battalion survived, many of the 1200 or so Indian warriors did, including such notables as Sitting Bull, Gall, Crazy Horse, and Black Elk (then 13 years old). Many of the Indian survivors were interviewed in the following years, and their accounts were used to draw Indian images of the battle.

The Indian images tell a different story, as shown in Figure 12-6. In the first place, they are far bloodier than the paintings by Paxson and others, who sanitized the gruesome details of hand-to-hand combat. The Indians' images are filled with blood and entrails, decapitation and dismemberment. More important, they show groups of men spread over the battlefield—some firing, others running for their lives. Unlike the images created by white artists, the Indians' images show no grand last stand. In fact, there is nothing glorious in their pictures at all; there is only confusion and carnage. Which image is accurate?

An Archaeological Perspective on the Battle

Today, the battlefield is a national monument, but it still remains a lonely and windswept place. In 1983, a brush fire burned the area, which led Douglas Scott (National Park Service) and Richard Fox (University of South Dakota) to conduct a survey of the entire battlefield. They checked a sample of the grave markers (individual gravestones marked where bodies were found some time after the battle) and systematically surveyed the battlefield using metal detectors for battle-related artifacts. They found plenty: gun parts, belt buckles, buttons, bridle pieces, human remains, and lots of spent cartridges and bullets. Each item was recorded and its location carefully mapped.

The cartridges and bullets were especially interesting, because they were amenable to forensic analyses. Scott and Fox knew that the cavalry was armed only with .45-caliber single-shot Springfield carbines and

Figure 12-6 *Battle of the Little Bighorn* (about 1898) by Kicking Bear (1846?–1904). Kicking Bear made this painting at the request of Frederic Remington; Custer appears in buckskins at the left.

.45-caliber Colt pistols. The Indians had these, too, but forensic studies showed they were also equipped with some 40 other types of weapons, from obsolete muzzleloaders to repeating rifles (acquired through the illegal arms trade of the day). Careful mapping allowed Scott and Fox to ascertain combatant positions (Indian and soldier alike) using cartridge case locations and bullet orientations (which revealed the direction from which the bullet was fired). Most important, in many instances they could use discharged cartridges to trace individual combatant movements by matching the distinctive "fingerprint" that a gun's firing pin makes on the cartridge. What did they learn?

Where Was Custer?

We know that Custer's body was found on the hilltop that bears his name, surrounded by most of his headquarters staff. But where was he during the battle? We know that Custer's battalion had broken into two wings. Previous scholars argued that Custer was with the right wing because brass cartridges had been found along the path taken by the right wing, and Custer's .50-caliber Remington rifle was thought to be the only weapon on the battlefield that used brass cartridges. But Scott and Fox found many brass cartridges at the site, with firing pin fingerprints indicating that

brass cartridges were fired from several different .50-caliber guns (by both soldiers and Indians). The brass cartridges, therefore, can't be used to pinpoint Custer's personal movements. We don't know where Custer himself fought; we only know where his body eventually came to rest.

Where Were the Indians and the Soldiers?

Scott and Fox also found cavalry cartridge cases on Custer Hill, on the low ridges running to the east and south, and on Calhoun Hill (to the south of Custer Hill). Many more *Indian* cartridges are found in these same places (as well as on the rise coming up from the river—the direction from which the Indians would have attacked). In addition, in some places expended government bullets were found next to government-issue cartridges. A cartridge drops to the ground as a rifle is reloaded, but obviously the corresponding bullet should appear at the target. Some of the bullets may have resulted from men shooting their horses to use them as shields. But others were probably fired by Indians, using guns they had claimed from Reno's unsuccessful attack or weapons taken from the bodies of Custer's men.

Also odd is the lack of evidence for formal military maneuvers. Army tactics at the time called for companies to form skirmish lines as a defensive measure. To form a skirmish line, a company's men stood about 5 yards apart, with about 15 yards between companies. Such a tactical maneuver leaves a distinctive trace: piles of government-issue cartridges spaced about 5 yards apart. Scott and Fox found only tentative evidence for one skirmish line, on Calhoun Hill. Otherwise, the archaeological evidence fit the Indian accounts of chaos and hand-to-hand fighting.

Eventually, about 100 soldiers made it to Custer Hill, where order was apparently restored, albeit briefly. More Indians slowly arrived. Eventually, about 45 men, 5 of them mounted, made a break down a ridge to the east of Custer Hill. But Scott and Fox found no evidence of a skirmish line there. Instead, the men were perhaps trying to distract the Indians from the mounted soldiers, who were probably trying to reach Benteen. But these men, even the riders, were quickly pursued.

Eventually, Custer Hill was overrun, and more men ran down the hill to the ravine. Indians recalled that some fired into the air, but others failed even to draw their revolvers. And many did what soldiers before (and after) have done when confronted with death: they froze, with little choice but to accept the inevitable.

The battle lasted less than 90 minutes, and the final part took place not on Custer Hill, as the paintings suggest, but in the ravine, where terrified soldiers who "shot like drunken men," according to Iron Hawk, were hunted down and killed in a terrifying game of hide-and-seek.

Fox argues that Custer was moving confidently in an offensive tactical maneuver when he was caught completely off-guard, forcing a rapid transition from an offensive to a defensive posture. But Custer and his men were so rapidly surrounded that they had no time to regroup and carry out formal tactical maneuvers. The coordination of Custer's offensive attack rapidly gave way to chaos. In fact, the distribution of Springfield cases suggests that men clustered together tightly in a nontactical maneuver—something that Indian eyewitnesses recalled years later—firing against the Indians who surrounded them.

To the Last Bullet?

The romantic image of the battle has the soldiers holding off the Indians until their last bullet was fired. In fact, less than a month after the battle, the Helena *Herald* reported the tragedy with the headline "Not Until Their Ammunition Was Gone Were Our Troops Butchered."

But there were almost no Colt .45 cartridge cases found on the battlefield—none, in fact, on Custer Hill. A soldier could fire a revolver six times before he had to reload (unlike the single-shot carbines, from which a soldier had to remove the empty cartridge before reloading). But with their limited accuracy, handguns were only good for close combat. The Indians recalled soldiers using their sidearms, but they said that the soldiers had no time to reload. The distribution of .45-caliber Colt cartridges confirms this account. Close combat came so quickly and with such overwhelming force that soldiers either had no time to use their revolvers or, more likely, had no time to reload them (and the Indians collected the revolvers, still filled with empty or usable cartridges, after the battle).

The romantic images of the battle suggest that Custer and his men were in calm control until the very end. But the archaeology agrees with the Indians' accounts: Custer was caught off-guard. Perhaps he didn't expect the warriors to be so motivated to protect their women and children. Perhaps he expected Reno and Benteen to cut through and assist them. We don't know. We do know, however, that the popular images of the battle are inaccurate. The Battle of the Little Bighorn did not end in a "glorious" last stand. Instead, it ended like most battles: in chaos, panic, horror, and carnage.

The Monument Today

A pillar was erected on Custer's Hill in 1881 as a tribute to the Seventh Cavalry. One hundred and ten years later, Congress recognized the more complex nature of the site's history and changed the name from Custer Battlefield to Little Bighorn Battlefield National Monument. At the same time, it authorized a memorial to honor the fallen Cheyenne, Lakota, and Arapaho warriors. The new memorial, dedicated in June 2003, consists of a low, circular, granite-lined earthwork and contains bronze silhouettes of mounted warriors. Its name: "Peace through Unity."

Reexamining America's History

We now come to perhaps the most divisive aspect of historical archaeology—reexamining history. A national narrative can be contentious, because a nation's history defines who its citizens are and, in no small way, creates their identity. No one wishes to identify with a history of dishonorable acts. This is why slavery was long ignored at reconstructed plantation sites and why revisionist histories of western settlement remain controversial. Going back in time, it seems, is like going deeper into a people's identity and soul. There are many, for example, who do not welcome reinterpretations of Custer's Last Stand, because the myth has become "their" history, right or wrong. Everyone wants their history to be uplifting; scholars also want it to be honest. Here's one example from Annapolis, Maryland.

Historical Archaeology in Annapolis

Working with the Historic Annapolis Foundation, Mark Leone (University of Maryland) has conducted "backyard archaeology" for decades, excavating in basements and backyards, beneath parking lots and pavements throughout Annapolis. By looking at floor plans, dishes, facades, architecture, silverware, furniture, and gardens, Leone is trying to demonstrate the degree to which our history is "constructed"—that is, written and presented for contemporary purposes. And in doing that, Leone has established the relevance of eighteenth-century Annapolis to ourselves and the way we understand not only our past, but also the present and the future.

Because of the explicit political agenda behind Leone's work, it is important to understand his theoretical perspective. Leone works within a postprocessual paradigm called *critical theory*. As applied to archaeology, critical theory emphasizes the importance of archaeologists' understanding of the specific contexts within which they work and of the notion that knowledge is situated within a cultural framework (as

we pointed out in Chapter 3) and that it consequently can serve special interests. Critical theory assumes that domination in some form is a central element of modern capitalist society.

Critical in this sense means that the relationship between the assumptions and discoveries of a scholarly discipline on the one hand and its ties to modern life on the other is a central concern and subject to examination. Such an approach relates the questions, methods, and discoveries of a science like anthropology to those of the anthropologist's own culture. Critical theorists seek simultaneously to explain the social world, to criticize it, and to empower their audience to deal with it more productively by advocating change.

Pre-1760 Colonial America: The Georgian Order

Before continuing, we must situate Leone's work in a larger context. Folklorist Henry Glassie (Indiana University) and archaeologist James Deetz (1930–2000) both explored the way in which changing cultural ideas were reflected in the material record of the American colonies. As such, they took a decidedly ideational (rather than materialist) approach to the past. Glassie examined early colonial houses in Virginia, while Deetz looked at the overall pattern of material culture in New England. Deetz argued that early British colonists in New England had a **medieval mindset** that encouraged a group-oriented, corporate, and relatively undifferentiated lifestyle. He found that by 1660, however, the culture of American colonies had changed. This particular culture is sometimes known as the **Georgian order.**

Glassie and Deetz found that material remains of the late seventeenth century reflect a culture of increasing individualism and control. In this regard, American colonial culture reflected elements of the Enlightenment, which focused on progress and on the ability of rational thought to control nature and improve human morality and spirituality. During the late seventeenth century, Deetz argued, Georgian attitudes created material culture patterns that emphasized control, often by partitioning space, and reflected a focus on the individual. These patterns in material culture were strikingly different from the previous "medieval" culture of the colonies. Here is how Deetz saw the differences:

- *Architecture.* Medieval houses had only one or two rooms, with asymmetrical floor plans. All

medieval mindset The culture of the early (pre-AD 1660) British colonies that emphasized the group rather than the individual and in which the line between culture and nature was blurred; people were seen as conforming to nature.

Georgian order A worldview (1660/1680–1820) arising in the European Age of Reason and implying that the world has a single, basic immutable order. Using the powers of reason, people can discover what that order is and can thereby control the environment as they wish. The Georgian order is informed by the rise of scientific thought and by the balance and order in Renaissance architecture and art.

domestic activity took place in these rooms, from sleeping and eating to working and socializing. But with the Georgian worldview, houses became functionally structured and compartmentalized, with more balanced floor plans.

- *Ceramics.* The medieval mindset was characterized by plain, utilitarian earthenware. Food was served directly from the cooking pot and consumed from "trenchers," wooden trays that were shared with one or more "trencher mates." During this period, ceramics played a small role in food consumption. Georgian culture entailed ceramics that were purchased as matched sets of plates and teacups. Serving vessels appeared, and one plate was allotted to each individual around the family table. And whereas medieval ceramics were natural-colored earthenwares, Georgian ceramics became progressively whiter as technology improved.

- *Mortuary art.* Gravestones also became white, replacing earlier green, black, blue, and red markers, and the backs were sculpted smooth, "denying their origin in the native stone." The messages engraved on the medieval tombstones reminded the living of their mortality with engraved death's heads and simple epitaphs such as "Here lies buried . . . ." But in Georgian culture, the typical inscription changed to "In memory of . . . ," and the urn and willow motif was used as a "symbol of commemoration." Georgian epitaphs praised the worldly achievements of individuals.

- *Food preparation.* Medieval diners usually attacked a portion of meat still articulated in joints, "showing in part at least the vestiges of the anatomy of the beast from which they came." But Georgian food was dominated by segmented cuts of meat that were more difficult to identify to anatomical part. Archaeologically, this change is seen as a shift from chopping bones to sawing them.

- *Refuse disposal.* During early medieval days, trash was simply tossed out of doors and windows, creating a sheet of refuse that domestic animals scavenged. By the mid-eighteenth century, however, trash was deposited in an orderly manner, in square pits up to 7 feet deep. Chamber pots also came into use, reflecting a desire for increased privacy.

These changes in material culture signal a shift to a culture that focused on the individual, rather than the group, and on the control of nature. Glassie and Deetz believe these patterns point to a simple cultural idea: culture was to nature as order was to chaos. This reflects a general Enlightenment theme: for nature to be controlled, it had to be ordered, and for it to be ordered, it had to be brought into the world of culture.

Capitalism and Power in Historic Annapolis

Leone was interested not just in the operation of the Georgian worldview, but also in how and why it came to exist. He chose to examine these questions in the community of Annapolis.

Annapolis has been a small community since it was founded about 1650. It became the capital of Maryland in 1695, later experiencing a "golden age" of wealth and fame that peaked between about 1760 and the end of the American Revolution. In a move designed to symbolically subordinate the military to civil authority, George Washington came to Annapolis to resign his command of the Continental Army. The Treaty of Paris, which officially ended the American Revolution, was also signed there. During the early days of the United States, even though Annapolis remained the state capital, the international, commercial, and industrial potential of nearby Baltimore attracted many of the area's wealthiest residents. Although the U.S. Naval Academy moved to Annapolis in 1845, the nineteenth century signaled an era of "gentle eclipse" for Annapolis. The 1950s saw the beginning of a commercial revival based on yachting, tourism, and new highways that defined Annapolis as a suburb of Washington, D.C., and Baltimore, less than 30 miles away.

Leone and his team consciously deconstructed the ideology behind the historical development of Annapolis and its environs: Why did some people become rich? Why were some poor? What was the relationship between the two? How did the American Revolution affect these inequalities?

Eventually, Leone developed a "theory of power" to explain the growth of Chesapeake society under the European and American systems. By 1720, a class structure had developed in which a few families of the gentry controlled most of the wealth. The social position of the rest of the population—poorer whites, Native and African Americans—remained the same before and after the American Revolution.

The Power Garden: Landscape Archaeology as Ideology

Leone paid special attention to the formal landscapes of Annapolis. Recognizing that formal gardens were a new addition to wealthy households, Leone wanted to understand what this piece of material culture had to say about the formation of the Georgian order.

Shown in Figure 12-7, the best known of Annapolis's formal gardens in the late eighteenth century was that of William Paca—a signer of

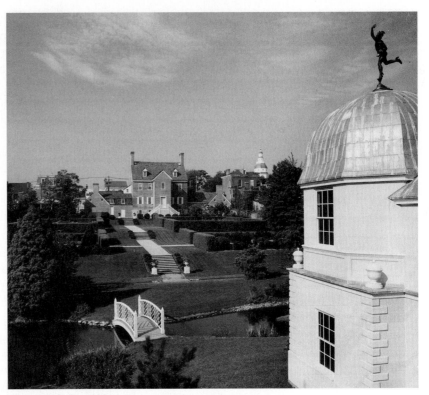

Figure 12-7 The William Paca garden (Annapolis).

the Declaration of Independence. If we could ask him, Paca would probably say that he built his garden in the style that he did because he "enjoyed" it or because it was fashionable. But this only raises the question of *why* this particular garden style was fashionable.

Paca's garden, once described as "the most elegant in Annapolis," was originally built in the 1760s, behind a large, five-part Georgian mansion—which sported a facade and a floor plan exhibiting bilateral symmetry.

The garden is likewise Georgian, with a central axis, and a straight, broad path that descends through several sets of steps as one leaves the house, dividing the space into two parts. These steps lead down over a series of small terraces, creating the same visual effect of bilateral symmetry as that of Georgian architecture.

The garden survived into the early twentieth century, when it was destroyed to make room for a 200-room hotel. When the hotel was torn down in 1968, Stanley South excavated in and around the standing house. Historical archaeologists then moved into the garden area, first testing and then excavating large areas. Original wall footings, documenting the terraces (which could be seen in stratigraphic profile), were

found; thus, the garden's basic topography was reconstructed. Trenching and examination of the profiles showed a canal and pond at the bottom of the garden, surrounded by a natural garden (in the terminology of the time, a "wilderness") in the lowest third of the garden. Foundations of a central pavilion and springhouse and of footings for a bridge over the ponds were discovered; 125 paleobotanical samples were recovered from the wet fill. These archaeological data were combined with a few period descriptions and with a contemporary portrait of William Paca that showed the garden as background. The pavilion, bathhouse, springhouse, and Chinese Chippendale bridge all have been restored. Today, the Paca garden is open to the public as both an archaeologically based reconstruction and a horticultural experiment.

Leone first visited the restored garden in the early 1980s, and his impressions remained the touchstone for his subsequent archaeological analyses. He later wrote,

As I began to walk through the garden from the top, which is 16 feet higher than the bottom, which is 270 feet away, I found it difficult to tell distances; I felt

RAPID REVIEW — Three Themes of Historical Archaeology

Theme	Characteristics
Hidden history	Seeks to rectify an injustice by documenting the experiences of minority or subjugated populations whose lack of access to literacy often left their voice out of traditional historical texts
Correcting inaccuracies	Seeks to set historical records of events straight in cases where the records may be biased
Reexamining history	Seeks to determine whether our explanations of the past, or whether national "stories" of how a nation came to be, are accurate or whether the story masks the processes that led to and propagate inequalities

I was being controlled, as paths, precise borders, openings, stairs, and objects that had to be stepped over operated everywhere to control me. This sensation was especially true regarding sight.

This effect is not simply the impact of fastidious design. Paca's sensibilities were affected by larger cultural ideas, and his garden expresses the Enlightenment idea of the power of Reason over Nature. By putting trees and shrubs into their "proper" places, Paca's landscape architect was demonstrating that nature controlled by culture was more lovely and desirable than wilderness—that is, than nature uncontrolled by culture.

After studying two other large gardens in Annapolis, Leone synthesized what he believed to be the rules behind the design. The Paca garden was constructed following the laws of perspective and used Baroque rules for creating optical illusions. Convergent or divergent lines of sight (to make distances appear shorter or longer, depending on the specific need in each garden) were created, and rows of beds or shrubs were formed into trapezoids and focal points (rather than strictly parallel lines) to manipulate the view. "The gardens are three-dimensional spaces," he wrote, "built consciously using rules which were well understood to create illusions for those who walked through them."

But why the illusion? Leone asked. And why would such Anglo-American gardens proliferate just before the American Revolution and then slowly disappear—like the rest of Georgian material culture—in the decades leading up to the Civil War?

For answers, Leone turned to the general body of materialist theory and formulated a hypothesis to explain governance through ostentatious displays. When money forms the only power base, Leone argued, those governing have little need to demonstrate their right or power to govern; they are in control and intend to stay that way. But ostentatious displays become important when factors other than simple wealth come into play, when it is necessary to convince the governed that those in power deserve to stay there. *Show* becomes important when those in authority do not necessarily control the purse strings or when the wealthy do not control the power structure.

The William Paca garden was built by a wealthy man who lived in a time of contradictions. Although not born to particular affluence, he married into plenty of it. Although a slave owner, he argued for the Bill of Rights. Although descended from planters and tied to merchants, he grew up and lived in economic circumstances in which he and everyone around him was facing serious economic and political change.

Paca could have built his garden anytime during his lifetime, but he chose to do so when his power to protect his wealth was being diminished by Britain. Parliamentary restrictions on trade and local office holding compromised profits and power in the 1760s. Paca was isolated socially and economically by a large and difficult-to-control slave population as well as by poor white farmers and day laborers who were anxious to learn who their future allies would be in the coming war with Britain.

Leone argues that the formal Anglo-American gardens were built deliberately to demonstrate a knowledge of—and control over—the laws of nature. Paca was trying to create the illusion that either (1) he still retained power over his own wealth or (2) he should be granted the political clout to do so. In this perspective, the garden was not a statement of what existed. Paca's garden both reflected and helped create an ideology, at a time when the wealth and prestige of his class were being undermined and diminished.

Leone points out that the Paca garden illustrates the principles that defined the layout of Annapolis as a whole. The early street patterns and building placements still dominate life in the city. This archaeological study of Paca's garden reveals that perspective and its power to invite attention are still actively used to manage relations of power in the city today. The relations among the prominence of the state capitol, the isolation of the Naval Academy, and the invisibility of the African American community are all managed using the same spatial principles exhibited in Paca's garden. Together, Leone argues, historical archaeological and critical theory illustrate the origins of modern—and exploitative—social relations that continue to the present.

Taking Critical Theory Public

As discussed in Chapter 2, archaeology's postprocessual critique calls attention to the important role played by local politics in archaeological interpretation—and particularly to interpretation within the field of historical archaeology.

Critical theorists argue that the proper role of the historian is to unearth the beginnings of contemporary class-based ideologies—distortions that rationalize forms of exploitation, such as slavery, sexism, and racism. Applied to historical archaeology, critical theory suggests that, once a repressed people can be shown a past in which things were different, they can use this knowledge to challenge and attempt to change the inequities of the present. From this position, the responsible historian (and historical archaeologist) should form alliances with members of oppressed classes and work toward social change to better the workers' condition. To the critical theorist, capitalism has negative social elements that should be confronted.

Leone grounded his research at Annapolis in the belief that archaeologists and historians should "stand up" against the oppressive excesses of capitalism. In other words, it was not enough for archaeologists simply to learn about abuse of power in the past; it was essential that this knowledge be brought forward into the present.

The call for historical archaeology to become more political comes from two directions. As archaeology becomes more public, individual archaeologists are increasingly called upon to interpret their findings for the public. Such interpretation takes many forms—traditional museum exhibits, outdoor history museums, site-specific tourist facilities, and television and other media interpretations of "the past." But the problem immediately surfaces—which and whose past?

Consider the case of Annapolis, where historical preservation has played a major role in the commercial renaissance of the city. Annually, more than 1 million people visit Annapolis, a city of only about 32,000 people. As in many other small, historical towns, local residents work hard to protect those things that attract visitors.

The encapsulated history of Annapolis has been peddled to generations of tourists who buy guidebooks, listen to tour guides, and saunter through the historic-house museums. Prominent are references to the ultimate first tourist, none other than George Washington himself. Discussing his many visits, conventional Annapolis history plays up the social and domestic aspects of Washington's jaunts into the city—going to the racetrack, attending social events and plays, and visiting a host of friends and family members. In effect, the image of Washington-in-Annapolis largely mirrored the profile of just the sort of visitor that Annapolis wanted to attract—the high-end tourist with some money to spend, but without an attitude.

Through the lens of critical theory, however, Leone and his colleagues noticed something interesting about the tourism process. As the tourists poured through, they were presented the history of Annapolis as a collection of disconnected units from different time periods and institutions. History-for-the-tourist was left in the hands of diverse groups and institutions, some overlapping, some in competition. Annapolis had no unified history to connect the different parts of the city. Black and white populations were presented as unconnected, as were the histories of the city of Annapolis and the Naval Academy.

As written and presented by whites, black history (viewed from the nineteenth-century perspective) was separated from white history (presented from the eighteenth-century perspective). Slavery was not seen as an antecedent to relationships between contemporary groups.

Leone and his associates—notably an archaeologist-cum-lawyer, Parker Potter—designed an on-site program for the 5,000 to 10,000 visitors who stopped by each year. Tourists visiting Historic Annapolis often have a chance to walk through the ongoing archaeological excavations. Well-prepared guides explain what the archaeologists are doing and why they are doing it.

Did Critical Theory Succeed at Annapolis?

The site excursions were enormously popular with tourists and residents in Annapolis, and they seemed to rally the city's support to protect the archaeological sites of Annapolis. But in regard to social change, Leone and Potter were frustrated with the results. Potter believed that the "Archaeology in Annapolis" tour program failed to effect any significant change in Annapolis. "As far as I can tell," Leone has written, "[the tours]changed consciousness not at all. . . . We were speaking to the wrong audience."

For a historical archaeology of capitalism to be fruitful, Leone realized, "there would have to be a dialogue with those who see knowledge about themselves as a way of dealing with their own oppression or victimization." This was disappointing in a sense because it suggested that critical theory—as a strategy for effecting social change (its avowed goal)—might not work as intended (at least not by itself).

On reflection, Leone still believed that the "Archaeology in Annapolis" program had successfully explored the histories of the white residents who lived there (even if the white tourists to Annapolis did not seem to pick up on the message to "stand up against capitalism").

But he also realized that, in its early stages, the archaeology program had overlooked a major portion of the city by not explicitly addressing the African American experience through archaeology. This realization led Leone and the public programming effort at Annapolis in another direction—into the contemporary African American community of Annapolis.

The dialogue between Annapolis archaeologists and the African American community immediately raised three related questions:

1. Was there, indeed, any way to tell whether archaeological material was associated with African Americans?
2. Does the African American community care about that record? (Some important questions: Can you tell us about freedom, not just about slavery? Is there anything left from Africa?)
3. What would an African American historical archaeology look like?

Faced with this entirely new direction, Leone realized, "We ourselves had to admit we did not know the answers."

So began a new interchange at Annapolis, between white archaeologists and African Americans. No longer was the archaeologist the "teacher," with the community serving only as "listener." In this dialogue, all participants defined themselves as professionals, informants, scholars, students, and fund-raisers. Everyone involved, according to Leone, admitted ignorance on some topics, but also expressed a willingness to learn. This experiment in historical archaeology is still ongoing.

Conclusion: Historical Archaeology's Future

Historical archaeology is the growth industry of Americanist archaeology in the twenty-first century. In part, cultural resource management and the large number of historical sites that are uncovered by the construction activities of a growing population drive this. But it is also driven by a desire to understand the colonial and postcolonial history of the United States and the roles played by all the peoples who have found a home in America. For this reason, historical archaeology will continue to occupy a prominent place in Americanist archaeology for years to come. We expect that the processual paradigm will continue to be important, but that postprocessual approaches will play a large and significant role as issues such as power, domination, class, and resistance figure prominently in the world's recent (colonial) history.

For this reason also, historical archaeology will continue to be the source of some heated disputes. Some of these disputes will focus on who has the right to study and interpret the material remains that document the history of those other groups—African, Asian, Native, Hispanic, and Euro-Americans. We predict that these debates will be less contentious and more productive if archaeologists maintain a dialogue with the public and descendant communities and yet do not withdraw from their scientific standards of excavation and interpretation.

Other disputes will focus on the proper place of politically motivated interpretations of the past. Leone,

for example, suggests that capitalism creates its own view of the past, which masks the formation of inequities that are essential to the operation of capitalism today—a bourgeois class of consumers and an economically and politically repressed group of workers. But some might legitimately argue that any archaeology pursuing a political position is biased from the start, and hence all its interpretations of the past are suspect. Those in historical archaeology who pursue the paradigm of critical theory will have to meet this challenge in the future by combining a passionate desire to use archaeology to effect social change with a dispassionate and thorough scientific analysis of archaeology's data.

Summary

- Historical archaeology looks at material remains from past societies that also left behind some form of written documentation ("history") about themselves. So defined, the first bona fide historical archaeology in America took place about 150 years ago.

- During the first half of the twentieth century, historical archaeologists labored mostly to supplement historical records, serving as a kind of "handmaiden to history." This perspective is evident in public interpretive projects, such as Plimouth Plantation, Colonial Williamsburg, and the Little Bighorn battlefield. Such projects tended to concentrate on a very few selected sites, particularly houses of the rich and famous, forts, and other military sites.

- Things changed in the 1960s, when some processual archaeologists realized that they could refine their archaeological methods and theories by working in the contexts of verifiable historical controls. Mainstream historical archaeology distanced itself from an emphasis on the "most historically significant" sites—looking instead at the larger social contexts.

- In the 1960s, historical archaeology began to focus on historically disenfranchised groups in our own culture, seeking to uncover the history of African Americans, Asian Americans, Native Americans during the historic period, and Hispanic Americans.

- Historical archaeology has also been fertile ground for postprocessual interests, because texts can provide data with which to place archaeological remains in context.

- The study of the symbolic meaning of material remains also proceeds more comfortably in historical archaeology, where documents can provide interpretations of material culture.

- Historical archaeology is today one of the most rapidly expanding and exciting directions in Americanist archaeology; current trends—challenges to existing histories and the recovery of the history of disenfranchised groups—will generate debates and dialogue for years to come.

Media Resources

The Companion Website for **Archaeology: Down to Earth,** *Third Edition*

http://anthropology.wadsworth.com/thomas_kelly3e_down/

Supplement your review of this chapter by going to the companion website to take one of the practice quizzes, use the flash cards to master key terms, and check out the many other study aids that are designed to help you succeed in your introductory archaeology course.

13 Caring for America's Cultural Heritage

Outline

Archaeologists in Wyoming excavate a site in the path of a railroad trestle, the other side of which is under construction in the background.

© Charles Reher

Preview

Throughout this book, we have tried to paint a realistic picture of what Americanist archaeology is all about. We have often reached into the past to demonstrate how today's archaeology has evolved over the past 150 years.

Now we look forward to address two of the key challenges facing Americanist archaeology in the twenty-first century:

1. How is archaeology relevant to the modern world?

2. How should archaeologists share control over knowledge of the past?

As we explore these related issues, you will probably find more questions than answers.

Introduction

We began this book by describing Kennewick Man, an important archaeological find that fostered an equally important legal case. The legalities of the Kennewick case highlight even larger issues surrounding the role of archaeology in modern society. But before we consider those issues, let's first recap some key concepts from earlier chapters.

We have emphasized throughout this text the "big picture" of archaeology: the place of archaeological objects in the modern world. We discussed archaeology's contribution to the larger field of anthropology and the ways that archaeologists think—the paradigms that we use to reconstruct and explain the past.

We then focused on the particulars of archaeological fieldwork and analysis: how to find and excavate sites; how to date and analyze artifacts and dirt; and how to interpret the remains of plants, animals, and people themselves. You have seen how archaeologists can extract an enormous amount of information from broken, dirty bits of ancient objects to reconstruct ancient cultural behavior—and archaeology is still a relatively young science, making progress each year.

Now it is time to examine the "business" of archaeology—cultural resource management—and its link to laws that govern the preservation of cultural resources. Before this chapter concludes, we revisit the Kennewick case and discuss the Native American Graves Protection and Repatriation Act (NAGPRA) of 1990, a law that, instead of protecting the *objects* of the past, is intended to protect the various *interests* in the past. This law explicitly recognizes that archaeologists are not the only ones interested in antiquity and that the past holds different meanings for different people. Through this chapter we revisit a point we made in the first chapter: Americanist archaeology is not just about the dead; it's also about the living. We devote part of this final chapter to exploring the implications of that statement.

What Is Cultural Resource Management?

Commercial development is going on all around us. Nearly everywhere you look, you see bridges, dams, roads, and buildings under construction. Pipelines, power lines, highways, and fiber optic cables slice across our landscape. Such development destroys as much as it constructs. New roads pave over the American past, and as new houses spring up, archaeological remains are carted away in dump trucks.

We should be concerned about the trade-offs that arise from such development. Most people benefit from improved transportation and better homes, but, at the same time, these projects destroy important parts of America's cultural heritage. Developers are not evil people, and neither are those who care about preserving our past. So this leaves us with a critical question: What part of our past must we save, and what part can we do without?

This question is hardly unique to the United States. Most modern nations try to balance economic development and heritage preservation through laws and regulations. In this country, **cultural resource management (CRM)** is the field that conducts activities related to compliance with legislation that protects cultural resources. It is difficult to emphasize the importance of CRM to contemporary archaeology. Prior to the 1960s, nearly all American archaeologists worked for universities and museums. Today, the number of archaeologists in the United States vastly exceeds those working in the 1960s. Well over half of them work in the framework of CRM; in fact, CRM projects account for about 90 percent of field archaeology conducted today in the United States.

How did this change come about?

Early Efforts to Protect America's Cultural Heritage

A concern with historic preservation extends to the earliest days of the United States. In 1789, for example, wealthy Bostonians formed the Massachusetts His-torical Society in response to the destruction of John Hancock's house. The society became a watchdog to ensure that other historically significant properties were not lost. And, in 1813, the federal government ordered the preservation of Independence Hall in Philadelphia. But a *systematic* concern for preserving America's cultural heritage developed rather slowly, coincident with the more broadly based environmental preservation movement. Both movements flourished in the 1960s and 1970s, but their roots extend back another century.

America's environmental movement can be traced to such late nineteenth-century writers as Henry David Thoreau, John Muir, and Ernest Thompson Seton, each of whom inspired generations to notice the natural world around them and to respond to increasing human impact on the landscape. Some worked to save the continent's indigenous wildlife, while others worked to preserve wild places.

Archaeology and the preservation of cultural and historic properties were swept along with the conservation movement nearly from its beginning. One of the first sites to be protected was Ohio's Serpent Mound, a 1400-foot-long snake effigy mound. Treasure hunters had heavily damaged the site by the 1870s, and it was probably not pristine even when Squier and Davis (the Moundbuilder investigators whom you met in Chapter 2) mapped it some 40 years earlier. Frederic Putnam (1838–1945), of Harvard University's Peabody Museum, realized that the nation would soon lose this unique site. So, he decided to save it the old-fashioned way: he bought it. Working with wealthy Bostonians, Putnam raised $6000 and purchased the site. Harvard University owned it until 1900, when it transferred title to the Ohio Historical Society, which owns and maintains the site today.

While this concern for preserving the past was sincere, the late nineteenth-century approach was piecemeal, and the looting and destruction of archaeological sites proceeded at an alarming pace. The cliff dwellings in the Mesa Verde area of southwestern Colorado (see Figure 13-1) were especially hard-hit by pothunters. Tucked beneath massive arches in sandstone cliffs, the large pueblos of the Mesa Verde region—and the tens of thousands of well-preserved artifacts they contain—had been protected from the elements since the dwellings were abandoned in the late thirteenth century. This fact did not escape the notice of skilled pothunters working the area. They tore the roofs off structures, and blasted

cultural resource management (CRM) A professional field that conducts activities, including archaeology, related to compliance with legislation aimed at conserving cultural resources.

Figure 13-1 The site known as Cliff Palace, in Mesa Verde National Park, was occupied in the late 1200s; it was among the first archaeological sites in the United States to be protected by the government.

holes through the stone and adobe walls to let sunlight in. Six-hundred-year-old roof beams disappeared in the looters' campfires, hundreds of purloined pots appeared on an expanding curios market, and sacred kivas were damaged beyond repair.

To prevent such destruction, in 1906 President Theodore Roosevelt signed into law the **Antiquities Act,** which contained three important provisions:

1. It made it illegal to excavate or collect remains from archaeological sites on public lands without a permit from the relevant government agency.
2. It stipulated that permits would be granted only to museums, universities, and other scientific or education institutions "with a view to increasing knowledge," and that objects gathered would only be "for permanent preservation in public museums."
3. It gave the president the authority to create national monuments on federal lands con-

taining "historic landmarks, historic and prehistoric structures, and other objects of historic or scientific interest."

The Antiquities Act of 1906 is the foundation of all subsequent archaeological legislation.

Historic Preservation Comes of Age

In the 1960s, a large portion of the American public recognized that wildlife refuges alone could not stem the effects of environmental degradation. Numerous demonstrations were held in the 1960s (Earth Day

Antiquities Act Passed in 1906, this act (1) requires federal permits before excavating or collecting artifacts on federal land, (2) established a permitting process, and (3) gave the president the authority to create national monuments.

PROFILE OF AN ARCHAEOLOGIST
A Federal Archaeologist

Terry Fifield is the archaeologist for the Prince of Wales Island Districts, Tongass National Forest, Alaska.

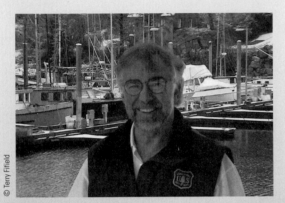

© Terry Fifield

Prince of Wales Island, in the southern portion of southeast Alaska's Alexander Archipelago, is an archaeological frontier.

In 1994, I moved my family to the Craig/Klawock area on the west coast of Prince of Wales Island. I was the first Forest Service archaeologist to live there, and the first to have the opportunity to get to know the residents and become familiar with the land and seascape.

During my first summer, Dave Putnam, a quaternary geologist/archaeologist working with me, spotted a scrap of spruce root basketry eroding from a muddy riverbed in the estuary of the Thorne River. Dave and I worked closely with the state of Alaska (on whose land the discovery was located), other Forest Service resource groups, the Alaska State Museum, and local tribal people. Within a few days, having assembled a small team and having received a lot of advice, we excavated a pedestal of mud containing the oldest example of spruce root basketry known from North America's Northwest Coast.

I made mistakes in that situation, especially in the area of consulting with Native Americans. Being new to the island, I was unfamiliar with clan and tribal boundaries and failed to locate the correct clan leaders for advice.

But I did try to make the contacts and we did one thing right. After preserving the basket in isopropyl alcohol–laced water, we invited local weavers to come view it. We did not know the basket's age then, but the site's stratigraphy suggested it was sev-

among them), and by the early 1970s an environmental movement was in full swing. The voter appeal of these popular movements was not lost on legislators, and many of them became "conservationists" as well. In fact, sufficient power came down on the side of the ecologists for laws to be drafted protecting the *nonrenewable resources* of the nation.

When most people think of nonrenewable resources, they think of redwoods, whooping cranes, and baby seals. Others think of energy-related assets, such as oil, coal, and uranium. But in the course of legally defining national resources, legislators realized that properties of historic value must also be included. After all, they reasoned, how many Monticellos do we have? Shouldn't archaeological and historic sites be considered nonrenewable resources?

The concern with historic preservation was largely about the destruction of historic buildings through urban renewal programs and the construction of national highways in the 1950s and 1960s. Nonetheless, archaeological sites were included in legislation and are now considered **cultural resources,** to be legally protected just like redwoods, whooping cranes, and shale oil fields. That legal protection came through various laws and established the framework within which archaeology in the United States operates today.

cultural resources Physical features, both natural and artificial, associated with human activity, including sites, structures, and objects possessing significance in history, architecture, or human development. Cultural properties are unique and nonrenewable resources.

eral thousand years old. The scene that played out in the Forest Service conference room over the next few days was a powerful one. Weavers from Klawock, Craig, and Hydaburg came by to study the 11 × 13-inch swatch of woven fabric. Haida and Tlingit alike saw the similarities between this ancient basket and the craft they had learned from their aunts and grandmothers.

Before the basket was hand-carried to the Alaska State Museum in Juneau for curation, the Forest Service conference room was host to a small but moving ceremony affirming the importance of this artifact to its people and place of origin.

Study of the Thorne River basket eventually revealed it to be a collecting basket woven of spruce root almost 6000 years ago. In 1998, the basket and its discovery were the subject of the Alaska Archaeology Week poster. The poster, featuring Margaret Davidson's technical drawing and watercolor reconstruction, was popular with Native American weavers all over southeast Alaska. People again imagined

the chain of knowledge linking 300 generations of women over nearly six millennia.

This important discovery provided tangible proof to today's subsistence-oriented residents that the lifeways and traditions of the island's native people extend deeply into the past.

Here on Prince of Wales Island, where many people are of Native American ancestry, there is widespread interest in studying and understanding the past. But there is also some apprehension about where archaeological specimens go, and perhaps more importantly, what happens to the knowledge that scientists draw from research. I believe an essential part of what we do as archaeologists must be to communicate what we have learned to the people most affected, to the public at large, and to our professional colleagues. As with most situations involving people, it's all about communication, in this case sharing information and the excitement of learning about the past.

The most important of these is the National Historic Preservation Act of 1966.

The National Historic Preservation Act

The Antiquities Act is a short, one-page piece of legislation, intelligible to just about anyone. The **National Historic Preservation Act (NHPA),** on the other hand, is lengthy, tedious, and shot through with bureaucratic jargon. But every archaeologist working in the United States must be intimately familiar with its details.

The NHPA formally stated the policy that lay behind the 1906 Antiquities Act: "It shall be the policy of the Federal Government . . . to foster conditions under which our modern society and our prehistoric and historic resources can exist in productive harmony. . . ." Three years later, Congress made this policy even more

explicit in the National Environmental Policy Act (NEPA): "It is the continuing policy of the Federal Government" to "preserve important historic, cultural, and natural aspects of our national heritage. . . ." Whereas the approach of previous legislation to historic preservation was reactive, the NHPA created a systematic, nationwide program of historic preservation.

It has therefore had far-reaching effects on American archaeology. The act created State Historic Preservation

 National Historic Preservation Act (NHPA) Passed in 1966, this act created (1) the National Register of Historic Places, (2) the Advisory Council on Historic Preservation, (3) State Historic Preservation Offices, as well as (4) a process to mitigate the impact of development; it also requires that government agencies provide good stewardship of their cultural resources..

Offices, headed by State Historic Preservation Officers. Subsequent amendments created Tribal Historic Preservation Offices on Indian reservations as well; many tribes, such as the Cherokee, Hopi, Zuni, and Navajo, now have large and successful historic preservation programs.

Historic preservation offices are tasked with creating state (or reservation) inventories of archaeological and historic properties, assisting federal agencies in complying with the State Historic Preservation Act, evaluating national register nominations (to give select sites special protection), and serving as repositories for resource information, such as state site files. The NHPA also created the national Advisory Council on Historic Preservation, which promotes the preservation of the nation's cultural resources and which advises the president and Congress on preservation policy.

The Archaeological Resources Protection Act

The Antiquities Act made it illegal to collect and/or excavate a site on federal property without a permit, and the penalties were pretty stiff for 1906: "a sum of not more than five hundred dollars" and/or imprisonment "for a period of not more than ninety days." But in today's world, where a single Mimbres bowl or Mississippian vessel can fetch thousands or even tens of thousands of dollars on the black market, looters see those penalties as a small cost of "doing business." As a result, looters have damaged or destroyed nearly all the nation's archaeological sites.

The **Archaeological Resources Protection Act (ARPA)** of 1979 tried to change this, making it a felony "to excavate, remove, damage, or otherwise alter or deface or attempt to excavate, remove, damage or otherwise alter or deface any archaeological resources located on public lands or Indian lands" without a per-

mit. ARPA also made it illegal to sell, receive, or transport artifacts illegally removed from federal lands. The penalties for violating ARPA can include prison sentences of up to 5 years and fines that can run into the millions of dollars. This may seem stiff, but looted sites are lost forever. Consider also that many looters are involved in other illegal activities as well—fencing stolen goods, drugs, burglary, and so on. ARPA, in fact, has proven to be a way to track down some serious criminals.

Even with the added protection of ARPA, however, it is difficult to police millions of acres of federal land, so looting continues to destroy the nation's cultural heritage. Numerous federal and private agencies have taken aggressive antilooting measures, such as site monitoring (using motion-sensitive cameras in some cases), substantial fencing, and more diligent law enforcement. And still, vandalism and looting continue to be the major threats to American archaeology today.

What about Private Land?

ARPA and NHPA apply to federal land. And some states protect cultural resources on state land. But these laws do not apply to private land. Some landowners are wary of archaeologists because they believe that the government will take their land away if they find something significant on it, but this is simply not true in the United States. The only exception concerns human burials. In many states (but not all), the *intentional* destruction of a burial, regardless of its age, is a violation of state law—even if that burial is on your property.

The sanctity of private land in the United States can be frustrating, however, because the lack of protection opens the door to commercial mining of terrestrial (and underwater) sites for artifacts. As a result, important sites on private land can be rapidly destroyed. Archaeologists in Kentucky learned this lesson the hard way.

The Slack Farm Incident

Slack Farm sits on a pleasant stretch of rich bottomland along the Ohio River in northern Kentucky. In the fifteenth century, the Ohio River valley was the center of a thriving chiefdom society, supported by maize agriculture. Several large sites, complete with flat-topped temple mounds similar to those we described at Moundville (see Chapter 10), were the centers of large populations. Some of these Mississippian com-

Archaeological Resources Protection Act (ARPA) Passed in 1979, this act (1) prohibits the excavation or removal of artifacts from federal property without a permit, (2) prohibits the sale, exchange, or transport of artifacts acquired illegally from federal property, and (3) increased the penalties for violations of the act over those of the Antiquities Act by allowing judges to take into account the value of the artifacts as well and the cost of restoration and repair of the site munities may have been even larger than the small towns that lie along the river today.

Prior to 1987, the Slack family protected a large fifteenth-century Mississippian site on their property. But when they sold the farm, the new owner was uninterested and, in fact, he leased the property to two men for $10,000. These men subleased portions of the land to eight others. Their intent was not to grow tobacco or maize, but to mine artifacts.

Using everything from shovels to bulldozers, the men mined their shares and paraded the skulls and pots they recovered from the 500-year-old cemetery around town. Within a few weeks, the field looked like a war zone—just look at Figure 13-2—pockmarked with craters. Human skeletal remains were strewn about alongside beer cans as the looters made a mad rush for valuable artifacts.

The police were alerted, but they could only charge the men with "desecration of a venerated object," which only carried a penalty of $500 and a maximum of 6 months in prison. Some of the recovered pots were probably sold on the black market for thousands of dollars, so the fine was a mere annoyance. Archaeologists later determined that more than 600 graves had been disinterred.

Outrage in the Native American community and the public brought a halt to the looting, and archaeologists tried to assess the damage and retrieve some information (all the skeletal remains were reburied in 1988). But because the crime was a misdemeanor, no one would prosecute, and the looters walked away. As a result, Kentucky revised its burial laws, upgrading the penalty for desecrating a grave, including those on private property, from a misdemeanor to a felony.

But the looting of archaeological sites on private land will continue unabated until the market for artifacts disappears. Given that this is unlikely, the alternative is that an educated public must simply refuse to accept it, as at Slack Farm.

Figure 13-2 Several hundred burials at the Slack Farm site, a fifteenth-century Mississippian burial ground, were looted and destroyed in the 1980s.

© David Pollack/Kentucky Heritage Council

Archaeological Science: Pure or Applied?

Anthropology is conventionally perceived as a **pure (basic) science,** as the systematic pursuit of knowledge for its own sake. And it is true that anthropologists, like many other scientists, are commonly motivated more by intellectual curiosity than by the practical applications of what they learn. Anthropologists have traditionally looked for answers to the larger, holistic questions regarding the human condition: How, where, and when did humanity arise? What is the relative importance of nature versus nurture? How (and why) did the major social institutions evolve? These are large-scale questions about the nature of the human condition, issues without immediate practical application or "relevance."

But anthropologists have long attempted to apply their findings to practical ends—that is, to do **applied science.** During World War II, for instance, some American anthropologists volunteered their services

pure (basic) science Systematic research directed toward acquisition of knowledge for its own sake.

applied science Research to acquire the knowledge necessary to solve a specific, recognized problem.

in the war effort. Several collaborated on "national character" studies—detailed memoranda on European and Asian countries that tried to characterize peoples who were either allies or enemies, or who lived in enemy-occupied territory. Working with knowledgeable people in the United States, these anthropologists eventually evolved their own research methods—the "cultures at a distance" approach—to generalize about countries inaccessible because of wartime conditions.

Applied anthropology is now a huge field. For example, applied anthropologists evaluate domestic social programs, improve corporate working conditions, develop culturally appropriate methods of delivering health care or agricultural assistance programs, and devise and implement international development programs.

Modern archaeology likewise attempts to apply its knowledge and insights to the modern world. Cultural resource management is applied archaeology, and other archaeologists are finding yet other ways to our knowledge of the human past and recovery techniques to concrete economic or social problems.

The Garbage Project

Emil Haury (1904–1992) was the senior archaeologist at the University of Arizona for decades. A specialist in southwestern prehistory, Haury continually taught his students that "if you want to know what is really going on in a community, look at its garbage."

Haury's earthy advice was not lost on his students and colleagues. In 1971, the University of Arizona launched a long-term study of a community's garbage. But it must have surprised Haury when the Garbage Project decided to focus on the garbage of contemporary Tucson.

The Garbage Project was begun by William Rathje (Stanford University), a Harvard-trained archaeologist who had previously specialized in Maya archaeology. Through the Garbage Project, however, Rathje applied archaeological methods to the analysis of modern American society.

Rathje was dissatisfied with available research techniques for dealing with contemporary society, particularly the dependence on interviews and questionnaires. Like many anthropologists, Rathje realized that they can be problematic because respondents might lie or give answers that they think are truthful, but actually are not.

Archaeologists, of course, have methods designed to reconstruct human behavior from trash. And so Rathje reasoned, "Why can't we use these methods to study modern human behavior?"

How Do Archaeologists Collect Trash?

Although it would eventually investigate community trash and landfills around the country (Figure 13-3), Rathje's Garbage Project began in Tucson, Arizona, in 1973. Garbage was picked up from randomly selected households, and a sampling design ensured that different socioeconomic neighborhoods were included. Student volunteers, with appropriate inoculations and wearing lab coats, masks, and gloves, sorted the garbage into 150 categories under the headings of food, drugs, sanitation products, amusement and educational items, communication, and pet-related products and recorded the data. The principles of archaeological classification provided objective, repeatable categories of data retrieval.

The Archaeology of Us

The Garbage Project has studied a number of contemporary social issues, such as alcohol consumption, that show the importance of its data collection methods. The Pima County Health Department once conducted interviews with a sample of Tucson households to discover how much beer people drank in a week. The sample was carefully chosen using conventional sociological procedures, and informant anonymity was ensured. Many took the health department's information as accurate measures of the rate of alcohol consumption in Tucson.

How did the questionnaires stack up against the material evidence—the beer bottles and cans that Rathje's volunteers recorded? It turned out that a large discrepancy existed between front-door answers given to interviewers and back-door behavior reflected in the contents of the trash. Garbage cans don't lie, and the differences from the health department questionnaire's results were striking: The Garbage Project found significantly heavier beer consumption—in the form of more drinkers and higher rates of drinking—than was reported to the interviewers.

This should astound nobody. People drink more beer than they own up to. But the degree of distortion is noteworthy. The skewing, it turns out, correlates

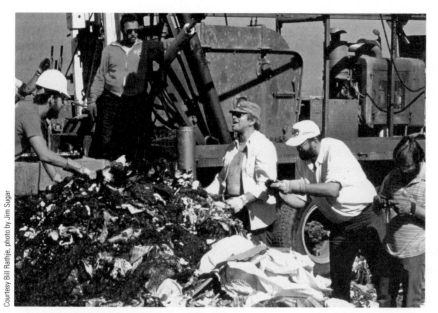

Figure 13-3 At California's Sunnyvale landfill, garbage project coordinators Bill Rathje (center) and Wilson Hughes (to Rathje's left) search for newspapers to date a landfill sample.

with socioeconomic factors. Low-income households typically distorted their interviews by reporting no beer consumption at all (low-income households may receive food stamps and, fearing the loss of support, might lie on surveys). By contrast, middle-income respondents admitted to drinking beer, but they underreported the amount they actually consumed. These individuals probably gave an honest, though inaccurate, estimate because they don't perceive themselves to be "beer drinkers." These findings provided future studies with a way to correct for this inevitable skewing in the data of health questionnaires.

Myths about America's Landfills

The Garbage Project also has something to say about landfills. Everyone knows that we produce a lot of trash. But it's hard to say how much we're producing and what it consists of. Formal landfills did not become a significant feature on the American landscape until after 1945, when the country's rural population shifted to the industrial cities. Today, more than 70 percent of our garbage—180 million tons annually—goes into some 5500 active landfills across the country. Landfills are the largest human-made structures in the world; some are many times the size of Khufu's Pyramid near Cairo. The twentieth century's lasting monuments for

posterity will be places like Staten Island's Fresh Kills landfill, which even before rubble from the World Trade Center was deposited there, covered 3000 acres and contained 3 billion cubic feet of trash.

But space for landfills is rapidly dwindling; New York City, for example, trucks some of its garbage as far away as New Mexico. One reason is that old landfills were simply holes in the ground, while new landfills are complex places governed by a host of regulations and technologies to control toxic substances and methane gas. As a result, the cost of garbage disposal is skyrocketing—$15 billion a year and rising. This means that we need to know as much about landfills as possible.

But surprisingly, prior to Rathje's studies, little was known about what is actually in landfills and what actually happens there. Rathje argues that "if we are making such a large contribution to future generations, we should know exactly what we are bequeathing them. The only way to unlock these entombed secrets is to excavate." And so Rathje dug, and his research exposed a number of myths about landfills.

The Garbage Project used systematic archaeological methods to explore nine landfills across the United States, recovering about 12 metric tons of debris deposited between 1952 and 1989.

Landfills are generally covered with layers of earth on a set schedule, so they are conveniently stratified. And these strata can be chronologically ordered using newspapers and magazines. But the size of modern landfills did not allow Rathje to sample them with a trowel and dustpan. Instead, he used backhoe trenches (up to 25 feet deep) and a 3-foot-diameter auger equipped with steel teeth that can cut through anything, including a car chassis. Each auger load was hand-sorted, allowing the Garbage Project personnel to calculate what's in America's landfills.

Let's first consider what Americans *think* is in their landfills. The Garbage Project's surveys showed that people think disposable diapers, plastic bottles, and large appliances take up most space in landfills. But Rathje's excavations show that these three items *together* take up *less than 5 percent* of a landfill's volume. All kinds of plastics take up less than 15 percent of landfills. And the percent volume of plastic appears to be going down over time as manufacturers continually "lightweight" packaging. Similarly, a survey conducted by the Audubon Society concluded that fast-food containers, polystyrene foam cups and packaging, and disposable diapers constituted most of the space, but Rathje's data show that these products *together* take up *less than 3 percent* of a landfill's volume.

So, what's in landfills? What fills up Fresh Kills' 3 billion cubic feet?

The main culprit, it turns out, is *paper*—packaging, newspapers, telephone books, magazines, and mail order catalogs. Paper takes up *40–50 percent* of the volume in American landfills. Despite the growing commitment to local recycling programs, the amount of paper is steadily rising—up from 35 percent in 1970. The rest of a landfill consists of, in descending order of volume, construction/demolition debris, metals, plastics, other materials, food and yard waste, and glass.

And here's the really bad news: Contrary to popular opinion, paper doesn't biodegrade in landfills. The Garbage Project has found 40-year-old newspapers, still fully readable (some with 40-year-old hot dogs wrapped in them). Our landfills are constructed on the belief that the nasty stuff inside will decompose on its own, like some kind of monumental compost heap.

But very little in our landfills actually biodegrades. Compost heaps work only when we chop up the organics, add fluids, and regularly churn the whole batch. This doesn't happen in landfills: nothing is chopped up, fluids are often prohibited, and debris is compacted, not churned. Methane production, a by-product of decomposition, ceases 15–20 years after a landfill is closed, indicating that decomposition has stopped. But Rathje's excavations show that after 20 years, from one-third to one-half of all organic materials are still recognizable. These remaining organics may eventually break down, but only after many more decades, if not longer.

Most of our knowledge about solid waste disposal and landfill design comes from laboratory experiments, but the inside workings of landfills—what actually happens—have remained almost entirely unknown.

Plenty of federal policies regulate landfills, but usually government planners work with "logical assumptions" about what landfills "should" contain.

Rathje doesn't assume, he digs. If we are interested in finding sensible ways to dispose of our trash, we need to know *exactly* what is being thrown away and what happens to it after it enters a landfill. By applying some archaeological approaches, Rathje has learned that many of the long-held assumptions about America's garbage are just that—rubbish.

Forensic Archaeology

When Thomas was a first-year curator at the American Museum of Natural History (in the early 1970s), he received a telephone call from a Sergeant McTigue of the New York City bomb squad. At the time, McTigue was working a series of New York City subway bombings. Nearly a dozen such attacks had occurred, killing one person and injuring several others. McTigue suspected that a political protest group was behind the bombings, and he had even identified a prime suspect ("I know the creep who's doin' it").

Before he could make an arrest, however, McTigue had to establish that, in fact, a crime had been committed. Otherwise, "the perp's lawyer will claim that it was a natural gas explosion, and we can't prove otherwise." To clinch his case, McTigue needed to produce parts of the actual detonating device that had triggered the explosion. Knowing this, McTigue kept sorting through the debris left by each underground explosion. But he never could find what he was looking for. So "the perps" remained free to bomb again, which they did with alarming regularity.

As he was investigating yet another ruined subway station, McTigue finally admitted to himself that he was a cop—trained in standard law enforcement techniques—and not an expert in sorting through trash and debris. But if he wasn't, who was? That's what archaeologists do, right?

That insight brought McTigue to Thomas's office. He explained the problem in simple terms: Suppose that he were to treat each crime scene as if it were an ancient archaeological site. What are the systematic, standardized techniques that archaeologists use to recover their data?

IN HIS OWN WORDS

Disaster Archaeology

By Richard A. Gould

Richard A. Gould is professor of anthropology at Brown University.

Archaeologists use their skills only to study past human cultures, or so it seemed to me until October 6, 2001. That was the day I first saw the World Trade Center (WTC) disaster scene. What I found there that day and on subsequent visits to the site and its surroundings changed my outlook toward archaeology and many other things.

As I walked the streets and alleys east of Ground Zero, I encountered fragmented human remains scattered in the gritty, gray matrix of ash and pulverized building materials that covered the fire escapes, sidewalks, and Dumpster tops of lower Manhattan. This initial encounter was followed by repeated visits to the area, reports to the authorities, and a rooftop survey with Brooklyn College archaeologist Sophia Perdikaris. The aftermath of this appalling disaster was initially marked by feelings of inadequacy, followed by a realization that archaeological skills could help the healing process for the victims' families and friends. By locating, recording, and recovering human remains and personal effects using archaeological methods and entering this evidence in a chain of custody, we could help victims' families and friends cope with their terrible loss.

The lessons from this experience guided further training. Eventually, we created a volunteer unit that included safety, medical, and public affairs experts, which we dubbed "Forensic Archaeology Recover" (FAR). We trained and prepared in a variety of ways based on advice from different agencies in Rhode Island. But we never expected what happened next.

Shortly after 11 p.m. on February 20, 2003, a fast-moving fire devastated the Station Nightclub in West Warwick, Rhode Island, killing 100 people and leaving others horribly burned. Almost exactly one year after our deployment to the WTC, our volunteer team was activated by the Rhode Island State Fire Marshall's Office and was at the disaster scene by February 26.

The medical examiner's staff had already recovered and identified the fire's victims. Our initial task was to recover, record, and enter as evidence hundreds of personal items for the R. I. State Medical Examiner's Office to repatriate to the victims' families. The winter conditions required that we dry-sieve the frozen remains. At the request of the fire marshal, we also watched for specific items related to the investigation. While maintaining its primary humanitarian activities, FAR also came to play an increasingly investigative role.

The work took place within a limited area surrounded by a chain-link fence covered with flowers, photographs, and messages. Hundreds of mourners, survivors, and the media viewed our activities through the fence. It was like working in a fish bowl, but the FAR team remained focused on the archaeological tasks. This in itself did much to comfort and reassure those watching, as I learned by speaking with my own friends, several of whom lost relatives or close friends in the fire. It was trying at times, for myself and other members of the team, but it taught us that victims' families and friends find it reassuring to know that there are people willing to engage in this kind of recovery effort on their behalf.

Disaster scenes are always complex and chaotic. Archaeology can bring a degree of order out of chaos to comfort the people affected and to help to understand the circumstances of the disaster.

IN HER OWN WORDS

The Journey of a Forensic Anthropologist

By Clea Koff

Figure 13-4 Clea Koff excavating a mass grave in Yugoslavia.

Clea Koff earned her MA in anthropology from the University of Nebraska–Lincoln in 1999; she is the author of The Bone Woman: A Forensic Anthropologist's Search for Truth in the Mass Graves of Rwanda, Bosnia, Croatia, and Kosovo.

My first experience with archaeology was at the age of 10, digging around in my backyard to find the dead bird I had buried the previous winter. I found the bird and an old hairpin. Years later, on a college-level archaeological dig in the Greek countryside, we found Athenian coins, stone foundations, and one human skeleton.

This was my first exposure to human bones and it was a profound experience. I became curious about what the bones could tell us about people, about how they lived and died.

In 1996, I joined a team of forensic experts brought together by Physicians for Human Rights to work on behalf of the United Nations International Criminal Tribunals for Rwanda and the former Yugoslavia, the international bodies prosecuting war criminals for genocide and crimes against humanity in those two countries. Our job was to locate, exhume, and analyze human remains from mass graves to provide evidence of the decedents' age, sex, and cause of death. For 6 months, I helped analyze five mass graves, each holding from 30 to over 400 remains. We worked long hours under the protection of military guards, and often lived in military compounds.

After the exhumation and analysis at the first site in Rwanda, Kibuye, was completed, a "Clothing Day"

So McTigue and Thomas spent 3 hours working through Archaeology 101: how to establish a three-dimensional grid system and datum point, map surface finds, remove archaeological strata, and use sifters and flotation devices. They went over note taking, photography, and cataloging. Armed with this new investigative strategy, McTigue said, "Thanks," and took off.

forensic archaeology The application of archaeological and bioarchaeological knowledge for legal purposes.

A few days later, there was the sergeant with his bomb squad on the six o'clock news. They were quickly yet efficiently digging and measuring, photographing and sifting the ruins of the latest subway bombing. Except for being a little older (and also heavily armed), the police looked no different from other novices on their first "dig class." After a week or two, Thomas got another call from Sergeant McTigue and, sure enough, they'd found the detonating device they were looking for. An arrest was quickly made, and New York's subway bombings came to an end.

This is an example of **forensic archaeology**—using established archaeological techniques to assist law was convened. It was publicized on the radio that our team would be displaying clothing from the grave, and we asked survivors to view the clothing in the hopes of providing leads to probable identifications.

I shall never forget one woman. She looked as though she was in her fifties, wearing a traditional kanga (a large, printed piece of cloth worn wrapped around the body) over a knit shirt. She was a dignified woman who held her head high, as though not wanting to be involved in this sordid business, but having no choice.

She recognized one of the jackets on display and assented to an interview about the clothing. I asked her for her name and to whom she thought the jacket belonged. She gave a man's name, adding that he could still be alive, having removed his jacket at some point and lent it to someone who was subsequently killed at Kibuye.

I then asked her if she knew if this man had any surviving relatives. Yes, she replied, he'd had a sister. I asked for the sister's name and she gave one, pointedly not looking at me. The name sounded familiar, so I flipped back to the first page of the witness statement and there was that name. It was her name. She was talking about her brother.

As this dawned on me, my eyes shifted to that dirty, empty jacket baking in the sun. I thought of her brother and of my brother, and what I would feel if that thing that had come out of a mass grave looked like my brother's jacket. I couldn't look her in the eye at first, so I looked at her hands—one hand on her purse and one hand grasping her other arm, holding herself together.

I finally looked at her face, unable to talk. Her eyes brimmed ever-so-slightly with tears as she looked out into the distance. I looked where she was looking and saw nothing. I wanted to apologize, to hug her, but I had no protocol. So I just capped my pen, and put my hand on her forearm. She said nothing, I said nothing, but she held her head high. As I held that woman's arm I had a true sensation of being on the continuum of history for the Rwandans affected by the genocide.

We are irretrievably part of their process of healing.

enforcement agencies. This has become increasingly common in the past 20 years—although, as you will see, for some tragic reasons.

Today, several archaeological organizations regularly conduct seminars and workshops for law enforcement personnel. For 20 years, the Oklahoma City Police Academy has sent trainees to an archaeological field program, now taught by Kent Buehler of the Oklahoma Archeological Survey. There, police trainees learn how to read a soil profile, probe the ground to find subsurface pits, read topographic maps and soil reports, as well as how to find and map surface evidence. Through the use of mock crime scenes, trainees acquire basic identification skills, such as distinguishing human from animal bones, and they learn basic mapping and evidence collection skills.

The Archaeology of Mass Disasters

As archaeologists become increasingly involved with criminal investigations domestically, they are also increasingly involved with international investigations. These are tragic cases, involving people lost in war, massacres, and assassinations. Professional archaeologists have joined investigatory teams to recover MIAs (personnel missing in action) in Vietnam, excavate mass graves in South and Central America, and work with United Nations investigatory teams to collect data for tribunals and courts from massacre sites in Croatia, El Salvador, and Rwanda. We look at the last of these.

The violence in Rwanda began in April 1994, shortly after Rwandan president Juvenal Habyarimana was killed in an airline crash (allegedly caused by a missile). An ethnic war broke out between the Hutus and Tutsis and, within months, more than 500,000 people were slaughtered. Many were rumored to be civilians, including women and children who were mercilessly clubbed, burned, or macheted to death. Seeking to determine whether the deaths resulted from civil war or genocide, United Nations investigators authorized archaeological investigations at key sites in central Rwanda.

One such excavation took place at Home St. Jean, where an estimated 4000 to 6000 people were killed. The Midwest Archeological Center, a branch of the National Park Service, assisted in the investigations. Working with forensic specialists, the archaeological team mapped and photographed surface skeletal materials, numbering each item and collecting it for analysis. Through this process, the team discovered six potential mass graves and began working on the largest. Once the stratigraphy was determined through hand excavation of several test trenches, the overburden was removed with a backhoe. The archaeologists then exposed human remains by standard archaeological procedures and photographed, mapped, and removed them from the grave.

The archaeologists recovered several hundred sets of remains using these procedures, making this one of the largest exhumations ever conducted in the investigation of human rights violations. Autopsies were conducted to determine sex, age, kind of trauma, and cause of death. Decomposition is rapid in tropical environments, and many of the identifications were made using the techniques discussed in Chapter 9.

Cut marks on bones showed that many individuals were killed by machetes from behind, as if they were fleeing their attackers; cut marks on the bones of hands and forearms showed that some people were merci-

lessly macheted to death, their arms raised in a desperate effort to ward off the blows. These were clearly unarmed civilians, murdered as part of a program of genocide. The meticulous archaeological documentation provided critical evidence for the United Nations tribunal, which quickly handed down numerous indictments.

Archaeologists are playing an increasingly important role in the investigation and documentation of human rights abuses (see "In Her Own Words: The Journey of a Forensic Anthropologist" by Clea Koff). In fact, as we write this, teams are at work uncovering mass graves in Iraq that could contain the remains of hundreds of thousands bodies of people whose deaths were allegedly ordered by Saddam Hussein.

Who Has the Authority to Study the Past?

At the same time that archaeology has found a new applied niche, it has found that its authority to investigate the past is increasingly being questioned. Who has the right to acquire data of the past? Who gets to analyze and use them? We have considered how these challenges to archaeology arise over the analysis of human skeletal remains; they are also seen in the study of Native American spiritual sites.

A Spiritual Site: The Bighorn Medicine Wheel

Look at Figure 13-5 and you will see the Bighorn Medicine Wheel, an ancient stone arrangement perched atop a 9640-foot windswept peak in Wyoming's Bighorn Mountains. There are actually quite a few medicine wheels in the mountains of the high plains, but the Bighorn Mountains site is by far the largest. Today, you reach it by driving up a gravel road to a parking lot and then walking 1.5 miles up the ridge. If you arrive in July or August, you might avoid trudging through snowdrifts.

The modern visitor is first struck by the simplicity of the structure: a stone circle, or "wheel," nearly 90 feet in diameter; in the background stretches the vast Bighorn Basin. Inside the stone circle, 28 stone "spokes" radiate out from a central "hub," which is marked by a stone **cairn** about 4.5 meters across. Five smaller cairns lie along the Wheel's periphery.

cairn An artificial mound of stones. May be deliberately constructed as an aid to navigation, as a memorial, or to mark the location of a grave.

Figure 13-5 An aerial view of the Bighorn Medicine Wheel (1974), when it was surrounded by a wire fence. Today it is protected by a log fence.

ducted by them to the underground chamber. He remained there for three days and three nights and was instructed in the arts of warfare and in leading his people. He was told that the Red Eagle would be his powerful medicine and would guide him and be his protector through life. He was told to wear always upon his person as an emblem of his medicine, the soft little feather which grows upon the back above the tail of the eagle. This little red plume gave him his name. Upon his death, after many years of successful warfare and leadership, he instructed his people that his spirit would occupy the shrine at the medicine wheel which is not connected with the rim, except by an extended spoke, and that they might at all times communicate with him there.

From its lofty perch, the Medicine Wheel is well suited for vision questing. Several contemporary Native American people say they have used it this way. Upslope winds whistle through countless crevices, creating a babel of moaning and shrieking voices. Some archaeological evidence suggests the rock cairns were protected by small enclosures during the early historic period, perhaps providing a modicum of shelter for those fasting, waiting, and seeking supernatural advice.

But there are other explanations. Astronomer John Eddy suggested that Native Americans constructed the Medicine Wheel as an astronomical observatory, to record the summer and winter solstices. Yet others suggest that it was built to aid travel, the rock piles left as directional aids to newcomers; or that it is a representation of the 28-raftered lodge built as part of the Sun Dance ceremony. Others suggest that the Medicine Wheel may have been a boundary marker, a depiction of a mythical turtle, or an enduring stone marker demonstrating geometrical expertise.

In brief, we don't know what the Medicine Wheel was in the past. But we do know what it is today.

But who built it (and why) is more controversial. Some suggest that the rock cairns were graves, each marking where a powerful person was buried. The lines of rocks (the spokes) show the different directions in which the departed ranged "on the warpath," recording the deeds of each dead chief. The rock piles at the ends of the lines may represent enemies killed in battle.

Drawing upon the ethnohistoric record, others suggested the site was for vision quests (see Chapter 11), the Plains Indian ritual whereby an individual sought communication with the spirit world. For example, the Crow gave an account of the Bighorn Medicine Wheel based on the experience of Red Plume (also known as Long Hair), a famous Crow chief who visited the wheel in the late 1700s:

Red Plume . . . obtained his inspiration and received his medicine and the token which resulted in the application of that name by him at the Medicine Wheel. As a young man, Red Plume visited the wheel in the hope of receiving a strong medicine which would make of him a great warrior and chief. Without food, water, or clothing, he remained for four days and nights awaiting recognition from the spirits. On the fourth night he was approached by the three little men and one woman who inhabited the underground passage to the wheel and was con-

The Medicine Wheel as a Modern Sacred Site

After taking in the simple majesty of the stone structure and the breathtaking view, the modern visitor is soon struck by the number of offerings left at the site, a scene reminiscent of the Vietnam memorial in Washington, D.C. Scattered among the cairns and stone spokes are medicine bundles, antlers, coins, beadwork, photographs, bundles of sage or sweetgrass, and strips of cloth tied to the heavy wooden fence that now surrounds the site. The prehistoric use of the Medicine Wheel may forever remain an enigma but, to many contemporary Indian people, the Medicine Wheel remains a holy place, one of many sacred sites where ceremonies are performed to this day.

And yet many of the most important sacred sites—places like the Bighorn Medicine Wheel—are visited each year by thousands of non-Indians: well-meaning tourists, scientific teams, and New Agers seeking a spiritual experience. Indians are concerned that the plants, paths, shrines, rocks, and other aspects of their sacred sites are being destroyed by the curious, and their power diffused by the insensitive.

North American archaeologists agree that the Bighorn Medicine Wheel is one of America's more intriguing ancient sites—and with its stunning setting and puzzling past, the Medicine Wheel is a natural for the heritage tourist. Or is it? Should tourists be encouraged to visit the Bighorn Medicine Wheel?

How do archaeologists balance the concerns of bringing American archaeology to the interested public while respecting the wishes of the descendant populations still involved with many of those sites? Some Native Americans claim that all prehistoric sites are sacred. Should they be closed to the public? Should only Indians get to visit these places? Should only Indians study and interpret them?

In the case of the Medicine Wheel, a coalition representing varied interests—tribal, scientific, ecological, and governmental—is trying to protect, preserve, and respect the site. One mutual decision was to close the last mile and a half of the road to the site (allowance is made for the disabled). This solution minimizes the negative impact of tourism, respects the religious freedom of Native people, and yet keeps this place accessible to those who wish to see firsthand the structure that has drawn people here for centuries.

William Tallbull (1921–1996), a Northern Cheyenne elder who had a deep and long-lasting personal relationship to the Medicine Wheel, felt it important to keep the site accessible. He believed it inappropriate to exclude anybody (see "In His Own Words: Archaeological Sites or Sacred Places? A Native American Perspective" by William Tallbull). In his perspective, if the educational and contemplative potential of sacred sites can be maintained, then they can offer an important opportunity for teaching tolerance and respect.

Who Owns the Past?

Whether we consider the Medicine Wheel or any other site, it is impossible for archaeologists to escape a central issue: Who owns the past? This is not a question of who owns a site—that's a matter of property law—but who has the authority to uncover, interpret, and present knowledge gained from the past?

The past can be a powerful place to visit and, for many, archaeological sites like the Medicine Wheel are strong symbolic reminders of identity and continuity. But is it appropriate that only "descendants" should be "owners" of their past? Is the ancestral perspective the only admissible one?

Leave aside the sticky issue of defining who is a "descendant," and just consider the extreme case—giving complete power to one group of people. Our point will be a familiar one: Power corrupts, and absolute power corrupts absolutely. It's true in politics, and it's true in archaeology. The Nazis provided a vivid example of this.

Nazi Archaeology: The Danger of Owning the Past

Gustav Kossinna (1858–1931) did not live to see Hitler's ascension to power in 1933, but his work was inspirational to the Nazi elite. A linguist-turned-prehistorian, Kossinna sought to link Germanic culture to particular types of artifacts. Bettina Arnold (University of Wisconsin, Milwaukee) notes that Kossinna's work was intended to help the Germans rebuild their country after the First World War. In fact, Kossinna's book on German prehistory was dedicated "to the German people, as a building block in the reconstruction of the externally as well as internally disintegrated fatherland."

Kossinna wrote that the presence of allegedly "Germanic" artifacts was archaeological proof demonstrat-

IN HIS OWN WORDS

Archaeological Sites or Sacred Places?
A Native American Perspective

By William Tallbull

The late William Tallbull was an elder of the Northern Cheyenne tribe.

To the Indigenous Peoples of North America, the archaeological sites found on North American soil are not "archaeological" sites. They are sites where our relatives lived and carried out their lives.

Sacred Sites such as the Medicine Wheel and Medicine Mountain are no different. To Native Americans they are living cultural sites from which help comes when "The People" needed or need help. They were/are places where tribal peoples went in times of famine and sickness, in periods of long drought when animals would leave, or in more current times when tribes are being torn apart by politics, alcohol, or other abuses.

The men make a pledge to go and vision quest at these places, seeking help. As we leave to go to these sites, our every breath is a prayer. We follow the path to the sites, observing a protocol that has been in place for thousands of years. The Native American approaching these sites must stop four times from the beginning of his or her journey to arrival at the site. A trip to a Sacred Site was/is not done just for curiosity, but only after much preparation and seeking.

Many blessings have come to "The Peoples" in this way. Many tribes have received covenants (bundles) from these sites. Some Tribes still carry the bundles that were received from a certain mountain or site.

These are considered no different than the covenants given Moses or the traditional law that went with it.

When Native Peoples have been blessed by a site or area, they go back to give thanks and leave offerings whenever they get a chance. These should be left undisturbed and not handled or tampered with.

Today many of our people are reconnecting with these sites after many years of being denied the privilege of practicing our own religion at these very sacred areas. In the past, trips were made in secret and hidden from curious eyes.

If you go to see a Sacred Site, remember you are walking on "holy ground," and we ask that you respect our culture and traditions. If you come to a site that is being used for a religious purpose, we hope you will understand.

---

ing Germany's prior claim to vast stretches of territory, including large parts of Poland. Kossinna and his acolytes argued that waves of Germanic people had emanated from a northern European core area, carrying with them major cultural achievements such as agriculture, pottery, and metallurgy (none of which fit with the archaeological evidence as we know it). In one of his dinnertime monologues, Arnold notes, Hitler even claimed that the ancient Greeks were Germans who had migrated south.

Prehistory was largely ignored in Germany prior to Hitler's rise to power, and Arnold suggests that this made it easy for the Nazis to appropriate the past for their own purposes. From the time Hitler rose to power in 1933 through the end of World War II, eight new chairs of archaeology were established at German universities, and considerable funding became available for excavation. Of course, new archaeologists were appointed and funded only if they were enthusiastic Nazi Party members.

The interest in prehistory went to the highest levels of Nazi political power. Heinrich Himmler—the leader of the SS, Hitler's terrifying personal army—formed a wing of the SS called the *Ahnenerbe* ("Ancestor

Heritage"). He looked to prehistory to establish an identity for the SS, using a Germanic-like rune as the source of the unit's double lightning-strike insignia. His archaeologists ventured as far as Tibet and Iceland searching for Atlantis, the Holy Grail, and Aryan kings (and providing the inspiration for Steven Spielberg's *Raiders of the Lost Ark*).

During the war, archaeologists were part of the *Sonderkommando Jankuhn,* a military organization led by SS-archaeologist Herbert Jankuhn, which looted museums and libraries in conquered lands in the search for artifacts that would demonstrate Germany's ancestral claim on virtually all of Europe. Posters exhorted Germans to preserve and report all archaeological finds to authorities because every potsherd was "a document of our ancestors." (This was not motivated by a love of prehistory, for although allegedly Germanic artifacts were preserved, unrelated archaeological sites in places such as Poland and Czechoslovakia were destroyed.)

Archaeological excavations in Germany were wildly misinterpreted to support claims for Aryan superiority, and contrary evidence was suppressed. Open-air theaters, known as *Thingstätten,* where Nazi propaganda plays were performed, were built only in places where the community could demonstrate prehistoric Germanic occupation. For many of these, Arnold points out that the archaeological data were grossly misinterpreted, if not outright fabricated.

Not all German scholars were complacent, but opposition was squashed, many books were banned, and scientists who would not toe the party line were ostracized. There were no open debates; the Nazi Party controlled discussion of the past.

Nazi archaeology is, to be sure, an extreme case. But even extreme cases have value because they warn what can happen when a single group appropriates complete control over the past.

It is precisely the issue of power and control—who determines exclusive access to the past—that created the conflict over Kennewick Man. In Chapter 1, we used the Kennewick case to raise some tough questions: *What gives archaeologists the right to poke into the past, to study the dead? Who owns the past, anyway? And who gets to decide?* We can now return to those questions and consider them in a broader context.

The Native American Graves Protection and Repatriation Act of 1990

The Kennewick Man controversy was sparked by a landmark piece of legislation that required the museums of America to return and even *rebury* some cultural resources that other legislation has long protected and preserved. The **Native American Graves Protection and Repatriation Act** (**NAGPRA**) moves cultural resource law away from the area of preservation into the field of human rights legislation. Obviously, NAGPRA has a huge impact on the practice of American archaeology.

In 1988, the Senate Select Committee on Indian Affairs was told by the American Association of Museums that thousands of individual Native American skeletons were held in United States museums. Some of these were skulls removed from battlefields—including heads taken from the 1864 Sand Creek Massacre in Colorado, where soldiers and militiamen massacred 150 Cheyenne and Arapaho, mostly women and children. Native Americans pointed out that, although Indian people represent less than 1 percent of the U.S. population, their bones constitute more than 50 percent of the skeletal collection in the Smithsonian Institution. Many senators were shocked.

And they should have been. Although archaeologists obviously had nothing to do with decapitating fallen Indian warriors, they had been aware for years that many Native Americans were upset by the excavation,

---

Native American Graves Protection and Repatriation Act (NAGPRA) Passed in 1990, this act (1) protects Indian graves on federal and tribal lands, (2) recognizes tribal authority over treatment of unmarked graves, (3) prohibits the commercial selling of native dead bodies, (4) requires an inventory and repatriation of human remains held by the federal government and institutions that receive federal funding, (5) requires these same institutions to return inappropriately acquired sacred objects and other important communally owned property to native owners, and (6) sets up a process to determine ownership of human remains found on federal and tribal property after November 16, 1990.

ARCHAEOLOGICAL ETHICS
Should Antiquities Be Returned to the Country of Origin?

Many of the world's major museums contain artifacts that come from many different countries. The majority of these were acquired through legal channels. But some pieces have more checkered pasts. The Rosetta Stone, for example, is a large basalt tablet inscribed in three scripts, which allowed French linguist Jean-François Champollion to decipher Egyptian hieroglyphics. It was found by a French soldier in 1799 during Napoleon's conquest of Egypt. Fortunes change quickly in war, however, and by 1801 the Rosetta Stone was in the British Museum, where it is today.

Britain scored another "victory" in nearly the same year in Greece, one that has caused considerable consternation between these two countries.

Atop the Acropolis in downtown Athens stands the Parthenon, built between 447 and 438 BC and dedicated to the goddess Athena. It has been a sacred place in Greek culture for more than 2500 years and has served as a Catholic church and, during Turkish rule, as a mosque.

The difficulties began about 1800, when Thomas Bruce (better known as Lord Elgin) was British ambassador to Turkey. At that time, Turkey ruled Greece as part of the Ottoman Empire. Elgin removed statues and portions of the 75-meter marble frieze from the Parthenon, sending them to England aboard British military vessels. Elgin had spent most of his fortune removing the marbles and many other Greek art treasures. Deeply in debt, he sold the marbles to the British Museum for a fraction of what they cost him.

Greece has been demanding the return of the marbles ever since. The late Greek minister of culture, Melina Mercouri, argued that they symbolize Greece itself, and many Greeks feel that the sculptures belong in Greece. But Sir David Wilson (former director of the British Museum) countered that the museum acquired the marbles legally, had done nothing wrong, and to return the marbles smacks of "cultural fascism." It is true that the museum purchased the sculptures legally; and Lord Elgin always claimed he had permission from the Turkish government to remove them. Greece counters that the Turks, as occupiers of Greece, did not have the right to give Greek patrimony away.

The British Museum thinks that Elgin probably saved these priceless treasures from the decay that political violence and pollution has visited upon the statues that remain on the Acropolis. Britain claims that the marbles are now part of the global, not just Greek, patrimony, and that many more people can enjoy them on display in the British Museum. If the museum returned the marbles to Greece, wouldn't the floodgates open up to countries everywhere demanding the return of art objects?

Greece points out that pollution is now under control in Athens, and that conservation measures protect the sculptures. The marbles themselves could be housed in a proposed museum at the base of the Acropolis.

These, then, are the arguments. Should treasures like the Parthenon's marbles be returned to their country of origin? Or should they be housed someplace where more of the world's people can enjoy them? Should we take into account the (often nefarious) ways in which artifacts were acquired when making this decision? Do we consider whether the country of origin is capable of caring for artifacts by itself? Seeking to defend the British Museum's claim to the marbles, the Parliamentary Assembly of the Council of Europe passed a resolution stressing "the unity of the European cultural heritage." Does keeping the marbles in Britain achieve this goal better than keeping them in Greece?

analysis, and display of their ancestors' skeletal remains. Walter Echo-Hawk (Pawnee) said, "We don't expect everyone to share our beliefs; but it doesn't take the wisdom of Solomon to understand that our dead deserve to rest in peace. . . . All we're asking for is a little common decency. . . . We're not asking for anything but to bury our dead." Such statements spurred Congress into action and the result, in 1990, was NAGPRA.

NAGPRA protects Indian graves on federal and tribal lands and prohibits the commercial sale or interstate transport of Native American bodies or body parts. It also requires that all institutions that receive federal funds inventory their collections of human skeletal remains. Those inventories showed that American institutions held more than 117,000 sets of human remains, most of which are from Native American burials. This inventory also covered funerary objects, sacred objects, and "objects of cultural patrimony" (objects that have ongoing historical, traditional, or cultural importance to a Native American group). For Native American human remains and objects, a museum must consult with the appropriate culturally affiliated tribal representatives regarding their repatriation. And for burials found after 1990 and in the future, NAGPRA requires that archaeologists that go through a rigorous process of consultation to determine if the remains are culturally affiliated with an existing tribe.

As of October 2003, 27,777 sets of human remains had been determined to be culturally affiliated and offered to the relevant tribe for repatriation, along with about 636,386 funerary objects, 1185 sacred objects, and 267 objects of cultural patrimony. Critical to the disposition of these remains and those found in the future is the definition of "Native American" and the concept of "cultural affiliation" in the law.

Native Americans and Cultural Affiliation

Once an institution determines that remains and covered objects are Native American, they then have to decide if they are to be repatriated. But to which tribe? Many tribes expressed a desire to have only *their* specific tribal ancestors returned to them. The Eastern Shoshone on the Wind River Reservation in Wyoming, for example, do not wish their ancestral remains repatriated because they question the accuracy of museum records.

And tribes have different ideas about what should be done with the remains. The Zuni asked that skeletons identified as Zuni remain under museum curation. California's Chumash elected to preserve their repatriated remains in their own repository. Other tribes rebury or cremate repatriated remains. These differences of opinion meant that the government needed a procedure to decide which tribes have control over which remains.

That decision rests on the concept of *cultural affiliation*. Tribes that are determined to be culturally affiliated with particular burials, funerary and sacred objects, and objects of cultural patrimony are entitled to have those burials and objects repatriated to them. If remains or objects cannot be culturally affiliated under the law, then they are classed as "unaffiliated." NAGPRA does not say what happens to those remains; for the time being, they remain in museums.

Although some archaeologists remain flatly opposed to NAGPRA, the vast majority recognize that the statute has forced a dialogue that was long overdue. But this does not mean that answers come easily.

Kennewick Man and Repatriation

In the legal saga of Kennewick Man, the courts eventually decided that the individual was *not* Native American as defined in the law, and that even if he were, he could *not* be culturally affiliated with the tribes who claimed him. Most people would probably assume that a 9400-year-old skeleton was Native American. And others might think it obvious that the remains should be returned to a tribe that requested them. How did the courts arrive at their decisions?

Is Kennewick Native American?

NAGPRA's definition of *Native American* is "of, or relating to, a tribe, people, or culture that is indigenous to the United States." According to the courts, the key word in the definition, believe it or not, is the word *is*. The courts argued that the definition requires showing a "general relationship to a *present-day* tribe, people, or culture" (emphasis added). Kennewick, the courts pointed out, had no artifacts associated with it; and, because it had eroded from a riverbank, the nature of any burial ritual, which is a cultural act, is gone. Thus, the judge concluded that the culture of Kennewick Man "is unknown and apparently unknowable."

RAPID REVIEW   Key Legislative Acts and Their Effects

1906 Antiquities Act

- Made unpermitted collection of artifacts from federal lands illegal
- Approved permits only to scientific or education institutions to increase knowledge; artifacts must reside in public institutions
- Gave the president the authority to create national monuments on federal lands
- Began U.S. protection of archaeological sites

1966 National Historic Preservation Act

- Mandated inventory of sites on government property
- Mandated that federal government consider effects of actions on federal land or federally supported projects
- Created the National Register of Historic Places
- Created State Historic Preservation Offices
- Made site protection the official U.S. policy

1979 Archaeological Resources Protection Act

- Increased penalties for removal of artifacts from federal lands
- Made illegal the interstate transport or sale of artifacts illegally obtained from federal lands
- Added teeth to existing legislation to halt looting and vandalism

1990 Native American Graves Protection and Repatriation Act

- Mandated inventory of institution's human skeletal remains
- Required consultation with tribes and it requires that you offer to repatriate culturally affiliated remains, funerary objects, sacred objects, and objects of cultural patrimony
- Gave Native Americans a large role in disposition of artifacts and skeletal remains

Recall from Chapter 1 that Kennewick's cranial morphology—the shape of his skull—is quite different from that of later Native Americans. No matter how you measure it, the Kennewick skull looks more like southeast Asians, Polynesians, or Japan's Ainu, not other Native Americans. For this reason, and although many archaeologists disagreed, the courts declared that Kennewick was not Native American.

Can Kennewick Be Culturally Affiliated with Modern Tribes?

But suppose the courts had ruled that Kennewick is Native American. NAGPRA then would have moved to the next question: is he culturally affiliated with a modern tribe? NAGPRA's definition of cultural affiliation is "a relationship of shared group identity which can be reasonably traced historically or prehistorically between a present-day tribe or Native Hawaiian organization and an identifiable earlier group." This is a more rigorous definition than that of *Native American*. Cultural affiliation requires that we establish an identifiable earlier group. With only one burial and no grave goods, it is impossible for archaeologists to identify Kennewick's social group. That alone means that Kennewick cannot meet the requirement of cultural affiliation under the law. In addition, archaeology tells the lifeways of Native Americans who lived on the Columbia Plateau for the past 13,000 years have dramatically changed over time, for example, in the style of projectile points and houses that were used, in burial rituals, in economy and trade patterns. In this particular case, archaeology cannot reasonably trace shared group identity over time.

What about Native American oral history? Is it possible that oral traditions preserve eyewitness accounts of the past? For example, oral traditions among Columbia Plateau tribes include tales in which bison turn to stone or mythical beings create valleys and hills by dragging huge fish across the landscape. Clearly, the tales do not relate eyewitness accounts, and thus they could be explanations of how a landscape came to be using observations made on that landscape long after the natural events that formed it actually took place. Oral traditions may be useful in some cases, but in Kennewick's case they cannot meet the legal standard of tracing "shared group identity" across time.

Taking all these data into account, the judge decided that, under the requirements of NAGPRA, Kennewick cannot be culturally affiliated with the tribes who claimed affiliation.

The Legacy of Kennewick Man

The controversy over Kennewick Man has been, to put it mildly, divisive. Many archaeologists in the past, and some today, are incensed that human burials and grave goods are reburied. To these archaeologists, Kennewick demonstrates what happens when communities that claim descent from an ancient person are provided exclusive control over ancient remains and objects: how does this differ, some ask, from Nazi book burnings?

A long-standing social policy in America emphasizes the common heritage of the citizenry. So viewed, the scientific community is responsible for understanding the human condition of all, including Indian people, ancient and living. By removing cultural materials from museums and reburying skeletal remains, selected elements of the common heritage are removed from the public domain. A vocal minority views NAGPRA as blatant destruction of archaeological collections and the common American heritage. They urge archaeologists to stand up for their duties as scientists. Repatriation and reburial efforts, in this sense, are viewed as censorship, undermining the ability of scientists to inspect the work of others for errors, a procedure that is basic to all modern, ethical science. How is it, some archaeologists ask, that we support laws to protect cultural heritage, yet we simultaneously condone repatriation? If the objects of the past are so important that the government must protect them, then why do we willingly lose some of the most important ones, forever? Decades from now, some archaeologists warn, we will condemn the archaeological and museum communities for caving in to political demands and allowing the destruction of irreplaceable scientific materials.

These archaeologists make some valid points. Given the far-reaching concern over the Kennewick case—in tribal, scientific, and mainstream venues—it seems clear that Americans are indeed interested in what ancient human remains have to say. And it is true that, once a skeleton is reburied, it is gone forever. Down the road of reburial, scientists claim, lays a balkanization of knowledge, a "tyranny of the minority" that ultimately will serve nobody.

Many American Indians and archaeologists take a different view. The human body is a powerful symbol, especially the human skeleton—the last vestige of what was once a living, breathing person. When federal troops forced Cherokee and Choctaw people to move from their homes in the southeastern United States to Oklahoma in 1838, some families dug up the bones of their relatives and took them along on the bitter Trail of Tears, burying them after their arrival in Oklahoma. Many Indians see archaeology as yet another colonial act, another way to deny Indians their basic humanity and rights—they took our land, our language and our culture, and now they've come for our dead!

This side also makes some valid points. How do we decide who is right? Should science trump all other concerns? What are the ethical and moral issues at stake here?

Seeking Common Ground

A growing number of American archaeologists have developed research programs that incorporate the perspectives of Indian and other descendant communities. Each year, we see more examples of archaeologists using archaeology to help communities reconnect to their past, to establish ties broken by past sociopolitical forces. Many archaeologists have worked hard to make participation in field projects financially possible for members of descendant communities. The Society for American Archaeology, for example, annually awards field school scholarships to Native American students.

More archaeologists are tackling projects in close consultation with tribal councils and descendant communities at the beginning, rather than the end, of a project, devising research in such a way that it is useful to the tribe or community. These projects often incorporate public education programs specifically designed for the descendant community.

On Alaska's Kodiak Island, for example, the repatriation of several hundred burials excavated in the 1930s resulted in the formation of a Native-driven archaeology program. Kodiak Island is the aboriginal home of the *Alutiiq*, an Eskimo people. The repatriation took years to negotiate, but because it empowered the Native community, the result was more not less interest in their past. So, while the repatriation struggle was going on, Amy Steffian (then a graduate student at the University of Michigan) was given permission and funding to dig further at the grave site. It turns out that the Alutiiq did not hate archaeology; they just hated an archaeology that implied that they could not be full partners, that their participation was not needed.

Today, Steffian serves as deputy director of the Alutiiq Museum, an outgrowth of the Kodiak Area Native Association's Culture and Heritage division. Recognizing that they were losing a record of their heritage to winter storms, vandalism and time, the Alutiiq founded the Heritage program in 1987 to create an islandwide strategy of archaeological research and to promote educational programs on Alutiiq culture, language, and arts. Eight native corporations today fund and govern the Alutiiq Museum; they also oversee their own archaeological research projects, employing professional archaeologists to work with crews of Native people, as shown in Figure 13-6, and community volunteers. The Alutiiq Museum curates the resulting collections and displays artifacts in a Native-governed repository. In fact, the repatriated artifacts are today stored and available for study in the Alutiiq Museum.

The museum also provides professional and technical support to the *Dig Afognak* archaeological program, which is organized and staffed through the Afognak Native Corporation. *Dig Afognak* offers the opportunity to live and work with Native people in the remote wilderness of the Kodiak archipelago. Its purpose is "to regain, restore, and carry forward the light of our culture" and "to make the circle complete" by inviting the interested public to join the effort.

The founding of the museum and the growth of archaeological programs produced new career opportunities for Native people. Many of the Alutiiq students involved in the archaeology program are now pursuing college degrees in history and anthropology. One of

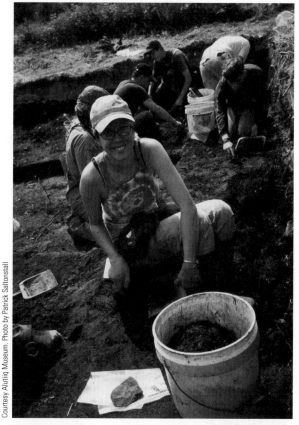

Courtesy Alutiiq Museum. Photo by Patrick Saltonstall

Figure 13-6 Alutiiq intern April Laktonen Counceller excavates at the Outlet Site on Kodiak Island, Alaska, during the Alutiiq Museum's Community Archaeology Program.

these, Sven Haakanson, Jr., became director of the museum after completing a PhD in anthropology at Harvard. Several other Alutiiq women, who were once interns on field projects, form a third of the museum's staff.

Oddly, the beginning of this new brand of archaeology on Kodiak Island was NAGPRA. This legislation forced archaeologists to consult with local communities over their research and to do some soul-searching. Although NAGPRA calls for the repatriation of many archaeological collections, in some cases the result has been increased protection of the unexcavated archaeological record. And, ironically, NAGPRA may have engendered changes within archaeology and the Native American community the end result of which will be the acquisition of more, not less information about the past.

Conclusion: Archaeology and America's Cultural Heritage

This chapter has discussed how archaeology operates in the modern, pragmatic world. We discussed how archaeology attempts to protect the past, which is a nonrenewable resource. It protects the past through legislative means that require archaeological study in advance of construction projects. It also tries to protect the past through legislative means to protect sites from looting and vandalism. Although archaeologists are willing to make some concessions to development, they make no concessions to looting. From these twin concerns has grown the large field of cultural resource management and the many legislative acts designed to protect archaeological sites.

Perhaps even more important, however, will be archaeology's role in knocking down the walls that so often divide people of the world. Archaeology can do this in part by the information that it gathers. Archaeology can show, for example, how different environmental and historical circumstances work together to create the diversity of human societies. In so doing, archaeology proves many racist assumptions to be wrong. But archaeology also contributes not only by *what* it learns about the past, but *how* it goes about learning it—the way in which it incorporates different perspectives, attitudes, and concerns of descendant communities and other stakeholders in the past.

Archaeology, as we have said, is not just about the dead; it's also about the living. And, it turns out, archaeology is not just about the past; it's also about the future.

Summary

- America has been concerned with preserving its cultural heritage for as long as it has existed as a country, but the first legislation to protect all sites on public lands was the 1906 Antiquities Act.

- A systematic effort to preserve cultural resources appeared in 1966 with the National Historic Preservation Act (NHPA); the 1979 Archaeological Resources Protection Act provided further safeguards against looting.

- But looting still continues to be the major threat to the nation's cultural resources.

- Although archaeology is conventionally perceived as a "pure" science, many archaeologists apply archaeological techniques to new problems, such as the analysis of contemporary landfills, and to the field of law enforcement.

- Cultural resource management (CRM) is today the most influential force in Americanist archaeology. The bulk of archaeological work being done has shifted from the academic side to the private and government sectors. CRM archaeologists are involved in the governmental decision making that requires environmental and cultural variables be considered side by side with technological and economic benefits when planning future construction.

- The 1990 Native American Graves Protection and Repatriation Act moved legislation from the area of historic preservation to the area of human rights.

- In the past 20 years, archaeology has become increasingly concerned with incorporating multiple voices into their research and educational efforts as they focus on the question of "Who owns the past?"

Media Resources

The Companion Website for Archaeology:
Down to Earth, *Third Edition*

http://anthropology.wadsworth.com/thomas_kelly3e_down/

Supplement your review of this chapter by going to the
companion website to take one of the practice quizzes,
use the flash cards to master key terms, and check out
the many other study aids that are designed to help you
succeed in your introductory archaeology course.

Glossary

absolute date A date expressed as specific units of scientific measurement, such as days, years, centuries, or millennia; absolute determinations attempting to pinpoint a discrete, known interval in time.

accelerator mass spectrometry (AMS) A method of radiocarbon dating that counts the proportion of carbon isotopes directly (rather than using the indirect Geiger counter method), thereby dramatically reducing the quantity of datable material required.

achieved status Rights, duties, and obligations that accrue to a person by virtue of what they accomplished in their life.

adaptive perspective A research perspective that emphasizes technology, ecology, demography, and economics in the definition of human behavior.

Americanist archaeology The brand of archaeology that evolved in close association with anthropology in the Americas; it is practiced throughout the world.

analogy Noting similarities between two entities and inferring from that similarity that an *additional* attribute of one (the ethnographic case) is also true of the other (the archaeological case).

androcentric A perspective that focuses on what men do in a society, to the exclusion of women.

anthropological linguistics A subdiscipline of anthropology that focuses on human language: its diversity in grammar, syntax, and lexicon; its historical development; and its relation to a culture's perception of the world.

anthropology The study of all aspects of humankind—biological, cultural, and linguistic; extant and extinct—employing an all-encompassing holistic approach.

antiquarian Originally, someone who studied antiquities (that is, ancient objects) largely for the sake of the objects themselves—not to understand the people or culture that produced them.

Antiquities Act Passed in 1906, this act (1) requires federal permits before excavating or collecting artifacts on federal land, (2) established a permitting process, and (3) gave the president the authority to create national monuments.

appendicular skeleton All parts of an animal excluding the axial skeleton.

applied science Research to acquire the knowledge necessary to solve a specific, recognized problem.

arbitrary level The basic vertical subdivision of an excavation square; used only when easily recognizable "natural" strata are lacking and when natural strata are more than 10 centimeters thick.

archaeofauna The animal bones found in an archaeological site.

archaeological context Once artifacts enter the ground, they are part of the archaeological context, where they can continue to be affected by human action, but where they also are affected by natural processes.

archaeological record The documentation of artifacts and other material remains, along with their contexts recovered from archaeological sites.

Archaeological Resources Protection Act (ARPA) Passed in 1979, this act (1) prohibits the excavation or removal of artifacts from federal property without a permit, (2) prohibits the sale, exchange, or transport of artifacts acquired illegally from federal property, and (3) increased the penalties for violations of the act over those of the Antiquities Act by allowing judges to take into account the value of the artifacts as well and the cost of restoration and repair of the site.

archaeological site Any place where material evidence exists about the human past. Usually, "site" refers to a concentration of such evidence.

archaeology The study of the past through the systematic recovery and analysis of material remains.

argilliturbation A natural formation process in which wet/dry cycles push artifacts upward as the sediment swells and then moves them down as cracks form during dry cycles.

argon-argon dating A high-precision method for estimating the relative quantities of argon-39 to argon-40 gas; used to date volcanic ashes that are between 500,000 and several million years old.

artifact Any movable object that has been used, modified, or manufactured by humans; artifacts include stone, bone, and metal tools; beads and other ornaments; pottery; artwork; religious and sacred items.

ascribed status Rights, duties, and obligations that accrue to a person by virtue of their parentage; ascribed status is inherited.

assemblage A collection of artifacts of one or several classes of materials (stone tools, ceramics, bones) that comes from a defined context, such as a site, feature, or stratum.

attribute An individual characteristic that distinguishes one artifact from another on the basis of its size, surface texture, form, material, method of manufacture, and design pattern.

axial skeleton The head, mandibles, vertebrae, ribs, sacrum, and tail of an animal skeleton.

band A residential group composed of a few nuclear families, but whose membership is neither permanent nor binding.

berdaches Among Plains Indian societies, men who elected to live life as women; they were recognized by their group as a third gender.

bilateral descent A kinship system in which relatives are traced equally on both the mother's and father's sides.

bioarchaeology The study of the human biological component evident in the archaeological record.

biological anthropology A subdiscipline of anthropology that views humans as biological organisms; also known as physical anthropology.

bone collagen The organic component of bone.

bonebed Archaeological and paleontological sites consisting of the remains of a large number of animals, often of the same species, and often representing a single moment in time—a mass kill or mass death.

bridging arguments Logical statements linking observations on the static archaeological record to the dynamic behavior or natural processes that produced it.

bundle burial Burial of a person's bones, bundled together, after the flesh has been removed or allowed to decay off the bones.

burial population A set of human burials that come from a limited region and a limited time period. The more limited the region and the time period, the more accurate will be inferences drawn from analysis of the burials.

cairn An artificial mound of stones. May be deliberately constructed as an aid to navigation, as a memorial, or to mark the location of a grave.

cargo system Part of the social organization found in many Central American communities in which a wealthy individual is named to carry out and bear the cost of important religious ceremonies throughout the year.

caries Cavities.

channel flake The longitudinal flake removed from the faces of Folsom and Clovis projectile points to create the flute.

ch'arki Native South American (Quechua) term for freeze-dried llama and alpaca meat.

charnel house A structure used by eastern North Americans to lay out the dead where the body would decompose. The bones would later be gathered and buried or cremated.

chiefdom A regional polity in which two or more local groups are organized under a single chief (who is the head of a ranked social hierarchy). Unlike autonomous bands and villages, chiefdoms consist of several more or less permanently aligned communities or settlements.

clans A group of matri- or patrilineages who see themselves as descended from a (sometimes-mythical) common ancestor.

classical archaeology The branch of archaeology that studies the "classical" civilizations of the Mediterranean, such as Greece and Rome, and the Near East.

Clovis The earliest well-established Native American culture, distributed throughout much of North America and dating 10,900 to 11,200 BC.

codices Maya texts, long strips of paper, many meters in length when unfolded, made of the pounded inner bark of certain trees; these texts helped analysts interpret Maya hieroglyphics on stelae.

cognitive archaeology The study of all those aspects of ancient culture that are the product of the human mind: the perception, description, and classification of the universe; the nature of the supernatural;

the principles, philosophies, ethics, and values by which human societies are governed; and the ways in which aspects of the world, the supernatural, or human values are conveyed in art.

comparative collection A skeletal collection of modern fauna of both sexes and different ages used to make identifications of archaeofaunas.

component An archaeological construct consisting of a stratum or set of strata that are presumed to be culturally homogeneous; a set of components from various sites in a region will make up a phase.

conjunctive approach As defined by Walter W. Taylor, using functional interpretations of artifacts and their contexts to reconstruct daily life of the past.

coprolite Desiccated feces, often containing macrobotanical remains, pollen, and the remains of small animals.

core A piece of stone that is worked ("knapped"). Cores sometimes serve merely as sources for raw materials; they also can serve as functional tools.

cosmology The study of the origin, large-scale structure, and future of the universe. A cosmological explanation demonstrates how the universe developed—both the totality and its constituent parts—and also describes what principles keep it together.

cribra orbitalia A symptom of iron deficiency anemia in which the bone of the upper eye sockets takes on a spongy appearance.

cultural anthropology A subdiscipline of anthropology that emphasizes nonbiological aspects: the learned social, linguistic, technological, and familial behaviors of humans.

cultural disturbance processes Human behaviors that modify artifacts in their archaeological context, for instance, digging pits, hearths, canals, and houses.

cultural materialism A research paradigm that takes a scientific approach and that emphasizes the importance of material factors—such as environment, population density, subsistence, and technology—in understanding change and diversity in human societies.

cultural resource management (CRM) A professional field that conducts activities, including archaeology, related to compliance with legislation aimed at conserving cultural resources.

cultural resources Physical features, both natural and artificial, associated with human activity, including sites, structures, and objects possessing significance in history, architecture, or human development. Cultural properties are unique and nonrenewable resources.

culture An integrated system of beliefs, traditions, and customs that govern or influence a person's behavior. Culture is learned, shared by members of a group, and based on the ability to think in terms of symbols.

culture history The kind of archaeology practiced mainly in the early to mid-twentieth century; it "explains" differences or changes over time in artifact frequencies by positing the diffusion of ideas between neighboring cultures or the migration of a people who had different mental templates for artifact styles.

data Relevant observations made on objects that then serve as the basis for study and discussion.

datum point The zero point, a fixed reference used to keep control on a dig; usually controls both the vertical and horizontal dimensions of provenience.

deconstruction Efforts to expose the assumptions behind the alleged objective and systematic search for knowledge. A primary tool of postmodernism.

deductive reasoning Reasoning from theory to account for specific observational or experimental results.

de Vries effects Fluctuations in the calibration curve produced by variations in the atmosphere's carbon-14 content; these can cause radiocarbon dates to calibrate to more than one calendar age.

direct acquisition A form of trade in which a person/group goes to the source area of an item to procure the raw material directly or to trade for it or finished products.

dosimeter A device to measure the amount of gamma radiation emitted by sediments. It is normally buried in a stratum for a year to record the annual dose of radiation. Dosimeters are often a short length of pure copper tubing filled with calcium sulfate.

down-the-line trade An exchange system in which goods are traded outward from a source area from group to group, resulting in a steady decline in the item's abundance in archaeological sites farther from the source.

eburnation A sign of osteoarthritis in which the epiphyses of long bones are worn smooth, causing them to take on a varnish-like appearance.

ecofact Plant or animal remains found in an archaeological site.

egalitarian societies Social systems that contain roughly as many valued positions as there are persons capable of filling them; in egalitarian societies, all people have nearly equal access to the critical resources needed to live.

electron spin resonance (ESR) A trapped charge technique used to date tooth enamel and burned stone tools; it can date teeth that are beyond the range of radiocarbon dating.

element In faunal analysis, a specific skeletal part of the body—for example, humerus or sternum.

enamel hypoplasias Horizontal linear defects in tooth enamel indicating episodes of physiological stress.

energy dispersive x-ray fluorescence (XRF) An analytical technique that uses obsidian's trace elements to "fingerprint" an artifact and trace it to its geologic source.

Enlightenment A Western philosophy that advocated ideas of linear progress, absolute truth, science, rational planning of ideal social orders, and the standardization of knowledge. It held that rational thought was the key to progress; that science and technology would free people from the oppression of historical traditions of myth, religion, and superstition; and that the control of nature through technology would permit the development of moral and spiritual virtues.

epiphyses The ends of bones that fuse to the main shaft or portion of bone at various ages; most bones are fused by age 25. This fact can be used to age skeletons of younger individuals.

ethnoarchaeology The study of contemporary peoples to determine how human behavior is translated into the archaeological record.

ethnology That branch of anthropology dealing chiefly with the comparative study of cultures.

exotics Material culture that was not produced locally and/or whose raw material is not found locally.

experimental archaeology Experiments designed to determine the archaeological correlates of ancient behavior; may overlap with both ethnoarchaeology and taphonomy.

faunal In archaeology, animal bones in archaeological sites.

faunal analysis Identification and interpretation of animal remains from an archaeological site.

faunalturbation A natural formation process in which animals, from large game to earthworms, affect the distribution of material within an archaeological site.

feature The nonportable evidence of technology; usually fire hearths, architectural elements, artifact clusters, garbage pits, soil stains, and so on.

flake A thin, sharp sliver of stone removed from a core during the knapping process.

floralturbation A natural formation process in which trees and other plants affect the distribution of artifacts within an archaeological site.

flotation The use of fluid suspension to recover tiny burned plant remains and bone fragments from archaeological sites.

flute Distinctive channel on the faces of Folsom and Clovis projectile points formed by removal of one or more flakes from the point's base.

forensic archaeology The application of archaeological and bioarchaeological knowledge for legal purposes.

formal analogies Analogies justified by similarities in the formal attributes of archaeological and ethnographic objects and features.

formation processes The ways in which human behaviors and natural actions operate to produce the archaeological record.

functional type A class of artifacts that performed the same function; these may or may not be temporal and/or morphological types.

gender ideology The culturally prescribed values assigned to the task and status of men and women; values can vary from society to society.

gender role The culturally prescribed behavior associated with men and women; roles can vary from society to society.

gene A unit of the chromosomes that controls inheritance of particular traits.

geographic information system (GIS) A computer program for storing, retrieving, analyzing, and displaying cartographic data.

georeferenced Data that are input to a GIS database using a common mapping reference—for example, the UTM grid—so that all data can be spatially analyzed.

Georgian order A worldview (1660/1680–1820) arising in the European Age of Reason and implying that the world has a single, basic immutable order. Using the powers of reason, people can discover what that order is and can thereby control the environment as they wish. The Georgian order is informed by the rise of scientific thought and by the balance and order in Renaissance architecture and art.

global positioning system (GPS) Hand-held devices that use triangulation from radio waves received from satellites to determine your current position in terms of either the UTM grid or latitude and longitude.

graviturbation A natural formation process in which artifacts are moved downslope through gravity, sometimes assisted by precipitation runoff.

ground-penetrating radar (GPR) A remote sensing technique in which radar pulses directed into the ground reflect back to the surface when they strike features or interfaces within the ground, showing the presence and depth of possible buried features.

haplogroup Genetic lineages defined by similar genes at a locus on a chromosome.

Harris lines Horizontal lines near the ends of long bones indicating episodes of physiological stress.

heat treatment A process whereby the flintknapping properties of stone tool raw material are improved by subjecting the material to heat.

high-level (or **general**) **theory** Theory that seeks to answer large "why" questions.

historical archaeology The study of human behavior through material remains, for which written history in some way affects its interpretation.

Homo erectus A hominid who lived in Africa, Asia, and Europe between 2 million and 500,000 years ago. These hominids walked upright, made simple stone tools, and may have used fire.

Hopewell A cultural tradition found primarily in the Ohio River valley and its tributaries, dating from 200 BC to AD 400. Hopewell societies engaged in hunting and gathering and in some horticulture of indigenous plants. They are known for their mortuary rituals, which included charnel houses and burial mounds; some central tombs contained exotics. They also constructed geometric earthworks as ceremonial enclosures and effigy mounds.

Hopewell Interaction Sphere The common set of symbols found in the midwestern United States between 200 BC and AD 400.

humanism A doctrine, attitude, or way of life that focuses on human interests and values. In general, a humanistic approach tends to reject a search for universals and stress instead the importance of the individual's lived experience.

hypothesis A proposition proposed as an explanation of some phenomena.

iconography Art forms or writing systems (such as Egyptian or Maya hieroglyphics) that symbolically represent ideas about religion or cosmology.

ideational perspective The research perspective that defines ideas, symbols, and mental structures as driving forces in shaping human behavior.

in situ From Latin, meaning "in position"; the place where an artifact, ecofact, or feature was found during excavation or survey.

index fossil concept The idea that strata containing similar fossil assemblages are of similar age. This concept enables archaeologists to characterize and date strata within sites using distinctive artifact forms that research shows to be diagnostic of a particular period of time.

inductive reasoning Working from specific observations to more general hypotheses.

infrastructure In cultural materialism, the elements most important to satisfying basic human survival and well-being—food, shelter, reproduction, health—that are assumed to lie at the causal heart of every sociocultural system.

instrumental neutron activation analysis An analytical technique that determines the trace element composition of the clay used to make a pot and trace the clay to its geological source.

kill sites Places where animals were killed in the past.

kinship Socially recognized network of relationships through which individuals are related to one another by ties of descent (real or imagined) and marriage.

kiva A Pueblo ceremonial structure that is usually round (but may be square or rectangular) and semi-subterranean. They appear in early Pueblo sites and perhaps even in the earlier (pre-AD 700) pithouse villages.

krotovina A filled-in animal burrow.

law of superposition The geological principle stating that, in any pile of sedimentary rocks that have not been disturbed by folding or overturning, each bed is older than the layers above and younger than the layers below; also known as Steno's law.

Libby half-life The time required for half of the carbon-14 available in an organic sample to decay; the standard is 5568 years, although it is known that the half-life is closer to 5730 years.

living floors A distinct buried surface on which people lived.

long bone cross-sections Cross-sections of the body's long bones (arms and legs) used to analyze bone shape and reconstruct the mechanical stresses placed on that bone—and hence activity patterns.

low-level theories The observations and interpretations that emerge from hands-on archaeological field and lab work.

macrobotanical remains Nonmicroscopic plant remains recovered from an archaeological site.

Magdalenian The last major culture of the European Upper Paleolithic period (about 16,000–10,000 BC); named after the rockshelter La Madeleine, in southwestern France. Magdalenian artisans crafted intricately carved tools of reindeer bone and antler; this was also the period during which Upper Paleolithic cave art in France and Spain reached its zenith.

mano A fist-sized, round, flat, hand-held stone used with a *metate* for grinding foods.

matrilineage Individuals who share a line of matrilineal descent.

matrilineal descent A unilineal descent system in which ancestry is traced through the female line.

matrix sorting The hand-sorting of processed bulk soil samples for minute artifacts and ecofacts.

medieval mindset The culture of the early (pre-AD 1660) British colonies that emphasized the group rather than the individual and in which the line between culture and nature was blurred; people were seen as conforming to nature.

mestizos Spanish term referring to people of mixed European and Native American ancestry.

metate A large, flat stone used as a stationary surface upon which seeds, tubers, and nuts are ground with a *mano*.

midden Refuse deposit resulting from human activities, generally consisting of sediment; food remains such as charred seeds, animal bone, and shell; and discarded artifacts.

middle-level (or **middle-range**) **theory** Hypothesis that links archaeological observations with the human behavior or natural processes that produced them.

minimum number of individuals (MNI) The smallest number of individuals necessary to account for all identified bones.

Mississippian A widespread cultural tradition across much of the eastern United States from AD 800 to 1500. Mississippian societies engaged in intensive village-based maize horticulture and constructed large, earthen platform mounds that served as sub-structures for temples, residences, and council buildings.

mitochondrial DNA (mtDNA) Genetic material found in the mitochondria of cells; it is inherited only from the mother and appears to mutate at a rate of 2–4 percent per 1 million years.

moieties Two groups of clans that perform reciprocal ceremonial obligations for one another; moieties often intermarry.

molecular archaeology The use of genetic information in ancient human remains to reconstruct the past.

morphological type A descriptive and abstract grouping of individual artifacts whose focus is on *overall* similarity rather than function or chronological significance.

mortality profiles Charts that depict the various ages at death of a burial population.

Mousterian A culture from the Middle Paleolithic ("Middle Old Stone Age") period that appeared throughout Europe after 250,000 and before 30,000 years ago. Mousterian artifacts are frequently associated with Neanderthal human remains.

National Historic Preservation Act (NHPA) Passed in 1966, this act created (1) the National Register of Historic Places, (2) the Advisory Council on Historic Preservation, (3) State Historic Preservation Offices, as well as (4) a process to mitigate the impact of development; it also requires that government agencies provide good stewardship of their cultural resources.

Native American Graves Protection and Repatriation Act (NAGPRA) Passed in 1990, this act (1) protects Indian graves on federal and tribal lands, (2) recognizes tribal authority over treatment of unmarked graves, (3) prohibits the commercial selling of native dead bodies, (4) requires an inventory and repatriation of human remains held by the federal government and institutions that receive federal funding, (5) requires these same institutions to return inappropriately acquired sacred objects and other important communally owned property to native owners, and (6) sets up a process to determine ownership of human remains found on federal and tribal property after November 16, 1990.

natural level A vertical subdivision of an excavation square that is based on natural breaks in the sediments (in terms of color, grain size, texture, hardness, or other characteristics).

Neanderthals (or **Neandertals**) An early form of humans who lived in Europe and the Near East about 300,000 to 30,000 years ago; biological anthropologists debate whether Neanderthals were in the direct evolutionary line leading to *Homo sapiens.*

new archaeology An approach to archaeology that arose in the 1960s, emphasizing the understanding of underlying cultural processes and the use of the scientific method; today's version of the "new archaeology" is sometimes called *processual archaeology.*

nuclear DNA Genetic material found in a cell's nuclei; this material is primarily responsible for an individual's inherited traits.

number of identified specimens (NISP) The raw number of identified bones (specimens) per species; a largely outmoded way of comparing archaeological bone frequencies.

objectivity The attempt to observe things as they actually are, without prejudging or falsifying observations in light of some preconceived view of the world—reducing subjective factors to a minimum.

old wood problem A potential problem with radiocarbon (or tree-ring) dating in which old wood has been scavenged and reused in a later archaeological site; the resulting date is not a true age of the associated human activity.

optically stimulated luminescence (OSL) A trapped charge dating technique used to date sediments; the age is the time elapsed between the last time a few moments' exposure to sunlight reset the clock to zero and the present.

oracle A shrine in which a deity reveals hidden knowledge or divine purpose.

osteoarthritis A disorder in which the cartilage between joints wears away, often because of overuse of the joint, resulting in osteophytes and eburnation.

osteology The study of bone.

osteophyte A sign of osteoarthritis in which bones develop a distinct "lipping" of bone at the point of articulation.

paleodemography The study of ancient demographic patterns and trends.

paleoethnobotanist An archaeologist who analyzes and interprets plant remains from archaeological sites in order to understand the past interactions between human populations and plants.

paleopathology The study of ancient patterns of disease and disorders.

palynology The technique through which the fossil pollen grains and spores from archaeological sites are studied.

paradigm The overarching framework, often unstated, for understanding a research problem. It is a researcher's "culture."

patrilineage Individuals who share a line of patrilineal descent.

patrilineal descent A unilineal descent system in which ancestry is traced through the male line.

patrilocal residence A cultural practice in which a newly married couple live in the groom's village of origin; it is often associated with patrilineal descent.

period A length of time distinguished by particular items of material culture, such as house form, pottery, or subsistence.

petrographic analysis An analytical technique that identifies the mineral composition of a pot's temper and clay through microscopic observation of thin sections.

phase An archaeological construct possessing traits sufficiently characteristic to distinguish it from other units similarly conceived; spatially limited to roughly a locality or region and chronologically limited to the briefest interval of time possible.

photosynthetic pathways The specific chemical process through which plants metabolize carbon; the three major pathways discriminate against carbon-13 in different ways, therefore similarly aged plants that use different pathways can produce different radiocarbon ages.

phytoliths Tiny silica particles contained in plants.

Pleistocene A geologic period from 2 million to 10 thousand years ago, which was characterized by multiple periods of extensive glaciation.

plow zone The upper portion of a soil profile that has been disturbed by repeated plowing or other agricultural activity.

political organization A society's formal and informal institutions that regulate a population's collective acts.

pollen diagram A chart showing the changing frequencies of different identified pollens through time from samples taken from archaeological or other sites.

porotic hyperostosis A symptom of iron deficiency anemia in which the skull takes on a porous appearance.

postmodernism A paradigm that rejects grand historical schemes in favor of humanistic approaches that appreciate the multiple voices of history. It seeks to see how colonialism created our vision of the world we occupy today; it eschews science and argues against the existence of objective truth.

postprocessual paradigm A paradigm that focuses on humanistic approaches and rejects scientific objectivity; it sees archaeology as inherently political and is more concerned with interpreting the past than with testing hypotheses. It sees change as arising largely from interactions between individuals operating within a symbolic and/or competitive system.

potassium-argon dating An absolute dating technique that monitors the decay of potassium (K-40) into argon gas (Ar-40).

potsherd Fragment of pottery.

principle of infrastructural determinism Argument that the infrastructure lies at the causal heart of every sociocultural system, that human society responds to factors that directly affect survival and well-being, and that such responses determine the rest of the sociocultural system.

principle of uniformitarianism The principle asserting that the processes now operating to modify the Earth's surface are the same processes that operated long ago in the geological past.

processual paradigm The paradigm that explains social, economic, and cultural change as primarily the result of adaptation to material conditions; external conditions (for example, the environment) are assumed to take causal priority over ideational factors in explaining change.

projectile points Arrowheads, dart points, or spear points.

proton precession magnetometer A remote sensing technique that measures the strength of magnetism between the Earth's magnetic core and a sensor controlled by the archaeologist. Magnetic anomalies can indicate the presence of buried walls or features.

provenience An artifact's location relative to a system of spatial data collection.

pubic symphysis Where the two halves of the pelvis meet in the groin area; the appearance of its articulating surface can be used to age skeletons.

puna Native American (Quechua) term for the treeless, windswept tablelands and basins of the higher Andes.

pure (basic) science Systematic research directed toward acquisition of knowledge for its own sake.

ranked societies Social systems in which a hierarchy of social status has been established, with a restricted number of valued positions available; in ranked societies, not everyone has the same access to the critical resources of life.

reclamation processes Human behaviors that result in artifacts moving from the archaeological context back to the systemic context, for example, scavenging beams from an abandoned structure to use them in a new one.

relational analogies Analogies justified on the basis of close cultural continuity between the archaeological and ethnographic cases or similarity in general cultural form.

relative dates Dates expressed relative to one another (for instance, earlier, later, more recent, and so forth) instead of in absolute terms.

religion A specific set of beliefs about one's relation to the supernatural; a society's mechanism for relating supernatural phenomena to the everyday world.

remote sensing The application of methods that employ some form of electromagnetic energy to detect and measure characteristics of an archaeological target.

reservoir effect When organisms take in carbon from a source that is depleted of or enriched in ^{14}C relative to the atmosphere; such samples may return ages that are considerably older or younger than they actually are.

reuse processes Human behaviors that recycle and reuse artifacts before the artifact enters an archaeological context.

ritual A succession of discrete behaviors that must be performed in a particular order under particular circumstances.

rockshelter A common type of archaeological site, consisting of a rock overhang that is deep enough to provide shelter but not deep enough to be called a cave (technically speaking, a cave must have an area of perpetual darkness).

sample fraction The percentage of the sample universe that is surveyed.

sample units Survey units of a standard size and shape, determined by the research question and practical considerations, used to obtain the sample.

sample universe The region that contains the statistical population and that will be sampled. Its size and shape are determined by the research question and practical considerations.

sciatic notch The angled edge of both halves of the posterior (rear) side of the pelvis; measurement of this angle is used to determine sex in human skeletons. Although its width varies among populations, narrow notches indicate a male and wider notches indicate a female.

science The search for universals by means of established scientific methods of inquiry.

scientific method Accepted principles and procedures for the systematic pursuit of secure knowledge. Established scientific procedures involve the following steps: define a relevant problem; establish one or more hypotheses; determine the empirical implications of the hypotheses; collect appropriate data through observation and/or experimentation; compare these data with the expected implications; and revise and/or retest hypotheses as necessary.

seasonality An estimate of what part of the year a particular archaeological site was occupied.

sedimentary rock Rock formed when the weathered products of preexisting rocks have been transported by and deposited in water and are turned once again to stone.

seriation A relative dating method that orders artifacts based on the assumption that one cultural style slowly replaces an earlier style over time; with a master seriation diagram, sites can be dated based on their frequency of several artifact (for instance, ceramic) styles.

shaman One who has the power to contact the spirit world through trance, possession, or visions. On the basis of this ability, the shaman invokes, manipulates, or coerces the power of the spirits for socially recognized ends—both good and ill.

shell midden The remnants of shellfish collecting; some shellfish middens can become many meters thick.

shovel testing A sample survey method used in regions where rapid soil buildup obscures buried archaeological remains; it entails digging shallow, systematic pits across the survey unit.

sipapu A Hopi word that loosely translates as "place of emergence." The original sipapu is the place where the Hopi are said to have emerged into this world from the underworld. Sipapus are also small pits in *kivas* through which communication with the supernatural world takes place.

size classes A categorization of faunal remains, not to taxon, but to one of five categories based on body size.

slash-and-burn A horticultural method used frequently in the tropics wherein a section of forest is cut, dried, and then burned, thus returning nutrients to the ground. This permits a plot of land to be farmed for a limited number of years.

Smithsonian number A unique catalog number given to sites; it consists of a number (the state's position alphabetically), a letter abbreviation of the county, and the site's sequential number within the county.

social organization The rules and structures that govern relations within a group of interacting people. Societies are divided into social units (groups) within which are recognized social positions (statuses), with appropriate behavior patterns prescribed for these positions (roles).

soil resistivity survey A remote sensing technique that monitors the electrical resistance of soils in a restricted volume near the surface of an archaeological site; buried walls or features can be detected by changes in the amount of resistance registered by the resistivity meter.

Southeastern Ceremonial Complex An assortment of ceremonial objects that occurs in the graves of high-status Mississippian individuals. Ritual exchange of these artifacts crosscut the boundaries of many distinctive local cultures.

space-time systematics The delineation of patterns in material culture through time and over space. These patterns are what the archaeologist will eventually try to explain or account for.

statistical population A set of counts, measurements, or characteristics about which relevant inquiries are to be made. Scientists use the term "statistical population" in a specialized way (quite different from "population" in the ordinary sense).

statistical sampling The principles that underlie sampling strategies that provide accurate measures of a statistical population.

status The rights, duties, privileges, powers, liabilities, and immunities that accrue to a recognized and named social position.

stelae Stone monuments erected by Maya rulers to record their history in rich images and hieroglyphic symbols. These symbols can be read and dated.

strata (singular, **stratum**) More or less homogeneous or gradational material, visually separable from other levels by a discrete change in the character of the material—texture, compactness, color, rock, organic content—and/or by a sharp break in the nature of deposition.

stratified random sample A survey universe divided into several sub-universes that are then sampled at potentially different sample fractions.

stratigraphy A site's physical structure produced by the deposition of geological and/or cultural sediments into layers, or strata.

structuralism A paradigm holding that human culture is the expression of unconscious modes of thought and reasoning, notably binary oppositions. Structuralism is most closely associated with the French anthropologist Claude Lévi-Strauss.

structure The behavior that supports choices made at the level of the infrastructure, including the organization of reproduction, production, exchange, family structure, division of labor, age and sex roles, political units, social organization, and warfare.

superstructure A group's values, aesthetics, rules, beliefs, religions, and symbols, which can be behaviorally manifested as art, music, dance, literature, advertising, religious rituals, sports, games, hobbies, and even science.

symbol An object or act (verbal or nonverbal) that, by cultural convention, stands for something else with which it has no necessary connection.

sympathetic magic Rituals in which doing something to an image of an object produces the desired effect on the real object.

systemic context A living behavioral system wherein artifacts are part of the ongoing system of manufacture, use, reuse, and discard.

taphonomy The study of how organisms become part of the fossil record; in archaeology it primarily refers to the study of how natural processes produce patterning in archaeological data.

taxon In faunal analysis, the classification of a skeletal element to a taxonomic category—species, genus, family, or order.

temper Material added to clay to give a ceramic item strength through the firing process.

temporal type A morphological type that has temporal significance; also known as a time marker or index fossil.

test excavation A small initial excavation to determine a site's potential for answering a research question.

testability The degree to which one's observations and experiments can be reproduced.

theory An explanation for observed, empirical phenomena. It is empirical and seeks to explain the relationships between variables; it is an answer to a "why" question.

thermal infrared multispectral scanner (TIMS) A remote sensing technique that uses equipment mounted in aircraft or satellite to measure infrared thermal radiation given off by the ground. Sensitive to differences as little as 0.1° Centigrade, it can locate subsurface structures by tracking how they affect surface thermal radiation.

thermoluminescence (TL) A trapped charge dating technique used on ceramics and burnt stone artifacts—anything mineral that has been heated to more than 500° C.

time markers Similar to index fossils in geology; artifact forms that research shows to be diagnostic of a particular period of time.

totem A natural object, often an animal, from which a lineage or clan believes itself to be descended and/or with which lineage or clan members have special relations.

trait list A simple listing of a culture's material and behavioral characteristics, for example, house and pottery styles, foods, degree of nomadism, particular rituals, or ornaments. Trait lists were used primarily to trace the movement of cultures across a landscape and through time.

trapped charge dating Forms of dating that rely upon the fact that electrons become trapped in minerals' crystal lattices as a function of background radiation; the age of the specimen is the total radiation received divided by the annual dose of radiation.

tree-ring dating (dendrochronology) The use of annual growth rings in trees to assign calendar ages to ancient wood samples.

type A class of archaeological artifacts defined by a consistent clustering of attributes.

typology The systematic arrangement of material culture into types.

Upper Paleolithic The last major division of the Old World Paleolithic, beginning about 40,000 years ago and lasting until the end of the Pleistocene (about 10,000 BC).

UTM grid Universal Transverse Mercator, a grid system whereby north and east coordinates provide a location anywhere in the world, precise to 1 meter.

vision quest A ritual in which an individual seeks visions through starvation, dehydration, and exposure; considered in some cultures to be a way to communicate with the supernatural world.

water screening A sieving process in which deposit is placed in a screen and the matrix washed away with hoses; essential where artifacts are expected to be small and/or difficult to find without washing.

zooarchaeologist (also faunal analyst) An individual who studies the faunal (animal) remains recovered from archaeological sites.

Bibliography

The following chapter-by-chapter bibliography contains the specific references used in each chapter as well as some additional references that can provide the student with more in-depth reading on particular subjects. We've arranged this bibliography by chapter so that the student can more easily locate additional readings on a particular subject. Where direct quotes have been used in the text, their source is indicated here at the end of the appropriate entry.

Chapter 1

Babcock, Barbara A., and Nancy J. Parezo. 1988. *Daughters of the Desert: Women Anthropologists and the Native American Southwest 1880–1980.* Albuquerque: University of New Mexico Press.

Benedict, Jeff. 2002. *No Bone Unturned: The Adventures of a Top Smithsonian Forensic Scientist and the Legal Battle for America's Oldest Skeletons.* New York: HarperCollins.

Binford, Lewis R. 1962. Archeology as anthropology. *American Antiquity* 28: 217–225.

———. 1972. *An Archaeological Perspective.* New York: Seminar Press.

———(Ed.). 1977. *For Theory Building in Archaeology.* New York: Academic Press.

———. 1983a. *In Pursuit of the Past: Decoding the Archaeological Record.* London: Thames and Hudson.

———(Ed.). 1983b. *Working at Archaeology.* New York: Academic Press.

———. 1989. *Debating Archaeology.* San Diego: Academic Press.

———. 2001. *Constructing Frames of Reference: An Analytical Method for Archaeological Theory Building Using Ethnographic and Environmental Data Sets.* Berkeley: University of California Press.

Binford, Sally R., and Lewis R. Binford (Eds.). 1968. *New Perspectives in Archeology.* Chicago: Aldine.

Brigham, Clarence S. 1937. Clarence Bloomfield Moore. *Proceedings of the American Antiquarian Society* (1936) 46: 13–14.

Brown, Ian W. 1978. *James Alfred Ford: The Man and His Works.* Southeastern Archaeological Conference, Special Publication no. 4.

Chatters, James C. 2001. *Ancient Encounters: Kennewick Man and the First Americans.* New York: Simon and Schuster.

Daniel, Glyn, and Colin Renfrew. 1988. *The Idea of Prehistory.* Edinburgh: University of Edinburgh Press.

Darwin, Charles. 1958 [1859]. *On the Origin of Species.* New York: Dutton.

Deagan, Kathleen. 1973. Mestizaje in colonial St. Augustine. *Ethnohistory* 20: 55–65.

———. 1980. Spanish St. Augustine: America's first "melting pot." *Archaeology* 33(5): 22–30.

———. 1982. Avenues of historical archaeology. In M. B. Schiffer (Ed.), *Advances in Archaeological Method and Theory,* Vol. 5 (pp. 151–177).

———. 1983. *Spanish St. Augustine: The Archaeology of a Colonial Creole Community.* New York: Academic Press.

———. 1987. *Artifacts of the Spanish Colonies of Florida and the Caribbean, 1500–1800,* Vol. 1, *Ceramics, Glassware, and Beads.* Washington, DC: Smithsonian Institution Press.

———. (Ed.). 1995. *Puerto Real: The Archaeology of a Sixteenth-Century Spanish Town in Hispaniola.* Gainesville: University Press of Florida.

———. 1996. Colonial transformation: Euro-American cultural genesis in the early Spanish-American colonies. *Journal of Anthropological Research* 52: 135–160.

Deagan, Kathleen, and José María Cruxent. 2002a. *Archaeology at La Isabela: America's First European Town.* New Haven: Yale University Press.

———. 2002b. *Columbus's Outpost among the Tainos.* New Haven: Yale University Press.

Dunnell, Robert C. 1986. Five decades of American archaeology. In David J. Meltzer, Don D. Fowler, and Jeremy A. Sabloff (Eds.), *American Archaeology Past and Future: A Celebration of the Society for American Archaeology 1935–1985* (pp. 23–49). Washington, DC: Smithsonian Institution Press.

Ford, James Alfred. 1949. Cultural dating of prehistoric sites in the Virú Valley, Peru. Pt. 2 of "Surface survey of the Virú Valley, Peru" by James Alfred Ford and Gordon R. Willey. *Anthropological Papers of the American Museum of Natural History* 43(1).

———. 1969. A comparison of formative cultures in the Americas: Diffusion or the psychic unity of man? *Smithsonian Contributions to Anthropology*, Vol. 2. Washington, DC.

Ford, James Alfred, and Clarence H. Webb. 1956. Poverty Point, a late Archaic site in Louisiana. *Anthropological Papers of the American Museum of Natural History* 46(1): 1–140.

Grayson, Donald K. 1983. *The Establishment of Human Antiquity.* New York: Academic Press.

Irwin-Williams, Cynthia. 1990. Women in the field: The role of women in archaeology before 1960. In G. Kass-Simon and Patricia Farnes (Eds.), *Women of Science: Righting the Record* (pp. 1–41). Bloomington: Indiana University Press.

Kidder, Alfred V. 1924. *An Introduction to the Study of Southwestern Archaeology.* New Haven: Yale University Press.

———. 1960. Reminiscences in Southwest archaeology, I. *Kiva* 25: 1–32.

Kidder, Alfred V., and Samuel J. Guernsey. 1921. Basketmaker caves of northeastern Arizona. *Papers of the Peabody Museum of American Archaeology and Ethnology* 8(2).

Kidder, Alfred V., Jesse D. Jennings, and Edwin M. Shook. 1946. *Excavations at Kaminaljuyu, Guatemala.* Carnegie Institution of Washington Publication no. 561. Washington, DC: Carnegie Institution.

Moore, Clarence B. 1905. Certain aboriginal remains of the Black Warrior River. *Journal of the Academy of Natural Sciences of Philadelphia.* Second Series, 13: 123–244.

———. 1907. Moundville revisited. *Journal of the Academy of Natural Sciences of Philadelphia.* Second Series, 13: 337–405.

Nelson, Nels C. 1909. Shellmounds of the San Francisco Bay region. *University of California Publications in American Archaeology and Ethnology* 7(4): 310–356.

———. 1914. Pueblo ruins of the Galisteo Basin, New Mexico. *Anthropological Papers of the American Museum of Natural History* 15(1).

Parezo, Nancy J. (Ed.). 1993. *Hidden Scholars: Women Anthropologists and the Native American Southwest.* Albuquerque: University of New Mexico Press.

Patterson, Thomas. 1995. *Toward a Social History of Archaeology in the United States.* Fort Worth: Harcourt Brace.

Taylor, Walter W. 1948. A study of archeology. *American Anthropological Association, Memoir,* 69.

Thomas, David Hurst. 2000. *Skull Wars: Kennewick Man, Archaeology, and the Battle for Native American Identity.* New York: Basic Books.

Trigger, Bruce G. 1999. *A History of Archaeological Thought,* 2d ed. Cambridge, UK: Cambridge University Press.

Wardle, H. Newell. 1956. Clarence Bloomfield Moore (1852–1936). *Bulletin of the Philadelphia Anthropological Society* 9(2): 9–11.

Webb, Clarence H. 1968. (Obituary of) James Alfred Ford, 1911–1968. *Texas Archaeological Society Bulletin* 38: 135–146.

White, Nancy M., Lynne P. Sullivan, and Rochelle A. Marrinan. 1999. *Grit-Tempered: Early Women Archaeologists in the Southeastern United States.* Knoxville: University of Tennessee Press.

Willey, Gordon R., and Jeremy A. Sabloff. 1993. *A History of American Archaeology,* 3d ed. New York: Freeman.

Woodbury, Richard B. 1960. Nels C. Nelson and chronological archaeology. *American Antiquity* 25: 400–401.

———. 1973. *Alfred V. Kidder.* New York: Columbia University Press.

Chapter 2

Anyon, Roger, and T. J. Ferguson. 1995. Cultural resources management at the Pueblo of Zuni, New Mexico, USA. *Antiquity* 69: 913–930.

Atwater, Caleb. 1820. Description of the antiquities discovered in the state of Ohio and other western states. *Archaeologia Americana: Transactions and*

Collections of the American Antiquarian Society 1: 105–267.

Baldwin, John. D. 1872. *Ancient America in Notes on American Archaeology.* New York: Harper.

Binford, Lewis R. 1983. *In Pursuit of the Past: Decoding the Archaeological Record.* London: Thames and Hudson.

Bintliff, John. 1991. Post-modernism, rhetoric, and scholasticism at TAG: The current state of British archaeological theory. *Antiquity* 65: 274–278.

Carrithers, Michael. 1990. Is anthropology art or science? *Current Anthropology* 31: 263–282.

Daniel, Glyn. 1991. Post-processual developments in Anglo-American archaeology. *Norwegian Archaeological Review* 24: 65–76.

———. 1995. Expanding middle-range theory. *Antiquity* 69: 449–458.

Dark, K. R. 1995. *Theoretical Archaeology.* Ithaca, NY: Cornell University Press.

Deetz, James. 1983. Scientific humanism and humanistic science: A plea for paradigmatic pluralism in historical archaeology. *Geoscience and Man* 23: 27–34.

Flannery, Kent V. 1967. Culture history vs. cultural process: A debate in American archaeology. *Scientific American* 217(2): 119–121.

———. 1973. Archeology with a capital S. In Charles L. Redman (Ed.), *Research and Theory in Current Archeology* (pp. 47–53). New York: Wiley.

Gibbon, Guy. 1989. *Explanation in Archaeology.* Oxford, UK: Basil Blackwell.

Harris, Marvin. 1968. *The Rise of Anthropological Theory.* New York: Thomas Y. Crowell.

———. 1979. *Cultural Materialism: The Struggle for a Science of Culture.* New York: Random House.

Hegmon, Michelle. 2003. Setting theoretical egos aside: Issues and theory in North American archaeology. *American Antiquity* 68: 213–244.

Hodder, Ian. 1985. Postprocessual archaeology. In Michael B. Schiffer (Ed.), *Advances in Archaeological Method and Theory,* Vol. 8 (pp. 1–26). Orlando, FL: Academic Press.

———. 1986. *Reading the Past: Current Approaches to Interpretation in Archaeology.* Cambridge: Cambridge University Press.

———. 1989a. Post-modernism, post-structuralism and post-processual archaeology. In Ian Hodder (Ed.), *The Meaning of Things.* One World Archaeology, no. 6 (pp. 64–78). London: Unwin Hyman.

———. 1989b. Writing archaeology: Site reports in context. *Antiquity* 63: 268–274.

———. 1990. Archaeology and the post-modern. *Anthropology Today* 6(5): 13–15.

———. 1995. *Theory and Practice in Archaeology.* London: Routledge.

———. 1999. *The Archaeological Process: An Introduction.* Oxford, UK: Blackwell.

———. (Ed.). 2001. *Archaeological Theory Today.* Oxford, UK: Blackwell.

Jefferson, Thomas. 1787. *Notes on the State of Virginia.* London: John Stockdale (rpt. Chapel Hill: University of North Carolina Press, 1954).

Johnson, Matthew. 1999. *Archaeological Theory: An Introduction.* Oxford, UK: Blackwell.

Kemeny, John G. 1959. *A Philosopher Looks at Science.* New York: Van Nostrand Reinhold.

Knapp, A. Bernard. 1996. Archaeology without gravity: Postmodernism and the past. *Journal of Archaeological Method and Theory* 3: 127–158.

Kroeber, Alfred, and Clyde Kluckholn. 1952. Culture: A critical review of concepts and definitions. *Papers of the Peabody Museum of American Archaeology and Ethnology* 47(1).

Kuznar, Lawrence. 1997. *Reclaiming a Scientific Anthropology.* Walnut Creek, CA: Altamira.

Mcgee, R. Jon, and Richard L. Williams. 2004. *Anthropological Theory: An Introductory History,* 3d ed. New York: McGraw Hill.

Preucel, R. W. (Ed.). 1991. *Processual and Postprocessual Archaeologies: Multiple Ways of Knowing the Past.* Center for Archaeological Investigations, Occasional Paper, no. 10. Carbondale: Southern Illinois University.

———. 1995. The postprocessual condition. *Journal of Archaeological Research* 3: 147–175.

Price, Barbara J. 1982. Cultural materialism: A theoretical review. *American Antiquity* 47: 709–741.

Salmon, Merrilee H. 1982. *Philosophy and Archaeology.* New York: Academic Press.

Skibo, James M., William H. Walker, and Axel E. Nielsen. (Eds.). 1995. *Expanding Archaeology.* Salt Lake City: University of Utah Press.

Squier, Ephraim G., and Edwin H. Davis. 1998. *Ancient Monuments of the Mississippi Valley,* edited and with an introduction by David J. Meltzer. Washington, DC: Smithsonian Institution Press.

Thomas, Cyrus. 1894. *Report on the Mound Explorations of the Bureau of Ethnology.* Washington, DC: Smithsonian Institution.

Tylor, Edward Burnett. 1871. *Primitive Culture,* Vols. 1 and 2. London: Murray (quote from p. 1).

Watson, Patty Jo. 1995. Archaeology, anthropology, and the culture concept. *American Anthropologist* 97: 683–694.

Wilk, Richard. 1985. The ancient Maya and the political present. *Journal of Anthropological Research* 41: 307–326.

Yoffee, Norman, and Andrew Sherratt (Eds.). 1993. *Archaeological Theory: Who Sets the Agenda?* Cambridge: Cambridge University Press.

Chapter 3

Aldenderfer, Mark, and Herbert Maschner (Eds.). 1996. *Anthropology, Space, and Geographic Information Systems.* New York: Oxford University Press.

Allen, K. M. S., S. W. Green, and E. B. W. Zubrow (Eds.). 1990. *Interpreting Space: GIS and Archaeology.* London: Taylor and Francis.

Bevan, Bruce W. 1983. Electromagnetics for mapping buried earth features. *Journal of Field Archaeology* 10: 47–54.

Binford, Lewis R. 1964. A consideration of archaeological research design. *American Antiquity* 29: 425–441.

Carr, Christopher. 1982. *Handbook on Soil Resistivity Surveying: Interpretation of Data from Earthen Archaeological Sites.* Evanston, IL: Center for American Archeology Press.

Clark, Anthony. 1990. *Seeing Beneath the Soil: Prospecting Methods in Archaeology.* London: Batsford.

Conyers, Lawrence B. 1995. The use of ground-penetrating radar to map the buried structures and landscape of the Cerén site, El Salvador. *Geoarchaeology* 10: 275–299.

Donoghue, D. N. M. 2001. Remote sensing. In D. Brothwell and A. Pollard (Eds.), *Handbook of Archaeological Sciences* (pp. 555–564). Chichester, UK: Wiley.

Ebert, James I. 1984. Remote sensing applications in archaeology. In Michael B. Schiffer (Ed.), *Advances in Archaeological Method and Theory,* Vol. 7 (pp. 293–362). New York: Academic Press.

Garrison, Ervan G., James G. Baker, and David Hurst Thomas. 1985. Magnetic prospection and the discovery of Mission Santa Catalina de Guale, Georgia. *Journal of Field Archaeology* 12: 299–313.

Goodman, Dean. 1994. Ground-penetrating radar simulation in engineering and archaeology. *Geophysics* 59: 224–232.

Kantner, John. 1997. Ancient roads, modern mapping: Evaluating prehistoric Chaco Anasazi roadways using GIS technology. *Expedition* 39: 4962.

———. 2004. Geographical approaches for reconstructing past human behavior from prehistoric roadways. In M. F. Goodchild and D. G. Janelle (Eds.), *Spatially Integrated Social Sciences: Examples in Best Practice* (pp. 323–344). Oxford, UK: Oxford University Press.

Kelly, Robert. 2001. *Prehistory of the Carson Desert and Stillwater Mountains, Nevada: Environment, Mobility, and Subsistence.* University of Utah Anthropological Papers 123.

Kvamme, Kenneth L. 1989. Geographic information systems in regional archaeological research and data management. In M. B. Schiffer (Ed.), *Archaeological Method and Theory,* Vol. 1 (pp. 139–204). Tucson: University of Arizona Press.

Lewarch, Dennis E., and Michael J. O'Brien. 1981. The expanding role of surface assemblages in archaeological research. In Michael B. Schiffer (Ed.), *Advances in Archaeological Method and Theory,* Vol. 4 (pp. 297–342). New York: Academic Press.

Lyons, T. R., and T. E. Avery. 1984. *Remote Sensing: A Handbook for Archaeologists and Cultural Resource Managers.* Washington, DC: National Park Service.

Mueller, James W. 1974. The use of sampling in archaeological survey. *Society for American Archaeology Memoir* 28.

———. (Ed.). 1975. *Sampling in Archaeology.* Tucson: University of Arizona Press.

Parrington, Michael. 1983. Remote sensing. *Annual Review of Anthropology* 12: 105–124.

Peck, Mary. 1994. *Chaco Canyon: A Center and Its World.* Santa Fe: Museum of New Mexico Press.

Plog, Stephen, Fred Plog, and Walter Wait. 1978. Decision making in modern surveys. In Michael B. Schiffer (Ed.), *Advances in Archaeological Method and Theory,* Vol. 1 (pp. 383–421). New York: Academic Press.

Riley, D. N. 1987. *Air Photography and Archaeology.* London: Duckworth.

Sabins, Floyd F., Jr. 1996. *Remote Sensing: Principles and Interpretation,* 3d ed. New York: W. H. Freeman.

Scollar, Irwin, A. Tabbagh, A. Hesse, and I. Herzog (Eds.). 1990. *Archaeological Prospecting and Remote Sensing.* Cambridge: Cambridge University Press.

Sheets, Payson D. 2002. *Before the Volcano Erupted: The Ancient Cerén Village in Central America.* Austin: University of Texas Press.

Sheets, Payson D., and Tom Sever. 1988. High-tech wizardry. *Archaeology* 41(6): 28–35.

Snead, J., and Preucel, R. 1999. The ideology of settlement: Ancestral Keres landscapes in the northern Rio Grande. In W. Ashmore and A. B. Knapp (Eds.), *Archaeologies of Landscape: Contemporary Perspectives* (pp. 169–197). Oxford, UK: Blackwell.

Thomas, David Hurst. 1983a. The archaeology of Monitor Valley: 1. Epistemology. *Anthropological Papers of the American Museum of Natural History* 58(1): 1–194.

———. 1983b. The archaeology of Monitor Valley: 2. Gatecliff Shelter. *Anthropological Papers of the American Museum of Natural History* 59(1): 1–552.

———. 1987. The archaeology of Mission Santa Catalina de Guale: 1. Search and discovery. *Anthropological Papers of the American Museum of Natural History* 63(2): 47–161.

———. 1988. The archaeology of Monitor Valley: 3. Survey and additional excavation. *Anthropological Papers of the American Museum of Natural History* 66(2): 131–633.

———. 1993. The archaeology of Mission Santa Catalina de Guale: Our first 15 years. In Bonnie G. McEwan (Ed.), *The Missions of La Florida* (pp. 1–34). Gainesville: University Press of Florida.

Weymouth, John W. 1986. Geophysical methods of archaeological site surveying. In Michael B. Schiffer (Ed.), *Advances in Archaeological Method and Theory,* Vol. 9 (pp. 311–395). Orlando, FL: Academic Press.

Wheatley, David, and Mark Gillings. 2002. *Spatial Technology and Archaeology: The Archaeological Applications of GIS.* London: Taylor and Francis.

Chapter 4

Collis, John. 2001. *Digging Up the Past: An Introduction to Archaeological Excavation.* Phoenix Mills, UK: Sutton.

Daugherty, Richard, and Ruth Kirk. 1976. Ancient Indian village where time stood still. *Smithsonian* 7(2): 68–75.

Folsom, Franklin. 1992. *The Black Cowboy.* Niwot, CO: Roberts Rinehart.

Fowler, Brenda. 2001. *Iceman: Uncovering the Life and Times of a Prehistoric Man Found in an Alpine Glacier.* Chicago: University of Chicago Press.

Kirk, Ruth, and Richard Daugherty. 1974. *Hunters of the Whale.* New York: William Morrow.

Lock, Gary. 2003. *Using Computers in Archaeology: Towards Virtual Pasts.* London: Routledge.

Loud, Lewellyn L., and Mark R. Harrington. 1929. Lovelock Cave. *University of California Publications in American Archaeology and Ethnology* 25: 1–183.

McMillon, Bill. 1991. *The Archaeology Handbook: A Field Manual and Resource Guide.* New York: Wiley.

Meltzer, David. 1993. *Search for the First Americans.* Washington, DC: Smithsonian Institution Press.

Purdy, Barbara A. 1996. *How to Do Archaeology the Right Way.* Gainesville: University Press of Florida.

Schiffer, Michael B. 1972. Archaeological context and systemic context. *American Antiquity* 37: 156–165.

———. 1987. *Formation Processes of the Archaeological Record.* Albuquerque: University of New Mexico Press.

Struever, Stuart. 1968. Flotation techniques for the recovery of small-scale archaeological remains. *American Antiquity* 33: 353–362.

Thomas, David Hurst. 1983. The archaeology of Monitor Valley: 2. Gatecliff Shelter. *Anthropological Papers of the American Museum of Natural History* 59(1): 1–552.

Wagner, Gail E. 1982. Testing flotation recovery rates. *American Antiquity* 47: 127–132.

Watson, Patty Jo. 1974. Flotation procedures used on Salts Cave sediments. In Patty Jo Watson (Ed.),

Archaeology of the Mammoth Cave Area (pp. 107–108). New York: Academic Press.

Chapter 5

Aitken, M. J. 1990. *Science-Based Dating in Archaeology.* London: Longman.

Baillie, M. G. L. 1995. *A Slice through Time: Dendrochronology and Precision Dating.* London: Batsford.

Bar-Yosef, O., and B. Vandermeersch. 1993. Modern humans in the Levant. *Scientific American* 268: 64–70.

Bowman, Sheridan. 1990. *Radiocarbon Dating.* Berkeley: University of California Press.

———. 1994. Using radiocarbon: An update. *Antiquity* 68: 838–843.

Douglass, Andrew Ellicott. 1929. The secret of the Southwest solved by talkative tree rings. *National Geographic* 56(6): 736–770.

Dunnell, Robert C. 1970. Seriation method and its evaluation. *American Antiquity* 35: 305–319.

Feathers, James. 2003. Use of luminescence dating in archaeology. *Measurement Science and Technology* 14: 1493–1509.

Grün, R. 1999. Trapped charge dating (ESR, TL, OSL). In D. Brothwell and A. Pollard (Eds.), *Handbook of Archaeological Sciences* (pp. 47–62). Chichester, UK: Wiley.

Haas, Herbert, James Devine, Robert Wenke, Mark Lehner, Willy Wolfli, and George Bonani. 1987. Radiocarbon chronology and the historical calendar in Egypt. In Oliver Aurenche, Jacques Evin, and Francis Hours (Eds.), *Chronologies in the Near East: Relative Chronologies and Absolute Chronology 16,000–4,000 BP* (pp. 585–606). British Archaeology Reports International Series 379. Oxford, UK.

Marquardt, William H. 1978. Advances in archaeological seriation. In Michael B. Schiffer (Ed.), *Advances in Archaeological Method and Theory,* Vol. 1 (pp. 257–314). New York: Academic Press.

Mayer-Oakes, William J. 1955. Prehistory of the upper Ohio Valley. *Annals of the Carnegie Museum,* vol. 34.

Nash, Stephen E. 1999. *Time, Trees, and Prehistory: Tree Ring Dating and the Development of North American Archaeology, 1914–1950.* Salt Lake City: University of Utah Press.

———. 2000. *It's about Time: A History of Archaeological Dating in North America.* Salt Lake City: University of Utah Press.

Nelson, Nels. 1916. Chronology of the Tano Ruins, New Mexico. *American Anthropologist* 18: 159–180 (Table 5-1 is from p. 166).

Roberts, R. G., M. Bird, J. Olley, R. Galbraith, E. Lawson, G. Laslett, H. Yoshida, R. Jones, R. L. K. Fullagar, G. Jacobsen, and Q. Hua. 1998. Optical and radiocarbon dating at Jinmium rock shelter in northern Australia. *Nature* 393: 358–362.

Stahle, David W., and Daniel Wolfman. 1985. The potential for archaeological tree-ring dating in eastern North America. In Michael B. Schiffer (Ed.), *Advances in Archaeological Method and Theory,* Vol. 8 (pp. 279–302). New York: Academic Press.

Stuiver, Minze, and Paula J. Reimer. 1993. Extended 14C database and revised CALIB 3.0 14C age calibration program. *Radiocarbon* 35: 215–230.

Swisher, C. C., III, G. H. Curtis, T. Jacob, A. G. Getty, and A. Suprijo Widasmoro. 1994. Age of the earliest known hominids in Java, Indonesia. *Science* 263: 1118–1121.

Taylor, R. E. 1985. The beginnings of radiocarbon dating in American antiquity: A historical perspective. *American Antiquity* 50: 309–325.

Taylor, R. E., and M. J. Aitken (Eds.). 1997. *Chronometric Dating in Archaeology.* New York: Plenum Press.

Taylor, R. E., Austin Long, and Renee S. Kra (Eds.). 1992. *Radiocarbon after Four Decades: An Interdisciplinary Perspective.* New York: Springer-Verlag.

van der Merwe, Nikolaas J. 1982. Carbon isotopes, photosynthesis, and archaeology. *American Scientist* 70: 596–606.

Wendorf, Fred, R. Schild, A. E. Close, D. J. Donahue, A. J. T. Jull, T. H. Zabel, H. Więcłowska, M. Kobusiewicz, B. Issawi, N. el Hadidi, and H. Haas. 1984. New radiocarbon dates on the cereals from Wadi Kubbaniua. *Science* 225: 645–646.

Wendorf, Fred, R. Schild, N. el Hadidi, A. E. Close, M. Kobusiewicz, H. Więcłowska, B. Issawi, and H. Haas. 1979. The use of barley in the Egyptian late Paleolithic. *Science* 205: 1341–1347.

Wintle, Ann G. 1996. Archaeologically relevant dating techniques for the next century. *Journal of Archaeological Science* 23: 123–138.

Chapter 6

Binford, Lewis R. 1973. Interassemblage variability—The Mousterian and the "functional" argument. In Colin Renfrew (Ed.), *The Explanation of Culture Change: Models in Prehistory* (pp. 227–254). London: Duckworth.

Cordell, Linda. 1984. *Prehistory of the Southwest.* New York: Academic Press.

Dunnell, Robert C. 1986. Methodological issues in Americanist artifact classification. In Michael B. Schiffer (Ed.), *Advances in Archaeological Method and Theory,* Vol. 9 (pp. 149–207). New York: Academic Press.

Ford, James. 1954. The type concept revisited. *American Anthropologist* 56: 42–54.

Haury, Emil W. 1950. *The Stratigraphy and Archaeology of Ventana Cave, Arizona.* Albuquerque: University of New Mexico Press; Tucson: University of Arizona Press (quote is from p. 329).

Lyman, R. Lee, and Michael O'Brien. 2003. *W. C. McKern and the Midwestern Taxonomic Method.* Tuscaloosa: University of Alabama Press.

Lyman, R. Lee, Michael O'Brien, and Robert C. Dunnell (Eds.). 1997. *Americanist Culture History: Fundamentals of Time, Space, and Form.* New York: Plenum.

Rouse, Irving. 1960. The classification of artifacts in archaeology. *American Antiquity* 25: 313–323.

Spaulding, Albert C. 1960. The dimensions of archaeology. In G. E. Dole and R. L. Carneiro (Eds.), *Essays in the Science of Culture in Honor of Leslie A. White* (pp. 437–456). New York: Thomas Y. Crowell.

Spier, Leslie. 1931. N. C. Nelson's stratigraphic technique in the reconstruction of prehistoric sequences in southwestern America. In S. A. Rice (Ed.), *Methods in Social Science* (pp. 275–283). Chicago: University of Chicago Press.

Steward, Julian H. 1954. Types of types. *American Anthropologist* 56: 54–57.

Sutton, Mark Q., and Brooke S. Arkush. 1996. *Archaeological Laboratory Methods: An Introduction.* Dubuque, IA: Kendall/Hunt.

Thomas, David Hurst. 1981. How to classify the projectile points from Monitor Valley, Nevada. *Journal of California and Great Basin Anthropology* 3: 7–43.

———. 1983. The Archaeology of Monitor Valley: 2. Gatecliff Shelter. *Anthropological Papers of the American Museum of Natural History,* Vol. 59, Part 1.

Willey, Gordon R., and Philip Phillips. 1958. *Method and Theory in American Archaeology.* Chicago: University of Chicago Press (quote is from p. 22).

Wissler, Clark. 1926. *The Relation of Nature to Man in Aboriginal America.* New York: Oxford University Press.

Chapter 7

Agenbroad, Larry. 1978. *The Hudson-Meng Site: An Alberta Bison Kill in the Nebraska High Plains.* Washington, DC: University Press of America.

Behrensmeyer, Anna K., and Susan M. Kidwell. 1985. Taphonomy's contributions to paleobiology. *Paleobiology* 1: 105–119.

Binford, Lewis R. 1967. Smudge pits and hide smoking: The use of analogy in archaeological reasoning. *American Antiquity* 32: 1–12.

———. 1978. *Nunamiut Ethnoarchaeology.* New York: Academic Press.

———. 1983. *In Pursuit of the Past: Decoding the Archaeological Record.* London: Thames and Hudson ("In His Own Words" text quoted is from pp. 98, 100–101).

Binford, Lewis R., and James F. O'Connell. 1984. An Alyawara day: The stone quarry. *Journal of Anthropological Research* 40: 406–432.

Brandt, Steve A., and Kathryn Weedman. 1997. The ethnoarchaeology of hideworking and flaked stonetool use in southern Ethiopia. In K. Fukui, E. Kuimoto, and M. Shigeta (Eds.), *Ethiopia in Broader Perspective: Papers of the XIIth International Conference of Ethiopian Studies* (pp. 351–361). Kyoto: Shokado Book Sellers.

Chaplin, R. E. 1971. *The Study of Animal Bones from Archaeological Sites.* New York: Seminar Press.

Coles, John M. 1973. *Archaeology by Experiment.* New York: Scribner's.

Crabtree, Don E. 1966. A stoneworker's approach to analyzing and replicating the Lindenmeier Folsom. *Tebiwa* 9: 3–39.

David, Nicholas, and Carol Kramer. 2001. *Ethnoarchaeology in Action.* Cambridge: Cambridge University Press.

Efremov, I. A. 1940. Taphonomy: A new branch of pale-ontology. *Pan-American Geologist* 74(2): 81–93.

Flenniken, J. Jeffrey. 1978. Reevaluation of the Linden-meier Folsom: A replication experiment in lithic technology. *American Antiquity* 43: 473–480.

Gamble, C. S., and W. A. Boismier (Eds.). 1991. *Eth-noarchaeological Approaches to Mobile Campsites.* International Monographs in Prehistory. Ann Arbor.

Gifford, Diane P. 1981. Taphonomy and paleoecology: A critical review of archaeology's sister disciplines. In Michael B. Schiffer (Ed.), *Advances in Archaeo-logical Method and Theory.* Vol. 4 (pp. 365–438). New York: Academic Press.

Gryba, Eugene M. 1988. A Stone Age pressure method of Folsom fluting. *Plains Anthropologist* 33: 53–66.

Hayden, Brian. 1979. *Palaeolithic Reflections: Lithic Technology and Ethnographic Excavation among Australian Aborigines.* Atlantic Highlands, NJ: Humanities Press.

Hayden, Brian, and Aubrey Cannon. 1984. The struc-ture of material systems: Ethnoarchaeology in the Maya highlands. *Society for American Archaeology Papers,* no. 3.

Hill, Andrew, and Anna Kay Behrensmeyer. 1984. Dis-articulation patterns of some modern East African mammals. *Paleobiology* 10: 366–376.

Hodder, Ian. 1982. *Symbols in Action.* Cambridge: Cambridge University Press.

———. 1987. The meaning of discard: Ash and domestic space in Baringo. In S. Kent (Ed.), *Method and Theory in Activity Area Research* (pp. 424–448). New York: Columbia University Press.

Kelly, Robert L., Lin Poyer, and Bram Tucker. 2005. An Ethnoarchaeological Study of Mobility, Architec-tural Investment, and Food Sharing among Mada-gascar's Mikea. *American Anthropologist* 107: 403–416.

Kelly, Robert, Jean-François Rabedimy, and Lin A. Poyer. 1999. The Mikea of southwestern Madagas-car. In R. B. Lee and R. Daly (Eds.), *The Cambridge Encyclopedia of Hunter-Gatherers* (pp. 215–219). Cambridge: Cambridge University Press.

Kramer, Carol. 1997. *Pottery in Rajasthan: Ethnoar-chaeology in Two Indian Cities.* Washington, DC: Smithsonian Institution Press.

Kroeber, Theodora. 1967. *Ishi in Two Worlds: A Biogra-phy of the Last Wild Indian in North America.* Berkeley: University of California Press.

Lehner, Mark. 1997. *The Complete Pyramids: Solving the Ancient Mysteries.* London: Thames and Hudson.

Longacre, William A. (Ed.). 1991. *Ceramic Ethnoar-chaeology.* Tucson: University of Arizona Press.

Longacre, William A., and James M. Skibo (Eds.). 1994. *Kalinga Ethnoarchaeology: Expanding Archaeological Method and Theory.* Washington, DC: Smithsonian Institution Press.

O'Connell, James F. 1995. Ethnoarchaeology needs a general theory of behavior. *Journal of Archaeologi-cal Research* 3: 205–255.

Perkins, D., Jr., and P. Daly. 1968. A hunter's village in Neolithic Turkey. *Scientific American* 219(5): 96–106.

Pope, Saxton T. 1974. Hunting with Ishi—the last Yana Indian. *Journal of California Anthropology* 1: 152–173.

Raab, L. Mark, and Albert C. Goodyear. 1984. Middle-range theory in archaeology: A critical review of origins and applications. *American Antiquity* 49: 255–268.

Stahl, Ann B. 1995. Has ethnoarchaeology come of age? *Antiquity* 69: 404–407.

Todd, Lawrence C., and David Rapson. 1999. Forma-tional analysis of bison bonebeds and interpreta-tion of Paleoindian subsistence. In J-P. Brugal, F. David, J. G. Enloe, and J. Jaubert (Eds.), *Le Bison: Gibier et Moyen de Subsistance des hommes du Paléolithique aux Paléoindiens des Grandes Plains* (pp. 479–499). Antibes, France: Association pour la promotion et la diffusion des Connaissances Archéologiques.

Trigger, Bruce G. 1981. Archaeology and the ethno-graphic present. *Anthropologica* 23: 3–17.

———. 1995. Expanding middle-range theory. *Antiq-uity* 69: 449–458.

Tunnell, C. 1977. Fluted projectile point production as revealed by lithic specimens from the Adair-Steadman site in northwest Texas. In Eileen John-son (Ed.), *Paleoindian Lifeways.* Lubbock: West Texas Museum Association, Texas Tech University. *The Museum Journal* 17: 140–168.

White, Theodore E. 1953. A method of calculating the dietary percentage of various food animals utilized by aboriginal peoples. *American Antiquity* 18: 396–398.

———. 1954. Observations on the butchering technique of some aboriginal peoples, nos. 3, 4, 5, and 6. *American Antiquity* 19: 254–264.

Wylie, Alison. 1985. The reaction against analogy. In M. B. Schiffer (Ed.), *Advances in Archaeological Method and Theory*. Vol. 8 (pp. 63–112). New York: Academic Press.

Yellen, John E. 1977. *Archaeological Approaches to the Present: Models for Reconstructing the Past*. New York: Academic Press.

Chapter 8

Binford, Lewis R. 1978. *Nunamiut Ethnoarchaeology*. New York: Academic Press.

———. 1981. *Bones: Ancient Men and Modern Myths*. New York: Academic Press.

Brewer, Douglas J. 1992. Zooarchaeology: Method, theory, and goals. In M. B. Schiffer (Ed.), *Archaeological Method and Theory*. Vol. 4 (pp. 195–244). Tucson: University of Arizona Press.

Brothwell, D., and A. Pollard (Eds.). 2001. *Handbook of Archaeological Sciences*. Chichester, UK: Wiley.

Bryant, Vaughn M., Jr., and Stephen A. Hall. 1993. Archaeological palynology in the United States: A critique. *American Antiquity* 58: 277–286.

Crabtree, Pam J. 1990. Zooarchaeology and complex societies: Some uses of faunal analysis for the study of trade, social status, and ethnicity. In M. B. Schiffer (Ed.), *Archaeological Method and Theory*. Vol. 2 (pp. 155–205). Tucson: University of Arizona Press.

Dincauze, Dena. 2000. *Environmental Archaeology: Principles and Practice*. Cambridge: Cambridge University Press.

Faegri, K., P. E. Kaland, and K. Krzywinski. 1989. *Textbook of Pollen Analysis*, 4th ed. New York: Wiley.

Frison, George C., and Dennis Stanford. 1982. *The Agate Basin Site: A Record of the Paleoindian Occupation of the Northwestern High Plains*. New York: Academic Press.

Gilbert, B. Miles. 1980. *Mammalian Osteology*. Laramie, W Y: Modern Printing.

Grayson, Donald K. 1984. *Quantitative Zooarchaeology: Topics in the Analysis of Archaeological Faunas*. Orlando, FL: Academic Press.

Hastorf, Christine A., and Sissel Johannessen. 1991. Understanding changing people/plant relationships in the prehispanic Andes. In Robert W. Preucel (Ed.), *Processual and Postprocessual Archaeologies: Multiple Ways of Knowing the Past* (pp. 140–155). Center for Archaeological Investigations, Occasional Paper, no. 10. Southern Illinois University at Carbondale.

Hastorf, Christine A., and Virginia S. Popper (Eds.). 1988. *Current Paleoethnobotany: Analytical Methods and Cultural Interpretations of Archaeological Plant Remains*. Chicago: University of Chicago Press.

Haury, Emil W., E. B. Sayles, and William W. Wasley. 1959. The Lehner mammoth site, southeastern Arizona. *American Antiquity* 25: 2–30.

Hill, K., and K. Hawkes. 1983. Neotropical Hunting among the Ache of Eastern Paraguay. In R. Hames and W. Vickers (Eds.), *Adaptive Responses of Native Amazonians* (pp. 139–188). New York: Academic Press.

Hill, Matthew G. 2001. *Paleoindian Diet and Subsistence Behavior on the Northwestern Great Plains of North America*. PhD dissertation, University of Wisconsin, Madison. (Table 8-1 is from p. 55.)

———. 2005. *Paleoindian Diet and Subsistence Behavior on the Northwestern Great Plains*. Boulder: University Press of Colorado.

Holden, T. G. 2001. Dietary evidence from the coprolites and the intestinal contents of ancient humans. In D. Brothwell and A. Pollard (Eds.), *Handbook of Archaeological Sciences* (pp. 403–414). Chichester, UK: Wiley.

Leroi-Gourhan, Arlette. 1975. The flowers found with Shanidar IV, a Neanderthal burial in Iraq. *Science* 190: 562–564.

Lyman, R. Lee. 1994. *Vertebrate Taphonomy*. Cambridge: Cambridge University Press.

Mehringer, Peter J., and Vance Haynes. 1965. The pollen evidence for the environment of early man and extinct mammals at the Lehner mammoth site, southeastern Arizona. *American Antiquity* 31: 17–23.

Miksicek, Charles H. 1987. Formation processes of the archaeobotanical record. In Michael B. Schiffer (Ed.), *Advances in Archaeological Method and Theory*. Vol. 10 (pp. 211–247). New York: Academic Press.

Explore more, understand more, and improve your performance in class with

The Wadsworth Anthropology Resource Center
http://anthropology.wadsworth.com

This hands-on resource center provides an exciting new way to learn about archaeology! Accessible 24 hours a day, **The Wadsworth Anthropology Resource Center** helps you experience the excitement of archaeology by getting you actively involved with the science. Simply choose your field of study and select from engaging activities and features that will enrich your understanding of course topics. Explore the science in ways not possible in lecture or with a textbook alone!

Log on today for fun and interactive explorations in archaeology, including:

- ■ **Interactive Anthropology** exercises that put archaeology in motion
- ■ **Map Exercises** that will heighten your understanding of various countries and issues relevant to you
- ■ **Video Exercises** that show archaeologists in the field interacting with other cultures and sharing their experiences
- ■ **Meet the Scientists** interviews with scientists who talk about their field research projects, including project goals, personal anecdotes, and discoveries
- ■ The **Researching Anthropology** online guide, which assists you in doing research on the Internet
- ■ **Breaking News in Anthropology**, which links you to many of the recent events and findings in archaeology
- ■ **Exploring Further** links to a variety of additional material, including Thomson Wadsworth's exclusive *EarthWatch Journal,* an online magazine that explores important anthropological themes
- ■ **Applying Anthropology**, a web tour that leads you to valuable information on careers, graduate school programs in applied anthropology, and internships

Get started today at **http://1pass.thomson.com**

If an access card came with this book, you can start using many of these resources right away by following the directions on the card.

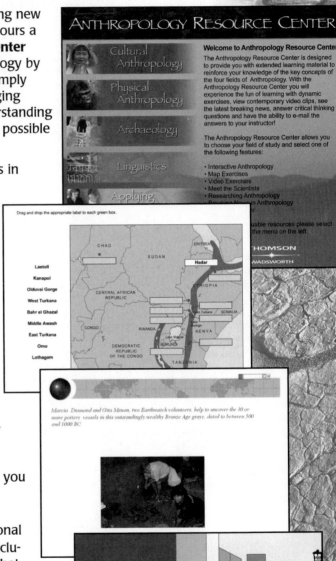